Precalculus

Part 1: Chapters 1–6

SENIOR CONTRIBUTING AUTHOR
JAY ABRAMSON, ARIZONA STATE UNIVERSITY

ISBN: 978-1-50669-812-0

OpenStax
Rice University
6100 Main Street MS-375
Houston, Texas 77005

To learn more about OpenStax, visit https://openstax.org.
Individual print copies and bulk orders can be purchased through our website.

HARDCOVER BOOK ISBN-13	978-1-938168-34-5
PAPERBACK BOOK ISBN-13	978-1-947 172-87-6
B&W PAPERBACK BOOK ISBN-13	978-1-50669-812-0
DIGITAL VERSION ISBN-13	978-1-947172-06-7
ENHANCED TEXTBOOK ISBN-13	978-0-9986257-5-1
Revision	PR-2015-002(03/17)-BW
Original Publication Year	2014

Printed by

XanEdu

4750 Venture Drive, Suite 400
Ann Arbor, MI 48108
800-562-2147
www.xanedu.com

OpenStax

OpenStax provides free, peer-reviewed, openly licensed textbooks for introductory college and Advanced Placement® courses and low-cost, personalized courseware that helps students learn. A nonprofit ed tech initiative based at Rice University, we're committed to helping students access the tools they need to complete their courses and meet their educational goals.

Rice University

OpenStax and OpenStax CNX are initiatives of Rice University. As a leading research university with a distinctive commitment to undergraduate education, Rice University aspires to path-breaking research, unsurpassed teaching, and contributions to the betterment of our world. It seeks to fulfill this mission by cultivating a diverse community of learning and discovery that produces leaders across the spectrum of human endeavor.

Foundation Support

OpenStax is grateful for the tremendous support of our sponsors. Without their strong engagement, the goal of free access to high-quality textbooks would remain just a dream.

Laura and John Arnold Foundation (LJAF) actively seeks opportunities to invest in organizations and thought leaders that have a sincere interest in implementing fundamental changes that not only yield immediate gains, but also repair broken systems for future generations. LJAF currently focuses its strategic investments on education, criminal justice, research integrity, and public accountability.

The William and Flora Hewlett Foundation has been making grants since 1967 to help solve social and environmental problems at home and around the world. The Foundation concentrates its resources on activities in education, the environment, global development and population, performing arts, and philanthropy, and makes grants to support disadvantaged communities in the San Francisco Bay Area.

Guided by the belief that every life has equal value, the Bill & Melinda Gates Foundation works to help all people lead healthy, productive lives. In developing countries, it focuses on improving people's health with vaccines and other life-saving tools and giving them the chance to lift themselves out of hunger and extreme poverty. In the United States, it seeks to signifi antly improve education so that all young people have the opportunity to reach their full potential. Based in Seattle, Washington, the foundation is led by CEO Jeff Raikes and Co-chair William H. Gates Sr., under the direction of Bill and Melinda Gates and Warren Buffett.

The Maxfield Foundation supports projects with potential for high impact in science, education, sustainability, and other areas of social importance.

Our mission at The Michelson 20MM Foundation is to grow access and success by eliminating unnecessary hurdles to affordabilitay. We support the creation, sharing, and proliferation of more effective, more affordable educational content by leveraging disruptive technologies, open educational resources, and new models for collaboration between for-profi , nonprofi , and public entities.

Calvin K. Kazanjian was the founder and president of Peter Paul (Almond Joy), Inc. He firmly believed that the more people understood about basic economics the happier and more prosperous they would be. Accordingly, he established the Calvin K. Kazanjian Economics Foundation Inc, in 1949 as a philanthropic, nonpolitical educational organization to support efforts that enhanced economic understanding.

The Bill and Stephanie Sick Fund supports innovative projects in the areas of Education, Art, Science and Engineering.

About Our Team

Senior Contributing Author

Jay Abramson has been teaching Precalculus for 33 years, the last 14 at Arizona State University, where he is a principal lecturer in the School of Mathematics and Statistics. His accomplishments at ASU include co-developing the university's first hybrid and online math courses as well as an extensive library of video lectures and tutorials. In addition, he has served as a contributing author for two of Pearson Education's math programs, NovaNet Precalculus and Trigonometry. Prior to coming to ASU, Jay taught at Texas State Technical College and Amarillo College. He received Teacher of the Year awards at both institutions.

Reviewers

Nina Alketa, Cecil College
Kiran Bhutani, Catholic University of America
Brandie Biddy, Cecil College
Lisa Blank, Lyme Central School
Bryan Blount, Kentucky Wesleyan College
Jessica Bolz, The Bryn Mawr School
Sheri Boyd, Rollins College
Sarah Brewer, Alabama School of Math and Science
Charles Buckley, St. Gregory's University
Michael Cohen, Hofstra University
Kenneth Crane, Texarkana College
Rachel Cywinski, Alamo Colleges
Nathan Czuba
Srabasti Dutta, Ashford University
Kristy Erickson, Cecil College
Nicole Fernandez, Georgetown University / Kent State University
David French, Tidewater Community College
Douglas Furman, SUNY Ulster
Lance Hemlow, Raritan Valley Community College
Erinn Izzo, Nicaragua Christian Academy
John Jaffe
Jerry Jared, Blue Ridge School
Stan Kopec, Mount Wachusett Community College
Kathy Kovacs
Cynthia Landrigan, Erie Community College
Sara Lenhart, Christopher Newport University
Wendy Lightheart, Lane Community College
Joanne Manville, Bunker Hill Community College
Karla McCavit, Albion College
Cynthia McGinnis, Northwest Florida State College
Lana Neal, University of Texas at Austin
Rhonda Porter, Albany State University
Steven Purtee, Valencia College
William Radulovich, Florida State College Jacksonville
Alice Ramos, Bethel College
Nick Reynolds, Montgomery Community College
Amanda Ross, A. A. Ross Consulting and Research, LLC
Erica Rutter, Arizona State University
Sutandra Sarkar, Georgia State University
Willy Schild, Wentworth Institute of Technology
Todd Stephen, Cleveland State University
Scott Sykes, University of West Georgia
Linda Tansil, Southeast Missouri State University
John Thomas, College of Lake County
Diane Valade, Piedmont Virginia Community College
Allen Wolmer, Atlanta Jewish Academy

Contributing Authors

Valeree Falduto, Palm Beach State College
Rachael Gross, Towson University
David Lippman, Pierce College
Melonie Rasmussen, Pierce College
Rick Norwood, East Tennessee State University
Nicholas Belloit, Florida State College Jacksonville
Jean-Marie Magnier, Springfield Technical Community College
Harold Whipple
Christina Fernandez

Brief Contents

Contents

Preface

Welcome to *Precalculus*, an OpenStax resource. This textbook was written to increase student access to high-quality learning materials, maintaining highest standards of academic rigor at little to no cost.

About OpenStax

OpenStax is a nonprofit based at Rice University, and it's our mission to improve student access to education. Our first openly licensed college textbook was published in 2012, and our library has since scaled to over 25 books for college and AP* courses used by hundreds of thousands of students. Our adaptive learning technology, designed to improve learning outcomes through personalized educational paths, is being piloted in college courses throughout the country. Through our partnerships with philanthropic foundations and our alliance with other educational resource organizations, OpenStax is breaking down the most common barriers to learning and empowering students and instructors to succeed.

About OpenStax's Resources

Customization

OpenStax is licensed under a Creative Commons Attribution 4.0 International (CC BY) license, which means that you can distribute, remix, and build upon the content, as long as you provide attribution to OpenStax and its content contributors.

Because our books are openly licensed, you are free to use the entire book or pick and choose the sections that are most relevant to the needs of your course. Feel free to remix the content by assigning your students certain chapters and sections in your syllabus, in the order that you prefer. You can even provide a direct link in your syllabus to the sections in the web view of your book.

Faculty also have the option of creating a customized version of their OpenStax book through the aerSelect platform. The custom version can be made available to students in low-cost print or digital form through their campus bookstore. Visit your book page on openstax.org for a link to your book on aerSelect.

Errata

All OpenStax textbooks undergo a rigorous review process. However, like any professional-grade textbook, errors sometimes occur. Since our books are web based, we can make updates periodically when deemed pedagogically necessary. If you have a correction to suggest, submit it through the link on your book page on openstax.org. Subject matter experts review all errata suggestions. OpenStax is committed to remaining transparent about all updates, so you will also find a list of past errata changes on your book page on openstax.org.

Format

You can access this textbook for free in web view or PDF through openstax.org, and for a low cost in print.

About *Precalculus*

Precalculus is adaptable and designed to fit the needs of a variety of precalculus courses. It is a comprehensive text that covers more ground than a typical one- or two-semester college-level precalculus course. The content is organized by clearly-defined learning objectives, and includes worked examples that demonstrate problem-solving approaches in an accessible way.

Coverage and Scope

Precalculus contains twelve chapters, roughly divided into three groups.

Chapters 1-4 discuss various types of functions, providing a foundation for the remainder of the course.

    Chapter 1: Functions
    Chapter 2: Linear Functions
    Chapter 3: Polynomial and Rational Functions
    Chapter 4: Exponential and Logarithmic Functions

Chapters 5-8 focus on Trigonometry. In *Precalculus*, we approach trigonometry by first introducing angles and the unit circle, as opposed to the right triangle approach more commonly used in College Algebra and Trigonometry courses.

    Chapter 5: Trigonometric Functions
    Chapter 6: Periodic Functions
    Chapter 7: Trigonometric Identities and Equations
    Chapter 8: Further Applications of Trigonometry

Chapters 9-12 present some advanced Precalculus topics that build on topics introduced in chapters 1-8. Most Precalculus syllabi include some of the topics in these chapters, but few include all. Instructors can select material as needed from this group of chapters, since they are not cumulative.

    Chapter 9: Systems of Equations and Inequalities
    Chapter 10: Analytic Geometry
    Chapter 11: Sequences, Probability and Counting Theory
    Chapter 12: Introduction to Calculus

All chapters are broken down into multiple sections, the titles of which can be viewed in the Table of Contents.

Development Overview

Precalculus is the product of a collaborative effort by a group of dedicated authors, editors, and instructors whose collective passion for this project has resulted in a text that is remarkably unified in purpose and voice. Special thanks is due to our Lead Author, Jay Abramson of Arizona State University, who provided the overall vision for the book and oversaw the development of each and every chapter, drawing up the initial blueprint, reading numerous drafts, and assimilating field reviews into actionable revision plans for our authors and editors.

The first eight chapters are built on the foundation of ***Precalculus: An Investigation of Functions*** by David Lippman and Melonie Rasmussen. Chapters 9-12 were written and developed from by our expert and highly experienced author team. All twelve chapters follow a new and innovative instructional design, and great care has been taken to maintain a consistent voice from cover to cover. New features have been introduced to flesh out the instruction, all of the graphics have been redone in a more contemporary style, and much of the content has been revised, replaced, or supplemented to bring the text more in line with mainstream approaches to teaching precalculus.

Accuracy of the Content

We have taken great pains to ensure the validity and accuracy of this text. Each chapter's manuscript underwent at least two rounds of review and revision by a panel of active precalculus instructors. Then, prior to publication, a separate team of experts checked all text, examples, and graphics for mathematical accuracy; multiple reviewers were assigned to each chapter to minimize the chances of any error escaping notice. A third team of experts was responsible for the accuracy of the Answer Key, dutifully reworking every solution to eradicate any lingering errors. Finally, the editorial team conducted a multi-round post-production review to ensure the integrity of the content in its final form was written and developed after the Student Edition, has also been rigorously checked for accuracy following a process similar to that described above. Incidentally, the act of writing out solutions step-by-step served as yet another round of validation for the Answer Key in the back of the Student Edition.

Pedagogical Foundations and Features

Learning Objectives

Each chapter is divided into multiple sections (or modules), each of which is organized around a set of learning objectives. The learning objectives are listed explicitly at the beginning of each section and are the focal point of every instructional element.

Narrative Text

Narrative text is used to introduce key concepts, terms, and definitions, to provide real-world context, and to provide transitions between topics and examples. Throughout this book, we rely on a few basic conventions to highlight the most important ideas:

- Key terms are boldfaced, typically when first introduced and/or when formally defined.
- Key concepts and definitions are called out in a blue box for easy reference.

Example

Each learning objective is supported by one or more worked examples that demonstrate the problem-solving approaches that students must master. Typically, we include multiple Examples for each learning objective in order to model different approaches to the same type of problem, or to introduce similar problems of increasing complexity. All told, there are more than 650 Examples, or an average of about 55 per chapter.

All Examples follow a simple two- or three-part format. First, we pose a problem or question. Next, we demonstrate the Solution, spelling out the steps along the way. Finally (for select Examples), we conclude with an Analysis reflecting on the broader implications of the Solution just shown.

Figures

Precalculus contains more than 2000 figures and illustrations, the vast majority of which are graphs and diagrams. Art throughout the text adheres to a clear, understated style, drawing the eye to the most important information in each figure while minimizing visual distractions. Color contrast is employed with discretion to distinguish between the different functions or features of a graph.

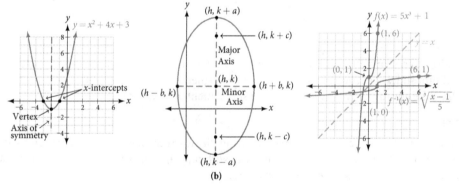

Supporting Features

Four small but important features, each marked by a distinctive icon, serve to support Examples.

A "*How To*" is a list of steps necessary to solve a certain type of problem. A How To typically precedes an Example that proceeds to demonstrate the steps in action.

A "*Try It*" exercise immediately follows an Example or a set of related Examples, providing the student with an immediate opportunity to solve a similar problem. In the Online version of the text, students can click an Answer link directly below the question to check their understanding. In other versions, answers to the Try-It exercises are located in the Answer Key.

A "*Q & A...*" may appear at any point in the narrative, but most often follows an Example. This feature pre-empts misconceptions by posing a commonly asked yes/no question, followed by a detailed answer and explanation.

The "Media" links appear at the conclusion of each section, just prior to the Section Exercises. These are a list of links to online video tutorials that reinforce the concepts and skills introduced in the section

While we have selected tutorials that closely align to our learning objectives, we did not produce these tutorials, nor were they specifically produced or tailored to accompany Precalculus.

Section Exercises

Each section of every chapter concludes with a well-rounded set of exercises that can be assigned as homework or used selectively for guided practice. With over 5,900 exercises across the 12 chapters, instructors should have plenty to choose from[i].

Section Exercises are organized by question type, and generally appear in the following order:

Verbal questions assess conceptual understanding of key terms and concepts.

Algebraic problems require students to apply algebraic manipulations demonstrated in the section.

Graphical problems assess students' ability to interpret or produce a graph.

Numeric problems require the student perform calculations or computations.

Technology problems encourage exploration through use of a graphing utility, either to visualize or verify algebraic results or to solve problems via an alternative to the methods demonstrated in the section.

Extensions pose problems more challenging than the Examples demonstrated in the section. They require students to synthesize multiple learning objectives or apply critical thinking to solve complex problems.

Real-World Applications present realistic problem scenarios from fields such as physics, geology, biology, finance, and the social sciences.

Chapter Review Features

Each chapter concludes with a review of the most important takeaways, as well as additional practice problems that students can use to prepare for exams.x

Key Terms provides a formal definition for each bold-faced term in the chapter.

Key Equations presents a compilation of formulas, theorems, and standard-form equations.

Key Concepts summarizes the most important ideas introduced in each section, linking back to the relevant Example(s) in case students need to review.

Chapter Review Exercises include 40-80 practice problems that recall the most important concepts from each section.

Practice Test includes 25-50 problems assessing the most important learning objectives from the chapter. Note that the practice test is not organized by section, and may be more heavily weighted toward cumulative objectives as opposed to the foundational objectives covered in the opening sections.

Additional Resources

Student and Instructor Resources

We've compiled additional resources for both students and instructors, including Getting Started Guides, instructor solution manual, and PowerPoint slides. Instructor resources require a verified instructor account, which can be requested on your openstax.org log-in. Take advantage of these resources to supplement your OpenStax book.

Partner Resources

OpenStax Partners are our allies in the mission to make high-quality learning materials affordable and accessible to students and instructors everywhere. Their tools integrate seamlessly with our OpenStax titles at a low cost. To access the partner resources for your text, visit your book page on openstax.org.

Online Homework

XYZ Homework
XYZ Homework is built using the fastest-growing mathematics cloud platform. XYZ Homework gives instructors access to the Precalculus aligned problems, organized in the Precalculus Course Template. Instructors have access to thousands of additional algorithmically-generated questions for unparalleled course customization. For one low annual price, students can take multiple classes through XYZ Homework. Learn more at www.xyzhomework.com/openstax.

WEBASSIGN
WebAssign is an independent online homework and assessment solution first launched at North Carolina State University in 1997. Today, WebAssign is an employee-owned benefit corporation and participates in the education of over a million students each year. WebAssign empowers faculty to deliver fully customizable assignments and high quality content to their students in an interactive online environment. WebAssign supports Precalculus with hundreds of problems covering every concept in the course, each containing algorithmically-generated values and links directly to the eBook providing a completely integrated online learning experience.

i. 5,924 total exercises. Includes Chapter Reviews and Practice Tests.

Functions

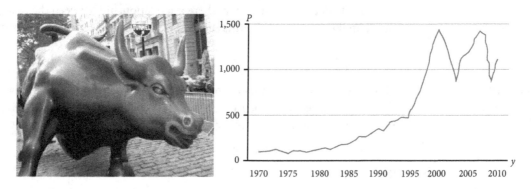

Figure 1 Standard and Poor's Index with dividends reinvested
(credit "bull": modification of work by Prayitno Hadinata; credit "graph": modification of work by MeasuringWorth)

CHAPTER OUTLINE

Introduction

Toward the end of the twentieth century, the values of stocks of internet and technology companies rose dramatically. As a result, the Standard and Poor's stock market average rose as well. **Figure 1** tracks the value of that initial investment of just under $100 over the 40 years. It shows that an investment that was worth less than $500 until about 1995 skyrocketed up to about $1,100 by the beginning of 2000. That five-year period became known as the "dot-com bubble" because so many internet startups were formed. As bubbles tend to do, though, the dot-com bubble eventually burst. Many companies grew too fast and then suddenly went out of business. The result caused the sharp decline represented on the graph beginning at the end of 2000.

Notice, as we consider this example, that there is a definite relationship between the year and stock market average. For any year we choose, we can determine the corresponding value of the stock market average. In this chapter, we will explore these kinds of relationships and their properties.

LEARNING OBJECTIVES

In this section, you will:

- Determine whether a relation represents a function.
- Find the value of a function.
- Determine whether a function is one-to-one.
- Use the vertical line test to identify functions.
- Graph the functions listed in the library of functions.

1.1   FUNCTIONS AND FUNCTION NOTATION

A jetliner changes altitude as its distance from the starting point of a flight increases. The weight of a growing child increases with time. In each case, one quantity depends on another. There is a relationship between the two quantities that we can describe, analyze, and use to make predictions. In this section, we will analyze such relationships.

Determining Whether a Relation Represents a Function

A **relation** is a set of ordered pairs. The set of the first components of each ordered pair is called the **domain** and the set of the second components of each ordered pair is called the **range**. Consider the following set of ordered pairs. The first numbers in each pair are the first five natural numbers. The second number in each pair is twice that of the first.

$$\{(1, 2), (2, 4), (3, 6), (4, 8), (5, 10)\}$$

The domain is $\{1, 2, 3, 4, 5\}$. The range is $\{2, 4, 6, 8, 10\}$.

Note that each value in the domain is also known as an **input** value, or **independent variable**, and is often labeled with the lowercase letter x. Each value in the range is also known as an **output** value, or **dependent variable**, and is often labeled lowercase letter y.

A function f is a relation that assigns a single value in the range to each value in the domain. In other words, no x-values are repeated. For our example that relates the first five natural numbers to numbers double their values, this relation is a function because each element in the domain, $\{1, 2, 3, 4, 5\}$, is paired with exactly one element in the range, $\{2, 4, 6, 8, 10\}$.

Now let's consider the set of ordered pairs that relates the terms "even" and "odd" to the first five natural numbers. It would appear as

$$\{(\text{odd}, 1), (\text{even}, 2), (\text{odd}, 3), (\text{even}, 4), (\text{odd}, 5)\}$$

Notice that each element in the domain, $\{\text{even}, \text{odd}\}$ is *not* paired with exactly one element in the range, $\{1, 2, 3, 4, 5\}$. For example, the term "odd" corresponds to three values from the domain, $\{1, 3, 5\}$ and the term "even" corresponds to two values from the range, $\{2, 4\}$. This violates the definition of a function, so this relation is not a function. **Figure 1** compares relations that are functions and not functions.

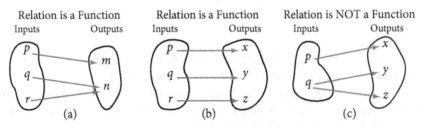

Figure 1 (a) This relationship is a function because each input is associated with a single output. Note that input q and r both give output n.
(b) This relationship is also a function. In this case, each input is associated with a single output.
(c) This relationship is not a function because input q is associated with two different outputs.

> *function*
> A **function** is a relation in which each possible input value leads to exactly one output value. We say "the output is a function of the input." The **input** values make up the **domain**, and the **output** values make up the **range**.

How To...

Given a relationship between two quantities, determine whether the relationship is a function.

1. Identify the input values.
2. Identify the output values.
3. If each input value leads to only one output value, classify the relationship as a function. If any input value leads to two or more outputs, do not classify the relationship as a function.

Example 1   **Determining If Menu Price Lists Are Functions**

The coffee shop menu, shown in **Figure 2** consists of items and their prices.

a. Is price a function of the item?   **b.** Is the item a function of the price?

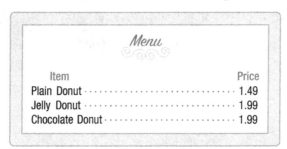

Figure 2

Solution

a. Let's begin by considering the input as the items on the menu. The output values are then the prices. See **Figure 3**.

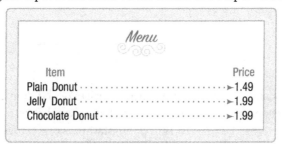

Figure 3

Each item on the menu has only one price, so the price is a function of the item.

b. Two items on the menu have the same price. If we consider the prices to be the input values and the items to be the output, then the same input value could have more than one output associated with it. See **Figure 4**.

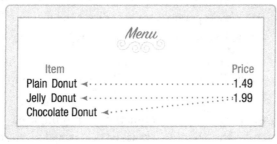

Figure 4

Therefore, the item is a not a function of price.

Example 2   **Determining If Class Grade Rules Are Functions**

In a particular math class, the overall percent grade corresponds to a grade point average. Is grade point average a function of the percent grade? Is the percent grade a function of the grade point average? **Table 1** shows a possible rule for assigning grade points.

Percent grade	0-56	57-61	62-66	67-71	72-77	78-86	87-91	92-100
Grade point average	0.0	1.0	1.5	2.0	2.5	3.0	3.5	4.0

Table 1

Solution　For any percent grade earned, there is an associated grade point average, so the grade point average is a function of the percent grade. In other words, if we input the percent grade, the output is a specific grade point average.

In the grading system given, there is a range of percent grades that correspond to the same grade point average. For example, students who receive a grade point average of 3.0 could have a variety of percent grades ranging from 78 all the way to 86. Thus, percent grade is not a function of grade point average

Try It #1

Table 2[1] lists the five greatest baseball players of all time in order of rank.

Player	Rank
Babe Ruth	1
Willie Mays	2
Ty Cobb	3
Walter Johnson	4
Hank Aaron	5

Table 2

a. Is the rank a function of the player name?
b. Is the player name a function of the rank?

Using Function Notation

Once we determine that a relationship is a function, we need to display and define the functional relationships so that we can understand and use them, and sometimes also so that we can program them into computers. There are various ways of representing functions. A standard function notation is one representation that facilitates working with functions.

To represent "height is a function of age," we start by identifying the descriptive variables h for height and a for age. The letters f, g, and h are often used to represent functions just as we use x, y, and z to represent numbers and A, B, and C to represent sets.

h is f of a	We name the function f; height is a function of age.
$h = f(a)$	We use parentheses to indicate the function input.
$f(a)$	We name the function f; the expression is read as "f of a."

Remember, we can use any letter to name the function; the notation $h(a)$ shows us that h depends on a. The value a must be put into the function h to get a result. The parentheses indicate that age is input into the function; they do not indicate multiplication.

We can also give an algebraic expression as the input to a function. For example $f(a + b)$ means "first add a and b, and the result is the input for the function f." The operations must be performed in this order to obtain the correct result.

> *function notation*
> The notation $y = f(x)$ defines a function named f. This is read as "y is a function of x." The letter x represents the input value, or independent variable. The letter y, or $f(x)$, represents the output value, or dependent variable.

1　http://www.baseball-almanac.com/legendary/lisn100.shtml. Accessed 3/24/2014.

Example 3   Using Function Notation for Days in a Month

Use function notation to represent a function whose input is the name of a month and output is the number of days in that month.

Solution   The number of days in a month is a function of the name of the month, so if we name the function f, we write days $= f(\text{month})$ or $d = f(m)$. The name of the month is the input to a "rule" that associates a specific number (the output) with each input.

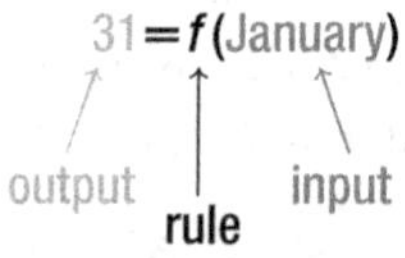

$$31 = f(\text{January})$$

output   rule   input

Figure 5

For example, $f(\text{March}) = 31$, because March has 31 days. The notation $d = f(m)$ reminds us that the number of days, d (the output), is dependent on the name of the month, m (the input).

Analysis   Note that the inputs to a function do not have to be numbers; function inputs can be names of people, labels of geometric objects, or any other element that determines some kind of output. However, most of the functions we will work with in this book will have numbers as inputs and outputs.

Example 4   Interpreting Function Notation

A function $N = f(y)$ gives the number of police officers, N, in a town in year y. What does $f(2005) = 300$ represent?

Solution   When we read $f(2005) = 300$, we see that the input year is 2005. The value for the output, the number of police officers (N), is 300. Remember $N = f(y)$. The statement $f(2005) = 300$ tells us that in the year 2005 there were 300 police officers in the town.

Try It #2

Use function notation to express the weight of a pig in pounds as a function of its age in days d.

Q & A...

Instead of a notation such as $y = f(x)$, could we use the same symbol for the output as for the function, such as $y = y(x)$, meaning "y is a function of x?"

Yes, this is often done, especially in applied subjects that use higher math, such as physics and engineering. However, in exploring math itself we like to maintain a distinction between a function such as f, which is a rule or procedure, and the output y we get by applying f to a particular input x. This is why we usually use notation such as $y = f(x)$, $P = W(d)$, and so on.

Representing Functions Using Tables

A common method of representing functions is in the form of a table. The table rows or columns display the corresponding input and output values. In some cases, these values represent all we know about the relationship; other times, the table provides a few select examples from a more complete relationship.

Table 3 lists the input number of each month (January = 1, February = 2, and so on) and the output value of the number of days in that month. This information represents all we know about the months and days for a given year (that is not a leap year). Note that, in this table, we define a days-in-a-month function f where $D = f(m)$ identifies months by an integer rather than by name.

Month number, m (input)	1	2	3	4	5	6	7	8	9	10	11	12
Days in month, D (output)	31	28	31	30	31	30	31	31	30	31	30	31

Table 3

Table 4 defines a function $Q = g(n)$. Remember, this notation tells us that g is the name of the function that takes the input n and gives the output Q.

n	1	2	3	4	5
Q	8	6	7	6	8

Table 4

Table 5 below displays the age of children in years and their corresponding heights. This table displays just some of the data available for the heights and ages of children. We can see right away that this table does not represent a function because the same input value, 5 years, has two different output values, 40 in. and 42 in.

Age in years, a (input)	5	5	6	7	8	9	10
Height in inches, h (output)	40	42	44	47	50	52	54

Table 5

How To...

Given a table of input and output values, determine whether the table represents a function.

1. Identify the input and output values.
2. Check to see if each input value is paired with only one output value. If so, the table represents a function.

Example 5   **Identifying Tables that Represent Functions**

Which table, **Table 6**, **Table 7**, or **Table 8**, represents a function (if any)?

Input	Output
2	1
5	3
8	6

Table 6

Input	Output
−3	5
0	1
4	5

Table 7

Input	Output
1	0
5	2
5	4

Table 8

Solution   **Table 6** and **Table 7** define functions. In both, each input value corresponds to exactly one output value. **Table 8** does not define a function because the input value of 5 corresponds to two different output values.

When a table represents a function, corresponding input and output values can also be specified using function notation.

The function represented by **Table 6** can be represented by writing

$$f(2) = 1, f(5) = 3, \text{ and } f(8) = 6$$

Similarly, the statements

$$g(-3) = 5, g(0) = 1, \text{ and } g(4) = 5$$

represent the function in table **Table 7.**

Table 8 cannot be expressed in a similar way because it does not represent a function.

Try It #3

Does **Table 9** represent a function?

Input	Output
1	10
2	100
3	1000

Table 9

Finding Input and Output Values of a Function

When we know an input value and want to determine the corresponding output value for a function, we evaluate the function. Evaluating will always produce one result because each input value of a function corresponds to exactly one output value.

When we know an output value and want to determine the input values that would produce that output value, we set the output equal to the function's formula and solve for the input. Solving can produce more than one solution because different input values can produce the same output value.

Evaluation of Functions in Algebraic Forms

When we have a function in formula form, it is usually a simple matter to evaluate the function. For example, the function $f(x) = 5 - 3x^2$ can be evaluated by squaring the input value, multiplying by 3, and then subtracting the product from 5.

How To...

Given the formula for a function, evaluate.

1. Replace the input variable in the formula with the value provided.
2. Calculate the result.

Example 6　**Evaluating Functions at Specific Values**

Evaluate $f(x) = x^2 + 3x - 4$ at:

a. 2　　**b.** a　　**c.** $a + h$　　**d.** $\dfrac{f(a+h) - f(a)}{h}$

Solution　Replace the x in the function with each specified value.

a. Because the input value is a number, 2, we can use simple algebra to simplify.

$$f(2) = 2^2 + 3(2) - 4$$
$$= 4 + 6 - 4$$
$$= 6$$

b. In this case, the input value is a letter so we cannot simplify the answer any further.

$$f(a) = a^2 + 3a - 4$$

c. With an input value of $a + h$, we must use the distributive property.

$$f(a + h) = (a + h)^2 + 3(a + h) - 4$$
$$= a^2 + 2ah + h^2 + 3a + 3h - 4$$

d. In this case, we apply the input values to the function more than once, and then perform algebraic operations on the result. We already found that

$$f(a + h) = a^2 + 2ah + h^2 + 3a + 3h - 4$$

and we know that

$$f(a) = a^2 + 3a - 4$$

Now we combine the results and simplify.

$$\frac{f(a+h) - f(a)}{h} = \frac{(a^2 + 2ah + h^2 + 3a + 3h - 4) - (a^2 + 3a - 4)}{h}$$
$$= \frac{2ah + h^2 + 3h}{h}$$
$$= \frac{h(2a + h + 3)}{h} \qquad \text{Factor out } h.$$
$$= 2a + h + 3 \qquad \text{Simplify.}$$

Example 7   **Evaluating Functions**

Given the function $h(p) = p^2 + 2p$, evaluate $h(4)$.

Solution   To evaluate $h(4)$, we substitute the value 4 for the input variable p in the given function.

$$h(p) = p^2 + 2p$$
$$h(4) = (4)^2 + 2(4)$$
$$= 16 + 8$$
$$= 24$$

Therefore, for an input of 4, we have an output of 24.

Try It #4

Given the function $g(m) = \sqrt{m - 4}$. Evaluate $g(5)$.

Example 8   **Solving Functions**

Given the function $h(p) = p^2 + 2p$, solve for $h(p) = 3$.

Solution

$$h(p) = 3$$
$$p^2 + 2p = 3 \qquad \text{Substitute the original function } h(p) = p^2 + 2p.$$
$$p^2 + 2p - 3 = 0 \qquad \text{Subtract 3 from each side.}$$
$$(p + 3)(p - 1) = 0 \qquad \text{Factor.}$$

If $(p + 3)(p - 1) = 0$, either $(p + 3) = 0$ or $(p - 1) = 0$ (or both of them equal 0). We will set each factor equal to 0 and solve for p in each case.

$$(p + 3) = 0, \quad p = -3$$
$$(p - 1) = 0, \quad p = 1$$

This gives us two solutions. The output $h(p) = 3$ when the input is either $p = 1$ or $p = -3$. We can also verify by graphing as in **Figure 6**. The graph verifies that $h(1) = h(-3) = 3$ and $h(4) = 24$.

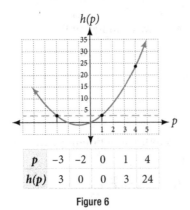

p	−3	−2	0	1	4
$h(p)$	3	0	0	3	24

Figure 6

Try It #5

Given the function $g(m) = \sqrt{m - 4}$, solve $g(m) = 2$.

Evaluating Functions Expressed in Formulas

Some functions are defined by mathematical rules or procedures expressed in equation form. If it is possible to express the function output with a formula involving the input quantity, then we can define a function in algebraic form. For example, the equation $2n + 6p = 12$ expresses a functional relationship between n and p. We can rewrite it to decide if p is a function of n.

How To...

Given a function in equation form, write its algebraic formula.

1. Solve the equation to isolate the output variable on one side of the equal sign, with the other side as an expression that involves *only* the input variable.
2. Use all the usual algebraic methods for solving equations, such as adding or subtracting the same quantity to or from both sides, or multiplying or dividing both sides of the equation by the same quantity.

Example 9   **Finding an Equation of a Function**

Express the relationship $2n + 6p = 12$ as a function $p = f(n)$, if possible.

Solution   To express the relationship in this form, we need to be able to write the relationship where p is a function of n, which means writing it as $p =$ [expression involving n].

$$2n + 6p = 12$$

$$6p = 12 - 2n \qquad \text{Subtract } 2n \text{ from both sides.}$$

$$p = \frac{12 - 2n}{6} \qquad \text{Divide both sides by 6 and simplify.}$$

$$p = \frac{12}{6} - \frac{2n}{6}$$

$$p = 2 - \frac{1}{3}n$$

Therefore, p as a function of n is written as

$$p = f(n) = 2 - \frac{1}{3}n$$

Analysis   It is important to note that not every relationship expressed by an equation can also be expressed as a function with a formula.

Example 10   **Expressing the Equation of a Circle as a Function**

Does the equation $x^2 + y^2 = 1$ represent a function with x as input and y as output? If so, express the relationship as a function $y = f(x)$.

Solution   First we subtract x^2 from both sides.

$$y^2 = 1 - x^2$$

We now try to solve for y in this equation.

$$y = \pm\sqrt{1 - x^2}$$

$$= +\sqrt{1 - x^2} \quad \text{and} \quad -\sqrt{1 - x^2}$$

We get two outputs corresponding to the same input, so this relationship cannot be represented as a single function $y = f(x)$.

Try It #6

If $x - 8y^3 = 0$, express y as a function of x.

Q & A...

Are there relationships expressed by an equation that do represent a function but which still cannot be represented by an algebraic formula?

Yes, this can happen. For example, given the equation $x = y + 2^y$, if we want to express y as a function of x, there is no simple algebraic formula involving only x that equals y. However, each x does determine a unique value for y, and there are mathematical procedures by which y can be found to any desired accuracy. In this case, we say that the equation gives an implicit (implied) rule for y as a function of x, even though the formula cannot be written explicitly.

Evaluating a Function Given in Tabular Form

As we saw above, we can represent functions in tables. Conversely, we can use information in tables to write functions, and we can evaluate functions using the tables. For example, how well do our pets recall the fond memories we share with them? There is an urban legend that a goldfish has a memory of 3 seconds, but this is just a myth. Goldfish can remember up to 3 months, while the beta fish has a memory of up to 5 months. And while a puppy's memory span is no longer than 30 seconds, the adult dog can remember for 5 minutes. This is meager compared to a cat, whose memory span lasts for 16 hours.

The function that relates the type of pet to the duration of its memory span is more easily visualized with the use of a table. See **Table 10**.[2]

Pet	Memory span in hours
Puppy	0.008
Adult dog	0.083
Cat	16
Goldfish	2160
Beta fish	3600

Table 10

At times, evaluating a function in table form may be more useful than using equations. Here let us call the function P. The domain of the function is the type of pet and the range is a real number representing the number of hours the pet's memory span lasts. We can evaluate the function P at the input value of "goldfish." We would write $P(\text{goldfish}) = 2160$. Notice that, to evaluate the function in table form, we identify the input value and the corresponding output value from the pertinent row of the table. The tabular form for function P seems ideally suited to this function, more so than writing it in paragraph or function form.

How To...

Given a function represented by a table, identify specific output and input values.

1. Find the given input in the row (or column) of input values.
2. Identify the corresponding output value paired with that input value.
3. Find the given output values in the row (or column) of output values, noting every time that output value appears.
4. Identify the input value(s) corresponding to the given output value.

Example 11   **Evaluating and Solving a Tabular Function**

Using **Table 11**,

    a. Evaluate $g(3)$ **b.** Solve $g(n) = 6$.

n	1	2	3	4	5
$g(n)$	8	6	7	6	8

Table 11

Solution

    a. Evaluating $g(3)$ means determining the output value of the function g for the input value of $n = 3$. The table output value corresponding to $n = 3$ is 7, so $g(3) = 7$.

    b. Solving $g(n) = 6$ means identifying the input values, n, that produce an output value of 6. **Table 11** shows two solutions: 2 and 4. When we input 2 into the function g, our output is 6. When we input 4 into the function g, our output is also 6.

2 http://www.kgbanswers.com/how-long-is-a-dogs-memory-span/4221590. Accessed 3/24/2014.

Try It #7

Using **Table 11**, evaluate $g(1)$.

Finding Function Values from a Graph

Evaluating a function using a graph also requires finding the corresponding output value for a given input value, only in this case, we find the output value by looking at the graph. Solving a function equation using a graph requires finding all instances of the given output value on the graph and observing the corresponding input value(s).

Example 12   **Reading Function Values from a Graph**

Given the graph in **Figure 7**,

   a. Evaluate $f(2)$.   **b.** Solve $f(x) = 4$.

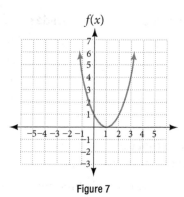

Figure 7

Solution

   a. To evaluate $f(2)$, locate the point on the curve where $x = 2$, then read the y-coordinate of that point. The point has coordinates $(2, 1)$, so $f(2) = 1$. See **Figure 8**.

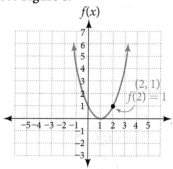

Figure 8

   b. To solve $f(x) = 4$, we find the output value 4 on the vertical axis. Moving horizontally along the line $y = 4$, we locate two points of the curve with output value 4: $(-1, 4)$ and $(3, 4)$. These points represent the two solutions to $f(x) = 4$: -1 or 3. This means $f(-1) = 4$ and $f(3) = 4$, or when the input is -1 or 3, the output is 4. See **Figure 9**.

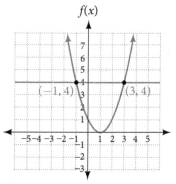

Figure 9

Try It #8

Using **Figure 7**, solve $f(x) = 1$.

Determining Whether a Function is One-to-One

Some functions have a given output value that corresponds to two or more input values. For example, in the stock chart shown in **Figure 1** at the beginning of this chapter, the stock price was $1,000 on five different dates, meaning that there were five different input values that all resulted in the same output value of $1,000.

However, some functions have only one input value for each output value, as well as having only one output for each input. We call these functions one-to-one functions. As an example, consider a school that uses only letter grades and decimal equivalents, as listed in **Table 12**.

Letter grade	Grade point average
A	4.0
B	3.0
C	2.0
D	1.0

Table 12

This grading system represents a one-to-one function, because each letter input yields one particular grade point average output and each grade point average corresponds to one input letter.

To visualize this concept, let's look again at the two simple functions sketched in **Figure 1(a)** and **Figure 1(b)**. The function in part (a) shows a relationship that is not a one-to-one function because inputs q and r both give output n. The function in part (b) shows a relationship that is a one-to-one function because each input is associated with a single output.

> **one-to-one function**
> A **one-to-one function** is a function in which each output value corresponds to exactly one input value.

Example 13   **Determining Whether a Relationship Is a One-to-One Function**

Is the area of a circle a function of its radius? If yes, is the function one-to-one?

Solution   A circle of radius r has a unique area measure given by $A = \pi r^2$, so for any input, r, there is only one output, A. The area is a function of radius r.

If the function is one-to-one, the output value, the area, must correspond to a unique input value, the radius. Any area measure A is given by the formula $A = \pi r^2$. Because areas and radii are positive numbers, there is exactly one solution: $r = \sqrt{\dfrac{A}{\pi}}$ So the area of a circle is a one-to-one function of the circle's radius.

Try It #9

a. Is a balance a function of the bank account number?
b. Is a bank account number a function of the balance?
c. Is a balance a one-to-one function of the bank account number?

Try It #10

a. If each percent grade earned in a course translates to one letter grade, is the letter grade a function of the percent grade?
b. If so, is the function one-to-one?

Using the Vertical Line Test

As we have seen in some examples above, we can represent a function using a graph. Graphs display a great many input-output pairs in a small space. The visual information they provide often makes relationships easier to understand. By convention, graphs are typically constructed with the input values along the horizontal axis and the output values along the vertical axis.

The most common graphs name the input value x and the output value y, and we say y is a function of x, or $y = f(x)$ when the function is named f. The graph of the function is the set of all points (x, y) in the plane that satisfies the equation $y = f(x)$. If the function is defined for only a few input values, then the graph of the function is only a few points, where the x-coordinate of each point is an input value and the y-coordinate of each point is the corresponding output value. For example, the black dots on the graph in **Figure 10** tell us that $f(0) = 2$ and $f(6) = 1$. However, the set of all points (x, y) satisfying $y = f(x)$ is a curve. The curve shown includes $(0, 2)$ and $(6, 1)$ because the curve passes through those points.

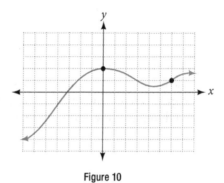

Figure 10

The **vertical line test** can be used to determine whether a graph represents a function. If we can draw any vertical line that intersects a graph more than once, then the graph does not define a function because a function has only one output value for each input value. See **Figure 11**.

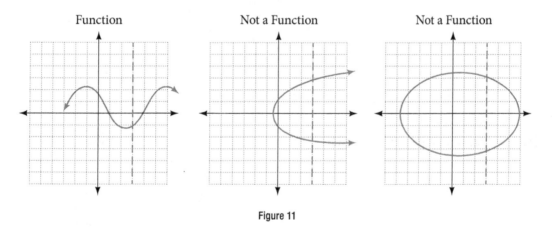

Figure 11

How To...

Given a graph, use the vertical line test to determine if the graph represents a function.

1. Inspect the graph to see if any vertical line drawn would intersect the curve more than once.
2. If there is any such line, determine that the graph does not represent a function.

Example 14   **Applying the Vertical Line Test**

Which of the graphs in **Figure 12** represent(s) a function $y = f(x)$?

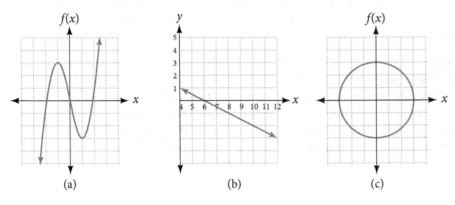

(a)   (b)   (c)

Figure 12

Solution   If any vertical line intersects a graph more than once, the relation represented by the graph is not a function. Notice that any vertical line would pass through only one point of the two graphs shown in parts (a) and (b) of **Figure 12**. From this we can conclude that these two graphs represent functions. The third graph does not represent a function because, at most x-values, a vertical line would intersect the graph at more than one point, as shown in **Figure 13**.

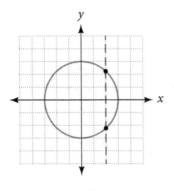

Figure 13

Try It #11

Does the graph in **Figure 14** represent a function?

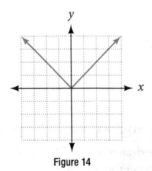

Figure 14

Using the Horizontal Line Test

Once we have determined that a graph defines a function, an easy way to determine if it is a one-to-one function is to use the **horizontal line test**. Draw horizontal lines through the graph. If any horizontal line intersects the graph more than once, then the graph does not represent a one-to-one function.

How To...

Given a graph of a function, use the horizontal line test to determine if the graph represents a one-to-one function.

1. Inspect the graph to see if any horizontal line drawn would intersect the curve more than once.
2. If there is any such line, determine that the function is not one-to-one.

Example 15 **Horizontal Line Test**

Consider the functions shown in **Figure 12(a)** and **Figure 12(b)**. Are either of the functions one-to-one?

Solution   The function in **Figure 12(a)** is not one-to-one. The horizontal line shown in **Figure 15** intersects the graph of the function at two points (and we can even find horizontal lines that intersect it at three points.)

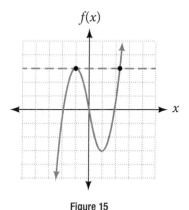

Figure 15

The function in **Figure 12(b)** is one-to-one. Any horizontal line will intersect a diagonal line at most once.

Try It #12

Is the graph shown here one-to-one?

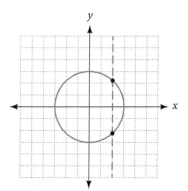

Identifying Basic Toolkit Functions

In this text, we will be exploring functions—the shapes of their graphs, their unique characteristics, their algebraic formulas, and how to solve problems with them. When learning to read, we start with the alphabet. When learning to do arithmetic, we start with numbers. When working with functions, it is similarly helpful to have a base set of building-block elements. We call these our "toolkit functions," which form a set of basic named functions for which we know the graph, formula, and special properties. Some of these functions are programmed to individual buttons on many calculators. For these definitions we will use x as the input variable and $y = f(x)$ as the output variable.

We will see these toolkit functions, combinations of toolkit functions, their graphs, and their transformations frequently throughout this book. It will be very helpful if we can recognize these toolkit functions and their features quickly by name, formula, graph, and basic table properties. The graphs and sample table values are included with each function shown in **Table 13**.

Toolkit Functions		
Name	**Function**	**Graph**
Constant	$f(x) = c$, where c is a constant	$\begin{array}{cc} x & f(x) \\ -2 & 2 \\ 0 & 2 \\ 2 & 2 \end{array}$
Identity	$f(x) = x$	$\begin{array}{cc} x & f(x) \\ -2 & -2 \\ 0 & 0 \\ 2 & 2 \end{array}$
Absolute value	$f(x) = \lvert x \rvert$	$\begin{array}{cc} x & f(x) \\ -2 & 2 \\ 0 & 0 \\ 2 & 2 \end{array}$
Quadratic	$f(x) = x^2$	$\begin{array}{cc} x & f(x) \\ -2 & 4 \\ -1 & 1 \\ 0 & 0 \\ 1 & 1 \\ 2 & 4 \end{array}$
Cubic	$f(x) = x^3$	$\begin{array}{cc} x & f(x) \\ -1 & -1 \\ -0.5 & -0.125 \\ 0 & 0 \\ 0.5 & 0.125 \\ 1 & 1 \end{array}$

Reciprocal	$f(x) = \dfrac{1}{x}$			
Reciprocal squared	$f(x) = \dfrac{1}{x^2}$			
Square root	$f(x) = \sqrt{x}$			
Cube root	$f(x) = \sqrt[3]{x}$			

Reciprocal table:

x	f(x)
−2	−0.5
−1	−1
−0.5	−2
0.5	2
1	1
2	0.5

Reciprocal squared table:

x	f(x)
−2	0.25
−1	1
−0.5	4
0.5	4
1	1
2	0.25

Square root table:

x	f(x)
0	0
1	1
4	2

Cube root table:

x	f(x)
−1	−1
−0.125	−0.5
0	0
0.125	0.5
1	1

Table 13

Access the following online resources for additional instruction and practice with functions.

- Determine if a Relation is a Function (http://openstaxcollege.org/l/relationfunction)
- Vertical Line Test (http://openstaxcollege.org/l/vertlinetest)
- Introduction to Functions (http://openstaxcollege.org/l/introtofunction)
- Vertical Line Test of Graph (http://openstaxcollege.org/l/vertlinegraph)
- One-to-one Functions (http://openstaxcollege.org/l/onetoone)
- Graphs as One-to-one Functions (http://openstaxcollege.org/l/graphonetoone)

1.1   SECTION EXERCISES

VERBAL

1. What is the difference between a relation and a function?

2. What is the difference between the input and the output of a function?

3. Why does the vertical line test tell us whether the graph of a relation represents a function?

4. How can you determine if a relation is a one-to-one function?

5. Why does the horizontal line test tell us whether the graph of a function is one-to-one?

ALGEBRAIC

For the following exercises, determine whether the relation represents a function.

6. $\{(a, b), (c, d), (a, c)\}$

7. $\{(a, b),(b, c),(c, c)\}$

For the following exercises, determine whether the relation represents y as a function of x.

8. $5x + 2y = 10$

9. $y = x^2$

10. $x = y^2$

11. $3x^2 + y = 14$

12. $2x + y^2 = 6$

13. $y = -2x^2 + 40x$

14. $y = \dfrac{1}{x}$

15. $x = \dfrac{3y + 5}{7y - 1}$

16. $x = \sqrt{1 - y^2}$

17. $y = \dfrac{3x + 5}{7x - 1}$

18. $x^2 + y^2 = 9$

19. $2xy = 1$

20. $x = y^3$

21. $y = x^3$

22. $y = \sqrt{1 - x^2}$

23. $x = \pm\sqrt{1 - y}$

24. $y = \pm\sqrt{1 - x}$

25. $y^2 = x^2$

26. $y^3 = x^2$

For the following exercises, evaluate the function f at the indicated values $f(-3), f(2), f(-a), -f(a), f(a + h)$.

27. $f(x) = 2x - 5$

28. $f(x) = -5x^2 + 2x - 1$

29. $f(x) = \sqrt{2 - x} + 5$

30. $f(x) = \dfrac{6x - 1}{5x + 2}$

31. $f(x) = |x - 1| - |x + 1|$

32. Given the function $g(x) = 5 - x^2$, evaluate $\dfrac{g(x + h) - g(x)}{h}, h \neq 0$

33. Given the function $g(x) = x^2 + 2x$, evaluate $\dfrac{g(x) - g(a)}{x - a}, \ x \neq a$

34. Given the function $k(t) = 2t - 1$:
    a. Evaluate $k(2)$.
    b. Solve $k(t) = 7$.

35. Given the function $f(x) = 8 - 3x$:
    a. Evaluate $f(-2)$.
    b. Solve $f(x) = -1$.

36. Given the function $p(c) = c^2 + c$:
    a. Evaluate $p(-3)$.
    b. Solve $p(c) = 2$.

37. Given the function $f(x) = x^2 - 3x$
    a. Evaluate $f(5)$.
    b. Solve $f(x) = 4$

38. Given the function $f(x) = \sqrt{x + 2}$:
    a. Evaluate $f(7)$.
    b. Solve $f(x) = 4$

39. Consider the relationship $3r + 2t = 18$.
    a. Write the relationship as a function $r = f(t)$.
    b. Evaluate $f(-3)$.
    c. Solve $f(t) = 2$.

GRAPHICAL

For the following exercises, use the vertical line test to determine which graphs show relations that are functions.

40.

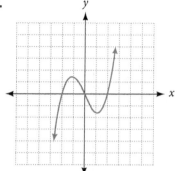

41.

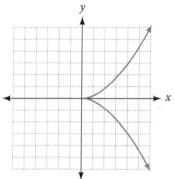

42.

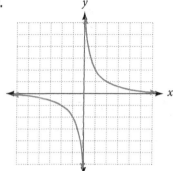

43.

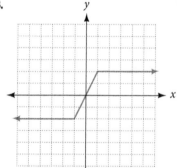

44.

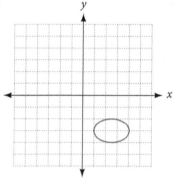

45.

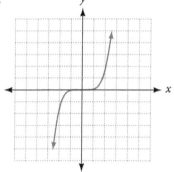

46.

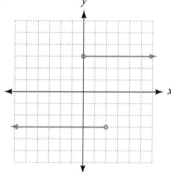

47.

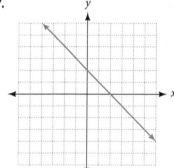

48.

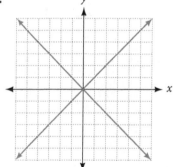

49.

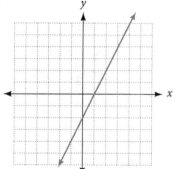

50.

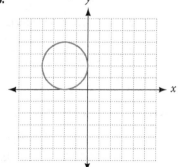

51.

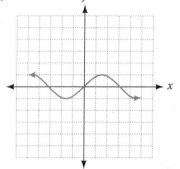

52. Given the following graph
   a. Evaluate $f(-1)$.
   b. Solve for $f(x) = 3$.

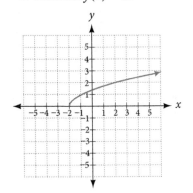

53. Given the following graph
   a. Evaluate $f(0)$.
   b. Solve for $f(x) = -3$.

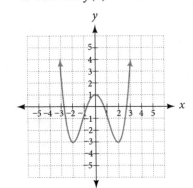

54. Given the following graph
   a. Evaluate $f(4)$.
   b. Solve for $f(x) = 1$.

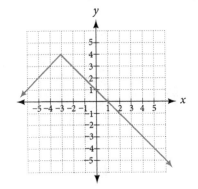

For the following exercises, determine if the given graph is a one-to-one function.

55.

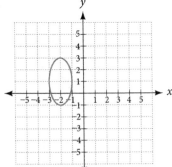

56.

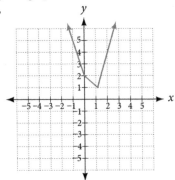

57.

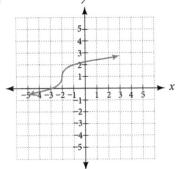

58.

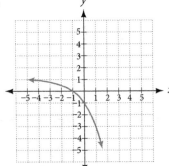

59.

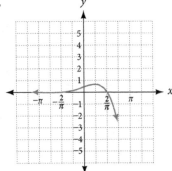

NUMERIC

For the following exercises, determine whether the relation represents a function.

60. $\{(-1, -1), (-2, -2), (-3, -3)\}$ **61.** $\{(3, 4), (4, 5), (5, 6)\}$ **62.** $\{(2, 5), (7, 11), (15, 8), (7, 9)\}$

For the following exercises, determine if the relation represented in table form represents y as a function of x.

63.

x	5	10	15
y	3	8	14

64.

x	5	10	15
y	3	8	8

65.

x	5	10	10
y	3	8	14

For the following exercises, use the function f represented in **Table 14** below.

x	0	1	2	3	4	5	6	7	8	9
$f(x)$	74	28	1	53	56	3	36	45	14	47

Table 14

66. Evaluate $f(3)$.   **67.** Solve $f(x) = 1$

For the following exercises, evaluate the function f at the values $f(-2), f(-1), f(0), f(1),$ and $f(2)$.

68. $f(x) = 4 - 2x$

69. $f(x) = 8 - 3x$

70. $f(x) = 8x^2 - 7x + 3$

71. $f(x) = 3 + \sqrt{x + 3}$

72. $f(x) = \dfrac{x - 2}{x + 3}$

73. $f(x) = 3^x$

For the following exercises, evaluate the expressions, given functions f, g, and h:

$$f(x) = 3x - 2 \qquad g(x) = 5 - x^2 \qquad h(x) = -2x^2 + 3x - 1$$

74. $3f(1) - 4g(-2)$

75. $f\left(\dfrac{7}{3}\right) - h(-2)$

TECHNOLOGY

For the following exercises, graph $y = x^2$ on the given viewing window. Determine the corresponding range for each viewing window. Show each graph.

76. $[-0.1, 0.1]$

77. $[-10, 10]$

78. $[-100, 100]$

For the following exercises, graph $y = x^3$ on the given viewing window. Determine the corresponding range for each viewing window. Show each graph.

79. $[-0.1, 0.1]$

80. $[-10, 10]$

81. $[-100, 100]$

For the following exercises, graph $y = \sqrt{x}$ on the given viewing window. Determine the corresponding range for each viewing window. Show each graph.

82. $[0, 0.01]$

83. $[0, 100]$

84. $[0, 10,000]$

For the following exercises, graph $y = \sqrt[3]{x}$ on the given viewing window. Determine the corresponding range for each viewing window. Show each graph.

85. $[-0.001, 0.001]$

86. $[-1,000, 1,000]$

87. $[-1,000,000, 1,000,000]$

REAL-WORLD APPLICATIONS

88. The amount of garbage, G, produced by a city with population p is given by $G = f(p)$. G is measured in tons per week, and p is measured in thousands of people.

   a. The town of Tola has a population of 40,000 and produces 13 tons of garbage each week. Express this information in terms of the function f.

   b. Explain the meaning of the statement $f(5) = 2$.

89. The number of cubic yards of dirt, D, needed to cover a garden with area a square feet is given by $D = g(a)$.

   a. A garden with area 5,000 ft² requires 50 yd³ of dirt. Express this information in terms of the function g.

   b. Explain the meaning of the statement $g(100) = 1$.

90. Let $f(t)$ be the number of ducks in a lake t years after 1990. Explain the meaning of each statement:

   a. $f(5) = 30$

   b. $f(10) = 40$

91. Let $h(t)$ be the height above ground, in feet, of a rocket t seconds after launching. Explain the meaning of each statement:

   a. $h(1) = 200$

   b. $h(2) = 350$

92. Show that the function $f(x) = 3(x - 5)^2 + 7$ is <u>not</u> one-to-one.

LEARNING OBJECTIVES

In this section, you will:

- Find the domain of a function defined by an equation.
- Graph piecewise-defined functions.

1.2   DOMAIN AND RANGE

If you're in the mood for a scary movie, you may want to check out one of the five most popular horror movies of all time—*I am Legend*, *Hannibal*, *The Ring*, *The Grudge*, and *The Conjuring*. **Figure 1** shows the amount, in dollars, each of those movies grossed when they were released as well as the ticket sales for horror movies in general by year. Notice that we can use the data to create a function of the amount each movie earned or the total ticket sales for all horror movies by year. In creating various functions using the data, we can identify different independent and dependent variables, and we can analyze the data and the functions to determine the domain and range. In this section, we will investigate methods for determining the domain and range of functions such as these.

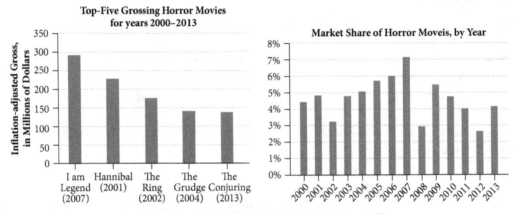

Figure 1 Based on data compiled by www.the-numbers.com.[3]

Finding the Domain of a Function Defined by an Equation

In **Functions and Function Notation**, we were introduced to the concepts of domain and range. In this section, we will practice determining domains and ranges for specific functions. Keep in mind that, in determining domains and ranges, we need to consider what is physically possible or meaningful in real-world examples, such as tickets sales and year in the horror movie example above. We also need to consider what is mathematically permitted. For example, we cannot include any input value that leads us to take an even root of a negative number if the domain and range consist of real numbers. Or in a function expressed as a formula, we cannot include any input value in the domain that would lead us to divide by 0.

We can visualize the domain as a "holding area" that contains "raw materials" for a "function machine" and the range as another "holding area" for the machine's products. See **Figure 2**.

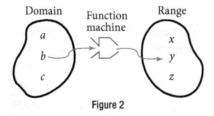

Figure 2

We can write the domain and range in **interval notation**, which uses values within brackets to describe a set of numbers. In interval notation, we use a square bracket [when the set includes the endpoint and a parenthesis (to indicate that the endpoint is either not included or the interval is unbounded. For example, if a person has $100 to spend, he or she would need to express the interval that is more than 0 and less than or equal to 100 and write (0, 100]. We will discuss interval notation in greater detail later.

3 The Numbers: Where Data and the Movie Business Meet. "Box Office History for Horror Movies." http://www.the-numbers.com/market/genre/Horror. Accessed 3/24/2014

Let's turn our attention to finding the domain of a function whose equation is provided. Oftentimes, finding the domain of such functions involves remembering three different forms. First, if the function has no denominator or an even root, consider whether the domain could be all real numbers. Second, if there is a denominator in the function's equation, exclude values in the domain that force the denominator to be zero. Third, if there is an even root, consider excluding values that would make the radicand negative.

Before we begin, let us review the conventions of interval notation:

- The smallest term from the interval is written first.
- The largest term in the interval is written second, following a comma.
- Parentheses, (or), are used to signify that an endpoint is not included, called exclusive.
- Brackets, [or], are used to indicate that an endpoint is included, called inclusive.

See **Figure 3** for a summary of interval notation.

Inequality	Interval Notation	Graph on Number Line	Description
$x > a$	(a, ∞)		x is greater than a
$x < a$	$(-\infty, a)$		x is less than a
$x \geq a$	$[a, \infty)$		x is greater than or equal to a
$x \leq a$	$(-\infty, a]$		x is less than or equal to a
$a < x < b$	(a, b)		x is strictly between a and b
$a \leq x < b$	$[a, b)$		x is between a and b, to include a
$a < x \leq b$	$(a, b]$		x is between a and b, to include b
$a \leq x \leq b$	$[a, b]$		x is between a and b, to include a and b

Figure 3

Example 1   Finding the Domain of a Function as a Set of Ordered Pairs

Find the domain of the following function: $\{(2, 10), (3, 10), (4, 20), (5, 30), (6, 40)\}$.

Solution   First identify the input values. The input value is the first coordinate in an ordered pair. There are no restrictions, as the ordered pairs are simply listed. The domain is the set of the first coordinates of the ordered pairs.

$$\{2, 3, 4, 5, 6\}$$

Try It #1

Find the domain of the function: $\{(-5, 4), (0, 0), (5, -4), (10, -8), (15, -12)\}$

How To...

Given a function written in equation form, find the domain.

1. Identify the input values.
2. Identify any restrictions on the input and exclude those values from the domain.
3. Write the domain in interval form, if possible.

Example 2   **Finding the Domain of a Function**

Find the domain of the function $f(x) = x^2 - 1$.

Solution   The input value, shown by the variable x in the equation, is squared and then the result is lowered by one. Any real number may be squared and then be lowered by one, so there are no restrictions on the domain of this function. The domain is the set of real numbers.

In interval form, the domain of f is $(-\infty, \infty)$.

Try It #2

Find the domain of the function: $f(x) = 5 - x + x^3$.

How To...

Given a function written in an equation form that includes a fraction, find the domain.

1. Identify the input values.
2. Identify any restrictions on the input. If there is a denominator in the function's formula, set the denominator equal to zero and solve for x. If the function's formula contains an even root, set the radicand greater than or equal to 0, and then solve.
3. Write the domain in interval form, making sure to exclude any restricted values from the domain.

Example 3   **Finding the Domain of a Function Involving a Denominator**

Find the domain of the function $f(x) = \dfrac{x+1}{2-x}$.

Solution   When there is a denominator, we want to include only values of the input that do not force the denominator to be zero. So, we will set the denominator equal to 0 and solve for x.

$$2 - x = 0$$
$$-x = -2$$
$$x = 2$$

Now, we will exclude 2 from the domain. The answers are all real numbers where $x < 2$ or $x > 2$. We can use a symbol known as the union, $\cup$, to combine the two sets. In interval notation, we write the solution: $(-\infty, 2) \cup (2, \infty)$.

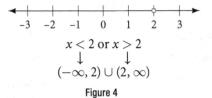

Figure 4

In interval form, the domain of f is $(-\infty, 2) \cup (2, \infty)$.

Try It #3

Find the domain of the function: $f(x) = \dfrac{1+4x}{2x-1}$.

How To...

Given a function written in equation form including an even root, find the domain.

1. Identify the input values.
2. Since there is an even root, exclude any real numbers that result in a negative number in the radicand. Set the radicand greater than or equal to zero and solve for x.
3. The solution(s) are the domain of the function. If possible, write the answer in interval form.

Example 4   **Finding the Domain of a Function with an Even Root**

Find the domain of the function $f(x) = \sqrt{7 - x}$.

Solution   When there is an even root in the formula, we exclude any real numbers that result in a negative number in the radicand.

Set the radicand greater than or equal to zero and solve for x.

$$7 - x \geq 0$$
$$-x \geq -7$$
$$x \leq 7$$

Now, we will exclude any number greater than 7 from the domain. The answers are all real numbers less than or equal to 7, or $(-\infty, 7]$.

Try It #4

Find the domain of the function $f(x) = \sqrt{5 + 2x}$.

Q & A...

Can there be functions in which the domain and range do not intersect at all?

Yes. For example, the function $f(x) = -\dfrac{1}{\sqrt{x}}$ has the set of all positive real numbers as its domain but the set of all negative real numbers as its range. As a more extreme example, a function's inputs and outputs can be completely different categories (for example, names of weekdays as inputs and numbers as outputs, as on an attendance chart), in such cases the domain and range have no elements in common.

Using Notations to Specify Domain and Range

In the previous examples, we used inequalities and lists to describe the domain of functions. We can also use inequalities, or other statements that might define sets of values or data, to describe the behavior of the variable in **set-builder notation**. For example, $\{x \mid 10 \leq x < 30\}$ describes the behavior of x in set-builder notation. The braces $\{\ \}$ are read as "the set of," and the vertical bar | is read as "such that," so we would read $\{x \mid 10 \leq x < 30\}$ as "the set of x-values such that 10 is less than or equal to x, and x is less than 30."

Figure 5 compares inequality notation, set-builder notation, and interval notation.

	Inequality Notation	Set-builder Notation	Interval Notation
	$5 < h \leq 10$	$\{h \mid 5 < h \leq 10\}$	$(5, 10]$
	$5 \leq h < 10$	$\{h \mid 5 \leq h < 10\}$	$[5, 10)$
	$5 < h < 10$	$\{h \mid 5 < h < 10\}$	$(5, 10)$
	$h < 10$	$\{h \mid h < 10\}$	$(-\infty, 10)$
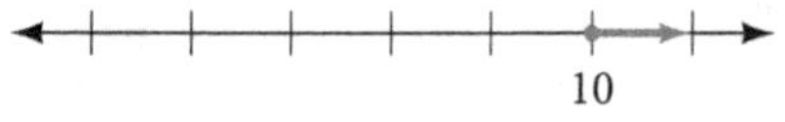	$h \geq 10$	$\{h \mid h \geq 10\}$	$[10, \infty)$
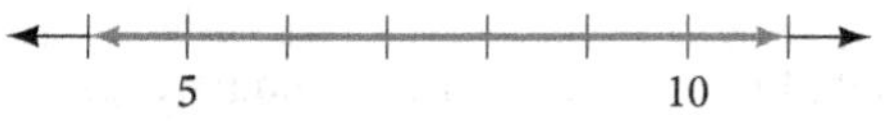	All real numbers	$\mathbb{R}$	$(-\infty, \infty)$

Figure 5

To combine two intervals using inequality notation or set-builder notation, we use the word "or." As we saw in earlier examples, we use the union symbol, ∪, to combine two unconnected intervals. For example, the union of the sets {2, 3, 5} and {4, 6} is the set {2, 3, 4, 5, 6}. It is the set of all elements that belong to one *or* the other (or both) of the original two sets. For sets with a finite number of elements like these, the elements do not have to be listed in ascending order of numerical value. If the original two sets have some elements in common, those elements should be listed only once in the union set. For sets of real numbers on intervals, another example of a union is

$$\{x \mid |x| \geq 3\} = (-\infty, -3] \cup [3, \infty)$$

---

set-builder notation and *interval notation*

Set-builder notation is a method of specifying a set of elements that satisfy a certain condition. It takes the form {x | statement about x} which is read as, "the set of all x such that the statement about x is true." For example,

$$\{x \mid 4 < x \leq 12\}$$

Interval notation is a way of describing sets that include all real numbers between a lower limit that may or may not be included and an upper limit that may or may not be included. The endpoint values are listed between brackets or parentheses. A square bracket indicates inclusion in the set, and a parenthesis indicates exclusion from the set. For example,

$$(4, 12]$$

How To...

Given a line graph, describe the set of values using interval notation.

1. Identify the intervals to be included in the set by determining where the heavy line overlays the real line.
2. At the left end of each interval, use [with each end value to be included in the set (solid dot) or (for each excluded end value (open dot).
3. At the right end of each interval, use] with each end value to be included in the set (filled dot) or) for each excluded end value (open dot).
4. Use the union symbol ∪ to combine all intervals into one set.

Example 5   **Describing Sets on the Real-Number Line**

Describe the intervals of values shown in **Figure 6** using inequality notation, set-builder notation, and interval notation.

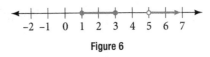

Figure 6

Solution   To describe the values, x, included in the intervals shown, we would say, "x is a real number greater than or equal to 1 and less than or equal to 3, or a real number greater than 5."

Inequality	$1 \leq x \leq 3$ or $x > 5$
Set-builder notation	$\{x \mid 1 \leq x \leq 3 \text{ or } x > 5\}$
Interval notation	$[1, 3] \cup (5, \infty)$

Remember that, when writing or reading interval notation, using a square bracket means the boundary is included in the set. Using a parenthesis means the boundary is not included in the set.

Try It #5

Given this figure, specify the graphed set in

a. words

b. set-builder notation

c. interval notation

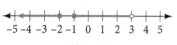

Figure 7

Finding Domain and Range from Graphs

Another way to identify the domain and range of functions is by using graphs. Because the domain refers to the set of possible input values, the domain of a graph consists of all the input values shown on the *x*-axis. The range is the set of possible output values, which are shown on the *y*-axis. Keep in mind that if the graph continues beyond the portion of the graph we can see, the domain and range may be greater than the visible values. See **Figure 8**.

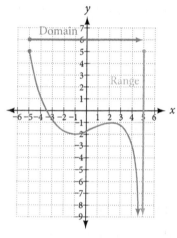

Figure 8

We can observe that the graph extends horizontally from -5 to the right without bound, so the domain is $[-5, \infty)$. The vertical extent of the graph is all range values 5 and below, so the range is $(-\infty, 5]$. Note that the domain and range are always written from smaller to larger values, or from left to right for domain, and from the bottom of the graph to the top of the graph for range.

Example 6   **Finding Domain and Range from a Graph**

Find the domain and range of the function *f* whose graph is shown in **Figure 9**.

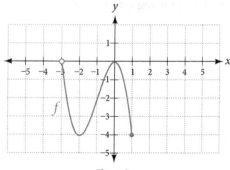

Figure 9

Solution   We can observe that the horizontal extent of the graph is −3 to 1, so the domain of *f* is (−3, 1].

The vertical extent of the graph is 0 to −4, so the range is [−4, 0]. See **Figure 10**.

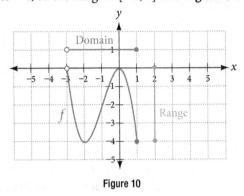

Figure 10

Example 7   **Finding Domain and Range from a Graph of Oil Production**

Find the domain and range of the function *f* whose graph is shown in **Figure 11**.

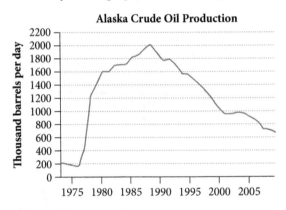

Figure 11   (credit: modification of work by the U.S. Energy Information Administration) [4]

Solution   The input quantity along the horizontal axis is "years," which we represent with the variable *t* for time. The output quantity is "thousands of barrels of oil per day," which we represent with the variable *b* for barrels. The graph may continue to the left and right beyond what is viewed, but based on the portion of the graph that is visible, we can determine the domain as $1973 \leq t \leq 2008$ and the range as approximately $180 \leq b \leq 2010$.

In interval notation, the domain is [1973, 2008], and the range is about [180, 2010]. For the domain and the range, we approximate the smallest and largest values since they do not fall exactly on the grid lines.

Try It #6

Given **Figure 12**, identify the domain and range using interval notation.

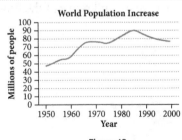

Figure 12

Q & A...

Can a function's domain and range be the same?

Yes. For example, the domain and range of the cube root function are both the set of all real numbers.

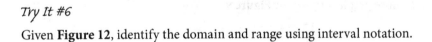

4   http://www.eia.gov/dnav/pet/hist/LeafHandler.ashx?n=PET&s=MCRFPAK2&f=A.

Finding Domains and Ranges of the Toolkit Functions

We will now return to our set of toolkit functions to determine the domain and range of each.

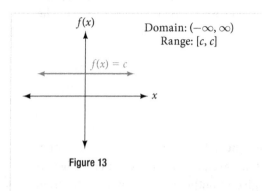

Figure 13

Domain: $(-\infty, \infty)$
Range: $[c, c]$

For the **constant function** $f(x) = c$, the domain consists of all real numbers; there are no restrictions on the input. The only output value is the constant c, so the range is the set $\{c\}$ that contains this single element. In interval notation, this is written as $[c, c]$, the interval that both begins and ends with c.

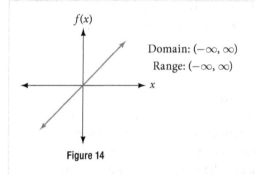

Figure 14

Domain: $(-\infty, \infty)$
Range: $(-\infty, \infty)$

For the **identity function** $f(x) = x$, there is no restriction on x. Both the domain and range are the set of all real numbers.

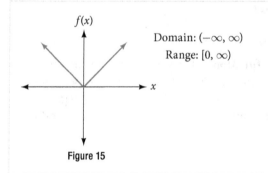

Figure 15

Domain: $(-\infty, \infty)$
Range: $[0, \infty)$

For the **absolute value function** $f(x) = |x|$, there is no restriction on x. However, because absolute value is defined as a distance from 0, the output can only be greater than or equal to 0.

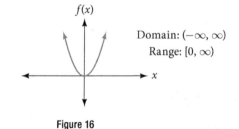

Figure 16

Domain: $(-\infty, \infty)$
Range: $[0, \infty)$

For the **quadratic function** $f(x) = x^2$, the domain is all real numbers since the horizontal extent of the graph is the whole real number line. Because the graph does not include any negative values for the range, the range is only nonnegative real numbers.

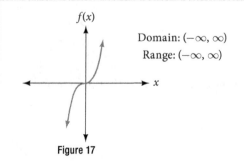

Figure 17

Domain: $(-\infty, \infty)$
Range: $(-\infty, \infty)$

For the **cubic function** $f(x) = x^3$, the domain is all real numbers because the horizontal extent of the graph is the whole real number line. The same applies to the vertical extent of the graph, so the domain and range include all real numbers.

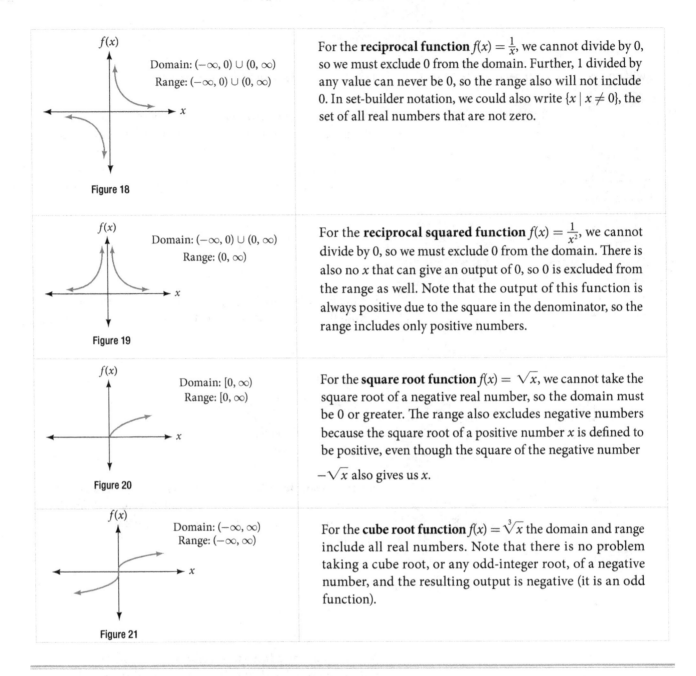

For the **reciprocal function** $f(x) = \frac{1}{x}$, we cannot divide by 0, so we must exclude 0 from the domain. Further, 1 divided by any value can never be 0, so the range also will not include 0. In set-builder notation, we could also write $\{x \mid x \neq 0\}$, the set of all real numbers that are not zero.

Domain: $(-\infty, 0) \cup (0, \infty)$
Range: $(-\infty, 0) \cup (0, \infty)$

Figure 18

For the **reciprocal squared function** $f(x) = \frac{1}{x^2}$, we cannot divide by 0, so we must exclude 0 from the domain. There is also no x that can give an output of 0, so 0 is excluded from the range as well. Note that the output of this function is always positive due to the square in the denominator, so the range includes only positive numbers.

Domain: $(-\infty, 0) \cup (0, \infty)$
Range: $(0, \infty)$

Figure 19

For the **square root function** $f(x) = \sqrt{x}$, we cannot take the square root of a negative real number, so the domain must be 0 or greater. The range also excludes negative numbers because the square root of a positive number x is defined to be positive, even though the square of the negative number $-\sqrt{x}$ also gives us x.

Domain: $[0, \infty)$
Range: $[0, \infty)$

Figure 20

For the **cube root function** $f(x) = \sqrt[3]{x}$ the domain and range include all real numbers. Note that there is no problem taking a cube root, or any odd-integer root, of a negative number, and the resulting output is negative (it is an odd function).

Domain: $(-\infty, \infty)$
Range: $(-\infty, \infty)$

Figure 21

How To...

Given the formula for a function, determine the domain and range.

1. Exclude from the domain any input values that result in division by zero.
2. Exclude from the domain any input values that have nonreal (or undefined) number outputs.
3. Use the valid input values to determine the range of the output values.
4. Look at the function graph and table values to confirm the actual function behavior.

Example 8   **Finding the Domain and Range Using Toolkit Functions**

Find the domain and range of $f(x) = 2x^3 - x$.

Solution   There are no restrictions on the domain, as any real number may be cubed and then subtracted from the result. The domain is $(-\infty, \infty)$ and the range is also $(-\infty, \infty)$.

Example 9   **Finding the Domain and Range**

Find the domain and range of $f(x) = \dfrac{2}{x+1}$.

Solution   We cannot evaluate the function at -1 because division by zero is undefined. The domain is $(-\infty, -1) \cup (-1, \infty)$. Because the function is never zero, we exclude 0 from the range. The range is $(-\infty, 0) \cup (0, \infty)$.

Example 10   **Finding the Domain and Range**

Find the domain and range of $f(x) = 2\sqrt{x+4}$.

Solution   We cannot take the square root of a negative number, so the value inside the radical must be nonnegative.

$$x + 4 \geq 0 \text{ when } x \geq -4$$

The domain of $f(x)$ is $[-4, \infty)$.

We then find the range. We know that $f(-4) = 0$, and the function value increases as x increases without any upper limit. We conclude that the range of f is $[0, \infty)$.

Analysis   **Figure 22** *represents the function f.*

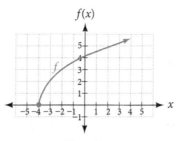

Figure 22

Try It #7

Find the domain and range of $f(x) = -\sqrt{2-x}$.

Graphing Piecewise-Defined Functions

Sometimes, we come across a function that requires more than one formula in order to obtain the given output. For example, in the toolkit functions, we introduced the absolute value function $f(x) = |x|$. With a domain of all real numbers and a range of values greater than or equal to 0, absolute value can be defined as the magnitude, or modulus, of a real number value regardless of sign. It is the distance from 0 on the number line. All of these definitions require the output to be greater than or equal to 0.

If we input 0, or a positive value, the output is the same as the input.

$$f(x) = x \text{ if } x \geq 0$$

If we input a negative value, the output is the opposite of the input.

$$f(x) = -x \text{ if } x < 0$$

Because this requires two different processes or pieces, the absolute value function is an example of a piecewise function. A **piecewise function** is a function in which more than one formula is used to define the output over different pieces of the domain.

We use piecewise functions to describe situations in which a rule or relationship changes as the input value crosses certain "boundaries." For example, we often encounter situations in business for which the cost per piece of a certain item is discounted once the number ordered exceeds a certain value. Tax brackets are another real-world example of piecewise functions. For example, consider a simple tax system in which incomes up to $10,000 are taxed at 10%, and any additional income is taxed at 20%. The tax on a total income S would be $0.1S$ if $S \leq \$10,000$ and $\$1000 + 0.2(S - \$10,000)$ if $S > \$10,000$.

> **piecewise function**
> A piecewise function is a function in which more than one formula is used to define the output. Each formula has its own domain, and the domain of the function is the union of all these smaller domains. We notate this idea like this:
>
> $$f(x) = \begin{cases} \text{formula 1} & \text{if } x \text{ is in domain 1} \\ \text{formula 2} & \text{if } x \text{ is in domain 2} \\ \text{formula 3} & \text{if } x \text{ is in domain 3} \end{cases}$$
>
> In piecewise notation, the absolute value function is
>
> $$|x| = \begin{cases} x & \text{if } x \geq 0 \\ -x & \text{if } x < 0 \end{cases}$$

How To…

Given a piecewise function, write the formula and identify the domain for each interval.

1. Identify the intervals for which different rules apply.
2. Determine formulas that describe how to calculate an output from an input in each interval.
3. Use braces and if-statements to write the function.

Example 11   **Writing a Piecewise Function**

A museum charges $5 per person for a guided tour with a group of 1 to 9 people or a fixed $50 fee for a group of 10 or more people. Write a function relating the number of people, *n*, to the cost, *C*.

Solution   Two different formulas will be needed. For *n*-values under 10, $C = 5n$. For values of *n* that are 10 or greater, $C = 50$.

$$C(n) = \begin{cases} 5n & \text{if } 0 < n < 10 \\ 50 & \text{if } n \geq 10 \end{cases}$$

Analysis   *The function is represented in* **Figure 23**. *The graph is a diagonal line from n = 0 to n = 10 and a constant after that. In this example, the two formulas agree at the meeting point where n = 10, but not all piecewise functions have this property.*

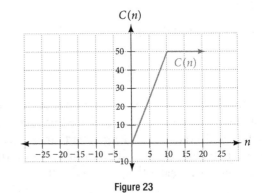

Figure 23

Example 12   **Working with a Piecewise Function**

A cell phone company uses the function below to determine the cost, *C*, in dollars for *g* gigabytes of data transfer.

$$C(g) = \begin{cases} 25 & \text{if } 0 < g < 2 \\ 25 + 10(g - 2) & \text{if } g \geq 2 \end{cases}$$

Find the cost of using 1.5 gigabytes of data and the cost of using 4 gigabytes of data.

Solution   To find the cost of using 1.5 gigabytes of data, $C(1.5)$, we first look to see which part of the domain our input falls in. Because 1.5 is less than 2, we use the first formula.

$$C(1.5) = \$25$$

To find the cost of using 4 gigabytes of data, $C(4)$, we see that our input of 4 is greater than 2, so we use the second formula.

$$C(4) = 25 + 10(4 - 2) = \$45$$

Analysis The function is represented in **Figure 24**. We can see where the function changes from a constant to a shifted and stretched identity at $g = 2$. We plot the graphs for the different formulas on a common set of axes, making sure each formula is applied on its proper domain.

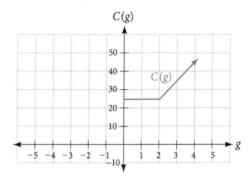

Figure 24

How To...

Given a piecewise function, sketch a graph.

1. Indicate on the x-axis the boundaries defined by the intervals on each piece of the domain.

2. For each piece of the domain, graph on that interval using the corresponding equation pertaining to that piece. Do not graph two functions over one interval because it would violate the criteria of a function.

Example 13 **Graphing a Piecewise Function**

Sketch a graph of the function.

$$f(x) = \begin{cases} x^2 & \text{if} & x \le 1 \\ 3 & \text{if} & 1 < x \le 2 \\ x & \text{if} & x > 2 \end{cases}$$

Solution Each of the component functions is from our library of toolkit functions, so we know their shapes. We can imagine graphing each function and then limiting the graph to the indicated domain. At the endpoints of the domain, we draw open circles to indicate where the endpoint is not included because of a less-than or greater-than inequality; we draw a closed circle where the endpoint is included because of a less-than-or-equal-to or greater-than-or-equal-to inequality.

Figure 25 shows the three components of the piecewise function graphed on separate coordinate systems.

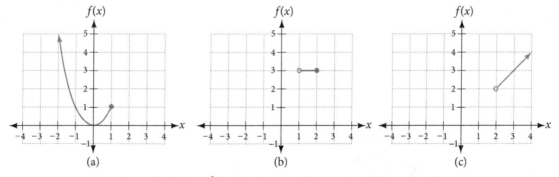

Figure 25 (a) $f(x) = x^2$ if $x \le 1$; (b) $f(x) = 3$ if $1 < x \le 2$; (c) $f(x) = x$ if $x > 2$

Now that we have sketched each piece individually, we combine them in the same coordinate plane. See **Figure 26**.

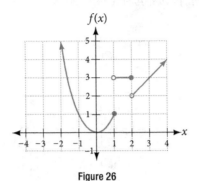

Figure 26

Analysis   Note that the graph does pass the vertical line test even at $x = 1$ and $x = 2$ because the points $(1, 3)$ and $(2, 2)$ are not part of the graph of the function, though $(1, 1)$ and $(2, 3)$ are.

Try It #8

Graph the following piecewise function.

$$f(x) = \begin{cases} x^3 & \text{if} & x < -1 \\ -2 & \text{if} & -1 < x < 4 \\ \sqrt{x} & \text{if} & x > 4 \end{cases}$$

Q & A...

Can more than one formula from a piecewise function be applied to a value in the domain?

No. Each value corresponds to one equation in a piecewise formula.

Access these online resources for additional instruction and practice with domain and range.

- Domain and Range of Square Root Functions (http://openstaxcollege.org/l/domainsqroot)
- Determining Domain and Range (http://openstaxcollege.org/l/determinedomain)
- Find Domain and Range Given the Graph (http://openstaxcollege.org/l/drgraph)
- Find Domain and Range Given a Table (http://openstaxcollege.org/l/drtable)
- Find Domain and Range Given Points on a Coordinate Plane (http://openstaxcollege.org/l/drcoordinate)

1.2 SECTION EXERCISES

VERBAL

1. Why does the domain differ for different functions?

2. How do we determine the domain of a function defined by an equation?

3. Explain why the domain of $f(x) = \sqrt[3]{x}$ is different from the domain of $f(x) = \sqrt{x}$.

4. When describing sets of numbers using interval notation, when do you use a parenthesis and when do you use a bracket?

5. How do you graph a piecewise function?

ALGEBRAIC

For the following exercises, find the domain of each function using interval notation.

6. $f(x) = -2x(x - 1)(x - 2)$

7. $f(x) = 5 - 2x^2$

8. $f(x) = 3\sqrt{x - 2}$

9. $f(x) = 3 - \sqrt{6 - 2x}$

10. $f(x) = \sqrt{4 - 3x}$

11. $f(x) = \sqrt{x^2 + 4}$

12. $f(x) = \sqrt[3]{1 - 2x}$

13. $f(x) = \sqrt[3]{x - 1}$

14. $f(x) = \dfrac{9}{x - 6}$

15. $f(x) = \dfrac{3x + 1}{4x + 2}$

16. $f(x) = \dfrac{\sqrt{x + 4}}{x - 4}$

17. $f(x) = \dfrac{x - 3}{x^2 + 9x - 22}$

18. $f(x) = \dfrac{1}{x^2 - x - 6}$

19. $f(x) = \dfrac{2x^3 - 250}{x^2 - 2x - 15}$

20. $f(x) = \dfrac{5}{\sqrt{x - 3}}$

21. $f(x) = \dfrac{2x + 1}{\sqrt{5 - x}}$

22. $f(x) = \dfrac{\sqrt{x - 4}}{\sqrt{x - 6}}$

23. $f(x) = \dfrac{\sqrt{x - 6}}{\sqrt{x - 4}}$

24. $f(x) = \dfrac{x}{x}$

25. $f(x) = \dfrac{x^2 - 9x}{x^2 - 81}$

26. Find the domain of the function $f(x) = \sqrt{2x^3 - 50x}$ by:

  a. using algebra.

  b. graphing the function in the radicand and determining intervals on the x-axis for which the radicand is nonnegative.

GRAPHICAL

For the following exercises, write the domain and range of each function using interval notation.

27.

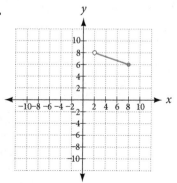

28.

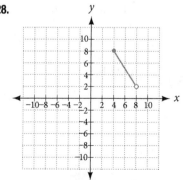

29.

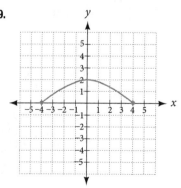

30.

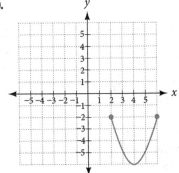

31.

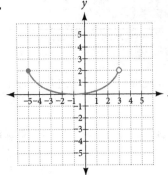

32.

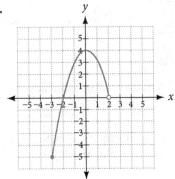

33.

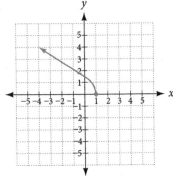

34.

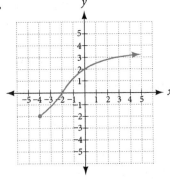

35.

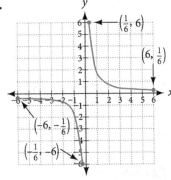

36.

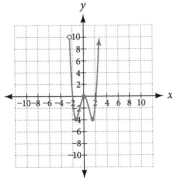

37.

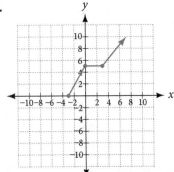

For the following exercises, sketch a graph of the piecewise function. Write the domain in interval notation.

38. $f(x) = \begin{cases} x+1 & \text{if } x < -2 \\ -2x - 3 & \text{if } x \geq -2 \end{cases}$

39. $f(x) = \begin{cases} 2x - 1 & \text{if } x < 1 \\ 1 + x & \text{if } x \geq 1 \end{cases}$

40. $f(x) = \begin{cases} x+1 & \text{if } x < 0 \\ x - 1 & \text{if } x > 0 \end{cases}$

41. $f(x) = \begin{cases} 3 & \text{if } x < 0 \\ \sqrt{x} & \text{if } x \geq 0 \end{cases}$

42. $f(x) = \begin{cases} x^2 & \text{if } x < 0 \\ 1 - x & \text{if } x > 0 \end{cases}$

43. $f(x) = \begin{cases} x^2 & \text{if } x < 0 \\ x + 2 & \text{if } x \geq 0 \end{cases}$

44. $f(x) = \begin{cases} x + 1 & \text{if } x < 1 \\ x^3 & \text{if } x \geq 1 \end{cases}$

45. $f(x) = \begin{cases} |x| & \text{if } x < 2 \\ 1 & \text{if } x \geq 2 \end{cases}$

NUMERIC

For the following exercises, given each function f, evaluate $f(-3), f(-2), f(-1)$, and $f(0)$.

46. $f(x) = \begin{cases} x+1 & \text{if } x < -2 \\ -2x-3 & \text{if } x \geq -2 \end{cases}$

47. $f(x) = \begin{cases} 1 & \text{if } x \leq -3 \\ 0 & \text{if } x > -3 \end{cases}$

48. $f(x) = \begin{cases} -2x^2+3 & \text{if } x \leq -1 \\ 5x-7 & \text{if } x > -1 \end{cases}$

For the following exercises, given each function f, evaluate $f(-1), f(0), f(2)$, and $f(4)$.

49. $f(x) = \begin{cases} 7x+3 & \text{if } x < 0 \\ 7x+6 & \text{if } x \geq 0 \end{cases}$

50. $f(x) = \begin{cases} x^2-2 & \text{if } x < 2 \\ 4+|x-5| & \text{if } x \geq 2 \end{cases}$

51. $f(x) = \begin{cases} 5x & \text{if } x < 0 \\ 3 & \text{if } 0 \leq x \leq 3 \\ x^2 & \text{if } x > 3 \end{cases}$

For the following exercises, write the domain for the piecewise function in interval notation.

52. $f(x) = \begin{cases} x+1 & \text{if } x < -2 \\ -2x-3 & \text{if } x \geq -2 \end{cases}$

53. $f(x) = \begin{cases} x^2-2 & \text{if } x < 1 \\ -x^2+2 & \text{if } x > 1 \end{cases}$

54. $f(x) = \begin{cases} 2x-3 & \text{if } x < 0 \\ -3x^2 & \text{if } x \geq 2 \end{cases}$

TECHNOLOGY

55. Graph $y = \dfrac{1}{x^2}$ on the viewing window $[-0.5, -0.1]$ and $[0.1, 0.5]$. Determine the corresponding range for the viewing window. Show the graphs.

56. Graph $y = \dfrac{1}{x}$ on the viewing window $[-0.5, -0.1]$ and $[0.1, 0.5]$. Determine the corresponding range for the viewing window. Show the graphs.

EXTENSION

57. Suppose the range of a function f is $[-5, 8]$. What is the range of $|f(x)|$?

58. Create a function in which the range is all nonnegative real numbers.

59. Create a function in which the domain is $x > 2$.

REAL-WORLD APPLICATIONS

60. The height h of a projectile is a function of the time t it is in the air. The height in feet for t seconds is given by the function $h(t) = -16t^2 + 96t$. What is the domain of the function? What does the domain mean in the context of the problem?

61. The cost in dollars of making x items is given by the function $C(x) = 10x + 500$.

    a. The fixed cost is determined when zero items are produced. Find the fixed cost for this item.

    b. What is the cost of making 25 items?

    c. Suppose the maximum cost allowed is $1500. What are the domain and range of the cost function, $C(x)$?

LEARNING OBJECTIVES

In this section, you will:

- Find the average rate of change of a function.
- Use a graph to determine where a function is increasing, decreasing, or constant.
- Use a graph to locate local maxima and local minima.
- Use a graph to locate the absolute maximum and absolute minimum.

1.3   RATES OF CHANGE AND BEHAVIOR OF GRAPHS

Gasoline costs have experienced some wild fluctuations over the last several decades. **Table 1**[5] lists the average cost, in dollars, of a gallon of gasoline for the years 2005–2012. The cost of gasoline can be considered as a function of year.

y	2005	2006	2007	2008	2009	2010	2011	2012
$C(y)$	2.31	2.62	2.84	3.30	2.41	2.84	3.58	3.68

Table 1

If we were interested only in how the gasoline prices changed between 2005 and 2012, we could compute that the cost per gallon had increased from \$2.31 to \$3.68, an increase of \$1.37. While this is interesting, it might be more useful to look at how much the price changed *per year*. In this section, we will investigate changes such as these.

Finding the Average Rate of Change of a Function

The price change per year is a **rate of change** because it describes how an output quantity changes relative to the change in the input quantity. We can see that the price of gasoline in **Table 1** did not change by the same amount each year, so the rate of change was not constant. If we use only the beginning and ending data, we would be finding the **average rate of change** over the specified period of time. To find the average rate of change, we divide the change in the output value by the change in the input value.

$$\text{Average rate of change} = \frac{\text{Change in output}}{\text{Change in input}}$$
$$= \frac{\Delta y}{\Delta x}$$
$$= \frac{y_2 - y_1}{x_2 - x_1}$$
$$= \frac{f(x_2) - f(x_1)}{x_2 - x_1}$$

The Greek letter Δ (delta) signifies the change in a quantity; we read the ratio as "delta-y over delta-x" or "the change in y divided by the change in x." Occasionally we write Δf instead of Δy, which still represents the change in the function's output value resulting from a change to its input value. It does not mean we are changing the function into some other function.

In our example, the gasoline price increased by \$1.37 from 2005 to 2012. Over 7 years, the average rate of change was

$$\frac{\Delta y}{\Delta x} = \frac{\$1.37}{7 \text{ years}} \approx 0.196 \text{ dollars per year}$$

On average, the price of gas increased by about 19.6¢ each year.

Other examples of rates of change include:

- A population of rats increasing by 40 rats per week
- A car traveling 68 miles per hour (distance traveled changes by 68 miles each hour as time passes)
- A car driving 27 miles per gallon (distance traveled changes by 27 miles for each gallon)
- The current through an electrical circuit increasing by 0.125 amperes for every volt of increased voltage
- The amount of money in a college account decreasing by \$4,000 per quarter

5 http://www.eia.gov/totalenergy/data/annual/showtext.cfm?t=ptb0524. Accessed 3/5/2014.

> ### rate of change
>
> A rate of change describes how an output quantity changes relative to the change in the input quantity. The units on a rate of change are "output units per input units."
>
> The average rate of change between two input values is the total change of the function values (output values) divided by the change in the input values.
>
> $$\frac{\Delta y}{\Delta x} = \frac{f(x_2) - f(x_1)}{x_2 - x_1}$$

How To...

Given the value of a function at different points, calculate the average rate of change of a function for the interval between two values x_1 and x_2.

1. Calculate the difference $y_2 - y_1 = \Delta y$.

2. Calculate the difference $x_2 - x_1 = \Delta x$.

3. Find the ratio $\dfrac{\Delta y}{\Delta x}$.

Example 1   **Computing an Average Rate of Change**

Using the data in **Table 1**, find the average rate of change of the price of gasoline between 2007 and 2009.

Solution   In 2007, the price of gasoline was $2.84. In 2009, the cost was $2.41. The average rate of change is

$$\frac{\Delta y}{\Delta x} = \frac{y_2 - y_1}{x_2 - x_1}$$

$$= \frac{\$2.41 - \$2.84}{2009 - 2007}$$

$$= \frac{-\$0.43}{2 \text{ years}}$$

$$= -\$0.22 \text{ per year}$$

Analysis   Note that a decrease is expressed by a negative change or "negative increase." A rate of change is negative when the output decreases as the input increases or when the output increases as the input decreases.

Try It #1

Using the data in **Table 1** at the beginning of this section, find the average rate of change between 2005 and 2010.

Example 2   **Computing Average Rate of Change from a Graph**

Given the function $g(t)$ shown in **Figure 1**, find the average rate of change on the interval $[-1, 2]$.

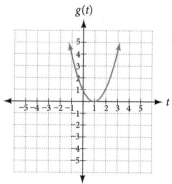

Figure 1

Solution   At $t = -1$, **Figure 2** shows $g(-1) = 4$. At $t = 2$, the graph shows $g(2) = 1$.

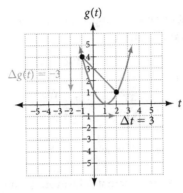

Figure 2

The horizontal change $\Delta t = 3$ is shown by the red arrow, and the vertical change $\Delta g(t) = -3$ is shown by the turquoise arrow. The output changes by -3 while the input changes by 3, giving an average rate of change of

$$\frac{1 - 4}{2 - (-1)} = \frac{-3}{3} = -1$$

Analysis   Note that the order we choose is very important. If, for example, we use $\dfrac{y_2 - y_1}{x_1 - x_2}$, we will not get the correct answer. Decide which point will be 1 and which point will be 2, and keep the coordinates fixed as (x_1, y_1) and (x_2, y_2).

Example 3   **Computing Average Rate of Change from a Table**

After picking up a friend who lives 10 miles away, Anna records her distance from home over time. The values are shown in **Table 2**. Find her average speed over the first 6 hours.

t (hours)	0	1	2	3	4	5	6	7
$D(t)$ (miles)	10	55	90	153	214	240	292	300

Table 2

Solution   Here, the average speed is the average rate of change. She traveled 282 miles in 6 hours, for an average speed of

$$\frac{292 - 10}{6 - 0} = \frac{282}{6}$$
$$= 47$$

The average speed is 47 miles per hour.

Analysis   Because the speed is not constant, the average speed depends on the interval chosen. For the interval $[2, 3]$, the average speed is 63 miles per hour.

Example 4   **Computing Average Rate of Change for a Function Expressed as a Formula**

Compute the average rate of change of $f(x) = x^2 - \dfrac{1}{x}$ on the interval $[2, 4]$.

Solution   We can start by computing the function values at each endpoint of the interval.

$$f(2) = 2^2 - \frac{1}{2} \qquad\qquad f(4) = 4^2 - \frac{1}{4}$$

$$= 4 - \frac{1}{2} \qquad\qquad\quad = 16 - \frac{1}{4}$$

$$= \frac{7}{2} \qquad\qquad\qquad\quad = \frac{63}{4}$$

Now we compute the average rate of change.

$$\text{Average rate of change} = \frac{f(4) - f(2)}{4 - 2}$$

$$= \frac{\frac{63}{4} - \frac{7}{2}}{4 - 2}$$

$$= \frac{\frac{49}{4}}{2}$$

$$= \frac{49}{8}$$

Try It #2

Find the average rate of change of $f(x) = x - 2\sqrt{x}$ on the interval $[1, 9]$.

Example 5   **Finding the Average Rate of Change of a Force**

The electrostatic force F, measured in newtons, between two charged particles can be related to the distance between the particles d, in centimeters, by the formula $F(d) = \frac{2}{d^2}$. Find the average rate of change of force if the distance between the particles is increased from 2 cm to 6 cm.

Solution   We are computing the average rate of change of $F(d) = \frac{2}{d^2}$ on the interval $[2, 6]$.

$$\text{Average rate of change} = \frac{F(6) - F(2)}{6 - 2}$$

$$= \frac{\frac{2}{6^2} - \frac{2}{2^2}}{6 - 2} \qquad \text{Simplify.}$$

$$= \frac{\frac{2}{36} - \frac{2}{4}}{4}$$

$$= \frac{-\frac{16}{36}}{4} \qquad \text{Combine numerator terms.}$$

$$= -\frac{1}{9} \qquad \text{Simplify.}$$

The average rate of change is $-\frac{1}{9}$ newton per centimeter.

Example 6   **Finding an Average Rate of Change as an Expression**

Find the average rate of change of $g(t) = t^2 + 3t + 1$ on the interval $[0, a]$. The answer will be an expression involving a.

Solution   We use the average rate of change formula.

$$\text{Average rate of change} = \frac{g(a) - g(0)}{a - 0} \qquad \text{Evaluate.}$$

$$= \frac{(a^2 + 3a + 1) - (0^2 + 3(0) + 1)}{a - 0} \qquad \text{Simplify.}$$

$$= \frac{a^2 + 3a + 1 - 1}{a} \qquad \text{Simplify and factor.}$$

$$= \frac{a(a + 3)}{a} \qquad \text{Divide by the common factor } a.$$

$$= a + 3$$

This result tells us the average rate of change in terms of a between $t = 0$ and any other point $t = a$. For example, on the interval $[0, 5]$, the average rate of change would be $5 + 3 = 8$.

Try It #3

Find the average rate of change of $f(x) = x^2 + 2x - 8$ on the interval $[5, a]$.

Using a Graph to Determine Where a Function is Increasing, Decreasing, or Constant

As part of exploring how functions change, we can identify intervals over which the function is changing in specific ways. We say that a function is increasing on an interval if the function values increase as the input values increase within that interval. Similarly, a function is decreasing on an interval if the function values decrease as the input values increase over that interval. The average rate of change of an increasing function is positive, and the average rate of change of a decreasing function is negative. **Figure 3** shows examples of increasing and decreasing intervals on a function.

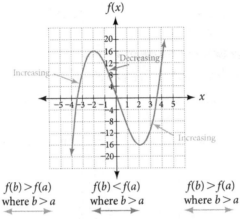

$f(b) > f(a)$ $f(b) < f(a)$ $f(b) > f(a)$
where $b > a$ where $b > a$ where $b > a$

Figure 3 The function $f(x) = x^3 - 12x$ is increasing on $(-\infty, -2) \cup (2, \infty)$ and is decreasing on $(-2, 2)$.

While some functions are increasing (or decreasing) over their entire domain, many others are not. A value of the input where a function changes from increasing to decreasing (as we go from left to right, that is, as the input variable increases) is called a **local maximum**. If a function has more than one, we say it has local maxima. Similarly, a value of the input where a function changes from decreasing to increasing as the input variable increases is called a **local minimum**. The plural form is "local minima." Together, local maxima and minima are called **local extrema**, or local extreme values, of the function. (The singular form is "extremum.") Often, the term *local* is replaced by the term *relative*. In this text, we will use the term *local*.

Clearly, a function is neither increasing nor decreasing on an interval where it is constant. A function is also neither increasing nor decreasing at extrema. Note that we have to speak of *local* extrema, because any given local extremum as defined here is not necessarily the highest maximum or lowest minimum in the function's entire domain.

For the function whose graph is shown in **Figure 4**, the local maximum is 16, and it occurs at $x = -2$. The local minimum is -16 and it occurs at $x = 2$.

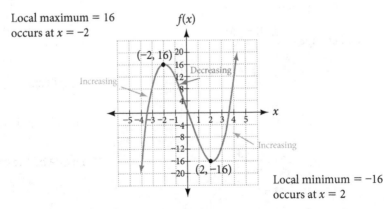

Figure 4

To locate the local maxima and minima from a graph, we need to observe the graph to determine where the graph attains its highest and lowest points, respectively, within an open interval. Like the summit of a roller coaster, the graph of a function is higher at a local maximum than at nearby points on both sides. The graph will also be lower at a local minimum than at neighboring points. **Figure 5** illustrates these ideas for a local maximum.

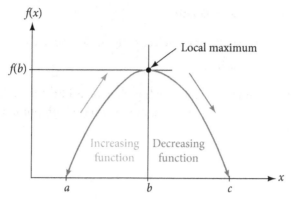

Figure 5 Definition of a local maximum

These observations lead us to a formal definition of local extrema.

---

local minima and local maxima

A function f is an **increasing function** on an open interval if $f(b) > f(a)$ for every two input values a and b in the interval where $b > a$.

A function f is a **decreasing function** on an open interval if $f(b) < f(a)$ for every two input values a and b in the interval where $b > a$.

A function f has a local maximum at a point b in an open interval (a, c) if $f(b) \geq f(x)$ for every point x (x does not equal b) in the interval. f has a local minimum at a point b in the interval (a, c) if $f(b) \leq f(x)$ for every point x (x does not equal both) in the interval.

Example 7 **Finding Increasing and Decreasing Intervals on a Graph**

Given the function $p(t)$ in **Figure 6**, identify the intervals on which the function appears to be increasing.

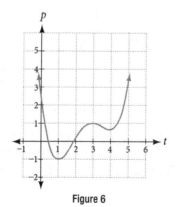

Figure 6

Solution   We see that the function is not constant on any interval. The function is increasing where it slants upward as we move to the right and decreasing where it slants downward as we move to the right. The function appears to be increasing from $t = 1$ to $t = 3$ and from $t = 4$ on.

In interval notation, we would say the function appears to be increasing on the interval $(1, 3)$ and the interval $(4, \infty)$.

Analysis Notice in this example that we used open intervals (intervals that do not include the endpoints), because the function is neither increasing nor decreasing at $t = 1$, $t = 3$, and $t = 4$. These points are the local extrema (two minima and a maximum).

Example 8   **Finding Local Extrema from a Graph**

Graph the function $f(x) = \dfrac{2}{x} + \dfrac{x}{3}$. Then use the graph to estimate the local extrema of the function and to determine the intervals on which the function is increasing.

Solution   Using technology, we find that the graph of the function looks like that in **Figure 7**. It appears there is a low point, or local minimum, between $x = 2$ and $x = 3$, and a mirror-image high point, or local maximum, somewhere between $x = -3$ and $x = -2$.

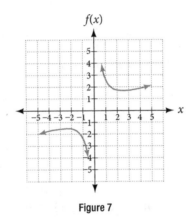

Figure 7

Analysis Most graphing calculators and graphing utilities can estimate the location of maxima and minima. **Figure 8** provides screen images from two different technologies, showing the estimate for the local maximum and minimum.

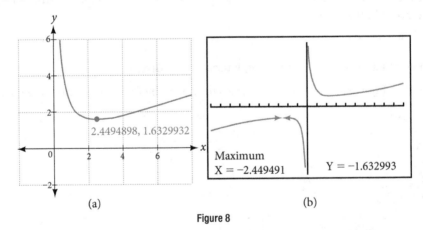

(a)   (b)

Figure 8

Based on these estimates, the function is increasing on the interval $(-\infty, -2.449)$ and $(2.449, \infty)$. Notice that, while we expect the extrema to be symmetric, the two different technologies agree only up to four decimals due to the differing approximation algorithms used by each. (The exact location of the extrema is at $\pm\sqrt{6}$, but determining this requires calculus.)

Try It #4

Graph the function $f(x) = x^3 - 6x^2 - 15x + 20$ to estimate the local extrema of the function. Use these to determine the intervals on which the function is increasing and decreasing.

Example 9   **Finding Local Maxima and Minima from a Graph**

For the function f whose graph is shown in **Figure 9**, find all local maxima and minima.

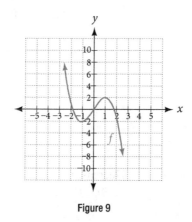

Figure 9

Solution   Observe the graph of f. The graph attains a local maximum at $x = 1$ because it is the highest point in an open interval around $x = 1$. The local maximum is the y-coordinate at $x = 1$, which is 2.

The graph attains a local minimum at $x = -1$ because it is the lowest point in an open interval around $x = -1$.

The local minimum is the y-coordinate at $x = -1$, which is -2.

Analyzing the Toolkit Functions for Increasing or Decreasing Intervals

We will now return to our toolkit functions and discuss their graphical behavior in **Figure 10**, **Figure 11**, and **Figure 12**.

Function	Increasing/Decreasing	Example
Constant Function $f(x) = c$	Neither increasing nor decreasing	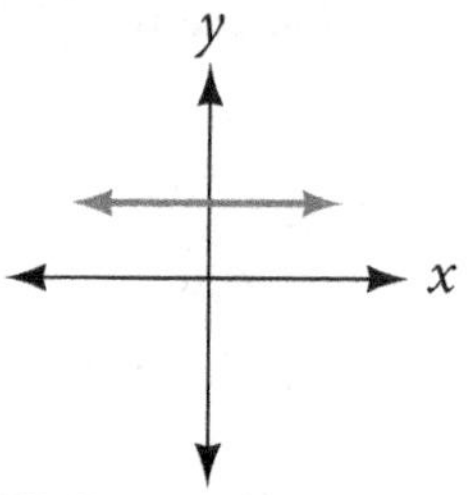
Identity Function $f(x) = x$	Increasing	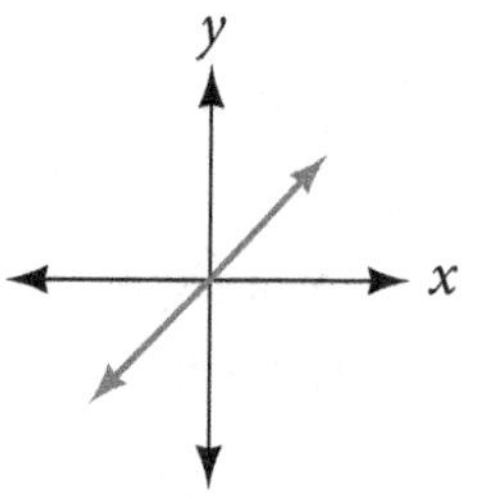
Quadratic Function $f(x) = x^2$	Increasing on $(0, \infty)$ Decreasing on $(-\infty, 0)$ Minimum at $x = 0$	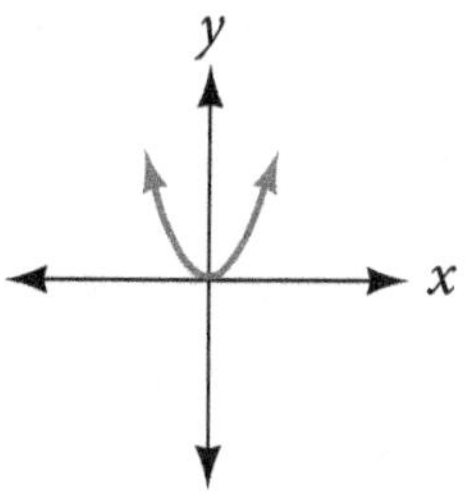

Figure 10

Function	Increasing/Decreasing	Example
Cubic Function $f(x) = x^3$	Increasing	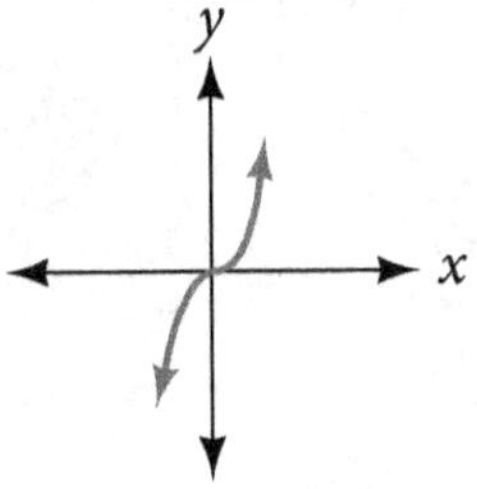
Reciprocal $f(x) = \dfrac{1}{x}$	Decreasing $(-\infty, 0) \cup (0, \infty)$	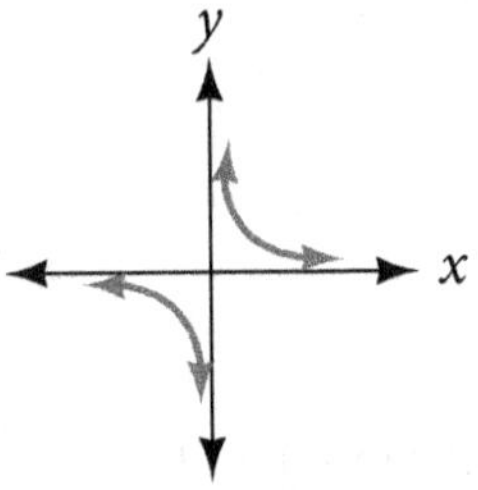
Reciprocal Squared $f(x) = \dfrac{1}{x^2}$	Increasing on $(-\infty, 0)$ Decreasing on $(0, \infty)$	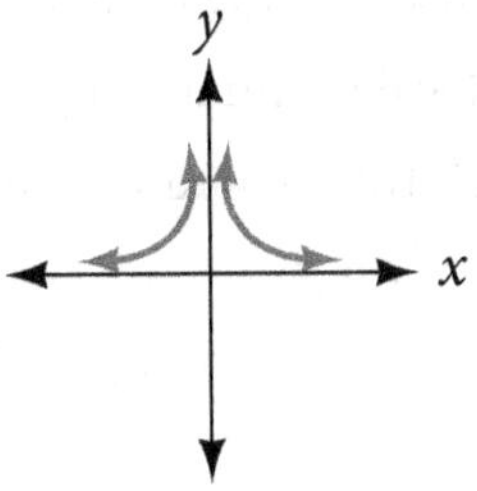

Figure 11

Function	Increasing/Decreasing	Example
Cube Root $f(x) = \sqrt[3]{x}$	Increasing	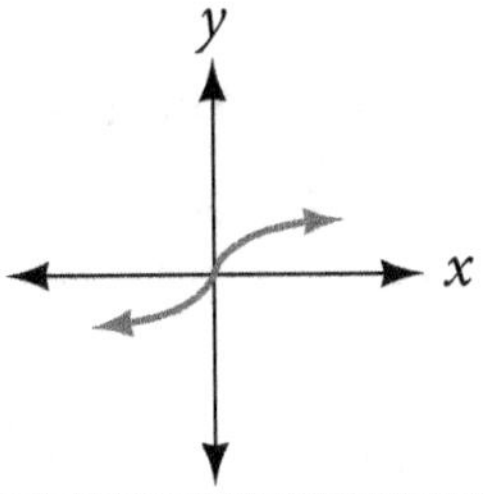
Square Root $f(x) = \sqrt{x}$	Increasing on $(0, \infty)$	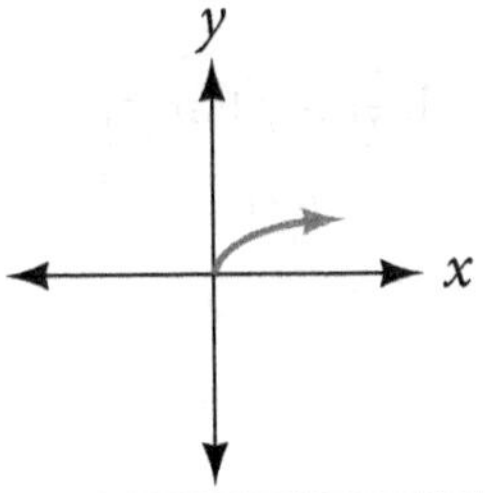
Absolute Value $f(x) = |x|$	Increasing on $(0, \infty)$ Decreasing on $(-\infty, 0)$	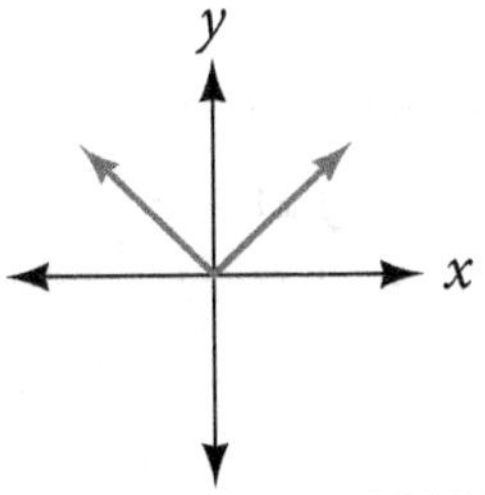

Figure 12

Use A Graph to Locate the Absolute Maximum and Absolute Minimum

There is a difference between locating the highest and lowest points on a graph in a region around an open interval (locally) and locating the highest and lowest points on the graph for the entire domain. The *y*-coordinates (output) at the highest and lowest points are called the **absolute maximum** and **absolute minimum**, respectively.

To locate absolute maxima and minima from a graph, we need to observe the graph to determine where the graph attains it highest and lowest points on the domain of the function. See **Figure 13**.

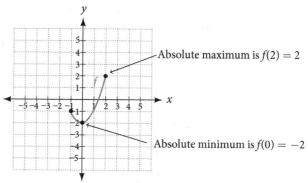

Figure 13

Not every function has an absolute maximum or minimum value. The toolkit function $f(x) = x^3$ is one such function.

absolute maxima and minima

The **absolute maximum** of f at $x = c$ is $f(c)$ where $f(c) \geq f(x)$ for all x in the domain of f.

The **absolute minimum** of f at $x = d$ is $f(d)$ where $f(d) \leq f(x)$ for all x in the domain of f.

Example 10 **Finding Absolute Maxima and Minima from a Graph**

For the function f shown in **Figure 14**, find all absolute maxima and minima.

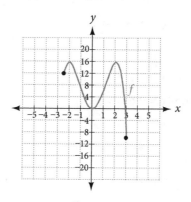

Figure 14

Solution Observe the graph of f. The graph attains an absolute maximum in two locations, $x = -2$ and $x = 2$, because at these locations, the graph attains its highest point on the domain of the function. The absolute maximum is the *y*-coordinate at $x = -2$ and $x = 2$, which is 16.

The graph attains an absolute minimum at $x = 3$, because it is the lowest point on the domain of the function's graph. The absolute minimum is the *y*-coordinate at $x = 3$, which is -10.

Access this online resource for additional instruction and practice with rates of change.

- Average Rate of Change (http://openstaxcollege.org/l/aroc)

1.3   SECTION EXERCISES

VERBAL

1. Can the average rate of change of a function be constant?

2. If a function f is increasing on (a, b) and decreasing on (b, c), then what can be said about the local extremum of f on (a, c)?

3. How are the absolute maximum and minimum similar to and different from the local extrema?

4. How does the graph of the absolute value function compare to the graph of the quadratic function, $y = x^2$, in terms of increasing and decreasing intervals?

ALGEBRAIC

For the following exercises, find the average rate of change of each function on the interval specified for real numbers b or h.

5. $f(x) = 4x^2 - 7$ on $[1, b]$

6. $g(x) = 2x^2 - 9$ on $[4, b]$

7. $p(x) = 3x + 4$ on $[2, 2 + h]$

8. $k(x) = 4x - 2$ on $[3, 3 + h]$

9. $f(x) = 2x^2 + 1$ on $[x, x + h]$

10. $g(x) = 3x^2 - 2$ on $[x, x + h]$

11. $a(t) = \dfrac{1}{t + 4}$ on $[9, 9 + h]$

12. $b(x) = \dfrac{1}{x + 3}$ on $[1, 1 + h]$

13. $j(x) = 3x^3$ on $[1, 1 + h]$

14. $r(t) = 4t^3$ on $[2, 2 + h]$

15. $\dfrac{f(x + h) - f(x)}{h}$ given $f(x) = 2x^2 - 3x$ on $[x, x + h]$

GRAPHICAL

For the following exercises, consider the graph of f shown in **Figure 15**.

16. Estimate the average rate of change from $x = 1$ to $x = 4$.

17. Estimate the average rate of change from $x = 2$ to $x = 5$.

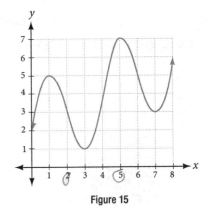

Figure 15

For the following exercises, use the graph of each function to estimate the intervals on which the function is increasing or decreasing.

18.

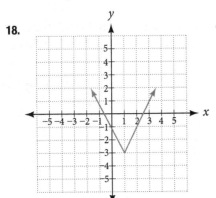

19.

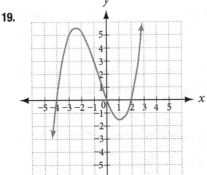

20.

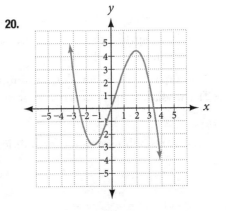

21.

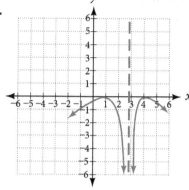

For the following exercises, consider the graph shown in **Figure 16**.

22. Estimate the intervals where the function is increasing or decreasing.

23. Estimate the point(s) at which the graph of *f* has a local maximum or a local minimum.

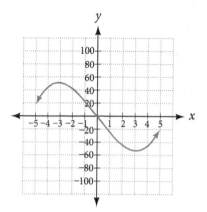

Figure 16

For the following exercises, consider the graph in **Figure 17.**

24. If the complete graph of the function is shown, estimate the intervals where the function is increasing or decreasing.

25. If the complete graph of the function is shown, estimate the absolute maximum and absolute minimum.

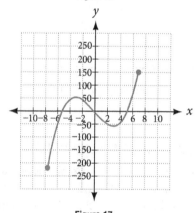

Figure 17

NUMERIC

26. Table 3 gives the annual sales (in millions of dollars) of a product from 1998 to 2006. What was the average rate of change of annual sales (**a**) between 2001 and 2002, and (**b**) between 2001 and 2004?

Year	1998	1999	2000	2001	2002	2003	2004	2005	2006
Sales (millions of dollars)	201	219	233	243	249	251	249	243	233

Table 3

27. Table 4 gives the population of a town (in thousands) from 2000 to 2008. What was the average rate of change of population (**a**) between 2002 and 2004, and (**b**) between 2002 and 2006?

Year	2000	2001	2002	2003	2004	2005	2006	2007	2008
Population (thousands)	87	84	83	80	77	76	78	81	85

Table 4

For the following exercises, find the average rate of change of each function on the interval specified.

28. $f(x) = x^2$ on $[1, 5]$

29. $h(x) = 5 - 2x^2$ on $[-2, 4]$

30. $q(x) = x^3$ on $[-4, 2]$

31. $g(x) = 3x^3 - 1$ on $[-3, 3]$

32. $y = \dfrac{1}{x}$ on $[1, 3]$

33. $p(t) = \dfrac{(t^2 - 4)(t + 1)}{t^2 + 3}$ on $[-3, 1]$

34. $k(t) = 6t^2 + \dfrac{4}{t^3}$ on $[-1, 3]$

TECHNOLOGY

For the following exercises, use a graphing utility to estimate the local extrema of each function and to estimate the intervals on which the function is increasing and decreasing.

35. $f(x) = x^4 - 4x^3 + 5$

36. $h(x) = x^5 + 5x^4 + 10x^3 + 10x^2 - 1$

37. $g(t) = t\sqrt{t + 3}$

38. $k(t) = 3t^{\frac{2}{3}} - t$

39. $m(x) = x^4 + 2x^3 - 12x^2 - 10x + 4$

40. $n(x) = x^4 - 8x^3 + 18x^2 - 6x + 2$

EXTENSION

41. The graph of the function f is shown in **Figure 18**.

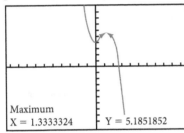

Maximum
X = 1.3333324   Y = 5.1851852

Figure 18

Based on the calculator screen shot, the point (1.333, 5.185) is which of the following?

a. a relative (local) maximum of the function

b. the vertex of the function

c. the absolute maximum of the function

d. a zero of the function

42. Let $f(x) = \dfrac{1}{x}$. Find a number c such that the average rate of change of the function f on the interval $(1, c)$ is $-\dfrac{1}{4}$

43. Let $f(x) = \dfrac{1}{x}$. Find the number b such that the average rate of change of f on the interval $(2, b)$ is $-\dfrac{1}{10}$.

REAL-WORLD APPLICATIONS

44. At the start of a trip, the odometer on a car read 21,395. At the end of the trip, 13.5 hours later, the odometer read 22,125. Assume the scale on the odometer is in miles. What is the average speed the car traveled during this trip?

45. A driver of a car stopped at a gas station to fill up his gas tank. He looked at his watch, and the time read exactly 3:40 p.m. At this time, he started pumping gas into the tank. At exactly 3:44, the tank was full and he noticed that he had pumped 10.7 gallons. What is the average rate of flow of the gasoline into the gas tank?

46. Near the surface of the moon, the distance that an object falls is a function of time. It is given by $d(t) = 2.6667t^2$, where t is in seconds and $d(t)$ is in feet. If an object is dropped from a certain height, find the average velocity of the object from $t = 1$ to $t = 2$.

47. The graph in **Figure 19** illustrates the decay of a radioactive substance over t days.

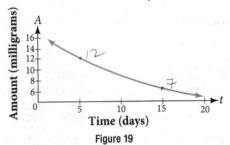

Figure 19

Use the graph to estimate the average decay rate from $t = 5$ to $t = 15$.

LEARNING OBJECTIVES

In this section, you will:

- Combine functions using algebraic operations.
- Create a new function by composition of functions.
- Evaluate composite functions.
- Find the domain of a composite function.
- Decompose a composite function into its component functions.

1.4 COMPOSITION OF FUNCTIONS

Suppose we want to calculate how much it costs to heat a house on a particular day of the year. The cost to heat a house will depend on the average daily temperature, and in turn, the average daily temperature depends on the particular day of the year. Notice how we have just defined two relationships: The cost depends on the temperature, and the temperature depends on the day.

Using descriptive variables, we can notate these two functions. The function $C(T)$ gives the cost C of heating a house for a given average daily temperature in T degrees Celsius. The function $T(d)$ gives the average daily temperature on day d of the year. For any given day, Cost $= C(T(d))$ means that the cost depends on the temperature, which in turns depends on the day of the year. Thus, we can evaluate the cost function at the temperature $T(d)$. For example, we could evaluate $T(5)$ to determine the average daily temperature on the 5th day of the year. Then, we could evaluate the cost function at that temperature. We would write $C(T(5))$.

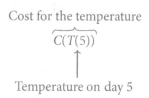

By combining these two relationships into one function, we have performed function composition, which is the focus of this section.

Combining Functions Using Algebraic Operations

Function composition is only one way to combine existing functions. Another way is to carry out the usual algebraic operations on functions, such as addition, subtraction, multiplication and division. We do this by performing the operations with the function outputs, defining the result as the output of our new function.

Suppose we need to add two columns of numbers that represent a husband and wife's separate annual incomes over a period of years, with the result being their total household income. We want to do this for every year, adding only that year's incomes and then collecting all the data in a new column. If $w(y)$ is the wife's income and $h(y)$ is the husband's income in year y, and we want T to represent the total income, then we can define a new function.

$$T(y) = h(y) + w(y)$$

If this holds true for every year, then we can focus on the relation between the functions without reference to a year and write

$$T = h + w$$

Just as for this sum of two functions, we can define difference, product, and ratio functions for any pair of functions that have the same kinds of inputs (not necessarily numbers) and also the same kinds of outputs (which do have to be numbers so that the usual operations of algebra can apply to them, and which also must have the same units or no units when we add and subtract). In this way, we can think of adding, subtracting, multiplying, and dividing functions.

For two functions $f(x)$ and $g(x)$ with real number outputs, we define new functions $f+g$, $f-g$, fg, and $\frac{f}{g}$ by the relations

$$(f+g)(x) = f(x) + g(x)$$

$$(f-g)(x) = f(x) - g(x)$$

$$(fg)(x) = f(x)g(x)$$

$$\left(\frac{f}{g}\right)(x) = \frac{f(x)}{g(x)}$$

Example 1   Performing Algebraic Operations on Functions

Find and simplify the functions $(g-f)(x)$ and $\left(\frac{g}{f}\right)(x)$, given $f(x) = x - 1$ and $g(x) = x^2 - 1$. Are they the same function?

Solution   Begin by writing the general form, and then substitute the given functions.

$$(g-f)(x) = g(x) - f(x)$$

$$(g-f)(x) = x^2 - 1 - (x - 1)$$

$$(g-f)(x) = x^2 - x$$

$$(g-f)(x) = x(x - 1)$$

$$\left(\frac{g}{f}\right)(x) = \frac{g(x)}{f(x)}$$

$$\left(\frac{g}{f}\right)(x) = \frac{x^2 - 1}{x - 1} \qquad \text{where } x \neq 1$$

$$\left(\frac{g}{f}\right)(x) = \frac{(x+1)(x-1)}{x - 1} \qquad \text{where } x \neq 1$$

$$\left(\frac{g}{f}\right)(x) = x + 1 \qquad \text{where } x \neq 1$$

No, the functions are not the same.

Note: For $\left(\frac{g}{f}\right)(x)$, the condition $x \neq 1$ is necessary because when $x = 1$, the denominator is equal to 0, which makes the function undefined.

Try It #1

Find and simplify the functions $(fg)(x)$ and $(f-g)(x)$.

$$f(x) = x - 1 \text{ and } g(x) = x^2 - 1$$

Are they the same function?

Create a Function by Composition of Functions

Performing algebraic operations on functions combines them into a new function, but we can also create functions by composing functions. When we wanted to compute a heating cost from a day of the year, we created a new function that takes a day as input and yields a cost as output. The process of combining functions so that the output of one function becomes the input of another is known as a composition of functions. The resulting function is known as a **composite function**. We represent this combination by the following notation:

$$(f \circ g)(x) = f(g(x))$$

We read the left-hand side as "f composed with g at x," and the right-hand side as "f of g of x." The two sides of the equation have the same mathematical meaning and are equal. The open circle symbol $\circ$ is called the composition operator. We use this operator mainly when we wish to emphasize the relationship between the functions themselves without referring to any particular input value. Composition is a binary operation that takes two functions and forms a new function, much as addition or multiplication takes two numbers and gives a new number. However, it is important not to confuse function composition with multiplication because, as we learned above, in most cases $f(g(x)) \neq f(x)g(x)$.

It is also important to understand the order of operations in evaluating a composite function. We follow the usual convention with parentheses by starting with the innermost parentheses first, and then working to the outside. In the equation above, the function g takes the input x first and yields an output $g(x)$. Then the function f takes $g(x)$ as an input and yields an output $f(g(x))$.

$$g(x), \text{ the output of } g$$
$$\text{is the input of } f$$
$$\downarrow$$
$$(f \circ g)(x) = f(\underline{g(x)})$$
$$\uparrow$$
$$x \text{ is the input of } g$$

In general, $f \circ g$ and $g \circ f$ are different functions. In other words, in many cases $f(g(x)) \neq g(f(x))$ for all x. We will also see that sometimes two functions can be composed only in one specific order.

For example, if $f(x) = x^2$ and $g(x) = x + 2$, then

$$f(g(x)) = f(x + 2)$$
$$= (x + 2)^2$$
$$= x^2 + 4x + 4$$

but

$$g(f(x)) = g(x^2)$$
$$= x^2 + 2$$

These expressions are not equal for all values of x, so the two functions are not equal. It is irrelevant that the expressions happen to be equal for the single input value $x = -\dfrac{1}{2}$.

Note that the range of the inside function (the first function to be evaluated) needs to be within the domain of the outside function. Less formally, the composition has to make sense in terms of inputs and outputs.

---

composition of functions

When the output of one function is used as the input of another, we call the entire operation a composition of functions. For any input x and functions f and g, this action defines a **composite function**, which we write as $f \circ g$ such that

$$(f \circ g)(x) = f(g(x))$$

The domain of the composite function $f \circ g$ is all x such that x is in the domain of g and $g(x)$ is in the domain of f. It is important to realize that the product of functions fg is not the same as the function composition $f(g(x))$, because, in general, $f(x)g(x) \neq f(g(x))$.

Example 2   **Determining whether Composition of Functions is Commutative**

Using the functions provided, find $f(g(x))$ and $g(f(x))$. Determine whether the composition of the functions is commutative.

$$f(x) = 2x + 1 \qquad g(x) = 3 - x$$

Solution   Let's begin by substituting $g(x)$ into $f(x)$.

$$f(g(x)) = 2(3 - x) + 1$$
$$= 6 - 2x + 1$$
$$= 7 - 2x$$

Now we can substitute $f(x)$ into $g(x)$.

$$g(f(x)) = 3 - (2x + 1)$$
$$= 3 - 2x - 1$$
$$= -2x + 2$$

We find that $g(f(x)) \neq f(g(x))$, so the operation of function composition is not commutative.

Example 3   Interpreting Composite Functions

The function $c(s)$ gives the number of calories burned completing s sit-ups, and $s(t)$ gives the number of sit-ups a person can complete in t minutes. Interpret $c(s(3))$.

Solution   The inside expression in the composition is $s(3)$. Because the input to the s-function is time, $t = 3$ represents 3 minutes, and $s(3)$ is the number of sit-ups completed in 3 minutes.

Using $s(3)$ as the input to the function $c(s)$ gives us the number of calories burned during the number of sit-ups that can be completed in 3 minutes, or simply the number of calories burned in 3 minutes (by doing sit-ups).

Example 4   Investigating the Order of Function Composition

Suppose $f(x)$ gives miles that can be driven in x hours and $g(y)$ gives the gallons of gas used in driving y miles. Which of these expressions is meaningful: $f(g(y))$ or $g(f(x))$?

Solution   The function $y = f(x)$ is a function whose output is the number of miles driven corresponding to the number of hours driven.

$$\text{number of miles} = f(\text{number of hours})$$

The function $g(y)$ is a function whose output is the number of gallons used corresponding to the number of miles driven. This means:

$$\text{number of gallons} = g\,(\text{number of miles})$$

The expression $g(y)$ takes miles as the input and a number of gallons as the output. The function $f(x)$ requires a number of hours as the input. Trying to input a number of gallons does not make sense. The expression $f(g(y))$ is meaningless.

The expression $f(x)$ takes hours as input and a number of miles driven as the output. The function $g(y)$ requires a number of miles as the input. Using $f(x)$ (miles driven) as an input value for $g(y)$, where gallons of gas depends on miles driven, does make sense. The expression $g(f(x))$ makes sense, and will yield the number of gallons of gas used, g, driving a certain number of miles, $f(x)$, in x hours.

Q & A...

Are there any situations where $f(g(y))$ and $g(f(x))$ would both be meaningful or useful expressions?

Yes. For many pure mathematical functions, both compositions make sense, even though they usually produce different new functions. In real-world problems, functions whose inputs and outputs have the same units also may give compositions that are meaningful in either order.

Try It #2

The gravitational force on a planet a distance r from the sun is given by the function $G(r)$. The acceleration of a planet subjected to any force F is given by the function $a(F)$. Form a meaningful composition of these two functions, and explain what it means.

Evaluating Composite Functions

Once we compose a new function from two existing functions, we need to be able to evaluate it for any input in its domain. We will do this with specific numerical inputs for functions expressed as tables, graphs, and formulas and with variables as inputs to functions expressed as formulas. In each case, we evaluate the inner function using the starting input and then use the inner function's output as the input for the outer function.

Evaluating Composite Functions Using Tables

When working with functions given as tables, we read input and output values from the table entries and always work from the inside to the outside. We evaluate the inside function first and then use the output of the inside function as the input to the outside function.

Example 5   **Using a Table to Evaluate a Composite Function**

Using **Table 1**, evaluate $f(g(3))$ and $g(f(3))$.

x	$f(x)$	$g(x)$
1	6	3
2	8	5
3	3	2
4	1	7

Table 1

Solution   To evaluate $f(g(3))$, we start from the inside with the input value 3. We then evaluate the inside expression $g(3)$ using the table that defines the function g: $g(3) = 2$. We can then use that result as the input to the function f, so $g(3)$ is replaced by 2 and we get $f(2)$. Then, using the table that defines the function f, we find that $f(2) = 8$.

$$g(3) = 2$$
$$f(g(3)) = f(2) = 8$$

To evaluate $g(f(3))$, we first evaluate the inside expression $f(3)$ using the first table: $f(3) = 3$. Then, using the table for g, we can evaluate

$$g(f(3)) = g(3) = 2$$

Table 2 shows the composite functions $f \circ g$ and $g \circ f$ as tables.

x	$g(x)$	$f(g(x))$	$f(x)$	$g(f(x))$
3	2	8	3	2

Table 2

Try It #3

Using **Table 1**, evaluate $f(g(1))$ and $g(f(4))$.

Evaluating Composite Functions Using Graphs

When we are given individual functions as graphs, the procedure for evaluating composite functions is similar to the process we use for evaluating tables. We read the input and output values, but this time, from the x- and y-axes of the graphs.

Given a composite function and graphs of its individual functions, evaluate it using the information provided by the graphs.

1. Locate the given input to the inner function on the *x*-axis of its graph.
2. Read off the output of the inner function from the *y*-axis of its graph.
3. Locate the inner function output on the *x*-axis of the graph of the outer function.
4. Read the output of the outer function from the *y*-axis of its graph. This is the output of the composite function.

Example 6   **Using a Graph to Evaluate a Composite Function**

Using **Figure 1**, evaluate $f(g(1))$.

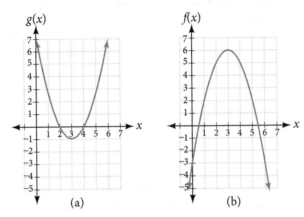

Figure 1

Solution   To evaluate $f(g(1))$, we start with the inside evaluation. See **Figure 2**.

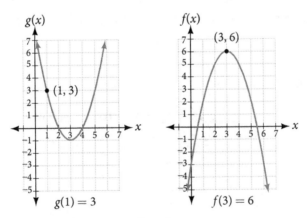

Figure 2

We evaluate $g(1)$ using the graph of $g(x)$, finding the input of 1 on the *x*-axis and finding the output value of the graph at that input. Here, $g(1) = 3$. We use this value as the input to the function f.

$$f(g(1)) = f(3)$$

We can then evaluate the composite function by looking to the graph of $f(x)$, finding the input of 3 on the *x*-axis and reading the output value of the graph at this input. Here, $f(3) = 6$, so $f(g(1)) = 6$.

Analysis **Figure 3** *shows how we can mark the graphs with arrows to trace the path from the input value to the output value.*

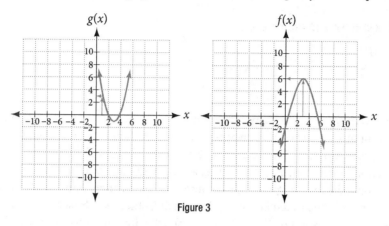

Figure 3

Try It #4

Using **Figure 1**, evaluate $g(f(2))$.

Evaluating Composite Functions Using Formulas

When evaluating a composite function where we have either created or been given formulas, the rule of working from the inside out remains the same. The input value to the outer function will be the output of the inner function, which may be a numerical value, a variable name, or a more complicated expression.

While we can compose the functions for each individual input value, it is sometimes helpful to find a single formula that will calculate the result of a composition $f(g(x))$. To do this, we will extend our idea of function evaluation. Recall that, when we evaluate a function like $f(t) = t^2 - t$, we substitute the value inside the parentheses into the formula wherever we see the input variable.

How To...

Given a formula for a composite function, evaluate the function.

1. Evaluate the inside function using the input value or variable provided.
2. Use the resulting output as the input to the outside function.

Example 7 **Evaluating a Composition of Functions Expressed as Formulas with a Numerical Input**

Given $f(t) = t^2 - t$ and $h(x) = 3x + 2$, evaluate $f(h(1))$.

Solution Because the inside expression is $h(1)$, we start by evaluating $h(x)$ at 1.

$$h(1) = 3(1) + 2$$

$$h(1) = 5$$

Then $f(h(1)) = f(5)$, so we evaluate $f(t)$ at an input of 5.

$$f(h(1)) = f(5)$$

$$f(h(1)) = 5^2 - 5$$

$$f(h(1)) = 20$$

Analysis *It makes no difference what the input variables t and x were called in this problem because we evaluated for specific numerical values.*

Finding the Domain of a Composite Function

As we discussed previously, the domain of a composite function such as $f \circ g$ is dependent on the domain of g and the domain of f. It is important to know when we can apply a composite function and when we cannot, that is, to know the domain of a function such as $f \circ g$. Let us assume we know the domains of the functions f and g separately. If we write the composite function for an input x as $f(g(x))$, we can see right away that x must be a member of the domain of g in order for the expression to be meaningful, because otherwise we cannot complete the inner function evaluation. However, we also see that $g(x)$ must be a member of the domain of f, otherwise the second function evaluation in $f(g(x))$ cannot be completed, and the expression is still undefined. Thus the domain of $f \circ g$ consists of only those inputs in the domain of g that produce outputs from g belonging to the domain of f. Note that the domain of f composed with g is the set of all x such that x is in the domain of g and $g(x)$ is in the domain of f.

---

domain of a composite function

The domain of a composite function $f(g(x))$ is the set of those inputs x in the domain of g for which $g(x)$ is in the domain of f.

How To...

Given a function composition $f(g(x))$, determine its domain.

1. Find the domain of g.
2. Find the domain of f.
3. Find those inputs x in the domain of g for which $g(x)$ is in the domain of f. That is, exclude those inputs x from the domain of g for which $g(x)$ is not in the domain of f. The resulting set is the domain of $f \circ g$.

Example 8   **Finding the Domain of a Composite Function**

Find the domain of

$$(f \circ g)(x) \text{ where } f(x) = \frac{5}{x-1} \text{ and } g(x) = \frac{4}{3x-2}$$

Solution   The domain of $g(x)$ consists of all real numbers except $x = \frac{2}{3}$, since that input value would cause us to divide by 0. Likewise, the domain of f consists of all real numbers except 1. So we need to exclude from the domain of $g(x)$ that value of x for which $g(x) = 1$.

$$\frac{4}{3x-2} = 1$$

$$4 = 3x - 2$$

$$6 = 3x$$

$$x = 2$$

So the domain of $f \circ g$ is the set of all real numbers except $\frac{2}{3}$ and 2. This means that

$$x \neq \frac{2}{3} \text{ or } x \neq 2$$

We can write this in interval notation as

$$\left(-\infty, \frac{2}{3}\right) \cup \left(\frac{2}{3}, 2\right) \cup (2, \infty)$$

Finding the Domain of a Composite Function Involving Radicals Find the domain of

$$(f \circ g)(x) \text{ where } f(x) = \sqrt{x + 2} \text{ and } g(x) = \sqrt{3 - x}$$

Solution   Because we cannot take the square root of a negative number, the domain of g is $(-\infty, 3]$. Now we check the domain of the composite function

$$(f \circ g)(x) = \sqrt{\sqrt{3 - x} + 2}$$

For $(f \circ g)(x) = \sqrt{\sqrt{3 - x} + 2}$, $\sqrt{3 - x} + 2 \geq 0$, since the radicand of a square root must be positive. Since the square roots are positive, $\sqrt{3 - x} \geq 0$, $3 - x \geq 0$, which gives a domain of $(-\infty, 3]$.

Analysis   This example shows that knowledge of the range of functions (specifically the inner function) can also be helpful in finding the domain of a composite function. It also shows that the domain of $f \circ g$ can contain values that are not in the domain of f, though they must be in the domain of g.

Try It #6

Find the domain of $(f \circ g)(x)$ where $f(x) = \dfrac{1}{x - 2}$ and $g(x) = \sqrt{x + 4}$

Decomposing a Composite Function into its Component Functions

In some cases, it is necessary to decompose a complicated function. In other words, we can write it as a composition of two simpler functions. There may be more than one way to decompose a composite function, so we may choose the decomposition that appears to be most expedient.

Example 9   **Decomposing a Function**

Write $f(x) = \sqrt{5 - x^2}$ as the composition of two functions.

Solution   We are looking for two functions, g and h, so $f(x) = g(h(x))$. To do this, we look for a function inside a function in the formula for $f(x)$. As one possibility, we might notice that the expression $5 - x^2$ is the inside of the square root. We could then decompose the function as

$$h(x) = 5 - x^2 \text{ and } g(x) = \sqrt{x}$$

We can check our answer by recomposing the functions.

$$g(h(x)) = g(5 - x^2) = \sqrt{5 - x^2}$$

Try It #7

Write $f(x) = \dfrac{4}{3 - \sqrt{4 + x^2}}$ as the composition of two functions.

Access these online resources for additional instruction and practice with composite functions.

- Composite Functions (http://openstaxcollege.org/l/compfunction)
- Composite Function Notation Application (http://openstaxcollege.org/l/compfuncnot)
- Composite Functions Using Graphs (http://openstaxcollege.org/l/compfuncgraph)
- Decompose Functions (http://openstaxcollege.org/l/decompfunction)
- Composite Function Values (http://openstaxcollege.org/l/compfuncvalue)

1.4   SECTION EXERCISES

VERBAL

1. How does one find the domain of the quotient of two functions, $\frac{f}{g}$?

2. What is the composition of two functions, $f \circ g$?

3. If the order is reversed when composing two functions, can the result ever be the same as the answer in the original order of the composition? If yes, give an example. If no, explain why not.

4. How do you find the domain for the composition of two functions, $f \circ g$?

ALGEBRAIC

5. Given $f(x) = x^2 + 2x$ and $g(x) = 6 - x^2$, find $f + g$, $f - g$, fg, and $\frac{f}{g}$. Determine the domain for each function in interval notation.

6. Given $f(x) = -3x^2 + x$ and $g(x) = 5$, find $f + g$, $f - g$, fg, and $\frac{f}{g}$. Determine the domain for each function in interval notation.

7. Given $f(x) = 2x^2 + 4x$ and $g(x) = \frac{1}{2x}$, find $f + g$, $f - g$, fg, and $\frac{f}{g}$. Determine the domain for each function in interval notation.

8. Given $f(x) = \frac{1}{x - 4}$ and $g(x) = \frac{1}{6 - x}$, find $f + g$, $f - g$, fg, and $\frac{f}{g}$. Determine the domain for each function in interval notation.

9. Given $f(x) = 3x^2$ and $g(x) = \sqrt{x - 5}$, find $f + g$, $f - g$, fg, and $\frac{f}{g}$. Determine the domain for each function in interval notation.

10. Given $f(x) = \sqrt{x}$ and $g(x) = |x - 3|$, find $\frac{g}{f}$. Determine the domain for each function in interval notation.

11. Given $f(x) = 2x^2 + 1$ and $g(x) = 3x - 5$, find the following:
    a. $f(g(2))$ b. $f(g(x))$ c. $g(f(x))$ d. $(g \circ g)(x)$ e. $(f \circ f)(-2)$

For the following exercises, use each pair of functions to find $f(g(x))$ and $g(f(x))$. Simplify your answers.

12. $f(x) = x^2 + 1, g(x) = \sqrt{x + 2}$

13. $f(x) = \sqrt{x} + 2, g(x) = x^2 + 3$

14. $f(x) = |x|, g(x) = 5x + 1$

15. $f(x) = \sqrt[3]{x}, g(x) = \frac{x + 1}{x^3}$

16. $f(x) = \frac{1}{x - 6}, g(x) = \frac{7}{x} + 6$

17. $f(x) = \frac{1}{x - 4}, g(x) = \frac{2}{x} + 4$

For the following exercises, use each set of functions to find $f(g(h(x)))$. Simplify your answers.

18. $f(x) = x^4 + 6, g(x) = x - 6$, and $h(x) = \sqrt{x}$

19. $f(x) = x^2 + 1, g(x) = \frac{1}{x}$, and $h(x) = x + 3$

20. Given $f(x) = \frac{1}{x}$, and $g(x) = x - 3$, find the following:
    a. $(f \circ g)(x)$
    b. the domain of $(f \circ g)(x)$ in interval notation
    c. $(g \circ f)(x)$
    d. the domain of $(g \circ f)(x)$
    e. $\left(\frac{f}{g}\right)x$

21. Given $f(x) = \sqrt{2 - 4x}$ and $g(x) = -\frac{3}{x}$, find the following:
    a. $(g \circ f)(x)$
    b. the domain of $(g \circ f)(x)$ in interval notation

22. Given the functions $f(x) = \dfrac{1-x}{x}$ and $g(x) = \dfrac{1}{1+x^2}$, find the following:

 a. $(g \circ f)(x)$

 b. $(g \circ f)(2)$

23. Given functions $p(x) = \dfrac{1}{\sqrt{x}}$ and $m(x) = x^2 - 4$, state the domain of each of the following functions using interval notation:

 a. $\dfrac{p(x)}{m(x)}$ **b.** $p(m(x))$ **c.** $m(p(x))$

24. Given functions $q(x) = \dfrac{1}{\sqrt{x}}$ and $h(x) = x^2 - 9$, state the domain of each of the following functions using interval notation.

 a. $\dfrac{q(x)}{h(x)}$ **b.** $q(h(x))$ **c.** $h(q(x))$

25. For $f(x) = \dfrac{1}{x}$ and $g(x) = \sqrt{x-1}$, write the domain of $(f \circ g)(x)$ in interval notation.

For the following exercises, find functions $f(x)$ and $g(x)$ so the given function can be expressed as $h(x) = f(g(x))$.

26. $h(x) = (x+2)^2$

27. $h(x) = (x-5)^3$

28. $h(x) = \dfrac{3}{x-5}$

29. $h(x) = \dfrac{4}{(x+2)^2}$

30. $h(x) = 4 + \sqrt[3]{x}$

31. $h(x) = \sqrt[3]{\dfrac{1}{2x-3}}$

32. $h(x) = \dfrac{1}{(3x^2-4)^{-3}}$

33. $h(x) = \sqrt[4]{\dfrac{3x-2}{x+5}}$

34. $h(x) = \left(\dfrac{8+x^3}{8-x^3}\right)^4$

35. $h(x) = \sqrt{2x+6}$

36. $h(x) = (5x-1)^3$

37. $h(x) = \sqrt[3]{x-1}$

38. $h(x) = |x^2+7|$

39. $h(x) = \dfrac{1}{(x-2)^3}$

40. $h(x) = \left(\dfrac{1}{2x-3}\right)^2$

41. $h(x) = \sqrt{\dfrac{2x-1}{3x+4}}$

GRAPHICAL

For the following exercises, use the graphs of f, shown in **Figure 4**, and g, shown in **Figure 5**, to evaluate the expressions.

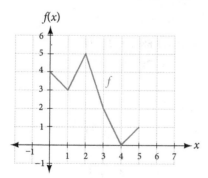

Figure 4

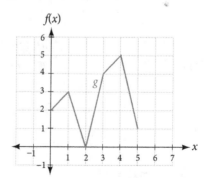

Figure 5

42. $f(g(3))$

43. $f(g(1))$

44. $g(f(1))$

45. $g(f(0))$

46. $f(f(5))$

47. $f(f(4))$

48. $g(g(2))$

49. $g(g(0))$

For the following exercises, use graphs of $f(x)$, shown in **Figure 6**, $g(x)$, shown in **Figure 7**, and $h(x)$, shown in **Figure 8**, to evaluate the expressions.

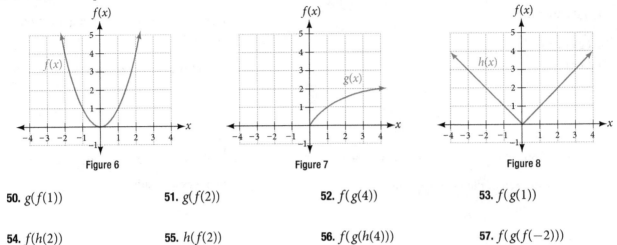

Figure 6   Figure 7   Figure 8

50. $g(f(1))$ **51.** $g(f(2))$ **52.** $f(g(4))$ **53.** $f(g(1))$

54. $f(h(2))$ **55.** $h(f(2))$ **56.** $f(g(h(4)))$ **57.** $f(g(f(-2)))$

NUMERIC

For the following exercises, use the function values for f and g shown in **Table 3** to evaluate each expression.

x	0	1	2	3	4	5	6	7	8	9
$f(x)$	7	6	5	8	4	0	2	1	9	3
$g(x)$	9	5	6	2	1	8	7	3	4	0

Table 3

58. $f(g(8))$ **59.** $f(g(5))$ **60.** $g(f(5))$ **61.** $g(f(3))$

62. $f(f(4))$ **63.** $f(f(1))$ **64.** $g(g(2))$ **65.** $g(g(6))$

For the following exercises, use the function values for f and g shown in **Table 4** to evaluate the expressions.

x	-3	-2	-1	0	1	2	3
$f(x)$	11	9	7	5	3	1	-1
$g(x)$	-8	-3	0	1	0	-3	-8

Table 4

66. $(f \circ g)(1)$ **67.** $(f \circ g)(2)$ **68.** $(g \circ f)(2)$

69. $(g \circ f)(3)$ **70.** $(g \circ g)(1)$ **71.** $(f \circ f)(3)$

For the following exercises, use each pair of functions to find $f(g(0))$ and $g(f(0))$.

72. $f(x) = 4x + 8, g(x) = 7 - x^2$ **73.** $f(x) = 5x + 7, g(x) = 4 - 2x^2$

74. $f(x) = \sqrt{x + 4}, g(x) = 12 - x^3$ **75.** $f(x) = \dfrac{1}{x + 2}, g(x) = 4x + 3$

For the following exercises, use the functions $f(x) = 2x^2 + 1$ and $g(x) = 3x + 5$ to evaluate or find the composite function as indicated.

76. $f(g(2))$ **77.** $f(g(x))$ **78.** $g(f(-3))$ **79.** $(g \circ g)(x)$

EXTENSIONS

For the following exercises, use $f(x) = x^3 + 1$ and $g(x) = \sqrt[3]{x - 1}$.

80. Find $(f \circ g)(x)$ and $(g \circ f)(x)$. Compare the two answers.

81. Find $(f \circ g)(2)$ and $(g \circ f)(2)$.

82. What is the domain of $(g \circ f)(x)$?

83. What is the domain of $(f \circ g)(x)$?

84. Let $f(x) = \dfrac{1}{x}$.

    a. Find $(f \circ f)(x)$.

    b. Is $(f \circ f)(x)$ for any function f the same result as the answer to part (a) for any function? Explain.

For the following exercises, let $F(x) = (x + 1)^5$, $f(x) = x^5$, and $g(x) = x + 1$.

85. True or False: $(g \circ f)(x) = F(x)$.

86. True or False: $(f \circ g)(x) = F(x)$.

For the following exercises, find the composition when $f(x) = x^2 + 2$ for all $x \geq 0$ and $g(x) = \sqrt{x - 2}$.

87. $(f \circ g)(6); (g \circ f)(6)$

88. $(g \circ f)(a); (f \circ g)(a)$

89. $(f \circ g)(11); (g \circ f)(11)$

REAL-WORLD APPLICATIONS

90. The function $D(p)$ gives the number of items that will be demanded when the price is p. The production cost $C(x)$ is the cost of producing x items. To determine the cost of production when the price is $6, you would do which of the following?

    a. Evaluate $D(C(6))$.

    b. Evaluate $C(D(6))$.

    c. Solve $D(C(x)) = 6$.

    d. Solve $C(D(p)) = 6$.

91. The function $A(d)$ gives the pain level on a scale of 0 to 10 experienced by a patient with d milligrams of a pain-reducing drug in her system. The milligrams of the drug in the patient's system after t minutes is modeled by $m(t)$. Which of the following would you do in order to determine when the patient will be at a pain level of 4?

    a. Evaluate $A(m(4))$.

    b. Evaluate $m(A(4))$.

    c. Solve $A(m(t)) = 4$.

    d. Solve $m(A(d)) = 4$.

92. A store offers customers a 30% discount on the price x of selected items. Then, the store takes off an additional 15% at the cash register. Write a price function $P(x)$ that computes the final price of the item in terms of the original price x. (Hint: Use function composition to find your answer.)

93. A rain drop hitting a lake makes a circular ripple. If the radius, in inches, grows as a function of time in minutes according to $r(t) = 25\sqrt{t + 2}$, find the area of the ripple as a function of time. Find the area of the ripple at $t = 2$.

94. A forest fire leaves behind an area of grass burned in an expanding circular pattern. If the radius of the circle of burning grass is increasing with time according to the formula $r(t) = 2t + 1$, express the area burned as a function of time, t (minutes).

95. Use the function you found in the previous exercise to find the total area burned after 5 minutes.

96. The radius r, in inches, of a spherical balloon is related to the volume, V, by $r(V) = \sqrt[3]{\dfrac{3V}{4\pi}}$. Air is pumped into the balloon, so the volume after t seconds is given by $V(t) = 10 + 20t$.

    a. Find the composite function $r(V(t))$.

    b. Find the *exact* time when the radius reaches 10 inches.

97. The number of bacteria in a refrigerated food product is given by

$$N(T) = 23T^2 - 56T + 1, 3 < T < 33,$$

where T is the temperature of the food. When the food is removed from the refrigerator, the temperature is given by $T(t) = 5t + 1.5$, where t is the time in hours.

    a. Find the composite function $N(T(t))$.

    b. Find the time (round to two decimal places) when the bacteria count reaches 6,752.

In this section, you will:

- Graph functions using vertical and horizontal shifts.
- Graph functions using reflections about the *x*-axis and the *y*-axis.
- Determine whether a function is even, odd, or neither from its graph.
- Graph functions using compressions and stretches.
- Combine transformations.

1.5   TRANSFORMATION OF FUNCTIONS

Figure 1 (credit: "Misko"/Flickr)

We all know that a flat mirror enables us to see an accurate image of ourselves and whatever is behind us. When we tilt the mirror, the images we see may shift horizontally or vertically. But what happens when we bend a flexible mirror? Like a carnival funhouse mirror, it presents us with a distorted image of ourselves, stretched or compressed horizontally or vertically. In a similar way, we can distort or transform mathematical functions to better adapt them to describing objects or processes in the real world. In this section, we will take a look at several kinds of transformations.

Graphing Functions Using Vertical and Horizontal Shifts

Often when given a problem, we try to model the scenario using mathematics in the form of words, tables, graphs, and equations. One method we can employ is to adapt the basic graphs of the toolkit functions to build new models for a given scenario. There are systematic ways to alter functions to construct appropriate models for the problems we are trying to solve.

Identifying Vertical Shifts

One simple kind of transformation involves shifting the entire graph of a function up, down, right, or left. The simplest shift is a **vertical shift**, moving the graph up or down, because this transformation involves adding a positive or negative constant to the function. In other words, we add the same constant to the output value of the function regardless of the input. For a function $g(x) = f(x) + k$, the function $f(x)$ is shifted vertically k units. See **Figure 2** for an example.

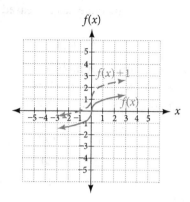

Figure 2 Vertical shift by $k = 1$ of the cube root function $f(x) = \sqrt[3]{x}$.

To help you visualize the concept of a vertical shift, consider that $y = f(x)$. Therefore, $f(x) + k$ is equivalent to $y + k$. Every unit of y is replaced by $y + k$, so the y-value increases or decreases depending on the value of k. The result is a shift upward or downward.

---

vertical shift

Given a function $f(x)$, a new function $g(x) = f(x) + k$, where k is a constant, is a **vertical shift** of the function $f(x)$. All the output values change by k units. If k is positive, the graph will shift up. If k is negative, the graph will shift down.

Example 1   **Adding a Constant to a Function**

To regulate temperature in a green building, airflow vents near the roof open and close throughout the day. **Figure 3** shows the area of open vents V (in square feet) throughout the day in hours after midnight, t. During the summer, the facilities manager decides to try to better regulate temperature by increasing the amount of open vents by 20 square feet throughout the day and night. Sketch a graph of this new function.

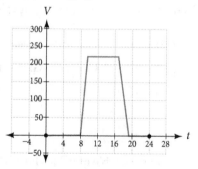

Figure 3

Solution   We can sketch a graph of this new function by adding 20 to each of the output values of the original function. This will have the effect of shifting the graph vertically up, as shown in **Figure 4**.

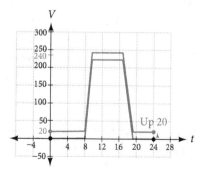

Figure 4

Notice that in **Figure 4**, for each input value, the output value has increased by 20, so if we call the new function $S(t)$, we could write

$$S(t) = V(t) + 20$$

This notation tells us that, for any value of t, $S(t)$ can be found by evaluating the function V at the same input and then adding 20 to the result. This defines S as a transformation of the function V, in this case a vertical shift up 20 units. Notice that, with a vertical shift, the input values stay the same and only the output values change. See **Table 1**.

t	0	8	10	17	19	24
$V(t)$	0	0	220	220	0	0
$S(t)$	20	20	240	240	20	20

Table 1

How To...

Given a tabular function, create a new row to represent a vertical shift.

1. Identify the output row or column.
2. Determine the magnitude of the shift.
3. Add the shift to the value in each output cell. Add a positive value for up or a negative value for down.

Example 2   **Shifting a Tabular Function Vertically**

A function $f(x)$ is given in **Table 2**. Create a table for the function $g(x) = f(x) - 3$.

x	2	4	6	8
$f(x)$	1	3	7	11

Table 2

Solution   The formula $g(x) = f(x) - 3$ tells us that we can find the output values of g by subtracting 3 from the output values of f. For example:

$$f(2) = 1 \qquad \text{Given}$$
$$g(x) = f(x) - 3 \qquad \text{Given transformation}$$
$$g(2) = f(2) - 3$$
$$= 1 - 3$$
$$= -2$$

Subtracting 3 from each $f(x)$ value, we can complete a table of values for $g(x)$ as shown in **Table 3**.

x	2	4	6	8
$f(x)$	1	3	7	11
$g(x)$	−2	0	4	8

Table 3

Analysis   As with the earlier vertical shift, notice the input values stay the same and only the output values change.

Try It #1

The function $h(t) = -4.9t^2 + 30t$ gives the height h of a ball (in meters) thrown upward from the ground after t seconds. Suppose the ball was instead thrown from the top of a 10-m building. Relate this new height function $b(t)$ to $h(t)$, and then find a formula for $b(t)$.

Identifying Horizontal Shifts

We just saw that the vertical shift is a change to the output, or outside, of the function. We will now look at how changes to input, on the inside of the function, change its graph and meaning. A shift to the input results in a movement of the graph of the function left or right in what is known as a **horizontal shift**, shown in **Figure 5**.

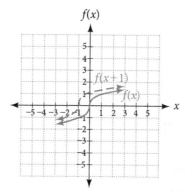

Figure 5 Horizontal shift of the function $f(x) = \sqrt[3]{x}$. Note that $h = +1$ shifts the graph to the left, that is, towards negative values of x.

For example, if $f(x) = x^2$, then $g(x) = (x - 2)^2$ is a new function. Each input is reduced by 2 prior to squaring the function. The result is that the graph is shifted 2 units to the right, because we would need to increase the prior input by 2 units to yield the same output value as given in f.

> ### horizontal shift
> Given a function f, a new function $g(x) = f(x - h)$, where h is a constant, is a **horizontal shift** of the function f. If h is positive, the graph will shift right. If h is negative, the graph will shift left.

Example 3 **Adding a Constant to an Input**

Returning to our building airflow example from **Figure 3**, suppose that in autumn the facilities manager decides that the original venting plan starts too late, and wants to begin the entire venting program 2 hours earlier. Sketch a graph of the new function.

Solution   We can set $V(t)$ to be the original program and $F(t)$ to be the revised program.

$$V(t) = \text{the original venting plan}$$

$$F(t) = \text{starting 2 hrs sooner}$$

In the new graph, at each time, the airflow is the same as the original function V was 2 hours later. For example, in the original function V, the airflow starts to change at 8 a.m., whereas for the function F, the airflow starts to change at 6 a.m. The comparable function values are $V(8) = F(6)$. See **Figure 6**. Notice also that the vents first opened to 220 ft² at 10 a.m. under the original plan, while under the new plan the vents reach 220 ft² at 8 a.m., so $V(10) = F(8)$.

In both cases, we see that, because $F(t)$ starts 2 hours sooner, $h = -2$. That means that the same output values are reached when $F(t) = V(t - (-2)) = V(t + 2)$.

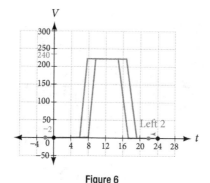

Figure 6

Analysis   Note that $V(t + 2)$ has the effect of shifting the graph to the left.

Horizontal changes or "inside changes" affect the domain of a function (the input) instead of the range and often seem counterintuitive. The new function $F(t)$ uses the same outputs as $V(t)$, but matches those outputs to inputs 2 hours earlier than those of $V(t)$. Said another way, we must add 2 hours to the input of V to find the corresponding output for F : $F(t) = V(t + 2)$.

How To...

Given a tabular function, create a new row to represent a horizontal shift.

1. Identify the input row or column.
2. Determine the magnitude of the shift.
3. Add the shift to the value in each input cell.

Example 4   **Shifting a Tabular Function Horizontally**

A function $f(x)$ is given in **Table 4**. Create a table for the function $g(x) = f(x - 3)$.

x	2	4	6	8
$f(x)$	1	3	7	11

Table 4

Solution   The formula $g(x) = f(x - 3)$ tells us that the output values of g are the same as the output value of f when the input value is 3 less than the original value. For example, we know that $f(2) = 1$. To get the same output from the function g, we will need an input value that is 3 *larger*. We input a value that is 3 larger for $g(x)$ because the function takes 3 away before evaluating the function f.

$$g(5) = f(5 - 3)$$
$$= f(2)$$
$$= 1$$

We continue with the other values to create **Table 5**.

x	5	7	9	11
$x - 3$	2	4	6	8
$f(x - 3)$	1	3	7	11
$g(x)$	1	3	7	11

Table 5

The result is that the function $g(x)$ has been shifted to the right by 3. Notice the output values for $g(x)$ remain the same as the output values for $f(x)$, but the corresponding input values, x, have shifted to the right by 3. Specifically, 2 shifted to 5, 4 shifted to 7, 6 shifted to 9, and 8 shifted to 11.

Analysis   **Figure 7 represents both of the functions. We can see the horizontal shift in each point.**

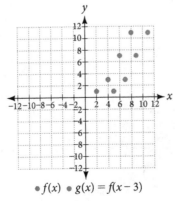

$\bullet f(x)$ $\bullet g(x) = f(x - 3)$

Figure 7

Example 5 Identifying a Horizontal Shift of a Toolkit Function

Figure 8 represents a transformation of the toolkit function $f(x) = x^2$. Relate this new function $g(x)$ to $f(x)$, and then find a formula for $g(x)$.

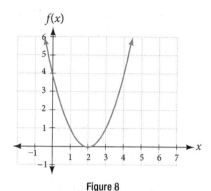

Figure 8

Solution   Notice that the graph is identical in shape to the $f(x) = x^2$ function, but the x-values are shifted to the right 2 units. The vertex used to be at $(0,0)$, but now the vertex is at $(2,0)$. The graph is the basic quadratic function shifted 2 units to the right, so

$$g(x) = f(x - 2)$$

Notice how we must input the value $x = 2$ to get the output value $y = 0$; the x-values must be 2 units larger because of the shift to the right by 2 units. We can then use the definition of the $f(x)$ function to write a formula for $g(x)$ by evaluating $f(x - 2)$.

$$f(x) = x^2$$
$$g(x) = f(x - 2)$$
$$g(x) = f(x - 2) = (x - 2)^2$$

Analysis   To determine whether the shift is $+2$ or -2, consider a single reference point on the graph. For a quadratic, looking at the vertex point is convenient. In the original function, $f(0) = 0$. In our shifted function, $g(2) = 0$. To obtain the output value of 0 from the function f, we need to decide whether a plus or a minus sign will work to satisfy $g(2) = f(x - 2) = f(0) = 0$. For this to work, we will need to subtract 2 units from our input values.

Example 6 Interpreting Horizontal versus Vertical Shifts

The function $G(m)$ gives the number of gallons of gas required to drive m miles. Interpret $G(m) + 10$ and $G(m + 10)$.

Solution $G(m) + 10$ can be interpreted as adding 10 to the output, gallons. This is the gas required to drive m miles, plus another 10 gallons of gas. The graph would indicate a vertical shift.

$G(m + 10)$ can be interpreted as adding 10 to the input, miles. So this is the number of gallons of gas required to drive 10 miles more than m miles. The graph would indicate a horizontal shift.

Try It #2

Given the function $f(x) = \sqrt{x}$, graph the original function $f(x)$ and the transformation $g(x) = f(x + 2)$ on the same axes. Is this a horizontal or a vertical shift? Which way is the graph shifted and by how many units?

Combining Vertical and Horizontal Shifts

Now that we have two transformations, we can combine them together. Vertical shifts are outside changes that affect the output (y-) axis values and shift the function up or down. Horizontal shifts are inside changes that affect the input (x-) axis values and shift the function left or right. Combining the two types of shifts will cause the graph of a function to shift up or down *and* right or left.

How To...

Given a function and both a vertical and a horizontal shift, sketch the graph.

1. Identify the vertical and horizontal shifts from the formula.
2. The vertical shift results from a constant added to the output. Move the graph up for a positive constant and down for a negative constant.
3. The horizontal shift results from a constant added to the input. Move the graph left for a positive constant and right for a negative constant.
4. Apply the shifts to the graph in either order.

Example 7   **Graphing Combined Vertical and Horizontal Shifts**

Given $f(x) = |x|$, sketch a graph of $h(x) = f(x + 1) - 3$.

Solution   The function f is our toolkit absolute value function. We know that this graph has a V shape, with the point at the origin. The graph of h has transformed f in two ways: $f(x + 1)$ is a change on the inside of the function, giving a horizontal shift left by 1, and the subtraction by 3 in $f(x + 1) - 3$ is a change to the outside of the function, giving a vertical shift down by 3. The transformation of the graph is illustrated in **Figure 9**.

Let us follow one point of the graph of $f(x) = |x|$.

- The point $(0, 0)$ is transformed first by shifting left 1 unit: $(0, 0) \rightarrow (-1, 0)$
- The point $(-1, 0)$ is transformed next by shifting down 3 units: $(-1, 0) \rightarrow (-1, -3)$

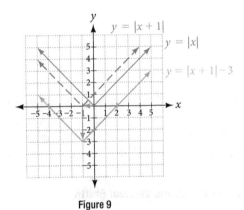

Figure 9

Figure 10 shows the graph of h.

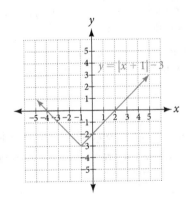

Figure 10

Try It #3

Given $f(x) = |x|$, sketch a graph of $h(x) = f(x - 2) + 4$.

Example 8   **Identifying Combined Vertical and Horizontal Shifts**

Write a formula for the graph shown in **Figure 11**, which is a transformation of the toolkit square root function.

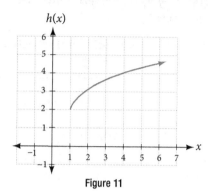

Figure 11

Solution   The graph of the toolkit function starts at the origin, so this graph has been shifted 1 to the right and up 2. In function notation, we could write that as

$$h(x) = f(x - 1) + 2$$

Using the formula for the square root function, we can write

$$h(x) = \sqrt{x - 1} + 2$$

Analysis   *Note that this transformation has changed the domain and range of the function. This new graph has domain $[1, \infty)$ and range $[2, \infty)$.*

Try It #4

Write a formula for a transformation of the toolkit reciprocal function $f(x) = \dfrac{1}{x}$ that shifts the function's graph one unit to the right and one unit up.

Graphing Functions Using Reflections about the Axes

Another transformation that can be applied to a function is a reflection over the *x*- or *y*-axis. A **vertical reflection** reflects a graph vertically across the *x*-axis, while a **horizontal reflection** reflects a graph horizontally across the *y*-axis. The reflections are shown in **Figure 12**.

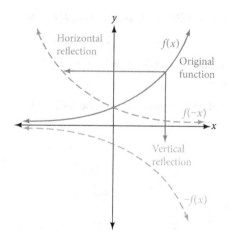

Figure 12 Vertical and horizontal reflections of a function.

Notice that the vertical reflection produces a new graph that is a mirror image of the base or original graph about the *x*-axis. The horizontal reflection produces a new graph that is a mirror image of the base or original graph about the *y*-axis.

> ### *reflections*
>
> Given a function $f(x)$, a new function $g(x) = -f(x)$ is a **vertical reflection** of the function $f(x)$, sometimes called a reflection about (or over, or through) the x-axis.
>
> Given a function $f(x)$, a new function $g(x) = f(-x)$ is a **horizontal reflection** of the function $f(x)$, sometimes called a reflection about the y-axis.

How To…

Given a function, reflect the graph both vertically and horizontally.

1. Multiply all outputs by −1 for a vertical reflection. The new graph is a reflection of the original graph about the x-axis.
2. Multiply all inputs by −1 for a horizontal reflection. The new graph is a reflection of the original graph about the y-axis.

Example 9   **Reflecting a Graph Horizontally and Vertically**

Reflect the graph of $s(t) = \sqrt{t}$ **a.** vertically and **b.** horizontally.

Solution

a. Reflecting the graph vertically means that each output value will be reflected over the horizontal t-axis as shown in **Figure 13**.

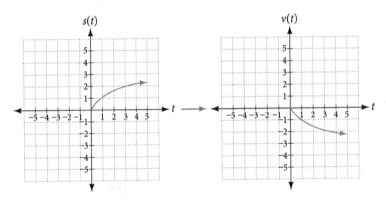

Figure 13 Vertical reflection of the square root function

Because each output value is the opposite of the original output value, we can write

$$V(t) = -s(t) \text{ or } V(t) = -\sqrt{t}$$

Notice that this is an outside change, or vertical shift, that affects the output $s(t)$ values, so the negative sign belongs outside of the function.

b. Reflecting horizontally means that each input value will be reflected over the vertical axis as shown in **Figure 14**.

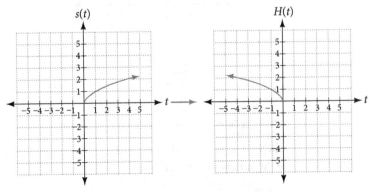

Figure 14 Horizontal reflection of the square root function

Because each input value is the opposite of the original input value, we can write

$$H(t) = s(-t) \text{ or } H(t) = \sqrt{-t}$$

Notice that this is an inside change or horizontal change that affects the input values, so the negative sign is on the inside of the function.

Note that these transformations can affect the domain and range of the functions. While the original square root function has domain $[0, \infty)$ and range $[0, \infty)$, the vertical reflection gives the $V(t)$ function the range $(-\infty, 0]$ and the horizontal reflection gives the $H(t)$ function the domain $(-\infty, 0]$.

Try It #5

Reflect the graph of $f(x) = |x - 1|$ **a.** vertically and **b.** horizontally.

Example 10 **Reflecting a Tabular Function Horizontally and Vertically**

A function $f(x)$ is given as **Table 6**. Create a table for the functions below.

   a. $g(x) = -f(x)$ **b.** $h(x) = f(-x)$

x	2	4	6	8
$f(x)$	1	3	7	11

Table 6

Solution

   a. For $g(x)$, the negative sign outside the function indicates a vertical reflection, so the x-values stay the same and each output value will be the opposite of the original output value. See **Table 7**.

x	2	4	6	8
$g(x)$	−1	−3	−7	−11

Table 7

   b. For $h(x)$, the negative sign inside the function indicates a horizontal reflection, so each input value will be the opposite of the original input value and the $h(x)$ values stay the same as the $f(x)$ values. See **Table 8**.

x	−2	−4	−6	−8
$h(x)$	1	3	7	11

Table 8

Try It #6

A function $f(x)$ is given as **Table 9**. Create a table for the functions below.

x	−2	0	2	4
$f(x)$	5	10	15	20

Table 9

a. $g(x) = -f(x)$

b. $h(x) = f(-x)$

Example 11   **Applying a Learning Model Equation**

A common model for learning has an equation similar to $k(t) = -2^{-t} + 1$, where k is the percentage of mastery that can be achieved after t practice sessions. This is a transformation of the function $f(t) = 2^t$ shown in **Figure 15**. Sketch a graph of $k(t)$.

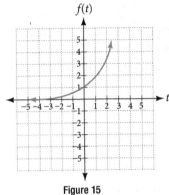

Figure 15

Solution   This equation combines three transformations into one equation.

- A horizontal reflection: $f(-t) = 2^{-t}$

- A vertical reflection: $-f(-t) = -2^{-t}$

- A vertical shift: $-f(-t) + 1 = -2^{-t} + 1$

We can sketch a graph by applying these transformations one at a time to the original function. Let us follow two points through each of the three transformations. We will choose the points $(0, 1)$ and $(1, 2)$.

1. First, we apply a horizontal reflection: $(0, 1)$ $(-1, 2)$.

2. Then, we apply a vertical reflection: $(0, -1)$ $(1, -2)$.

3. Finally, we apply a vertical shift: $(0, 0)$ $(1, 1)$.

This means that the original points, $(0,1)$ and $(1,2)$ become $(0,0)$ and $(1,1)$ after we apply the transformations.

In **Figure 16**, the first graph results from a horizontal reflection. The second results from a vertical reflection. The third results from a vertical shift up 1 unit.

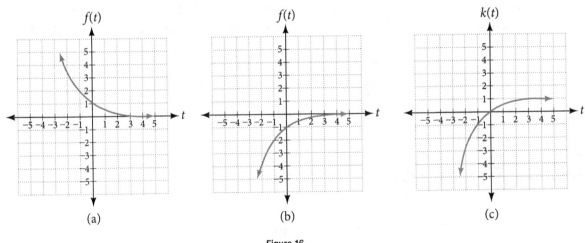

Figure 16

Analysis   *As a model for learning, this function would be limited to a domain of $t \geq 0$, with corresponding range $[0, 1)$.*

Try It #7

Given the toolkit function $f(x) = x^2$, graph $g(x) = -f(x)$ and $h(x) = f(-x)$. Take note of any surprising behavior for these functions.

Determining Even and Odd Functions

Some functions exhibit symmetry so that reflections result in the original graph. For example, horizontally reflecting the toolkit functions $f(x) = x^2$ or $f(x) = |x|$ will result in the original graph. We say that these types of graphs are symmetric about the y-axis. Functions whose graphs are symmetric about the y-axis are called **even functions**.

If the graphs of $f(x) = x^3$ or $f(x) = \frac{1}{x}$ were reflected over *both* axes, the result would be the original graph, as shown in **Figure 17**.

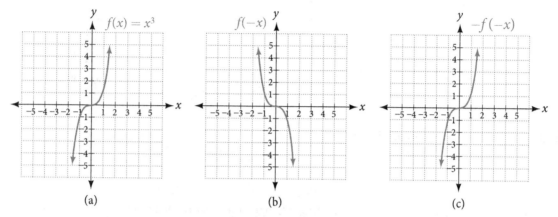

(a)   (b)   (c)

Figure 17 (a) The cubic toolkit function (b) Horizontal reflection of the cubic toolkit function
(c) Horizontal and vertical reflections reproduce the original cubic function.

We say that these graphs are symmetric about the origin. A function with a graph that is symmetric about the origin is called an **odd function**.

Note: A function can be neither even nor odd if it does not exhibit either symmetry. For example, $f(x) = 2^x$ is neither even nor odd. Also, the only function that is both even and odd is the constant function $f(x) = 0$.

---

even and odd functions

A function is called an **even function** if for every input x: $f(x) = f(-x)$

The graph of an even function is symmetric about the y-axis.

A function is called an **odd function** if for every input x: $f(x) = -f(-x)$

The graph of an odd function is symmetric about the origin.

How To…

Given the formula for a function, determine if the function is even, odd, or neither.

1. Determine whether the function satisfies $f(x) = f(-x)$. If it does, it is even.
2. Determine whether the function satisfies $f(x) = -f(-x)$. If it does, it is odd.
3. If the function does not satisfy either rule, it is neither even nor odd.

Example 12 **Determining whether a Function Is Even, Odd, or Neither**

Is the function $f(x) = x^3 + 2x$ even, odd, or neither?

Solution   Without looking at a graph, we can determine whether the function is even or odd by finding formulas for the reflections and determining if they return us to the original function. Let's begin with the rule for even functions.

$$f(-x) = (-x)^3 + 2(-x) = -x^3 - 2x$$

This does not return us to the original function, so this function is not even. We can now test the rule for odd functions.

$$-f(-x) = -(-x^3 - 2x) = x^3 + 2x$$

Because $-f(-x) = f(x)$, this is an odd function.

Analysis Consider the graph of *f* in **Figure 18**. Notice that the graph is symmetric about the origin. For every point (*x*, *y*) on the graph, the corresponding point (−*x*, −*y*) is also on the graph. For example, (1, 3) is on the graph of *f*, and the corresponding point (−1, −3) is also on the graph.

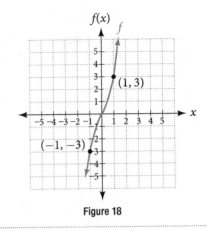

Figure 18

Try It #8

Is the function $f(s) = s^4 + 3s^2 + 7$ even, odd, or neither?

Graphing Functions Using Stretches and Compressions

Adding a constant to the inputs or outputs of a function changed the position of a graph with respect to the axes, but it did not affect the shape of a graph. We now explore the effects of multiplying the inputs or outputs by some quantity.

We can transform the inside (input values) of a function or we can transform the outside (output values) of a function. Each change has a specific effect that can be seen graphically.

Vertical Stretches and Compressions

When we multiply a function by a positive constant, we get a function whose graph is stretched or compressed vertically in relation to the graph of the original function. If the constant is greater than 1, we get a **vertical stretch**; if the constant is between 0 and 1, we get a **vertical compression**. **Figure 19** shows a function multiplied by constant factors 2 and 0.5 and the resulting vertical stretch and compression.

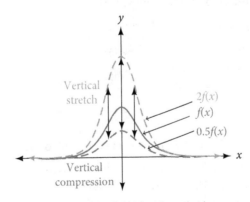

Figure 19 Vertical stretch and compression

---

vertical stretches and compressions

Given a function $f(x)$, a new function $g(x) = af(x)$, where *a* is a constant, is a **vertical stretch** or **vertical compression** of the function $f(x)$.

- If $a > 1$, then the graph will be stretched.

- If $0 < a < 1$, then the graph will be compressed.

- If $a < 0$, then there will be combination of a vertical stretch or compression with a vertical reflection.

Given a function, graph its vertical stretch.

1. Identify the value of a.

2. Multiply all range values by a.

3. If $a > 1$, the graph is stretched by a factor of a.
If $0 < a < 1$, the graph is compressed by a factor of a.
If $a < 0$, the graph is either stretched or compressed and also reflected about the x-axis.

Example 13   **Graphing a Vertical Stretch**

A function $P(t)$ models the population of fruit flies. The graph is shown in **Figure 20**.

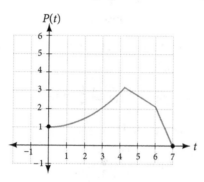

Figure 20

A scientist is comparing this population to another population, Q, whose growth follows the same pattern, but is twice as large. Sketch a graph of this population.

Solution   Because the population is always twice as large, the new population's output values are always twice the original function's output values. Graphically, this is shown in **Figure 21**.

If we choose four reference points, $(0, 1)$, $(3, 3)$, $(6, 2)$ and $(7, 0)$ we will multiply all of the outputs by 2.

The following shows where the new points for the new graph will be located.

$(0, 1) \rightarrow (0, 2)$

$(3, 3) \rightarrow (3, 6)$

$(6, 2) \rightarrow (6, 4)$

$(7, 0) \rightarrow (7, 0)$

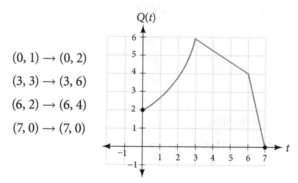

Figure 21

Symbolically, the relationship is written as

$$Q(t) = 2P(t)$$

This means that for any input t, the value of the function Q is twice the value of the function P. Notice that the effect on the graph is a vertical stretching of the graph, where every point doubles its distance from the horizontal axis. The input values, t, stay the same while the output values are twice as large as before.

How To…

Given a tabular function and assuming that the transformation is a vertical stretch or compression, create a table for a vertical compression.

1. Determine the value of a.
2. Multiply all of the output values by a.

Example 14   **Finding a Vertical Compression of a Tabular Function**

A function f is given as **Table 10**. Create a table for the function $g(x) = \frac{1}{2}f(x)$.

x	2	4	6	8
$f(x)$	1	3	7	11

Table 10

Solution   The formula $g(x) = \frac{1}{2}f(x)$ tells us that the output values of g are half of the output values of f with the same inputs. For example, we know that $f(4) = 3$. Then

$$g(4) = \frac{1}{2}f(4) = \frac{1}{2}(3) = \frac{3}{2}$$

We do the same for the other values to produce **Table 11**.

x	2	4	6	8
$g(x)$	$\frac{1}{2}$	$\frac{3}{2}$	$\frac{7}{2}$	$\frac{11}{2}$

Table 11

Analysis   *The result is that the function $g(x)$ has been compressed vertically by $\frac{1}{2}$. Each output value is divided in half, so the graph is half the original height.*

Try It #9

A function f is given as **Table 12**. Create a table for the function $g(x) = \frac{3}{4}f(x)$.

x	2	4	6	8
$f(x)$	12	16	20	0

Table 12

Example 15   **Recognizing a Vertical Stretch**

The graph in **Figure 22** is a transformation of the toolkit function $f(x) = x^3$. Relate this new function $g(x)$ to $f(x)$, and then find a formula for $g(x)$.

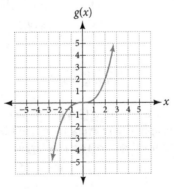

Figure 22

Solution   When trying to determine a vertical stretch or shift, it is helpful to look for a point on the graph that is relatively clear. In this graph, it appears that $g(2) = 2$. With the basic cubic function at the same input, $f(2) = 2^3 = 8$. Based on that, it appears that the outputs of g are $\frac{1}{4}$ the outputs of the function f because $g(2) = \frac{1}{4} f(2)$. From this we can fairly safely conclude that $g(x) = \frac{1}{4} f(x)$.

We can write a formula for g by using the definition of the function f.

$$g(x) = \frac{1}{4} f(x) = \frac{1}{4} x^3$$

Try It #10

Write the formula for the function that we get when we stretch the identity toolkit function by a factor of 3, and then shift it down by 2 units.

Horizontal Stretches and Compressions

Now we consider changes to the inside of a function. When we multiply a function's input by a positive constant, we get a function whose graph is stretched or compressed horizontally in relation to the graph of the original function. If the constant is between 0 and 1, we get a **horizontal stretch**; if the constant is greater than 1, we get a **horizontal compression** of the function.

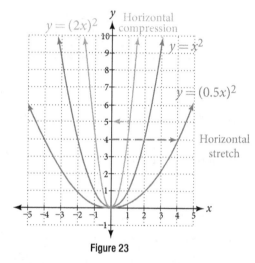

Figure 23

Given a function $y = f(x)$, the form $y = f(bx)$ results in a horizontal stretch or compression. Consider the function $y = x^2$. Observe **Figure 23**. The graph of $y = (0.5x)^2$ is a horizontal stretch of the graph of the function $y = x^2$ by a factor of 2. The graph of $y = (2x)^2$ is a horizontal compression of the graph of the function $y = x^2$ by a factor of 2.

---

horizontal stretches and compressions

Given a function $f(x)$, a new function $g(x) = f(bx)$, where b is a constant, is a **horizontal stretch** or **horizontal compression** of the function $f(x)$.

- If $b > 1$, then the graph will be compressed by $\frac{1}{b}$.

- If $0 < b < 1$, then the graph will be stretched by $\frac{1}{b}$.

- If $b < 0$, then there will be combination of a horizontal stretch or compression with a horizontal reflection.

How To...

Given a description of a function, sketch a horizontal compression or stretch.

1. Write a formula to represent the function.

2. Set $g(x) = f(bx)$ where $b > 1$ for a compression or $0 < b < 1$ for a stretch.

Example 16   **Graphing a Horizontal Compression**

Suppose a scientist is comparing a population of fruit flies to a population that progresses through its lifespan twice as fast as the original population. In other words, this new population, R, will progress in 1 hour the same amount as the original population does in 2 hours, and in 2 hours, it will progress as much as the original population does in 4 hours. Sketch a graph of this population.

Solution   Symbolically, we could write

$$R(1) = P(2),$$

$$R(2) = P(4), \text{ and in general,}$$

$$R(t) = P(2t).$$

See **Figure 24** for a graphical comparison of the original population and the compressed population.

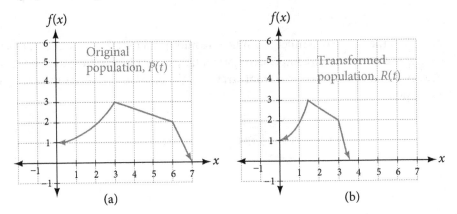

Figure 24 (a) Original population graph (b) Compressed population graph

Analysis   Note that the effect on the graph is a horizontal compression where all input values are half of their original distance from the vertical axis.

Example 17   **Finding a Horizontal Stretch for a Tabular Function**

A function $f(x)$ is given as **Table 13**. Create a table for the function $g(x) = f\left(\frac{1}{2}x\right)$.

x	2	4	6	8
$f(x)$	1	3	7	11

Table 13

Solution   The formula $g(x) = f\left(\frac{1}{2}x\right)$ tells us that the output values for g are the same as the output values for the function f at an input half the size. Notice that we do not have enough information to determine $g(2)$ because $g(2) = f\left(\frac{1}{2} \cdot 2\right) = f(1)$, and we do not have a value for $f(1)$ in our table. Our input values to g will need to be twice as large to get inputs for f that we can evaluate. For example, we can determine $g(4)$.

$$g(4) = f\left(\frac{1}{2} \cdot 4\right) = f(2) = 1$$

We do the same for the other values to produce **Table 14**.

x	4	8	12	16
$g(x)$	1	3	7	11

Table 14

Figure 25 shows the graphs of both of these sets of points.

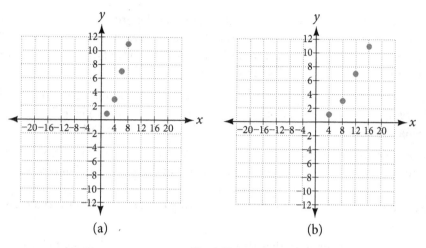

(a)   (b)

Figure 25

Analysis   *Because each input value has been doubled, the result is that the function g(x) has been stretched horizontally by a factor of 2.*

Example 18   Recognizing a Horizontal Compression on a Graph

Relate the function $g(x)$ to $f(x)$ in **Figure 26**.

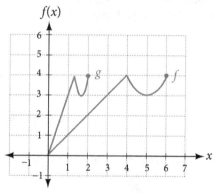

Figure 26

Solution   The graph of $g(x)$ looks like the graph of $f(x)$ horizontally compressed. Because $f(x)$ ends at $(6, 4)$ and $g(x)$ ends at $(2, 4)$, we can see that the x-values have been compressed by $\frac{1}{3}$, because $6\left(\frac{1}{3}\right) = 2$. We might also notice that $g(2) = f(6)$ and $g(1) = f(3)$. Either way, we can describe this relationship as $g(x) = f(3x)$. This is a horizontal compression by $\frac{1}{3}$.

Analysis   *Notice that the coefficient needed for a horizontal stretch or compression is the reciprocal of the stretch or compression. So to stretch the graph horizontally by a scale factor of 4, we need a coefficient of $\frac{1}{4}$ in our function: $f\left(\frac{1}{4}x\right)$. This means that the input values must be four times larger to produce the same result, requiring the input to be larger, causing the horizontal stretching.*

Try It #11

Write a formula for the toolkit square root function horizontally stretched by a factor of 3.

Performing a Sequence of Transformations

When combining transformations, it is very important to consider the order of the transformations. For example, vertically shifting by 3 and then vertically stretching by 2 does not create the same graph as vertically stretching by 2 and then vertically shifting by 3, because when we shift first, both the original function and the shift get stretched, while only the original function gets stretched when we stretch first.

When we see an expression such as $2f(x) + 3$, which transformation should we start with? The answer here follows nicely from the order of operations. Given the output value of $f(x)$, we first multiply by 2, causing the vertical stretch, and then add 3, causing the vertical shift. In other words, multiplication before addition.

Horizontal transformations are a little trickier to think about. When we write $g(x) = f(2x + 3)$, for example, we have to think about how the inputs to the function g relate to the inputs to the function f. Suppose we know $f(7) = 12$. What input to g would produce that output? In other words, what value of x will allow $g(x) = f(2x + 3) = 12$? We would need $2x + 3 = 7$. To solve for x, we would first subtract 3, resulting in a horizontal shift, and then divide by 2, causing a horizontal compression.

This format ends up being very difficult to work with, because it is usually much easier to horizontally stretch a graph before shifting. We can work around this by factoring inside the function.

$$f(bx + p) = f\left(b\left(x + \frac{p}{b}\right)\right)$$

Let's work through an example.

$$f(x) = (2x + 4)^2$$

We can factor out a 2.

$$f(x) = (2(x + 2))^2$$

Now we can more clearly observe a horizontal shift to the left 2 units and a horizontal compression. Factoring in this way allows us to horizontally stretch first and then shift horizontally.

---

combining transformations

When combining vertical transformations written in the form $af(x) + k$, first vertically stretch by a and then vertically shift by k.

When combining horizontal transformations written in the form $f(bx - h)$, first horizontally shift by h and then horizontally stretch by $\frac{1}{b}$.

When combining horizontal transformations written in the form $f(b(x - h))$, first horizontally stretch by $\frac{1}{b}$ and then horizontally shift by h.

Horizontal and vertical transformations are independent. It does not matter whether horizontal or vertical transformations are performed first.

Example 19   **Finding a Triple Transformation of a Tabular Function**

Given **Table 15** for the function $f(x)$, create a table of values for the function $g(x) = 2f(3x) + 1$.

x	6	12	18	24
$f(x)$	10	14	15	17

Table 15

Solution   There are three steps to this transformation, and we will work from the inside out. Starting with the horizontal transformations, $f(3x)$ is a horizontal compression by $\frac{1}{3}$, which means we multiply each x-value by $\frac{1}{3}$. See **Table 16**.

x	2	4	6	8
$f(3x)$	10	14	15	17

Table 16

Looking now to the vertical transformations, we start with the vertical stretch, which will multiply the output values by 2. We apply this to the previous transformation. See **Table 17**.

x	2	4	6	8
$2f(3x)$	20	28	30	34

Table 17

Finally, we can apply the vertical shift, which will add 1 to all the output values. See **Table 18**.

x	2	4	6	8
$g(x) = 2f(3x) + 1$	21	29	31	35

Table 18

Example 20 **Finding a Triple Transformation of a Graph**

Use the graph of $f(x)$ in **Figure 27** to sketch a graph of $k(x) = f\left(\dfrac{1}{2}x + 1\right) - 3$.

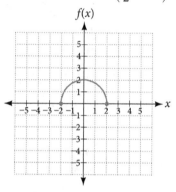

Figure 27

Solution To simplify, let's start by factoring out the inside of the function.

$$f\left(\frac{1}{2}x + 1\right) - 3 = f\left(\frac{1}{2}(x + 2)\right) - 3$$

By factoring the inside, we can first horizontally stretch by 2, as indicated by the $\dfrac{1}{2}$ on the inside of the function. Remember that twice the size of 0 is still 0, so the point (0, 2) remains at (0, 2) while the point (2, 0) will stretch to (4, 0). See **Figure 28**.

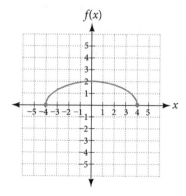

Figure 28

Next, we horizontally shift left by 2 units, as indicated by $x + 2$. See **Figure 29**.

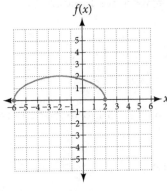

Figure 29

Last, we vertically shift down by 3 to complete our sketch, as indicated by the -3 on the outside of the function. See **Figure 30**.

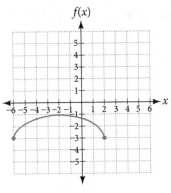

Figure 30

Access this online resource for additional instruction and practice with transformation of functions.

- Function Transformations (http://openstaxcollege.org/l/functrans)

1.5   SECTION EXERCISES

VERBAL

1. When examining the formula of a function that is the result of multiple transformations, how can you tell a horizontal shift from a vertical shift?

2. When examining the formula of a function that is the result of multiple transformations, how can you tell a horizontal stretch from a vertical stretch?

3. When examining the formula of a function that is the result of multiple transformations, how can you tell a horizontal compression from a vertical compression?

4. When examining the formula of a function that is the result of multiple transformations, how can you tell a reflection with respect to the x-axis from a reflection with respect to the y-axis?

5. How can you determine whether a function is odd or even from the formula of the function?

ALGEBRAIC

6. Write a formula for the function obtained when the graph of $f(x) = \sqrt{x}$ is shifted up 1 unit and to the left 2 units.

7. Write a formula for the function obtained when the graph of $f(x) = |x|$ is shifted down 3 units and to the right 1 unit.

8. Write a formula for the function obtained when the graph of $f(x) = \frac{1}{x}$ is shifted down 4 units and to the right 3 units.

9. Write a formula for the function obtained when the graph of $f(x) = \frac{1}{x^2}$ is shifted up 2 units and to the left 4 units.

For the following exercises, describe how the graph of the function is a transformation of the graph of the original function f.

10. $y = f(x - 49)$

11. $y = f(x + 43)$

12. $y = f(x + 3)$

13. $y = f(x - 4)$

14. $y = f(x) + 5$

15. $y = f(x) + 8$

16. $y = f(x) - 2$

17. $y = f(x) - 7$

18. $y = f(x - 2) + 3$

19. $y = f(x + 4) - 1$

For the following exercises, determine the interval(s) on which the function is increasing and decreasing.

20. $f(x) = 4(x + 1)^2 - 5$

21. $g(x) = 5(x + 3)^2 - 2$

22. $a(x) = \sqrt{-x + 4}$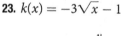

23. $k(x) = -3\sqrt{x} - 1$

y

Figure 31

GRAPHICAL

For the following exercises, use the graph of $f(x) = 2^x$ shown in **Figure 31** to sketch a graph of each transformation of $f(x)$.

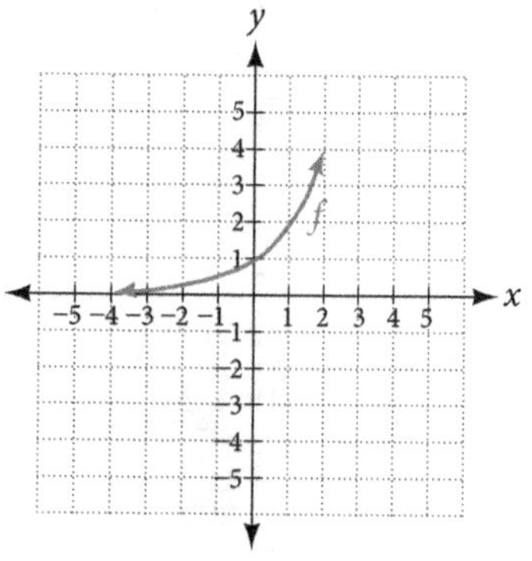

24. $g(x) = 2^x + 1$

25. $h(x) = 2^x - 3$

26. $w(x) = 2^{x-1}$

For the following exercises, sketch a graph of the function as a transformation of the graph of one of the toolkit functions.

27. $f(t) = (t + 1)^2 - 3$

28. $h(x) = |x - 1| + 4$

29. $k(x) = (x - 2)^3 - 1$

30. $m(t) = 3 + \sqrt{t + 2}$

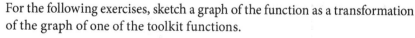

NUMERIC

31. Tabular representations for the functions f, g, and h are given below. Write $g(x)$ and $h(x)$ as transformations of $f(x)$.

x	-2	-1	0	1	2
$f(x)$	-2	-1	-3	1	2

x	-1	0	1	2	3
$g(x)$	-2	-1	-3	1	2

x	-2	-1	0	1	2
$h(x)$	-1	0	-2	2	3

32. Tabular representations for the functions f, g, and h are given below. Write $g(x)$ and $h(x)$ as transformations of $f(x)$.

x	-2	-1	0	1	2
$f(x)$	-1	-3	4	2	1

x	-3	-2	-1	0	1
$g(x)$	-1	-3	4	2	1

x	-2	-1	0	1	2
$h(x)$	-2	-4	3	1	0

For the following exercises, write an equation for each graphed function by using transformations of the graphs of one of the toolkit functions.

33.

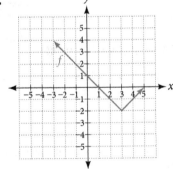

34.

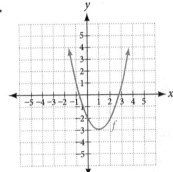

35.

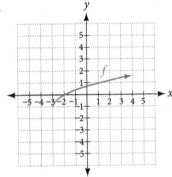

36.

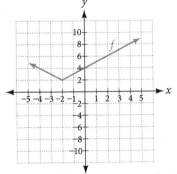

37.

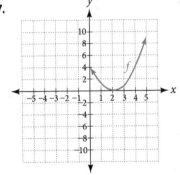

38.

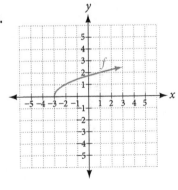

39.
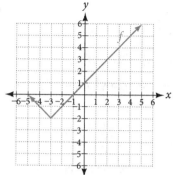

40.
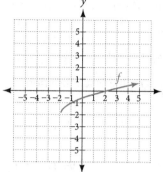

For the following exercises, use the graphs of transformations of the square root function to find a formula for each of the functions.

41.
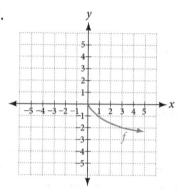

42.
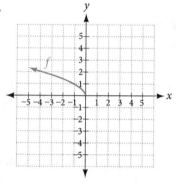

For the following exercises, use the graphs of the transformed toolkit functions to write a formula for each of the resulting functions.

43.
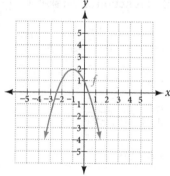

44.
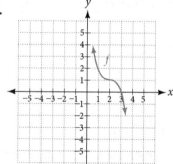

45.
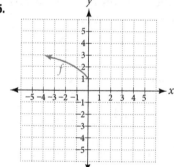

46.
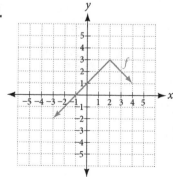

For the following exercises, determine whether the function is odd, even, or neither.

47. $f(x) = 3x^4$

48. $g(x) = \sqrt{x}$

49. $h(x) = \dfrac{1}{x} + 3x$

50. $f(x) = (x - 2)^2$

51. $g(x) = 2x^4$

52. $h(x) = 2x - x^3$

For the following exercises, describe how the graph of each function is a transformation of the graph of the original function f.

53. $g(x) = -f(x)$

54. $g(x) = f(-x)$

55. $g(x) = 4f(x)$

56. $g(x) = 6f(x)$

57. $g(x) = f(5x)$

58. $g(x) = f(2x)$

59. $g(x) = f\left(\dfrac{1}{3}x\right)$

60. $g(x) = f\left(\dfrac{1}{5}x\right)$

61. $g(x) = 3f(-x)$

62. $g(x) = -f(3x)$

For the following exercises, write a formula for the function g that results when the graph of a given toolkit function is transformed as described.

63. The graph of $f(x) = |x|$ is reflected over the y-axis and horizontally compressed by a factor of $\dfrac{1}{4}$.

64. The graph of $f(x) = \sqrt{x}$ is reflected over the x-axis and horizontally stretched by a factor of 2.

65. The graph of $f(x) = \dfrac{1}{x^2}$ is vertically compressed by a factor of $\dfrac{1}{3}$, then shifted to the left 2 units and down 3 units.

66. The graph of $f(x) = \dfrac{1}{x}$ is vertically stretched by a factor of 8, then shifted to the right 4 units and up 2 units.

67. The graph of $f(x) = x^2$ is vertically compressed by a factor of $\dfrac{1}{2}$, then shifted to the right 5 units and up 1 unit.

68. The graph of $f(x) = x^2$ is horizontally stretched by a factor of 3, then shifted to the left 4 units and down 3 units.

For the following exercises, describe how the formula is a transformation of a toolkit function. Then sketch a graph of the transformation.

69. $g(x) = 4(x + 1)^2 - 5$

70. $g(x) = 5(x + 3)^2 - 2$

71. $h(x) = -2|x - 4| + 3$

72. $k(x) = -3\sqrt{x} - 1$

73. $m(x) = \dfrac{1}{2}x^3$

74. $n(x) = \dfrac{1}{3}|x - 2|$

75. $p(x) = \left(\dfrac{1}{3}x\right)^3 - 3$

76. $q(x) = \left(\dfrac{1}{4}x\right)^3 + 1$

77. $a(x) = \sqrt{-x + 4}$

For the following exercises, use the graph in **Figure 32** to sketch the given transformations.

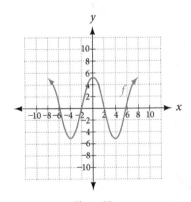

Figure 32

78. $g(x) = f(x) - 2$

79. $g(x) = -f(x)$

80. $g(x) = f(x + 1)$

81. $g(x) = f(x - 2)$

LEARNING OBJECTIVES

In this section you will:

- Graph an absolute value function.
- Solve an absolute value equation.
- Solve an absolute value inequality.

1.6   ABSOLUTE VALUE FUNCTIONS

Figure 1 Distances in deep space can be measured in all directions. As such, it is useful to consider distance in terms of absolute values. (credit: "s58y"/Flickr)

Until the 1920s, the so-called spiral nebulae were believed to be clouds of dust and gas in our own galaxy, some tens of thousands of light years away. Then, astronomer Edwin Hubble proved that these objects are galaxies in their own right, at distances of millions of light years. Today, astronomers can detect galaxies that are billions of light years away. Distances in the universe can be measured in all directions. As such, it is useful to consider distance as an absolute value function. In this section, we will investigate absolute value functions.

Understanding Absolute Value

Recall that in its basic form $f(x) = |x|$, the absolute value function, is one of our toolkit functions. The absolute value function is commonly thought of as providing the distance the number is from zero on a number line. Algebraically, for whatever the input value is, the output is the value without regard to sign.

> ***absolute value function***
> The absolute value function can be defined as a piecewise function
> $$f(x) = |x| = \begin{cases} x & \text{if } x \geq 0 \\ -x & \text{if } x < 0 \end{cases}$$

Example 1   **Determine a Number within a Prescribed Distance**

Describe all values x within or including a distance of 4 from the number 5.

Solution   We want the distance between x and 5 to be less than or equal to 4. We can draw a number line, such as the one in **Figure 2**, to represent the condition to be satisfied.

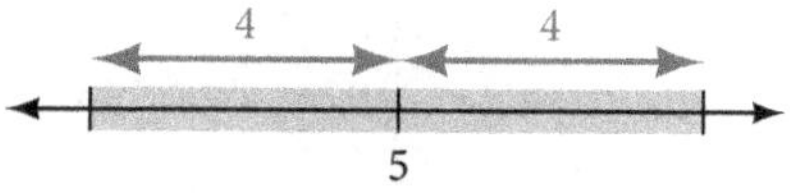

4   4

5

Figure 2

The distance from x to 5 can be represented using the absolute value as $|x - 5|$. We want the values of x that satisfy the condition $|x - 5| \leq 4$.

Analysis   *Note that*

$$-4 \leq x - 5 \qquad x - 5 \leq 4$$
$$1 \leq x \qquad\qquad x \leq 9$$

So $|x - 5| \leq 4$ *is equivalent to* $1 \leq x \leq 9$. *However, mathematicians generally prefer absolute value notation.*

Try It #1

Describe all values x within a distance of 3 from the number 2.

Example 2   **Resistance of a Resistor**

Electrical parts, such as resistors and capacitors, come with specified values of their operating parameters: resistance, capacitance, etc. However, due to imprecision in manufacturing, the actual values of these parameters vary somewhat from piece to piece, even when they are supposed to be the same. The best that manufacturers can do is to try to guarantee that the variations will stay within a specified range, often ±1%, ±5%, or ±10%.

Suppose we have a resistor rated at 680 ohms, ±5%. Use the absolute value function to express the range of possible values of the actual resistance.

Solution   5% of 680 ohms is 34 ohms. The absolute value of the difference between the actual and nominal resistance should not exceed the stated variability, so, with the resistance R in ohms,

$$|R - 680| \leq 34$$

Try It #2

Students who score within 20 points of 80 will pass a test. Write this as a distance from 80 using absolute value notation.

Graphing an Absolute Value Function

The most significant feature of the absolute value graph is the corner point at which the graph changes direction. This point is shown at the origin in **Figure 3**.

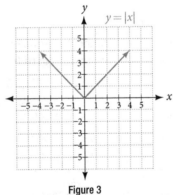

Figure 3

Figure 4 shows the graph of $y = 2|x - 3| + 4$. The graph of $y = |x|$ has been shifted right 3 units, vertically stretched by a factor of 2, and shifted up 4 units. This means that the corner point is located at (3, 4) for this transformed function.

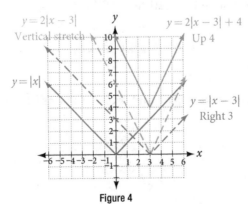

Figure 4

Example 3   **Writing an Equation for an Absolute Value Function**

Write an equation for the function graphed in **Figure 5**.

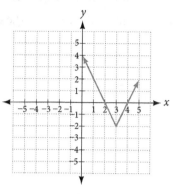

Figure 5

Solution   The basic absolute value function changes direction at the origin, so this graph has been shifted to the right 3 units and down 2 units from the basic toolkit function. See **Figure 6**.

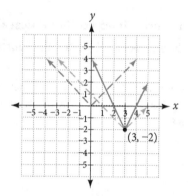

Figure 6

We also notice that the graph appears vertically stretched, because the width of the final graph on a horizontal line is not equal to 2 times the vertical distance from the corner to this line, as it would be for an unstretched absolute value function. Instead, the width is equal to 1 times the vertical distance as shown in **Figure 7**.

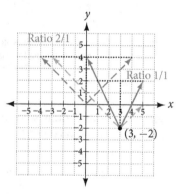

Figure 7

From this information we can write the equation

$$f(x) = 2|x - 3| - 2, \text{ treating the stretch as a vertical stretch, or}$$

$$f(x) = |2(x - 3)| - 2, \text{ treating the stretch as a horizontal compression.}$$

Analysis   Note that these equations are algebraically equivalent—the stretch for an absolute value function can be written interchangeably as a vertical or horizontal stretch or compression.

Q & A...

If we couldn't observe the stretch of the function from the graphs, could we algebraically determine it?

Yes. If we are unable to determine the stretch based on the width of the graph, we can solve for the stretch factor by putting in a known pair of values for x and $f(x)$.

$$f(x) = a|x - 3| - 2$$

Now substituting in the point (1, 2)

$$2 = a|1 - 3| - 2$$
$$4 = 2a$$
$$a = 2$$

Try It #3

Write the equation for the absolute value function that is horizontally shifted left 2 units, is vertically flipped, and vertically shifted up 3 units.

Q & A...

Do the graphs of absolute value functions always intersect the vertical axis? The horizontal axis?

Yes, they always intersect the vertical axis. The graph of an absolute value function will intersect the vertical axis when the input is zero.

No, they do not always intersect the horizontal axis. The graph may or may not intersect the horizontal axis, depending on how the graph has been shifted and reflected. It is possible for the absolute value function to intersect the horizontal axis at zero, one, or two points (see **Figure 8**).

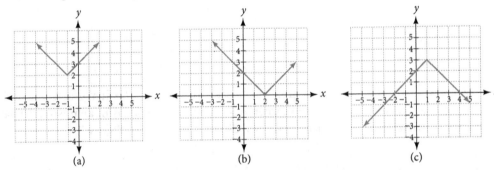

(a)   (b)   (c)

Figure 8 (a) The absolute value function does not intersect the horizontal axis. (b) The absolute value function intersects the horizontal axis at one point. (c) The absolute value function intersects the horizontal axis at two points.

Solving an Absolute Value Equation

Now that we can graph an absolute value function, we will learn how to solve an absolute value equation. To solve an equation such as $8 = |2x - 6|$, we notice that the absolute value will be equal to 8 if the quantity inside the absolute value is 8 or -8. This leads to two different equations we can solve independently.

$$2x - 6 = 8 \text{ or } 2x - 6 = -8$$
$$2x = 14 \qquad 2x = -2$$
$$x = 7 \qquad x = -1$$

Knowing how to solve problems involving absolute value functions is useful. For example, we may need to identify numbers or points on a line that are at a specified distance from a given reference point.

An **absolute value equation** is an equation in which the unknown variable appears in absolute value bars. For example,

$$|x| = 4,$$
$$|2x - 1| = 3$$
$$|5x + 2| - 4 = 9$$

> **solutions to absolute value equations**
> For real numbers A and B, an equation of the form $|A| = B$, with $B \geq 0$, will have solutions when $A = B$ or $A = -B$. If $B < 0$, the equation $|A| = B$ has no solution.

How To...

Given the formula for an absolute value function, find the horizontal intercepts of its graph.

1. Isolate the absolute value term.
2. Use $|A| = B$ to write $A = B$ or $-A = B$, assuming $B > 0$.
3. Solve for x.

Example 4 **Finding the Zeros of an Absolute Value Function**

For the function $f(x) = |4x + 1| - 7$, find the values of x such that $f(x) = 0$.

Solution

$$0 = |4x + 1| - 7 \qquad \text{Substitute 0 for } f(x).$$

$$7 = |4x + 1| \qquad \text{Isolate the absolute value on one side of the equation.}$$

$$7 = 4x + 1 \text{ or } -7 = 4x + 1 \qquad \text{Break into two separate equations and solve.}$$

$$6 = 4x \qquad\qquad -8 = 4x$$

$$x = \frac{6}{4} = 1.5 \qquad x = \frac{-8}{4} = -2$$

The function outputs 0 when $x = 1.5$ or $x = -2$. See **Figure 9**.

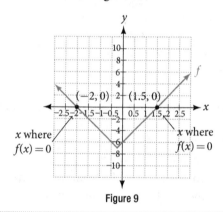

Figure 9

Try It #4

For the function $f(x) = |2x - 1| - 3$, find the values of x such that $f(x) = 0$.

Q & A...

Should we always expect two answers when solving $|A| = B$?

No. We may find one, two, or even no answers. For example, there is no solution to $2 + |3x - 5| = 1$.

How To...

Given an absolute value equation, solve it.

1. Isolate the absolute value term.
2. Use $|A| = B$ to write $A = B$ or $A = -B$.
3. Solve for x.

Example 5   **Solving an Absolute Value Equation**

Solve $1 = 4|x - 2| + 2$.

Solution   Isolating the absolute value on one side of the equation gives the following.

$$1 = 4|x - 2| + 2$$
$$-1 = 4|x - 2|$$
$$-\frac{1}{4} = |x - 2|$$

The absolute value always returns a positive value, so it is impossible for the absolute value to equal a negative value. At this point, we notice that this equation has no solutions.

Q & A...

In Example 5, if $f(x) = 1$ and $g(x) = 4|x - 2| + 2$ were graphed on the same set of axes, would the graphs intersect?

No. The graphs of f and g would not intersect, as shown in **Figure 10**. This confirms, graphically, that the equation $1 = 4|x - 2| + 2$ has no solution.

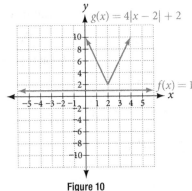

Figure 10

Try It #5

Find where the graph of the function $f(x) = -|x + 2| + 3$ intersects the horizontal and vertical axes.

Solving an Absolute Value Inequality

Absolute value equations may not always involve equalities. Instead, we may need to solve an equation within a range of values. We would use an absolute value inequality to solve such an equation. An **absolute value inequality** is an equation of the form

$$|A| < B, |A| \le B, |A| \ge B, \text{ or } |A| \ge B,$$

where an expression A (and possibly but not usually B) depends on a variable x. Solving the inequality means finding the set of all x that satisfy the inequality. Usually this set will be an interval or the union of two intervals.

There are two basic approaches to solving absolute value inequalities: graphical and algebraic. The advantage of the graphical approach is we can read the solution by interpreting the graphs of two functions. The advantage of the algebraic approach is it yields solutions that may be difficult to read from the graph.

For example, we know that all numbers within 200 units of 0 may be expressed as

$$|x| < 200 \text{ or } -200 < x < 200$$

Suppose we want to know all possible returns on an investment if we could earn some amount of money within \$200 of \$600. We can solve algebraically for the set of values x such that the distance between x and 600 is less than 200. We represent the distance between x and 600 as $|x - 600|$.

$$|x - 600| < 200 \text{ or } -200 < x - 600 < 200$$

$$-200 + 600 < x - 600 + 600 < 200 + 600$$

$$400 < x < 800$$

This means our returns would be between $400 and $800.

Sometimes an absolute value inequality problem will be presented to us in terms of a shifted and/or stretched or compressed absolute value function, where we must determine for which values of the input the function's output will be negative or positive.

How To…

Given an absolute value inequality of the form $|x - A| \leq B$ for real numbers a and b where b is positive, solve the absolute value inequality algebraically.

1. Find boundary points by solving $|x - A| = B$.
2. Test intervals created by the boundary points to determine where $|x - A| \leq B$.
3. Write the interval or union of intervals satisfying the inequality in interval, inequality, or set-builder notation.

Example 6   **Solving an Absolute Value Inequality**

Solve $|x - 5| < 4$.

Solution   With both approaches, we will need to know first where the corresponding equality is true. In this case we first will find where $|x - 5| = 4$. We do this because the absolute value is a function with no breaks, so the only way the function values can switch from being less than 4 to being greater than 4 is by passing through where the values equal 4. Solve $|x - 5| = 4$.

$$x - 5 = 4 \text{ or } x - 5 = -4$$
$$x = 9 \qquad x = 1$$

After determining that the absolute value is equal to 4 at $x = 1$ and $x = 9$, we know the graph can change only from being less than 4 to greater than 4 at these values. This divides the number line up into three intervals:

$$x < 1, 1 < x < 9, \text{ and } x > 9.$$

To determine when the function is less than 4, we could choose a value in each interval and see if the output is less than or greater than 4, as shown in **Table 1**.

Interval test x	$f(x)$	< 4 or > 4?	
$x < 1$	0	$\lvert 0 - 5 \rvert = 5$	Greater than
$1 < x < 9$	6	$\lvert 6 - 5 \rvert = 1$	Less than
$x > 9$	11	$\lvert 11 - 5 \rvert = 6$	Greater than

Table 1

Because $1 \leq x \leq 9$ is the only interval in which the output at the test value is less than 4, we can conclude that the solution to $|x - 5| \leq 4$ is $1 \leq x \leq 9$, or $[1, 9]$.

To use a graph, we can sketch the function $f(x) = |x - 5|$. To help us see where the outputs are 4, the line $g(x) = 4$ could also be sketched as in **Figure 11**.

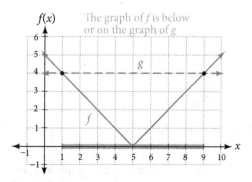

Figure 11 Graph to find the points satisfying an absolute value inequality.

We can see the following:

- The output values of the absolute value are equal to 4 at $x = 1$ and $x = 9$.
- The graph of f is below the graph of g on $1 < x < 9$. This means the output values of $f(x)$ are less than the output values of $g(x)$.
- The absolute value is less than or equal to 4 between these two points, when $1 \leq x \leq 9$. In interval notation, this would be the interval $[1, 9]$.

Analysis   *For absolute value inequalities,*

$$|x - A| < C, \qquad\qquad |x - A| > C,$$
$$-C < x - A < C, \qquad\qquad x - A < -C \text{ or } x - A > C.$$

The $<$ or $>$ symbol may be replaced by $\leq$ or $\geq$.

So, for this example, we could use this alternative approach.

$$|x - 5| \leq 4$$
$$-4 \leq x - 5 \leq 4 \qquad \text{Rewrite by removing the absolute value bars.}$$
$$-4 + 5 \leq x - 5 + 5 \leq 4 + 5 \qquad \text{Isolate the } x.$$
$$1 \leq x \leq 9$$

Try It #6

Solve $|x + 2| \leq 6$.

How To...

Given an absolute value function, solve for the set of inputs where the output is positive (or negative).

1. Set the function equal to zero, and solve for the boundary points of the solution set.
2. Use test points or a graph to determine where the function's output is positive or negative.

Example 7   **Using a Graphical Approach to Solve Absolute Value Inequalities**

Given the function $f(x) = -\dfrac{1}{2}|4x - 5| + 3$, determine the x-values for which the function values are negative.

Solution   We are trying to determine where $f(x) < 0$, which is when $-\dfrac{1}{2}|4x - 5| + 3 < 0$. We begin by isolating the absolute value.

$$-\frac{1}{2}\left|4x - 5\right| < -3 \qquad \text{Multiply both sides by } -2, \text{ and reverse the inequality.}$$
$$|4x - 5| > 6$$

Next we solve for the equality $|4x - 5| = 6$.

$$4x - 5 = 6 \quad \text{or} \quad 4x - 5 = -6$$
$$4x - 5 = 6 \qquad\qquad 4x = -1$$
$$x = \frac{11}{4} \qquad\qquad\qquad x = -\frac{1}{4}$$

Now, we can examine the graph of f to observe where the output is negative. We will observe where the branches are below the x-axis. Notice that it is not even important exactly what the graph looks like, as long as we know that it crosses the horizontal axis at $x = -\dfrac{1}{4}$ and $x = \dfrac{11}{4}$ and that the graph has been reflected vertically. See **Figure 12**.

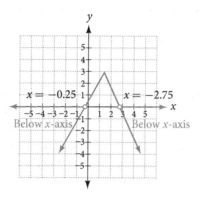

Figure 12

We observe that the graph of the function is below the *x*-axis left of $x = -\frac{1}{4}$ and right of $x = \frac{11}{4}$ This means the function values are negative to the left of the first horizontal intercept at $x = -\frac{1}{4}$, and negative to the right of the second intercept at $x = \frac{11}{4}$. This gives us the solution to the inequality.

$$x < -\frac{1}{4} \text{ or } x > \frac{11}{4}$$

In interval notation, this would be $(-\infty, -0.25) \cup (2.75, \infty)$.

Try It #7

Solve $-2|k - 4| \le -6$.

Access these online resources for additional instruction and practice with absolute value.

- Graphing Absolute Value Functions (http://openstaxcollege.org/l/graphabsvalue)
- Graphing Absolute Value Functions 2 (http://openstaxcollege.org/l/graphabsvalue2)
- Equations of Absolute Value Function (http://openstaxcollege.org/l/findeqabsval)
- Equations of Absolute Value Function 2 (http://openstaxcollege.org/l/findeqabsval2)
- Solving Absolute Value Equations (http://openstaxcollege.org/l/solveabsvalueeq)

1.6   SECTION EXERCISES

VERBAL

1. How do you solve an absolute value equation?

2. How can you tell whether an absolute value function has two x-intercepts without graphing the function?

3. When solving an absolute value function, the isolated absolute value term is equal to a negative number. What does that tell you about the graph of the absolute value function?

4. How can you use the graph of an absolute value function to determine the x-values for which the function values are negative?

5. How do you solve an absolute value inequality algebraically?

ALGEBRAIC

6. Describe all numbers x that are at a distance of 4 from the number 8. Express this using absolute value notation.

7. Describe all numbers x that are at a distance of $\frac{1}{2}$ from the number -4. Express this using absolute value notation.

8. Describe the situation in which the distance that point x is from 10 is at least 15 units. Express this using absolute value notation.

9. Find all function values $f(x)$ such that the distance from $f(x)$ to the value 8 is less than 0.03 units. Express this using absolute value notation.

For the following exercises, solve the equations below and express the answer using set notation.

10. $|x+3| = 9$

11. $|6-x| = 5$

12. $|5x-2| = 11$

13. $|4x-2| = 11$

14. $2|4-x| = 7$

15. $3|5-x| = 5$

16. $3|x+1|-4 = 5$

17. $5|x-4|-7 = 2$

18. $0 = -|x-3|+2$

19. $2|x-3|+1 = 2$

20. $|3x-2| = 7$

21. $|3x-2| = -7$

22. $\left|\frac{1}{2}x-5\right| = 11$

23. $\left|\frac{1}{3}x+5\right| = 14$

24. $-\left|\frac{1}{3}x+5\right|+14 = 0$

For the following exercises, find the x- and y-intercepts of the graphs of each function.

25. $f(x) = 2|x+1|-10$

26. $f(x) = 4|x-3|+4$

27. $f(x) = -3|x-2|-1$

28. $f(x) = -2|x+1|+6$

For the following exercises, solve each inequality and write the solution in interval notation.

29. $|x-2| > 10$

30. $2|v-7|-4 \geq 42$

31. $|3x-4| \leq 8$

32. $|x-4| \geq 8$

33. $|3x-5| \geq 13$

34. $|3x-5| \geq -13$

35. $\left|\frac{3}{4}x-5\right| \geq 7$

36. $\left|\frac{3}{4}x-5\right|+1 \leq 16$

GRAPHICAL

For the following exercises, graph the absolute value function. Plot at least five points by hand for each graph.

37. $y = |x - 1|$ **38.** $y = |x + 1|$ **39.** $y = |x| + 1$

For the following exercises, graph the given functions by hand.

40. $y = |x| - 2$ **41.** $y = -|x|$ **42.** $y = -|x| - 2$

43. $y = -|x - 3| - 2$ **44.** $f(x) = -|x - 1| - 2$ **45.** $f(x) = -|x + 3| + 4$

46. $f(x) = 2|x + 3| + 1$ **47.** $f(x) = 3|x - 2| + 3$ **48.** $f(x) = |2x - 4| - 3$

49. $f(x) = |3x + 9| + 2$ **50.** $f(x) = -|x - 1| - 3$ **51.** $f(x) = -|x + 4| - 3$

52. $f(x) = \dfrac{1}{2}|x + 4| - 3$

TECHNOLOGY

53. Use a graphing utility to graph $f(x) = 10|x - 2|$ on the viewing window $[0, 4]$. Identify the corresponding range. Show the graph.

54. Use a graphing utility to graph $f(x) = -100|x| + 100$ on the viewing window $[-5, 5]$. Identify the corresponding range. Show the graph.

For the following exercises, graph each function using a graphing utility. Specify the viewing window.

55. $f(x) = -0.1|0.1(0.2 - x)| + 0.3$

56. $f(x) = 4 \times 10^9 |x - (5 \times 10^9)| + 2 \times 10^9$

EXTENSIONS

For the following exercises, solve the inequality.

57. $\left| -2x - \dfrac{2}{3}(x + 1) \right| + 3 > -1$

58. If possible, find all values of a such that there are no x-intercepts for $f(x) = 2|x + 1| + a$.

59. If possible, find all values of a such that there are no y-intercepts for $f(x) = 2|x + 1| + a$.

REAL-WORLD APPLICATIONS

60. Cities A and B are on the same east-west line. Assume that city A is located at the origin. If the distance from city A to city B is at least 100 miles and x represents the distance from city B to city A, express this using absolute value notation.

61. The true proportion p of people who give a favorable rating to Congress is 8% with a margin of error of 1.5%. Describe this statement using an absolute value equation.

62. Students who score within 18 points of the number 82 will pass a particular test. Write this statement using absolute value notation and use the variable x for the score.

63. A machinist must produce a bearing that is within 0.01 inches of the correct diameter of 5.0 inches. Using x as the diameter of the bearing, write this statement using absolute value notation.

64. The tolerance for a ball bearing is 0.01. If the true diameter of the bearing is to be 2.0 inches and the measured value of the diameter is x inches, express the tolerance using absolute value notation.

LEARNING OBJECTIVES

In this section, you will:

- Verify inverse functions.
- Determine the domain and range of an inverse function, and restrict the domain of a function to make it one-to-one.
- Find or evaluate the inverse of a function.
- Use the graph of a one-to-one function to graph its inverse function on the same axes.

1.7   INVERSE FUNCTIONS

A reversible heat pump is a climate-control system that is an air conditioner and a heater in a single device. Operated in one direction, it pumps heat out of a house to provide cooling. Operating in reverse, it pumps heat into the building from the outside, even in cool weather, to provide heating. As a heater, a heat pump is several times more efficient than conventional electrical resistance heating.

If some physical machines can run in two directions, we might ask whether some of the function "machines" we have been studying can also run backwards. **Figure 1** provides a visual representation of this question. In this section, we will consider the reverse nature of functions.

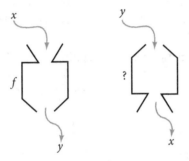

Figure 1 Can a function "machine" operate in reverse?

Verifying That Two Functions Are Inverse Functions

Suppose a fashion designer traveling to Milan for a fashion show wants to know what the temperature will be. He is not familiar with the Celsius scale. To get an idea of how temperature measurements are related, he asks his assistant, Betty, to convert 75 degrees Fahrenheit to degrees Celsius. She finds the formula

$$C = \frac{5}{9}(F - 32)$$

and substitutes 75 for F to calculate

$$\frac{5}{9}(75 - 32) \approx 24°C.$$

Knowing that a comfortable 75 degrees Fahrenheit is about 24 degrees Celsius, he sends his assistant the week's weather forecast from **Figure 2** for Milan, and asks her to convert all of the temperatures to degrees Fahrenheit.

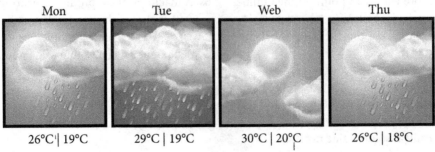

Mon	Tue	Web	Thu
26°C | 19°C	29°C | 19°C	30°C | 20°C	26°C | 18°C

Figure 2

At first, Betty considers using the formula she has already found to complete the conversions. After all, she knows her algebra, and can easily solve the equation for F after substituting a value for C. For example, to convert 26 degrees Celsius, she could write

$$26 = \frac{5}{9}(F - 32)$$

$$26 \cdot \frac{9}{5} = F - 32$$

$$F = 26 \cdot \frac{9}{5} + 32 \approx 79$$

After considering this option for a moment, however, she realizes that solving the equation for each of the temperatures will be awfully tedious. She realizes that since evaluation is easier than solving, it would be much more convenient to have a different formula, one that takes the Celsius temperature and outputs the Fahrenheit temperature.

The formula for which Betty is searching corresponds to the idea of an **inverse function**, which is a function for which the input of the original function becomes the output of the inverse function and the output of the original function becomes the input of the inverse function.

Given a function $f(x)$, we represent its inverse as $f^{-1}(x)$, read as "f inverse of x." The raised -1 is part of the notation. It is not an exponent; it does not imply a power of -1. In other words, $f^{-1}(x)$ does *not* mean $\frac{1}{f(x)}$ because $\frac{1}{f(x)}$ is the reciprocal of f and not the inverse.

The "exponent-like" notation comes from an analogy between function composition and multiplication: just as a^{-1} $a = 1$ (1 is the identity element for multiplication) for any nonzero number a, so $f^{-1} \circ f$ equals the identity function, that is,

$$(f^{-1} \circ f)(x) = f^{-1}(f(x)) = f^{-1}(y) = x$$

This holds for all x in the domain of f. Informally, this means that inverse functions "undo" each other. However, just as zero does not have a reciprocal, some functions do not have inverses.

Given a function $f(x)$, we can verify whether some other function $g(x)$ is the inverse of $f(x)$ by checking whether either $g(f(x)) = x$ or $f(g(x)) = x$ is true. We can test whichever equation is more convenient to work with because they are logically equivalent (that is, if one is true, then so is the other.)

For example, $y = 4x$ and $y = \frac{1}{4}x$ are inverse functions.

$$(f^{-1} \circ f)(x) = f^{-1}(4x) = \frac{1}{4}(4x) = x$$

and

$$(f \circ f^{-1})(x) = f\left(\frac{1}{4}x\right) = 4\left(\frac{1}{4}x\right) = x$$

A few coordinate pairs from the graph of the function $y = 4x$ are $(-2, -8)$, $(0, 0)$, and $(2, 8)$. A few coordinate pairs from the graph of the function $y = \frac{1}{4}x$ are $(-8, -2)$, $(0, 0)$, and $(8, 2)$. If we interchange the input and output of each coordinate pair of a function, the interchanged coordinate pairs would appear on the graph of the inverse function.

---

inverse function

For any one-to-one function $f(x) = y$, a function $f^{-1}(x)$ is an **inverse function** of f if $f^{-1}(y) = x$. This can also be written as $f^{-1}(f(x)) = x$ for all x in the domain of f. It also follows that $f(f^{-1}(x)) = x$ for all x in the domain of f^{-1} if f^{-1} is the inverse of f.

The notation f^{-1} is read "f inverse." Like any other function, we can use any variable name as the input for f^{-1}, so we will often write $f^{-1}(x)$, which we read as "f inverse of x." Keep in mind that

$$f^{-1}(x) \neq \frac{1}{f(x)}$$

and not all functions have inverses.

Example 1   **Identifying an Inverse Function for a Given Input-Output Pair**

If for a particular one-to-one function $f(2) = 4$ and $f(5) = 12$, what are the corresponding input and output values for the inverse function?

Solution   The inverse function reverses the input and output quantities, so if

$$f(2) = 4, \text{ then } f^{-1}(4) = 2;$$
$$f(5) = 12, \text{ then } f^{-1}(12) = 5.$$

Alternatively, if we want to name the inverse function g, then $g(4) = 2$ and $g(12) = 5$.

Analysis Notice that if we show the coordinate pairs in a table form, the input and output are clearly reversed. See **Table 1**.

$(x, f(x))$	$(x, g(x))$
(2, 4)	(4, 2)
(5, 12)	(12, 5)

Table 1

Try It #1

Given that $h^{-1}(6) = 2$, what are the corresponding input and output values of the original function h?

How To...

Given two functions $f(x)$ and $g(x)$, test whether the functions are inverses of each other.

1. Determine whether $f(g(x)) = x$ or $g(f(x)) = x$.
2. If both statements are true, then $g = f^{-1}$ and $f = g^{-1}$. If either statement is false, then both are false, and $g \neq f^{-1}$ and $f \neq g^{-1}$.

Example 2   **Testing Inverse Relationships Algebraically**

If $f(x) = \dfrac{1}{x+2}$ and $g(x) = \dfrac{1}{x} - 2$, is $g = f^{-1}$?

Solution
$$g(f(x)) = \dfrac{1}{\left(\dfrac{1}{x+2}\right)} - 2$$
$$= x + 2 - 2$$
$$= x$$

so
$$g = f^{-1} \text{ and } f = g^{-1}$$

This is enough to answer yes to the question, but we can also verify the other formula.

$$f(g(x)) = \dfrac{1}{\dfrac{1}{x} - 2 + 2}$$
$$= \dfrac{1}{\dfrac{1}{x}}$$
$$= x$$

Analysis Notice the inverse operations are in reverse order of the operations from the original function.

Try It #2

If $f(x) = x^3 - 4$ and $g(x) = \sqrt[3]{x - 4}$, is $g = f^{-1}$?

Example 3   **Determining Inverse Relationships for Power Functions**

If $f(x) = x^3$ (the cube function) and $g(x) = \frac{1}{3}x$, is $g = f^{-1}$?

Solution $f(g(x)) = \frac{x^3}{27} \neq x$

No, the functions are not inverses.

Analysis   The correct inverse to the cube is, of course, the cube root $\sqrt[3]{x} = x^{1/3}$ that is, the one-third is an exponent, not a multiplier.

Try It #3

If $f(x) = (x-1)^3$ and $g(x) = \sqrt[3]{x} + 1$, is $g = f^{-1}$?

Finding Domain and Range of Inverse Functions

The outputs of the function f are the inputs to f^{-1}, so the range of f is also the domain of f^{-1}. Likewise, because the inputs to f are the outputs of f^{-1}, the domain of f is the range of f^{-1}. We can visualize the situation as in **Figure 3**.

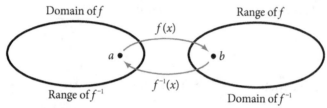

Figure 3 Domain and range of a function and its inverse

When a function has no inverse function, it is possible to create a new function where that new function on a limited domain does have an inverse function. For example, the inverse of $f(x) = \sqrt{x}$ is $f^{-1}(x) = x^2$, because a square "undoes" a square root; but the square is only the inverse of the square root on the domain $[0, \infty)$, since that is the range of $f(x) = \sqrt{x}$.

We can look at this problem from the other side, starting with the square (toolkit quadratic) function $f(x) = x^2$. If we want to construct an inverse to this function, we run into a problem, because for every given output of the quadratic function, there are two corresponding inputs (except when the input is 0). For example, the output 9 from the quadratic function corresponds to the inputs 3 and –3. But an output from a function is an input to its inverse; if this inverse input corresponds to more than one inverse output (input of the original function), then the "inverse" is not a function at all! To put it differently, the quadratic function is not a one-to-one function; it fails the horizontal line test, so it does not have an inverse function. In order for a function to have an inverse, it must be a one-to-one function.

In many cases, if a function is not one-to-one, we can still restrict the function to a part of its domain on which it is one-to-one. For example, we can make a restricted version of the square function $f(x) = x^2$ with its domain limited to $[0, \infty)$, which is a one-to-one function (it passes the horizontal line test) and which has an inverse (the square-root function).

If $f(x) = (x-1)^2$ on $[1, \infty)$, then the inverse function is $f^{-1}(x) = \sqrt{x} + 1$.

- The domain of f = range of f^{-1} = $[1, \infty)$.
- The domain of f^{-1} = range of f = $[0, \infty)$.

Q & A...

Is it possible for a function to have more than one inverse?

No. If two supposedly different functions, say, g and h, both meet the definition of being inverses of another function f, then you can prove that $g = h$. We have just seen that some functions only have inverses if we restrict the domain of the original function. In these cases, there may be more than one way to restrict the domain, leading to different inverses. However, on any one domain, the original function still has only one unique inverse.

> **domain and range of inverse functions**
>
> The range of a function $f(x)$ is the domain of the inverse function $f^{-1}(x)$. The domain of $f(x)$ is the range of $f^{-1}(x)$.

How To…

Given a function, find the domain and range of its inverse.

1. If the function is one-to-one, write the range of the original function as the domain of the inverse, and write the domain of the original function as the range of the inverse.
2. If the domain of the original function needs to be restricted to make it one-to-one, then this restricted domain becomes the range of the inverse function.

Example 4   **Finding the Inverses of Toolkit Functions**

Identify which of the toolkit functions besides the quadratic function are not one-to-one, and find a restricted domain on which each function is one-to-one, if any. The toolkit functions are reviewed in **Table 2**. We restrict the domain in such a fashion that the function assumes all y-values exactly once.

Constant	Identity	Quadratic	Cubic	Reciprocal
$f(x) = c$	$f(x) = x$	$f(x) = x^2$	$f(x) = x^3$	$f(x) = \frac{1}{x}$

Reciprocal squared	Cube root	Square root	Absolute value	
$f(x) = \frac{1}{x^2}$	$f(x) = \sqrt[3]{x}$	$f(x) = \sqrt{x}$	$f(x) = |x|$	

Table 2

Solution   The constant function is not one-to-one, and there is no domain (except a single point) on which it could be one-to-one, so the constant function has no meaningful inverse.

The absolute value function can be restricted to the domain $[0, \infty)$, where it is equal to the identity function.

The reciprocal-squared function can be restricted to the domain $(0, \infty)$.

*Analysis   We can see that these functions (if unrestricted) are not one-to-one by looking at their graphs, shown in **Figure 4**. They both would fail the horizontal line test. However, if a function is restricted to a certain domain so that it passes the horizontal line test, then in that restricted domain, it can have an inverse.*

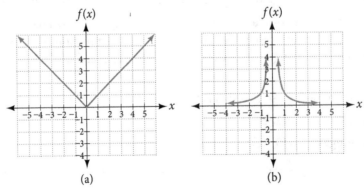

Figure 4 (a) Absolute value (b) Reciprocal squared

Try It #4

The domain of function f is $(1, \infty)$ and the range of function f is $(-\infty, -2)$. Find the domain and range of the inverse function.

Finding and Evaluating Inverse Functions

Once we have a one-to-one function, we can evaluate its inverse at specific inverse function inputs or construct a complete representation of the inverse function in many cases.

Inverting Tabular Functions

Suppose we want to find the inverse of a function represented in table form. Remember that the domain of a function is the range of the inverse and the range of the function is the domain of the inverse. So we need to interchange the domain and range.

Each row (or column) of inputs becomes the row (or column) of outputs for the inverse function. Similarly, each row (or column) of outputs becomes the row (or column) of inputs for the inverse function.

Example 5 Interpreting the Inverse of a Tabular Function

A function $f(t)$ is given in **Table 3**, showing distance in miles that a car has traveled in t minutes. Find and interpret $f^{-1}(70)$.

t (minutes)	30	50	70	90
$f(t)$ (miles)	20	40	60	70

Table 3

Solution The inverse function takes an output of f and returns an input for f. So in the expression $f^{-1}(70)$, 70 is an output value of the original function, representing 70 miles. The inverse will return the corresponding input of the original function f, 90 minutes, so $f^{-1}(70) = 90$. The interpretation of this is that, to drive 70 miles, it took 90 minutes.

Alternatively, recall that the definition of the inverse was that if $f(a) = b$, then $f^{-1}(b) = a$. By this definition, if we are given $f^{-1}(70) = a$, then we are looking for a value a so that $f(a) = 70$. In this case, we are looking for a t so that $f(t) = 70$, which is when $t = 90$.

Try It #5

Using **Table 4**, find and interpret **a.** $f(60)$, and **b.** $f^{-1}(60)$.

t (minutes)	30	50	60	70	90
$f(t)$ (miles)	20	40	50	60	70

Table 4

Evaluating the Inverse of a Function, Given a Graph of the Original Function

We saw in **Functions and Function Notation** that the domain of a function can be read by observing the horizontal extent of its graph. We find the domain of the inverse function by observing the *vertical* extent of the graph of the original function, because this corresponds to the horizontal extent of the inverse function. Similarly, we find the range of the inverse function by observing the *horizontal* extent of the graph of the original function, as this is the vertical extent of the inverse function. If we want to evaluate an inverse function, we find its input within its domain, which is all or part of the vertical axis of the original function's graph.

How To...

Given the graph of a function, evaluate its inverse at specific points.

1. Find the desired input on the y-axis of the given graph.
2. Read the inverse function's output from the x-axis of the given graph.

Example 6   **Evaluating a Function and Its Inverse from a Graph at Specific Points**

A function $g(x)$ is given in **Figure 5**. Find $g(3)$ and $g^{-1}(3)$.

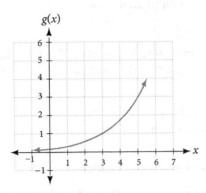

Figure 5

Solution   To evaluate $g(3)$, we find 3 on the x-axis and find the corresponding output value on the y-axis. The point $(3, 1)$ tells us that $g(3) = 1$.

To evaluate $g^{-1}(3)$, recall that by definition $g^{-1}(3)$ means the value of x for which $g(x) = 3$. By looking for the output value 3 on the vertical axis, we find the point $(5, 3)$ on the graph, which means $g(5) = 3$, so by definition, $g^{-1}(3) = 5$. See **Figure 6**.

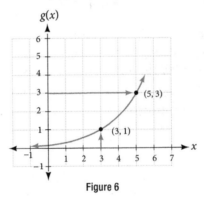

Figure 6

Try It #6

Using the graph in **Figure 6**, **a.** find $g^{-1}(1)$, and **b.** estimate $g^{-1}(4)$.

Finding Inverses of Functions Represented by Formulas

Sometimes we will need to know an inverse function for all elements of its domain, not just a few. If the original function is given as a formula—for example, y as a function of x—we can often find the inverse function by solving to obtain x as a function of y.

How To...

Given a function represented by a formula, find the inverse.

1. Make sure f is a one-to-one function.
2. Solve for x.
3. Interchange x and y.

Example 7   **Inverting the Fahrenheit-to-Celsius Function**

Find a formula for the inverse function that gives Fahrenheit temperature as a function of Celsius temperature.

$$C = \frac{5}{9}(F - 32)$$

Solution

$$C = \frac{5}{9}(F - 32)$$

$$C \cdot \frac{9}{5} = F - 32$$

$$F = \frac{9}{5}C + 32$$

By solving in general, we have uncovered the inverse function. If

$$C = h(F) = \frac{5}{9}(F - 32),$$

then

$$F = h^{-1}(C) = \frac{9}{5}C + 32.$$

In this case, we introduced a function h to represent the conversion because the input and output variables are descriptive, and writing C^{-1} could get confusing.

Try It #7

Solve for x in terms of y given $y = \frac{1}{3}(x - 5)$

Example 8 Solving to Find an Inverse Function

Find the inverse of the function $f(x) = \frac{2}{x - 3} + 4.$

Solution

$$y = \frac{2}{x - 3} + 4 \quad \text{Set up an equation.}$$

$$y - 4 = \frac{2}{x - 3} \quad \text{Subtract 4 from both sides.}$$

$$x - 3 = \frac{2}{y - 4} \quad \text{Multiply both sides by } x - 3 \text{ and divide by } y - 4.$$

$$x = \frac{2}{y - 4} + 3 \quad \text{Add 3 to both sides.}$$

So $f^{-1}(y) = \frac{2}{y - 4} + 3$ or $f^{-1}(x) = \frac{2}{x - 4} + 3.$

Analysis *The domain and range of f exclude the values 3 and 4, respectively. f and f^{-1} are equal at two points but are not the same function, as we can see by creating* **Table 5**.

x	1	2	5	$f^{-1}(y)$
$f(x)$	3	2	5	y

Table 5

Example 9 Solving to Find an Inverse with Radicals

Find the inverse of the function $f(x) = 2 + \sqrt{x - 4}.$

Solution $y = 2 + \sqrt{x - 4}$

$$(y - 2)^2 = x - 4$$

$$x = (y - 2)^2 + 4$$

So $f^{-1}(x) = (x - 2)^2 + 4.$

The domain of f is $[4, \infty)$. Notice that the range of f is $[2, \infty)$, so this means that the domain of the inverse function f^{-1} is also $[2, \infty)$.

Analysis *The formula we found for $f^{-1}(x)$ looks like it would be valid for all real x. However, f^{-1} itself must have an inverse (namely, f) so we have to restrict the domain of f^{-1} to $[2, \infty)$ in order to make f^{-1} a one-to-one function. This domain of f^{-1} is exactly the range of f.*

Try It #8

What is the inverse of the function $f(x) = 2 - \sqrt{x}$? State the domains of both the function and the inverse function.

Finding Inverse Functions and Their Graphs

Now that we can find the inverse of a function, we will explore the graphs of functions and their inverses. Let us return to the quadratic function $f(x) = x^2$ restricted to the domain $[0, \infty)$, on which this function is one-to-one, and graph it as in **Figure 7**.

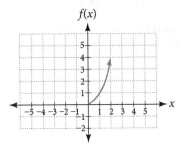

Figure 7 Quadratic function with domain restricted to $[0, \infty)$.

Restricting the domain to $[0, \infty)$ makes the function one-to-one (it will obviously pass the horizontal line test), so it has an inverse on this restricted domain.

We already know that the inverse of the toolkit quadratic function is the square root function, that is, $f^{-1}(x) = \sqrt{x}$. What happens if we graph both f and f^{-1} on the same set of axes, using the x-axis for the input to both f and f^{-1}?

We notice a distinct relationship: The graph of $f^{-1}(x)$ is the graph of $f(x)$ reflected about the diagonal line $y = x$, which we will call the identity line, shown in **Figure 8**.

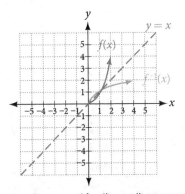

Figure 8 Square and square-root functions on the non-negative domain

This relationship will be observed for all one-to-one functions, because it is a result of the function and its inverse swapping inputs and outputs. This is equivalent to interchanging the roles of the vertical and horizontal axes.

Example 10 **Finding the Inverse of a Function Using Reflection about the Identity Line**

Given the graph of $f(x)$ in **Figure 9**, sketch a graph of $f^{-1}(x)$.

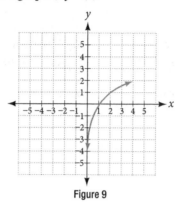

Figure 9

Solution   This is a one-to-one function, so we will be able to sketch an inverse. Note that the graph shown has an apparent domain of $(0, \infty)$ and range of $(-\infty, \infty)$, so the inverse will have a domain of $(-\infty, \infty)$ and range of $(0, \infty)$.

If we reflect this graph over the line $y = x$, the point $(1, 0)$ reflects to $(0, 1)$ and the point $(4, 2)$ reflects to $(2, 4)$. Sketching the inverse on the same axes as the original graph gives **Figure 10**.

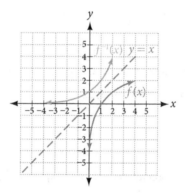

Figure 10 The function and its inverse, showing reflection about the identity line

Try It #9

Draw graphs of the functions f and f^{-1} from **Example 8**.

Q & A...

Is there any function that is equal to its own inverse?

Yes. If $f = f^{-1}$, then $f(f(x)) = x$, and we can think of several functions that have this property. The identity function does, and so does the reciprocal function, because

$$\frac{1}{\frac{1}{x}} = x$$

Any function $f(x) = c - x$, where c is a constant, is also equal to its own inverse.

Access these online resources for additional instruction and practice with inverse functions.

- Inverse Functions (http://openstaxcollege.org/l/inversefunction)
- Inverse Function Values Using Graph (http://openstaxcollege.org/l/inversfuncgraph)
- Restricting the Domain and Finding the Inverse (http://openstaxcollege.org/l/restrictdomain)

1.7   SECTION EXERCISES

VERBAL

1. Describe why the horizontal line test is an effective way to determine whether a function is one-to-one?

2. Why do we restrict the domain of the function $f(x) = x^2$ to find the function's inverse?

3. Can a function be its own inverse? Explain.

4. Are one-to-one functions either always increasing or always decreasing? Why or why not?

5. How do you find the inverse of a function algebraically?

ALGEBRAIC

6. Show that the function $f(x) = a - x$ is its own inverse for all real numbers a.

For the following exercises, find $f^{-1}(x)$ for each function.

7. $f(x) = x + 3$

8. $f(x) = x + 5$

9. $f(x) = 2 - x$

10. $f(x) = 3 - x$

11. $f(x) = \dfrac{x}{x + 2}$

12. $f(x) = \dfrac{2x + 3}{5x + 4}$

For the following exercises, find a domain on which each function f is one-to-one and non-decreasing. Write the domain in interval notation. Then find the inverse of f restricted to that domain.

13. $f(x) = (x + 7)^2$

14. $f(x) = (x - 6)^2$

15. $f(x) = x^2 - 5$

16. Given $f(x) = \dfrac{x}{2 + x}$ and $g(x) = \dfrac{2x}{1 - x}$:

 a. Find $f(g(x))$ and $g(f(x))$.

 b. What does the answer tell us about the relationship between $f(x)$ and $g(x)$?

For the following exercises, use function composition to verify that $f(x)$ and $g(x)$ are inverse functions.

17. $f(x) = \sqrt[3]{x - 1}$ and $g(x) = x^3 + 1$

18. $f(x) = -3x + 5$ and $g(x) = \dfrac{x - 5}{-3}$

GRAPHICAL

For the following exercises, use a graphing utility to determine whether each function is one-to-one.

19. $f(x) = \sqrt{x}$

20. $f(x) = \sqrt[3]{3x + 1}$

21. $f(x) = -5x + 1$

22. $f(x) = x^3 - 27$

For the following exercises, determine whether the graph represents a one-to-one function.

23.

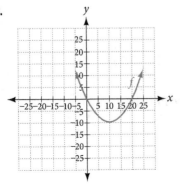

24.

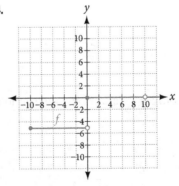

For the following exercises, use the graph of f shown in **Figure 11**.

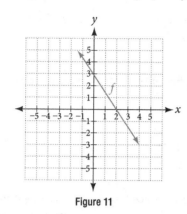

Figure 11

25. Find $f(0)$.

26. Solve $f(x) = 0$.

27. Find $f^{-1}(0)$.

28. Solve $f^{-1}(x) = 0$.

For the following exercises, use the graph of the one-to-one function shown in **Figure 12**.

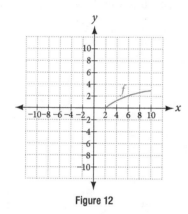

Figure 12

29. Sketch the graph of f^{-1}.

30. Find $f(6)$ and $f^{-1}(2)$.

31. If the complete graph of f is shown, find the domain of f.

32. If the complete graph of f is shown, find the range of f.

NUMERIC

For the following exercises, evaluate or solve, assuming that the function f is one-to-one.

33. If $f(6) = 7$, find $f^{-1}(7)$.

34. If $f(3) = 2$, find $f^{-1}(2)$.

35. If $f^{-1}(-4) = -8$, find $f(-8)$.

36. If $f^{-1}(-2) = -1$, find $f(-1)$.

For the following exercises, use the values listed in **Table 6** to evaluate or solve.

x	0	1	2	3	4	5	6	7	8	9
$f(x)$	8	0	7	4	2	6	5	3	9	1

Table 6

37. Find $f(1)$.

38. Solve $f(x) = 3$.

39. Find $f^{-1}(0)$.

40. Solve $f^{-1}(x) = 7$.

41. Use the tabular representation of f in **Table 7** to create a table for $f^{-1}(x)$.

x	3	6	9	13	14
$f(x)$	1	4	7	12	16

Table 7

TECHNOLOGY

For the following exercises, find the inverse function. Then, graph the function and its inverse.

42. $f(x) = \dfrac{3}{x-2}$

43. $f(x) = x^3 - 1$

44. Find the inverse function of $f(x) = \dfrac{1}{x-1}$. Use a graphing utility to find its domain and range. Write the domain and range in interval notation.

REAL-WORLD APPLICATIONS

45. To convert from x degrees Celsius to y degrees Fahrenheit, we use the formula $f(x) = \dfrac{9}{5}x + 32$. Find the inverse function, if it exists, and explain its meaning.

46. The circumference C of a circle is a function of its radius given by $C(r) = 2\pi r$. Express the radius of a circle as a function of its circumference. Call this function $r(C)$. Find $r(36\pi)$ and interpret its meaning.

47. A car travels at a constant speed of 50 miles per hour. The distance the car travels in miles is a function of time, t, in hours given by $d(t) = 50t$. Find the inverse function by expressing the time of travel in terms of the distance traveled. Call this function $t(d)$. Find $t(180)$ and interpret its meaning.

CHAPTER 1 REVIEW

Key Terms

absolute maximum the greatest value of a function over an interval

absolute minimum the lowest value of a function over an interval

absolute value equation an equation of the form $|A| = B$, with $B \geq 0$; it will have solutions when $A = B$ or $A = -B$

absolute value inequality a relationship in the form $|A| < B$, $|A| \leq B$, $|A| > B$, or $|A| \geq B$

average rate of change the difference in the output values of a function found for two values of the input divided by the difference between the inputs

composite function the new function formed by function composition, when the output of one function is used as the input of another

decreasing function a function is decreasing in some open interval if $f(b) < f(a)$ for any two input values a and b in the given interval where $b > a$

dependent variable an output variable

domain the set of all possible input values for a relation

even function a function whose graph is unchanged by horizontal reflection, $f(x) = f(-x)$, and is symmetric about the y-axis

function a relation in which each input value yields a unique output value

horizontal compression a transformation that compresses a function's graph horizontally, by multiplying the input by a constant $b > 1$

horizontal line test a method of testing whether a function is one-to-one by determining whether any horizontal line intersects the graph more than once

horizontal reflection a transformation that reflects a function's graph across the y-axis by multiplying the input by -1

horizontal shift a transformation that shifts a function's graph left or right by adding a positive or negative constant to the input

horizontal stretch a transformation that stretches a function's graph horizontally by multiplying the input by a constant $0 < b < 1$

increasing function a function is increasing in some open interval if $f(b) > f(a)$ for any two input values a and b in the given interval where $b > a$

independent variable an input variable

input each object or value in a domain that relates to another object or value by a relationship known as a function

interval notation a method of describing a set that includes all numbers between a lower limit and an upper limit; the lower and upper values are listed between brackets or parentheses, a square bracket indicating inclusion in the set, and a parenthesis indicating exclusion

inverse function for any one-to-one function $f(x)$, the inverse is a function $f^{-1}(x)$ such that $f^{-1}(f(x)) = x$ for all x in the domain of f; this also implies that $f(f^{-1}(x)) = x$ for all x in the domain of f^{-1}

local extrema collectively, all of a function's local maxima and minima

local maximum a value of the input where a function changes from increasing to decreasing as the input value increases.

local minimum a value of the input where a function changes from decreasing to increasing as the input value increases.

odd function a function whose graph is unchanged by combined horizontal and vertical reflection, $f(x) = -f(-x)$, and is symmetric about the origin

one-to-one function a function for which each value of the output is associated with a unique input value

output each object or value in the range that is produced when an input value is entered into a function

piecewise function a function in which more than one formula is used to define the output

range the set of output values that result from the input values in a relation

rate of change the change of an output quantity relative to the change of the input quantity

relation a set of ordered pairs

set-builder notation a method of describing a set by a rule that all of its members obey; it takes the form $\{x \mid \text{statement about } x\}$

vertical compression a function transformation that compresses the function's graph vertically by multiplying the output by a constant $0 < a < 1$

vertical line test a method of testing whether a graph represents a function by determining whether a vertical line intersects the graph no more than once

vertical reflection a transformation that reflects a function's graph across the x-axis by multiplying the output by -1

vertical shift a transformation that shifts a function's graph up or down by adding a positive or negative constant to the output

vertical stretch a transformation that stretches a function's graph vertically by multiplying the output by a constant $a > 1$

Key Equations

Constant function	$f(x) = c$, where c is a constant
Identity function	$f(x) = x$
Absolute value function	$f(x) = |x|$
Quadratic function	$f(x) = x^2$
Cubic function	$f(x) = x^3$
Reciprocal function	$f(x) = \dfrac{1}{x}$
Reciprocal squared function	$f(x) = \dfrac{1}{x^2}$
Square root function	$f(x) = \sqrt{x}$
Cube root function	$f(x) = \sqrt[3]{x}$
Average rate of change	$\dfrac{\Delta y}{\Delta x} = \dfrac{f(x_2) - f(x_1)}{x_2 - x_1}$
Composite function	$(f \circ g)(x) = f(g(x))$
Vertical shift	$g(x) = f(x) + k$ (up for $k > 0$)
Horizontal shift	$g(x) = f(x - h)$ (right for $h > 0$)
Vertical reflection	$g(x) = -f(x)$
Horizontal reflection	$g(x) = f(-x)$
Vertical stretch	$g(x) = af(x)$ $(a > 0)$
Vertical compression	$g(x) = af(x)$ $(0 < a < 1)$
Horizontal stretch	$g(x) = f(bx)$ $(0 < b < 1)$
Horizontal compression	$g(x) = f(bx)$ $(b > 1)$

Key Concepts

1.1 Functions and Function Notation

- A relation is a set of ordered pairs. A function is a specific type of relation in which each domain value, or input, leads to exactly one range value, or output. See **Example 1** and **Example 2**.

- Function notation is a shorthand method for relating the input to the output in the form $y = f(x)$. See **Example 3** and **Example 4**.

- In tabular form, a function can be represented by rows or columns that relate to input and output values. See **Example 5**.

- To evaluate a function, we determine an output value for a corresponding input value. Algebraic forms of a function can be evaluated by replacing the input variable with a given value. See **Example 6** and **Example 7**.

- To solve for a specific function value, we determine the input values that yield the specific output value. See **Example 8**.

- An algebraic form of a function can be written from an equation. See **Example 9** and **Example 10**.

- Input and output values of a function can be identified from a table. See **Example 11**.

- Relating input values to output values on a graph is another way to evaluate a function. See **Example 12**.

- A function is one-to-one if each output value corresponds to only one input value. See **Example 13**.

- A graph represents a function if any vertical line drawn on the graph intersects the graph at no more than one point. See **Example 14**.

- The graph of a one-to-one function passes the horizontal line test. See **Example 15**.

1.2 Domain and Range

- The domain of a function includes all real input values that would not cause us to attempt an undefined mathematical operation, such as dividing by zero or taking the square root of a negative number.

- The domain of a function can be determined by listing the input values of a set of ordered pairs. See **Example 1**.

- The domain of a function can also be determined by identifying the input values of a function written as an equation. See **Example 2**, **Example 3**, and **Example 4**.

- Interval values represented on a number line can be described using inequality notation, set-builder notation, and interval notation. See **Example 5**.

- For many functions, the domain and range can be determined from a graph. See **Example 6** and **Example 7**.

- An understanding of toolkit functions can be used to find the domain and range of related functions. See **Example 8**, **Example 9**, and **Example 10**.

- A piecewise function is described by more than one formula. See **Example 11** and **Example 12**.

- A piecewise function can be graphed using each algebraic formula on its assigned subdomain. See **Example 13**.

1.3 Rates of Change and Behavior of Graphs

- A rate of change relates a change in an output quantity to a change in an input quantity. The average rate of change is determined using only the beginning and ending data. See **Example 1**.

- Identifying points that mark the interval on a graph can be used to find the average rate of change. See **Example 2**.

- Comparing pairs of input and output values in a table can also be used to find the average rate of change. See **Example 3**.

- An average rate of change can also be computed by determining the function values at the endpoints of an interval described by a formula. See **Example 4** and **Example 5**.

- The average rate of change can sometimes be determined as an expression. See **Example 6**.

- A function is increasing where its rate of change is positive and decreasing where its rate of change is negative. See **Example 7**.

- A local maximum is where a function changes from increasing to decreasing and has an output value larger (more positive or less negative) than output values at neighboring input values.

- A local minimum is where the function changes from decreasing to increasing (as the input increases) and has an output value smaller (more negative or less positive) than output values at neighboring input values.
- Minima and maxima are also called extrema.
- We can find local extrema from a graph. See **Example 8** and **Example 9**.
- The highest and lowest points on a graph indicate the maxima and minima. See **Example 10**.

1.4 Composition of Functions

- We can perform algebraic operations on functions. See **Example 1**.
- When functions are combined, the output of the first (inner) function becomes the input of the second (outer) function.
- The function produced by combining two functions is a composite function. See **Example 2** and **Example 3**.
- The order of function composition must be considered when interpreting the meaning of composite functions. See **Example 4**.
- A composite function can be evaluated by evaluating the inner function using the given input value and then evaluating the outer function taking as its input the output of the inner function.
- A composite function can be evaluated from a table. See **Example 5**.
- A composite function can be evaluated from a graph. See **Example 6**.
- A composite function can be evaluated from a formula. See **Example 7**.
- The domain of a composite function consists of those inputs in the domain of the inner function that correspond to outputs of the inner function that are in the domain of the outer function. See **Example 8** and **Example 9**.
- Just as functions can be combined to form a composite function, composite functions can be decomposed into simpler functions.
- Functions can often be decomposed in more than one way. See **Example 10**.

1.5 Transformation of Functions

- A function can be shifted vertically by adding a constant to the output. See **Example 1** and **Example 2**.
- A function can be shifted horizontally by adding a constant to the input. See **Example 3**, **Example 4**, and **Example 5**.
- Relating the shift to the context of a problem makes it possible to compare and interpret vertical and horizontal shifts. See **Example 6**.
- Vertical and horizontal shifts are often combined. See **Example 7** and **Example 8**.
- A vertical reflection reflects a graph about the x-axis. A graph can be reflected vertically by multiplying the output by -1.
- A horizontal reflection reflects a graph about the y-axis. A graph can be reflected horizontally by multiplying the input by -1.
- A graph can be reflected both vertically and horizontally. The order in which the reflections are applied does not affect the final graph. See **Example 9**.
- A function presented in tabular form can also be reflected by multiplying the values in the input and output rows or columns accordingly. See **Example 10**.
- A function presented as an equation can be reflected by applying transformations one at a time. See **Example 11**.
- Even functions are symmetric about the y-axis, whereas odd functions are symmetric about the origin.
- Even functions satisfy the condition $f(x) = f(-x)$.
- Odd functions satisfy the condition $f(x) = -f(-x)$.
- A function can be odd, even, or neither. See **Example 12**.
- A function can be compressed or stretched vertically by multiplying the output by a constant. See **Example 13**, **Example 14**, and **Example 15**.
- A function can be compressed or stretched horizontally by multiplying the input by a constant. See **Example 16**, **Example 17**, and **Example 18**.

- The order in which different transformations are applied does affect the final function. Both vertical and horizontal transformations must be applied in the order given. However, a vertical transformation may be combined with a horizontal transformation in any order. See **Example 19** and **Example 20**.

1.6 Absolute Value Functions

- The absolute value function is commonly used to measure distances between points. See **Example 1**.

- Applied problems, such as ranges of possible values, can also be solved using the absolute value function. See **Example 2**.

- The graph of the absolute value function resembles a letter V. It has a corner point at which the graph changes direction. See **Example 3**.

- In an absolute value equation, an unknown variable is the input of an absolute value function.

- If the absolute value of an expression is set equal to a positive number, expect two solutions for the unknown variable. See **Example 4**.

- An absolute value equation may have one solution, two solutions, or no solutions. See **Example 5**.

- An absolute value inequality is similar to an absolute value equation but takes the form $|A| < B$, $|A| \leq B$, $|A| > B$, or $|A| \geq B$. It can be solved by determining the boundaries of the solution set and then testing which segments are in the set. See **Example 6**.

- Absolute value inequalities can also be solved graphically. See **Example 7**.

1.7 Inverse Functions

- If $g(x)$ is the inverse of $f(x)$, then $g(f(x)) = f(g(x)) = x$. See **Example 1**, **Example 2**, and **Example 3**.

- Each of the toolkit functions has an inverse. See **Example 4**.

- For a function to have an inverse, it must be one-to-one (pass the horizontal line test).

- A function that is not one-to-one over its entire domain may be one-to-one on part of its domain.

- For a tabular function, exchange the input and output rows to obtain the inverse. See **Example 5**.

- The inverse of a function can be determined at specific points on its graph. See **Example 6**.

- To find the inverse of a formula, solve the equation $y = f(x)$ for x as a function of y. Then exchange the labels x and y. See **Example 7**, **Example 8**, and **Example 9**.

- The graph of an inverse function is the reflection of the graph of the original function across the line $y = x$. See **Example 10**.

CHAPTER 1 REVIEW EXERCISES

FUNCTIONS AND FUNCTION NOTATION

For the following exercises, determine whether the relation is a function.

1. $\{(a, b), (c, d), (e, d)\}$

2. $\{(5, 2), (6, 1), (6, 2), (4, 8)\}$

3. $y^2 + 4 = x$, for x the independent variable and y the dependent variable

4. Is the graph in **Figure 1** a function?

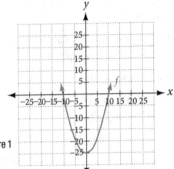

Figure 1

For the following exercises, evaluate the function at the indicated values: $f(-3); f(2); f(-a); -f(a); f(a+h)$.

5. $f(x) = -2x^2 + 3x$

6. $f(x) = 2|3x - 1|$

For the following exercises, determine whether the functions are one-to-one.

7. $f(x) = -3x + 5$

8. $f(x) = |x - 3|$

For the following exercises, use the vertical line test to determine if the relation whose graph is provided is a function.

9.

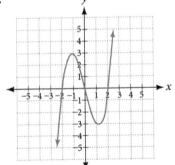

10.

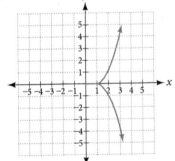

11.

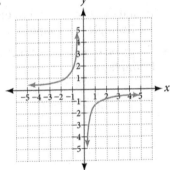

For the following exercises, graph the functions.

12. $f(x) = |x + 1|$

13. $f(x) = x^2 - 2$

For the following exercises, use **Figure 2** to approximate the values.

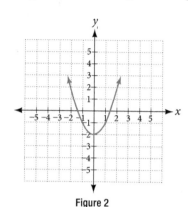

Figure 2

14. $f(2)$

15. $f(-2)$

16. If $f(x) = -2$, then solve for x.

17. If $f(x) = 1$, then solve for x.

For the following exercises, use the function $h(t) = -16t^2 + 80t$ to find the values.

18. $\dfrac{h(2) - h(1)}{2 - 1}$

19. $\dfrac{h(a) - h(1)}{a - 1}$

DOMAIN AND RANGE

For the following exercises, find the domain of each function, expressing answers using interval notation.

20. $f(x) = \dfrac{2}{3x + 2}$

21. $f(x) = \dfrac{x - 3}{x^2 - 4x - 12}$

22. $f(x) = \dfrac{\sqrt{x - 6}}{\sqrt{x - 4}}$

23. Graph this piecewise function: $f(x) = \begin{cases} x + 1 & x < -2 \\ -2x - 3 & x \geq -2 \end{cases}$

RATES OF CHANGE AND BEHAVIOR OF GRAPHS

For the following exercises, find the average rate of change of the functions from $x = 1$ to $x = 2$.

24. $f(x) = 4x - 3$

25. $f(x) = 10x^2 + x$

26. $f(x) = -\dfrac{2}{x^2}$

For the following exercises, use the graphs to determine the intervals on which the functions are increasing, decreasing, or constant.

27.

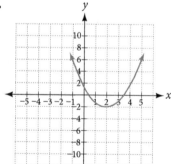

28.

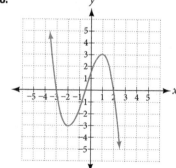

29.

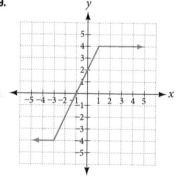

30. Find the local minimum of the function graphed in **Exercise 27**.

31. Find the local extrema for the function graphed in **Exercise 28**.

32. For the graph in **Figure 3**, the domain of the function is $[-3, 3]$. The range is $[-10, 10]$. Find the absolute minimum of the function on this interval.

33. Find the absolute maximum of the function graphed in **Figure 3**.

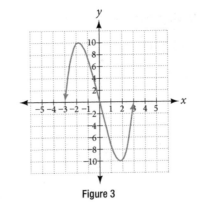

Figure 3

COMPOSITION OF FUNCTIONS

For the following exercises, find $(f \circ g)(x)$ and $(g \circ f)(x)$ for each pair of functions.

34. $f(x) = 4 - x$, $g(x) = -4x$

35. $f(x) = 3x + 2$, $g(x) = 5 - 6x$

36. $f(x) = x^2 + 2x$, $g(x) = 5x + 1$

37. $f(x) = \sqrt{x + 2}$, $g(x) = \frac{1}{x}$

38. $f(x) = \frac{x + 3}{2}$, $g(x) = \sqrt{1 - x}$

For the following exercises, find $(f \circ g)$ and the domain for $(f \circ g)(x)$ for each pair of functions.

39. $f(x) = \frac{x + 1}{x + 4}$, $g(x) = \frac{1}{x}$

40. $f(x) = \frac{1}{x + 3}$, $g(x) = \frac{1}{x - 9}$

41. $f(x) = \frac{1}{x}$, $g(x) = \sqrt{x}$

42. $f(x) = \frac{1}{x^2 - 1}$, $g(x) = \sqrt{x + 1}$

For the following exercises, express each function H as a composition of two functions f and g where $H(x) = (f \circ g)(x)$.

43. $H(x) = \sqrt{\dfrac{2x - 1}{3x + 4}}$

44. $H(x) = \dfrac{1}{(3x^2 - 4)^{-3}}$

TRANSFORMATION OF FUNCTIONS

For the following exercises, sketch a graph of the given function.

45. $f(x) = (x - 3)^2$

46. $f(x) = (x + 4)^3$

47. $f(x) = \sqrt{x} + 5$

48. $f(x) = -x^3$

49. $f(x) = \sqrt[3]{-x}$

50. $f(x) = 5\sqrt{-x} - 4$

51. $f(x) = 4[|x - 2| - 6]$

52. $f(x) = -(x + 2)^2 - 1$

For the following exercises, sketch the graph of the function g if the graph of the function f is shown in **Figure 4**.

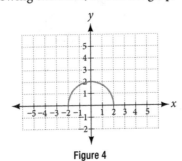

Figure 4

53. $g(x) = f(x - 1)$

54. $g(x) = 3f(x)$

For the following exercises, write the equation for the standard function represented by each of the graphs below.

55.

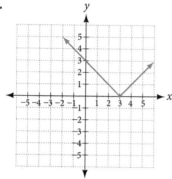

56.

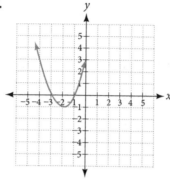

For the following exercises, determine whether each function below is even, odd, or neither.

57. $f(x) = 3x^4$

58. $g(x) = \sqrt{x}$

59. $h(x) = \dfrac{1}{x} + 3x$

For the following exercises, analyze the graph and determine whether the graphed function is even, odd, or neither.

60.

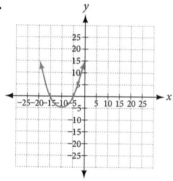

61.

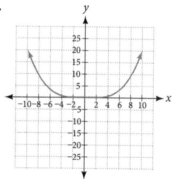

62.

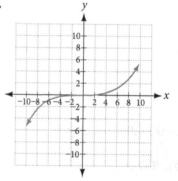

ABSOLUTE VALUE FUNCTIONS

For the following exercises, write an equation for the transformation of $f(x) = |x|$.

63.

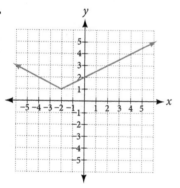

64.

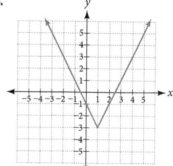

65.

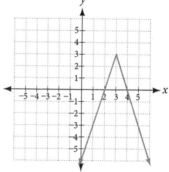

For the following exercises, graph the absolute value function.

66. $f(x) = |x - 5|$

67. $f(x) = -|x - 3|$

68. $f(x) = |2x - 4|$

For the following exercises, solve the absolute value equation.

69. $|x + 4| = 18$

70. $\left|\dfrac{1}{3}x + 5\right| = \left|\dfrac{3}{4}x - 2\right|$

For the following exercises, solve the inequality and express the solution using interval notation.

71. $|3x - 2| < 7$

72. $\left|\dfrac{1}{3}x - 2\right| \le 7$

INVERSE FUNCTIONS

For the following exercises, find $f^{-1}(x)$ for each function.

73. $f(x) = 9 + 10x$

74. $f(x) = \dfrac{x}{x + 2}$

For the following exercise, find a domain on which the function f is one-to-one and non-decreasing. Write the domain in interval notation. Then find the inverse of f restricted to that domain.

75. $f(x) = x^2 + 1$

76. Given $f(x) = x^3 - 5$ and $g(x) = \sqrt[3]{x + 5}$:

    a. Find $f(g(x))$ and $g(f(x))$.

    b. What does the answer tell us about the relationship between $f(x)$ and $g(x)$?

For the following exercises, use a graphing utility to determine whether each function is one-to-one.

77. $f(x) = \dfrac{1}{x}$

78. $f(x) = -3x^2 + x$

79. If $f(5) = 2$, find $f^{-1}(2)$.

80. If $f(1) = 4$, find $f^{-1}(4)$.

CHAPTER 1 PRACTICE TEST

For the following exercises, determine whether each of the following relations is a function.

1. $y = 2x + 8$

2. $\{(2, 1), (3, 2), (-1, 1), (0, -2)\}$

For the following exercises, evaluate the function $f(x) = -3x^2 + 2x$ at the given input.

3. $f(-2)$

4. $f(a)$

5. Show that the function $f(x) = -2(x - 1)^2 + 3$ is not one-to-one.

6. Write the domain of the function $f(x) = \sqrt{3 - x}$ in interval notation.

7. Given $f(x) = 2x^2 - 5x$, find $f(a + 1) - f(1)$.

8. Graph the function $f(x) = \begin{cases} x + 1 & \text{if } -2 < x < 3 \\ -x & \text{if } \quad x \geq 3 \end{cases}$

9. Find the average rate of change of the function $f(x) = 3 - 2x^2 + x$ by finding $\dfrac{f(b) - f(a)}{b - a}$.

For the following exercises, use the functions $f(x) = 3 - 2x^2 + x$ and $g(x) = \sqrt{x}$ to find the composite functions.

10. $(g \circ f)(x)$

11. $(g \circ f)(1)$

12. Express $H(x) = \sqrt[3]{5x^2 - 3x}$ as a composition of two functions, f and g, where $(f \circ g)(x) = H(x)$.

For the following exercises, graph the functions by translating, stretching, and/or compressing a toolkit function.

13. $f(x) = \sqrt{x + 6} - 1$

14. $f(x) = \dfrac{1}{x + 2} - 1$

For the following exercises, determine whether the functions are even, odd, or neither.

15. $f(x) = -\dfrac{5}{x^2} + 9x^6$

16. $f(x) = -\dfrac{5}{x^3} + 9x^5$

17. $f(x) = \dfrac{1}{x}$

18. Graph the absolute value function $f(x) = -2|x - 1| + 3$.

19. Solve $|2x - 3| = 17$.

20. Solve $-\left|\dfrac{1}{3}x - 3\right| \geq 17$. Express the solution in interval notation.

For the following exercises, find the inverse of the function.

21. $f(x) = 3x - 5$

22. $f(x) = \dfrac{4}{x + 7}$

For the following exercises, use the graph of g shown in **Figure 1**.

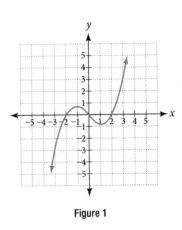

Figure 1

23. On what intervals is the function increasing?

24. On what intervals is the function decreasing?

25. Approximate the local minimum of the function. Express the answer as an ordered pair.

26. Approximate the local maximum of the function. Express the answer as an ordered pair.

For the following exercises, use the graph of the piecewise function shown in **Figure 2**.

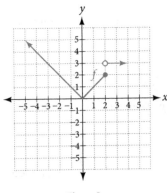

Figure 2

27. Find $f(2)$.

28. Find $f(-2)$.

29. Write an equation for the piecewise function.

For the following exercises, use the values listed in **Table 1**.

x	0	1	2	3	4	5	6	7	8
$F(x)$	1	3	5	7	9	11	13	15	17

Table 1

30. Find $F(6)$.

31. Solve the equation $F(x) = 5$.

32. Is the graph increasing or decreasing on its domain?

33. Is the function represented by the graph one-to-one?

34. Find $F^{-1}(15)$.

35. Given $f(x) = -2x + 11$, find $f^{-1}(x)$.

Linear Functions

Figure 1 A bamboo forest in China (credit: "JFXie"/Flickr)

CHAPTER OUTLINE

Introduction

Imagine placing a plant in the ground one day and finding that it has doubled its height just a few days later. Although it may seem incredible, this can happen with certain types of bamboo species. These members of the grass family are the fastest-growing plants in the world. One species of bamboo has been observed to grow nearly 1.5 inches every hour.[6] In a twenty-four hour period, this bamboo plant grows about 36 inches, or an incredible 3 feet! A constant rate of change, such as the growth cycle of this bamboo plant, is a linear function.

Recall from **Functions and Function Notation** that a function is a relation that assigns to every element in the domain exactly one element in the range. Linear functions are a specific type of function that can be used to model many real-world applications, such as plant growth over time. In this chapter, we will explore linear functions, their graphs, and how to relate them to data.

6 http://www.guinnessworldrecords.com/records-3000/fastest-growing-plant/

LEARNING OBJECTIVES

In this section, you will:

- Represent a linear function.
- Determine whether a linear function is increasing, decreasing, or constant.
- Calculate and interpret slope.
- Write the point-slope form of an equation.
- Write and interpret a linear function.

2.1 LINEAR FUNCTIONS

Figure 1 Shanghai MagLev Train (credit: "kanegen"/Flickr)

Just as with the growth of a bamboo plant, there are many situations that involve constant change over time. Consider, for example, the first commercial maglev train in the world, the Shanghai MagLev Train (**Figure 1**). It carries passengers comfortably for a 30-kilometer trip from the airport to the subway station in only eight minutes.[7]

Suppose a maglev train were to travel a long distance, and that the train maintains a constant speed of 83 meters per second for a period of time once it is 250 meters from the station. How can we analyze the train's distance from the station as a function of time? In this section, we will investigate a kind of function that is useful for this purpose, and use it to investigate real-world situations such as the train's distance from the station at a given point in time.

Representing Linear Functions

The function describing the train's motion is a **linear function**, which is defined as a function with a constant rate of change, that is, a polynomial of degree 1. There are several ways to represent a linear function, including word form, function notation, tabular form, and graphical form. We will describe the train's motion as a function using each method.

Representing a Linear Function in Word Form

Let's begin by describing the linear function in words. For the train problem we just considered, the following word sentence may be used to describe the function relationship.

- *The train's distance from the station is a function of the time during which the train moves at a constant speed plus its original distance from the station when it began moving at constant speed.*

The speed is the rate of change. Recall that a rate of change is a measure of how quickly the dependent variable changes with respect to the independent variable. The rate of change for this example is constant, which means that it is the same for each input value. As the time (input) increases by 1 second, the corresponding distance (output) increases by 83 meters. The train began moving at this constant speed at a distance of 250 meters from the station.

7 http://www.chinahighlights.com/shanghai/transportation/maglev-train.htm

Representing a Linear Function in Function Notation

Another approach to representing linear functions is by using function notation. One example of function notation is an equation written in the form known as the **slope-intercept form** of a line, where x is the input value, m is the rate of change, and b is the initial value of the dependent variable.

$$\text{Equation form} \qquad y = mx + b$$

$$\text{Equation notation} \qquad f(x) = mx + b$$

In the example of the train, we might use the notation $D(t)$ in which the total distance D is a function of the time t. The rate, m, is 83 meters per second. The initial value of the dependent variable b is the original distance from the station, 250 meters. We can write a generalized equation to represent the motion of the train.

$$D(t) = 83t + 250$$

Representing a Linear Function in Tabular Form

A third method of representing a linear function is through the use of a table. The relationship between the distance from the station and the time is represented in **Figure 2**. From the table, we can see that the distance changes by 83 meters for every 1 second increase in time.

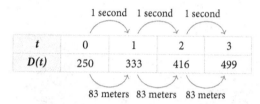

t	0	1	2	3
$D(t)$	250	333	416	499

Figure 2 Tabular representation of the function D showing selected input and output values

Q & A...

Can the input in the previous example be any real number?

No. The input represents time, so while nonnegative rational and irrational numbers are possible, negative real numbers are not possible for this example. The input consists of non-negative real numbers.

Representing a Linear Function in Graphical Form

Another way to represent linear functions is visually, using a graph. We can use the function relationship from above, $D(t) = 83t + 250$, to draw a graph, represented in **Figure 3**. Notice the graph is a line. When we plot a linear function, the graph is always a line.

The rate of change, which is constant, determines the slant, or **slope** of the line. The point at which the input value is zero is the vertical intercept, or **y-intercept**, of the line. We can see from the graph in **Figure 3** that the y-intercept in the train example we just saw is (0, 250) and represents the distance of the train from the station when it began moving at a constant speed.

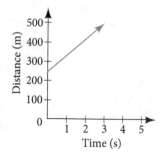

Figure 3 The graph of $D(t) = 83t + 250$. Graphs of linear functions are lines because the rate of change is constant.

Notice that the graph of the train example is restricted, but this is not always the case. Consider the graph of the line $f(x) = 2x + 1$. Ask yourself what numbers can be input to the function, that is, what is the domain of the function? The domain is comprised of all real numbers because any number may be doubled, and then have one added to the product.

> **linear function**
>
> A **linear function** is a function whose graph is a line. Linear functions can be written in the slope-intercept form of a line
>
> $$f(x) = mx + b$$
>
> where b is the initial or starting value of the function (when input, $x = 0$), and m is the constant rate of change, or **slope** of the function. The **y-intercept** is at $(0, b)$.

Example 1   **Using a Linear Function to Find the Pressure on a Diver**

The pressure, P, in pounds per square inch (PSI) on the diver in **Figure 4** depends upon her depth below the water surface, d, in feet. This relationship may be modeled by the equation, $P(d) = 0.434d + 14.696$. Restate this function in words.

Figure 4 (credit: Ilse Reijs and Jan-Noud Hutten)

Solution   To restate the function in words, we need to describe each part of the equation. The pressure as a function of depth equals four hundred thirty-four thousandths times depth plus fourteen and six hundred ninety-six thousandths.

Analysis   *The initial value, 14.696, is the pressure in PSI on the diver at a depth of 0 feet, which is the surface of the water. The rate of change, or slope, is 0.434 PSI per foot. This tells us that the pressure on the diver increases 0.434 PSI for each foot her depth increases.*

Determining Whether a Linear Function Is Increasing, Decreasing, or Constant

The linear functions we used in the two previous examples increased over time, but not every linear function does. A linear function may be increasing, decreasing, or constant. For an increasing function, as with the train example, the output values increase as the input values increase. The graph of an increasing function has a positive slope. A line with a positive slope slants upward from left to right as in **Figure 5(a)**. For a decreasing function, the slope is negative. The output values decrease as the input values increase. A line with a negative slope slants downward from left to right as in **Figure 5(b)**. If the function is constant, the output values are the same for all input values so the slope is zero. A line with a slope of zero is horizontal as in **Figure 5(c)**.

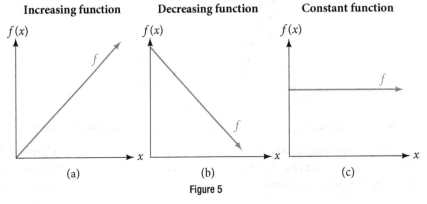

Figure 5

> ### increasing and decreasing functions
>
> The slope determines if the function is an **increasing linear function**, a **decreasing linear function**, or a constant function.
>
> - $f(x) = mx + b$ is an increasing function if $m > 0$.
> - $f(x) = mx + b$ is an decreasing function if $m < 0$.
> - $f(x) = mx + b$ is a constant function if $m = 0$.

Example 2 **Deciding Whether a Function Is Increasing, Decreasing, or Constant**

Some recent studies suggest that a teenager sends an average of 60 texts per day.[8] For each of the following scenarios, find the linear function that describes the relationship between the input value and the output value. Then, determine whether the graph of the function is increasing, decreasing, or constant.

    a. The total number of texts a teen sends is considered a function of time in days. The input is the number of days, and output is the total number of texts sent. **b.** A teen has a limit of 500 texts per month in his or her data plan. The input is the number of days, and output is the total number of texts remaining for the month.

    c. A teen has an unlimited number of texts in his or her data plan for a cost of $50 per month. The input is the number of days, and output is the total cost of texting each month.

Solution   Analyze each function.

    a. The function can be represented as $f(x) = 60x$ where x is the number of days. The slope, 60, is positive so the function is increasing. This makes sense because the total number of texts increases with each day.

    b. The function can be represented as $f(x) = 500 - 60x$ where x is the number of days. In this case, the slope is negative so the function is decreasing. This makes sense because the number of texts remaining decreases each day and this function represents the number of texts remaining in the data plan after x days.

    c. The cost function can be represented as $f(x) = 50$ because the number of days does not affect the total cost. The slope is 0 so the function is constant.

Calculating and Interpreting Slope

In the examples we have seen so far, we have had the slope provided for us. However, we often need to calculate the slope given input and output values. Given two values for the input, x_1 and x_2, and two corresponding values for the output, y_1 and y_2 —which can be represented by a set of points, (x_1, y_1) and (x_2, y_2) —we can calculate the slope m, as follows

$$m = \frac{\text{change in output (rise)}}{\text{change in input (run)}} = \frac{\Delta y}{\Delta x} = \frac{y_2 - y_1}{x_2 - x_1}$$

where Δy is the vertical displacement and Δx is the horizontal displacement. Note in function notation two corresponding values for the output y_1 and y_2 for the function f, $y_1 = f(x_1)$ and $y_2 = f(x_2)$, so we could equivalently write

$$m = \frac{f(x_2) - f(x_1)}{x_2 - x_1}$$

Figure 6 indicates how the slope of the line between the points, (x_1, y_1) and (x_2, y_2), is calculated. Recall that the slope measures steepness. The greater the absolute value of the slope, the steeper the line is.

---

8 http://www.cbsnews.com/8301-501465_162-57400228-501465/teens-are-sending-60-texts-a-day-study-says/

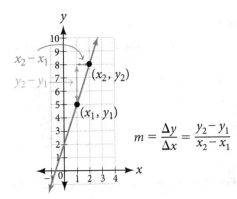

Figure 6 The slope of a function is calculated by the change in y divided by the change in x. It does not matter which coordinate is used as the (x_2, y_2) and which is the (x_1, y_1), as long as each calculation is started with the elements from the same coordinate pair.

Q & A...

Are the units for slope always $\dfrac{\textbf{units for the output}}{\textbf{units for the input}}$ **?**

Yes. Think of the units as the change of output value for each unit of change in input value. An example of slope could be miles per hour or dollars per day. Notice the units appear as a ratio of units for the output per units for the input.

---

calculate slope

The slope, or rate of change, of a function m can be calculated according to the following:

$$m = \frac{\text{change in output (rise)}}{\text{change in input (run)}} = \frac{\Delta y}{\Delta x} = \frac{y_2 - y_1}{x_2 - x_1}$$

where x_1 and x_2 are input values, y_1 and y_2 are output values.

How To...

Given two points from a linear function, calculate and interpret the slope.

1. Determine the units for output and input values.
2. Calculate the change of output values and change of input values.
3. Interpret the slope as the change in output values per unit of the input value.

Example 3   **Finding the Slope of a Linear Function**

If $f(x)$ is a linear function, and $(3, -2)$ and $(8, 1)$ are points on the line, find the slope. Is this function increasing or decreasing?

Solution   The coordinate pairs are $(3, -2)$ and $(8, 1)$. To find the rate of change, we divide the change in output by the change in input.

$$m = \frac{\text{change in output}}{\text{change in input}} = \frac{1 - (-2)}{8 - 3} = \frac{3}{5}$$

We could also write the slope as $m = 0.6$. The function is increasing because $m > 0$.

Analysis   As noted earlier, the order in which we write the points does not matter when we compute the slope of the line as long as the first output value, or y-coordinate, used corresponds with the first input value, or x-coordinate, used.

Try It #1

If $f(x)$ is a linear function, and $(2, 3)$ and $(0, 4)$ are points on the line, find the slope. Is this function increasing or decreasing?

Example 4   **Finding the Population Change from a Linear Function**

The population of a city increased from 23,400 to 27,800 between 2008 and 2012. Find the change of population per year if we assume the change was constant from 2008 to 2012.

Solution   The rate of change relates the change in population to the change in time. The population increased by $27,800 - 23,400 = 4,400$ people over the four-year time interval. To find the rate of change, divide the change in the number of people by the number of years.

$$\frac{4,400 \text{ people}}{4 \text{ years}} = \frac{1,100 \text{ people}}{\text{year}}$$

So the population increased by 1,100 people per year.

Analysis   *Because we are told that the population increased, we would expect the slope to be positive. This positive slope we calculated is therefore reasonable.*

Try It #2

The population of a small town increased from 1,442 to 1,868 between 2009 and 2012. Find the change of population per year if we assume the change was constant from 2009 to 2012.

Writing the Point-Slope Form of a Linear Equation

Up until now, we have been using the slope-intercept form of a linear equation to describe linear functions. Here, we will learn another way to write a linear function, the **point-slope form**.

$$y - y_1 = m(x - x_1)$$

The point-slope form is derived from the slope formula.

$$m = \frac{y - y_1}{x - x_1} \qquad \text{Assuming } x \neq x_1$$

$$m(x - x_1) = \frac{y - y_1}{x - x_1}(x - x_1) \qquad \text{Multiply both sides by } (x - x_1).$$

$$m(x - x_1) = y - y_1 \qquad \text{Simplify.}$$

$$y - y_1 = m(x - x_1) \qquad \text{Rearrange.}$$

Keep in mind that the slope-intercept form and the point-slope form can be used to describe the same function. We can move from one form to another using basic algebra. For example, suppose we are given an equation in point-slope form, $y - 4 = -\frac{1}{2}(x - 6)$.

We can convert it to the slope-intercept form as shown.

$$y - 4 = -\frac{1}{2}(x - 6)$$

$$y - 4 = -\frac{1}{2}x + 3 \qquad \text{Distribute the } -\frac{1}{2}.$$

$$y = -\frac{1}{2}x + 7 \qquad \text{Add 4 to each side.}$$

Therefore, the same line can be described in slope-intercept form as $y = -\frac{1}{2}x + 7$.

---

point-slope form of a linear equation

The **point-slope form** of a linear equation takes the form

$$y - y_1 = m(x - x_1)$$

where m is the slope, x_1 and y_1 are the x- and y-coordinates of a specific point through which the line passes.

Writing the Equation of a Line Using a Point and the Slope

The point-slope form is particularly useful if we know one point and the slope of a line. Suppose, for example, we are told hat a line has a slope of 2 and passes through the point (4, 1). We know that $m = 2$ and that $x_1 = 4$ and $y_1 = 1$. We can substitute these values into the general point-slope equation.

$$y - y_1 = m(x - x_1)$$
$$y - 1 = 2(x - 4)$$

If we wanted to then rewrite the equation in slope-intercept form, we apply algebraic techniques.

$$y - 1 = 2(x - 4)$$
$$y - 1 = 2x - 8 \qquad \text{Distribute the 2.}$$
$$y = 2x - 7 \qquad \text{Add 1 to each side.}$$

Both equations, $y - 1 = 2(x - 4)$ and $y = 2x - 7$, describe the same line. See **Figure 7**.

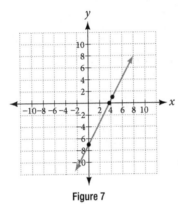

Figure 7

Example 5   Writing Linear Equations Using a Point and the Slope

Write the point-slope form of an equation of a line with a slope of 3 that passes through the point (6, −1). Then rewrite it in the slope-intercept form.

Solution   Let's figure out what we know from the given information. The slope is 3, so $m = 3$. We also know one point, so we know $x_1 = 6$ and $y_1 = -1$. Now we can substitute these values into the general point-slope equation.

$$y - y_1 = m(x - x_1)$$
$$y - (-1) = 3(x - 6) \qquad \text{Substitute known values.}$$
$$y + 1 = 3(x - 6) \qquad \text{Distribute } -1 \text{ to find point-slope form.}$$

Then we use algebra to find the slope-intercept form.

$$y + 1 = 3(x - 6)$$
$$y + 1 = 3x - 18 \qquad \text{Distribute 3.}$$
$$y = 3x - 19 \qquad \text{Simplify to slope-intercept form.}$$

Try It #3

Write the point-slope form of an equation of a line with a slope of −2 that passes through the point (−2, 2). Then rewrite it in the slope-intercept form.

Writing the Equation of a Line Using Two Points

The point-slope form of an equation is also useful if we know any two points through which a line passes. Suppose, for example, we know that a line passes through the points (0, 1) and (3, 2). We can use the coordinates of the two points to find the slope.

$$m = \frac{y_2 - y_1}{x_2 - x_1}$$

$$= \frac{2 - 1}{3 - 0}$$

$$= \frac{1}{3}$$

Now we can use the slope we found and the coordinates of one of the points to find the equation for the line. Let use (0, 1) for our point.

$$y - y_1 = m(x - x_1)$$

$$y - 1 = \frac{1}{3}(x - 0)$$

As before, we can use algebra to rewrite the equation in the slope-intercept form.

$$y - 1 = \frac{1}{3}(x - 0)$$

$$y - 1 = \frac{1}{3}x \qquad \text{Distribute the } \frac{1}{3}.$$

$$y = \frac{1}{3}x + 1 \qquad \text{Add 1 to each side.}$$

Both equations describe the line shown in **Figure 8**.

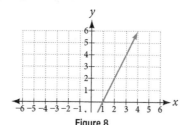

Figure 8

Example 6   **Writing Linear Equations Using Two Points**

Write the point-slope form of an equation of a line that passes through the points (5, 1) and (8, 7). Then rewrite it in the slope-intercept form.

Solution Let's begin by finding the slope.

$$m = \frac{y_2 - y_1}{x_2 - x_1}$$

$$= \frac{7 - 1}{8 - 5}$$

$$= \frac{6}{3}$$

$$= 2$$

So $m = 2$. Next, we substitute the slope and the coordinates for one of the points into the general point-slope equation. We can choose either point, but we will use (5, 1).

$$y - y_1 = m(x - x_1)$$

$$y - 1 = 2(x - 5)$$

The point-slope equation of the line is $y_2 - 1 = 2(x_2 - 5)$. To rewrite the equation in slope-intercept form, we use algebra.

$$y - 1 = 2(x - 5)$$

$$y - 1 = 2x - 10$$

$$y = 2x - 9$$

The slope-intercept equation of the line is $y = 2x - 9$.

Try It #4

Write the point-slope form of an equation of a line that passes through the points $(-1, 3)$ and $(0, 0)$. Then rewrite it in the slope-intercept form.

Writing and Interpreting an Equation for a Linear Function

Now that we have written equations for linear functions in both the slope-intercept form and the point-slope form, we can choose which method to use based on the information we are given. That information may be provided in the form of a graph, a point and a slope, two points, and so on. Look at the graph of the function f in **Figure 9.**

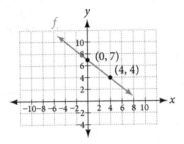

Figure 9

We are not given the slope of the line, but we can choose any two points on the line to find the slope. Let's choose $(0, 7)$ and $(4, 4)$. We can use these points to calculate the slope.

$$m = \frac{y_2 - y_1}{x_2 - x_1}$$

$$= \frac{4 - 7}{4 - 0}$$

$$= -\frac{3}{4}$$

Now we can substitute the slope and the coordinates of one of the points into the point-slope form.

$$y - y_1 = m(x - x_1)$$

$$y - 4 = -\frac{3}{4}(x - 4)$$

If we want to rewrite the equation in the slope-intercept form, we would find

$$y - 4 = -\frac{3}{4}(x - 4)$$

$$y - 4 = -\frac{3}{4}x + 3$$

$$y = -\frac{3}{4}x + 7$$

If we wanted to find the slope-intercept form without first writing the point-slope form, we could have recognized that the line crosses the y-axis when the output value is 7. Therefore, $b = 7$. We now have the initial value b and the slope m so we can substitute m and b into the slope-intercept form of a line.

$$f(x) = mx + b$$
$$\quad\quad\uparrow\quad\uparrow$$
$$\quad -\frac{3}{4}\quad 7$$

$$f(x) = -\frac{3}{4}x + 7$$

So the function is $f(x) = -\frac{3}{4}x + 7$, and the linear equation would be $y = -\frac{3}{4}x + 7$.

How To…

Given the graph of a linear function, write an equation to represent the function.

1. Identify two points on the line.
2. Use the two points to calculate the slope.
3. Determine where the line crosses the y-axis to identify the y-intercept by visual inspection.
4. Substitute the slope and y-intercept into the slope-intercept form of a line equation.

Example 7 **Writing an Equation for a Linear Function**

Write an equation for a linear function given a graph of f shown in **Figure 10**.

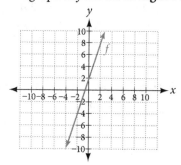

Figure 10

Solution Identify two points on the line, such as $(0, 2)$ and $(-2, -4)$. Use the points to calculate the slope.

$$m = \frac{y_2 - y_1}{x_2 - x_1}$$

$$= \frac{-4 - 2}{-2 - 0}$$

$$= \frac{-6}{-2}$$

$$= 3$$

Substitute the slope and the coordinates of one of the points into the point-slope form.

$$y - y_1 = m(x - x_1)$$
$$y - (-4) = 3(x - (-2))$$
$$y + 4 = 3(x + 2)$$

We can use algebra to rewrite the equation in the slope-intercept form.

$$y + 4 = 3(x + 2)$$
$$y + 4 = 3x + 6$$
$$y = 3x + 2$$

Analysis *This makes sense because we can see from* ***Figure 11*** *that the line crosses the y-axis at the point $(0, 2)$, which is the y-intercept, so $b = 2$.*

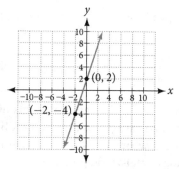

Figure 11

Example 8   **Writing an Equation for a Linear Cost Function**

Suppose Ben starts a company in which he incurs a fixed cost of $1,250 per month for the overhead, which includes his office rent. His production costs are $37.50 per item. Write a linear function C where $C(x)$ is the cost for x items produced in a given month.

Solution   The fixed cost is present every month, $1,250. The costs that can vary include the cost to produce each item, which is $37.50 for Ben. The variable cost, called the marginal cost, is represented by 37.5. The cost Ben incurs is the sum of these two costs, represented by $C(x) = 1250 + 37.5x$.

Analysis   *If Ben produces 100 items in a month, his monthly cost is represented by*

$$C(100) = 1250 + 37.5(100)$$
$$= 5000$$

So his monthly cost would be $5,000.

Example 9   **Writing an Equation for a Linear Function Given Two Points**

If f is a linear function, with $f(3) = -2$, and $f(8) = 1$, find an equation for the function in slope-intercept form.

Solution   We can write the given points using coordinates.

$$f(3) = -2 \rightarrow (3, -2)$$
$$f(8) = 1 \rightarrow (8, 1)$$

We can then use the points to calculate the slope.

$$m = \frac{y_2 - y_1}{x_2 - x_1}$$
$$= \frac{1 - (-2)}{8 - 3}$$
$$= \frac{3}{5}$$

Substitute the slope and the coordinates of one of the points into the point-slope form.

$$y - y_1 = m(x - x_1)$$
$$y - (-2) = \frac{3}{5}(x - 3)$$

We can use algebra to rewrite the equation in the slope-intercept form.

$$y + 2 = \frac{3}{5}(x - 3)$$
$$y + 2 = \frac{3}{5}x - \frac{9}{5}$$
$$y = \frac{3}{5}x - \frac{19}{5}$$

Try It #5

If $f(x)$ is a linear function, with $f(2) = -11$, and $f(4) = -25$, find an equation for the function in slope-intercept form.

Modeling Real-World Problems with Linear Functions

In the real world, problems are not always explicitly stated in terms of a function or represented with a graph. Fortunately, we can analyze the problem by first representing it as a linear function and then interpreting the components of the function. As long as we know, or can figure out, the initial value and the rate of change of a linear function, we can solve many different kinds of real-world problems.

How To...

Given a linear function f and the initial value and rate of change, evaluate $f(c)$.

1. Determine the initial value and the rate of change (slope).
2. Substitute the values into $f(x) = mx + b$.
3. Evaluate the function at $x = c$.

Example 10 **Using a Linear Function to Determine the Number of Songs in a Music Collection**

Marcus currently has 200 songs in his music collection. Every month, he adds 15 new songs. Write a formula for the number of songs, N, in his collection as a function of time, t, the number of months. How many songs will he own in a year?

Solution The initial value for this function is 200 because he currently owns 200 songs, so $N(0) = 200$, which means that $b = 200$.

The number of songs increases by 15 songs per month, so the rate of change is 15 songs per month. Therefore we know that $m = 15$. We can substitute the initial value and the rate of change into the slope-intercept form of a line.

$$f(x) = mx + b$$
$$\uparrow \quad \uparrow$$
$$15 \quad 200$$

$$N(t) = 15t + 200$$

Figure 12

We can write the formula $N(t) = 15t + 200$.

With this formula, we can then predict how many songs Marcus will have in 1 year (12 months). In other words, we can evaluate the function at $t = 12$.

$$N(12) = 15(12) + 200$$
$$= 180 + 200$$
$$= 380$$

Marcus will have 380 songs in 12 months.

Analysis Notice that N is an increasing linear function. As the input (the number of months) increases, the output (number of songs) increases as well.

Example 11 **Using a Linear Function to Calculate Salary Plus Commission**

Working as an insurance salesperson, Ilya earns a base salary plus a commission on each new policy. Therefore, Ilya's weekly income, I, depends on the number of new policies, n, he sells during the week. Last week he sold 3 new policies, and earned \$760 for the week. The week before, he sold 5 new policies and earned \$920. Find an equation for $I(n)$, and interpret the meaning of the components of the equation.

Solution The given information gives us two input-output pairs: (3,760) and (5,920). We start by finding the rate of change.

$$m = \frac{920 - 760}{5 - 3}$$
$$= \frac{\$160}{2 \text{ policies}}$$
$$= \$80 \text{ per policy}$$

Keeping track of units can help us interpret this quantity. Income increased by \$160 when the number of policies increased by 2, so the rate of change is \$80 per policy. Therefore, Ilya earns a commission of \$80 for each policy sold during the week.

We can then solve for the initial value.

$$I(n) = 80n + b$$

$$760 = 80(3) + b \text{ when } n = 3, \quad I(3) = 760$$

$$760 - 80(3) = b$$

$$520 = b$$

The value of b is the starting value for the function and represents Ilya's income when $n = 0$, or when no new policies are sold. We can interpret this as Ilya's base salary for the week, which does not depend upon the number of policies sold.

We can now write the final equation.

$$I(n) = 80n + 520$$

Our final interpretation is that Ilya's base salary is $520 per week and he earns an additional $80 commission for each policy sold.

Example 12   **Using Tabular Form to Write an Equation for a Linear Function**

Table 1 relates the number of rats in a population to time, in weeks. Use the table to write a linear equation.

w, number of weeks	0	2	4	6
$P(w)$, number of rats	1,000	1,080	1,160	1,240

Table 1

Solution   We can see from the table that the initial value for the number of rats is 1000, so $b = 1000$.

Rather than solving for m, we can tell from looking at the table that the population increases by 80 for every 2 weeks that pass. This means that the rate of change is 80 rats per 2 weeks, which can be simplified to 40 rats per week.

$$P(w) = 40w + 1000$$

If we did not notice the rate of change from the table we could still solve for the slope using any two points from the table. For example, using (2, 1080) and (6, 1240)

$$m = \frac{1240 - 1080}{6 - 2}$$

$$= \frac{160}{4}$$

$$= 40$$

Q & A...

Is the initial value always provided in a table of values like Table 1?

No. Sometimes the initial value is provided in a table of values, but sometimes it is not. If you see an input of 0, then the initial value would be the corresponding output. If the initial value is not provided because there is no value of input on the table equal to 0, find the slope, substitute one coordinate pair and the slope into $f(x) = mx + b$, and solve for b.

Try It #6

A new plant food was introduced to a young tree to test its effect on the height of the tree. **Table 2** shows the height of the tree, in feet, x months since the measurements began. Write a linear function, $H(x)$, where x is the number of months since the start of the experiment.

x	0	2	4	8	12
$H(x)$	12.5	13.5	14.5	16.5	18.5

Table 2

Access this online resource for additional instruction and practice with linear functions.

- Linear Functions (http://openstaxcollege.org/l/linearfunctions)

2.1 SECTION EXERCISES

VERBAL

1. Terry is skiing down a steep hill. Terry's elevation, $E(t)$, in feet after t seconds is given by $E(t) = 3000 - 70t$. Write a complete sentence describing Terry's starting elevation and how it is changing over time.

2. Maria is climbing a mountain. Maria's elevation, $E(t)$, in feet after t minutes is given by $E(t) = 1200 + 40t$. Write a complete sentence describing Maria's starting elevation and how it is changing over time.

3. Jessica is walking home from a friend's house. After 2 minutes she is 1.4 miles from home. Twelve minutes after leaving, she is 0.9 miles from home. What is her rate in miles per hour?

4. Sonya is currently 10 miles from home and is walking farther away at 2 miles per hour. Write an equation for her distance from home t hours from now.

5. A boat is 100 miles away from the marina, sailing directly toward it at 10 miles per hour. Write an equation for the distance of the boat from the marina after t hours.

6. Timmy goes to the fair with $40. Each ride costs $2. How much money will he have left after riding n rides?

ALGEBRAIC

For the following exercises, determine whether the equation of the curve can be written as a linear function.

7. $y = \dfrac{1}{4}x + 6$

8. $y = 3x - 5$

9. $y = 3x^2 - 2$

10. $3x + 5y = 15$

11. $3x^2 + 5y = 15$

12. $3x + 5y^2 = 15$

13. $-2x^2 + 3y^2 = 6$

14. $-\dfrac{x-3}{5} = 2y$

For the following exercises, determine whether each function is increasing or decreasing.

15. $f(x) = 4x + 3$

16. $g(x) = 5x + 6$

17. $a(x) = 5 - 2x$

18. $b(x) = 8 - 3x$

19. $h(x) = -2x + 4$

20. $k(x) = -4x + 1$

21. $j(x) = \dfrac{1}{2}x - 3$

22. $p(x) = \dfrac{1}{4}x - 5$

23. $n(x) = -\dfrac{1}{3}x - 2$

24. $m(x) = -\dfrac{3}{8}x + 3$

For the following exercises, find the slope of the line that passes through the two given points.

25. $(2, 4)$ and $(4, 10)$

26. $(1, 5)$ and $(4, 11)$

27. $(-1, 4)$ and $(5, 2)$

28. $(8, -2)$ and $(4, 6)$

29. $(6, 11)$ and $(-4, 3)$

For the following exercises, given each set of information, find a linear equation satisfying the conditions, if possible.

30. $f(-5) = -4$, and $f(5) = 2$

31. $f(-1) = 4$ and $f(5) = 1$

32. $(2, 4)$ and $(4, 10)$

33. Passes through $(1, 5)$ and $(4, 11)$

34. Passes through $(-1, 4)$ and $(5, 2)$

35. Passes through $(-2, 8)$ and $(4, 6)$

36. x-intercept at $(-2, 0)$ and y-intercept at $(0, -3)$

37. x-intercept at $(-5, 0)$ and y-intercept at $(0, 4)$

GRAPHICAL

For the following exercises, find the slope of the lines graphed.

38.

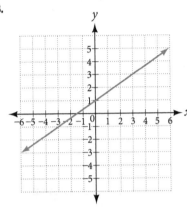

39.

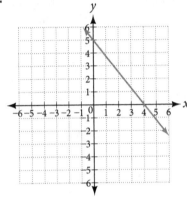

40.

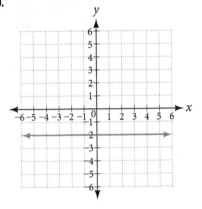

For the following exercises, write an equation for the lines graphed.

41.

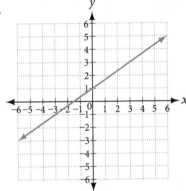

42.

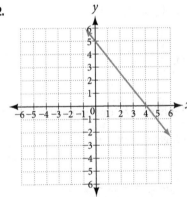

43.

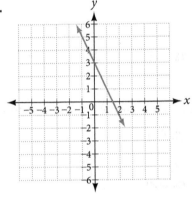

44.

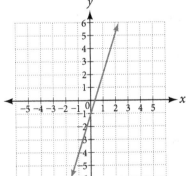

45.

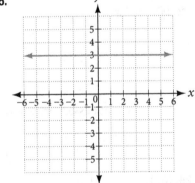

46.

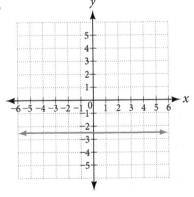

NUMERIC

For the following exercises, which of the tables could represent a linear function? For each that could be linear, find a linear equation that models the data.

47.

x	0	5	10	15
$g(x)$	5	-10	-25	-40

48.

x	0	5	10	15
$h(x)$	5	30	105	230

49.

x	0	5	10	15
$f(x)$	-5	20	45	70

50.

x	5	10	20	25
$k(x)$	13	28	58	73

51.

x	0	2	4	6
$g(x)$	6	-19	-44	-69

52.

x	2	4	6	8
$f(x)$	13	23	43	53

53.

x	2	4	6	8
$f(x)$	-4	16	36	56

54.

x	0	2	6	8
$k(x)$	6	31	106	231

TECHNOLOGY

55. If f is a linear function, $f(0.1) = 11.5$, and $f(0.4) = -5.9$, find an equation for the function.

56. Graph the function f on a domain of $[-10, 10]$: $f(x) = 0.02x - 0.01$. Enter the function in a graphing utility. For the viewing window, set the minimum value of x to be -10 and the maximum value of x to be 10.

57. Graph the function f on a domain of $[-10, 10]$: $f(x) = 2{,}500x + 4{,}000$

58. Table 3 shows the input, w, and output, k, for a linear function k. **a.** Fill in the missing values of the table. **b.** Write the linear function k, round to 3 decimal places.

w	-10	5.5	67.5	b
k	30	-26	a	-44

Table 3

59. Table 4 shows the input, p, and output, q, for a linear function q. **a.** Fill in the missing values of the table. **b.** Write the linear function k.

p	0.5	0.8	12	b
q	400	700	a	1,000,000

Table 4

60. Graph the linear function f on a domain of $[-10, 10]$ for the function whose slope is $\frac{1}{8}$ and y-intercept is $\frac{31}{16}$. Label the points for the input values of -10 and 10.

61. Graph the linear function f on a domain of $[-0.1, 0.1]$ for the function whose slope is 75 and y-intercept is -22.5. Label the points for the input values of -0.1 and 0.1.

62. Graph the linear function f where $f(x) = ax + b$ on the same set of axes on a domain of $[-4, 4]$ for the following values of a and b.

  a. $a = 2; b = 3$ **b.** $a = 2; b = 4$ **c.** $a = 2; b = -4$ **d.** $a = 2; b = -5$

EXTENSIONS

63. Find the value of x if a linear function goes through the following points and has the following slope: $(x, 2), (-4, 6), m = 3$

64. Find the value of y if a linear function goes through the following points and has the following slope: $(10, y), (25, 100), m = -5$

65. Find the equation of the line that passes through the following points: (a, b) and $(a, b + 1)$

66. Find the equation of the line that passes through the following points: $(2a, b)$ and $(a, b + 1)$

67. Find the equation of the line that passes through the following points: $(a, 0)$ and (c, d)

REAL-WORLD APPLICATIONS

68. At noon, a barista notices that she has $20 in her tip jar. If she makes an average of $0.50 from each customer, how much will she have in her tip jar if she serves n more customers during her shift?

69. A gym membership with two personal training sessions costs $125, while gym membership with five personal training sessions costs $260. What is cost per session?

70. A clothing business finds there is a linear relationship between the number of shirts, n, it can sell and the price, p, it can charge per shirt. In particular, historical data shows that 1,000 shirts can be sold at a price of $30, while 3,000 shirts can be sold at a price of $22. Find a linear equation in the form $p(n) = mn + b$ that gives the price p they can charge for n shirts.

71. A phone company charges for service according to the formula: $C(n) = 24 + 0.1n$, where n is the number of minutes talked, and $C(n)$ is the monthly charge, in dollars. Find and interpret the rate of change and initial value.

72. A farmer finds there is a linear relationship between the number of bean stalks, n, she plants and the yield, y, each plant produces. When she plants 30 stalks, each plant yields 30 oz of beans. When she plants 34 stalks, each plant produces 28 oz of beans. Find a linear relationship in the form $y = mn + b$ that gives the yield when n stalks are planted.

73. A city's population in the year 1960 was 287,500. In 1989 the population was 275,900. Compute the rate of growth of the population and make a statement about the population rate of change in people per year.

74. A town's population has been growing linearly. In 2003, the population was 45,000, and the population has been growing by 1,700 people each year. Write an equation, $P(t)$, for the population t years after 2003.

75. Suppose that average annual income (in dollars) for the years 1990 through 1999 is given by the linear function: $I(x) = 1,054x + 23,286$, where x is the number of years after 1990. Which of the following interprets the slope in the context of the problem?

   a. As of 1990, average annual income was $23,286.

   b. In the ten-year period from 1990–1999, average annual income increased by a total of $1,054.

   c. Each year in the decade of the 1990s, average annual income increased by $1,054.

   d. Average annual income rose to a level of $23,286 by the end of 1999.

76. When temperature is 0 degrees Celsius, the Fahrenheit temperature is 32. When the Celsius temperature is 100, the corresponding Fahrenheit temperature is 212. Express the Fahrenheit temperature as a linear function of C, the Celsius temperature, $F(C)$.

   a. Find the rate of change of Fahrenheit temperature for each unit change temperature of Celsius.

   b. Find and interpret $F(28)$.

   c. Find and interpret $F(-40)$.

LEARNING OBJECTIVES

In this section, you will:

- Graph linear functions.
- Write the equation for a linear function from the graph of a line.
- Given the equations of two lines, determine whether their graphs are parallel or perpendicular.
- Write the equation of a line parallel or perpendicular to a given line.
- Solve a system of linear equations.

2.2 GRAPHS OF LINEAR FUNCTIONS

Two competing telephone companies offer different payment plans. The two plans charge the same rate per long distance minute, but charge a different monthly flat fee. A consumer wants to determine whether the two plans will ever cost the same amount for a given number of long distance minutes used. The total cost of each payment plan can be represented by a linear function. To solve the problem, we will need to compare the functions. In this section, we will consider methods of comparing functions using graphs.

Graphing Linear Functions

In **Linear Functions**, we saw that the graph of a linear function is a straight line. We were also able to see the points of the function as well as the initial value from a graph. By graphing two functions, then, we can more easily compare their characteristics.

There are three basic methods of graphing linear functions. The first is by plotting points and then drawing a line through the points. The second is by using the y-intercept and slope. And the third is by using transformations of the identity function $f(x) = x$.

Graphing a Function by Plotting Points

To find points of a function, we can choose input values, evaluate the function at these input values, and calculate output values. The input values and corresponding output values form coordinate pairs. We then plot the coordinate pairs on a grid. In general, we should evaluate the function at a minimum of two inputs in order to find at least two points on the graph. For example, given the function, $f(x) = 2x$, we might use the input values 1 and 2. Evaluating the function for an input value of 1 yields an output value of 2, which is represented by the point (1, 2). Evaluating the function for an input value of 2 yields an output value of 4, which is represented by the point (2, 4). Choosing three points is often advisable because if all three points do not fall on the same line, we know we made an error.

How To…

Given a linear function, graph by plotting points.

1. Choose a minimum of two input values.

2. Evaluate the function at each input value.

3. Use the resulting output values to identify coordinate pairs.

4. Plot the coordinate pairs on a grid.

5. Draw a line through the points.

Example 1   **Graphing by Plotting Points**

Graph $f(x) = -\dfrac{2}{3}x + 5$ by plotting points.

Solution   Begin by choosing input values. This function includes a fraction with a denominator of 3, so let's choose multiples of 3 as input values. We will choose 0, 3, and 6.

Evaluate the function at each input value, and use the output value to identify coordinate pairs.

$$x = 0 \qquad f(0) = -\frac{2}{3}(0) + 5 = 5 \qquad (0, 5)$$

$$x = 3 \qquad f(3) = -\frac{2}{3}(3) + 5 = 3 \qquad (3, 3)$$

$$x = 6 \qquad f(6) = -\frac{2}{3}(6) + 5 = 1 \qquad (6, 1)$$

Plot the coordinate pairs and draw a line through the points. **Figure 1** represents the graph of the function $f(x) = -\frac{2}{3}x + 5$.

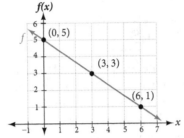

Figure 1 The graph of the linear function $f(x) = -\frac{2}{3}x + 5$.

Analysis 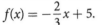 The graph of the function is a line as expected for a linear function. In addition, the graph has a downward slant, which indicates a negative slope. This is also expected from the negative constant rate of change in the equation for the function.

Try It #1

Graph $f(x) = -\frac{3}{4}x + 6$ by plotting points.

Graphing a Function Using *y*-intercept and Slope

Another way to graph linear functions is by using specific characteristics of the function rather than plotting points. The first characteristic is its *y*-intercept, which is the point at which the input value is zero. To find the *y*-intercept, we can set $x = 0$ in the equation.

The other characteristic of the linear function is its slope *m*, which is a measure of its steepness. Recall that the slope is the rate of change of the function. The slope of a function is equal to the ratio of the change in outputs to the change in inputs. Another way to think about the slope is by dividing the vertical difference, or rise, by the horizontal difference, or run. We encountered both the *y*-intercept and the slope in **Linear Functions**.

Let's consider the following function.

$$f(x) = \frac{1}{2}x + 1$$

The slope is $\frac{1}{2}$. Because the slope is positive, we know the graph will slant upward from left to right. The *y*-intercept is the point on the graph when $x = 0$. The graph crosses the *y*-axis at (0, 1). Now we know the slope and the *y*-intercept. We can begin graphing by plotting the point (0, 1). We know that the slope is rise over run, $m = \frac{\text{rise}}{\text{run}}$.

From our example, we have $m = \frac{1}{2}$, which means that the rise is 1 and the run is 2. So starting from our *y*-intercept (0, 1), we can rise 1 and then run 2, or run 2 and then rise 1. We repeat until we have a few points, and then we draw a line through the points as shown in **Figure 2**.

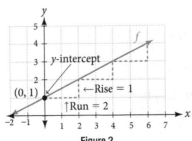

Figure 2

---

graphical interpretation of a linear function

In the equation $f(x) = mx + b$

- b is the y-intercept of the graph and indicates the point $(0, b)$ at which the graph crosses the y-axis.

- m is the slope of the line and indicates the vertical displacement (rise) and horizontal displacement (run) between each successive pair of points. Recall the formula for the slope:

$$m = \frac{\text{change in output (rise)}}{\text{change in input (run)}} = \frac{\Delta y}{\Delta x} = \frac{y_2 - y_1}{x_2 - x_1}$$

Q & A...

Do all linear functions have y-intercepts?

Yes. All linear functions cross the y-axis and therefore have y-intercepts. (*Note*: A vertical line parallel to the y-axis does not have a y-intercept, but it is not a function.)

How To...

Given the equation for a linear function, graph the function using the y-intercept and slope.

1. Evaluate the function at an input value of zero to find the y-intercept.
2. Identify the slope as the rate of change of the input value.
3. Plot the point represented by the y-intercept.
4. Use $\frac{\text{rise}}{\text{run}}$ to determine at least two more points on the line.
5. Sketch the line that passes through the points.

Example 2   **Graphing by Using the y-intercept and Slope**

Graph $f(x) = -\frac{2}{3}x + 5$ using the y-intercept and slope.

Solution   Evaluate the function at $x = 0$ to find the y-intercept. The output value when $x = 0$ is 5, so the graph will cross the y-axis at $(0, 5)$.

According to the equation for the function, the slope of the line is $-\frac{2}{3}$. This tells us that for each vertical decrease in the "rise" of -2 units, the "run" increases by 3 units in the horizontal direction. We can now graph the function by first plotting the y-intercept on the graph in **Figure 3**. From the initial value $(0, 5)$ we move down 2 units and to the right 3 units. We can extend the line to the left and right by repeating, and then draw a line through the points.

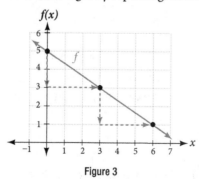

Figure 3

Analysis   The graph slants downward from left to right, which means it has a negative slope as expected.

Try It #2

Find a point on the graph we drew in **Example 2** that has a negative x-value.

Graphing a Function Using Transformations

Another option for graphing is to use transformations of the identity function $f(x) = x$. A function may be transformed by a shift up, down, left, or right. A function may also be transformed using a reflection, stretch, or compression.

Vertical Stretch or Compression

In the equation $f(x) = mx$, the m is acting as the vertical stretch or compression of the identity function. When m is negative, there is also a vertical reflection of the graph. Notice in **Figure 4** that multiplying the equation of $f(x) = x$ by m stretches the graph of f by a factor of m units if $m > 1$ and compresses the graph of f by a factor of m units if $0 < m < 1$. This means the larger the absolute value of m, the steeper the slope.

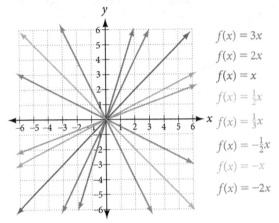

Figure 4 Vertical stretches and compressions and reflections on the function $f(x) = x$.

Vertical Shift

In $f(x) = mx + b$, the b acts as the vertical shift, moving the graph up and down without affecting the slope of the line. Notice in **Figure 5** that adding a value of b to the equation of $f(x) = x$ shifts the graph of f a total of b units up if b is positive and $|b|$ units down if b is negative.

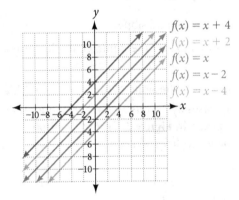

Figure 5 This graph illustrates vertical shifts of the function $f(x) = x$.

Using vertical stretches or compressions along with vertical shifts is another way to look at identifying different types of linear functions. Although this may not be the easiest way to graph this type of function, it is still important to practice each method.

How To...

Given the equation of a linear function, use transformations to graph the linear function in the form $f(x) = mx + b$.

1. Graph $f(x) = x$.
2. Vertically stretch or compress the graph by a factor m.
3. Shift the graph up or down b units.

Example 3 Graphing by Using Transformations

Graph $f(x) = \dfrac{1}{2}x - 3$ using transformations.

Solution The equation for the function shows that $m = \dfrac{1}{2}$ so the identity function is vertically compressed by $\dfrac{1}{2}$. The equation for the function also shows that $b = -3$ so the identity function is vertically shifted down 3 units. First, graph the identity function, and show the vertical compression as in **Figure 6**.

Then show the vertical shift as in **Figure 7**.

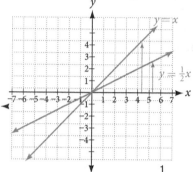

Figure 6 The function, $y = x$, compressed by a factor of $\dfrac{1}{2}$.

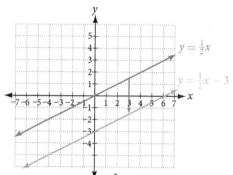

Figure 7 The function $y = \dfrac{1}{2}x$, shifted down 3 units.

Try It #3

Graph $f(x) = 4 + 2x$, using transformations.

Q & A...

In Example 3, could we have sketched the graph by reversing the order of the transformations?

No. The order of the transformations follows the order of operations. When the function is evaluated at a given input, the corresponding output is calculated by following the order of operations. This is why we performed the compression first. For example, following the order: Let the input be 2.

$$f(2) = \frac{1}{2}(2) - 3$$
$$= 1 - 3$$
$$= -2$$

Writing the Equation for a Function from the Graph of a Line

Recall that in **Linear Functions**, we wrote the equation for a linear function from a graph. Now we can extend what we know about graphing linear functions to analyze graphs a little more closely. Begin by taking a look at **Figure 8**. We can see right away that the graph crosses the y-axis at the point $(0, 4)$ so this is the y-intercept.

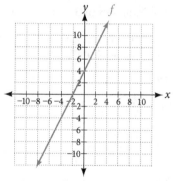

Figure 8

Then we can calculate the slope by finding the rise and run. We can choose any two points, but let's look at the point $(-2, 0)$. To get from this point to the y-intercept, we must move up 4 units (rise) and to the right 2 units (run). So the slope must be

$$m = \frac{\text{rise}}{\text{run}} = \frac{4}{2} = 2$$

Substituting the slope and y-intercept into the slope-intercept form of a line gives

$$y = 2x + 4$$

How To...

Given a graph of linear function, find the equation to describe the function.

1. Identify the y-intercept of an equation.
2. Choose two points to determine the slope.
3. Substitute the y-intercept and slope into the slope-intercept form of a line.

Example 4   **Matching Linear Functions to Their Graphs**

Match each equation of the linear functions with one of the lines in **Figure 9**.

 a. $f(x) = 2x + 3$ **b.** $g(x) = 2x - 3$ **c.** $h(x) = -2x + 3$ **d.** $j(x) = \dfrac{1}{2}x + 3$

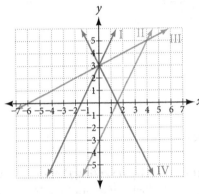

Figure 9

Solution   Analyze the information for each function.

a. This function has a slope of 2 and a y-intercept of 3. It must pass through the point $(0, 3)$ and slant upward from left to right. We can use two points to find the slope, or we can compare it with the other functions listed. Function g has the same slope, but a different y-intercept. Lines I and III have the same slant because they have the same slope. Line III does not pass through $(0, 3)$ so f must be represented by line I.

b. This function also has a slope of 2, but a y-intercept of -3. It must pass through the point $(0, -3)$ and slant upward from left to right. It must be represented by line III.

c. This function has a slope of -2 and a y-intercept of 3. This is the only function listed with a negative slope, so it must be represented by line IV because it slants downward from left to right.

d. This function has a slope of $\dfrac{1}{2}$ and a y-intercept of 3. It must pass through the point $(0, 3)$ and slant upward from left to right. Lines I and II pass through $(0, 3)$, but the slope of j is less than the slope of f so the line for j must be flatter. This function is represented by Line II.

Now we can re-label the lines as in **Figure 10**.

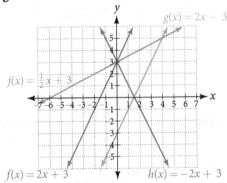

Figure 10

Finding the x-intercept of a Line

So far, we have been finding the y-intercepts of a function: the point at which the graph of the function crosses the y-axis. A function may also have an **x-intercept**, which is the x-coordinate of the point where the graph of the function crosses the x-axis. In other words, it is the input value when the output value is zero.

To find the x-intercept, set a function $f(x)$ equal to zero and solve for the value of x. For example, consider the function shown.

$$f(x) = 3x - 6$$

Set the function equal to 0 and solve for x.

$$0 = 3x - 6$$
$$6 = 3x$$
$$2 = x$$
$$x = 2$$

The graph of the function crosses the x-axis at the point (2, 0).

Q & A...

Do all linear functions have x-intercepts?

No. However, linear functions of the form $y = c$, where c is a nonzero real number are the only examples of linear functions with no x-intercept. For example, $y = 5$ is a horizontal line 5 units above the x-axis. This function has no x-intercepts, as shown in **Figure 11**.

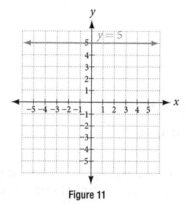

Figure 11

---

x-intercept

The **x-intercept** of the function is value of x when $f(x) = 0$. It can be solved by the equation $0 = mx + b$.

Example 5 **Finding an x-intercept**

Find the x-intercept of $f(x) = \frac{1}{2}x - 3$.

Solution Set the function equal to zero to solve for x.

$$0 = \frac{1}{2}x - 3$$

$$3 = \frac{1}{2}x$$

$$6 = x$$

$$x = 6$$

The graph crosses the x-axis at the point $(6, 0)$.

Analysis   *A graph of the function is shown in* **Figure 12**. *We can see that the x-intercept is $(6, 0)$ as we expected.*

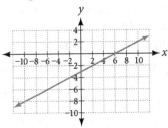

Figure 12 The graph of the linear function $f(x) = \frac{1}{2}x - 3$.

Try It #4

Find the x-intercept of $f(x) = \frac{1}{4}x - 4$.

Describing Horizontal and Vertical Lines

There are two special cases of lines on a graph—horizontal and vertical lines. A **horizontal line** indicates a constant output, or y-value. In **Figure 13**, we see that the output has a value of 2 for every input value. The change in outputs between any two points, therefore, is 0. In the slope formula, the numerator is 0, so the slope is 0. If we use $m = 0$ in the equation $f(x) = mx + b$, the equation simplifies to $f(x) = b$. In other words, the value of the function is a constant. This graph represents the function $f(x) = 2$.

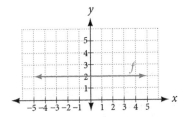

x	-4	-2	0	2	4
y	2	2	2	2	2

Figure 13 A horizontal line representing the function $f(x) = 2$.

A **vertical line** indicates a constant input, or x-value. We can see that the input value for every point on the line is 2, but the output value varies. Because this input value is mapped to more than one output value, a vertical line does not represent a function. Notice that between any two points, the change in the input values is zero. In the slope formula, the denominator will be zero, so the slope of a vertical line is undefined.

$$m = \frac{\text{change of output}}{\text{change of input}} \begin{array}{l} \leftarrow \text{Non-zero real number} \\ \leftarrow 0 \end{array}$$

Notice that a vertical line, such as the one in **Figure 14**, has an x-intercept, but no y-intercept unless it's the line $x = 0$. This graph represents the line $x = 2$.

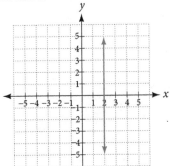

x	2	2	2	2	2
y	-4	-2	0	2	4

Figure 14 The vertical line, $x = 2$, which does not represent a function.

---

horizontal and vertical lines

Lines can be horizontal or vertical.

A **horizontal line** is a line defined by an equation in the form $f(x) = b$.

A **vertical line** is a line defined by an equation in the form $x = a$.

Example 6   **Writing the Equation of a Horizontal Line**

Write the equation of the line graphed in **Figure 15**.

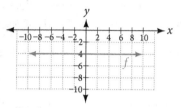

Figure 15

Solution   For any x-value, the y-value is -4, so the equation is $y = -4$.

Example 7   **Writing the Equation of a Vertical Line**

Write the equation of the line graphed in **Figure 16**.

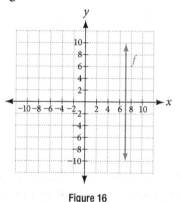

Figure 16

Solution   The constant x-value is 7, so the equation is $x = 7$.

Determining Whether Lines are Parallel or Perpendicular

The two lines in **Figure 17** are **parallel lines**: they will never intersect. Notice that they have exactly the same steepness, which means their slopes are identical. The only difference between the two lines is the y-intercept. If we shifted one line vertically toward the y-intercept of the other, they would become the same line.

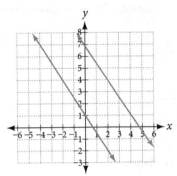

Figure 17 Parallel lines

We can determine from their equations whether two lines are parallel by comparing their slopes. If the slopes are the same and the y-intercepts are different, the lines are parallel. If the slopes are different, the lines are not parallel.

$$\left.\begin{array}{l} f(x) = -2x + 6 \\ f(x) = -2x - 4 \end{array}\right\} \text{ parallel} \qquad \left.\begin{array}{l} f(x) = 3x + 2 \\ f(x) = 2x + 2 \end{array}\right\} \text{ not parallel}$$

Unlike parallel lines, **perpendicular lines** do intersect. Their intersection forms a right, or 90-degree, angle. The two lines in **Figure 18** are perpendicular.

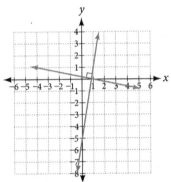

Figure 18 Perpendicular lines

Perpendicular lines do not have the same slope. The slopes of perpendicular lines are different from one another in a specific way. The slope of one line is the negative reciprocal of the slope of the other line. The product of a number and its reciprocal is 1. So, if m_1 and m_2 are negative reciprocals of one another, they can be multiplied together to yield -1.

$$m_1 m_2 = -1$$

To find the reciprocal of a number, divide 1 by the number. So the reciprocal of 8 is $\frac{1}{8}$, and the reciprocal of $\frac{1}{8}$ is 8. To find the negative reciprocal, first find the reciprocal and then change the sign.

As with parallel lines, we can determine whether two lines are perpendicular by comparing their slopes, assuming that the lines are neither horizontal nor perpendicular. The slope of each line below is the negative reciprocal of the other so the lines are perpendicular.

$$f(x) = \frac{1}{4}x + 2 \quad \text{negative reciprocal of } \frac{1}{4} \text{ is } -4$$

$$f(x) = -4x + 3 \quad \text{negative reciprocal of } -4 \text{ is } \frac{1}{4}$$

The product of the slopes is -1.

$$-4\left(\frac{1}{4}\right) = -1$$

---

parallel and perpendicular lines

Two lines are **parallel lines** if they do not intersect. The slopes of the lines are the same.

$$f(x) = m_1 x + b_1 \text{ and } g(x) = m_2 x + b_2 \text{ are parallel if } m_1 = m_2.$$

If and only if $b_1 = b_2$ and $m_1 = m_2$, we say the lines coincide. Coincident lines are the same line.

Two lines are **perpendicular lines** if they intersect at right angles.

$f(x) = m_1 x + b_1$ and $g(x) = m_2 x + b_2$ are perpendicular if $m_1 m_2 = -1$, and so $m_2 = -\dfrac{1}{m_1}$.

Example 8   **Identifying Parallel and Perpendicular Lines**

Given the functions below, identify the functions whose graphs are a pair of parallel lines and a pair of perpendicular lines.

$$f(x) = 2x + 3 \qquad\qquad h(x) = -2x + 2$$

$$g(x) = \frac{1}{2}x - 4 \qquad\qquad j(x) = 2x - 6$$

Solution   Parallel lines have the same slope. Because the functions $f(x) = 2x + 3$ and $j(x) = 2x - 6$ each have a slope of 2, they represent parallel lines. Perpendicular lines have negative reciprocal slopes. Because -2 and $\dfrac{1}{2}$ are negative reciprocals, the equations, $g(x) = \dfrac{1}{2}x - 4$ and $h(x) = -2x + 2$ represent perpendicular lines.

Analysis   *A graph of the lines is shown in* **Figure 19**.

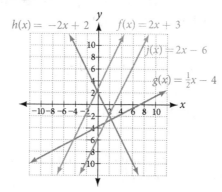

Figure 19

The graph shows that the lines $f(x) = 2x + 3$ and $j(x) = 2x - 6$ are parallel, and the lines $g(x) = \dfrac{1}{2}x - 4$ and $h(x) = -2x + 2$ are perpendicular.

Writing the Equation of a Line Parallel or Perpendicular to a Given Line

If we know the equation of a line, we can use what we know about slope to write the equation of a line that is either parallel or perpendicular to the given line.

Writing Equations of Parallel Lines

Suppose for example, we are given the following equation.

$$f(x) = 3x + 1$$

We know that the slope of the line formed by the function is 3. We also know that the y-intercept is $(0, 1)$. Any other line with a slope of 3 will be parallel to $f(x)$. So the lines formed by all of the following functions will be parallel to $f(x)$.

$$g(x) = 3x + 6$$

$$h(x) = 3x + 1$$

$$p(x) = 3x + \frac{2}{3}$$

Suppose then we want to write the equation of a line that is parallel to f and passes through the point $(1, 7)$. We already know that the slope is 3. We just need to determine which value for b will give the correct line. We can begin with the point-slope form of an equation for a line, and then rewrite it in the slope-intercept form.

$$y - y_1 = m(x - x_1)$$
$$y - 7 = 3(x - 1)$$
$$y - 7 = 3x - 3$$
$$y = 3x + 4$$

So $g(x) = 3x + 4$ is parallel to $f(x) = 3x + 1$ and passes through the point $(1, 7)$.

How To...

Given the equation of a function and a point through which its graph passes, write the equation of a line parallel to the given line that passes through the given point.

1. Find the slope of the function.
2. Substitute the given values into either the general point-slope equation or the slope-intercept equation for a line.
3. Simplify.

Example 9   **Finding a Line Parallel to a Given Line**

Find a line parallel to the graph of $f(x) = 3x + 6$ that passes through the point $(3, 0)$.

Solution   The slope of the given line is 3. If we choose the slope-intercept form, we can substitute $m = 3$, $x = 3$, and $f(x) = 0$ into the slope-intercept form to find the y-intercept.

$$g(x) = 3x + b$$
$$0 = 3(3) + b$$
$$b = -9$$

The line parallel to $f(x)$ that passes through $(3, 0)$ is $g(x) = 3x - 9$.

Analysis   *We can confirm that the two lines are parallel by graphing them.* **Figure 20** *shows that the two lines will never intersect.*

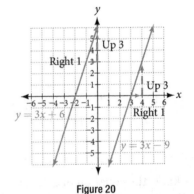

Figure 20

Writing Equations of Perpendicular Lines

We can use a very similar process to write the equation for a line perpendicular to a given line. Instead of using the same slope, however, we use the negative reciprocal of the given slope. Suppose we are given the following function:

$$f(x) = 2x + 4$$

The slope of the line is 2, and its negative reciprocal is $-\frac{1}{2}$. Any function with a slope of $-\frac{1}{2}$ will be perpendicular to $f(x)$. So the lines formed by all of the following functions will be perpendicular to $f(x)$.

$$g(x) = -\frac{1}{2}x + 4 \qquad h(x) = -\frac{1}{2}x + 2 \qquad p(x) = -\frac{1}{2}x - \frac{1}{2}$$

As before, we can narrow down our choices for a particular perpendicular line if we know that it passes through a given point. Suppose then we want to write the equation of a line that is perpendicular to $f(x)$ and passes through the point $(4, 0)$. We already know that the slope is $-\frac{1}{2}$. Now we can use the point to find the y-intercept by substituting the given values into the slope-intercept form of a line and solving for b.

$$g(x) = mx + b$$
$$0 = -\frac{1}{2}(4) + b$$
$$0 = -2 + b$$
$$2 = b$$
$$b = 2$$

The equation for the function with a slope of $-\frac{1}{2}$ and a y-intercept of 2 is

$$g(x) = -\frac{1}{2}x + 2.$$

So $g(x) = -\frac{1}{2}x + 2$ is perpendicular to $f(x) = 2x + 4$ and passes through the point $(4, 0)$. Be aware that perpendicular lines may not look obviously perpendicular on a graphing calculator unless we use the square zoom feature.

Q & A...

A horizontal line has a slope of zero and a vertical line has an undefined slope. These two lines are perpendicular, but the product of their slopes is not −1. Doesn't this fact contradict the definition of perpendicular lines?

No. For two perpendicular linear functions, the product of their slopes is −1. However, a vertical line is not a function so the definition is not contradicted.

How To...

Given the equation of a function and a point through which its graph passes, write the equation of a line perpendicular to the given line.

1. Find the slope of the function.
2. Determine the negative reciprocal of the slope.
3. Substitute the new slope and the values for x and y from the coordinate pair provided into $g(x) = mx + b$.
4. Solve for b.
5. Write the equation for the line.

Example 10   **Finding the Equation of a Perpendicular Line**

Find the equation of a line perpendicular to $f(x) = 3x + 3$ that passes through the point $(3, 0)$.

Solution   The original line has slope $m = 3$, so the slope of the perpendicular line will be its negative reciprocal, or $-\frac{1}{3}$. Using this slope and the given point, we can find the equation for the line.

$$g(x) = -\frac{1}{3}x + b$$
$$0 = -\frac{1}{3}(3) + b$$
$$1 = b$$
$$b = 1$$

The line perpendicular to $f(x)$ that passes through $(3, 0)$ is $g(x) = -\frac{1}{3}x + 1$.

Analysis   *A graph of the two lines is shown in **Figure 21**.*

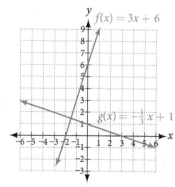

Figure 21

Try It #5

Given the function $h(x) = 2x - 4$, write an equation for the line passing through $(0, 0)$ that is

a. parallel to $h(x)$ **b.** perpendicular to $h(x)$

How To...

Given two points on a line and a third point, write the equation of the perpendicular line that passes through the point.

1. Determine the slope of the line passing through the points.
2. Find the negative reciprocal of the slope.
3. Use the slope-intercept form or point-slope form to write the equation by substituting the known values.
4. Simplify.

Example 11   **Finding the Equation of a Line Perpendicular to a Given Line Passing through a Point**

A line passes through the points $(-2, 6)$ and $(4, 5)$. Find the equation of a perpendicular line that passes through the point $(4, 5)$.

Solution   From the two points of the given line, we can calculate the slope of that line.

$$m_1 = \frac{5 - 6}{4 - (-2)}$$

$$= \frac{-1}{6}$$

$$= -\frac{1}{6}$$

Find the negative reciprocal of the slope.

$$m_2 = \frac{-1}{-\frac{1}{6}}$$

$$= -1\left(-\frac{6}{1}\right)$$

$$= 6$$

We can then solve for the y-intercept of the line passing through the point $(4, 5)$.

$$g(x) = 6x + b$$

$$5 = 6(4) + b$$

$$5 = 24 + b$$

$$-19 = b$$

$$b = -19$$

The equation for the line that is perpendicular to the line passing through the two given points and also passes through point $(4, 5)$ is

$$y = 6x - 19$$

Try It #6

A line passes through the points, $(-2, -15)$ and $(2, -3)$. Find the equation of a perpendicular line that passes through the point, $(6, 4)$.

Solving a System of Linear Equations Using a Graph

A system of linear equations includes two or more linear equations. The graphs of two lines will intersect at a single point if they are not parallel. Two parallel lines can also intersect if they are coincident, which means they are the same line and they intersect at every point. For two lines that are not parallel, the single point of intersection will satisfy both equations and therefore represent the solution to the system.

To find this point when the equations are given as functions, we can solve for an input value so that $f(x) = g(x)$. In other words, we can set the formulas for the lines equal to one another, and solve for the input that satisfies the equation.

Example 12 **Finding a Point of Intersection Algebraically**

Find the point of intersection of the lines $h(t) = 3t - 4$ and $j(t) = 5 - t$.

Solution   Set $h(t) = j(t)$.

$$3t - 4 = 5 - t$$

$$4t = 9$$

$$t = \frac{9}{4}$$

This tells us the lines intersect when the input is $\frac{9}{4}$.

We can then find the output value of the intersection point by evaluating either function at this input.

$$j\left(\frac{9}{4}\right) = 5 - \frac{9}{4}$$

$$= \frac{11}{4}$$

These lines intersect at the point $\left(\frac{9}{4}, \frac{11}{4}\right)$.

*Analysis   Looking at **Figure 22**, this result seems reasonable.*

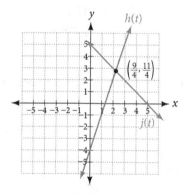

Figure 22

Q & A...

If we were asked to find the point of intersection of two distinct parallel lines, should something in the solution process alert us to the fact that there are no solutions?

Yes. After setting the two equations equal to one another, the result would be the contradiction "0 = non-zero real number."

Try It #7

Look at the graph in **Figure 22** and identify the following for the function $j(t)$:

a. y-intercept   **b.** x-intercept(s)   **c.** slope

d. Is $j(t)$ parallel or perpendicular to $h(t)$ (or neither)?

e. Is $j(t)$ an increasing or decreasing function (or neither)?

f. Write a transformation description for $j(t)$ from the identity toolkit function $f(x) = x$.

Example 13   **Finding a Break-Even Point**

A company sells sports helmets. The company incurs a one-time fixed cost for $250,000. Each helmet costs $120 to produce, and sells for $140.

    a. Find the cost function, C, to produce x helmets, in dollars.

    b. Find the revenue function, R, from the sales of x helmets, in dollars.

    c. Find the break-even point, the point of intersection of the two graphs C and R.

Solution

    a. The cost function in the sum of the fixed cost, $250,000, and the variable cost, $120 per helmet.

$$C(x) = 120x + 250,000$$

    b. The revenue function is the total revenue from the sale of x helmets, $R(x) = 140x$.

    c. The break-even point is the point of intersection of the graph of the cost and revenue functions. To find the x-coordinate of the coordinate pair of the point of intersection, set the two equations equal, and solve for x.

$$C(x) = R(x)$$
$$250,000 + 120x = 140x$$
$$250,000 = 20x$$
$$12,500 = x$$
$$x = 12,500$$

To find y, evaluate either the revenue or the cost function at 12,500.

$$R(x) = 140(12,500)$$
$$= \$1,750,000$$

The break-even point is (12,500, 1,750,000).

Analysis   *This means if the company sells 12,500 helmets, they break even; both the sales and cost incurred equaled 1.75 million dollars. See* **Figure 23.**

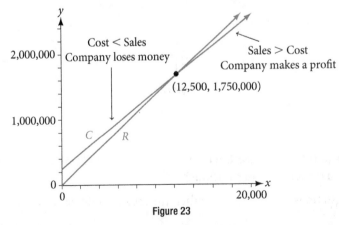

Figure 23

Access these online resources for additional instruction and practice with graphs of linear functions.

- Finding Input of Function from the Output and Graph (http://openstaxcollege.org/l/findinginput)
- Graphing Functions Using Tables (http://openstaxcollege.org/l/graphwithtable)

2.2   SECTION EXERCISES

VERBAL

1. If the graphs of two linear functions are parallel, describe the relationship between the slopes and the y-intercepts.

2. If the graphs of two linear functions are perpendicular, describe the relationship between the slopes and the y-intercepts.

3. If a horizontal line has the equation $f(x) = a$ and a vertical line has the equation $x = a$, what is the point of intersection? Explain why what you found is the point of intersection.

4. Explain how to find a line parallel to a linear function that passes through a given point.

5. Explain how to find a line perpendicular to a linear function that passes through a given point.

ALGEBRAIC

For the following exercises, determine whether the lines given by the equations below are parallel, perpendicular, or neither parallel nor perpendicular:

6. $4x - 7y = 10$
   $7x + 4y = 1$

7. $3y + x = 12$
   $-y = 8x + 1$

8. $3y + 4x = 12$
   $-6y = 8x + 1$

9. $6x - 9y = 10$
   $3x + 2y = 1$

10. $y = \dfrac{2}{3}x + 1$
    $3x + 2y = 1$

11. $y = \dfrac{3}{4}x + 1$
    $-3x + 4y = 1$

For the following exercises, find the x- and y-intercepts of each equation

12. $f(x) = -x + 2$

13. $g(x) = 2x + 4$

14. $h(x) = 3x - 5$

15. $k(x) = -5x + 1$

16. $-2x + 5y = 20$

17. $7x + 2y = 56$

For the following exercises, use the descriptions of each pair of lines given below to find the slopes of Line 1 and Line 2. Is each pair of lines parallel, perpendicular, or neither?

18. Line 1: Passes through $(0, 6)$ and $(3, -24)$
    Line 2: Passes through $(-1, 19)$ and $(8, -71)$

19. Line 1: Passes through $(-8, -55)$ and $(10, 89)$
    Line 2: Passes through $(9, -44)$ and $(4, -14)$

20. Line 1: Passes through $(2, 3)$ and $(4, -1)$
    Line 2: Passes through $(6, 3)$ and $(8, 5)$

21. Line 1: Passes through $(1, 7)$ and $(5, 5)$
    Line 2: Passes through $(-1, -3)$ and $(1, 1)$

22. Line 1: Passes through $(0, 5)$ and $(3, 3)$
    Line 2: Passes through $(1, -5)$ and $(3, -2)$

23. Line 1: Passes through $(2, 5)$ and $(5, -1)$
    Line 2: Passes through $(-3, 7)$ and $(3, -5)$

24. Write an equation for a line parallel to $f(x) = -5x - 3$ and passing through the point $(2, -12)$.

25. Write an equation for a line parallel to $g(x) = 3x - 1$ and passing through the point $(4, 9)$.

26. Write an equation for a line perpendicular to $h(t) = -2t + 4$ and passing through the point $(-4, -1)$.

27. Write an equation for a line perpendicular to $p(t) = 3t + 4$ and passing through the point $(3, 1)$.

28. Find the point at which the line $f(x) = -2x - 1$ intersects the line $g(x) = -x$.

29. Find the point at which the line $f(x) = 2x + 5$ intersects the line $g(x) = -3x - 5$.

30. Use algebra to find the point at which the line $f(x) = -\dfrac{4}{5}x + \dfrac{274}{25}$ intersects $h(x) = \dfrac{9}{4}x + \dfrac{73}{10}$.

31. Use algebra to find the point at which the line $f(x) = \dfrac{7}{4}x + \dfrac{457}{60}$ intersects $g(x) = \dfrac{4}{3}x + \dfrac{31}{5}$.

GRAPHICAL

For the following exercises, match the given linear equation with its graph in **Figure 24**.

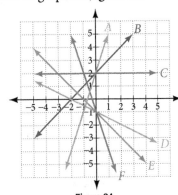

Figure 24

32. $f(x) = -x - 1$

33. $f(x) = -2x - 1$

34. $f(x) = -\dfrac{1}{2}x - 1$

35. $f(x) = 2$

36. $f(x) = 2 + x$

37. $f(x) = 3x + 2$

For the following exercises, sketch a line with the given features.

38. An x-intercept of $(-4, 0)$ and y-intercept of $(0, -2)$

39. An x-intercept of $(-2, 0)$ and y-intercept of $(0, 4)$

40. A y-intercept of $(0, 7)$ and slope $-\dfrac{3}{2}$

41. A y-intercept of $(0, 3)$ and slope $\dfrac{2}{5}$

42. Passing through the points $(-6, -2)$ and $(6, -6)$

43. Passing through the points $(-3, -4)$ and $(3, 0)$

For the following exercises, sketch the graph of each equation.

44. $f(x) = -2x - 1$

45. $g(x) = -3x + 2$

46. $h(x) = \dfrac{1}{3}x + 2$

47. $k(x) = \dfrac{2}{3}x - 3$

48. $f(t) = 3 + 2t$

49. $p(t) = -2 + 3t$

50. $x = 3$

51. $x = -2$

52. $r(x) = 4$

53. $q(x) = 3$

54. $4x = -9y + 36$

55. $\dfrac{x}{3} - \dfrac{y}{4} = 1$

56. $3x - 5y = 15$

57. $3x = 15$

58. $3y = 12$

59. If $g(x)$ is the transformation of $f(x) = x$ after a vertical compression by $\dfrac{3}{4}$, a shift right by 2, and a shift down by 4
  a. Write an equation for $g(x)$.
  b. What is the slope of this line?
  c. Find the y-intercept of this line.

60. If $g(x)$ is the transformation of $f(x) = x$ after a vertical compression by $\dfrac{1}{3}$, a shift left by 1, and a shift up by 3
  a. Write an equation for $g(x)$.
  b. What is the slope of this line?
  c. Find the y-intercept of this line.

For the following exercises, write the equation of the line shown in the graph.

61.

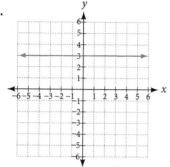

62.

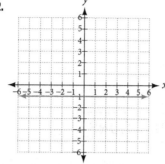

63.

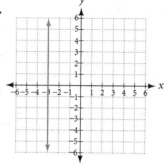

64.

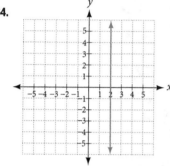

For the following exercises, find the point of intersection of each pair of lines if it exists. If it does not exist, indicate that there is no point of intersection.

65.
$$y = \frac{3}{4}x + 1$$
$$-3x + 4y = 12$$

66. $2x - 3y = 12$
$$5y + x = 30$$

67. $2x = y - 3$
$$y + 4x = 15$$

68. $x - 2y + 2 = 3$
$$x - y = 3$$

69. $5x + 3y = -65$
$$x - y = -5$$

EXTENSIONS

70. Find the equation of the line parallel to the line $g(x) = -0.01x + 2.01$ through the point $(1, 2)$.

71. Find the equation of the line perpendicular to the line $g(x) = -0.01x + 2.01$ through the point $(1, 2)$.

For the following exercises, use the functions $f(x) = -0.1x + 200$ and $g(x) = 20x + 0.1$.

72. Find the point of intersection of the lines f and g.

73. Where is $f(x)$ greater than $g(x)$? Where is $g(x)$ greater than $f(x)$?

REAL-WORLD APPLICATIONS

74. A car rental company offers two plans for renting a car.
Plan A: $30 per day and $0.18 per mile
Plan B: $50 per day with free unlimited mileage
How many miles would you need to drive for plan B to save you money?

75. A cell phone company offers two plans for minutes.
Plan A: $20 per month and $1 for every one hundred texts.
Plan B: $50 per month with free unlimited texts.
How many texts would you need to send per month for plan B to save you money?

76. A cell phone company offers two plans for minutes.
Plan A: $15 per month and $2 for every 300 texts.
Plan B: $25 per month and $0.50 for every 100 texts.
How many texts would you need to send per month for plan B to save you money?

LEARNING OBJECTIVES

In this section, you will:

- Identify steps for modeling and solving.
- Build linear models from verbal descriptions.
- Build systems of linear models.

2.3　MODELING WITH LINEAR FUNCTIONS

Figure 1 (credit: EEK Photography/Flickr)

Emily is a college student who plans to spend a summer in Seattle. She has saved $3,500 for her trip and anticipates spending $400 each week on rent, food, and activities. How can we write a linear model to represent her situation? What would be the *x*-intercept, and what can she learn from it? To answer these and related questions, we can create a model using a linear function. Models such as this one can be extremely useful for analyzing relationships and making predictions based on those relationships. In this section, we will explore examples of linear function models.

Identifying Steps to Model and Solve Problems

When modeling scenarios with linear functions and solving problems involving quantities with a constant rate of change, we typically follow the same problem strategies that we would use for any type of function. Let's briefly review them:

1. Identify changing quantities, and then define descriptive variables to represent those quantities. When appropriate, sketch a picture or define a coordinate system.

2. Carefully read the problem to identify important information. Look for information that provides values for the variables or values for parts of the functional model, such as slope and initial value.

3. Carefully read the problem to determine what we are trying to find, identify, solve, or interpret.

4. Identify a solution pathway from the provided information to what we are trying to find. Often this will involve checking and tracking units, building a table, or even finding a formula for the function being used to model the problem.

5. When needed, write a formula for the function.

6. Solve or evaluate the function using the formula.

7. Reflect on whether your answer is reasonable for the given situation and whether it makes sense mathematically.

8. Clearly convey your result using appropriate units, and answer in full sentences when necessary.

Building Linear Models

Now let's take a look at the student in Seattle. In her situation, there are two changing quantities: time and money. The amount of money she has remaining while on vacation depends on how long she stays. We can use this information to define our variables, including units.

- Output: M, money remaining, in dollars
- Input: t, time, in weeks

So, the amount of money remaining depends on the number of weeks: $M(t)$

We can also identify the initial value and the rate of change.

- Initial Value: She saved $3,500, so $3,500 is the initial value for M.
- Rate of Change: She anticipates spending $400 each week, so −$400 per week is the rate of change, or slope.

Notice that the unit of dollars per week matches the unit of our output variable divided by our input variable. Also, because the slope is negative, the linear function is decreasing. This should make sense because she is spending money each week.

The rate of change is constant, so we can start with the linear model $M(t) = mt + b$. Then we can substitute the intercept and slope provided.

$$M(t) = mt + b$$
$$\uparrow \quad \uparrow$$
$$-400 \quad 3500$$

$$M(t) = -400t + 3500$$

To find the x-intercept, we set the output to zero, and solve for the input.

$$0 = -400t + 3500$$

$$t = \frac{3500}{400}$$

$$= 8.75$$

The x-intercept is 8.75 weeks. Because this represents the input value when the output will be zero, we could say that Emily will have no money left after 8.75 weeks.

When modeling any real-life scenario with functions, there is typically a limited domain over which that model will be valid—almost no trend continues indefinitely. Here the domain refers to the number of weeks. In this case, it doesn't make sense to talk about input values less than zero. A negative input value could refer to a number of weeks before she saved $3,500, but the scenario discussed poses the question once she saved $3,500 because this is when her trip and subsequent spending starts. It is also likely that this model is not valid after the x-intercept, unless Emily will use a credit card and goes into debt. The domain represents the set of input values, so the reasonable domain for this function is $0 \leq t \leq 8.75$.

In the above example, we were given a written description of the situation. We followed the steps of modeling a problem to analyze the information. However, the information provided may not always be the same. Sometimes we might be provided with an intercept. Other times we might be provided with an output value. We must be careful to analyze the information we are given, and use it appropriately to build a linear model.

Using a Given Intercept to Build a Model

Some real-world problems provide the y-intercept, which is the constant or initial value. Once the y-intercept is known, the x-intercept can be calculated. Suppose, for example, that Hannah plans to pay off a no-interest loan from her parents. Her loan balance is $1,000. She plans to pay $250 per month until her balance is $0. The y-intercept is the initial amount of her debt, or $1,000. The rate of change, or slope, is −$250 per month. We can then use the slope-intercept form and the given information to develop a linear model.

$$f(x) = mx + b$$

$$= -250x + 1000$$

Now we can set the function equal to 0, and solve for x to find the x-intercept.

$$0 = -250x + 1000$$

$$1000 = 250x$$

$$4 = x$$

$$x = 4$$

The x-intercept is the number of months it takes her to reach a balance of $0. The x-intercept is 4 months, so it will take Hannah four months to pay off her loan.

Using a Given Input and Output to Build a Model

Many real-world applications are not as direct as the ones we just considered. Instead they require us to identify some aspect of a linear function. We might sometimes instead be asked to evaluate the linear model at a given input or set the equation of the linear model equal to a specified output.

How To...

Given a word problem that includes two pairs of input and output values, use the linear function to solve a problem.

1. Identify the input and output values.
2. Convert the data to two coordinate pairs.
3. Find the slope.
4. Write the linear model.
5. Use the model to make a prediction by evaluating the function at a given x-value.
6. Use the model to identify an x-value that results in a given y-value.
7. Answer the question posed.

Example 1   **Using a Linear Model to Investigate a Town's Population**

A town's population has been growing linearly. In 2004 the population was 6,200. By 2009 the population had grown to 8,100. Assume this trend continues.

    a. Predict the population in 2013.

    b. Identify the year in which the population will reach 15,000.

Solution   The two changing quantities are the population size and time. While we could use the actual year value as the input quantity, doing so tends to lead to very cumbersome equations because the y-intercept would correspond to the year 0, more than 2,000 years ago!

To make computation a little nicer, we will define our input as the number of years since 2004:

- Input: t, years since 2004

- Output: $P(t)$, the town's population

To predict the population in 2013 ($t = 9$), we would first need an equation for the population. Likewise, to find when the population would reach 15,000, we would need to solve for the input that would provide an output of 15,000. To write an equation, we need the initial value and the rate of change, or slope.

To determine the rate of change, we will use the change in output per change in input.

$$m = \frac{\text{change in output}}{\text{change in input}}$$

The problem gives us two input-output pairs. Converting them to match our defined variables, the year 2004 would correspond to $t = 0$, giving the point $(0, 6200)$. Notice that through our clever choice of variable definition, we have "given" ourselves the y-intercept of the function. The year 2009 would correspond to $t = 5$, giving the point $(5, 8100)$.

The two coordinate pairs are $(0, 6200)$ and $(5, 8100)$. Recall that we encountered examples in which we were provided two points earlier in the chapter. We can use these values to calculate the slope.

$$m = \frac{8100 - 6200}{5 - 0}$$

$$= \frac{1900}{5}$$

$$= 380 \text{ people per year}$$

We already know the y-intercept of the line, so we can immediately write the equation:

$$P(t) = 380t + 6200$$

To predict the population in 2013, we evaluate our function at $t = 9$.

$$P(9) = 380(9) + 6{,}200$$

$$= 9{,}620$$

If the trend continues, our model predicts a population of 9,620 in 2013.

To find when the population will reach 15,000, we can set $P(t) = 15000$ and solve for t.

$$15000 = 380t + 6200$$

$$8800 = 380t$$

$$t \approx 23.158$$

Our model predicts the population will reach 15,000 in a little more than 23 years after 2004, or somewhere around the year 2027.

Try It #1

A company sells doughnuts. They incur a fixed cost of $25,000 for rent, insurance, and other expenses. It costs $0.25 to produce each doughnut.

a. Write a linear model to represent the cost C of the company as a function of x, the number of doughnuts produced.

b. Find and interpret the y-intercept.

Try It #2

A city's population has been growing linearly. In 2008, the population was 28,200. By 2012, the population was 36,800. Assume this trend continues.

a. Predict the population in 2014.

b. Identify the year in which the population will reach 54,000.

Using a Diagram to Model a Problem

It is useful for many real-world applications to draw a picture to gain a sense of how the variables representing the input and output may be used to answer a question. To draw the picture, first consider what the problem is asking for. Then, determine the input and the output. The diagram should relate the variables. Often, geometrical shapes or figures are drawn. Distances are often traced out. If a right triangle is sketched, the Pythagorean Theorem relates the sides. If a rectangle is sketched, labeling width and height is helpful.

Example 2　**Using a Diagram to Model Distance Walked**

Anna and Emanuel start at the same intersection. Anna walks east at 4 miles per hour while Emanuel walks south at 3 miles per hour. They are communicating with a two-way radio that has a range of 2 miles. How long after they start walking will they fall out of radio contact?

Solution　In essence, we can partially answer this question by saying they will fall out of radio contact when they are 2 miles apart, which leads us to ask a new question:

"How long will it take them to be 2 miles apart?"

In this problem, our changing quantities are time and position, but ultimately we need to know how long will it take for them to be 2 miles apart. We can see that time will be our input variable, so we'll define our input and output variables.

- Input: t, time in hours.

- Output: $A(t)$, distance in miles, and $E(t)$, distance in miles

Because it is not obvious how to define our output variable, we'll start by drawing a picture such as **Figure 2**.

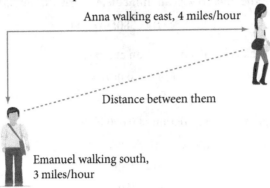

Anna walking east, 4 miles/hour

Distance between them

Emanuel walking south, 3 miles/hour

Figure 2

Initial Value: They both start at the same intersection so when $t = 0$, the distance traveled by each person should also be 0. Thus the initial value for each is 0.

Rate of Change: Anna is walking 4 miles per hour and Emanuel is walking 3 miles per hour, which are both rates of change. The slope for A is 4 and the slope for E is 3.

Using those values, we can write formulas for the distance each person has walked.

$$A(t) = 4t$$

$$E(t) = 3t$$

For this problem, the distances from the starting point are important. To notate these, we can define a coordinate system, identifying the "starting point" at the intersection where they both started. Then we can use the variable, A, which we introduced above, to represent Anna's position, and define it to be a measurement from the starting point in the eastward direction. Likewise, can use the variable, E, to represent Emanuel's position, measured from the starting point in the southward direction. Note that in defining the coordinate system, we specified both the starting point of the measurement and the direction of measure.

We can then define a third variable, D, to be the measurement of the distance between Anna and Emanuel.

Showing the variables on the diagram is often helpful, as we can see from **Figure 3**.

Recall that we need to know how long it takes for D, the distance between them, to equal 2 miles. Notice that for any given input t, the outputs $A(t)$, $E(t)$, and $D(t)$ represent distances.

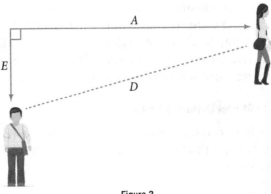

A

E

D

Figure 3

Figure 3 shows us that we can use the Pythagorean Theorem because we have drawn a right angle.

Using the Pythagorean Theorem, we get:

$$D(t)^2 = A(t)^2 + E(t)^2$$
$$= (4t)^2 + (3t)^2$$
$$= 16t^2 + 9t^2$$
$$= 25t^2$$
$$D(t) = \pm\sqrt{25t^2} \qquad \text{Solve for } D(t) \text{ using the square root.}$$
$$= \pm 5|t|$$

In this scenario we are considering only positive values of t, so our distance $D(t)$ will always be positive. We can simplify this answer to $D(t) = 5t$. This means that the distance between Anna and Emanuel is also a linear function. Because D is a linear function, we can now answer the question of when the distance between them will reach 2 miles. We will set the output $D(t) = 2$ and solve for t.

$$D(t) = 2$$
$$5t = 2$$
$$t = \frac{2}{5} = 0.4$$

They will fall out of radio contact in 0.4 hours, or 24 minutes.

Q & A...

Should I draw diagrams when given information based on a geometric shape?

Yes. Sketch the figure and label the quantities and unknowns on the sketch.

Example 3   **Using a Diagram to Model Distance Between Cities**

There is a straight road leading from the town of Westborough to Agritown 30 miles east and 10 miles north. Partway down this road, it junctions with a second road, perpendicular to the first, leading to the town of Eastborough. If the town of Eastborough is located 20 miles directly east of the town of Westborough, how far is the road junction from Westborough?

Solution   It might help here to draw a picture of the situation. See **Figure 4**. It would then be helpful to introduce a coordinate system. While we could place the origin anywhere, placing it at Westborough seems convenient. This puts Agritown at coordinates (30, 10), and Eastborough at (20, 0).

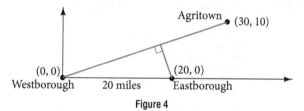

Figure 4

Using this point along with the origin, we can find the slope of the line from Westborough to Agritown:

$$m = \frac{10 - 0}{30 - 0} = \frac{1}{3}$$

The equation of the road from Westborough to Agritown would be

$$W(x) = \frac{1}{3}x$$

From this, we can determine the perpendicular road to Eastborough will have slope $m = -3$. Because the town of Eastborough is at the point (20, 0), we can find the equation:

$$E(x) = -3x + b$$
$$0 = -3(20) + b \qquad \text{Substitute in (20, 0).}$$
$$b = 60$$
$$E(x) = -3x + 60$$

We can now find the coordinates of the junction of the roads by finding the intersection of these lines. Setting them equal,

$$\frac{1}{3}x = -3x + 60$$

$$\frac{10}{3}x = 60$$

$$10x = 180$$

$$x = 18 \qquad\qquad \text{Substitute this back into } W(x).$$

$$y = W(18)$$

$$= \frac{1}{3}(18)$$

$$= 6$$

The roads intersect at the point (18, 6). Using the distance formula, we can now find the distance from Westborough to the junction.

$$\text{distance} = \sqrt{(x_2 - x_1)^2 + (y_2 - y_1)^2}$$

$$= \sqrt{(18 - 0)^2 + (6 - 0)^2}$$

$$\approx 18.974 \text{ miles}$$

Analysis   *One nice use of linear models is to take advantage of the fact that the graphs of these functions are lines. This means real-world applications discussing maps need linear functions to model the distances between reference points.*

Try It #3

There is a straight road leading from the town of Timpson to Ashburn 60 miles east and 12 miles north. Partway down the road, it junctions with a second road, perpendicular to the first, leading to the town of Garrison. If the town of Garrison is located 22 miles directly east of the town of Timpson, how far is the road junction from Timpson?

Building Systems of Linear Models

Real-world situations including two or more linear functions may be modeled with a system of linear equations. Remember, when solving a system of linear equations, we are looking for points the two lines have in common. Typically, there are three types of answers possible, as shown in **Figure 5**.

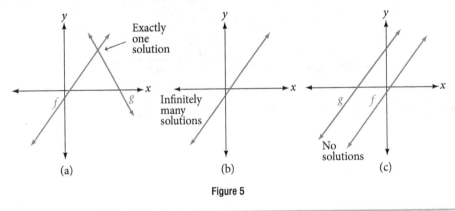

Figure 5

How To...

Given a situation that represents a system of linear equations, write the system of equations and identify the solution.

1. Identify the input and output of each linear model.
2. Identify the slope and *y*-intercept of each linear model.
3. Find the solution by setting the two linear functions equal to one another and solving for *x*, or find the point of intersection on a graph.

Example 4   **Building a System of Linear Models to Choose a Truck Rental Company**

Jamal is choosing between two truck-rental companies. The first, Keep on Trucking, Inc., charges an up-front fee of $20, then 59 cents a mile. The second, Move It Your Way, charges an up-front fee of $16, then 63 cents a mile[9]. When will Keep on Trucking, Inc. be the better choice for Jamal?

Solution   The two important quantities in this problem are the cost and the number of miles driven. Because we have two companies to consider, we will define two functions.

Input	d, distance driven in miles
Outputs	$K(d)$: cost, in dollars, for renting from Keep on Trucking $M(d)$ cost, in dollars, for renting from Move It Your Way
Initial Value	Up-front fee: $K(0) = 20$ and $M(0) = 16$
Rate of Change	$K(d) = \$0.59$/mile and $P(d) = \$0.63$/mile

Table 1

A linear function is of the form $f(x) = mx + b$. Using the rates of change and initial charges, we can write the equations

$$K(d) = 0.59d + 20$$

$$M(d) = 0.63d + 16$$

Using these equations, we can determine when Keep on Trucking, Inc., will be the better choice. Because all we have to make that decision from is the costs, we are looking for when Move It Your Way, will cost less, or when $K(d) < M(d)$. The solution pathway will lead us to find the equations for the two functions, find the intersection, and then see where the $K(d)$ function is smaller.

These graphs are sketched in **Figure 6**, with $K(d)$ in red.

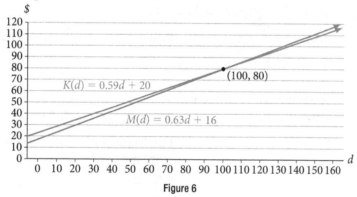

Figure 6

To find the intersection, we set the equations equal and solve:

$$K(d) = M(d)$$

$$0.59d + 20 = 0.63d + 16$$

$$4 = 0.04d$$

$$100 = d$$

$$d = 100$$

This tells us that the cost from the two companies will be the same if 100 miles are driven. Either by looking at the graph, or noting that $K(d)$ is growing at a slower rate, we can conclude that Keep on Trucking, Inc. will be the cheaper price when more than 100 miles are driven, that is $d > 100$.

Access this online resources for additional instruction and practice with linear function models.

• Interpreting a Linear Function (http://openstaxcollege.org/l/interpretlinear)

9 Rates retrieved Aug 2, 2010 from http://www.budgettruck.com and http://www.uhaul.com/

2.3   SECTION EXERCISES

VERBAL

1. Explain how to find the input variable in a word problem that uses a linear function.

2. Explain how to find the output variable in a word problem that uses a linear function.

3. Explain how to interpret the initial value in a word problem that uses a linear function.

4. Explain how to determine the slope in a word problem that uses a linear function.

ALGEBRAIC

5. Find the area of a parallelogram bounded by the y-axis, the line $x = 3$, the line $f(x) = 1 + 2x$, and the line parallel to $f(x)$ passing through $(2, 7)$.

6. Find the area of a triangle bounded by the x-axis, the line $f(x) = 12 - \frac{1}{3}x$, and the line perpendicular to $f(x)$ that passes through the origin.

7. Find the area of a triangle bounded by the y-axis, the line $f(x) = 9 - \frac{6}{7}x$, and the line perpendicular to $f(x)$ that passes through the origin.

8. Find the area of a parallelogram bounded by the x-axis, the line $g(x) = 2$, the line $f(x) = 3x$, and the line parallel to $f(x)$ passing through $(6, 1)$.

For the following exercises, consider this scenario: A town's population has been decreasing at a constant rate. In 2010 the population was 5,900. By 2012 the population had dropped 4,700. Assume this trend continues.

9. Predict the population in 2016.

10. Identify the year in which the population will reach 0.

For the following exercises, consider this scenario: A town's population has been increased at a constant rate. In 2010 the population was 46,020. By 2012 the population had increased to 52,070. Assume this trend continues.

11. Predict the population in 2016.

12. Identify the year in which the population will reach 75,000.

For the following exercises, consider this scenario: A town has an initial population of 75,000. It grows at a constant rate of 2,500 per year for 5 years.

13. Find the linear function that models the town's population P as a function of the year, t, where t is the number of years since the model began.

14. Find a reasonable domain and range for the function P.

15. If the function P is graphed, find and interpret the x-and y-intercepts.

16. If the function P is graphed, find and interpret the slope of the function.

17. When will the output reached 100,000?

18. What is the output in the year 12 years from the onset of the model?

For the following exercises, consider this scenario: The weight of a newborn is 7.5 pounds. The baby gained one-half pound a month for its first year.

19. Find the linear function that models the baby's weight, W, as a function of the age of the baby, in months, t.

20. Find a reasonable domain and range for the function W.

21. If the function W is graphed, find and interpret the x- and y-intercepts.

22. If the function W is graphed, find and interpret the slope of the function.

23. When did the baby weight 10.4 pounds?

24. What is the output when the input is 6.2? Interpret your answer.

For the following exercises, consider this scenario: The number of people afflicted with the common cold in the winter months steadily decreased by 205 each year from 2005 until 2010. In 2005, 12,025 people were afflicted.

25. Find the linear function that models the number of people inflicted with the common cold, C, as a function of the year, t.

26. Find a reasonable domain and range for the function C.

27. If the function C is graphed, find and interpret the x-and y-intercepts.

28. If the function C is graphed, find and interpret the slope of the function.

29. When will the output reach 0?

30. In what year will the number of people be 9,700?

GRAPHICAL

For the following exercises, use the graph in **Figure 7**, which shows the profit, y, in thousands of dollars, of a company in a given year, t, where t represents the number of years since 1980.

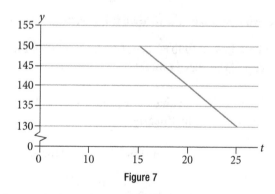

Figure 7

31. Find the linear function y, where y depends on t, the number of years since 1980.

32. Find and interpret the y-intercept.

33. Find and interpret the x-intercept.

34. Find and interpret the slope.

For the following exercises, use the graph in **Figure 8**, which shows the profit, *y*, in thousands of dollars, of a company in a given year, *t*, where *t* represents the number of years since 1980.

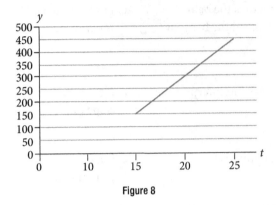

Figure 8

35. Find the linear function *y*, where *y* depends on *t*, the number of years since 1980.

36. Find and interpret the *y*-intercept.

37. Find and interpret the *x*-intercept.

38. Find and interpret the slope.

NUMERIC

For the following exercises, use the median home values in Mississippi and Hawaii (adjusted for inflation) shown in **Table 2**. Assume that the house values are changing linearly.

Year	Mississippi	Hawaii
1950	$25,200	$74,400
2000	$71,400	$272,700

Table 2

39. In which state have home values increased at a higher rate?

40. If these trends were to continue, what would be the median home value in Mississippi in 2010?

41. If we assume the linear trend existed before 1950 and continues after 2000, the two states' median house values will be (or were) equal in what year? (The answer might be absurd.)

For the following exercises, use the median home values in Indiana and Alabama (adjusted for inflation) shown in **Table 3**. Assume that the house values are changing linearly.

Year	Indiana	Alabama
1950	$37,700	$27,100
2000	$94,300	$85,100

Table 3

42. In which state have home values increased at a higher rate?

43. If these trends were to continue, what would be the median home value in Indiana in 2010?

44. If we assume the linear trend existed before 1950 and continues after 2000, the two states' median house values will be (or were) equal in what year? (The answer might be absurd.)

REAL-WORLD APPLICATIONS

45. In 2004, a school population was 1,001. By 2008 the population had grown to 1,697. Assume the population is changing linearly.

    a. How much did the population grow between the year 2004 and 2008?

    b. How long did it take the population to grow from 1,001 students to 1,697 students?

    c. What is the average population growth per year?

    d. What was the population in the year 2000?

    e. Find an equation for the population, P, of the school t years after 2000.

    f. Using your equation, predict the population of the school in 2011.

46. In 2003, a town's population was 1,431. By 2007 the population had grown to 2,134. Assume the population is changing linearly.

    a. How much did the population grow between the year 2003 and 2007?

    b. How long did it take the population to grow from 1,431 people to 2,134 people?

    c. What is the average population growth per year?

    d. What was the population in the year 2000?

    e. Find an equation for the population, P of the town t years after 2000.

    f. Using your equation, predict the population of the town in 2014.

47. A phone company has a monthly cellular plan where a customer pays a flat monthly fee and then a certain amount of money per minute used on the phone. If a customer uses 410 minutes, the monthly cost will be $71.50. If the customer uses 720 minutes, the monthly cost will be $118.

    a. Find a linear equation for the monthly cost of the cell plan as a function of x, the number of monthly minutes used.

    b. Interpret the slope and y-intercept of the equation.

    c. Use your equation to find the total monthly cost if 687 minutes are used.

48. A phone company has a monthly cellular data plan where a customer pays a flat monthly fee of $10 and then a certain amount of money per megabyte (MB) of data used on the phone. If a customer uses 20 MB, the monthly cost will be $11.20. If the customer uses 130 MB, the monthly cost will be $17.80.

    a. Find a linear equation for the monthly cost of the data plan as a function of x, the number of MB used.

    b. Interpret the slope and y-intercept of the equation.

    c. Use your equation to find the total monthly cost if 250 MB are used.

49. In 1991, the moose population in a park was measured to be 4,360. By 1999, the population was measured again to be 5,880. Assume the population continues to change linearly.

    a. Find a formula for the moose population, P since 1990.

    b. What does your model predict the moose population to be in 2003?

50. In 2003, the owl population in a park was measured to be 340. By 2007, the population was measured again to be 285. The population changes linearly. Let the input be years since 1990.

    a. Find a formula for the owl population, P. Let the input be years since 2003.

    b. What does your model predict the owl population to be in 2012?

51. The Federal Helium Reserve held about 16 billion cubic feet of helium in 2010 and is being depleted by about 2.1 billion cubic feet each year.

    a. Give a linear equation for the remaining federal helium reserves, R, in terms of t, the number of years since 2010.

    b. In 2015, what will the helium reserves be?

    c. If the rate of depletion doesn't change, in what year will the Federal Helium Reserve be depleted?

52. Suppose the world's oil reserves in 2014 are 1,820 billion barrels. If, on average, the total reserves are decreasing by 25 billion barrels of oil each year:

    a. Give a linear equation for the remaining oil reserves, R, in terms of t, the number of years since now.

    b. Seven years from now, what will the oil reserves be?

    c. If the rate at which the reserves are decreasing is constant, when will the world's oil reserves be depleted?

53. You are choosing between two different prepaid cell phone plans. The first plan charges a rate of 26 cents per minute. The second plan charges a monthly fee of $19.95 *plus* 11 cents per minute. How many minutes would you have to use in a month in order for the second plan to be preferable?

54. You are choosing between two different window washing companies. The first charges $5 per window. The second charges a base fee of $40 plus $3 per window. How many windows would you need to have for the second company to be preferable?

55. When hired at a new job selling jewelry, you are given two pay options:
- Option A: Base salary of $17,000 a year with a commission of 12% of your sales
- Option B: Base salary of $20,000 a year with a commission of 5% of your sales

How much jewelry would you need to sell for option A to produce a larger income?

56. When hired at a new job selling electronics, you are given two pay options:
- Option A: Base salary of $14,000 a year with a commission of 10% of your sales
- Option B: Base salary of $19,000 a year with a commission of 4% of your sales

How much electronics would you need to sell for option A to produce a larger income?

57. When hired at a new job selling electronics, you are given two pay options:
- Option A: Base salary of $20,000 a year with a commission of 12% of your sales
- Option B: Base salary of $26,000 a year with a commission of 3% of your sales

How much electronics would you need to sell for option A to produce a larger income?

58. When hired at a new job selling electronics, you are given two pay options:
- Option A: Base salary of $10,000 a year with a commission of 9% of your sales
- Option B: Base salary of $20,000 a year with a commission of 4% of your sales

How much electronics would you need to sell for option A to produce a larger income?

LEARNING OBJECTIVES

In this section, you will:

- Draw and interpret scatter plots.
- Find the line of best fit.
- Distinguish between linear and nonlinear relations.
- Use a linear model to make predictions.

2.4 FITTING LINEAR MODELS TO DATA

A professor is attempting to identify trends among final exam scores. His class has a mixture of students, so he wonders if there is any relationship between age and final exam scores. One way for him to analyze the scores is by creating a diagram that relates the age of each student to the exam score received. In this section, we will examine one such diagram known as a scatter plot.

Drawing and Interpreting Scatter Plots

A scatter plot is a graph of plotted points that may show a relationship between two sets of data. If the relationship is from a linear model, or a model that is nearly linear, the professor can draw conclusions using his knowledge of linear functions. **Figure 1** shows a sample scatter plot.

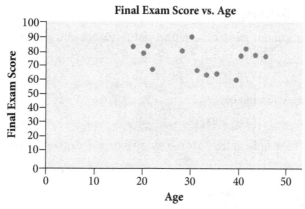

Figure 1 A scatter plot of age and final exam score variables.

Notice this scatter plot does *not* indicate a linear relationship. The points do not appear to follow a trend. In other words, there does not appear to be a relationship between the age of the student and the score on the final exam.

Example 1   **Using a Scatter Plot to Investigate Cricket Chirps**

Table 1 shows the number of cricket chirps in 15 seconds, for several different air temperatures, in degrees Fahrenheit[10]. Plot this data, and determine whether the data appears to be linearly related.

Chirps	44	35	20.4	33	31	35	18.5	37	26
Temperature	80.5	70.5	57	66	68	72	52	73.5	53

Table 1

Solution   Plotting this data, as depicted in **Figure 2** suggests that there may be a trend. We can see from the trend in the data that the number of chirps increases as the temperature increases. The trend appears to be roughly linear, though certainly not perfectly so.

10 Selected data from http://classic.globe.gov/fsl/scientistsblog/2007/10/. Retrieved Aug 3, 2010.

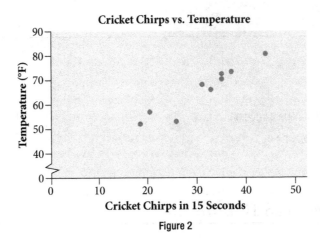

Figure 2

Finding the Line of Best Fit

Once we recognize a need for a linear function to model that data, the natural follow-up question is "what is that linear function?" One way to approximate our linear function is to sketch the line that seems to best fit the data. Then we can extend the line until we can verify the y-intercept. We can approximate the slope of the line by extending it until we can estimate the $\dfrac{\text{rise}}{\text{run}}$.

Example 2   Finding a Line of Best Fit

Find a linear function that fits the data in **Table 1** by "eyeballing" a line that seems to fit.

Solution   On a graph, we could try sketching a line.

Using the starting and ending points of our hand drawn line, points (0, 30) and (50, 90), this graph has a slope of

$$m = \frac{60}{50} = 1.2$$

and a y-intercept at 30. This gives an equation of

$$T(c) = 1.2c + 30$$

where c is the number of chirps in 15 seconds, and $T(c)$ is the temperature in degrees Fahrenheit. The resulting equation is represented in **Figure 3**.

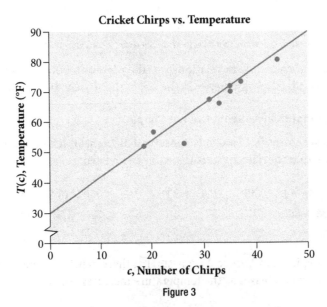

Figure 3

Analysis   *This linear equation can then be used to approximate answers to various questions we might ask about the trend.*

Recognizing Interpolation or Extrapolation

While the data for most examples does not fall perfectly on the line, the equation is our best guess as to how the relationship will behave outside of the values for which we have data. We use a process known as **interpolation** when we predict a value inside the domain and range of the data. The process of **extrapolation** is used when we predict a value outside the domain and range of the data.

Figure 4 compares the two processes for the cricket-chirp data addressed in **Example 2**. We can see that interpolation would occur if we used our model to predict temperature when the values for chirps are between 18.5 and 44. Extrapolation would occur if we used our model to predict temperature when the values for chirps are less than 18.5 or greater than 44.

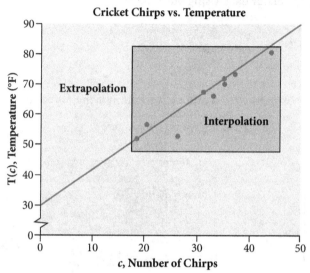

Figure 4 Interpolation occurs within the domain and range of the provided data whereas extrapolation occurs outside.

There is a difference between making predictions inside the domain and range of values for which we have data and outside that domain and range. Predicting a value outside of the domain and range has its limitations. When our model no longer applies after a certain point, it is sometimes called **model breakdown**. For example, predicting a cost function for a period of two years may involve examining the data where the input is the time in years and the output is the cost. But if we try to extrapolate a cost when $x = 50$, that is in 50 years, the model would not apply because we could not account for factors fifty years in the future.

---

interpolation and extrapolation

Different methods of making predictions are used to analyze data.

- The method of **interpolation** involves predicting a value inside the domain and/or range of the data.

- The method of **extrapolation** involves predicting a value outside the domain and/or range of the data.

- **Model breakdown** occurs at the point when the model no longer applies.

Example 3   **Understanding Interpolation and Extrapolation**

Use the cricket data from **Table 1** to answer the following questions:

   a. Would predicting the temperature when crickets are chirping 30 times in 15 seconds be interpolation or extrapolation? Make the prediction, and discuss whether it is reasonable.

   b. Would predicting the number of chirps crickets will make at 40 degrees be interpolation or extrapolation? Make the prediction, and discuss whether it is reasonable.

Solution

a. The number of chirps in the data provided varied from 18.5 to 44. A prediction at 30 chirps per 15 seconds is inside the domain of our data, so would be interpolation. Using our model:

$$T(30) = 30 + 1.2(30)$$
$$= 66 \text{ degrees}$$

Based on the data we have, this value seems reasonable.

b. The temperature values varied from 52 to 80.5. Predicting the number of chirps at 40 degrees is extrapolation because 40 is outside the range of our data. Using our model:

$$40 = 30 + 1.2c$$
$$10 = 1.2c$$
$$c \approx 8.33$$

We can compare the regions of interpolation and extrapolation using **Figure 5**.

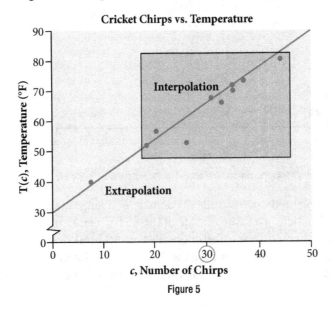

Figure 5

Analysis Our model predicts the crickets would chirp 8.33 times in 15 seconds. While this might be possible, we have no reason to believe our model is valid outside the domain and range. In fact, generally crickets stop chirping altogether below around 50 degrees.

Try It #1

According to the data from **Table 1**, what temperature can we predict it is if we counted 20 chirps in 15 seconds?

Finding the Line of Best Fit Using a Graphing Utility

While eyeballing a line works reasonably well, there are statistical techniques for fitting a line to data that minimize the differences between the line and data values[11]. One such technique is called **least squares regression** and can be computed by many graphing calculators, spreadsheet software, statistical software, and many web-based calculators[12]. Least squares regression is one means to determine the line that best fits the data, and here we will refer to this method as linear regression.

---

11 Technically, the method minimizes the sum of the squared differences in the vertical direction between the line and the data values.

12 For example, http://www.shodor.org/unchem/math/lls/leastsq.html

Given data of input and corresponding outputs from a linear function, find the best fit line using linear regression.

1. Enter the input in **List 1 (L1)**.
2. Enter the output in **List 2 (L2)**.
3. On a graphing utility, select **Linear Regression (LinReg)**.

Example 4 **Finding a Least Squares Regression Line**

Find the least squares regression line using the cricket-chirp data in **Table 1**.

Solution

1. Enter the input (chirps) in **List 1 (L1)**.
2. Enter the output (temperature) in **List 2 (L2)**. See **Table 2**.

L1	44	35	20.4	33	31	35	18.5	37	26
L2	80.5	70.5	57	66	68	72	52	73.5	53

Table 2

3. On a graphing utility, select **Linear Regression (LinReg)**. Using the cricket chirp data from earlier, with technology we obtain the equation:

$$T(c) = 30.281 + 1.143c$$

Analysis *Notice that this line is quite similar to the equation we "eyeballed" but should fit the data better. Notice also that using this equation would change our prediction for the temperature when hearing 30 chirps in 15 seconds from 66 degrees to:*

$$T(30) = 30.281 + 1.143(30)$$

$$= 64.571$$

$$\approx 64.6 \text{ degrees}$$

The graph of the scatter plot with the least squares regression line is shown in **Figure 6***.*

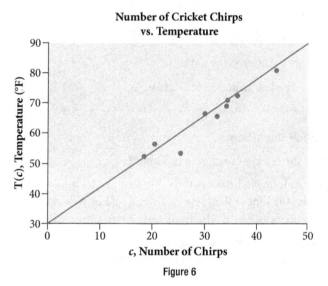

Number of Cricket Chirps vs. Temperature

Figure 6

Will there ever be a case where two different lines will serve as the best fit for the data?

No. There is only one best fit line.

Distinguishing Between Linear and Non-Linear Models

As we saw above with the cricket-chirp model, some data exhibit strong linear trends, but other data, like the final exam scores plotted by age, are clearly nonlinear. Most calculators and computer software can also provide us with the **correlation coefficient**, which is a measure of how closely the line fits the data. Many graphing calculators require the user to turn a "diagnostic on" selection to find the correlation coefficient, which mathematicians label as r. The correlation coefficient provides an easy way to get an idea of how close to a line the data falls.

We should compute the correlation coefficient only for data that follows a linear pattern or to determine the degree to which a data set is linear. If the data exhibits a nonlinear pattern, the correlation coefficient for a linear regression is meaningless. To get a sense for the relationship between the value of r and the graph of the data, **Figure 7** shows some large data sets with their correlation coefficients. Remember, for all plots, the horizontal axis shows the input and the vertical axis shows the output.

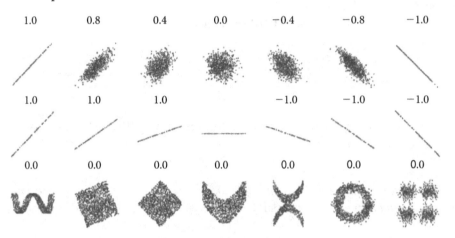

Figure 7 Plotted data and related correlation coefficients. (credit: "DenisBoigelot," Wikimedia Commons)

> ***correlation coefficient***
>
> The **correlation coefficient** is a value, r, between -1 and 1.
>
> - $r > 0$ suggests a positive (increasing) relationship
> - $r < 0$ suggests a negative (decreasing) relationship
> - The closer the value is to 0, the more scattered the data.
> - The closer the value is to 1 or -1, the less scattered the data is.

Example 5   **Finding a Correlation Coefficient**

Calculate the correlation coefficient for cricket-chirp data in **Table 1**.

Solution   Because the data appear to follow a linear pattern, we can use technology to calculate r. Enter the inputs and corresponding outputs and select the Linear Regression. The calculator will also provide you with the correlation coefficient, $r = 0.9509$. This value is very close to 1, which suggests a strong increasing linear relationship.

Note: For some calculators, the Diagnostics must be turned "on" in order to get the correlation coefficient when linear regression is performed: [**2nd**]>[**0**]>[**alpha**][$x-1$], then scroll to **DIAGNOSTICSON**.

Predicting with a Regression Line

Once we determine that a set of data is linear using the correlation coefficient, we can use the regression line to make predictions. As we learned above, a regression line is a line that is closest to the data in the scatter plot, which means that only one such line is a best fit for the data.

Example 6   **Using a Regression Line to Make Predictions**

Gasoline consumption in the United States has been steadily increasing. Consumption data from 1994 to 2004 is shown in **Table 3**[13]. Determine whether the trend is linear, and if so, find a model for the data. Use the model to predict the consumption in 2008.

Year	'94	'95	'96	'97	'98	'99	'00	'01	'02	'03	'04
Consumption (billions of gallons)	113	116	118	119	123	125	126	128	131	133	136

Table 3

The scatter plot of the data, including the least squares regression line, is shown in **Figure 8**.

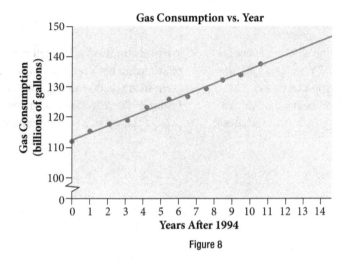

Figure 8

Solution   We can introduce new input variable, t, representing years since 1994.

The least squares regression equation is:

$$C(t) = 113.318 + 2.209t$$

Using technology, the correlation coefficient was calculated to be 0.9965, suggesting a very strong increasing linear trend.

Using this to predict consumption in 2008 ($t = 14$),

$$C(14) = 113.318 + 2.209(14)$$

$$= 144.244$$

The model predicts 144.244 billion gallons of gasoline consumption in 2008.

Try It #2

Use the model we created using technology in **Example 6** to predict the gas consumption in 2011. Is this an interpolation or an extrapolation?

Access these online resources for additional instruction and practice with fitting linear models to data.

- Introduction to Regression Analysis (http://openstaxcollege.org/l/introregress)
- Linear Regression (http://openstaxcollege.org/l/linearregress)

13 http://www.bts.gov/publications/national_transportation_statistics/2005/html/table_04_10.html

2.4   SECTION EXERCISES

VERBAL

1. Describe what it means if there is a model breakdown when using a linear model.

2. What is interpolation when using a linear model?

3. What is extrapolation when using a linear model?

4. Explain the difference between a positive and a negative correlation coefficient.

5. Explain how to interpret the absolute value of a correlation coefficient.

ALGEBRAIC

6. A regression was run to determine whether there is a relationship between hours of TV watched per day (x) and number of sit-ups a person can do (y). The results of the regression are given below. Use this to predict the number of situps a person who watches 11 hours of TV can do.

$$y = ax + b$$
$$a = -1.341$$
$$b = 32.234$$
$$r = -0.896$$

7. A regression was run to determine whether there is a relationship between the diameter of a tree (x, in inches) and the tree's age (y, in years). The results of the regression are given below. Use this to predict the age of a tree with diameter 10 inches.

$$y = ax + b$$
$$a = 6.301$$
$$b = -1.044$$
$$r = -0.970$$

For the following exercises, draw a scatter plot for the data provided. Does the data appear to be linearly related?

8.

0	2	4	6	8	10
−22	−19	−15	−11	−6	−2

9.

1	2	3	4	5	6
46	50	59	75	100	136

10.

100	250	300	450	600	750
12	12.6	13.1	14	14.5	15.2

11.

1	3	5	7	9	11
1	9	28	65	125	216

12. For the following data, draw a scatter plot. If we wanted to know when the population would reach 15,000, would the answer involve interpolation or extrapolation? Eyeball the line, and estimate the answer.

Year	1990	1995	2000	2005	2010
Population	11,500	12,100	12,700	13,000	13,750

13. For the following data, draw a scatter plot. If we wanted to know when the temperature would reach 28°F, would the answer involve interpolation or extrapolation? Eyeball the line and estimate the answer.

Temperature, °F	16	18	20	25	30
Time, seconds	46	50	54	55	62

GRAPHICAL

For the following exercises, match each scatterplot with one of the four specified correlations in **Figure 9** and **Figure 10**.

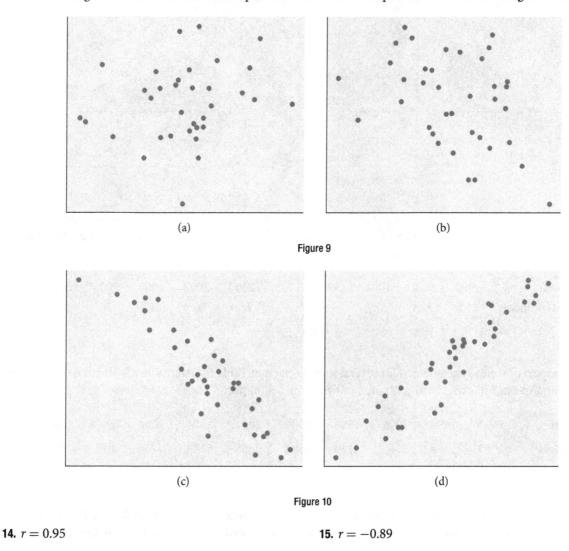

(a)   (b)

Figure 9

(c)   (d)

Figure 10

14. $r = 0.95$ **15.** $r = -0.89$

16. $r = 0.26$ **17.** $r = -0.39$

For the following exercises, draw a best-fit line for the plotted data.

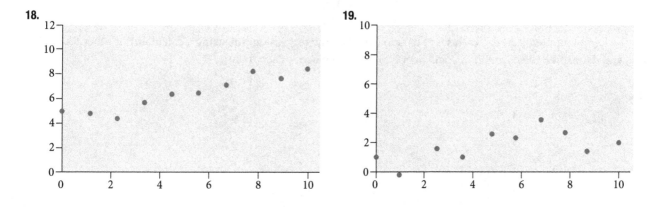

18.

19.

20.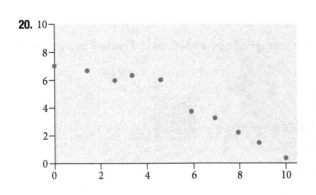

21.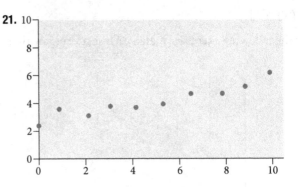

NUMERIC

22. The U.S. Census tracks the percentage of persons 25 years or older who are college graduates. That data for several years is given in **Table 4**[14]. Determine whether the trend appears linear. If so, and assuming the trend continues, in what year will the percentage exceed 35%?

Year	1990	1992	1994	1996	1998	2000	2002	2004	2006	2008
Percent Graduates	21.3	21.4	22.2	23.6	24.4	25.6	26.7	27.7	28	29.4

Table 4

23. The U.S. import of wine (in hectoliters) for several years is given in **Table 5**. Determine whether the trend appears linear. If so, and assuming the trend continues, in what year will imports exceed 12,000 hectoliters?

Year	1992	1994	1996	1998	2000	2002	2004	2006	2008	2009
Imports	2665	2688	3565	4129	4584	5655	6549	7950	8487	9462

Table 5

24. **Table 6** shows the year and the number of people unemployed in a particular city for several years. Determine whether the trend appears linear. If so, and assuming the trend continues, in what year will the number of unemployed reach 5 people?

Year	1990	1992	1994	1996	1998	2000	2002	2004	2006	2008
Number Unemployed	750	670	650	605	550	510	460	420	380	320

Table 6

TECHNOLOGY

For the following exercises, use each set of data to calculate the regression line using a calculator or other technology tool, and determine the correlation coefficient to 3 decimal places of accuracy.

25.

x	8	15	26	31	56
y	23	41	53	72	103

26.

x	5	7	10	12	15
y	4	12	17	22	24

14 http://www.census.gov/hhes/socdemo/education/data/cps/historical/index.html. Accessed 5/1/2014.

27.

x	3	4	5	6	7	8	9	10
y	21.9	22.22	22.74	22.26	20.78	17.6	16.52	18.54

x	11	12	13	14	15	16	17	18
y	15.76	13.68	14.1	14.02	11.94	12.76	11.28	9.1

28.

x	4	5	6	7	8	9	10	11	12	13
y	44.8	43.1	38.8	39	38	32.7	30.1	29.3	27	25.8

29.

x	21	25	30	31	40	50
y	17	11	2	−1	−18	−40

30.

x	100	80	60	55	40	20
y	2000	1798	1589	1580	1390	1202

31.

x	900	988	1000	1010	1200	1205
y	70	80	82	84	105	108

EXTENSIONS

32. Graph $f(x) = 0.5x + 10$. Pick a set of 5 ordered pairs using inputs $x = -2, 1, 5, 6, 9$ and use linear regression to verify that the function is a good fit for the data.

33. Graph $f(x) = -2x - 10$. Pick a set of 5 ordered pairs using inputs $x = -2, 1, 5, 6, 9$ and use linear regression to verify the function.

For the following exercises, consider this scenario: The profit of a company decreased steadily over a ten-year span. The following ordered pairs shows dollars and the number of units sold in hundreds and the profit in thousands of over the ten-year span, (number of units sold, profit) for specific recorded years:

(46, 600), (48, 550), (50, 505), (52, 540), (54, 495).

34. Use linear regression to determine a function P where the profit in thousands of dollars depends on the number of units sold in hundreds.

35. Find to the nearest tenth and interpret the x-intercept.

36. Find to the nearest tenth and interpret the y-intercept.

REAL-WORLD APPLICATIONS

For the following exercises, consider this scenario: The population of a city increased steadily over a ten-year span. The following ordered pairs shows the population and the year over the ten-year span, (population, year) for specific recorded years:

(2500, 2000), (2650, 2001), (3000, 2003), (3500, 2006), (4200, 2010)

37. Use linear regression to determine a function y, where the year depends on the population. Round to three decimal places of accuracy.

38. Predict when the population will hit 8,000.

For the following exercises, consider this scenario: The profit of a company increased steadily over a ten-year span. The following ordered pairs show the number of units sold in hundreds and the profit in thousands of over the ten-year span, (number of units sold, profit) for specific recorded years:

(46, 250), (48, 305), (50, 350), (52, 390), (54, 410).

39. Use linear regression to determine a function y, where the profit in thousands of dollars depends on the number of units sold in hundreds.

40. Predict when the profit will exceed one million dollars.

For the following exercises, consider this scenario: The profit of a company decreased steadily over a ten-year span. The following ordered pairs show dollars and the number of units sold in hundreds and the profit in thousands of over the ten-year span (number of units sold, profit) for specific recorded years:

(46, 250), (48, 225), (50, 205), (52, 180), (54, 165).

41. Use linear regression to determine a function y, where the profit in thousands of dollars depends on the number of units sold in hundreds.

42. Predict when the profit will dip below the $25,000 threshold.

CHAPTER 2 REVIEW

Key Terms

correlation coefficient a value, r, between -1 and 1 that indicates the degree of linear correlation of variables, or how closely a regression line fits a data set.

decreasing linear function a function with a negative slope: If $f(x) = mx + b$, then $m < 0$.

extrapolation predicting a value outside the domain and range of the data

horizontal line a line defined by $f(x) = b$, where b is a real number. The slope of a horizontal line is 0.

increasing linear function a function with a positive slope: If $f(x) = mx + b$, then $m > 0$.

interpolation predicting a value inside the domain and range of the data

least squares regression a statistical technique for fitting a line to data in a way that minimizes the differences between the line and data values

linear function a function with a constant rate of change that is a polynomial of degree 1, and whose graph is a straight line

model breakdown when a model no longer applies after a certain point

parallel lines two or more lines with the same slope

perpendicular lines two lines that intersect at right angles and have slopes that are negative reciprocals of each other

point-slope form the equation for a line that represents a linear function of the form $y - y_1 = m(x - x_1)$

slope the ratio of the change in output values to the change in input values; a measure of the steepness of a line

slope-intercept form the equation for a line that represents a linear function in the form $f(x) = mx + b$

vertical line a line defined by $x = a$, where a is a real number. The slope of a vertical line is undefined.

x-intercept the point on the graph of a linear function when the output value is 0; the point at which the graph crosses the horizontal axis

y-intercept the value of a function when the input value is zero; also known as initial value

Key Equations

slope-intercept form of a line $f(x) = mx + b$

slope $m = \dfrac{\text{change in output (rise)}}{\text{change in input (run)}} = \dfrac{\Delta y}{\Delta x} = \dfrac{y_2 - y_1}{x_2 - x_1}$

point-slope form of a line $y - y_1 = m(x - x_1)$

Key Concepts

2.1 Linear Functions

- The ordered pairs given by a linear function represent points on a line.
- Linear functions can be represented in words, function notation, tabular form, and graphical form. See **Example 1**.
- The rate of change of a linear function is also known as the slope.
- An equation in the slope-intercept form of a line includes the slope and the initial value of the function.
- The initial value, or y-intercept, is the output value when the input of a linear function is zero. It is the y-value of the point at which the line crosses the y-axis.
- An increasing linear function results in a graph that slants upward from left to right and has a positive slope.
- A decreasing linear function results in a graph that slants downward from left to right and has a negative slope.
- A constant linear function results in a graph that is a horizontal line.

- Analyzing the slope within the context of a problem indicates whether a linear function is increasing, decreasing, or constant. See **Example 2**.

- The slope of a linear function can be calculated by dividing the difference between y-values by the difference in corresponding x-values of any two points on the line. See **Example 3** and **Example 4**.

- The slope and initial value can be determined given a graph or any two points on the line.

- One type of function notation is the slope-intercept form of an equation.

- The point-slope form is useful for finding a linear equation when given the slope of a line and one point. See **Example 5**.

- The point-slope form is also convenient for finding a linear equation when given two points through which a line passes. See **Example 6**.

- The equation for a linear function can be written if the slope m and initial value b are known. See **Example 7**, **Example 8**, and **Example 9**.

- A linear function can be used to solve real-world problems. See **Example 10** and **Example 11**.

- A linear function can be written from tabular form. See **Example 12**.

2.2 Graphs of Linear Functions

- Linear functions may be graphed by plotting points or by using the y-intercept and slope. See **Example 1** and **Example 2**.

- Graphs of linear functions may be transformed by using shifts up, down, left, or right, as well as through stretches, compressions, and reflections. See **Example 3**.

- The y-intercept and slope of a line may be used to write the equation of a line.

- The x-intercept is the point at which the graph of a linear function crosses the x-axis. See **Example 4** and **Example 5**.

- Horizontal lines are written in the form, $f(x) = b$. See **Example 6**.

- Vertical lines are written in the form, $x = b$. See **Example 7**.

- Parallel lines have the same slope.

- Perpendicular lines have negative reciprocal slopes, assuming neither is vertical. See **Example 8**.

- A line parallel to another line, passing through a given point, may be found by substituting the slope value of the line and the x- and y-values of the given point into the equation, $f(x) = mx + b$, and using the b that results. Similarly, the point-slope form of an equation can also be used. See **Example 9**.

- A line perpendicular to another line, passing through a given point, may be found in the same manner, with the exception of using the negative reciprocal slope. See **Example 10** and **Example 11**.

- A system of linear equations may be solved setting the two equations equal to one another and solving for x. The y-value may be found by evaluating either one of the original equations using this x-value.

- A system of linear equations may also be solved by finding the point of intersection on a graph. See **Example 12** and **Example 13**.

2.3 Modeling with Linear Functions

- We can use the same problem strategies that we would use for any type of function.

- When modeling and solving a problem, identify the variables and look for key values, including the slope and y-intercept. See **Example 1**.

- Draw a diagram, where appropriate. See **Example 2** and **Example 3**.

- Check for reasonableness of the answer.

- Linear models may be built by identifying or calculating the slope and using the y-intercept.

- The x-intercept may be found by setting $y = 0$, which is setting the expression $mx + b$ equal to 0.

- The point of intersection of a system of linear equations is the point where the x- and y-values are the same. See **Example 4**.

- A graph of the system may be used to identify the points where one line falls below (or above) the other line.

2.4 Fitting Linear Models to Data

- Scatter plots show the relationship between two sets of data. See **Example 1**.

- Scatter plots may represent linear or non-linear models.

- The line of best fit may be estimated or calculated, using a calculator or statistical software. See **Example 2**.

- Interpolation can be used to predict values inside the domain and range of the data, whereas extrapolation can be used to predict values outside the domain and range of the data. See **Example 3**.

- The correlation coefficient, r, indicates the degree of linear relationship between data. See **Example 5**.

- A regression line best fits the data. See **Example 6**.

- The least squares regression line is found by minimizing the squares of the distances of points from a line passing through the data and may be used to make predictions regarding either of the variables. See **Example 4**.

CHAPTER 2 REVIEW EXERCISES

LINEAR FUNCTIONS

1. Determine whether the algebraic equation is linear.
$2x + 3y = 7$

2. Determine whether the algebraic equation is linear.
$6x^2 - y = 5$

3. Determine whether the function is increasing or decreasing. $f(x) = 7x - 2$

4. Determine whether the function is increasing or decreasing. $g(x) = -x + 2$

5. Given each set of information, find a linear equation that satisfies the given conditions, if possible. Passes through $(7, 5)$ and $(3, 17)$

6. Given each set of information, find a linear equation that satisfies the given conditions, if possible. x-intercept at $(6, 0)$ and y-intercept at $(0, 10)$

7. Find the slope of the line shown in the graph.

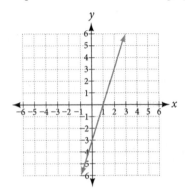

8. Find the slope of the line shown in the graph.

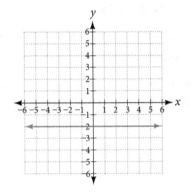

9. Write an equation in slope-intercept form for the line shown.

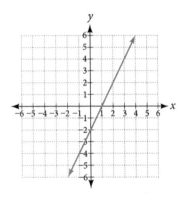

10. Does the following table represent a linear function? If so, find the linear equation that models the data.

x	-4	0	2	10
$g(x)$	18	-2	-12	-52

11. Does the following table represent a linear function? If so, find the linear equation that models the data.

x	6	8	12	26
$g(x)$	-8	-12	-18	-46

12. On June 1st, a company has $4,000,000 profit. If the company then loses 150,000 dollars per day thereafter in the month of June, what is the company's profit nth day after June 1st?

GRAPHS OF LINEAR FUNCTIONS

For the following exercises, determine whether the lines given by the equations below are parallel, perpendicular, or neither parallel nor perpendicular:

13. $2x - 6y = 12$
$-x + 3y = 1$

14. $y = \dfrac{1}{3}x - 2$
$3x + y = -9$

For the following exercises, find the x- and y-intercepts of the given equation

15. $7x + 9y = -63$ **16.** $f(x) = 2x - 1$

For the following exercises, use the descriptions of the pairs of lines to find the slopes of Line 1 and Line 2. Is each pair of lines parallel, perpendicular, or neither?

17. Line 1: Passes through $(5, 11)$ and $(10, 1)$
Line 2: Passes through $(-1, 3)$ and $(-5, 11)$

18. Line 1: Passes through $(8, -10)$ and $(0, -26)$
Line 2: Passes through $(2, 5)$ and $(4, 4)$

19. Write an equation for a line perpendicular to $f(x) = 5x - 1$ and passing through the point $(5, 20)$.

20. Find the equation of a line with a y-intercept of $(0, 2)$ and slope $-\dfrac{1}{2}$.

21. Sketch a graph of the linear function $f(t) = 2t - 5$.

22. Find the point of intersection for the 2 linear functions: $x = y + 6$
$2x - y = 13$

23. A car rental company offers two plans for renting a car.
Plan A: 25 dollars per day and 10 cents per mile
Plan B: 50 dollars per day with free unlimited mileage
How many miles would you need to drive for plan B to save you money?

MODELING WITH LINEAR FUNCTIONS

24. Find the area of a triangle bounded by the y-axis, the line $f(x) = 10 - 2x$, and the line perpendicular to f that passes through the origin.

25. A town's population increases at a constant rate. In 2010 the population was 55,000. By 2012 the population had increased to 76,000. If this trend continues, predict the population in 2016.

26. The number of people afflicted with the common cold in the winter months dropped steadily by 50 each year since 2004 until 2010. In 2004, 875 people were inflicted.

Find the linear function that models the number of people afflicted with the common cold C as a function of the year, t. When will no one be afflicted?

For the following exercises, use the graph in **Figure 1** showing the profit, y, in thousands of dollars, of a company in a given year, x, where x represents years since 1980.

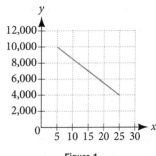

Figure 1

27. Find the linear function y, where y depends on x, the number of years since 1980.

28. Find and interpret the y-intercept.

For the following exercise, consider this scenario: In 2004, a school population was 1,700. By 2012 the population had grown to 2,500.

29. Assume the population is changing linearly.
   a. How much did the population grow between the year 2004 and 2012?
   b. What is the average population growth per year?
   c. Find an equation for the population, P, of the school t years after 2004.

For the following exercises, consider this scenario: In 2000, the moose population in a park was measured to be 6,500. By 2010, the population was measured to be 12,500. Assume the population continues to change linearly.

30. Find a formula for the moose population, P.

31. What does your model predict the moose population to be in 2020?

For the following exercises, consider this scenario: The median home values in subdivisions Pima Central and East Valley (adjusted for inflation) are shown in **Table 1**. Assume that the house values are changing linearly.

Year	Pima Central	East Valley
1970	32,000	120,250
2010	85,000	150,000

Table 1

32. In which subdivision have home values increased at a higher rate?

33. If these trends were to continue, what would be the median home value in Pima Central in 2015?

FITTING LINEAR MODELS TO DATA

34. Draw a scatter plot for the data in **Table 2**. Then determine whether the data appears to be linearly related.

0	2	4	6	8	10
−105	−50	1	55	105	160

Table 2

35. Draw a scatter plot for the data in **Table 3**. If we wanted to know when the population would reach 15,000, would the answer involve interpolation or extrapolation?

Year	1990	1995	2000	2005	2010
Population	5,600	5,950	6,300	6,600	6,900

Table 3

36. Eight students were asked to estimate their score on a 10-point quiz. Their estimated and actual scores are given in **Table 4**. Plot the points, then sketch a line that fits the data.

Predicted	6	7	7	8	7	9	10	10
Actual	6	7	8	8	9	10	10	9

Table 4

37. Draw a best-fit line for the plotted data.

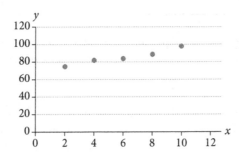

For the following exercises, consider the data in **Table 5**, which shows the percent of unemployed in a city of people 25 years or older who are college graduates is given below, by year.

Year	2000	2002	2005	2007	2010
Percent Graduates	6.5	7.0	7.4	8.2	9.0

Table 5

38. Determine whether the trend appears to be linear. If so, and assuming the trend continues, find a linear regression model to predict the percent of unemployed in a given year to three decimal places.

39. In what year will the percentage exceed 12%?

40. Based on the set of data given in **Table 6**, calculate the regression line using a calculator or other technology tool, and determine the correlation coefficient to three decimal places.

x	17	20	23	26	29
y	15	25	31	37	40

Table 6

41. Based on the set of data given in **Table 7**, calculate the regression line using a calculator or other technology tool, and determine the correlation coefficient to three decimal places.

x	10	12	15	18	20
y	36	34	30	28	22

Table 7

For the following exercises, consider this scenario: The population of a city increased steadily over a ten-year span. The following ordered pairs show the population and the year over the ten-year span (population, year) for specific recorded years:

(3,600, 2000); (4,000, 2001); (4,700, 2003); (6,000, 2006)

42. Use linear regression to determine a function y, where the year depends on the population, to three decimal places of accuracy.

43. Predict when the population will hit 12,000.

44. What is the correlation coefficient for this model to three decimal places of accuracy?

45. According to the model, what is the population in 2014?

CHAPTER 2 PRACTICE TEST

1. Determine whether the following algebraic equation can be written as a linear function.
$2x + 3y = 7$

2. Determine whether the following function is increasing or decreasing. $f(x) = -2x + 5$

3. Determine whether the following function is increasing or decreasing. $f(x) = 7x + 9$

4. Given the following set of information, find a linear equation satisfying the conditions, if possible. Passes through $(5, 1)$ and $(3, -9)$

5. Given the following set of information, find a linear equation satisfying the conditions, if possible.
x-intercept at $(-4, 0)$ and y-intercept at $(0, -6)$

6. Find the slope of the line in **Figure 1**.

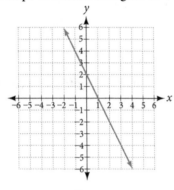

Figure 1

7. Write an equation for line in **Figure 2**.

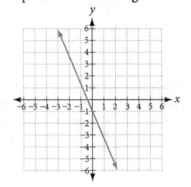

Figure 2

8. Does **Table 1** represent a linear function? If so, find a linear equation that models the data.

x	-6	0	2	4
$g(x)$	14	32	38	44

Table 1

9. Does **Table 2** represent a linear function? If so, find a linear equation that models the data.

x	1	3	7	11
$g(x)$	4	9	19	12

Table 2

10. At 6 am, an online company has sold 120 items that day. If the company sells an average of 30 items per hour for the remainder of the day, write an expression to represent the number of items that were sold n after 6 am.

For the following exercises, determine whether the lines given by the equations below are parallel, perpendicular, or neither parallel nor perpendicular:

11. $y = \dfrac{3}{4}x - 9$
$-4x - 3y = 8$

12. $-2x + y = 3$
$3x + \dfrac{3}{2}y = 5$

13. Find the x- and y-intercepts of the equation $2x + 7y = -14$.

14. Given below are descriptions of two lines. Find the slopes of Line 1 and Line 2. Is the pair of lines parallel, perpendicular, or neither?
Line 1: Passes through $(-2, -6)$ and $(3, 14)$
Line 2: Passes through $(2, 6)$ and $(4, 14)$

15. Write an equation for a line perpendicular to $f(x) = 4x + 3$ and passing through the point $(8, 10)$.

16. Sketch a line with a y-intercept of $(0, 5)$ and slope $-\frac{5}{2}$.

17. Graph of the linear function $f(x) = -x + 6$.

18. For the two linear functions, find the point of intersection: $x = y + 2$
$$2x - 3y = -1$$

19. A car rental company offers two plans for renting a car.

Plan A: $25 per day and $0.10 per mile
Plan B: $40 per day with free unlimited mileage

How many miles would you need to drive for plan B to save you money?

20. Find the area of a triangle bounded by the y-axis, the line $f(x) = 12 - 4x$, and the line perpendicular to f that passes through the origin.

21. A town's population increases at a constant rate. In 2010 the population was 65,000. By 2012 the population had increased to 90,000. Assuming this trend continues, predict the population in 2018.

22. The number of people afflicted with the common cold in the winter months dropped steadily by 25 each year since 2002 until 2012. In 2002, 8,040 people were inflicted. Find the linear function that models the number of people afflicted with the common cold C as a function of the year, t. When will less than 6,000 people be afflicted?

For the following exercises, use the graph in **Figure 3**, showing the profit, y, in thousands of dollars, of a company in a given year, x, where x represents years since 1980.

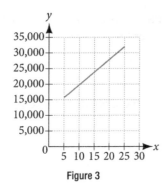
Figure 3

23. Find the linear function y, where y depends on x, the number of years since 1980.

24. Find and interpret the y-intercept.

25. In 2004, a school population was 1250. By 2012 the population had dropped to 875. Assume the population is changing linearly.
  a. How much did the population drop between the year 2004 and 2012?
  b. What is the average population decline per year?
  c. Find an equation for the population, P, of the school t years after 2004.

26. Draw a scatter plot for the data provided in **Table 3**. Then determine whether the data appears to be linearly related.

0	2	4	6	8	10
−450	−200	10	265	500	755

Table 3

27. Draw a best-fit line for the plotted data.

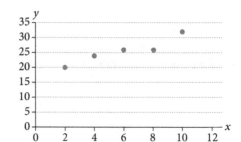

For the following exercises, use **Table 4** which shows the percent of unemployed persons 25 years or older who are college graduates in a particular city, by year.

Year	2000	2002	2005	2007	2010
Percent Graduates	8.5	8.0	7.2	6.7	6.4

Table 4

28. Determine whether the trend appears linear. If so, and assuming the trend continues, find a linear regression model to predict the percent of unemployed in a given year to three decimal places.

29. In what year will the percentage drop below 4%?

30. Based on the set of data given in **Table 5**, calculate the regression line using a calculator or other technology tool, and determine the correlation coefficient. Round to three decimal places of accuracy.

x	16	18	20	24	26
y	106	110	115	120	125

Table 5

For the following exercises, consider this scenario: The population of a city increased steadily over a ten-year span. The following ordered pairs shows the population (in hundreds) and the year over the ten-year span, (population, year) for specific recorded years:

(4,500, 2000); (4,700, 2001); (5,200, 2003); (5,800, 2006)

31. Use linear regression to determine a function y, where the year depends on the population. Round to three decimal places of accuracy.

32. Predict when the population will hit 20,000.

33. What is the correlation coefficient for this model?

3

Polynomial and Rational Functions

Figure 1 35-mm film, once the standard for capturing photographic images, has been made largely obsolete by digital photography. (credit "film": modification of work by Horia Varlan; credit "memory cards": modification of work by Paul Hudson)

CHAPTER OUTLINE

Introduction

Digital photography has dramatically changed the nature of photography. No longer is an image etched in the emulsion on a roll of film. Instead, nearly every aspect of recording and manipulating images is now governed by mathematics. An image becomes a series of numbers, representing the characteristics of light striking an image sensor. When we open an image file, software on a camera or computer interprets the numbers and converts them to a visual image. Photo editing software uses complex polynomials to transform images, allowing us to manipulate the image in order to crop details, change the color palette, and add special effects. Inverse functions make it possible to convert from one file format to another. In this chapter, we will learn about these concepts and discover how mathematics can be used in such applications.

LEARNING OBJECTIVES

In this section, you will:

- Express square roots of negative numbers as multiples of *i*.
- Plot complex numbers on the complex plane.
- Add and subtract complex numbers.
- Multiply and divide complex numbers.

3.1   COMPLEX NUMBERS

The study of mathematics continuously builds upon itself. Negative integers, for example, fill a void left by the set of positive integers. The set of rational numbers, in turn, fills a void left by the set of integers. The set of real numbers fills a void left by the set of rational numbers. Not surprisingly, the set of real numbers has voids as well. For example, we still have no solution to equations such as

$$x^2 + 4 = 0$$

Our best guesses might be $+2$ or -2. But if we test $+2$ in this equation, it does not work. If we test -2, it does not work. If we want to have a solution for this equation, we will have to go farther than we have so far. After all, to this point we have described the square root of a negative number as undefined. Fortunately, there is another system of numbers that provides solutions to problems such as these. In this section, we will explore this number system and how to work within it.

Expressing Square Roots of Negative Numbers as Multiples of *i*

We know how to find the square root of any positive real number. In a similar way, we can find the square root of a negative number. The difference is that the root is not real. If the value in the radicand is negative, the root is said to be an **imaginary number**. The imaginary number *i* is defined as the square root of negative 1.

$$\sqrt{-1} = i$$

So, using properties of radicals,

$$i^2 = (\sqrt{-1})^2 = -1$$

We can write the square root of any negative number as a multiple of *i*. Consider the square root of -25.

$$\sqrt{-25} = \sqrt{25 \cdot (-1)}$$
$$= \sqrt{25}\sqrt{-1}$$
$$= 5i$$

We use $5i$ and not $-5i$ because the principal root of 25 is the positive root.

A **complex number** is the sum of a real number and an imaginary number. A complex number is expressed in standard form when written $a + bi$ where a is the real part and bi is the imaginary part. For example, $5 + 2i$ is a complex number. So, too, is $3 + 4\sqrt{3}i$.

$$5 + 2i$$

Real part   Imaginary part

Imaginary numbers are distinguished from real numbers because a squared imaginary number produces a negative real number. Recall, when a positive real number is squared, the result is a positive real number and when a negative real number is squared, again, the result is a positive real number. Complex numbers are a combination of real and imaginary numbers.

---

imaginary and complex numbers

A **complex number** is a number of the form $a + bi$ where

- a is the real part of the complex number.

- bi is the imaginary part of the complex number.

If $b = 0$, then $a + bi$ is a real number. If $a = 0$ and b is not equal to 0, the complex number is called an **imaginary number**. An imaginary number is an even root of a negative number.

How To...

Given an imaginary number, express it in standard form.

1. Write $\sqrt{-a}$ as $\sqrt{a}\ \sqrt{-1}$.

2. Express $\sqrt{-1}$ as i.

3. Write $\sqrt{a}\cdot i$ in simplest form.

Example 1   **Expressing an Imaginary Number in Standard Form**

Express $\sqrt{-9}$ in standard form.

Solution $\sqrt{-9} = \sqrt{9}\ \sqrt{-1} = 3i$

In standard form, this is $0 + 3i$.

Try It #1

Express $\sqrt{-24}$ in standard form.

Plotting a Complex Number on the Complex Plane

We cannot plot complex numbers on a number line as we might real numbers. However, we can still represent them graphically. To represent a complex number we need to address the two components of the number. We use the **complex plane**, which is a coordinate system in which the horizontal axis represents the real component and the vertical axis represents the imaginary component. Complex numbers are the points on the plane, expressed as ordered pairs (a, b), where a represents the coordinate for the horizontal axis and b represents the coordinate for the vertical axis.

Let's consider the number $-2 + 3i$. The real part of the complex number is -2 and the imaginary part is $3i$. We plot the ordered pair $(-2, 3)$ to represent the complex number $-2 + 3i$ as shown in **Figure 1**.

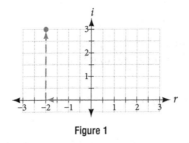

Figure 1

---

complex plane

In the **complex plane**, the horizontal axis is the real axis, and the vertical axis is the imaginary axis as shown in **Figure 2**.

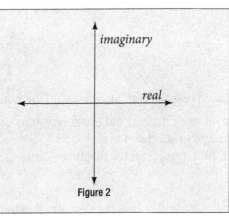

Figure 2

How To...

Given a complex number, represent its components on the complex plane.

1. Determine the real part and the imaginary part of the complex number.
2. Move along the horizontal axis to show the real part of the number.
3. Move parallel to the vertical axis to show the imaginary part of the number.
4. Plot the point.

Example 2   **Plotting a Complex Number on the Complex Plane**

Plot the complex number $3 - 4i$ on the complex plane.

Solution   The real part of the complex number is 3, and the imaginary part is $-4i$. We plot the ordered pair $(3, -4)$ as shown in **Figure 3**.

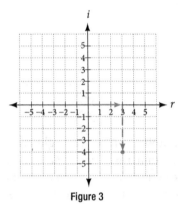

Figure 3

Try It #2

Plot the complex number $-4 - i$ on the complex plane.

Adding and Subtracting Complex Numbers

Just as with real numbers, we can perform arithmetic operations on complex numbers. To add or subtract complex numbers, we combine the real parts and combine the imaginary parts.

---

complex numbers: addition and subtraction

Adding complex numbers:
$$(a + bi) + (c + di) = (a + c) + (b + d)i$$

Subtracting complex numbers:
$$(a + bi) - (c + di) = (a - c) + (b - d)i$$

How To...

Given two complex numbers, find the sum or difference.

1. Identify the real and imaginary parts of each number.
2. Add or subtract the real parts.
3. Add or subtract the imaginary parts.

Example 3   **Adding Complex Numbers**

Add $3 - 4i$ and $2 + 5i$.

Solution   We add the real parts and add the imaginary parts.

$$(a + bi) + (c + di) = (a + c) + (b + d)i$$
$$(3 - 4i) + (2 + 5i) = (3 + 2) + (-4 + 5)i$$
$$= 5 + i$$

Try It #3

Subtract $2 + 5i$ from $3 - 4i$.

Multiplying Complex Numbers

Multiplying complex numbers is much like multiplying binomials. The major difference is that we work with the real and imaginary parts separately.

Multiplying a Complex Numbers by a Real Number

Let's begin by multiplying a complex number by a real number. We distribute the real number just as we would with a binomial. So, for example:

$$3(6 + 2i) = (3 \cdot 6) + (3 \cdot 2i) \quad \text{Distribute.}$$
$$= 18 + 6i \qquad\qquad \text{Simplify.}$$

How To...

Given a complex number and a real number, multiply to find the product.

1. Use the distributive property.
2. Simplify.

Example 4   **Multiplying a Complex Number by a Real Number**

Find the product $4(2 + 5i)$.

Solution   Distribute the 4.

$$4(2 + 5i) = (4 \cdot 2) + (4 \cdot 5i)$$
$$= 8 + 20i$$

Try It #4

Find the product $-4(2 + 6i)$.

Multiplying Complex Numbers Together

Now, let's multiply two complex numbers. We can use either the distributive property or the FOIL method. Recall that FOIL is an acronym for multiplying First, Outer, Inner, and Last terms together. Using either the distributive property or the FOIL method, we get

$$(a + bi)(c + di) = ac + adi + bci + bdi^2$$

Because $i^2 = -1$, we have

$$(a + bi)(c + di) = ac + adi + bci - bd$$

To simplify, we combine the real parts, and we combine the imaginary parts.

$$(a + bi)(c + di) = (ac - bd) + (ad + bc)i$$

How To...

Given two complex numbers, multiply to find the product.

1. Use the distributive property or the FOIL method.

2. Simplify.

Example 5   **Multiplying a Complex Number by a Complex Number**

Multiply $(4 + 3i)(2 - 5i)$.

Solution   Use $(a + bi)(c + di) = (ac - bd) + (ad + bc)i$

$$(4 + 3i)(2 - 5i) = (4 \cdot 2 - 3 \cdot (-5)) + (4 \cdot (-5) + 3 \cdot 2)i$$

$$= (8 + 15) + (-20 + 6)i$$

$$= 23 - 14i$$

Try It #5

Multiply $(3 - 4i)(2 + 3i)$.

Dividing Complex Numbers

Division of two complex numbers is more complicated than addition, subtraction, and multiplication because we cannot divide by an imaginary number, meaning that any fraction must have a real-number denominator. We need to find a term by which we can multiply the numerator and the denominator that will eliminate the imaginary portion of the denominator so that we end up with a real number as the denominator. This term is called the **complex conjugate** of the denominator, which is found by changing the sign of the imaginary part of the complex number. In other words, the complex conjugate of $a + bi$ is $a - bi$.

Note that complex conjugates have a reciprocal relationship: The complex conjugate of $a + bi$ is $a - bi$, and the complex conjugate of $a - bi$ is $a + bi$. Further, when a quadratic equation with real coefficients has complex solutions, the solutions are always complex conjugates of one another.

Suppose we want to divide $c + di$ by $a + bi$, where neither a nor b equals zero. We first write the division as a fraction, then find the complex conjugate of the denominator, and multiply.

$$\frac{c + di}{a + bi} \text{ where } a \neq 0 \text{ and } b \neq 0$$

Multiply the numerator and denominator by the complex conjugate of the denominator.

$$\frac{(c + di)}{(a + bi)} \cdot \frac{(a - bi)}{(a - bi)} = \frac{(c + di)(a - bi)}{(a + bi)(a - bi)}$$

Apply the distributive property.

$$= \frac{ca - cbi + adi - bdi^2}{a^2 - abi + abi - b^2i^2}$$

Simplify, remembering that $i^2 = -1$.

$$= \frac{ca - cbi + adi - bd(-1)}{a^2 - abi + abi - b^2(-1)}$$

$$= \frac{(ca + bd) + (ad - cb)i}{a^2 + b^2}$$

> **the complex conjugate**
>
> The **complex conjugate** of a complex number $a + bi$ is $a - bi$. It is found by changing the sign of the imaginary part of the complex number. The real part of the number is left unchanged.
> - When a complex number is multiplied by its complex conjugate, the result is a real number.
> - When a complex number is added to its complex conjugate, the result is a real number.

Example 6   **Finding Complex Conjugates**

Find the complex conjugate of each number.

    a. $2 + i\sqrt{5}$　**b.** $-\dfrac{1}{2}i$

Solution

    a. The number is already in the form $a + bi$. The complex conjugate is $a - bi$, or $2 - i\sqrt{5}$.

    b. We can rewrite this number in the form $a + bi$ as $0 - \dfrac{1}{2}i$. The complex conjugate is $a - bi$, or $0 + \dfrac{1}{2}i$. This can be written simply as $\dfrac{1}{2}i$.

Analysis   *Although we have seen that we can find the complex conjugate of an imaginary number, in practice we generally find the complex conjugates of only complex numbers with both a real and an imaginary component. To obtain a real number from an imaginary number, we can simply multiply by i.*

How To...

Given two complex numbers, divide one by the other.

1. Write the division problem as a fraction.
2. Determine the complex conjugate of the denominator.
3. Multiply the numerator and denominator of the fraction by the complex conjugate of the denominator.
4. Simplify.

Example 7   **Dividing Complex Numbers**

Divide $(2 + 5i)$ by $(4 - i)$.

Solution   We begin by writing the problem as a fraction.

$$\frac{(2 + 5i)}{(4 - i)}$$

Then we multiply the numerator and denominator by the complex conjugate of the denominator.

$$\frac{(2 + 5i)}{(4 - i)} \cdot \frac{(4 + i)}{(4 + i)}$$

To multiply two complex numbers, we expand the product as we would with polynomials (the process commonly called FOIL).

$$\frac{(2 + 5i)}{(4 - i)} \cdot \frac{(4 + i)}{(4 + i)} = \frac{8 + 2i + 20i + 5i^2}{16 + 4i - 4i - i^2}$$

$$= \frac{8 + 2i + 20i + 5(-1)}{16 + 4i - 4i - (-1)} \quad \text{Because } i^2 = -1$$

$$= \frac{3 + 22i}{17}$$

$$= \frac{3}{17} + \frac{22}{17}i \qquad \text{Separate real and imaginary parts.}$$

Note that this expresses the quotient in standard form.

Example 8   **Substituting a Complex Number into a Polynomial Function**

Let $f(x) = x^2 - 5x + 2$. Evaluate $f(3 + i)$.

Solution   Substitute $x = 3 + i$ into the function $f(x) = x^2 - 5x + 2$ and simplify.

$$f(3 + i) = (3 + i)^2 - 5(3 + i) + 2 \qquad \text{Substitute } 3 + i \text{ for } x.$$

$$= (3 + 6i + i^2) - (15 + 5i) + 2 \qquad \text{Multiply.}$$

$$= 9 + 6i + (-1) - 15 - 5i + 2 \qquad \text{Substitute } -1 \text{ for } i^2.$$

$$= -5 + i \qquad \text{Combine like terms.}$$

Analysis   We write $f(3 + i) = -5 + i$. Notice that the input is $3 + i$ and the output is $-5 + i$.

Try It #6

Let $f(x) = 2x^2 - 3x$. Evaluate $f(8 - i)$.

Example 9   **Substituting an Imaginary Number in a Rational Function**

Let $f(x) = \dfrac{2 + x}{x + 3}$. Evaluate $f(10i)$.

Solution   Substitute $x = 10i$ and simplify.

$$\frac{2 + 10i}{10i + 3} \qquad \text{Substitute } 10i \text{ for } x.$$

$$\frac{2 + 10i}{3 + 10i} \qquad \text{Rewrite the denominator in standard form.}$$

$$\frac{2 + 10i}{3 + 10i} \cdot \frac{3 - 10i}{3 - 10i} \qquad \text{Prepare to multiply the numerator and denominator by the complex conjugate of the denominator.}$$

$$\frac{6 - 20i + 30i - 100i^2}{9 - 30i + 30i - 100i^2} \qquad \text{Multiply using the distributive property or the FOIL method.}$$

$$\frac{6 - 20i + 30i - 100(-1)}{9 - 30i + 30i - 100(-1)} \qquad \text{Substitute } -1 \text{ for } i^2.$$

$$\frac{106 + 10i}{109} \qquad \text{Simplify.}$$

$$\frac{106}{109} + \frac{10}{109}i \qquad \text{Separate the real and imaginary parts.}$$

Try It #7

Let $f(x) = \dfrac{x + 1}{x - 4}$. Evaluate $f(-i)$.

Simplifying Powers of i

The powers of i are cyclic. Let's look at what happens when we raise i to increasing powers.

$$i^1 = i$$

$$i^2 = -1$$

$$i^3 = i^2 \cdot i = -1 \cdot i = -i$$

$$i^4 = i^3 \cdot i = -i \cdot i = -i^2 = -(-1) = 1$$

$$i^5 = i^4 \cdot i = 1 \cdot i = i$$

We can see that when we get to the fifth power of i, it is equal to the first power. As we continue to multiply i by itself for increasing powers, we will see a cycle of 4. Let's examine the next 4 powers of i.

$$i^6 = i^5 \cdot i = i \cdot i = i^2 = -1$$
$$i^7 = i^6 \cdot i = i^2 \cdot i = i^3 = -i$$
$$i^8 = i^7 \cdot i = i^3 \cdot i = i^4 = 1$$
$$i^9 = i^8 \cdot i = i^4 \cdot i = i^5 = i$$

Example 10 **Simplifying Powers of i**

Evaluate i^{35}.

Solution Since $i^4 = 1$, we can simplify the problem by factoring out as many factors of i^4 as possible. To do so, first determine how many times 4 goes into 35: $35 = 4 \cdot 8 + 3$.

$$i^{35} = i^{4 \cdot 8 + 3} = i^{4 \cdot 8} \cdot i^3 = (i^4)^8 \cdot i^3 = 1^8 \cdot i^3 = i^3 = -i$$

Q & A...

Can we write i^{35} in other helpful ways?

As we saw in **Example 10**, we reduced i^{35} to i^3 by dividing the exponent by 4 and using the remainder to find the simplified form. But perhaps another factorization of i^{35} may be more useful. **Table 1** shows some other possible factorizations.

Factorization of i^{35}	$i^{34} \cdot i$	$i^{33} \cdot i^2$	$i^{31} \cdot i^4$	$i^{19} \cdot i^{16}$
Reduced form	$(i^2)^{17} \cdot i$	$i^{33} \cdot (-1)$	$i^{31} \cdot 1$	$i^{19} \cdot (i^4)^4$
Simplified form	$(-1)^{17} \cdot i$	$-i^{33}$	i^{31}	i^{19}

Table 1

Each of these will eventually result in the answer we obtained above but may require several more steps than our earlier method.

Access these online resources for additional instruction and practice with complex numbers.

- Adding and Subtracting Complex Numbers (http://openstaxcollege.org/l/addsubcomplex)
- Multiply Complex Numbers (http://openstaxcollege.org/l/multiplycomplex)
- Multiplying Complex Conjugates (http://openstaxcollege.org/l/multcompconj)
- Raising i to Powers (http://openstaxcollege.org/l/raisingi)

3.1   SECTION EXERCISES

VERBAL

1. Explain how to add complex numbers.

2. What is the basic principle in multiplication of complex numbers?

3. Give an example to show the product of two imaginary numbers is not always imaginary.

4. What is a characteristic of the plot of a real number in the complex plane?

ALGEBRAIC

For the following exercises, evaluate the algebraic expressions.

5. If $f(x) = x^2 + x - 4$, evaluate $f(2i)$.

6. If $f(x) = x^3 - 2$, evaluate $f(i)$.

7. If $f(x) = x^2 + 3x + 5$, evaluate $f(2 + i)$.

8. If $f(x) = 2x^2 + x - 3$, evaluate $f(2 - 3i)$.

9. If $f(x) = \dfrac{x + 1}{2 - x}$, evaluate $f(5i)$.

10. If $f(x) = \dfrac{1 + 2x}{x + 3}$, evaluate $f(4i)$.

GRAPHICAL

For the following exercises, determine the number of real and nonreal solutions for each quadratic function shown.

11.

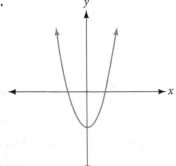

12.

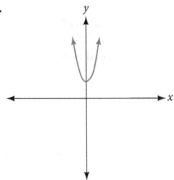

For the following exercises, plot the complex numbers on the complex plane.

13. $1 - 2i$

14. $-2 + 3i$

15. i

16. $-3 - 4i$

NUMERIC

For the following exercises, perform the indicated operation and express the result as a simplified complex number.

17. $(3 + 2i) + (5 - 3i)$

18. $(-2 - 4i) + (1 + 6i)$

19. $(-5 + 3i) - (6 - i)$

20. $(2 - 3i) - (3 + 2i)$

21. $(-4 + 4i) - (-6 + 9i)$

22. $(2 + 3i)(4i)$

23. $(5 - 2i)(3i)$

24. $(6 - 2i)(5)$

25. $(-2 + 4i)(8)$

26. $(2 + 3i)(4 - i)$

27. $(-1 + 2i)(-2 + 3i)$

28. $(4 - 2i)(4 + 2i)$

29. $(3 + 4i)(3 - 4i)$

30. $\dfrac{3 + 4i}{2}$

31. $\dfrac{6 - 2i}{3}$

32. $\dfrac{-5 + 3i}{2i}$

33. $\dfrac{6 + 4i}{i}$

34. $\dfrac{2 - 3i}{4 + 3i}$

35. $\dfrac{3+4i}{2-i}$

36. $\dfrac{2+3i}{2-3i}$

37. $\sqrt{-9}+3\sqrt{-16}$

38. $-\sqrt{-4}-4\sqrt{-25}$

39. $\dfrac{2+\sqrt{-12}}{2}$

40. $\dfrac{4+\sqrt{-20}}{2}$

41. i^8

42. i^{15}

43. i^{22}

TECHNOLOGY

For the following exercises, use a calculator to help answer the questions.

44. Evaluate $(1+i)^k$ for $k = 4, 8,$ and 12. Predict the value if $k = 16$.

45. Evaluate $(1-i)^k$ for $k = 2, 6,$ and 10. Predict the value if $k = 14$.

46. Evaluate $(1+i)^k - (1-i)^k$ for $k = 4, 8,$ and 12. Predict the value for $k = 16$.

47. Show that a solution of $x^6 + 1 = 0$ is $\dfrac{\sqrt{3}}{2} + \dfrac{1}{2}i$.

48. Show that a solution of $x^8 - 1 = 0$ is $\dfrac{\sqrt{2}}{2} + \dfrac{\sqrt{2}}{2}i$.

EXTENSIONS

For the following exercises, evaluate the expressions, writing the result as a simplified complex number.

49. $\dfrac{1}{i} + \dfrac{4}{i^3}$

50. $\dfrac{1}{i^{11}} - \dfrac{1}{i^{21}}$

51. $i^7(1 + i^2)$

52. $i^{-3} + 5i^7$

53. $\dfrac{(2+i)(4-2i)}{(1+i)}$

54. $\dfrac{(1+3i)(2-4i)}{(1+2i)}$

55. $\dfrac{(3+i)^2}{(1+2i)^2}$

56. $\dfrac{3+2i}{2+i} + (4+3i)$

57. $\dfrac{4+i}{i} + \dfrac{3-4i}{1-i}$

58. $\dfrac{3+2i}{1+2i} - \dfrac{2-3i}{3+i}$

In this section, you will:

- Recognize characteristics of parabolas.
- Understand how the graph of a parabola is related to its quadratic function.
- Determine a quadratic function's minimum or maximum value.
- Solve problems involving a quadratic function's minimum or maximum value.

3.2   QUADRATIC FUNCTIONS

Figure 1 An array of satellite dishes. (credit: Matthew Colvin de Valle, Flickr)

Curved antennas, such as the ones shown in **Figure 1** are commonly used to focus microwaves and radio waves to transmit television and telephone signals, as well as satellite and spacecraft communication. The cross-section of the antenna is in the shape of a parabola, which can be described by a quadratic function.

In this section, we will investigate quadratic functions, which frequently model problems involving area and projectile motion. Working with quadratic functions can be less complex than working with higher degree functions, so they provide a good opportunity for a detailed study of function behavior.

Recognizing Characteristics of Parabolas

The graph of a quadratic function is a U-shaped curve called a parabola. One important feature of the graph is that it has an extreme point, called the **vertex**. If the parabola opens up, the vertex represents the lowest point on the graph, or the minimum value of the quadratic function. If the parabola opens down, the vertex represents the highest point on the graph, or the maximum value. In either case, the vertex is a turning point on the graph. The graph is also symmetric with a vertical line drawn through the vertex, called the **axis of symmetry**. These features are illustrated in **Figure 2**.

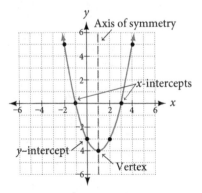

Figure 2

The y-intercept is the point at which the parabola crosses the y-axis. The x-intercepts are the points at which the parabola crosses the x-axis. If they exist, the x-intercepts represent the **zeros**, or **roots**, of the quadratic function, the values of x at which $y = 0$.

Example 1   **Identifying the Characteristics of a Parabola**

Determine the vertex, axis of symmetry, zeros, and y-intercept of the parabola shown in **Figure 3**.

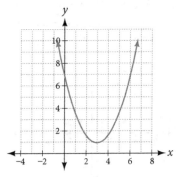

Figure 3

Solution   The vertex is the turning point of the graph. We can see that the vertex is at $(3, 1)$. Because this parabola opens upward, the axis of symmetry is the vertical line that intersects the parabola at the vertex. So the axis of symmetry is $x = 3$. This parabola does not cross the x-axis, so it has no zeros. It crosses the y-axis at $(0, 7)$ so this is the y-intercept.

Understanding How the Graphs of Parabolas are Related to Their Quadratic Functions

The **general form of a quadratic function** presents the function in the form

$$f(x) = ax^2 + bx + c$$

where a, b, and c are real numbers and $a \neq 0$. If $a > 0$, the parabola opens upward. If $a < 0$, the parabola opens downward. We can use the general form of a parabola to find the equation for the axis of symmetry.

The axis of symmetry is defined by $x = -\dfrac{b}{2a}$. If we use the quadratic formula, $x = \dfrac{-b \pm \sqrt{b^2 - 4ac}}{2a}$, to solve $ax^2 + bx + c = 0$ for the x-intercepts, or zeros, we find the value of x halfway between them is always $x = -\dfrac{b}{2a}$, the equation for the axis of symmetry.

Figure 4 represents the graph of the quadratic function written in general form as $y = x^2 + 4x + 3$. In this form, $a = 1$, $b = 4$, and $c = 3$. Because $a > 0$, the parabola opens upward. The axis of symmetry is $x = -\dfrac{4}{2(1)} = -2$. This also makes sense because we can see from the graph that the vertical line $x = -2$ divides the graph in half. The vertex always occurs along the axis of symmetry. For a parabola that opens upward, the vertex occurs at the lowest point on the graph, in this instance, $(-2, -1)$. The x-intercepts, those points where the parabola crosses the x-axis, occur at $(-3, 0)$ and $(-1, 0)$.

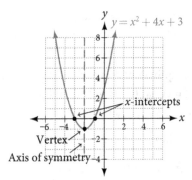

Figure 4

The **standard form of a quadratic function** presents the function in the form

$$f(x) = a(x - h)^2 + k$$

where (h, k) is the vertex. Because the vertex appears in the standard form of the quadratic function, this form is also known as the **vertex form of a quadratic function**.

As with the general form, if $a > 0$, the parabola opens upward and the vertex is a minimum. If $a < 0$, the parabola opens downward, and the vertex is a maximum. **Figure 5** represents the graph of the quadratic function written in standard form as $y = -3(x + 2)^2 + 4$. Since $x - h = x + 2$ in this example, $h = -2$. In this form, $a = -3$, $h = -2$, and $k = 4$. Because $a < 0$, the parabola opens downward. The vertex is at $(-2, 4)$.

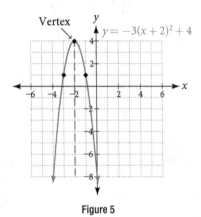

Figure 5

The standard form is useful for determining how the graph is transformed from the graph of $y = x^2$. **Figure 6** is the graph of this basic function.

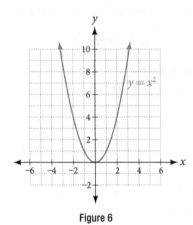

Figure 6

If $k > 0$, the graph shifts upward, whereas if $k < 0$, the graph shifts downward. In **Figure 5**, $k > 0$, so the graph is shifted 4 units upward. If $h > 0$, the graph shifts toward the right and if $h < 0$, the graph shifts to the left. In **Figure 5**, $h < 0$, so the graph is shifted 2 units to the left. The magnitude of a indicates the stretch of the graph. If $|a| > 1$, the point associated with a particular x-value shifts farther from the x-axis, so the graph appears to become narrower, and there is a vertical stretch. But if $|a| < 1$, the point associated with a particular x-value shifts closer to the x-axis, so the graph appears to become wider, but in fact there is a vertical compression. In **Figure 5**, $|a| > 1$, so the graph becomes narrower.

The standard form and the general form are equivalent methods of describing the same function. We can see this by expanding out the general form and setting it equal to the standard form.

$$a(x - h)^2 + k = ax^2 + bx + c$$

$$ax^2 - 2ahx + (ah^2 + k) = ax^2 + bx + c$$

For the linear terms to be equal, the coefficients must be equal.

$$-2ah = b, \text{ so } h = -\frac{b}{2a}.$$

This is the axis of symmetry we defined earlier. Setting the constant terms equal:

$$ah^2 + k = c$$

$$k = c - ah^2$$

$$= c - a\left(-\frac{b}{2a}\right)^2$$

$$= c - \frac{b^2}{4a}$$

In practice, though, it is usually easier to remember that k is the output value of the function when the input is h, so $f(h) = k$.

> ### *forms of quadratic functions*
>
> A quadratic function is a function of degree two. The graph of a quadratic function is a parabola. The **general form of a quadratic function** is $f(x) = ax^2 + bx + c$ where a, b, and c are real numbers and $a \neq 0$.
>
> The **standard form of a quadratic function** is $f(x) = a(x - h)^2 + k$.
>
> The vertex (h, k) is located at
>
> $$h = -\frac{b}{2a}, k = f(h) = f\left(\frac{-b}{2a}\right).$$

How To...

Given a graph of a quadratic function, write the equation of the function in general form.

1. Identify the horizontal shift of the parabola; this value is h. Identify the vertical shift of the parabola; this value is k.
2. Substitute the values of the horizontal and vertical shift for h and k. in the function $f(x) = a(x - h)^2 + k$.
3. Substitute the values of any point, other than the vertex, on the graph of the parabola for x and $f(x)$.
4. Solve for the stretch factor, $|a|$.
5. If the parabola opens up, $a > 0$. If the parabola opens down, $a < 0$ since this means the graph was reflected about the x-axis.
6. Expand and simplify to write in general form.

Example 2   **Writing the Equation of a Quadratic Function from the Graph**

Write an equation for the quadratic function g in **Figure 7** as a transformation of $f(x) = x^2$, and then expand the formula, and simplify terms to write the equation in general form.

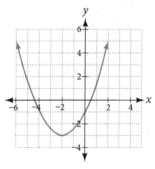

Figure 7

Solution   We can see the graph of g is the graph of $f(x) = x^2$ shifted to the left 2 and down 3, giving a formula in the form $g(x) = a(x + 2)^2 - 3$.

Substituting the coordinates of a point on the curve, such as $(0, -1)$, we can solve for the stretch factor.

$$-1 = a(0 + 2)^2 - 3$$
$$2 = 4a$$
$$a = \frac{1}{2}$$

In standard form, the algebraic model for this graph is $g(x) = \frac{1}{2}(x + 2)^2 - 3$.

To write this in general polynomial form, we can expand the formula and simplify terms.

$$g(x) = \frac{1}{2}(x + 2)^2 - 3$$
$$= \frac{1}{2}(x + 2)(x + 2) - 3$$
$$= \frac{1}{2}(x^2 + 4x + 4) - 3$$
$$= \frac{1}{2}x^2 + 2x + 2 - 3$$
$$= \frac{1}{2}x^2 + 2x - 1$$

Notice that the horizontal and vertical shifts of the basic graph of the quadratic function determine the location of the vertex of the parabola; the vertex is unaffected by stretches and compressions.

Analysis We can check our work using the table feature on a graphing utility. First enter $Y1 = \frac{1}{2}(x + 2)^2 - 3$. Next, select **TBLSET**, then use **TblStart** $= -6$ and Δ**Tbl** $= 2$, and select **TABLE**. See **Table 1**.

x	-6	-4	-2	0	2
y	5	-1	-3	-1	5

Table 1

The ordered pairs in the table correspond to points on the graph.

Try It #1

A coordinate grid has been superimposed over the quadratic path of a basketball in **Figure 8** Find an equation for the path of the ball. Does the shooter make the basket?

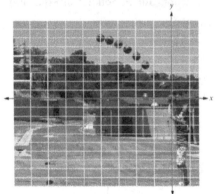

Figure 8 (credit: modification of work by Dan Meyer)

How To...

Given a quadratic function in general form, find the vertex of the parabola.

1. Identify a, b, and c.

2. Find h, the x-coordinate of the vertex, by substituting a and b into $h = -\dfrac{b}{2a}$.

3. Find k, the y-coordinate of the vertex, by evaluating $k = f(h) = f\left(-\dfrac{b}{2a}\right)$.

Example 3   **Finding the Vertex of a Quadratic Function**

Find the vertex of the quadratic function $f(x) = 2x^2 - 6x + 7$. Rewrite the quadratic in standard form (vertex form).

Solution   The horizontal coordinate of the vertex will be at

$$h = -\frac{b}{2a}$$

$$= -\frac{-6}{2(2)}$$

$$= \frac{6}{4}$$

$$= \frac{3}{2}$$

The vertical coordinate of the vertex will be at

$$k = f(h)$$

$$= f\left(\frac{3}{2}\right)$$

$$= 2\left(\frac{3}{2}\right)^2 - 6\left(\frac{3}{2}\right) + 7$$

$$= \frac{5}{2}$$

Rewriting into standard form, the stretch factor will be the same as the a in the original quadratic.

$$f(x) = ax^2 + bx + c$$

$$f(x) = 2x^2 - 6x + 7$$

Using the vertex to determine the shifts,

$$f(x) = 2\left(x - \frac{3}{2}\right)^2 + \frac{5}{2}$$

Analysis   One reason we may want to identify the vertex of the parabola is that this point will inform us where the maximum or minimum value of the output occurs, (k), and where it occurs, (x).

Try It #2

Given the equation $g(x) = 13 + x^2 - 6x$, write the equation in general form and then in standard form.

Finding the Domain and Range of a Quadratic Function

Any number can be the input value of a quadratic function. Therefore, the domain of any quadratic function is all real numbers. Because parabolas have a maximum or a minimum point, the range is restricted. Since the vertex of a parabola will be either a maximum or a minimum, the range will consist of all y-values greater than or equal to the y-coordinate at the turning point or less than or equal to the y-coordinate at the turning point, depending on whether the parabola opens up or down.

> ***domain and range of a quadratic function***
>
> The domain of any quadratic function is all real numbers.
>
> The range of a quadratic function written in general form $f(x) = ax^2 + bx + c$ with a positive a value is $f(x) \geq f\left(-\frac{b}{2a}\right)$, or $\left[f\left(-\frac{b}{2a}\right), \infty\right)$.
>
> The range of a quadratic function written in general form with a negative a value is $f(x) \leq f\left(-\frac{b}{2a}\right)$, or $\left(-\infty, f\left(-\frac{b}{2a}\right)\right]$.
>
> The range of a quadratic function written in standard form $f(x) = a(x - h)^2 + k$ with a positive a value is $f(x) \geq k$; the range of a quadratic function written in standard form with a negative a value is $f(x) \leq k$.

How To...

Given a quadratic function, find the domain and range.

1. Identify the domain of any quadratic function as all real numbers.
2. Determine whether a is positive or negative. If a is positive, the parabola has a minimum. If a is negative, the parabola has a maximum.
3. Determine the maximum or minimum value of the parabola, k.
4. If the parabola has a minimum, the range is given by $f(x) \geq k$, or $[k, \infty)$. If the parabola has a maximum, the range is given by $f(x) \leq k$, or $(-\infty, k]$.

Example 4   **Finding the Domain and Range of a Quadratic Function**

Find the domain and range of $f(x) = -5x^2 + 9x - 1$.

Solution   As with any quadratic function, the domain is all real numbers.

Because a is negative, the parabola opens downward and has a maximum value. We need to determine the maximum value. We can begin by finding the x-value of the vertex.

$$h = -\frac{b}{2a}$$

$$= -\frac{9}{2(-5)}$$

$$= \frac{9}{10}$$

The maximum value is given by $f(h)$.

$$f\left(\frac{9}{10}\right) = -5\left(\frac{9}{10}\right)^2 + 9\left(\frac{9}{10}\right) - 1$$

$$= \frac{61}{20}$$

The range is $f(x) \leq \frac{61}{20}$, or $\left(-\infty, \frac{61}{20}\right]$.

Try It #3

Find the domain and range of $f(x) = 2\left(x - \frac{4}{7}\right)^2 + \frac{8}{11}$.

Determining the Maximum and Minimum Values of Quadratic Functions

The output of the quadratic function at the vertex is the maximum or minimum value of the function, depending on the orientation of the parabola. We can see the maximum and minimum values in **Figure 9**.

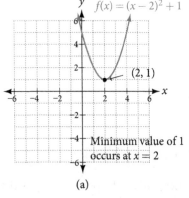

(a)

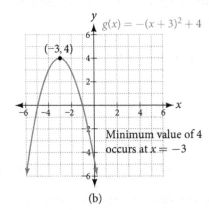

(b)

Figure 9

There are many real-world scenarios that involve finding the maximum or minimum value of a quadratic function, such as applications involving area and revenue.

Example 5   Finding the Maximum Value of a Quadratic Function

A backyard farmer wants to enclose a rectangular space for a new garden within her fenced backyard. She has purchased 80 feet of wire fencing to enclose three sides, and she will use a section of the backyard fence as the fourth side.

    a. Find a formula for the area enclosed by the fence if the sides of fencing perpendicular to the existing fence have length L.

    b. What dimensions should she make her garden to maximize the enclosed area?

Solution   Let's use a diagram such as **Figure 10** to record the given information. It is also helpful to introduce a temporary variable, W, to represent the width of the garden and the length of the fence section parallel to the backyard fence.

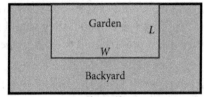

Figure 10

    a. We know we have only 80 feet of fence available, and $L + W + L = 80$, or more simply, $2L + W = 80$. This allows us to represent the width, W, in terms of L.

$$W = 80 - 2L$$

Now we are ready to write an equation for the area the fence encloses. We know the area of a rectangle is length multiplied by width, so

$$A = LW = L(80 - 2L)$$
$$A(L) = 80L - 2L^2$$

This formula represents the area of the fence in terms of the variable length L. The function, written in general form, is

$$A(L) = -2L^2 + 80L.$$

    b. The quadratic has a negative leading coefficient, so the graph will open downward, and the vertex will be the maximum value for the area. In finding the vertex, we must be careful because the equation is not written in standard polynomial form with decreasing powers. This is why we rewrote the function in general form above. Since a is the coefficient of the squared term, $a = -2$, $b = 80$, and $c = 0$.

    To find the vertex:

$$h = -\frac{80}{2(-2)} \qquad\qquad k = A(20)$$
$$= 20 \qquad \text{and} \qquad = 80(20) - 2(20)^2$$
$$= 800$$

The maximum value of the function is an area of 800 square feet, which occurs when $L = 20$ feet. When the shorter sides are 20 feet, there is 40 feet of fencing left for the longer side. To maximize the area, she should enclose the garden so the two shorter sides have length 20 feet and the longer side parallel to the existing fence has length 40 feet.

*Analysis This problem also could be solved by graphing the quadratic function. We can see where the maximum area occurs on a graph of the quadratic function in **Figure 11**.*

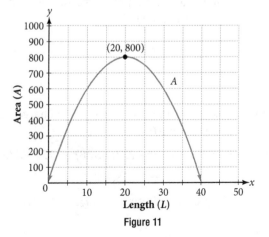

Figure 11

How To...

Given an application involving revenue, use a quadratic equation to find the maximum.

1. Write a quadratic equation for revenue.
2. Find the vertex of the quadratic equation.
3. Determine the y-value of the vertex.

Example 6   **Finding Maximum Revenue**

The unit price of an item affects its supply and demand. That is, if the unit price goes up, the demand for the item will usually decrease. For example, a local newspaper currently has 84,000 subscribers at a quarterly charge of $30. Market research has suggested that if the owners raise the price to $32, they would lose 5,000 subscribers. Assuming that subscriptions are linearly related to the price, what price should the newspaper charge for a quarterly subscription to maximize their revenue?

Solution   Revenue is the amount of money a company brings in. In this case, the revenue can be found by multiplying the price per subscription times the number of subscribers, or quantity. We can introduce variables, p for price per subscription and Q for quantity, giving us the equation Revenue $= pQ$.

Because the number of subscribers changes with the price, we need to find a relationship between the variables. We know that currently $p = 30$ and $Q = 84,000$. We also know that if the price rises to $32, the newspaper would lose 5,000 subscribers, giving a second pair of values, $p = 32$ and $Q = 79,000$. From this we can find a linear equation relating the two quantities. The slope will be

$$m = \frac{79,000 - 84,000}{32 - 30}$$

$$= \frac{-5,000}{2}$$

$$= -2,500$$

This tells us the paper will lose 2,500 subscribers for each dollar they raise the price. We can then solve for the y-intercept.

$$Q = -2,500p + b \qquad \text{Substitute in the point } Q = 84,000 \text{ and } p = 30$$

$$84,000 = -2,500(30) + b \qquad \text{Solve for } b$$

$$b = 159,000$$

This gives us the linear equation $Q = -2,500p + 159,000$ relating cost and subscribers. We now return to our revenue equation.

$$\text{Revenue} = pQ$$

$$\text{Revenue} = p(-2,500p + 159,000)$$

$$\text{Revenue} = -2,500p^2 + 159,000p$$

We now have a quadratic function for revenue as a function of the subscription charge. To find the price that will maximize revenue for the newspaper, we can find the vertex.

$$h = -\frac{159,000}{2(-2,500)}$$

$$= 31.8$$

The model tells us that the maximum revenue will occur if the newspaper charges $31.80 for a subscription. To find what the maximum revenue is, we evaluate the revenue function.

$$\text{maximum revenue} = -2,500(31.8)^2 + 159,000(31.8)$$

$$= 2,528,100$$

*Analysis   This could also be solved by graphing the quadratic as in **Figure 12**. We can see the maximum revenue on a graph of the quadratic function.*

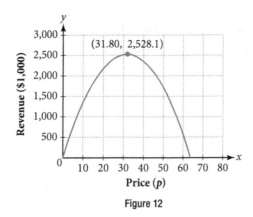

Figure 12

Finding the x- and y-Intercepts of a Quadratic Function

Much as we did in the application problems above, we also need to find intercepts of quadratic equations for graphing parabolas. Recall that we find the y-intercept of a quadratic by evaluating the function at an input of zero, and we find the x-intercepts at locations where the output is zero. Notice in **Figure 13** that the number of x-intercepts can vary depending upon the location of the graph.

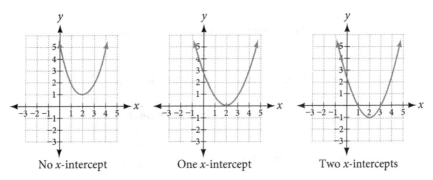

No x-intercept   One x-intercept   Two x-intercepts

Figure 13 Number of x-intercepts of a parabola

How To...

Given a quadratic function $f(x)$, find the y- and x-intercepts.

1. Evaluate $f(0)$ to find the y-intercept.
2. Solve the quadratic equation $f(x) = 0$ to find the x-intercepts.

Example 7   **Finding the y- and x-Intercepts of a Parabola**

Find the y- and x-intercepts of the quadratic $f(x) = 3x^2 + 5x - 2$.

Solution   We find the y-intercept by evaluating $f(0)$.

$$f(0) = 3(0)^2 + 5(0) - 2$$
$$= -2$$

So the y-intercept is at $(0, -2)$.

For the x-intercepts, we find all solutions of $f(x) = 0$.

$$0 = 3x^2 + 5x - 2$$

In this case, the quadratic can be factored easily, providing the simplest method for solution.

$$0 = (3x - 1)(x + 2)$$

$$0 = 3x - 1 \qquad 0 = x + 2$$

$$x = \frac{1}{3} \qquad \text{or} \qquad x = -2$$

So the x-intercepts are at $\left(\frac{1}{3}, 0\right)$ and $(-2, 0)$.

Analysis By graphing the function, we can confirm that the graph crosses the *y*-axis at $(0, -2)$. We can also confirm that the graph crosses the *x*-axis at $\left(\frac{1}{3}, 0\right)$ and $(-2, 0)$. See **Figure 14.**

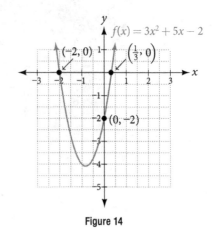

Figure 14

Rewriting Quadratics in Standard Form

In **Example 7**, the quadratic was easily solved by factoring. However, there are many quadratics that cannot be factored. We can solve these quadratics by first rewriting them in standard form.

How To...

Given a quadratic function, find the *x*-intercepts by rewriting in standard form.

1. Substitute a and b into $h = -\dfrac{b}{2a}$.
2. Substitute $x = h$ into the general form of the quadratic function to find k.
3. Rewrite the quadratic in standard form using h and k.
4. Solve for when the output of the function will be zero to find the *x*-intercepts.

Example 8   Finding the *x*-Intercepts of a Parabola

Find the *x*-intercepts of the quadratic function $f(x) = 2x^2 + 4x - 4$.

Solution We begin by solving for when the output will be zero.

$$0 = 2x^2 + 4x - 4$$

Because the quadratic is not easily factorable in this case, we solve for the intercepts by first rewriting the quadratic in standard form.

$$f(x) = a(x - h)^2 + k$$

We know that $a = 2$. Then we solve for h and k.

$$h = -\frac{b}{2a} \qquad\qquad k = f(-1)$$
$$= -\frac{4}{2(2)} \qquad\qquad = 2(-1)^2 + 4(-1) - 4$$
$$= -1 \qquad\qquad = -6$$

So now we can rewrite in standard form.

$$f(x) = 2(x + 1)^2 - 6$$

We can now solve for when the output will be zero.

$$0 = 2(x + 1)^2 - 6$$
$$6 = 2(x + 1)^2$$
$$3 = (x + 1)^2$$
$$x + 1 = \pm\sqrt{3}$$
$$x = -1 \pm \sqrt{3}$$

The graph has *x*-intercepts at $(-1 - \sqrt{3}, 0)$ and $(-1 + \sqrt{3}, 0)$.

Analysis We can check our work by graphing the given function on a graphing utility and observing the x-intercepts. See **Figure 15**.

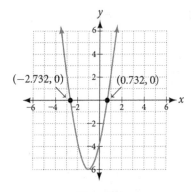

$(-2.732, 0)$ $(0.732, 0)$

Figure 15

Try It #4

In a separate **Try It**, we found the standard and general form for the function $g(x) = 13 + x^2 - 6x$. Now find the y- and x-intercepts (if any).

Example 9 **Solving a Quadratic Equation with the Quadratic Formula**

Solve $x^2 + x + 2 = 0$.

Solution Let's begin by writing the quadratic formula: $x = \dfrac{-b \pm \sqrt{b^2 - 4ac}}{2a}$.

When applying the quadratic formula, we identify the coefficients a, b and c. For the equation $x^2 + x + 2 = 0$, we have $a = 1$, $b = 1$, and $c = 2$. Substituting these values into the formula we have:

$$x = \frac{-b \pm \sqrt{b^2 - 4ac}}{2a}$$

$$= \frac{-1 \pm \sqrt{1^2 - 4 \cdot 1 \cdot (2)}}{2 \cdot 1}$$

$$= \frac{-1 \pm \sqrt{1 - 8}}{2}$$

$$= \frac{-1 \pm \sqrt{-7}}{2}$$

$$= \frac{-1 \pm i\sqrt{7}}{2}$$

The solutions to the equation are $\dfrac{-1 + i\sqrt{7}}{2}$ and $\dfrac{-1 - i\sqrt{7}}{2}$ or $\dfrac{-1}{2} + \dfrac{i\sqrt{7}}{2}$ and $\dfrac{-1}{2} - \dfrac{i\sqrt{7}}{2}$.

Example 10 **Applying the Vertex and x-Intercepts of a Parabola**

A ball is thrown upward from the top of a 40 foot high building at a speed of 80 feet per second. The ball's height above ground can be modeled by the equation $H(t) = -16t^2 + 80t + 40$.

    a. When does the ball reach the maximum height?
    b. What is the maximum height of the ball?
    c. When does the ball hit the ground?

Solution

    a. The ball reaches the maximum height at the vertex of the parabola.

$$h = -\frac{80}{2(-16)}$$

$$= \frac{80}{32}$$

$$= \frac{5}{2}$$

$$= 2.5$$

The ball reaches a maximum height after 2.5 seconds.

b. To find the maximum height, find the y-coordinate of the vertex of the parabola.

$$k = H\left(-\frac{b}{2a}\right)$$

$$= H(2.5)$$

$$= -16(2.5)^2 + 80(2.5) + 40$$

$$= 140$$

The ball reaches a maximum height of 140 feet.

c. To find when the ball hits the ground, we need to determine when the height is zero, $H(t) = 0$. We use the quadratic formula.

$$t = \frac{-80 \pm \sqrt{80^2 - 4(-16)(40)}}{2(-16)}$$

$$= \frac{-80 \pm \sqrt{8960}}{-32}$$

Because the square root does not simplify nicely, we can use a calculator to approximate the values of the solutions.

$$t = \frac{-80 - \sqrt{8960}}{-32} \approx 5.458 \text{ or } t = \frac{-80 + \sqrt{8960}}{-32} \approx -0.458$$

The second answer is outside the reasonable domain of our model, so we conclude the ball will hit the ground after about 5.458 seconds. See **Figure 16.**

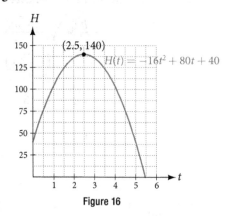

Figure 16

Try It #5

A rock is thrown upward from the top of a 112-foot high cliff overlooking the ocean at a speed of 96 feet per second. The rock's height above ocean can be modeled by the equation $H(t) = -16t^2 + 96t + 112$.

a. When does the rock reach the maximum height?

b. What is the maximum height of the rock?

c. When does the rock hit the ocean?

Access these online resources for additional instruction and practice with quadratic equations.

- Graphing Quadratic Functions in General Form (http://openstaxcollege.org/l/graphquadgen)
- Graphing Quadratic Functions in Standard Form (http://openstaxcollege.org/l/graphquadstan)
- Quadratic Function Review (http://openstaxcollege.org/l/quadfuncrev)
- Characteristics of a Quadratic Function (http://openstaxcollege.org/l/characterquad)

3.2   SECTION EXERCISES

VERBAL

1. Explain the advantage of writing a quadratic function in standard form.

3. Explain why the condition of $a \neq 0$ is imposed in the definition of the quadratic function.

5. What two algebraic methods can be used to find the horizontal intercepts of a quadratic function?

2. How can the vertex of a parabola be used in solving real world problems?

4. What is another name for the standard form of a quadratic function?

ALGEBRAIC

For the following exercises, rewrite the quadratic functions in standard form and give the vertex.

6. $f(x) = x^2 - 12x + 32$

7. $g(x) = x^2 + 2x - 3$

8. $f(x) = x^2 - x$

9. $f(x) = x^2 + 5x - 2$

10. $h(x) = 2x^2 + 8x - 10$

11. $k(x) = 3x^2 - 6x - 9$

12. $f(x) = 2x^2 - 6x$

13. $f(x) = 3x^2 - 5x - 1$

For the following exercises, determine whether there is a minimum or maximum value to each quadratic function. Find the value and the axis of symmetry.

14. $y(x) = 2x^2 + 10x + 12$

15. $f(x) = 2x^2 - 10x + 4$

16. $f(x) = -x^2 + 4x + 3$

17. $f(x) = 4x^2 + x - 1$

18. $h(t) = -4t^2 + 6t - 1$

19. $f(x) = \frac{1}{2}x^2 + 3x + 1$

20. $f(x) = -\frac{1}{3}x^2 - 2x + 3$

For the following exercises, determine the domain and range of the quadratic function.

21. $f(x) = (x - 3)^2 + 2$

22. $f(x) = -2(x + 3)^2 - 6$

23. $f(x) = x^2 + 6x + 4$

24. $f(x) = 2x^2 - 4x + 2$

25. $k(x) = 3x^2 - 6x - 9$

For the following exercises, solve the equations over the complex numbers.

26. $x^2 = -25$

27. $x^2 = -8$

28. $x^2 + 36 = 0$

29. $x^2 + 27 = 0$

30. $x^2 + 2x + 5 = 0$

31. $x^2 - 4x + 5 = 0$

32. $x^2 + 8x + 25 = 0$

33. $x^2 - 4x + 13 = 0$

34. $x^2 + 6x + 25 = 0$

35. $x^2 - 10x + 26 = 0$

36. $x^2 - 6x + 10 = 0$

37. $x(x - 4) = 20$

38. $x(x - 2) = 10$

39. $2x^2 + 2x + 5 = 0$

40. $5x^2 - 8x + 5 = 0$

41. $5x^2 + 6x + 2 = 0$

42. $2x^2 - 6x + 5 = 0$

43. $x^2 + x + 2 = 0$

44. $x^2 - 2x + 4 = 0$

For the following exercises, use the vertex (h, k) and a point on the graph (x, y) to find the general form of the equation of the quadratic function.

45. $(h, k) = (2, 0), (x, y) = (4, 4)$

46. $(h, k) = (-2, -1), (x, y) = (-4, 3)$

47. $(h, k) = (0, 1), (x, y) = (2, 5)$

48. $(h, k) = (2, 3), (x, y) = (5, 12)$

49. $(h, k) = (-5, 3), (x, y) = (2, 9)$

50. $(h, k) = (3, 2), (x, y) = (10, 1)$

51. $(h, k) = (0, 1), (x, y) = (1, 0)$

52. $(h, k) = (1, 0), (x, y) = (0, 1)$

GRAPHICAL

For the following exercises, sketch a graph of the quadratic function and give the vertex, axis of symmetry, and intercepts.

53. $f(x) = x^2 - 2x$

54. $f(x) = x^2 - 6x - 1$

55. $f(x) = x^2 - 5x - 6$

56. $f(x) = x^2 - 7x + 3$

57. $f(x) = -2x^2 + 5x - 8$

58. $f(x) = 4x^2 - 12x - 3$

For the following exercises, write the equation for the graphed function.

59.
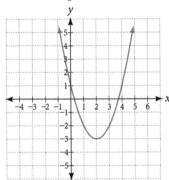

60.
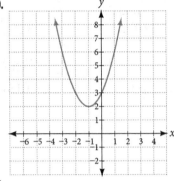

61.
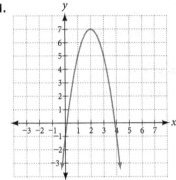

62.
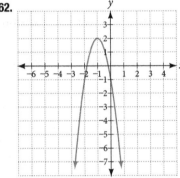

63.
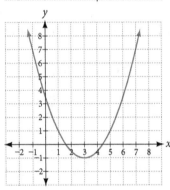

64.
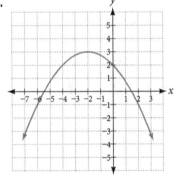

NUMERIC

For the following exercises, use the table of values that represent points on the graph of a quadratic function. By determining the vertex and axis of symmetry, find the general form of the equation of the quadratic function.

65.

x	-2	-1	0	1	2
y	5	2	1	2	5

66.

x	-2	-1	0	1	2
y	1	0	1	4	9

67.

x	-2	-1	0	1	2
y	-2	1	2	1	-2

68.

x	-2	-1	0	1	2
y	-8	-3	0	1	0

69.

x	-2	-1	0	1	2
y	8	2	0	2	8

TECHNOLOGY

For the following exercises, use a calculator to find the answer.

70. Graph on the same set of axes the functions $f(x) = x^2, f(x) = 2x^2,$ and $f(x) = \frac{1}{3}x^2$. What appears to be the effect of changing the coefficient?

71. Graph on the same set of axes $f(x) = x^2, f(x) = x^2 + 2$ and $f(x) = x^2, f(x) = x^2 + 5$ and $f(x) = x^2 - 3$. What appears to be the effect of adding a constant?

72. Graph on the same set of axes $f(x) = x^2$, $f(x) = (x - 2)^2, f(x - 3)^2,$ and $f(x) = (x + 4)^2$. What appears to be the effect of adding or subtracting those numbers?

73. The path of an object projected at a 45 degree angle with initial velocity of 80 feet per second is given by the function $h(x) = \frac{-32}{(80)^2}x^2 + x$ where x is the horizontal distance traveled and $h(x)$ is the height in feet. Use the [**TRACE**] feature of your calculator to determine the height of the object when it has traveled 100 feet away horizontally.

74. A suspension bridge can be modeled by the quadratic function $h(x) = 0.0001x^2$ with $-2000 \leq x \leq 2000$ where $|x|$ is the number of feet from the center and $h(x)$ is height in feet. Use the [**TRACE**] feature of your calculator to estimate how far from the center does the bridge have a height of 100 feet.

EXTENSIONS

For the following exercises, use the vertex of the graph of the quadratic function and the direction the graph opens to find the domain and range of the function.

75. Vertex $(1, -2)$, opens up.

76. Vertex $(-1, 2)$ opens down.

77. Vertex $(-5, 11)$, opens down.

78. Vertex $(-100, 100)$, opens up.

For the following exercises, write the equation of the quadratic function that contains the given point and has the same shape as the given function.

79. Contains $(1, 1)$ and has shape of $f(x) = 2x^2$. Vertex is on the y-axis.

80. Contains $(-1, 4)$ and has the shape of $f(x) = 2x^2$. Vertex is on the y-axis.

81. Contains $(2, 3)$ and has the shape of $f(x) = 3x^2$. Vertex is on the y-axis.

82. Contains $(1, -3)$ and has the shape of $f(x) = -x^2$. Vertex is on the y-axis.

83. Contains $(4, 3)$ and has the shape of $f(x) = 5x^2$. Vertex is on the y-axis.

84. Contains $(1, -6)$ has the shape of $f(x) = 3x^2$. Vertex has x-coordinate of -1.

REAL-WORLD APPLICATIONS

85. Find the dimensions of the rectangular corral producing the greatest enclosed area given 200 feet of fencing.

86. Find the dimensions of the rectangular corral split into 2 pens of the same size producing the greatest possible enclosed area given 300 feet of fencing.

87. Find the dimensions of the rectangular corral producing the greatest enclosed area split into 3 pens of the same size given 500 feet of fencing.

88. Among all of the pairs of numbers whose sum is 6, find the pair with the largest product. What is the product?

89. Among all of the pairs of numbers whose difference is 12, find the pair with the smallest product. What is the product?

90. Suppose that the price per unit in dollars of a cell phone production is modeled by $p = \$45 - 0.0125x$, where x is in thousands of phones produced, and the revenue represented by thousands of dollars is $R = x \cdot p$. Find the production level that will maximize revenue.

91. A rocket is launched in the air. Its height, in meters above sea level, as a function of time, in seconds, is given by $h(t) = -4.9t^2 + 229t + 234$. Find the maximum height the rocket attains.

92. A ball is thrown in the air from the top of a building. Its height, in meters above ground, as a function of time, in seconds, is given by $h(t) = -4.9t^2 + 24t + 8$. How long does it take to reach maximum height?

93. A soccer stadium holds 62,000 spectators. With a ticket price of $11, the average attendance has been 26,000. When the price dropped to $9, the average attendance rose to 31,000. Assuming that attendance is linearly related to ticket price, what ticket price would maximize revenue?

94. A farmer finds that if she plants 75 trees per acre, each tree will yield 20 bushels of fruit. She estimates that for each additional tree planted per acre, the yield of each tree will decrease by 3 bushels. How many trees should she plant per acre to maximize her harvest?

LEARNING OBJECTIVES

In this section, you will:

- Identify power functions.
- Identify end behavior of power functions.
- Identify polynomial functions.
- Identify the degree and leading coefficient of polynomial functions.

3.3   POWER FUNCTIONS AND POLYNOMIAL FUNCTIONS

Figure 1 (credit: Jason Bay, Flickr)

Suppose a certain species of bird thrives on a small island. Its population over the last few years is shown in **Table 1**.

Year	2009	2010	2011	2012	2013
Bird Population	800	897	992	1,083	1,169

Table 1

The population can be estimated using the function $P(t) = -0.3t^3 + 97t + 800$, where $P(t)$ represents the bird population on the island t years after 2009. We can use this model to estimate the maximum bird population and when it will occur. We can also use this model to predict when the bird population will disappear from the island. In this section, we will examine functions that we can use to estimate and predict these types of changes.

Identifying Power Functions

In order to better understand the bird problem, we need to understand a specific type of function. A **power function** is a function with a single term that is the product of a real number, a **coefficient**, and a variable raised to a fixed real number. (A number that multiplies a variable raised to an exponent is known as a coefficient.)

As an example, consider functions for area or volume. The function for the area of a circle with radius r is

$$A(r) = \pi r^2$$

and the function for the volume of a sphere with radius r is

$$V(r) = \frac{4}{3}\pi r^3$$

Both of these are examples of power functions because they consist of a coefficient, π or $\frac{4}{3}\pi$, multiplied by a variable r raised to a power.

> **power function**
> A **power function** is a function that can be represented in the form
> $$f(x) = kx^p$$
> where k and p are real numbers, and k is known as the **coefficient**.

Is $f(x) = 2^x$ a power function?

No. A power function contains a variable base raised to a fixed power. This function has a constant base raised to a variable power. This is called an exponential function, not a power function.

Example 1   **Identifying Power Functions**

Which of the following functions are power functions?

$f(x) = 1$	Constant function
$f(x) = x$	Identify function
$f(x) = x^2$	Quadratic function
$f(x) = x^3$	Cubic function
$f(x) = \dfrac{1}{x}$	Reciprocal function
$f(x) = \dfrac{1}{x^2}$	Reciprocal squared function
$f(x) = \sqrt{x}$	Square root function
$f(x) = \sqrt[3]{x}$	Cube root function

Solution   All of the listed functions are power functions.

The constant and identity functions are power functions because they can be written as $f(x) = x^0$ and $f(x) = x^1$ respectively.

The quadratic and cubic functions are power functions with whole number powers $f(x) = x^2$ and $f(x) = x^3$.

The reciprocal and reciprocal squared functions are power functions with negative whole number powers because they can be written as $f(x) = x^{-1}$ and $f(x) = x^{-2}$.

The square and cube root functions are power functions with fractional powers because they can be written as $f(x) = x^{1/2}$ or $f(x) = x^{1/3}$.

Try It #1

Which functions are power functions?

$$f(x) = 2x^2 \cdot 4x^3 \qquad g(x) = -x^5 + 5x^3 - 4x \qquad h(x) = \frac{2x^5 - 1}{3x^2 + 4}$$

Identifying End Behavior of Power Functions

Figure 2 shows the graphs of $f(x) = x^2$, $g(x) = x^4$ and $h(x) = x^6$, which are all power functions with even, whole-number powers. Notice that these graphs have similar shapes, very much like that of the quadratic function in the toolkit. However, as the power increases, the graphs flatten somewhat near the origin and become steeper away from the origin.

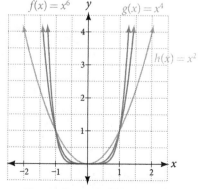

Figure 2 Even-power functions

To describe the behavior as numbers become larger and larger, we use the idea of infinity. We use the symbol ∞ for positive infinity and $-\infty$ for negative infinity. When we say that "x approaches infinity," which can be symbolically written as $x \to \infty$, we are describing a behavior; we are saying that x is increasing without bound.

With the even-power function, as the input increases or decreases without bound, the output values become very large, positive numbers. Equivalently, we could describe this behavior by saying that as x approaches positive or negative infinity, the $f(x)$ values increase without bound. In symbolic form, we could write

$$\text{as } x \to \pm\infty, \quad f(x) \to \infty$$

Figure 3 shows the graphs of $f(x) = x^3$, $g(x) = x^5$, and $h(x) = x^7$, which are all power functions with odd, whole-number powers. Notice that these graphs look similar to the cubic function in the toolkit. Again, as the power increases, the graphs flatten near the origin and become steeper away from the origin.

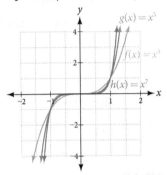

Figure 3 Odd-power functions

These examples illustrate that functions of the form $f(x) = x^n$ reveal symmetry of one kind or another. First, in **Figure 2** we see that even functions of the form $f(x) = x^n$, n even, are symmetric about the y-axis. In **Figure 3** we see that odd functions of the form $f(x) = x^n$, n odd, are symmetric about the origin.

For these odd power functions, as x approaches negative infinity, $f(x)$ decreases without bound. As x approaches positive infinity, $f(x)$ increases without bound. In symbolic form we write

$$\text{as } x \to -\infty, \quad f(x) \to -\infty \qquad \text{as } x \to \infty, \quad f(x) \to \infty$$

The behavior of the graph of a function as the input values get very small ($x \to -\infty$) and get very large ($x \to \infty$) is referred to as the **end behavior** of the function. We can use words or symbols to describe end behavior.

Figure 4 shows the end behavior of power functions in the form $f(x) = kx^n$ where n is a non-negative integer depending on the power and the constant.

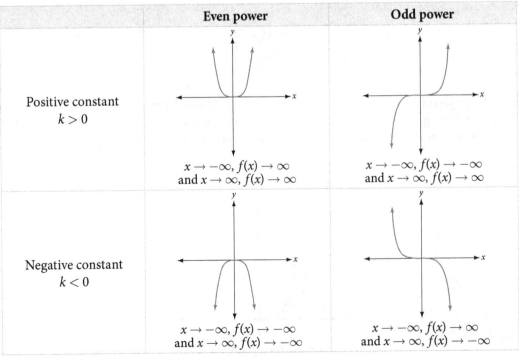

Figure 4

How To...

Given a power function $f(x) = kx^n$ where n is a non-negative integer, identify the end behavior.

1. Determine whether the power is even or odd.
2. Determine whether the constant is positive or negative.
3. Use **Figure 4** to identify the end behavior.

Example 2   **Identifying the End Behavior of a Power Function**

Describe the end behavior of the graph of $f(x) = x^8$.

Solution   The coefficient is 1 (positive) and the exponent of the power function is 8 (an even number). As x approaches infinity, the output (value of $f(x)$) increases without bound. We write as $x \to \infty$, $f(x) \to \infty$. As x approaches negative infinity, the output increases without bound. In symbolic form, as $x \to -\infty$, $f(x) \to \infty$. We can graphically represent the function as shown in **Figure 5**.

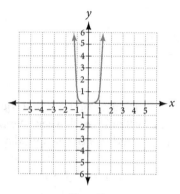

Figure 5

Example 3   **Identifying the End Behavior of a Power Function**

Describe the end behavior of the graph of $f(x) = -x^9$.

Solution   The exponent of the power function is 9 (an odd number). Because the coefficient is -1 (negative), the graph is the reflection about the x-axis of the graph of $f(x) = x^9$. **Figure 6** shows that as x approaches infinity, the output decreases without bound. As x approaches negative infinity, the output increases without bound. In symbolic form, we would write

$$\text{as } x \to -\infty, \quad f(x) \to \infty$$
$$\text{as } x \to \infty, \quad f(x) \to -\infty$$

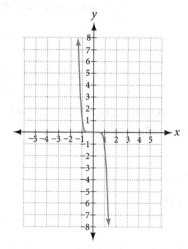

Figure 6

Analysis   We can check our work by using the table feature on a graphing utility.

x	$f(x)$
-10	1,000,000,000
-5	1,953,125
0	0
5	$-1,953,125$
10	$-1,000,000,000$

Table 2

We can see from **Table 2** that, when we substitute very small values for x, the output is very large, and when we substitute very large values for x, the output is very small (meaning that it is a very large negative value).

Try It #2

Describe in words and symbols the end behavior of $f(x) = -5x^4$.

Identifying Polynomial Functions

An oil pipeline bursts in the Gulf of Mexico, causing an oil slick in a roughly circular shape. The slick is currently 24 miles in radius, but that radius is increasing by 8 miles each week. We want to write a formula for the area covered by the oil slick by combining two functions. The radius r of the spill depends on the number of weeks w that have passed. This relationship is linear.

$$r(w) = 24 + 8w$$

We can combine this with the formula for the area A of a circle.

$$A(r) = \pi r^2$$

Composing these functions gives a formula for the area in terms of weeks.

$$A(w) = A(r(w))$$
$$= A(24 + 8w)$$
$$= \pi(24 + 8w)^2$$

Multiplying gives the formula.

$$A(w) = 576\pi + 384\pi w + 64\pi w^2$$

This formula is an example of a **polynomial function**. A polynomial function consists of either zero or the sum of a finite number of non-zero terms, each of which is a product of a number, called the coefficient of the term, and a variable raised to a non-negative integer power.

---

polynomial functions

Let n be a non-negative integer. A **polynomial function** is a function that can be written in the form
$$f(x) = a_n x^n + \ldots + a_2 x^2 + a_1 x + a_0$$

This is called the general form of a polynomial function. Each a_i is a coefficient and can be any real number, but a_n cannot $= 0$. Each product $a_i x^i$ is a **term of a polynomial function**.

Example 4   **Identifying Polynomial Functions**

Which of the following are polynomial functions?

$$f(x) = 2x^3 \cdot 3x + 4 \qquad g(x) = -x(x^2 - 4) \qquad h(x) = 5\sqrt{x} + 2$$

Solution   The first two functions are examples of polynomial functions because they can be written in the form $f(x) = a_n x^n + \ldots + a_2 x^2 + a_1 x + a_0$, where the powers are non-negative integers and the coefficients are real numbers.

- $f(x)$ can be written as $f(x) = 6x^4 + 4$.
- $g(x)$ can be written as $g(x) = -x^3 + 4x$.
- $h(x)$ cannot be written in this form and is therefore not a polynomial function.

Identifying the Degree and Leading Coefficient of a Polynomial Function

Because of the form of a polynomial function, we can see an infinite variety in the number of terms and the power of the variable. Although the order of the terms in the polynomial function is not important for performing operations, we typically arrange the terms in descending order of power, or in general form. The **degree** of the polynomial is the highest power of the variable that occurs in the polynomial; it is the power of the first variable if the function is in general form. The **leading term** is the term containing the highest power of the variable, or the term with the highest degree. The **leading coefficient** is the coefficient of the leading term.

---

terminology of polynomial functions

We often rearrange polynomials so that the powers are descending.

Leading coefficient   Degree

$$f(x) = a_n x^n + \ldots + a_2 x^2 + a_1 x + a_0$$

Leading term

When a polynomial is written in this way, we say that it is in general form.

How To...

Given a polynomial function, identify the degree and leading coefficient.

1. Find the highest power of x to determine the degree function.
2. Identify the term containing the highest power of x to find the leading term.
3. Identify the coefficient of the leading term.

Example 5   **Identifying the Degree and Leading Coefficient of a Polynomial Function**

Identify the degree, leading term, and leading coefficient of the following polynomial functions.

$$f(x) = 3 + 2x^2 - 4x^3$$
$$g(t) = 5t^5 - 2t^3 + 7t$$
$$h(p) = 6p - p^3 - 2$$

Solution   For the function $f(x)$, the highest power of x is 3, so the degree is 3. The leading term is the term containing that degree, $-4x^3$. The leading coefficient is the coefficient of that term, -4.

For the function $g(t)$, the highest power of t is 5, so the degree is 5. The leading term is the term containing that degree, $5t^5$. The leading coefficient is the coefficient of that term, 5.

For the function $h(p)$, the highest power of p is 3, so the degree is 3. The leading term is the term containing that degree, $-p^3$; the leading coefficient is the coefficient of that term, -1.

Try It #3

Identify the degree, leading term, and leading coefficient of the polynomial $f(x) = 4x^2 - x^6 + 2x - 6$.

Identifying End Behavior of Polynomial Functions

Knowing the degree of a polynomial function is useful in helping us predict its end behavior. To determine its end behavior, look at the leading term of the polynomial function. Because the power of the leading term is the highest, that term will grow significantly faster than the other terms as x gets very large or very small, so its behavior will dominate the graph. For any polynomial, the end behavior of the polynomial will match the end behavior of the term of highest degree. See **Table 3**.

Polynomial Function	Leading Term	Graph of Polynomial Function
$f(x) = 5x^4 + 2x^3 - x - 4$	$5x^4$	
$f(x) = -2x^6 - x^5 + 3x^4 + x^3$	$-2x^6$	
$f(x) = 3x^5 - 4x^4 + 2x^2 + 1$	$3x^5$	
$f(x) = -6x^3 + 7x^2 + 3x + 1$	$-6x^3$	

Table 3

Example 6   Identifying End Behavior and Degree of a Polynomial Function

Example 6   **Identifying End Behavior and Degree of a Polynomial Function**

Describe the end behavior and determine a possible degree of the polynomial function in **Figure 7**.

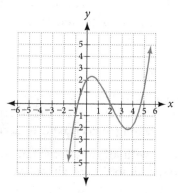

Figure 7

Solution   As the input values x get very large, the output values $f(x)$ increase without bound. As the input values x get very small, the output values $f(x)$ decrease without bound. We can describe the end behavior symbolically by writing

$$\text{as } x \to -\infty, \quad f(x) \to -\infty$$
$$\text{as } x \to \infty, \qquad f(x) \to \infty$$

In words, we could say that as x values approach infinity, the function values approach infinity, and as x values approach negative infinity, the function values approach negative infinity.

We can tell this graph has the shape of an odd degree power function that has not been reflected, so the degree of the polynomial creating this graph must be odd and the leading coefficient must be positive.

Try It #4

Describe the end behavior, and determine a possible degree of the polynomial function in **Figure 8**.

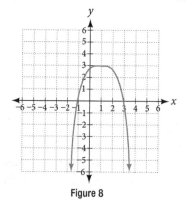

Figure 8

Example 7   **Identifying End Behavior and Degree of a Polynomial Function**

Given the function $f(x) = -3x^2(x - 1)(x + 4)$, express the function as a polynomial in general form, and determine the leading term, degree, and end behavior of the function.

Solution   Obtain the general form by expanding the given expression for $f(x)$.

$$f(x) = -3x^2(x - 1)(x + 4)$$
$$= -3x^2(x^2 + 3x - 4)$$
$$= -3x^4 - 9x^3 + 12x^2$$

The general form is $f(x) = -3x^4 - 9x^3 + 12x^2$. The leading term is $-3x^4$; therefore, the degree of the polynomial is 4. The degree is even (4) and the leading coefficient is negative (-3), so the end behavior is

$$\text{as } x \to -\infty, \quad f(x) \to -\infty$$
$$\text{as } x \to \infty, \qquad f(x) \to -\infty$$

Try It #5

Given the function $f(x) = 0.2(x - 2)(x + 1)(x - 5)$, express the function as a polynomial in general form and determine the leading term, degree, and end behavior of the function.

Identifying Local Behavior of Polynomial Functions

In addition to the end behavior of polynomial functions, we are also interested in what happens in the "middle" of the function. In particular, we are interested in locations where graph behavior changes. A **turning point** is a point at which the function values change from increasing to decreasing or decreasing to increasing.

We are also interested in the intercepts. As with all functions, the y-intercept is the point at which the graph intersects the vertical axis. The point corresponds to the coordinate pair in which the input value is zero. Because a polynomial is a function, only one output value corresponds to each input value so there can be only one y-intercept $(0, a_0)$. The x-intercepts occur at the input values that correspond to an output value of zero. It is possible to have more than one x-intercept. See **Figure 9**.

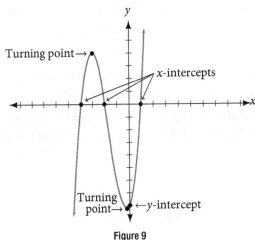

Figure 9

---

intercepts and turning points of polynomial functions

A **turning point** of a graph is a point at which the graph changes direction from increasing to decreasing or decreasing to increasing. The y-intercept is the point at which the function has an input value of zero. The x-intercepts are the points at which the output value is zero.

How To...

Given a polynomial function, determine the intercepts.

1. Determine the y-intercept by setting $x = 0$ and finding the corresponding output value.

2. Determine the x-intercepts by solving for the input values that yield an output value of zero.

Example 8   **Determining the Intercepts of a Polynomial Function**

Given the polynomial function $f(x) = (x - 2)(x + 1)(x - 4)$, written in factored form for your convenience, determine the y- and x-intercepts.

Solution   The y-intercept occurs when the input is zero so substitute 0 for x.

$$f(0) = (0 - 2)(0 + 1)(0 - 4)$$
$$= (-2)(1)(-4)$$
$$= 8$$

The y-intercept is $(0, 8)$.

The x-intercepts occur when the output is zero.

$$0 = (x - 2)(x + 1)(x - 4)$$
$$x - 2 = 0 \quad \text{or} \quad x + 1 = 0 \quad \text{or} \quad x - 4 = 0$$
$$x = 2 \quad \text{or} \quad x = -1 \quad \text{or} \quad x = 4$$

The x-intercepts are $(2, 0)$, $(-1, 0)$, and $(4, 0)$.

We can see these intercepts on the graph of the function shown in **Figure 10**.

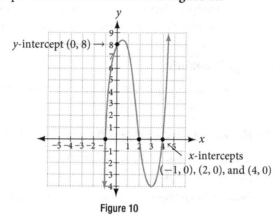

Figure 10

Example 9   Determining the Intercepts of a Polynomial Function with Factoring

Given the polynomial function $f(x) = x^4 - 4x^2 - 45$, determine the y- and x-intercepts.

Solution   The y-intercept occurs when the input is zero.

$$f(0) = (0)^4 - 4(0)^2 - 45$$
$$= -45$$

The y-intercept is $(0, -45)$.

The x-intercepts occur when the output is zero. To determine when the output is zero, we will need to factor the polynomial.

$$f(x) = x^4 - 4x^2 - 45$$
$$= (x^2 - 9)(x^2 + 5)$$
$$= (x - 3)(x + 3)(x^2 + 5)$$
$$0 = (x - 3)(x + 3)(x^2 + 5)$$
$$x - 3 = 0 \quad \text{or} \quad x + 3 = 0 \quad \text{or} \quad x^2 + 5 = 0$$
$$x = 3 \quad \text{or} \quad x = -3 \text{ or} \quad \text{(no real solution)}$$

The x-intercepts are $(3, 0)$ and $(-3, 0)$.

We can see these intercepts on the graph of the function shown in **Figure 11**. We can see that the function is even because $f(x) = f(-x)$.

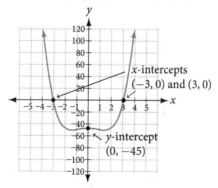

Figure 11

Try It #6

Given the polynomial function $f(x) = 2x^3 - 6x^2 - 20x$, determine the y- and x-intercepts.

Comparing Smooth and Continuous Graphs

The degree of a polynomial function helps us to determine the number of x-intercepts and the number of turning points. A polynomial function of nth degree is the product of n factors, so it will have at most n roots or zeros, or x-intercepts. The graph of the polynomial function of degree n must have at most $n - 1$ turning points. This means the graph has at most one fewer turning point than the degree of the polynomial or one fewer than the number of factors.

A **continuous function** has no breaks in its graph: the graph can be drawn without lifting the pen from the paper. A **smooth curve** is a graph that has no sharp corners. The turning points of a smooth graph must always occur at rounded curves. The graphs of polynomial functions are both continuous and smooth.

> ### intercepts and turning points of polynomials
>
> A polynomial of degree n will have, at most, n x-intercepts and $n - 1$ turning points.

Example 10   Determining the Number of Intercepts and Turning Points of a Polynomial

Without graphing the function, determine the local behavior of the function by finding the maximum number of x-intercepts and turning points for $f(x) = -3x^{10} + 4x^7 - x^4 + 2x^3$.

Solution   The polynomial has a degree of 10, so there are at most 10 x-intercepts and at most $10 - 1 = 9$ turning points.

Try It #7

Without graphing the function, determine the maximum number of x-intercepts and turning points for $f(x) = 108 - 13x^9 - 8x^4 + 14x^{12} + 2x^3$

Example 11   Drawing Conclusions about a Polynomial Function from the Graph

What can we conclude about the polynomial represented by the graph shown in **Figure 12** based on its intercepts and turning points?

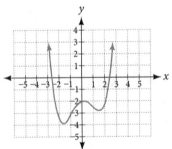

Figure 12

Solution   The end behavior of the graph tells us this is the graph of an even-degree polynomial. See **Figure 13**.

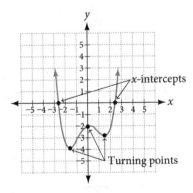

Figure 13

The graph has 2 x-intercepts, suggesting a degree of 2 or greater, and 3 turning points, suggesting a degree of 4 or greater. Based on this, it would be reasonable to conclude that the degree is even and at least 4.

Try It #8

What can we conclude about the polynomial represented by the graph shown in **Figure 14** based on its intercepts and turning points?

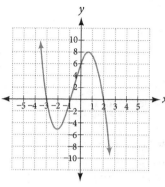

Figure 14

Example 12 **Drawing Conclusions about a Polynomial Function from the Factors**

Given the function $f(x) = -4x(x + 3)(x - 4)$, determine the local behavior.

Solution The *y*-intercept is found by evaluating $f(0)$.

$$f(0) = -4(0)(0 + 3)(0 - 4)$$
$$= 0$$

The *y*-intercept is $(0, 0)$.

The *x*-intercepts are found by determining the zeros of the function.

$$0 = -4x(x + 3)(x - 4)$$
$$x = 0 \quad \text{or} \quad x + 3 = 0 \quad \text{or } x - 4 = 0$$
$$x = 0 \quad \text{or} \quad x = -3 \quad \text{or} \quad x = 4$$

The *x*-intercepts are $(0, 0)$, $(-3, 0)$, and $(4, 0)$.

The degree is 3 so the graph has at most 2 turning points.

Try It #9

Given the function $f(x) = 0.2(x - 2)(x + 1)(x - 5)$, determine the local behavior.

Access these online resources for additional instruction and practice with power and polynomial functions.

- Find Key Information about a Given Polynomial Function (http://openstaxcollege.org/l/keyinfopoly)
- End Behavior of a Polynomial Function (http://openstaxcollege.org/l/endbehavior)
- Turning Points and *x*-Intercepts of Polynomial Functions (http://openstaxcollege.org/l/turningpoints)
- Least Possible Degree of a Polynomial Function (http://openstaxcollege.org/l/leastposdegree)

3.3   SECTION EXERCISES

VERBAL

1. Explain the difference between the coefficient of a power function and its degree.

2. If a polynomial function is in factored form, what would be a good first step in order to determine the degree of the function?

3. In general, explain the end behavior of a power function with odd degree if the leading coefficient is positive.

4. What is the relationship between the degree of a polynomial function and the maximum number of turning points in its graph?

5. What can we conclude if, in general, the graph of a polynomial function exhibits the following end behavior? As $x \to -\infty$, $f(x) \to -\infty$ and as $x \to \infty$, $f(x) \to -\infty$.

ALGEBRAIC

For the following exercises, identify the function as a power function, a polynomial function, or neither.

6. $f(x) = x^5$

7. $f(x) = (x^2)^3$

8. $f(x) = x - x^4$

9. $f(x) = \dfrac{x^2}{x^2 - 1}$

10. $f(x) = 2x(x + 2)(x - 1)^2$

11. $f(x) = 3^{x+1}$

For the following exercises, find the degree and leading coefficient for the given polynomial.

12. $-3x$

13. $7 - 2x^2$

14. $-2x^2 - 3x^5 + x - 6$

15. $x(4 - x^2)(2x + 1)$

16. $x^2(2x - 3)^2$

For the following exercises, determine the end behavior of the functions.

17. $f(x) = x^4$

18. $f(x) = x^3$

19. $f(x) = -x^4$

20. $f(x) = -x^9$

21. $f(x) = -2x^4 - 3x^2 + x - 1$

22. $f(x) = 3x^2 + x - 2$

23. $f(x) = x^2(2x^3 - x + 1)$

24. $f(x) = (2 - x)^7$

For the following exercises, find the intercepts of the functions.

25. $f(t) = 2(t - 1)(t + 2)(t - 3)$

26. $g(n) = -2(3n - 1)(2n + 1)$

27. $f(x) = x^4 - 16$

28. $f(x) = x^3 + 27$

29. $f(x) = x(x^2 - 2x - 8)$

30. $f(x) = (x + 3)(4x^2 - 1)$

GRAPHICAL

For the following exercises, determine the least possible degree of the polynomial function shown.

31.

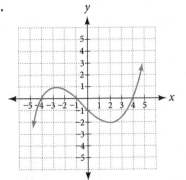

32.

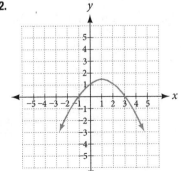

33.

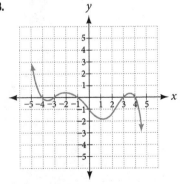

34.

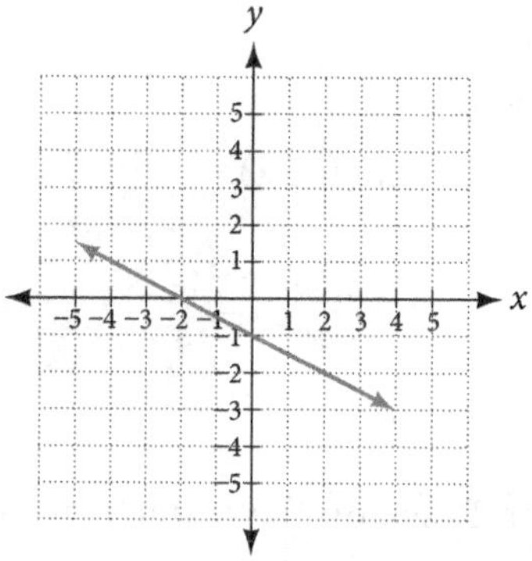

35.

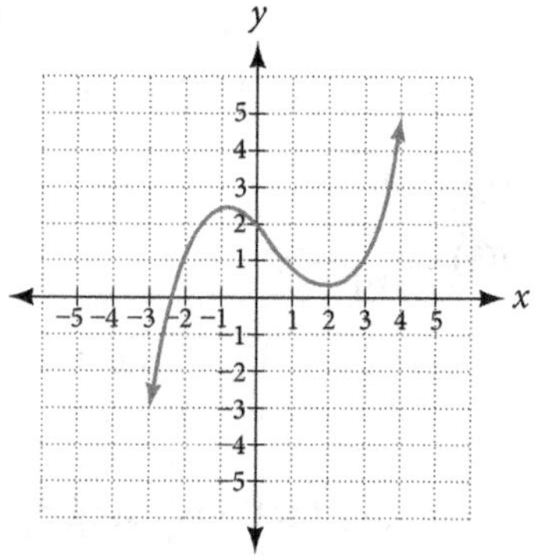

36.

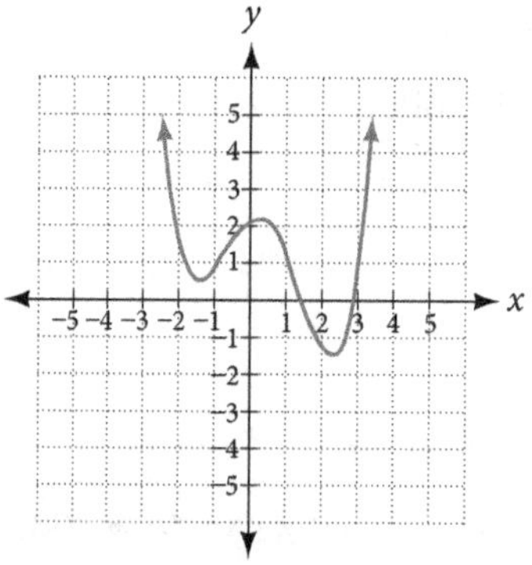

37.

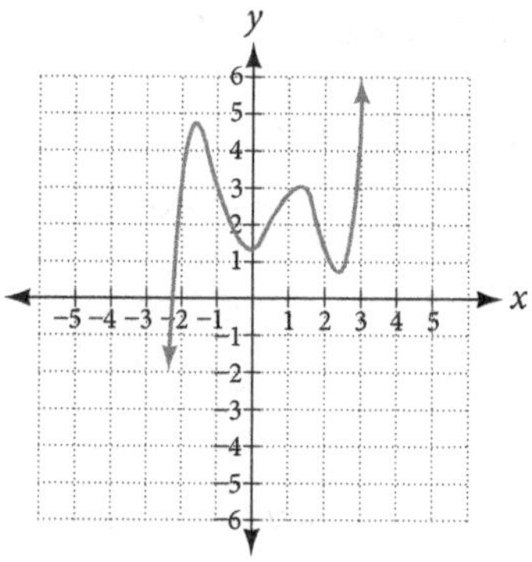

38.

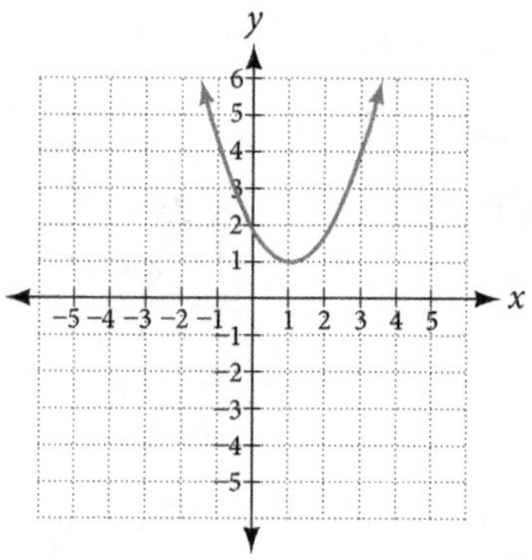

For the following exercises, determine whether the graph of the function provided is a graph of a polynomial function. If so, determine the number of turning points and the least possible degree for the function.

39.

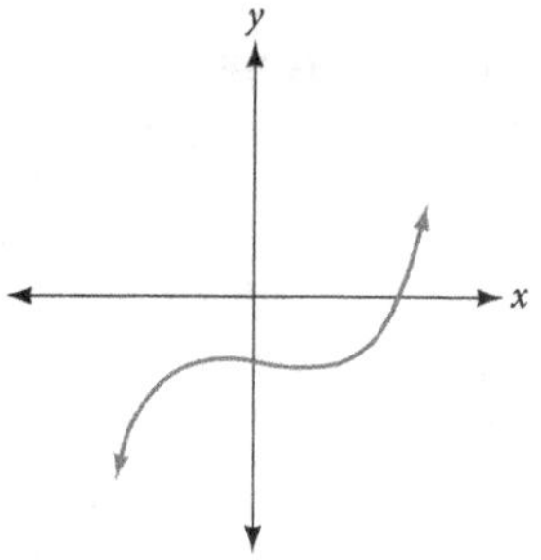

40.

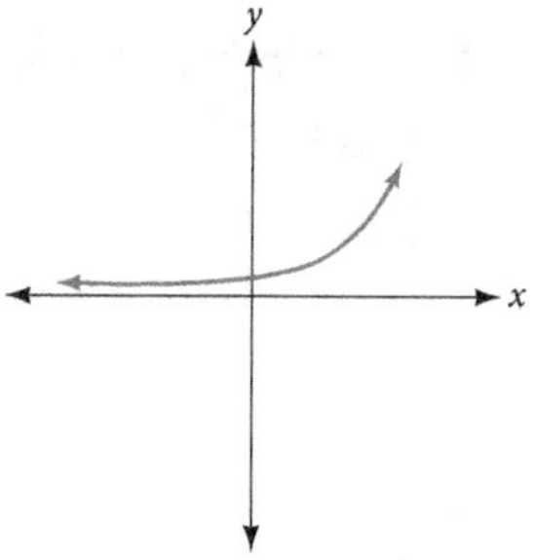

41.

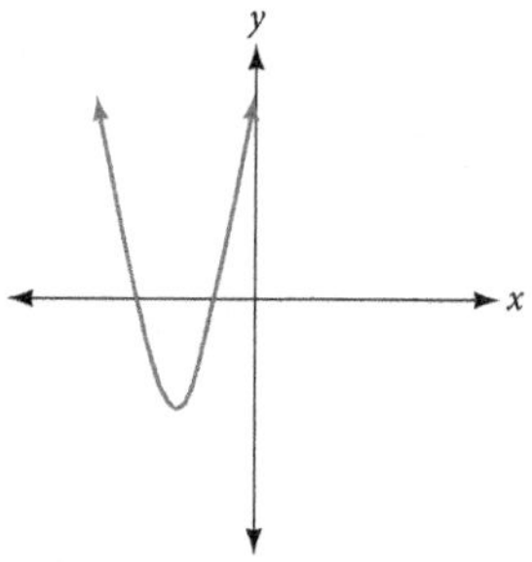

42.

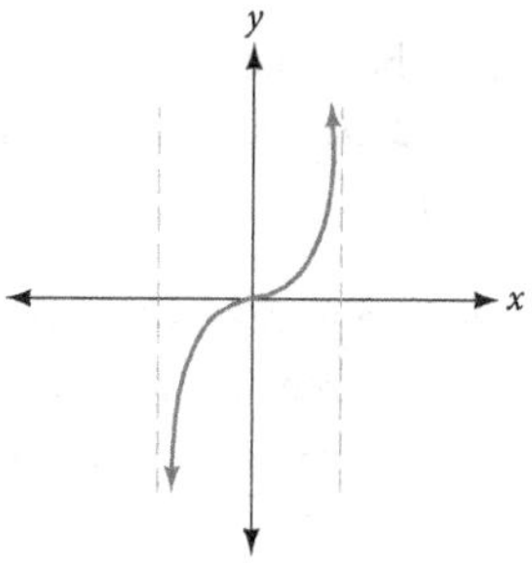

43.

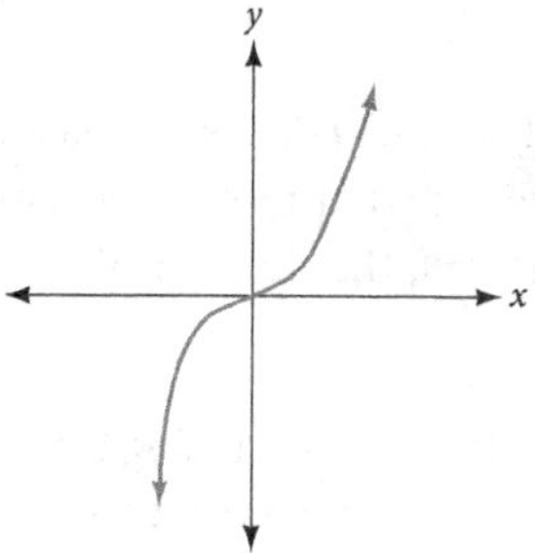

44.

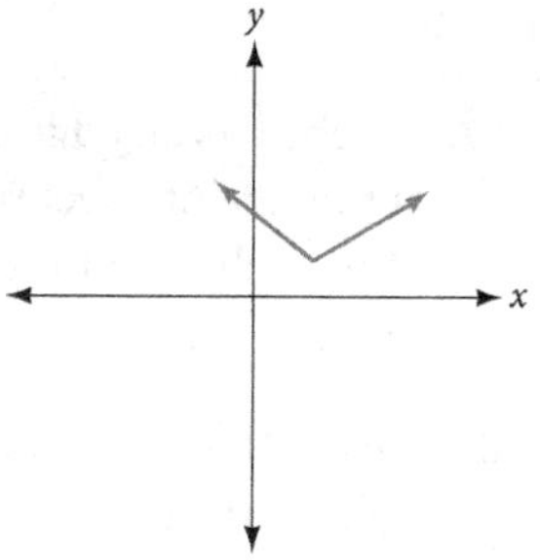

45.

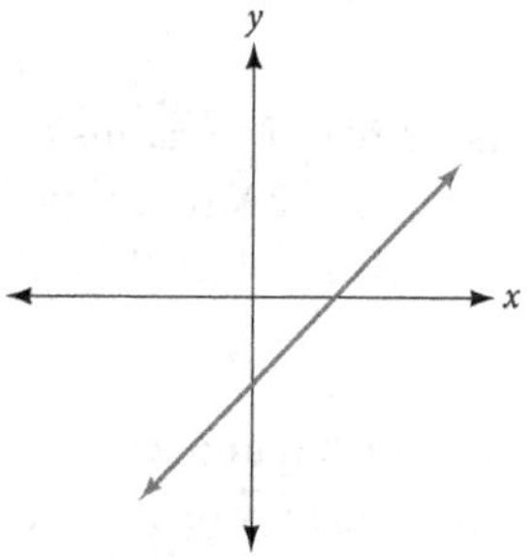

NUMERIC

For the following exercises, make a table to confirm the end behavior of the function.

46. $f(x) = -x^3$

47. $f(x) = x^4 - 5x^2$

48. $f(x) = x^2(1 - x)^2$

49. $f(x) = (x - 1)(x - 2)(3 - x)$

50. $f(x) = \dfrac{x^5}{10} - x^4$

TECHNOLOGY

For the following exercises, graph the polynomial functions using a calculator. Based on the graph, determine the intercepts and the end behavior.

51. $f(x) = x^3(x - 2)$

52. $f(x) = x(x - 3)(x + 3)$

53. $f(x) = x(14 - 2x)(10 - 2x)$

54. $f(x) = x(14 - 2x)(10 - 2x)^2$

55. $f(x) = x^3 - 16x$

56. $f(x) = x^3 - 27$

57. $f(x) = x^4 - 81$

58. $f(x) = -x^3 + x^2 + 2x$

59. $f(x) = x^3 - 2x^2 - 15x$

60. $f(x) = x^3 - 0.01x$

EXTENSIONS

For the following exercises, use the information about the graph of a polynomial function to determine the function. Assume the leading coefficient is 1 or −1. There may be more than one correct answer.

61. The y-intercept is $(0, -4)$. The x-intercepts are $(-2, 0)$, $(2, 0)$. Degree is 2. End behavior: as $x \to -\infty$, $f(x) \to \infty$, as $x \to \infty, f(x) \to \infty$.

62. The y-intercept is $(0, 9)$. The x-intercepts are $(-3, 0)$, $(3, 0)$. Degree is 2. End behavior: as $x \to -\infty$, $f(x) \to -\infty$, as $x \to \infty, f(x) \to -\infty$.

63. The y-intercept is $(0, 0)$. The x-intercepts are $(0, 0)$, $(2, 0)$. Degree is 3. End behavior: as $x \to -\infty$, $f(x) \to -\infty$, as $x \to \infty, f(x) \to \infty$.

64. The y-intercept is $(0, 1)$. The x-intercept is $(1, 0)$. Degree is 3. End behavior: as $x \to -\infty, f(x) \to \infty$, as $x \to \infty, f(x) \to -\infty$.

65. The y-intercept is $(0, 1)$. There is no x-intercept. Degree is 4. End behavior: as $x \to -\infty, f(x) \to \infty$, as $x \to \infty, f(x) \to \infty$.

REAL-WORLD APPLICATIONS

For the following exercises, use the written statements to construct a polynomial function that represents the required information.

66. An oil slick is expanding as a circle. The radius of the circle is increasing at the rate of 20 meters per day. Express the area of the circle as a function of d, the number of days elapsed.

67. A cube has an edge of 3 feet. The edge is increasing at the rate of 2 feet per minute. Express the volume of the cube as a function of m, the number of minutes elapsed.

68. A rectangle has a length of 10 inches and a width of 6 inches. If the length is increased by x inches and the width increased by twice that amount, express the area of the rectangle as a function of x.

69. An open box is to be constructed by cutting out square corners of x-inch sides from a piece of cardboard 8 inches by 8 inches and then folding up the sides. Express the volume of the box as a function of x.

70. A rectangle is twice as long as it is wide. Squares of side 2 feet are cut out from each corner. Then the sides are folded up to make an open box. Express the volume of the box as a function of the width (x).

LEARNING OBJECTIVES

In this section, you will:

- Recognize characteristics of graphs of polynomial functions.
- Use factoring to find zeros of polynomial functions.
- Identify zeros and their multiplicities.
- Determine end behavior.
- Understand the relationship between degree and turning points.
- Graph polynomial functions.
- Use the Intermediate Value Theorem.

3.4 GRAPHS OF POLYNOMIAL FUNCTIONS

The revenue in millions of dollars for a fictional cable company from 2006 through 2013 is shown in **Table 1**.

Year	2006	2007	2008	2009	2010	2011	2012	2013
Revenues	52.4	52.8	51.2	49.5	48.6	48.6	48.7	47.1

Table 1

The revenue can be modeled by the polynomial function

$$R(t) = -0.037t^4 + 1.414t^3 - 19.777t^2 + 118.696t - 205.332$$

where R represents the revenue in millions of dollars and t represents the year, with $t = 6$ corresponding to 2006. Over which intervals is the revenue for the company increasing? Over which intervals is the revenue for the company decreasing? These questions, along with many others, can be answered by examining the graph of the polynomial function. We have already explored the local behavior of quadratics, a special case of polynomials. In this section we will explore the local behavior of polynomials in general.

Recognizing Characteristics of Graphs of Polynomial Functions

Polynomial functions of degree 2 or more have graphs that do not have sharp corners; recall that these types of graphs are called smooth curves. Polynomial functions also display graphs that have no breaks. Curves with no breaks are called continuous. **Figure 1** shows a graph that represents a polynomial function and a graph that represents a function that is not a polynomial.

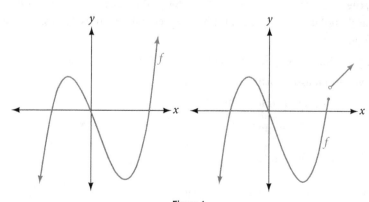

Figure 1

Example 1   **Recognizing Polynomial Functions**

Which of the graphs in **Figure 2** represents a polynomial function?

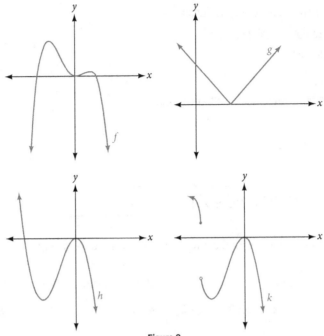

Figure 2

Solution   The graphs of f and h are graphs of polynomial functions. They are smooth and continuous.

The graphs of g and k are graphs of functions that are not polynomials. The graph of function g has a sharp corner. The graph of function k is not continuous.

Q & A...

Do all polynomial functions have as their domain all real numbers?

Yes. Any real number is a valid input for a polynomial function.

Using Factoring to Find Zeros of Polynomial Functions

Recall that if f is a polynomial function, the values of x for which $f(x) = 0$ are called zeros of f. If the equation of the polynomial function can be factored, we can set each factor equal to zero and solve for the zeros.

We can use this method to find x-intercepts because at the x-intercepts we find the input values when the output value is zero. For general polynomials, this can be a challenging prospect. While quadratics can be solved using the relatively simple quadratic formula, the corresponding formulas for cubic and fourth-degree polynomials are not simple enough to remember, and formulas do not exist for general higher-degree polynomials. Consequently, we will limit ourselves to three cases in this section:

1. The polynomial can be factored using known methods: greatest common factor and trinomial factoring.
2. The polynomial is given in factored form.
3. Technology is used to determine the intercepts.

How To...

Given a polynomial function f, find the x-intercepts by factoring.

1. Set $f(x) = 0$.
2. If the polynomial function is not given in factored form:
   a. Factor out any common monomial factors.
   b. Factor any factorable binomials or trinomials.
3. Set each factor equal to zero and solve to find the x-intercepts.

Example 2   **Finding the x-Intercepts of a Polynomial Function by Factoring**

Find the x-intercepts of $f(x) = x^6 - 3x^4 + 2x^2$.

Solution   We can attempt to factor this polynomial to find solutions for $f(x) = 0$.

$$x^6 - 3x^4 + 2x^2 = 0 \qquad \text{Factor out the greatest common factor.}$$
$$x^2(x^4 - 3x^2 + 2) = 0 \qquad \text{Factor the trinomial.}$$
$$x^2(x^2 - 1)(x^2 - 2) = 0 \qquad \text{Set each factor equal to zero.}$$
$$(x^2 - 1) = 0 \qquad (x^2 - 2) = 0$$
$$x^2 = 0 \quad \text{or} \quad x^2 = 1 \quad \text{or} \quad x^2 = 2$$
$$x = 0 \qquad x = \pm 1 \qquad x = \pm\sqrt{2}$$

This gives us five x-intercepts: $(0, 0)$, $(1, 0)$, $(-1, 0)$, $(\sqrt{2}, 0)$, and $(-\sqrt{2}, 0)$. See **Figure 3**. We can see that this is an even function.

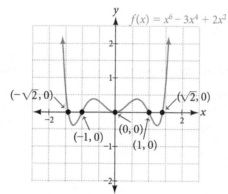

Figure 3

Example 3   **Finding the x-Intercepts of a Polynomial Function by Factoring**

Find the x-intercepts of $f(x) = x^3 - 5x^2 - x + 5$.

Solution   Find solutions for $f(x) = 0$ by factoring.

$$x^3 - 5x^2 - x + 5 = 0 \qquad \text{Factor by grouping.}$$
$$x^2(x - 5) - (x - 5) = 0 \qquad \text{Factor out the common factor.}$$
$$(x^2 - 1)(x - 5) = 0 \qquad \text{Factor the difference of squares.}$$
$$(x + 1)(x - 1)(x - 5) = 0 \qquad \text{Set each factor equal to zero.}$$
$$x + 1 = 0 \quad \text{or} \quad x - 1 = 0 \quad \text{or} \quad x - 5 = 0$$
$$x = -1 \qquad x = 1 \qquad x = 5$$

There are three x-intercepts: $(-1, 0)$, $(1, 0)$, and $(5, 0)$. See **Figure 4**.

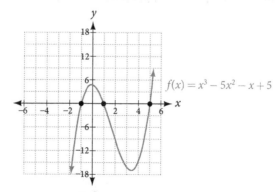

Figure 4

Example 4   **Finding the *y*- and *x*-Intercepts of a Polynomial in Factored Form**

Find the *y*- and *x*-intercepts of $g(x) = (x - 2)^2(2x + 3)$.

Solution   The *y*-intercept can be found by evaluating $g(0)$.

$$g(0) = (0 - 2)^2(2(0) + 3)$$
$$= 12$$

So the *y*-intercept is (0, 12).

The *x*-intercepts can be found by solving $g(x) = 0$.

$$(x - 2)^2(2x + 3) = 0$$

$$(x - 2)^2 = 0 \qquad (2x + 3) = 0$$
$$x - 2 = 0 \quad \text{or} \quad x = -\frac{3}{2}$$
$$x = 2$$

So the *x*-intercepts are (2, 0) and $\left(-\frac{3}{2}, 0\right)$.

Analysis   *We can always check that our answers are reasonable by using a graphing calculator to graph the polynomial as shown in **Figure 5**.*

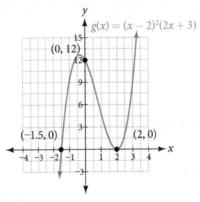

Figure 5

Example 5   **Finding the *x*-Intercepts of a Polynomial Function Using a Graph**

Find the *x*-intercepts of $h(x) = x^3 + 4x^2 + x - 6$.

Solution   This polynomial is not in factored form, has no common factors, and does not appear to be factorable using techniques previously discussed. Fortunately, we can use technology to find the intercepts. Keep in mind that some values make graphing difficult by hand. In these cases, we can take advantage of graphing utilities.

Looking at the graph of this function, as shown in **Figure 6**, it appears that there are *x*-intercepts at $x = -3, -2,$ and 1.

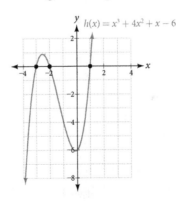

Figure 6

We can check whether these are correct by substituting these values for x and verifying that

$$h(-3) = h(-2) = h(1) = 0.$$

Since $h(x) = x^3 + 4x^2 + x - 6$, we have:

$$h(-3) = (-3)^3 + 4(-3)^2 + (-3) - 6 = -27 + 36 - 3 - 6 = 0$$
$$h(-2) = (-2)^3 + 4(-2)^2 + (-2) - 6 = -8 + 16 - 2 - 6 = 0$$
$$h(1) = (1)^3 + 4(1)^2 + (1) - 6 = 1 + 4 + 1 - 6 = 0$$

Each x-intercept corresponds to a zero of the polynomial function and each zero yields a factor, so we can now write the polynomial in factored form.

$$h(x) = x^3 + 4x^2 + x - 6$$
$$= (x + 3)(x + 2)(x - 1)$$

Try It #1

Find the y- and x-intercepts of the function $f(x) = x^4 - 19x^2 + 30x$.

Identifying Zeros and Their Multiplicities

Graphs behave differently at various x-intercepts. Sometimes, the graph will cross over the horizontal axis at an intercept. Other times, the graph will touch the horizontal axis and bounce off.

Suppose, for example, we graph the function

$$f(x) = (x + 3)(x - 2)^2(x + 1)^3.$$

Notice in **Figure 7** that the behavior of the function at each of the x-intercepts is different.

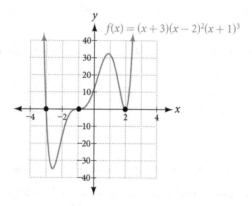

Figure 7 Identifying the behavior of the graph at an x-intercept by examining the multiplicity of the zero.

The x-intercept $x = -3$ is the solution of equation $(x + 3) = 0$. The graph passes directly through the x-intercept at $x = -3$. The factor is linear (has a degree of 1), so the behavior near the intercept is like that of a line—it passes directly through the intercept. We call this a single zero because the zero corresponds to a single factor of the function.

The x-intercept $x = 2$ is the repeated solution of equation $(x - 2)^2 = 0$. The graph touches the axis at the intercept and changes direction. The factor is quadratic (degree 2), so the behavior near the intercept is like that of a quadratic—it bounces off of the horizontal axis at the intercept.

$$(x - 2)^2 = (x - 2)(x - 2)$$

The factor is repeated, that is, the factor $(x - 2)$ appears twice. The number of times a given factor appears in the factored form of the equation of a polynomial is called the **multiplicity**. The zero associated with this factor, $x = 2$, has multiplicity 2 because the factor $(x - 2)$ occurs twice.

The x-intercept $x = -1$ is the repeated solution of factor $(x + 1)^3 = 0$. The graph passes through the axis at the intercept, but flattens out a bit first. This factor is cubic (degree 3), so the behavior near the intercept is like that of a cubic—with the same S-shape near the intercept as the toolkit function $f(x) = x^3$. We call this a triple zero, or a zero with multiplicity 3.

For zeros with even multiplicities, the graphs *touch* or are tangent to the x-axis. For zeros with odd multiplicities, the graphs *cross* or intersect the x-axis. See **Figure 8** for examples of graphs of polynomial functions with multiplicity 1, 2, and 3.

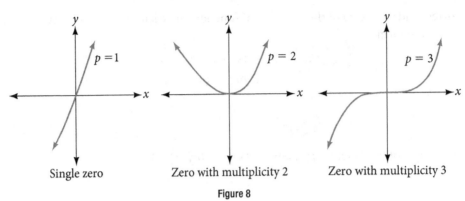

Figure 8

For higher even powers, such as 4, 6, and 8, the graph will still touch and bounce off of the horizontal axis but, for each increasing even power, the graph will appear flatter as it approaches and leaves the x-axis.

For higher odd powers, such as 5, 7, and 9, the graph will still cross through the horizontal axis, but for each increasing odd power, the graph will appear flatter as it approaches and leaves the x-axis.

---

graphical behavior of polynomials at x-intercepts

If a polynomial contains a factor of the form $(x - h)^p$, the behavior near the x-intercept h is determined by the power p. We say that $x = h$ is a zero of **multiplicity** p.

The graph of a polynomial function will touch the x-axis at zeros with even multiplicities. The graph will cross the x-axis at zeros with odd multiplicities.

The sum of the multiplicities is the degree of the polynomial function.

How To...

Given a graph of a polynomial function of degree n, identify the zeros and their multiplicities.

1. If the graph crosses the x-axis and appears almost linear at the intercept, it is a single zero.
2. If the graph touches the x-axis and bounces off of the axis, it is a zero with even multiplicity.
3. If the graph crosses the x-axis at a zero, it is a zero with odd multiplicity.
4. The sum of the multiplicities is n.

Example 6   **Identifying Zeros and Their Multiplicities**

Use the graph of the function of degree 6 in **Figure 9** to identify the zeros of the function and their possible multiplicities.

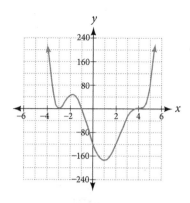

Figure 9

Solution   The polynomial function is of degree n. The sum of the multiplicities must be n.

Starting from the left, the first zero occurs at $x = -3$. The graph touches the x-axis, so the multiplicity of the zero must be even. The zero of -3 has multiplicity 2.

The next zero occurs at $x = -1$. The graph looks almost linear at this point. This is a single zero of multiplicity 1.

The last zero occurs at $x = 4$. The graph crosses the x-axis, so the multiplicity of the zero must be odd. We know that the multiplicity is likely 3 and that the sum of the multiplicities is likely 6.

Try It #2

Use the graph of the function of degree 5 in **Figure 10** to identify the zeros of the function and their multiplicities.

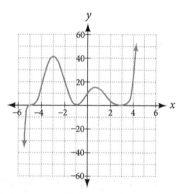

Figure 10

Determining End Behavior

As we have already learned, the behavior of a graph of a polynomial function of the form

$$f(x) = a_n x^n + ... + a_2 x^2 + a_1 x + a_0$$

will either ultimately rise or fall as x increases without bound and will either rise or fall as x decreases without bound. This is because for very large inputs, say 100 or 1,000, the leading term dominates the size of the output. The same is true for very small inputs, say -100 or $-1,000$.

Recall that we call this behavior the *end behavior* of a function. As we pointed out when discussing quadratic equations, when the leading term of a polynomial function, $a_n x^n$, is an even power function, as x increases or decreases without bound, $f(x)$ increases without bound. When the leading term is an odd power function, as x decreases without bound, $f(x)$ also decreases without bound; as x increases without bound, $f(x)$ also increases without bound. If the leading term is negative, it will change the direction of the end behavior. **Figure 11** summarizes all four cases.

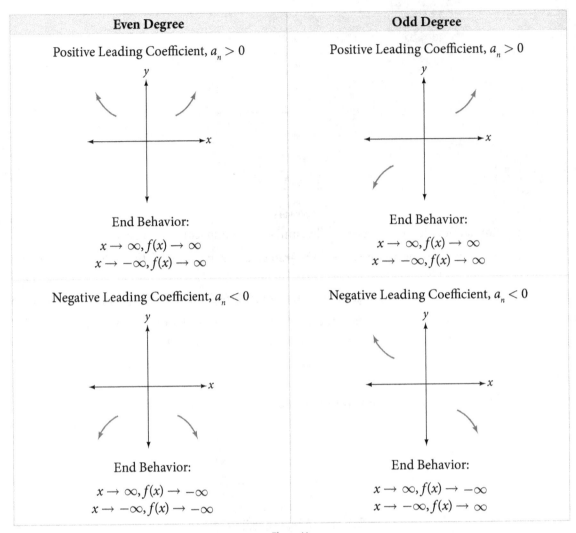

Even Degree	Odd Degree

Positive Leading Coefficient, $a_n > 0$

Positive Leading Coefficient, $a_n > 0$

End Behavior:

$$x \to \infty, f(x) \to \infty$$
$$x \to -\infty, f(x) \to \infty$$

End Behavior:

$$x \to \infty, f(x) \to \infty$$
$$x \to -\infty, f(x) \to \infty$$

Negative Leading Coefficient, $a_n < 0$

Negative Leading Coefficient, $a_n < 0$

End Behavior:

$$x \to \infty, f(x) \to -\infty$$
$$x \to -\infty, f(x) \to -\infty$$

End Behavior:

$$x \to \infty, f(x) \to -\infty$$
$$x \to -\infty, f(x) \to \infty$$

Figure 11

Understanding the Relationship Between Degree and Turning Points

In addition to the end behavior, recall that we can analyze a polynomial function's local behavior. It may have a turning point where the graph changes from increasing to decreasing (rising to falling) or decreasing to increasing (falling to rising). Look at the graph of the polynomial function $f(x) = x^4 - x^3 - 4x^2 + 4x$ in **Figure 12**. The graph has three turning points.

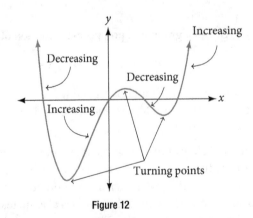

Figure 12

This function f is a 4th degree polynomial function and has 3 turning points. The maximum number of turning points of a polynomial function is always one less than the degree of the function.

---

interpreting turning points

A turning point is a point of the graph where the graph changes from increasing to decreasing (rising to falling) or decreasing to increasing (falling to rising).

A polynomial of degree n will have at most $n - 1$ turning points.

Example 7 **Finding the Maximum Number of Turning Points Using the Degree of a Polynomial Function**

Find the maximum number of turning points of each polynomial function.

a. $f(x) = -x^3 + 4x^5 - 3x^2 + 1$ **b.** $f(x) = -(x - 1)^2(1 + 2x^2)$

Solution

a. $f(x) = -x^3 + 4x^5 - 3x^2 + 1$

First, rewrite the polynomial function in descending order: $f(x) = 4x^5 - x^3 - 3x^2 + 1$
Identify the degree of the polynomial function. This polynomial function is of degree 5.
The maximum number of turning points is $5 - 1 = 4$.

b. $f(x) = -(x - 1)^2(1 + 2x^2)$

First, identify the leading term of the polynomial function if the function were expanded.

$$f(x) = -(x - 1)^2(1 + 2x^2)$$
$$a_n = -(x^2)(2x^2) - 2x^4$$

Then, identify the degree of the polynomial function. This polynomial function is of degree 4.

The maximum number of turning points is $4 - 1 = 3$.

Graphing Polynomial Functions

We can use what we have learned about multiplicities, end behavior, and turning points to sketch graphs of polynomial functions. Let us put this all together and look at the steps required to graph polynomial functions.

How To...

Given a polynomial function, sketch the graph.

1. Find the intercepts.
2. Check for symmetry. If the function is an even function, its graph is symmetrical about the y-axis, that is, $f(-x) = f(x)$. If a function is an odd function, its graph is symmetrical about the origin, that is, $f(-x) = -f(x)$.
3. Use the multiplicities of the zeros to determine the behavior of the polynomial at the x-intercepts.
4. Determine the end behavior by examining the leading term.
5. Use the end behavior and the behavior at the intercepts to sketch a graph.
6. Ensure that the number of turning points does not exceed one less than the degree of the polynomial.
7. Optionally, use technology to check the graph.

Example 8 **Sketching the Graph of a Polynomial Function**

Sketch a graph of $f(x) = -2(x + 3)^2(x - 5)$.

Solution This graph has two x-intercepts. At $x = -3$, the factor is squared, indicating a multiplicity of 2. The graph will bounce at this x-intercept. At $x = 5$, the function has a multiplicity of one, indicating the graph will cross through the axis at this intercept.

The y-intercept is found by evaluating $f(0)$.

$$f(0) = -2(0 + 3)^2(0 - 5)$$
$$= -2 \cdot 9 \cdot (-5)$$
$$= 90$$

The y-intercept is (0, 90).

Additionally, we can see the leading term, if this polynomial were multiplied out, would be $-2x^3$, so the end behavior is that of a vertically reflected cubic, with the outputs decreasing as the inputs approach infinity, and the outputs increasing as the inputs approach negative infinity. See **Figure 13**.

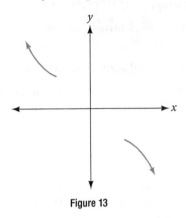

Figure 13

To sketch this, we consider that:

- As $x \to -\infty$ the function $f(x) \to \infty$, so we know the graph starts in the second quadrant and is decreasing toward the x-axis.
- Since $f(-x) = -2(-x + 3)^2 (-x - 5)$ is not equal to $f(x)$, the graph does not display symmetry.
- At $(-3, 0)$, the graph bounces off of the x-axis, so the function must start increasing. At $(0, 90)$, the graph crosses the y-axis at the y-intercept. See **Figure 14**.

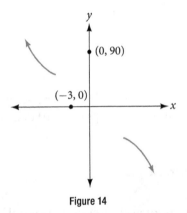

Figure 14

Somewhere after this point, the graph must turn back down or start decreasing toward the horizontal axis because the graph passes through the next intercept at $(5, 0)$. See **Figure 15**.

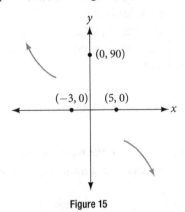

Figure 15

As $x \to \infty$ the function $f(x) \to -\infty$, so we know the graph continues to decrease, and we can stop drawing the graph in the fourth quadrant.

Using technology, we can create the graph for the polynomial function, shown in **Figure 16**, and verify that the resulting graph looks like our sketch in **Figure 15**.

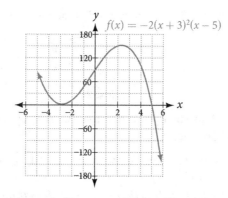

Figure 16 The complete graph of the polynomial function $f(x) = -2(x+3)^2(x-5)$

Try It #3

Sketch a graph of $f(x) = \frac{1}{4}x(x-1)^4(x+3)^3$.

Using the Intermediate Value Theorem

In some situations, we may know two points on a graph but not the zeros. If those two points are on opposite sides of the x-axis, we can confirm that there is a zero between them. Consider a polynomial function f whose graph is smooth and continuous. The **Intermediate Value Theorem** states that for two numbers a and b in the domain of f, if $a < b$ and $f(a) \neq f(b)$, then the function f takes on every value between $f(a)$ and $f(b)$. We can apply this theorem to a special case that is useful in graphing polynomial functions. If a point on the graph of a continuous function f at $x = a$ lies above the x-axis and another point at $x = b$ lies below the x-axis, there must exist a third point between $x = a$ and $x = b$ where the graph crosses the x-axis. Call this point $(c, f(c))$. This means that we are assured there is a solution c where $f(c) = 0$.

In other words, the Intermediate Value Theorem tells us that when a polynomial function changes from a negative value to a positive value, the function must cross the x-axis. **Figure 17** shows that there is a zero between a and b.

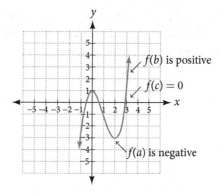

Figure 17 Using the Intermediate Value Theorem to show there exists a zero

Intermediate Value Theorem

Let f be a polynomial function. The **Intermediate Value Theorem** states that if $f(a)$ and $f(b)$ have opposite signs, then there exists at least one value c between a and b for which $f(c) = 0$.

Example 9   **Using the Intermediate Value Theorem**

Show that the function $f(x) = x^3 - 5x^2 + 3x + 6$ has at least two real zeros between $x = 1$ and $x = 4$.

Solution   As a start, evaluate $f(x)$ at the integer values $x = 1, 2, 3,$ and 4. See **Table 2**.

x	1	2	3	4
$f(x)$	5	0	-3	2

Table 2

We see that one zero occurs at $x = 2$. Also, since $f(3)$ is negative and $f(4)$ is positive, by the Intermediate Value Theorem, there must be at least one real zero between 3 and 4.

We have shown that there are at least two real zeros between $x = 1$ and $x = 4$.

Analysis   *We can also see on the graph of the function in* **Figure 18** *that there are two real zeros between $x = 1$ and $x = 4$.*

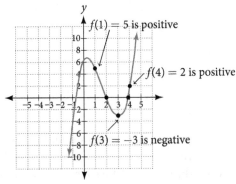

Figure 18

Try It #4

Show that the function $f(x) = 7x^5 - 9x^4 - x^2$ has at least one real zero between $x = 1$ and $x = 2$.

Writing Formulas for Polynomial Functions

Now that we know how to find zeros of polynomial functions, we can use them to write formulas based on graphs. Because a polynomial function written in factored form will have an x-intercept where each factor is equal to zero, we can form a function that will pass through a set of x-intercepts by introducing a corresponding set of factors.

factored form of polynomials

If a polynomial of lowest degree p has horizontal intercepts at $x = x_1, x_2, \ldots, x_n$, then the polynomial can be written in the factored form: $f(x) = a(x - x_1)^{p_1}(x - x_2)^{p_2} \ldots (x - x_n)^{p_n}$ where the powers p_i on each factor can be determined by the behavior of the graph at the corresponding intercept, and the stretch factor a can be determined given a value of the function other than the x-intercept.

How To...

Given a graph of a polynomial function, write a formula for the function.

1. Identify the x-intercepts of the graph to find the factors of the polynomial.
2. Examine the behavior of the graph at the x-intercepts to determine the multiplicity of each factor.
3. Find the polynomial of least degree containing all the factors found in the previous step.
4. Use any other point on the graph (the y-intercept may be easiest) to determine the stretch factor.

Example 10 **Writing a Formula for a Polynomial Function from the Graph**

Write a formula for the polynomial function shown in **Figure 19**.

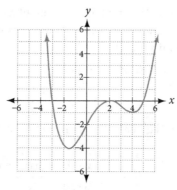

Figure 19

Solution   This graph has three x-intercepts: $x = -3$, 2, and 5. The y-intercept is located at $(0, -2)$. At $x = -3$ and $x = 5$, the graph passes through the axis linearly, suggesting the corresponding factors of the polynomial will be linear. At $x = 2$, the graph bounces at the intercept, suggesting the corresponding factor of the polynomial will be second degree (quadratic). Together, this gives us

$$f(x) = a(x + 3)(x - 2)^2(x - 5)$$

To determine the stretch factor, we utilize another point on the graph. We will use the y-intercept $(0, -2)$, to solve for a.

$$f(0) = a(0 + 3)(0 - 2)^2(0 - 5)$$
$$-2 = a(0 + 3)(0 - 2)^2(0 - 5)$$
$$-2 = -60a$$
$$a = \frac{1}{30}$$

The graphed polynomial appears to represent the function $f(x) = \frac{1}{30}(x + 3)(x - 2)^2(x - 5)$.

Try It #5

Given the graph shown in **Figure 20**, write a formula for the function shown.

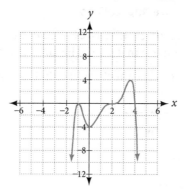

Figure 20

Using Local and Global Extrema

With quadratics, we were able to algebraically find the maximum or minimum value of the function by finding the vertex. For general polynomials, finding these turning points is not possible without more advanced techniques from calculus. Even then, finding where extrema occur can still be algebraically challenging. For now, we will estimate the locations of turning points using technology to generate a graph.

Each turning point represents a local minimum or maximum. Sometimes, a turning point is the highest or lowest point on the entire graph. In these cases, we say that the turning point is a **global maximum** or a **global minimum**. These are also referred to as the absolute maximum and absolute minimum values of the function.

local and global extrema

A local maximum or local minimum at $x = a$ (sometimes called the relative maximum or minimum, respectively) is the output at the highest or lowest point on the graph in an open interval around $x = a$. If a function has a local maximum at a, then $f(a) \geq f(x)$ for all x in an open interval around $x = a$. If a function has a local minimum at a, then $f(a) \leq f(x)$ for all x in an open interval around $x = a$.

A **global maximum** or **global minimum** is the output at the highest or lowest point of the function. If a function has a global maximum at a, then $f(a) \geq f(x)$ for all x. If a function has a global minimum at a, then $f(a) \leq f(x)$ for all x.

We can see the difference between local and global extrema in **Figure 21**.

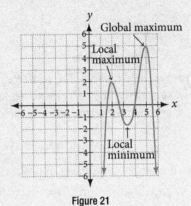

Figure 21

Q & A...

Do all polynomial functions have a global minimum or maximum?

No. Only polynomial functions of even degree have a global minimum or maximum. For example, $f(x) = x$ has neither a global maximum nor a global minimum.

Example 11   **Using Local Extrema to Solve Applications**

An open-top box is to be constructed by cutting out squares from each corner of a 14 cm by 20 cm sheet of plastic then folding up the sides. Find the size of squares that should be cut out to maximize the volume enclosed by the box.

Solution   We will start this problem by drawing a picture like that in **Figure 22**, labeling the width of the cut-out squares with a variable, w.

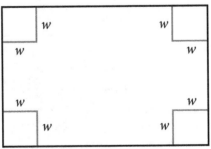

Figure 22

Notice that after a square is cut out from each end, it leaves a $(14 - 2w)$ cm by $(20 - 2w)$ cm rectangle for the base of the box, and the box will be w cm tall. This gives the volume

$$V(w) = (20 - 2w)(14 - 2w)w$$

$$= 280w - 68w^2 + 4w^3$$

Notice, since the factors are w, $20 - 2w$ and $14 - 2w$, the three zeros are 10, 7, and 0, respectively. Because a height of 0 cm is not reasonable, we consider the only the zeros 10 and 7. The shortest side is 14 and we are cutting off two squares, so values w may take on are greater than zero or less than 7. This means we will restrict the domain of this function to $0 < w < 7$. Using technology to sketch the graph of $V(w)$ on this reasonable domain, we get a graph like that in **Figure 23**. We can use this graph to estimate the maximum value for the volume, restricted to values for w that are reasonable for this problem—values from 0 to 7.

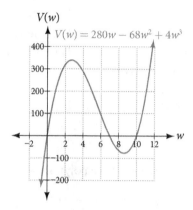

Figure 23

From this graph, we turn our focus to only the portion on the reasonable domain, $[0, 7]$. We can estimate the maximum value to be around 340 cubic cm, which occurs when the squares are about 2.75 cm on each side. To improve this estimate, we could use advanced features of our technology, if available, or simply change our window to zoom in on our graph to produce **Figure 24**.

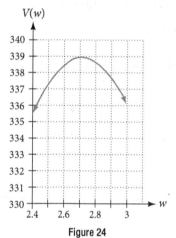

Figure 24

From this zoomed-in view, we can refine our estimate for the maximum volume to about 339 cubic cm, when the squares measure approximately 2.7 cm on each side.

Try It #6

Use technology to find the maximum and minimum values on the interval $[-1, 4]$ of the function $f(x) = -0.2(x - 2)^3(x + 1)^2(x - 4)$.

Access the following online resource for additional instruction and practice with graphing polynomial functions.

- Intermediate Value Theorem (http://openstaxcollege.org/l/ivt)

3.4   SECTION EXERCISES

VERBAL

1. What is the difference between an x-intercept and a zero of a polynomial function f?

2. If a polynomial function of degree n has n distinct zeros, what do you know about the graph of the function?

3. Explain how the Intermediate Value Theorem can assist us in finding a zero of a function.

4. Explain how the factored form of the polynomial helps us in graphing it.

5. If the graph of a polynomial just touches the x-axis and then changes direction, what can we conclude about the factored form of the polynomial?

ALGEBRAIC

For the following exercises, find the x- or t-intercepts of the polynomial functions.

6. $C(t) = 2(t-4)(t+1)(t-6)$

7. $C(t) = 3(t+2)(t-3)(t+5)$

8. $C(t) = 4t(t-2)^2(t+1)$

9. $C(t) = 2t(t-3)(t+1)^2$

10. $C(t) = 2t^4 - 8t^3 + 6t^2$

11. $C(t) = 4t^4 + 12t^3 - 40t^2$

12. $f(x) = x^4 - x^2$

13. $f(x) = x^3 + x^2 - 20x$

14. $f(x) = x^3 + 6x^2 - 7x$

15. $f(x) = x^3 + x^2 - 4x - 4$

16. $f(x) = x^3 + 2x^2 - 9x - 18$

17. $f(x) = 2x^3 - x^2 - 8x + 4$

18. $f(x) = x^6 - 7x^3 - 8$

19. $f(x) = 2x^4 + 6x^2 - 8$

20. $f(x) = x^3 - 3x^2 - x + 3$

21. $f(x) = x^6 - 2x^4 - 3x^2$

22. $f(x) = x^6 - 3x^4 - 4x^2$

23. $f(x) = x^5 - 5x^3 + 4x$

For the following exercises, use the Intermediate Value Theorem to confirm that the given polynomial has at least one zero within the given interval.

24. $f(x) = x^3 - 9x$, between $x = -4$ and $x = -2$.

25. $f(x) = x^3 - 9x$, between $x = 2$ and $x = 4$.

26. $f(x) = x^5 - 2x$, between $x = 1$ and $x = 2$.

27. $f(x) = -x^4 + 4$, between $x = 1$ and $x = 3$.

28. $f(x) = -2x^3 - x$, between $x = -1$ and $x = 1$.

29. $f(x) = x^3 - 100x + 2$, between $x = 0.01$ and $x = 0.1$

For the following exercises, find the zeros and give the multiplicity of each.

30. $f(x) = (x+2)^3(x-3)^2$

31. $f(x) = x^2(2x+3)^5(x-4)^2$

32. $f(x) = x^3(x-1)^3(x+2)$

33. $f(x) = x^2(x^2 + 4x + 4)$

34. $f(x) = (2x+1)^3(9x^2 - 6x + 1)$

35. $f(x) = (3x+2)^5(x^2 - 10x + 25)$

36. $f(x) = x(4x^2 - 12x + 9)(x^2 + 8x + 16)$

37. $f(x) = x^6 - x^5 - 2x^4$

38. $f(x) = 3x^4 + 6x^3 + 3x^2$

39. $f(x) = 4x^5 - 12x^4 + 9x^3$

40. $f(x) = 2x^4(x^3 - 4x^2 + 4x)$

41. $f(x) = 4x^4(9x^4 - 12x^3 + 4x^2)$

GRAPHICAL

For the following exercises, graph the polynomial functions. Note x- and y-intercepts, multiplicity, and end behavior.

42. $f(x) = (x+3)^2(x-2)$

43. $g(x) = (x+4)(x-1)^2$

44. $h(x) = (x-1)^3(x+3)^2$

45. $k(x) = (x-3)^3(x-2)^2$

46. $m(x) = -2x(x-1)(x+3)$

47. $n(x) = -3x(x+2)(x-4)$

For the following exercises, use the graphs to write the formula for a polynomial function of least degree.

48. *f(x)*

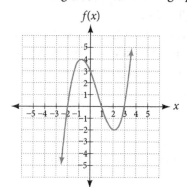

49. *f(x)*

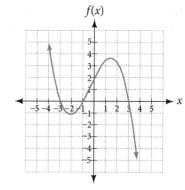

50. *f(x)*

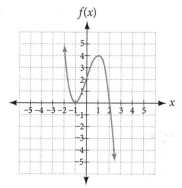

51. *f(x)*

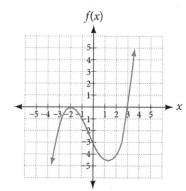

52. *f(x)*

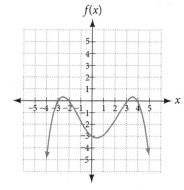

For the following exercises, use the graph to identify zeros and multiplicity.

53. *y*

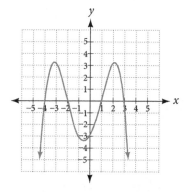

54. *y*

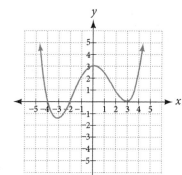

55. *y*

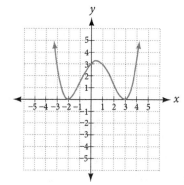

56. *y*

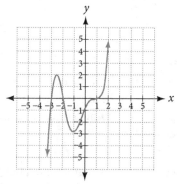

For the following exercises, use the given information about the polynomial graph to write the equation.

57. Degree 3. Zeros at $x = -2$, $x = 1$, and $x = 3$. *y*-intercept at $(0, -4)$.

58. Degree 3. Zeros at $x = -5$, $x = -2$, and $x = 1$. *y*-intercept at $(0, 6)$

59. Degree 5. Roots of multiplicity 2 at $x = 3$ and $x = 1$, and a root of multiplicity 1 at $x = -3$. *y*-intercept at $(0, 9)$

60. Degree 4. Root of multiplicity 2 at $x = 4$, and roots of multiplicity 1 at $x = 1$ and $x = -2$. *y*-intercept at $(0, -3)$.

61. Degree 5. Double zero at $x = 1$, and triple zero at $x = 3$. Passes through the point $(2, 15)$.

62. Degree 3. Zeros at $x = 4$, $x = 3$, and $x = 2$. y-intercept at $(0, -24)$.

63. Degree 3. Zeros at $x = -3$, $x = -2$ and $x = 1$. y-intercept at $(0, 12)$.

64. Degree 5. Roots of multiplicity 2 at $x = -3$ and $x = 2$ and a root of multiplicity 1 at $x = -2$. y-intercept at $(0, 4)$.

65. Degree 4. Roots of multiplicity 2 at $x = \frac{1}{2}$ and roots of multiplicity 1 at $x = 6$ and $x = -2$. y-intercept at $(0,18)$.

66. Double zero at $x = -3$ and triple zero at $x = 0$. Passes through the point $(1, 32)$.

TECHNOLOGY

For the following exercises, use a calculator to approximate local minima and maxima or the global minimum and maximum.

67. $f(x) = x^3 - x - 1$

68. $f(x) = 2x^3 - 3x - 1$

69. $f(x) = x^4 + x$

70. $f(x) = -x^4 + 3x - 2$

71. $f(x) = x^4 - x^3 + 1$

EXTENSIONS

For the following exercises, use the graphs to write a polynomial function of least degree.

72.

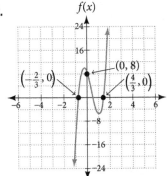

73.

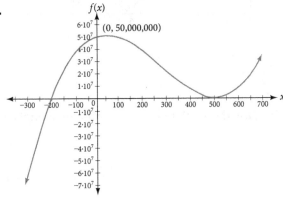

74.

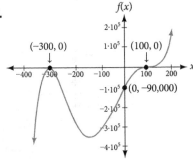

REAL-WORLD APPLICATIONS

For the following exercises, write the polynomial function that models the given situation.

75. A rectangle has a length of 10 units and a width of 8 units. Squares of x by x units are cut out of each corner, and then the sides are folded up to create an open box. Express the volume of the box as a polynomial function in terms of x.

76. Consider the same rectangle of the preceding problem. Squares of $2x$ by $2x$ units are cut out of each corner. Express the volume of the box as a polynomial in terms of x.

77. A square has sides of 12 units. Squares $x + 1$ by $x + 1$ units are cut out of each corner, and then the sides are folded up to create an open box. Express the volume of the box as a function in terms of x.

78. A cylinder has a radius of $x + 2$ units and a height of 3 units greater. Express the volume of the cylinder as a polynomial function.

79. A right circular cone has a radius of $3x + 6$ and a height 3 units less. Express the volume of the cone as a polynomial function. The volume of a cone is $V = \frac{1}{3}\pi r^2 h$ for radius r and height h.

LEARNING OBJECTIVES

In this section, you will:

- Use long division to divide polynomials.
- Use synthetic division to divide polynomials.

3.5   DIVIDING POLYNOMIALS

Figure 1 Lincoln Memorial, Washington, D.C. (credit: Ron Cogswell, Flickr)

The exterior of the Lincoln Memorial in Washington, D.C., is a large rectangular solid with length 61.5 meters (m), width 40 m, and height 30 m.[15] We can easily find the volume using elementary geometry.

$$V = l \cdot w \cdot h$$
$$= 61.5 \cdot 40 \cdot 30$$
$$= 73,800$$

So the volume is 73,800 cubic meters (m³). Suppose we knew the volume, length, and width. We could divide to find the height.

$$h = \frac{V}{l \cdot w}$$
$$= \frac{73,800}{61.5 \cdot 40}$$
$$= 30$$

As we can confirm from the dimensions above, the height is 30 m. We can use similar methods to find any of the missing dimensions. We can also use the same method if any or all of the measurements contain variable expressions. For example, suppose the volume of a rectangular solid is given by the polynomial $3x^4 - 3x^3 - 33x^2 + 54x$. The length of the solid is given by $3x$; the width is given by $x - 2$. To find the height of the solid, we can use polynomial division, which is the focus of this section.

Using Long Division to Divide Polynomials

We are familiar with the long division algorithm for ordinary arithmetic. We begin by dividing into the digits of the dividend that have the greatest place value. We divide, multiply, subtract, include the digit in the next place value position, and repeat. For example, let's divide 178 by 3 using long division.

Long Division

$$
\begin{array}{r}
59 \\
3{\overline{)178}} \\
-15 \\
\hline
28 \\
-27 \\
\hline
1
\end{array}
$$

Step 1: $5 \times 3 = 15$ and $17 - 15 = 2$

Step 2:   Bring down the 8

Step 3: $9 \times 3 = 27$ and $28 - 27 = 1$

Answer: $59 \, R \, 1$ or $59\frac{1}{3}$

15. National Park Service. "Lincoln Memorial Building Statistics." http://www.nps.gov/linc/historyculture/lincoln-memorial-building-statistics.htm. Accessed 4/3/2014/

Another way to look at the solution is as a sum of parts. This should look familiar, since it is the same method used to check division in elementary arithmetic.

$$\text{dividend} = (\text{divisor} \cdot \text{quotient}) + \text{remainder}$$
$$178 = (3 \cdot 59) + 1$$
$$= 177 + 1$$
$$= 178$$

We call this the **Division Algorithm** and will discuss it more formally after looking at an example.

Division of polynomials that contain more than one term has similarities to long division of whole numbers. We can write a polynomial dividend as the product of the divisor and the quotient added to the remainder. The terms of the polynomial division correspond to the digits (and place values) of the whole number division. This method allows us to divide two polynomials. For example, if we were to divide $2x^3 - 3x^2 + 4x + 5$ by $x + 2$ using the long division algorithm, it would look like this:

$$x + 2 \overline{)2x^3 - 3x^2 + 4x + 5}$$ Set up the division problem.

$$\begin{array}{r} 2x^2 \\ x + 2 \overline{)2x^3 - 3x^2 + 4x + 5} \end{array}$$ $2x^3$ divided by x is $2x^2$.

$$\begin{array}{r} 2x^2 \\ x + 2 \overline{)2x^3 - 3x^2 + 4x + 5} \\ -(2x^3 + 4x^2) \\ \hline -7x^2 + 4x \end{array}$$ Multiply $x + 2$ by $2x^2$.
Subtract.
Bring down the next term.

$$\begin{array}{r} 2x^2 - 7x \\ x + 2 \overline{)2x^3 - 3x^2 + 4x + 5} \\ -(2x^3 + 4x^2) \\ \hline -7x^2 + 4x \\ -(-7x^2 + 14x) \\ \hline 18x + 5 \end{array}$$ $-7x^2$ divided by x is $-7x$.
Multiply $x + 2$ by $-7x$.
Subtract. Bring down the next term.

$$\begin{array}{r} 2x^2 - 7x + 18 \\ x + 2 \overline{)2x^3 - 3x^2 + 4x + 5} \\ -(2x^3 + 4x^2) \\ \hline -7x^2 + 4x \\ -(-7x^2 + 14x) \\ \hline 18x + 5 \\ -18x + 36 \\ \hline -31 \end{array}$$ $18x$ divided by x is 18.
Multiply $x + 2$ by 18.
Subtract.

We have found

$$\frac{2x^3 - 3x^2 + 4x + 5}{x + 2} = 2x^2 - 7x + 18 - \frac{31}{x + 2}$$

or

$$\frac{2x^3 - 3x^2 + 4x + 5}{x + 2} = (x + 2)(2x^2 - 7x + 18) - 31$$

We can identify the dividend, the divisor, the quotient, and the remainder.

$$\underset{\text{Dividend}}{2x^3 - 3x^2 + 4x + 5} = \underset{\text{Divisor}}{(x + 2)} \ \underset{\text{Quotient}}{(2x^2 - 7x + 18)} + \underset{\text{Remainder}}{(-31)}$$

Writing the result in this manner illustrates the Division Algorithm.

> ### the Division Algorithm
>
> The **Division Algorithm** states that, given a polynomial dividend $f(x)$ and a non-zero polynomial divisor $d(x)$ where the degree of $d(x)$ is less than or equal to the degree of $f(x)$, there exist unique polynomials $q(x)$ and $r(x)$ such that
>
> $$f(x) = d(x)q(x) + r(x)$$
>
> $q(x)$ is the quotient and $r(x)$ is the remainder. The remainder is either equal to zero or has degree strictly less than $d(x)$.
>
> If $r(x) = 0$, then $d(x)$ divides evenly into $f(x)$. This means that, in this case, both $d(x)$ and $q(x)$ are factors of $f(x)$.

How To...

Given a polynomial and a binomial, use long division to divide the polynomial by the binomial.

1. Set up the division problem.
2. Determine the first term of the quotient by dividing the leading term of the dividend by the leading term of the divisor.
3. Multiply the answer by the divisor and write it below the like terms of the dividend.
4. Subtract the bottom binomial from the top binomial.
5. Bring down the next term of the dividend.
6. Repeat steps 2–5 until reaching the last term of the dividend.
7. If the remainder is non-zero, express as a fraction using the divisor as the denominator.

Example 1   **Using Long Division to Divide a Second-Degree Polynomial**

Divide $5x^2 + 3x - 2$ by $x + 1$.

Solution

$$x + 1 \overline{)5x^2 + 3x - 2} \qquad \text{Set up division problem.}$$

$$\begin{array}{r} 5x \\ x + 1 \overline{)5x^2 + 3x - 2} \end{array} \qquad 5x^2 \text{ divided by } x \text{ is } 5x.$$

$$\begin{array}{r} 5x \\ x + 1 \overline{)5x^2 + 3x - 2} \\ \underline{-(5x^2 + 5x)} \\ -2x - 2 \end{array} \qquad \begin{array}{l} \text{Multiply } x + 1 \text{ by } 5x. \\ \text{Subtract. Bring down the next term.} \end{array}$$

$$\begin{array}{r} 5x - 2 \\ x + 1 \overline{)5x^2 + 3x - 2} \\ \underline{-(5x^2 + 5x)} \\ -2x - 2 \\ \underline{-(-2x - 2)} \\ 0 \end{array} \qquad \begin{array}{l} -2x \text{ divided by } x \text{ is } -2. \\ \\ \\ \text{Multiply } x + 1 \text{ by } -2. \\ \text{Subtract.} \end{array}$$

The quotient is $5x - 2$. The remainder is 0. We write the result as

$$\frac{5x^2 + 3x - 2}{x + 1} = 5x - 2$$

or

$$5x^2 + 3x - 2 = (x + 1)(5x - 2)$$

Analysis This division problem had a remainder of 0. This tells us that the dividend is divided evenly by the divisor, and that the divisor is a factor of the dividend.

Example 2   **Using Long Division to Divide a Third-Degree Polynomial**

Divide $6x^3 + 11x^2 - 31x + 15$ by $3x - 2$.

Solution

$$
\begin{array}{r}
2x^2 + 5x - 7 \\
3x - 2\overline{)6x^3 + 11x^2 - 31x + 1} \\
\underline{-(6x^3 - 4x^2)} \\
15x^2 - 31x \\
\underline{-(15x^2 - 10x)} \\
-21x + 15 \\
\underline{-(-21x + 14)} \\
1
\end{array}
$$

$6x^3$ divided by $3x$ is $2x^2$.

Multiply $3x - 2$ by $2x^2$.

Subtract. Bring down the next term. $15x^2$ divided by $3x$ is $5x$.
Multiply $3x - 2$ by $5x$.

Subtract. Bring down the next term. $-21x$ divided by $3x$ is -7.
Multiply $3x - 2$ by -7.

Subtract. The remainder is 1.

There is a remainder of 1. We can express the result as:

$$\frac{6x^3 + 11x^2 - 31x + 15}{3x - 2} = 2x^2 + 5x - 7 + \frac{1}{3x - 2}$$

Analysis   *We can check our work by using the Division Algorithm to rewrite the solution. Then multiply.*

$$(3x - 2)(2x^2 + 5x - 7) + 1 = 6x^3 + 11x^2 - 31x + 15$$

Notice, as we write our result,

- *the dividend is $6x^3 + 11x^2 - 31x + 15$*

- *the divisor is $3x - 2$*

- *the quotient is $2x^2 + 5x - 7$*

- *the remainder is 1*

Try It #1

Divide $16x^3 - 12x^2 + 20x - 3$ by $4x + 5$.

Using Synthetic Division to Divide Polynomials

As we've seen, long division of polynomials can involve many steps and be quite cumbersome. **Synthetic division** is a shorthand method of dividing polynomials for the special case of dividing by a linear factor whose leading coefficient is 1.

To illustrate the process, recall the example at the beginning of the section.

Divide $2x^3 - 3x^2 + 4x + 5$ by $x + 2$ using the long division algorithm.

The final form of the process looked like this:

$$
\begin{array}{r}
2x^2 + x + 18 \\
x + 2\overline{)2x^3 - 3x^2 + 4x + 5} \\
\underline{-(2x^3 + 4x^2)} \\
-7x^2 + 4x \\
\underline{-(-7x^2 - 14x)} \\
18x + 5 \\
\underline{-(18x + 36)} \\
-31
\end{array}
$$

There is a lot of repetition in the table. If we don't write the variables but, instead, line up their coefficients in columns under the division sign and also eliminate the partial products, we already have a simpler version of the entire problem.

$$
\begin{array}{r}
2\overline{)2 \quad -3 \quad 4 \quad 5} \\
-2 \quad -4 \\
\hline
-7 \quad 14 \\
18 \; -36 \\
\hline
-31
\end{array}
$$

Synthetic division carries this simplification even a few more steps. Collapse the table by moving each of the rows up to fill any vacant spots. Also, instead of dividing by 2, as we would in division of whole numbers, then multiplying and subtracting the middle product, we change the sign of the "divisor" to −2, multiply and add. The process starts by bringing down the leading coefficient.

$$
\begin{array}{r|rrrr}
-2 & 2 & -3 & 4 & 5 \\
& & -4 & 14 & -36 \\
\hline
& 2 & -7 & 18 & -31
\end{array}
$$

We then multiply it by the "divisor" and add, repeating this process column by column, until there are no entries left. The bottom row represents the coefficients of the quotient; the last entry of the bottom row is the remainder. In this case, the quotient is $2x^2 - 7x + 18$ and the remainder is −31. The process will be made more clear in **Example 3**.

---

synthetic division

Synthetic division is a shortcut that can be used when the divisor is a binomial in the form $x - k$. In **synthetic division**, only the coefficients are used in the division process.

How To…

Given two polynomials, use synthetic division to divide.

1. Write k for the divisor.
2. Write the coefficients of the dividend.
3. Bring the lead coefficient down.
4. Multiply the lead coefficient by k. Write the product in the next column.
5. Add the terms of the second column.
6. Multiply the result by k. Write the product in the next column.
7. Repeat steps 5 and 6 for the remaining columns.
8. Use the bottom numbers to write the quotient. The number in the last column is the remainder and has degree 0, the next number from the right has degree 1, the next number from the right has degree 2, and so on.

Example 3   **Using Synthetic Division to Divide a Second-Degree Polynomial**

Use synthetic division to divide $5x^2 - 3x - 36$ by $x - 3$.

Solution Begin by setting up the synthetic division. Write k and the coefficients.

$$
\begin{array}{r|rrr}
3 & 5 & -3 & -36
\end{array}
$$

Bring down the lead coefficient. Multiply the lead coefficient by k.

$$
\begin{array}{r|rrr}
3 & 5 & -3 & -36 \\
& & 15 & \\
\hline
& 5 & &
\end{array}
$$

Continue by adding the numbers in the second column. Multiply the resulting number by k. Write the result in the next column. Then add the numbers in the third column.

$$
\begin{array}{r|rrr}
3 & 5 & -3 & -36 \\
& & 15 & -36 \\
\hline
& 5 & 12 & 0
\end{array}
$$

The result is $5x + 12$. The remainder is 0. So $x - 3$ is a factor of the original polynomial.

Analysis Just as with long division, we can check our work by multiplying the quotient by the divisor and adding the remainder.

$$(x - 3)(5x + 12) + 0 = 5x^2 - 3x - 36$$

Example 4   **Using Synthetic Division to Divide a Third-Degree Polynomial**

Use synthetic division to divide $4x^3 + 10x^2 - 6x - 20$ by $x + 2$.

Solution The binomial divisor is $x + 2$ so $k = -2$. Add each column, multiply the result by -2, and repeat until the last column is reached.

$$
\begin{array}{r|rrrr}
-2 & 4 & 10 & -6 & -20 \\
   &   & -8 & -4 & 20 \\
\hline
   & 4 & 2 & -10 & 0
\end{array}
$$

The result is $4x^2 + 2x - 10$. The remainder is 0. Thus, $x + 2$ is a factor of $4x^3 + 10x^2 - 6x - 20$.

Analysis The graph of the polynomial function $f(x) = 4x^3 + 10x^2 - 6x - 20$ in **Figure 2** shows a zero at $x = k = -2$. This confirms that $x + 2$ is a factor of $4x^3 + 10x^2 - 6x - 20$.

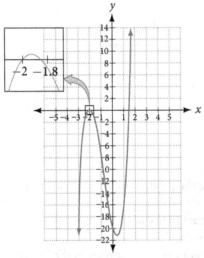

Figure 2

Example 5   **Using Synthetic Division to Divide a Fourth-Degree Polynomial**

Use synthetic division to divide $-9x^4 + 10x^3 + 7x^2 - 6$ by $x - 1$.

Solution Notice there is no x-term. We will use a zero as the coefficient for that term.

$$
\begin{array}{r|rrrrr}
1 & -9 & 10 & 7 & 0 & -6 \\
  &   & -9 & 1 & 8 & 8 \\
\hline
  & -9 & 1 & 8 & 8 & 2
\end{array}
$$

The result is $-9x^3 + x^2 + 8x + 8 + \dfrac{2}{x - 1}$.

Try It #2

Use synthetic division to divide $3x^4 + 18x^3 - 3x + 40$ by $x + 7$.

Using Polynomial Division to Solve Application Problems

Polynomial division can be used to solve a variety of application problems involving expressions for area and volume. We looked at an application at the beginning of this section. Now we will solve that problem in the following example.

Example 6   **Using Polynomial Division in an Application Problem**

The volume of a rectangular solid is given by the polynomial $3x^4 - 3x^3 - 33x^2 + 54x$. The length of the solid is given by $3x$ and the width is given by $x - 2$. Find the height of the solid.

Solution   There are a few ways to approach this problem. We need to divide the expression for the volume of the solid by the expressions for the length and width. Let us create a sketch as in **Figure 3**.

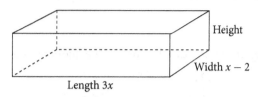

Figure 3

We can now write an equation by substituting the known values into the formula for the volume of a rectangular solid.

$$V = l \cdot w \cdot h$$

$$3x^4 - 3x^3 - 33x^2 + 54x = 3x \cdot (x - 2) \cdot h$$

To solve for h, first divide both sides by $3x$.

$$\frac{3x \cdot (x - 2) \cdot h}{3x} = \frac{3x^4 - 3x^3 - 33x^2 + 54x}{3x}$$

$$(x - 2)h = x^3 - x^2 - 11x + 18$$

Now solve for h using synthetic division.

$$h = \frac{x^3 - x^2 - 11x + 18}{x - 2}$$

$$
\begin{array}{r|rrrr}
2 & 1 & -1 & -11 & 18 \\
  &   & 2 & 2   & -18 \\
\hline
  & 1 & 1 & -9 & 0
\end{array}
$$

The quotient is $x^2 + x - 9$ and the remainder is 0. The height of the solid is $x^2 + x - 9$.

Try It #3

The area of a rectangle is given by $3x^3 + 14x^2 - 23x + 6$. The width of the rectangle is given by $x + 6$. Find an expression for the length of the rectangle.

Access these online resources for additional instruction and practice with polynomial division.

- Dividing a Trinomial by a Binomial Using Long Division (http://openstaxcollege.org/l/dividetribild)
- Dividing a Polynomial by a Binomial Using Long Division (http://openstaxcollege.org/l/dividepolybild)
- Ex 2: Dividing a Polynomial by a Binomial Using Synthetic Division (http://openstaxcollege.org/l/dividepolybisd2)
- Ex 4: Dividing a Polynomial by a Binomial Using Synthetic Division (http://openstaxcollege.org/l/dividepolybisd4)

3.5   SECTION EXERCISES

VERBAL

1. If division of a polynomial by a binomial results in a remainder of zero, what can be conclude?

2. If a polynomial of degree n is divided by a binomial of degree 1, what is the degree of the quotient?

ALGEBRAIC

For the following exercises, use long division to divide. Specify the quotient and the remainder.

3. $(x^2 + 5x - 1) \div (x - 1)$

4. $(2x^2 - 9x - 5) \div (x - 5)$

5. $(3x^2 + 23x + 14) \div (x + 7)$

6. $(4x^2 - 10x + 6) \div (4x + 2)$

7. $(6x^2 - 25x - 25) \div (6x + 5)$

8. $(-x^2 - 1) \div (x + 1)$

9. $(2x^2 - 3x + 2) \div (x + 2)$

10. $(x^3 - 126) \div (x - 5)$

11. $(3x^2 - 5x + 4) \div (3x + 1)$

12. $(x^3 - 3x^2 + 5x - 6) \div (x - 2)$

13. $(2x^3 + 3x^2 - 4x + 15) \div (x + 3)$

For the following exercises, use synthetic division to find the quotient.

14. $(3x^3 - 2x^2 + x - 4) \div (x + 3)$

15. $(2x^3 - 6x^2 - 7x + 6) \div (x - 4)$

16. $(6x^3 - 10x^2 - 7x - 15) \div (x + 1)$

17. $(4x^3 - 12x^2 - 5x - 1) \div (2x + 1)$

18. $(9x^3 - 9x^2 + 18x + 5) \div (3x - 1)$

19. $(3x^3 - 2x^2 + x - 4) \div (x + 3)$

20. $(-6x^3 + x^2 - 4) \div (2x - 3)$

21. $(2x^3 + 7x^2 - 13x - 3) \div (2x - 3)$

22. $(3x^3 - 5x^2 + 2x + 3) \div (x + 2)$

23. $(4x^3 - 5x^2 + 13) \div (x + 4)$

24. $(x^3 - 3x + 2) \div (x + 2)$

25. $(x^3 - 21x^2 + 147x - 343) \div (x - 7)$

26. $(x^3 - 15x^2 + 75x - 125) \div (x - 5)$

27. $(9x^3 - x + 2) \div (3x - 1)$

28. $(6x^3 - x^2 + 5x + 2) \div (3x + 1)$

29. $(x^4 + x^3 - 3x^2 - 2x + 1) \div (x + 1)$

30. $(x^4 - 3x^2 + 1) \div (x - 1)$

31. $(x^4 + 2x^3 - 3x^2 + 2x + 6) \div (x + 3)$

32. $(x^4 - 10x^3 + 37x^2 - 60x + 36) \div (x - 2)$

33. $(x^4 - 8x^3 + 24x^2 - 32x + 16) \div (x - 2)$

34. $(x^4 + 5x^3 - 3x^2 - 13x + 10) \div (x + 5)$

35. $(x^4 - 12x^3 + 54x^2 - 108x + 81) \div (x - 3)$

36. $(4x^4 - 2x^3 - 4x + 2) \div (2x - 1)$

37. $(4x^4 + 2x^3 - 4x^2 + 2x + 2) \div (2x + 1)$

For the following exercises, use synthetic division to determine whether the first expression is a factor of the second. If it is, indicate the factorization.

38. $x - 2, 4x^3 - 3x^2 - 8x + 4$

39. $x - 2, 3x^4 - 6x^3 - 5x + 10$

40. $x + 3, -4x^3 + 5x^2 + 8$

41. $x - 2, 4x^4 - 15x^2 - 4$

42. $x - \frac{1}{2}, 2x^4 - x^3 + 2x - 1$

43. $x + \frac{1}{3}, 3x^4 + x^3 - 3x + 1$

GRAPHICAL

For the following exercises, use the graph of the third-degree polynomial and one factor to write the factored form of the polynomial suggested by the graph. The leading coefficient is one.

44. Factor is $x^2 - x + 3$

45. Factor is $x^2 + 2x + 4$

46. Factor is $x^2 + 2x + 5$

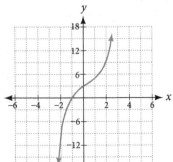

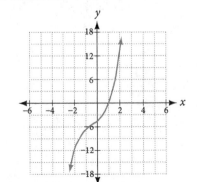

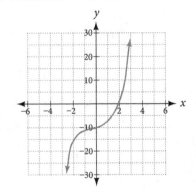

47. Factor is $x^2 + x + 1$

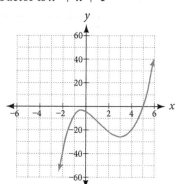

48. Factor is $x^2 + 2x + 2$

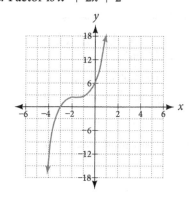

For the following exercises, use synthetic division to find the quotient and remainder.

49. $\dfrac{4x^3 - 33}{x - 2}$

50. $\dfrac{2x^3 + 25}{x + 3}$

51. $\dfrac{3x^3 + 2x - 5}{x - 1}$

52. $\dfrac{-4x^3 - x^2 - 12}{x + 4}$

53. $\dfrac{x^4 - 22}{x + 2}$

TECHNOLOGY

For the following exercises, use a calculator with CAS to answer the questions.

54. Consider $\dfrac{x^k - 1}{x - 1}$ with $k = 1, 2, 3$. What do you expect the result to be if $k = 4$?

55. Consider $\dfrac{x^k + 1}{x + 1}$ for $k = 1, 3, 5$. What do you expect the result to be if $k = 7$?

56. Consider $\dfrac{x^4 - k^4}{x - k}$ for $k = 1, 2, 3$. What do you expect the result to be if $k = 4$?

57. Consider $\dfrac{x^k}{x + 1}$ with $k = 1, 2, 3$. What do you expect the result to be if $k = 4$?

58. Consider $\dfrac{x^k}{x - 1}$ with $k = 1, 2, 3$. What do you expect the result to be if $k = 4$?

EXTENSIONS

For the following exercises, use synthetic division to determine the quotient involving a complex number.

59. $\dfrac{x + 1}{x - i}$

60. $\dfrac{x^2 + 1}{x - i}$

61. $\dfrac{x + 1}{x + i}$

62. $\dfrac{x^2 + 1}{x + i}$

63. $\dfrac{x^3 + 1}{x - i}$

REAL-WORLD APPLICATIONS

For the following exercises, use the given length and area of a rectangle to express the width algebraically.

64. Length is $x + 5$, area is $2x^2 + 9x - 5$.

65. Length is $2x + 5$, area is $4x^3 + 10x^2 + 6x + 15$

66. Length is $3x - 4$, area is $6x^4 - 8x^3 + 9x^2 - 9x - 4$

For the following exercises, use the given volume of a box and its length and width to express the height of the box algebraically.

67. Volume is $12x^3 + 20x^2 - 21x - 36$, length is $2x + 3$, width is $3x - 4$.

68. Volume is $18x^3 - 21x^2 - 40x + 48$, length is $3x - 4$, width is $3x - 4$.

69. Volume is $10x^3 + 27x^2 + 2x - 24$, length is $5x - 4$, width is $2x + 3$.

70. Volume is $10x^3 + 30x^2 - 8x - 24$, length is 2, width is $x + 3$.

For the following exercises, use the given volume and radius of a cylinder to express the height of the cylinder algebraically.

71. Volume is $\pi(25x^3 - 65x^2 - 29x - 3)$, radius is $5x + 1$.

72. Volume is $\pi(4x^3 + 12x^2 - 15x - 50)$, radius is $2x + 5$.

73. Volume is $\pi(3x^4 + 24x^3 + 46x^2 - 16x - 32)$, radius is $x + 4$.

LEARNING OBJECTIVES

In this section, you will:

- Evaluate a polynomial using the Remainder Theorem.
- Use the Factor Theorem to solve a polynomial equation.
- Use the Rational Zero Theorem to find rational zeros.
- Find zeros of a polynomial function.
- Use the Linear Factorization Theorem to find polynomials with given zeros.
- Use Decartes' Rule of Signs.
- Solve real-world applications of polynomial equations.

3.6   ZEROS OF POLYNOMIAL FUNCTIONS

A new bakery offers decorated sheet cakes for children's birthday parties and other special occasions. The bakery wants the volume of a small cake to be 351 cubic inches. The cake is in the shape of a rectangular solid. They want the length of the cake to be four inches longer than the width of the cake and the height of the cake to be one-third of the width. What should the dimensions of the cake pan be?

This problem can be solved by writing a cubic function and solving a cubic equation for the volume of the cake. In this section, we will discuss a variety of tools for writing polynomial functions and solving polynomial equations.

Evaluating a Polynomial Using the Remainder Theorem

In the last section, we learned how to divide polynomials. We can now use polynomial division to evaluate polynomials using the **Remainder Theorem**. If the polynomial is divided by $x - k$, the remainder may be found quickly by evaluating the polynomial function at k, that is, $f(k)$ Let's walk through the proof of the theorem.

Recall that the Division Algorithm states that, given a polynomial dividend $f(x)$ and a non-zero polynomial divisor $d(x)$ where the degree of $d(x)$ is less than or equal to the degree of $f(x)$, there exist unique polynomials $q(x)$ and $r(x)$ such that

$$f(x) = d(x)q(x) + r(x)$$

If the divisor, $d(x)$, is $x - k$, this takes the form

$$f(x) = (x - k)q(x) + r$$

Since the divisor $x - k$ is linear, the remainder will be a constant, r. And, if we evaluate this for $x = k$, we have

$$f(k) = (k - k)q(k) + r$$
$$= 0 \cdot q(k) + r$$
$$= r$$

In other words, $f(k)$ is the remainder obtained by dividing $f(x)$ by $x - k$.

---

the Remainder Theorem

If a polynomial $f(x)$ is divided by $x - k$, then the remainder is the value $f(k)$.

How To...

Given a polynomial function f, evaluate $f(x)$ at $x = k$ using the Remainder Theorem.

1. Use synthetic division to divide the polynomial by $x - k$.
2. The remainder is the value $f(k)$.

Example 1   Using the Remainder Theorem to Evaluate a Polynomial

Use the Remainder Theorem to evaluate $f(x) = 6x^4 - x^3 - 15x^2 + 2x - 7$ at $x = 2$.

Solution   To find the remainder using the Remainder Theorem, use synthetic division to divide the polynomial by $x - 2$.

$$
\begin{array}{r|rrrrr}
2 & 6 & -1 & -15 & 2 & -7 \\
  &   & 12 & 22 & 14 & 32 \\
\hline
  & 6 & 11 & 7 & 16 & 25
\end{array}
$$

The remainder is 25. Therefore, $f(2) = 25$.

Analysis *We can check our answer by evaluating $f(2)$.*

$$f(x) = 6x^4 - x^3 - 15x^2 + 2x - 7$$
$$f(2) = 6(2)^4 - (2)^3 - 15(2)^2 + 2(2) - 7$$
$$= 25$$

Try It #1

Use the Remainder Theorem to evaluate $f(x) = 2x^5 - 3x^4 - 9x^3 + 8x^2 + 2$ at $x = -3$.

Using the Factor Theorem to Solve a Polynomial Equation

The **Factor Theorem** is another theorem that helps us analyze polynomial equations. It tells us how the zeros of a polynomial are related to the factors. Recall that the Division Algorithm tells us

$$f(x) = (x - k)q(x) + r.$$

If k is a zero, then the remainder r is $f(k) = 0$ and $f(x) = (x - k)q(x) + 0$ or $f(x) = (x - k)q(x)$.

Notice, written in this form, $x - k$ is a factor of $f(x)$. We can conclude if k is a zero of $f(x)$, then $x - k$ is a factor of $f(x)$.

Similarly, if $x - k$ is a factor of $f(x)$, then the remainder of the Division Algorithm $f(x) = (x - k)q(x) + r$ is 0. This tells us that k is a zero.

This pair of implications is the Factor Theorem. As we will soon see, a polynomial of degree n in the complex number system will have n zeros. We can use the Factor Theorem to completely factor a polynomial into the product of n factors. Once the polynomial has been completely factored, we can easily determine the zeros of the polynomial.

> **the Factor Theorem**
>
> According to the **Factor Theorem**, k is a zero of $f(x)$ if and only if $(x - k)$ is a factor of $f(x)$.

How To...

Given a factor and a third-degree polynomial, use the Factor Theorem to factor the polynomial.

1. Use synthetic division to divide the polynomial by $(x - k)$.
2. Confirm that the remainder is 0.
3. Write the polynomial as the product of $(x - k)$ and the quadratic quotient.
4. If possible, factor the quadratic.
5. Write the polynomial as the product of factors.

Example 2   Using the Factor Theorem to Solve a Polynomial Equation

Show that $(x + 2)$ is a factor of $x^3 - 6x^2 - x + 30$. Find the remaining factors. Use the factors to determine the zeros of the polynomial.

Solution   We can use synthetic division to show that $(x + 2)$ is a factor of the polynomial.

$$
\begin{array}{r|rrrr}
-2 & 1 & -6 & -1 & 30 \\
& & -2 & 16 & -30 \\
\hline
& 1 & -8 & 15 & 0
\end{array}
$$

The remainder is zero, so $(x + 2)$ is a factor of the polynomial. We can use the Division Algorithm to write the polynomial as the product of the divisor and the quotient:

$$(x + 2)(x^2 - 8x + 15)$$

We can factor the quadratic factor to write the polynomial as

$$(x + 2)(x - 3)(x - 5)$$

By the Factor Theorem, the zeros of $x^3 - 6x^2 - x + 30$ are -2, 3, and 5.

Try It #2

Use the Factor Theorem to find the zeros of $f(x) = x^3 + 4x^2 - 4x - 16$ given that $(x - 2)$ is a factor of the polynomial.

Using the Rational Zero Theorem to Find Rational Zeros

Another use for the Remainder Theorem is to test whether a rational number is a zero for a given polynomial. But first we need a pool of rational numbers to test. The **Rational Zero Theorem** helps us to narrow down the number of possible rational zeros using the ratio of the factors of the constant term and factors of the leading coefficient of the polynomial.

Consider a quadratic function with two zeros, $x = \dfrac{2}{5}$ and $x = \dfrac{3}{4}$. By the Factor Theorem, these zeros have factors associated with them. Let us set each factor equal to 0, and then construct the original quadratic function absent its stretching factor.

$x - \dfrac{2}{5} = 0$ or $x - \dfrac{3}{4} = 0$	Set each factor equal to 0.
$5x - 2 = 0$ or $4x - 3 = 0$	Multiply both sides of the equation to eliminate fractions.
$f(x) = (5x - 2)(4x - 3)$	Create the quadratic function, multiplying the factors.
$f(x) = 20x^2 - 23x + 6$	Expand the polynomial.
$f(x) = (5 \cdot 4)x^2 - 23x + (2 \cdot 3)$	

Notice that two of the factors of the constant term, 6, are the two numerators from the original rational roots: 2 and 3. Similarly, two of the factors from the leading coefficient, 20, are the two denominators from the original rational roots: 5 and 4.

We can infer that the numerators of the rational roots will always be factors of the constant term and the denominators will be factors of the leading coefficient. This is the essence of the Rational Zero Theorem; it is a means to give us a pool of possible rational zeros.

> **the Rational Zero Theorem**
>
> The **Rational Zero Theorem** states that, if the polynomial $f(x) = a_n x^n + a_{n-1} x^{n-1} + \ldots + a_1 x + a_0$ has integer coefficients, then every rational zero of $f(x)$ has the form $\dfrac{p}{q}$ where p is a factor of the constant term a_0 and q is a factor of the leading coefficient a_n.
>
> When the leading coefficient is 1, the possible rational zeros are the factors of the constant term.

How To...

Given a polynomial function $f(x)$, use the Rational Zero Theorem to find rational zeros.

1. Determine all factors of the constant term and all factors of the leading coefficient.

2. Determine all possible values of $\dfrac{p}{q}$, where p is a factor of the constant term and q is a factor of the leading coefficient. Be sure to include both positive and negative candidates.

3. Determine which possible zeros are actual zeros by evaluating each case of $f\left(\dfrac{p}{q}\right)$.

Example 3 **Listing All Possible Rational Zeros**

List all possible rational zeros of $f(x) = 2x^4 - 5x^3 + x^2 - 4$.

Solution   The only possible rational zeros of $f(x)$ are the quotients of the factors of the last term, -4, and the factors of the leading coefficient, 2.

The constant term is -4; the factors of -4 are $p = \pm 1, \pm 2, \pm 4$.

The leading coefficient is 2; the factors of 2 are $q = \pm 1, \pm 2$.

If any of the four real zeros are rational zeros, then they will be of one of the following factors of -4 divided by one of the factors of 2.

$$\frac{p}{q} = \pm\frac{1}{1}, \pm\frac{1}{2} \quad \frac{p}{q} = \pm\frac{2}{1}, \pm\frac{2}{2} \quad \frac{p}{q} = \pm\frac{4}{1}, \pm\frac{4}{2}$$

Note that $\dfrac{2}{2} = 1$ and $\dfrac{4}{2} = 2$, which have already been listed. So we can shorten our list.

$$\frac{p}{q} = \frac{\text{Factors of the last}}{\text{Factors of the first}} = \pm 1, \pm 2, \pm 4, \pm\frac{1}{2}$$

Example 4 **Using the Rational Zero Theorem to Find Rational Zeros**

Use the Rational Zero Theorem to find the rational zeros of $f(x) = 2x^3 + x^2 - 4x + 1$.

Solution   The Rational Zero Theorem tells us that if $\dfrac{p}{q}$ is a zero of $f(x)$, then p is a factor of 1 and q is a factor of 2.

$$\frac{p}{q} = \frac{\text{factor of constant term}}{\text{factor of leading coefficient}}$$

$$= \frac{\text{factor of 1}}{\text{factor of 2}}$$

The factors of 1 are ± 1 and the factors of 2 are ± 1 and ± 2. The possible values for $\dfrac{p}{q}$ are ± 1 and $\pm\dfrac{1}{2}$. These are the possible rational zeros for the function. We can determine which of the possible zeros are actual zeros by substituting these values for x in $f(x)$.

$$f(-1) = 2(-1)^3 + (-1)^2 - 4(-1) + 1 = 4$$

$$f(1) = 2(1)^3 + (1)^2 - 4(1) + 1 = 0$$

$$f\left(-\frac{1}{2}\right) = 2\left(-\frac{1}{2}\right)^3 + \left(-\frac{1}{2}\right)^2 - 4\left(-\frac{1}{2}\right) + 1 = 3$$

$$f\left(\frac{1}{2}\right) = 2\left(\frac{1}{2}\right)^3 + \left(\frac{1}{2}\right)^2 - 4\left(\frac{1}{2}\right) + 1 = -\frac{1}{2}$$

Of those, -1, $-\dfrac{1}{2}$, and $\dfrac{1}{2}$ are not zeros of $f(x)$. 1 is the only rational zero of $f(x)$.

Try It #3

Use the Rational Zero Theorem to find the rational zeros of $f(x) = x^3 - 5x^2 + 2x + 1$.

Finding the Zeros of Polynomial Functions

The Rational Zero Theorem helps us to narrow down the list of possible rational zeros for a polynomial function. Once we have done this, we can use synthetic division repeatedly to determine all of the **zeros** of a polynomial function.

How To…

Given a polynomial function f, use synthetic division to find its zeros.

1. Use the Rational Zero Theorem to list all possible rational zeros of the function.
2. Use synthetic division to evaluate a given possible zero by synthetically dividing the candidate into the polynomial. If the remainder is 0, the candidate is a zero. If the remainder is not zero, discard the candidate.
3. Repeat step two using the quotient found with synthetic division. If possible, continue until the quotient is a quadratic.
4. Find the zeros of the quadratic function. Two possible methods for solving quadratics are factoring and using the quadratic formula.

Example 5   Finding the Zeros of a Polynomial Function with Repeated Real Zeros

Find the zeros of $f(x) = 4x^3 - 3x - 1$.

Solution   The Rational Zero Theorem tells us that if $\frac{p}{q}$ is a zero of $f(x)$, then p is a factor of -1 and q is a factor of 4.

$$\frac{p}{q} = \frac{\text{factor of constant term}}{\text{factor of leading coefficient}}$$

$$= \frac{\text{factor of} -1}{\text{factor of } 4}$$

The factors of -1 are ± 1 and the factors of 4 are $\pm 1, \pm 2,$ and ± 4. The possible values for $\frac{p}{q}$ are $\pm 1, \pm \frac{1}{2},$ and $\pm \frac{1}{4}$. These are the possible rational zeros for the function. We will use synthetic division to evaluate each possible zero until we find one that gives a remainder of 0. Let's begin with 1.

$$
\begin{array}{r|rrrr}
1 & 4 & 0 & -3 & -1 \\
  &   & 4 & 4 & 1 \\
\hline
  & 4 & 4 & 1 & 0 \\
\end{array}
$$

Dividing by $(x - 1)$ gives a remainder of 0, so 1 is a zero of the function. The polynomial can be written as

$$(x - 1)(4x^2 + 4x + 1).$$

The quadratic is a perfect square. $f(x)$ can be written as

$$(x - 1)(2x + 1)^2.$$

We already know that 1 is a zero. The other zero will have a multiplicity of 2 because the factor is squared. To find the other zero, we can set the factor equal to 0.

$$2x + 1 = 0$$
$$x = -\frac{1}{2}$$

The zeros of the function are 1 and $-\frac{1}{2}$ with multiplicity 2.

Analysis   *Look at the graph of the function f in* **Figure 1.** *Notice, at x = −0.5, the graph bounces off the x-axis, indicating the even multiplicity (2, 4, 6…) for the zero −0.5. At x = 1, the graph crosses the x-axis, indicating the odd multiplicity (1, 3, 5…) for the zero x = 1.*

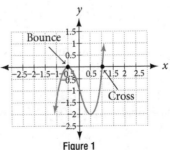

Figure 1

Using the Fundamental Theorem of Algebra

Now that we can find rational zeros for a polynomial function, we will look at a theorem that discusses the number of complex zeros of a polynomial function. The **Fundamental Theorem of Algebra** tells us that every polynomial function has at least one complex zero. This theorem forms the foundation for solving polynomial equations.

Suppose f is a polynomial function of degree four, and $f(x) = 0$. The Fundamental Theorem of Algebra states that there is at least one complex solution, call it c_1. By the Factor Theorem, we can write $f(x)$ as a product of $x - c_1$ and a polynomial quotient. Since $x - c_1$ is linear, the polynomial quotient will be of degree three. Now we apply the Fundamental Theorem of Algebra to the third-degree polynomial quotient. It will have at least one complex zero, call it c_2. So we can write the polynomial quotient as a product of $x - c_2$ and a new polynomial quotient of degree two. Continue to apply the Fundamental Theorem of Algebra until all of the zeros are found. There will be four of them and each one will yield a factor of $f(x)$.

> **The Fundamental Theorem of Algebra**
>
> The Fundamental Theorem of Algebra states that, if $f(x)$ is a polynomial of degree $n > 0$, then $f(x)$ has at least one complex zero. We can use this theorem to argue that, if $f(x)$ is a polynomial of degree $n > 0$, and a is a non-zero real number, then $f(x)$ has exactly n linear factors
>
> $$f(x) = a(x - c_1)(x - c_2)...(x - c_n)$$
>
> where $c_1, c_2, ..., c_n$ are complex numbers. Therefore, $f(x)$ has n roots if we allow for multiplicities.

Q & A...

Does every polynomial have at least one imaginary zero?

No. A complex number is not necessarily imaginary. Real numbers are also complex numbers.

Example 6 **Finding the Zeros of a Polynomial Function with Complex Zeros**

Find the zeros of $f(x) = 3x^3 + 9x^2 + x + 3$.

Solution The Rational Zero Theorem tells us that if $\frac{p}{q}$ is a zero of $f(x)$, then p is a factor of 3 and q is a factor of 3.

$$\frac{p}{q} = \frac{\text{factor of constant term}}{\text{factor of leading coefficient}}$$

$$= \frac{\text{factor of 3}}{\text{factor of 3}}$$

The factors of 3 are ± 1 and ± 3. The possible values for $\frac{p}{q}$, and therefore the possible rational zeros for the function, are $\pm 3, \pm 1,$ and $\pm \frac{1}{3}$. We will use synthetic division to evaluate each possible zero until we find one that gives a remainder of 0. Let's begin with -3.

$$
\begin{array}{r|rrrr}
-3 & 3 & 9 & 1 & 3 \\
   &   & -9 & 0 & -3 \\
\hline
   & 3 & 0 & 1 & 0 \\
\end{array}
$$

Dividing by $(x + 3)$ gives a remainder of 0, so -3 is a zero of the function. The polynomial can be written as

$$(x + 3)(3x^2 + 1)$$

We can then set the quadratic equal to 0 and solve to find the other zeros of the function.

$$3x^2 + 1 = 0$$

$$x^2 = -\frac{1}{3}$$

$$x = \pm\sqrt{-\frac{1}{3}} = \pm\frac{i\sqrt{3}}{3}$$

The zeros of $f(x)$ are -3 and $\pm\dfrac{i\sqrt{3}}{3}$.

Analysis   Look at the graph of the function *f* in **Figure 2**. Notice that, at $x = -3$, the graph crosses the x-axis, indicating an odd multiplicity (1) for the zero $x = -3$. Also note the presence of the two turning points. This means that, since there is a 3rd degree polynomial, we are looking at the maximum number of turning points. So, the end behavior of increasing without bound to the right and decreasing without bound to the left will continue. Thus, all the x-intercepts for the function are shown. So either the multiplicity of $x = -3$ is 1 and there are two complex solutions, which is what we found, or the multiplicity at $x = -3$ is three. Either way, our result is correct.

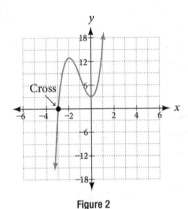

Figure 2

Try It #4

Find the zeros of $f(x) = 2x^3 + 5x^2 - 11x + 4$.

Using the Linear Factorization Theorem to Find Polynomials with Given Zeros

A vital implication of the Fundamental Theorem of Algebra, as we stated above, is that a polynomial function of degree *n* will have *n* zeros in the set of complex numbers, if we allow for multiplicities. This means that we can factor the polynomial function into *n* factors. The **Linear Factorization Theorem** tells us that a polynomial function will have the same number of factors as its degree, and that each factor will be in the form $(x - c)$, where *c* is a complex number.

Let *f* be a polynomial function with real coefficients, and suppose $a + bi$, $b \neq 0$, is a zero of $f(x)$. Then, by the Factor Theorem, $x - (a + bi)$ is a factor of $f(x)$. For *f* to have real coefficients, $x - (a - bi)$ must also be a factor of $f(x)$. This is true because any factor other than $x - (a - bi)$, when multiplied by $x - (a + bi)$, will leave imaginary components in the product. Only multiplication with conjugate pairs will eliminate the imaginary parts and result in real coefficients. In other words, if a polynomial function *f* with real coefficients has a complex zero $a + bi$, then the complex conjugate $a - bi$ must also be a zero of $f(x)$. This is called the Complex Conjugate Theorem.

> **complex conjugate theorem**
>
> According to the **Linear Factorization Theorem,** a polynomial function will have the same number of factors as its degree, and each factor will be in the form $(x - c)$, where *c* is a complex number.
>
> If the polynomial function *f* has real coefficients and a complex zero in the form $a + bi$, then the complex conjugate of the zero, $a - bi$, is also a zero.

How To...

Given the zeros of a polynomial function *f* and a point $(c, f(c))$ on the graph of *f*, use the Linear Factorization Theorem to find the polynomial function.

1. Use the zeros to construct the linear factors of the polynomial.
2. Multiply the linear factors to expand the polynomial.
3. Substitute $(c, f(c))$ into the function to determine the leading coefficient.
4. Simplify.

Example 7   **Using the Linear Factorization Theorem to Find a Polynomial with Given Zeros**

Find a fourth degree polynomial with real coefficients that has zeros of $-3, 2, i$, such that $f(-2) = 100$.

Solution   Because $x = i$ is a zero, by the Complex Conjugate Theorem $x = -i$ is also a zero. The polynomial must have factors of $(x + 3)$, $(x - 2)$, $(x - i)$, and $(x + i)$. Since we are looking for a degree 4 polynomial, and now have four zeros, we have all four factors. Let's begin by multiplying these factors.

$$f(x) = a(x + 3)(x - 2)(x - i)(x + i)$$

$$f(x) = a(x^2 + x - 6)(x^2 + 1)$$

$$f(x) = a(x^4 + x^3 - 5x^2 + x - 6)$$

We need to find a to ensure $f(-2) = 100$. Substitute $x = -2$ and $f(2) = 100$ into $f(x)$.

$$100 = a((-2)^4 + (-2)^3 - 5(-2)^2 + (-2) - 6)$$

$$100 = a(-20)$$

$$-5 = a$$

So the polynomial function is

$$f(x) = -5(x^4 + x^3 - 5x^2 + x - 6)$$

or

$$f(x) = -5x^4 - 5x^3 + 25x^2 - 5x + 30$$

Analysis   *We found that both i and $-i$ were zeros, but only one of these zeros needed to be given. If i is a zero of a polynomial with real coefficients, then $-i$ must also be a zero of the polynomial because $-i$ is the complex conjugate of i.*

Q & A...

If $2 + 3i$ were given as a zero of a polynomial with real coefficients, would $2 - 3i$ also need to be a zero?

Yes. When any complex number with an imaginary component is given as a zero of a polynomial with real coefficients, the conjugate must also be a zero of the polynomial.

Try It #5

Find a third degree polynomial with real coefficients that has zeros of 5 and $-2i$ such that $f(1) = 10$.

Using Descartes' Rule of Signs

There is a straightforward way to determine the possible numbers of positive and negative real zeros for any polynomial function. If the polynomial is written in descending order, **Descartes' Rule of Signs** tells us of a relationship between the number of sign changes in $f(x)$ and the number of positive real zeros. For example, the polynomial function below has one sign change.

$$f(x) = x^4 + x^3 + x^2 + x - 1$$

This tells us that the function must have 1 positive real zero.

There is a similar relationship between the number of sign changes in $f(-x)$ and the number of negative real zeros.

$$f(-x) = (-x)^4 + (-x)^3 + (-x)^2 + (-x) - 1$$

$$f(-x) = +x^4 - x^3 + x^2 - x - 1$$

In this case, $f(-x)$ has 3 sign changes. This tells us that $f(x)$ could have 3 or 1 negative real zeros.

Descartes' Rule of Signs

According to **Descartes' Rule of Signs**, if we let $f(x) = a_n x^n + a_{n-1} x^{n-1} + \ldots + a_1 x + a_0$ be a polynomial function with real coefficients:

- The number of positive real zeros is either equal to the number of sign changes of $f(x)$ or is less than the number of sign changes by an even integer.
- The number of negative real zeros is either equal to the number of sign changes of $f(-x)$ or is less than the number of sign changes by an even integer.

Example 8   **Using Descartes' Rule of Signs**

Use Descartes' Rule of Signs to determine the possible numbers of positive and negative real zeros for $f(x) = -x^4 - 3x^3 + 6x^2 - 4x - 12$.

Solution   Begin by determining the number of sign changes.

$$f(x) = -x^4 - 3x^3 + 6x^2 - 4x - 12$$

Figure 3

There are two sign changes, so there are either 2 or 0 positive real roots. Next, we examine $f(-x)$ to determine the number of negative real roots.

$$f(-x) = -(-x)^4 - 3(-x)^3 + 6(-x)^2 - 4(-x) - 12$$
$$f(-x) = -x^4 + 3x^3 + 6x^2 + 4x - 12$$
$$f(-x) = -x^4 + 3x^3 + 6x^2 + 4x - 12$$

Figure 4

Again, there are two sign changes, so there are either 2 or 0 negative real roots.

There are four possibilities, as we can see in **Table 1**.

Positive Real Zeros	Negative Real Zeros	Complex Zeros	Total Zeros
2	2	0	4
2	0	2	4
0	2	2	4
0	0	4	4

Table 1

Analysis   *We can confirm the numbers of positive and negative real roots by examining a graph of the function. See* **Figure 5**. *We can see from the graph that the function has 0 positive real roots and 2 negative real roots.*

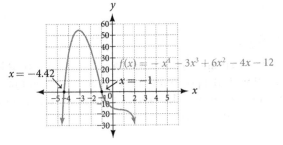

Figure 5

Try It #6

Use Descartes' Rule of Signs to determine the maximum possible numbers of positive and negative real zeros for $f(x) = 2x^4 - 10x^3 + 11x^2 - 15x + 12$. Use a graph to verify the numbers of positive and negative real zeros for the function.

Solving Real-World Applications

We have now introduced a variety of tools for solving polynomial equations. Let's use these tools to solve the bakery problem from the beginning of the section.

Example 9   **Solving Polynomial Equations**

A new bakery offers decorated sheet cakes for children's birthday parties and other special occasions. The bakery wants the volume of a small cake to be 351 cubic inches. The cake is in the shape of a rectangular solid. They want the length of the cake to be four inches longer than the width of the cake and the height of the cake to be one-third of the width. What should the dimensions of the cake pan be?

Solution   Begin by writing an equation for the volume of the cake. The volume of a rectangular solid is given by $V = lwh$. We were given that the length must be four inches longer than the width, so we can express the length of the cake as $l = w + 4$. We were given that the height of the cake is one-third of the width, so we can express the height of the cake as $h = \frac{1}{3}w$. Let's write the volume of the cake in terms of width of the cake.

$$V = (w + 4)(w)\left(\frac{1}{3}w\right)$$
$$V = \frac{1}{3}w^3 + \frac{4}{3}w^2$$

Substitute the given volume into this equation.

$$351 = \frac{1}{3}w^3 + \frac{4}{3}w^2 \qquad \text{Substitute 351 for } V.$$
$$1053 = w^3 + 4w^2 \qquad \text{Multiply both sides by 3.}$$
$$0 = w^3 + 4w^2 - 1053 \qquad \text{Subtract 1053 from both sides.}$$

Descartes' rule of signs tells us there is one positive solution. The Rational Zero Theorem tells us that the possible rational zeros are $\pm1, \pm3, \pm9, \pm13, \pm27, \pm39, \pm81, \pm117, \pm351,$ and ±1053. We can use synthetic division to test these possible zeros. Only positive numbers make sense as dimensions for a cake, so we need not test any negative values. Let's begin by testing values that make the most sense as dimensions for a small sheet cake. Use synthetic division to check $x = 1$.

$$
\begin{array}{r|rrrr}
1 & 1 & 4 & 0 & -1053 \\
  &   & 1 & 5 & 5 \\
\hline
  & 1 & 5 & 5 & -1048 \\
\end{array}
$$

Since 1 is not a solution, we will check $x = 3$.

$$
\begin{array}{r|rrrr}
3 & 1 & 4 & 0 & -1053 \\
  &   & 3 & 21 & 63 \\
\hline
  & 1 & 7 & 21 & -990 \\
\end{array}
$$

Since 3 is not a solution either, we will test $x = 9$.

$$
\begin{array}{r|rrrr}
9 & 1 & 4 & 0 & -1053 \\
  &   & 9 & 117 & 1053 \\
\hline
  & 1 & 13 & 117 & 0 \\
\end{array}
$$

Synthetic division gives a remainder of 0, so 9 is a solution to the equation. We can use the relationships between the width and the other dimensions to determine the length and height of the sheet cake pan.

$$l = w + 4 = 9 + 4 = 13 \text{ and } h = \frac{1}{3}w = \frac{1}{3}(9) = 3$$

The sheet cake pan should have dimensions 13 inches by 9 inches by 3 inches.

Try It #7

A shipping container in the shape of a rectangular solid must have a volume of 84 cubic meters. The client tells the manufacturer that, because of the contents, the length of the container must be one meter longer than the width, and the height must be one meter greater than twice the width. What should the dimensions of the container be?

Access these online resources for additional instruction and practice with zeros of polynomial functions.

- Real Zeros, Factors, and Graphs of Polynomial Functions (http://openstaxcollege.org/l/realzeros)
- Complex Factorization Theorem (http://openstaxcollege.org/l/factortheorem)
- Find the Zeros of a Polynomial Function (http://openstaxcollege.org/l/findthezeros)
- Find the Zeros of a Polynomial Function 2 (http://openstaxcollege.org/l/findthezeros2)
- Find the Zeros of a Polynomial Function 3 (http://openstaxcollege.org/l/findthezeros3)

3.6　SECTION EXERCISES

VERBAL

1. Describe a use for the Remainder Theorem.

2. Explain why the Rational Zero Theorem does not guarantee finding zeros of a polynomial function.

3. What is the difference between rational and real zeros?

4. If Descartes' Rule of Signs reveals a no change of signs or one sign of changes, what specific conclusion can be drawn?

5. If synthetic division reveals a zero, why should we try that value again as a possible solution?

ALGEBRAIC

For the following exercises, use the Remainder Theorem to find the remainder.

6. $(x^4 - 9x^2 + 14) \div (x - 2)$

7. $(3x^3 - 2x^2 + x - 4) \div (x + 3)$

8. $(x^4 + 5x^3 - 4x - 17) \div (x + 1)$

9. $(-3x^2 + 6x + 24) \div (x - 4)$

10. $(5x^5 - 4x^4 + 3x^3 - 2x^2 + x - 1) \div (x + 6)$

11. $(x^4 - 1) \div (x - 4)$

12. $(3x^3 + 4x^2 - 8x + 2) \div (x - 3)$

13. $(4x^3 + 5x^2 - 2x + 7) \div (x + 2)$

For the following exercises, use the Factor Theorem to find all real zeros for the given polynomial function and one factor.

14. $f(x) = 2x^3 - 9x^2 + 13x - 6;\ x - 1$

15. $f(x) = 2x^3 + x^2 - 5x + 2;\ x + 2$

16. $f(x) = 3x^3 + x^2 - 20x + 12;\ x + 3$

17. $f(x) = 2x^3 + 3x^2 + x + 6;\ x + 2$

18. $f(x) = -5x^3 + 16x^2 - 9;\ x - 3$

19. $x^3 + 3x^2 + 4x + 12;\ x + 3$

20. $4x^3 - 7x + 3;\ x - 1$

21. $2x^3 + 5x^2 - 12x - 30,\ 2x + 5$

For the following exercises, use the Rational Zero Theorem to find all real zeros.

22. $x^3 - 3x^2 - 10x + 24 = 0$

23. $2x^3 + 7x^2 - 10x - 24 = 0$

24. $x^3 + 2x^2 - 9x - 18 = 0$

25. $x^3 + 5x^2 - 16x - 80 = 0$

26. $x^3 - 3x^2 - 25x + 75 = 0$

27. $2x^3 - 3x^2 - 32x - 15 = 0$

28. $2x^3 + x^2 - 7x - 6 = 0$

29. $2x^3 - 3x^2 - x + 1 = 0$

30. $3x^3 - x^2 - 11x - 6 = 0$

31. $2x^3 - 5x^2 + 9x - 9 = 0$

32. $2x^3 - 3x^2 + 4x + 3 = 0$

33. $x^4 - 2x^3 - 7x^2 + 8x + 12 = 0$

34. $x^4 + 2x^3 - 9x^2 - 2x + 8 = 0$

35. $4x^4 + 4x^3 - 25x^2 - x + 6 = 0$

36. $2x^4 - 3x^3 - 15x^2 + 32x - 12 = 0$

37. $x^4 + 2x^3 - 4x^2 - 10x - 5 = 0$

38. $4x^3 - 3x + 1 = 0$

39. $8x^4 + 26x^3 + 39x^2 + 26x + 6$

For the following exercises, find all complex solutions (real and non-real).

40. $x^3 + x^2 + x + 1 = 0$

41. $x^3 - 8x^2 + 25x - 26 = 0$

42. $x^3 + 13x^2 + 57x + 85 = 0$

43. $3x^3 - 4x^2 + 11x + 10 = 0$

44. $x^4 + 2x^3 + 22x^2 + 50x - 75 = 0$

45. $2x^3 - 3x^2 + 32x + 17 = 0$

GRAPHICAL

For the following exercises, use Descartes' Rule to determine the possible number of positive and negative solutions. Then graph to confirm which of those possibilities is the actual combination.

46. $f(x) = x^3 - 1$

47. $f(x) = x^4 - x^2 - 1$

48. $f(x) = x^3 - 2x^2 - 5x + 6$

49. $f(x) = x^3 - 2x^2 + x - 1$

50. $f(x) = x^4 + 2x^3 - 12x^2 + 14x - 5$

51. $f(x) = 2x^3 + 37x^2 + 200x + 300$

52. $f(x) = x^3 - 2x^2 - 16x + 32$ **53.** $f(x) = 2x^4 - 5x^3 - 5x^2 + 5x + 3$ **54.** $f(x) = 2x^4 - 5x^3 - 14x^2 + 20x + 8$

55. $f(x) = 10x^4 - 21x^2 + 11$

NUMERIC

For the following exercises, list all possible rational zeros for the functions.

56. $f(x) = x^4 + 3x^3 - 4x + 4$ **57.** $f(x) = 2x^3 + 3x^2 - 8x + 5$ **58.** $f(x) = 3x^3 + 5x^2 - 5x + 4$

59. $f(x) = 6x^4 - 10x^2 + 13x + 1$ **60.** $f(x) = 4x^5 - 10x^4 + 8x^3 + x^2 - 8$

TECHNOLOGY

For the following exercises, use your calculator to graph the polynomial function. Based on the graph, find the rational zeros. All real solutions are rational.

61. $f(x) = 6x^3 - 7x^2 + 1$ **62.** $f(x) = 4x^3 - 4x^2 - 13x - 5$

63. $f(x) = 8x^3 - 6x^2 - 23x + 6$ **64.** $f(x) = 12x^4 + 55x^3 + 12x^2 - 117x + 54$

65. $f(x) = 16x^4 - 24x^3 + x^2 - 15x + 25$

EXTENSIONS

For the following exercises, construct a polynomial function of least degree possible using the given information.

66. Real roots: $-1, 1, 3$ and $(2, f(2)) = (2, 4)$ **67.** Real roots: $-1, 1$ (with multiplicity 2 and 1) and $(2, f(2)) = (2, 4)$

68. Real roots: $-2, \frac{1}{2}$ (with multiplicity 2) and $(-3, f(-3)) = (-3, 5)$ **69.** Real roots: $-\frac{1}{2}, 0, \frac{1}{2}$ and $(-2, f(-2)) = (-2, 6)$

70. Real roots: $-4, -1, 1, 4$ and $(-2, f(-2)) = (-2, 10)$

REAL-WORLD APPLICATIONS

For the following exercises, find the dimensions of the box described.

71. The length is twice as long as the width. The height is 2 inches greater than the width. The volume is 192 cubic inches.

72. The length, width, and height are consecutive whole numbers. The volume is 120 cubic inches.

73. The length is one inch more than the width, which is one inch more than the height. The volume is 86.625 cubic inches.

74. The length is three times the height and the height is one inch less than the width. The volume is 108 cubic inches.

75. The length is 3 inches more than the width. The width is 2 inches more than the height. The volume is 120 cubic inches.

For the following exercises, find the dimensions of the right circular cylinder described.

76. The radius is 3 inches more than the height. The volume is 16π cubic meters.

77. The height is one less than one half the radius. The volume is 72π cubic meters.

78. The radius and height differ by one meter. The radius is larger and the volume is 48π cubic meters.

79. The radius and height differ by two meters. The height is greater and the volume is 28.125π cubic meters.

80. The radius is $\frac{1}{3}$ meter greater than the height. The volume is $\frac{98}{9\pi}\pi$ cubic meters.

LEARNING OBJECTIVES

In this section, you will:

- Use arrow notation.
- Solve applied problems involving rational functions.
- Find the domains of rational functions.
- Identify vertical asymptotes.
- Identify horizontal asymptotes.
- Graph rational functions.

3.7   RATIONAL FUNCTIONS

Suppose we know that the cost of making a product is dependent on the number of items, x, produced. This is given by the equation $C(x) = 15{,}000x - 0.1x^2 + 1000$. If we want to know the average cost for producing x items, we would divide the cost function by the number of items, x.

The average cost function, which yields the average cost per item for x items produced, is

$$f(x) = \frac{15{,}000x - 0.1x^2 + 1000}{x}$$

Many other application problems require finding an average value in a similar way, giving us variables in the denominator. Written without a variable in the denominator, this function will contain a negative integer power.

In the last few sections, we have worked with polynomial functions, which are functions with non-negative integers for exponents. In this section, we explore rational functions, which have variables in the denominator.

Using Arrow Notation

We have seen the graphs of the basic reciprocal function and the squared reciprocal function from our study of toolkit functions. Examine these graphs, as shown in **Figure 1**, and notice some of their features.

Graphs of Toolkit Functions

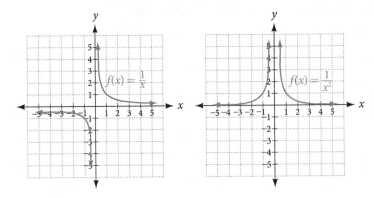

Figure 1

Several things are apparent if we examine the graph of $f(x) = \frac{1}{x}$.

1. On the left branch of the graph, the curve approaches the x-axis $(y = 0)$ as $x \to -\infty$.
2. As the graph approaches $x = 0$ from the left, the curve drops, but as we approach zero from the right, the curve rises.
3. Finally, on the right branch of the graph, the curves approaches the x-axis $(y = 0)$ as $x \to \infty$.

To summarize, we use **arrow notation** to show that x or $f(x)$ is approaching a particular value. See **Table 1**.

Symbol	Meaning
$x \to a^-$	x approaches a from the left ($x < a$ but close to a)
$x \to a^+$	x approaches a from the right ($x > a$ but close to a)
$x \to \infty$	x approaches infinity (x increases without bound)
$x \to -\infty$	x approaches negative infinity (x decreases without bound)
$f(x) \to \infty$	The output approaches infinity (the output increases without bound)
$f(x) \to -\infty$	The output approaches negative infinity (the output decreases without bound)
$f(x) \to a$	The output approaches a

Table 1 Arrow Notation

Local Behavior of $f(x) = \dfrac{1}{x}$

Let's begin by looking at the reciprocal function, $f(x) = \dfrac{1}{x}$. We cannot divide by zero, which means the function is undefined at $x = 0$; so zero is not in the domain. As the input values approach zero from the left side (becoming very small, negative values), the function values decrease without bound (in other words, they approach negative infinity). We can see this behavior in **Table 2**.

x	-0.1	-0.01	-0.001	-0.0001
$f(x) = \frac{1}{x}$	-10	-100	-1000	$-10,000$

Table 2

We write in arrow notation

$$\text{as } x \to 0^-, \ f(x) \to -\infty$$

As the input values approach zero from the right side (becoming very small, positive values), the function values increase without bound (approaching infinity). We can see this behavior in **Table 3**.

x	0.1	0.01	0.001	0.0001
$f(x) = \frac{1}{x}$	10	100	1000	$10,000$

Table 3

We write in arrow notation

$$\text{As } x \to 0^+, \ f(x) \to \infty.$$

See **Figure 2**.

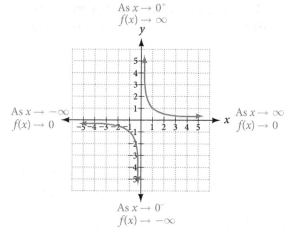

Figure 2

This behavior creates a **vertical asymptote**, which is a vertical line that the graph approaches but never crosses. In this case, the graph is approaching the vertical line $x = 0$ as the input becomes close to zero. See **Figure 3**.

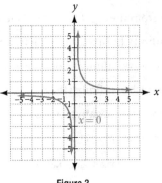

Figure 3

> ### *vertical asymptote*
>
> A **vertical asymptote** of a graph is a vertical line $x = a$ where the graph tends toward positive or negative infinity as the inputs approach a. We write
>
> $$\text{As } x \to a, f(x) \to \infty, \text{ or as } x \to a, f(x) \to -\infty.$$

End Behavior of $f(x) = \dfrac{1}{x}$

As the values of x approach infinity, the function values approach 0. As the values of x approach negative infinity, the function values approach 0. See **Figure 4**. Symbolically, using arrow notation

$$\text{As } x \to \infty, f(x) \to 0, \text{ and as } x \to -\infty, f(x) \to 0.$$

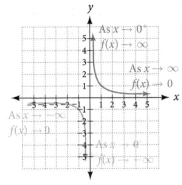

Figure 4

Based on this overall behavior and the graph, we can see that the function approaches 0 but never actually reaches 0; it seems to level off as the inputs become large. This behavior creates a **horizontal asymptote**, a horizontal line that the graph approaches as the input increases or decreases without bound. In this case, the graph is approaching the horizontal line $y = 0$. See **Figure 5**.

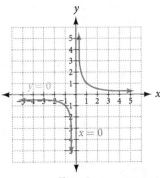

Figure 5

Example 1   **Using Arrow Notation**

Use arrow notation to describe the end behavior and local behavior of the function graphed in **Figure 6**.

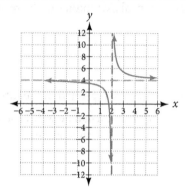

Figure 6

Solution   Notice that the graph is showing a vertical asymptote at $x = 2$, which tells us that the function is undefined at $x = 2$.

$$\text{As } x \to 2^-, f(x) \to -\infty, \text{ and as } x \to 2^+, \ f(x) \to \infty.$$

And as the inputs decrease without bound, the graph appears to be leveling off at output values of 4, indicating a horizontal asymptote at $y = 4$. As the inputs increase without bound, the graph levels off at 4.

$$\text{As } x \to \infty, f(x) \to 4 \text{ and as } x \to -\infty, f(x) \to 4.$$

Try It #1

Use arrow notation to describe the end behavior and local behavior for the reciprocal squared function.

Example 2   **Using Transformations to Graph a Rational Function**

Sketch a graph of the reciprocal function shifted two units to the left and up three units. Identify the horizontal and vertical asymptotes of the graph, if any.

Solution   Shifting the graph left 2 and up 3 would result in the function

$$f(x) = \frac{1}{x + 2} + 3$$

or equivalently, by giving the terms a common denominator,

$$f(x) = \frac{3x + 7}{x + 2}$$

The graph of the shifted function is displayed in **Figure 7**.

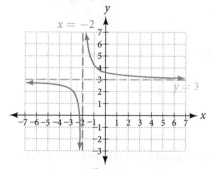

Figure 7

Notice that this function is undefined at $x = -2$, and the graph also is showing a vertical asymptote at $x = -2$.

$$\text{As } x \to -2^-, f(x) \to -\infty, \text{ and as } x \to -2^+, f(x) \to \infty.$$

As the inputs increase and decrease without bound, the graph appears to be leveling off at output values of 3, indicating a horizontal asymptote at $y = 3$.

$$\text{As } x \to \pm\infty, f(x) \to 3.$$

Analysis Notice that horizontal and vertical asymptotes are shifted left 2 and up 3 along with the function.

Try It #2

Sketch the graph, and find the horizontal and vertical asymptotes of the reciprocal squared function that has been shifted right 3 units and down 4 units.

Solving Applied Problems Involving Rational Functions

In **Example 2**, we shifted a toolkit function in a way that resulted in the function $f(x) = \dfrac{3x + 7}{x + 2}$. This is an example of a rational function. A **rational function** is a function that can be written as the quotient of two polynomial functions. Many real-world problems require us to find the ratio of two polynomial functions. Problems involving rates and concentrations often involve rational functions.

> **rational function**
>
> A **rational function** is a function that can be written as the quotient of two polynomial functions $P(x)$ and $Q(x)$.
>
> $$f(x) = \frac{P(x)}{Q(x)} = \frac{a_p x^p + a_{p-1} x^{p-1} + \dots + a_1 x + a_0}{b_q x^q + b_{q-1} x^{q-1} + \dots + b_1 x + b_0}, \quad Q(x) \neq 0$$

Example 3   **Solving an Applied Problem Involving a Rational Function**

A large mixing tank currently contains 100 gallons of water into which 5 pounds of sugar have been mixed. A tap will open pouring 10 gallons per minute of water into the tank at the same time sugar is poured into the tank at a rate of 1 pound per minute. Find the concentration (pounds per gallon) of sugar in the tank after 12 minutes. Is that a greater concentration than at the beginning?

Solution   Let t be the number of minutes since the tap opened. Since the water increases at 10 gallons per minute, and the sugar increases at 1 pound per minute, these are constant rates of change. This tells us the amount of water in the tank is changing linearly, as is the amount of sugar in the tank. We can write an equation independently for each:

$$\text{water: } W(t) = 100 + 10t \text{ in gallons}$$

$$\text{sugar: } S(t) = 5 + 1t \text{ in pounds}$$

The concentration, C, will be the ratio of pounds of sugar to gallons of water

$$C(t) = \frac{5 + t}{100 + 10t}$$

The concentration after 12 minutes is given by evaluating $C(t)$ at $t = 12$.

$$C(12) = \frac{5 + 12}{100 + 10(12)}$$

$$= \frac{17}{220}$$

This means the concentration is 17 pounds of sugar to 220 gallons of water.

At the beginning, the concentration is

$$C(0) = \frac{5 + 0}{100 + 10(0)}$$

$$= \frac{1}{20}$$

Since $\dfrac{17}{220} \approx 0.08 > \dfrac{1}{20} = 0.05$, the concentration is greater after 12 minutes than at the beginning.

Analysis To find the horizontal asymptote, divide the leading coefficient in the numerator by the leading coefficient in the denominator:

$$\frac{1}{10} = 0.1$$

Notice the horizontal asymptote is $y = 0.1$. This means the concentration, C, the ratio of pounds of sugar to gallons of water, will approach 0.1 in the long term.

Try It #3

There are 1,200 freshmen and 1,500 sophomores at a prep rally at noon. After 12 p.m., 20 freshmen arrive at the rally every five minutes while 15 sophomores leave the rally. Find the ratio of freshmen to sophomores at 1 p.m.

Finding the Domains of Rational Functions

A vertical asymptote represents a value at which a rational function is undefined, so that value is not in the domain of the function. A reciprocal function cannot have values in its domain that cause the denominator to equal zero. In general, to find the domain of a rational function, we need to determine which inputs would cause division by zero.

> **domain of a rational function**
>
> The domain of a rational function includes all real numbers except those that cause the denominator to equal zero.

How To...

Given a rational function, find the domain.

1. Set the denominator equal to zero.
2. Solve to find the x-values that cause the denominator to equal zero.
3. The domain is all real numbers except those found in Step 2.

Example 4 **Finding the Domain of a Rational Function**

Find the domain of $f(x) = \dfrac{x + 3}{x^2 - 9}$.

Solution Begin by setting the denominator equal to zero and solving.

$$x^2 - 9 = 0$$
$$x^2 = 9$$
$$x = \pm 3$$

The denominator is equal to zero when $x = \pm 3$. The domain of the function is all real numbers except $x = \pm 3$.

Analysis A graph of this function, as shown in **Figure 8**, confirms that the function is not defined when $x = \pm 3$.

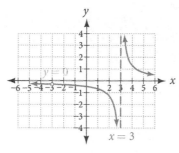

Figure 8

There is a vertical asymptote at $x = 3$ and a hole in the graph at $x = -3$. We will discuss these types of holes in greater detail later in this section.

Try It #4

Find the domain of $f(x) = \dfrac{4x}{5(x-1)(x-5)}$.

Identifying Vertical Asymptotes of Rational Functions

By looking at the graph of a rational function, we can investigate its local behavior and easily see whether there are asymptotes. We may even be able to approximate their location. Even without the graph, however, we can still determine whether a given rational function has any asymptotes, and calculate their location.

Vertical Asymptotes

The vertical asymptotes of a rational function may be found by examining the factors of the denominator that are not common to the factors in the numerator. Vertical asymptotes occur at the zeros of such factors.

How To...

Given a rational function, identify any vertical asymptotes of its graph.

1. Factor the numerator and denominator.
2. Note any restrictions in the domain of the function.
3. Reduce the expression by canceling common factors in the numerator and the denominator.
4. Note any values that cause the denominator to be zero in this simplified version. These are where the vertical asymptotes occur.
5. Note any restrictions in the domain where asymptotes do not occur. These are removable discontinuities.

Example 5   Identifying Vertical Asymptotes

Find the vertical asymptotes of the graph of $k(x) = \dfrac{5 + 2x^2}{2 - x - x^2}$.

Solution   First, factor the numerator and denominator.

$$k(x) = \frac{5 + 2x^2}{2 - x - x^2}$$

$$= \frac{5 + 2x^2}{(2 + x)(1 - x)}$$

To find the vertical asymptotes, we determine where this function will be undefined by setting the denominator equal to zero:

$$(2 + x)(1 - x) = 0$$

$$x = -2, 1$$

Neither $x = -2$ nor $x = 1$ are zeros of the numerator, so the two values indicate two vertical asymptotes. The graph in **Figure 9** confirms the location of the two vertical asymptotes.

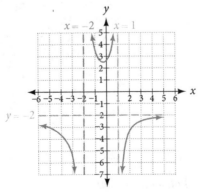

Figure 9

Removable Discontinuities

Occasionally, a graph will contain a hole: a single point where the graph is not defined, indicated by an open circle. We call such a hole a **removable discontinuity**.

For example, the function $f(x) = \dfrac{x^2 - 1}{x^2 - 2x - 3}$ may be re-written by factoring the numerator and the denominator.

$$f(x) = \frac{(x + 1)(x - 1)}{(x + 1)(x - 3)}$$

Notice that $x + 1$ is a common factor to the numerator and the denominator. The zero of this factor, $x = -1$, is the location of the removable discontinuity. Notice also that $x - 3$ is not a factor in both the numerator and denominator. The zero of this factor, $x = 3$, is the vertical asymptote. See **Figure 10.**

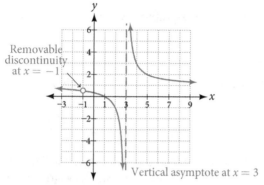

Figure 10

---

removable discontinuities of rational functions

A **removable discontinuity** occurs in the graph of a rational function at $x = a$ if a is a zero for a factor in the denominator that is common with a factor in the numerator. We factor the numerator and denominator and check for common factors. If we find any, we set the common factor equal to 0 and solve. This is the location of the removable discontinuity. This is true if the multiplicity of this factor is greater than or equal to that in the denominator. If the multiplicity of this factor is greater in the denominator, then there is still an asymptote at that value.

Example 6   **Identifying Vertical Asymptotes and Removable Discontinuities for a Graph**

Find the vertical asymptotes and removable discontinuities of the graph of $k(x) = \dfrac{x - 2}{x^2 - 4}$.

Solution   Factor the numerator and the denominator.

$$k(x) = \frac{x - 2}{(x - 2)(x + 2)}$$

Notice that there is a common factor in the numerator and the denominator, $x - 2$. The zero for this factor is $x = 2$. This is the location of the removable discontinuity.

Notice that there is a factor in the denominator that is not in the numerator, $x + 2$. The zero for this factor is $x = -2$. The vertical asymptote is $x = -2$. See **Figure 11**.

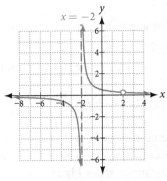

Figure 11

The graph of this function will have the vertical asymptote at $x = -2$, but at $x = 2$ the graph will have a hole.

Try It #5

Find the vertical asymptotes and removable discontinuities of the graph of $f(x) = \dfrac{x^2 - 25}{x^3 - 6x^2 + 5x}$.

Identifying Horizontal Asymptotes of Rational Functions

While vertical asymptotes describe the behavior of a graph as the *output* gets very large or very small, horizontal asymptotes help describe the behavior of a graph as the *input* gets very large or very small. Recall that a polynomial's end behavior will mirror that of the leading term. Likewise, a rational function's end behavior will mirror that of the ratio of the leading terms of the numerator and denominator functions.

There are three distinct outcomes when checking for horizontal asymptotes:

Case 1: If the degree of the denominator > degree of the numerator, there is a horizontal asymptote at $y = 0$.

$$\text{Example: } f(x) = \frac{4x + 2}{x^2 + 4x - 5}$$

In this case, the end behavior is $f(x) \approx \dfrac{4x}{x^2} = \dfrac{4}{x}$. This tells us that, as the inputs increase or decrease without bound, this function will behave similarly to the function $g(x) = \dfrac{4}{x}$, and the outputs will approach zero, resulting in a horizontal asymptote at $y = 0$. See **Figure 12**. Note that this graph crosses the horizontal asymptote.

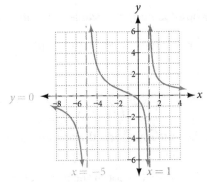

Figure 12 Horizontal Asymptote $y = 0$ when $f(x) = \frac{p(x)}{q(x)}$, $q(x) \neq 0$ where degree of $p <$ degree of q.

Case 2: If the degree of the denominator < degree of the numerator by one, we get a slant asymptote.

$$\text{Example: } f(x) = \frac{3x^2 - 2x + 1}{x - 1}$$

In this case, the end behavior is $f(x) \approx \dfrac{3x^2}{x} = 3x$. This tells us that as the inputs increase or decrease without bound, this function will behave similarly to the function $g(x) = 3x$. As the inputs grow large, the outputs will grow and not level off, so this graph has no horizontal asymptote. However, the graph of $g(x) = 3x$ looks like a diagonal line, and since f will behave similarly to g, it will approach a line close to $y = 3x$. This line is a slant asymptote.

To find the equation of the slant asymptote, divide $\dfrac{3x^2 - 2x + 1}{x - 1}$. The quotient is $3x + 1$, and the remainder is 2. The slant asymptote is the graph of the line $g(x) = 3x + 1$. See **Figure 13**.

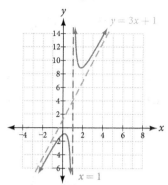

Figure 13 Slant Asymptote when $f(x) = \dfrac{p(x)}{q(x)}$, $q(x) \neq 0$ where degree of $p >$ degree of q by 1.

Case 3: If the degree of the denominator = degree of the numerator, there is a horizontal asymptote at $y = \dfrac{a_n}{b_n}$, where a_n and b_n are the leading coefficients of $p(x)$ and $q(x)$ for $f(x) = \dfrac{p(x)}{q(x)}$, $q(x) \neq 0$.

$$\text{Example: } f(x) = \frac{3x^2 + 2}{x^2 + 4x - 5}$$

In this case, the end behavior is $f(x) \approx \dfrac{3x^2}{x^2} = 3$. This tells us that as the inputs grow large, this function will behave like the function $g(x) = 3$, which is a horizontal line. As $x \to \pm\infty$, $f(x) \to 3$, resulting in a horizontal asymptote at $y = 3$. See **Figure 14**. Note that this graph crosses the horizontal asymptote.

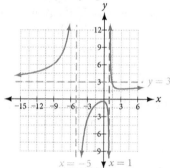

Figure 14 Horizontal Asymptote when $f(x) = \dfrac{p(x)}{q(x)}$, $q(x) \neq 0$ where degree of $p =$ degree of q.

Notice that, while the graph of a rational function will never cross a vertical asymptote, the graph may or may not cross a horizontal or slant asymptote. Also, although the graph of a rational function may have many vertical asymptotes, the graph will have at most one horizontal (or slant) asymptote.

It should be noted that, if the degree of the numerator is larger than the degree of the denominator by more than one, the end behavior of the graph will mimic the behavior of the reduced end behavior fraction. For instance, if we had the function

$$f(x) = \frac{3x^5 - x^2}{x + 3}$$

with end behavior

$$f(x) \approx \frac{3x^5}{x} = 3x^4,$$

the end behavior of the graph would look similar to that of an even polynomial with a positive leading coefficient.

$$x \to \pm\infty, \; f(x) \to \infty$$

---

horizontal asymptotes of rational functions

The horizontal asymptote of a rational function can be determined by looking at the degrees of the numerator and denominator.

- Degree of numerator *is less than* degree of denominator: horizontal asymptote at $y = 0$.
- Degree of numerator *is greater than degree of denominator by one*: no horizontal asymptote; slant asymptote.
- Degree of numerator *is equal to* degree of denominator: horizontal asymptote at ratio of leading coefficients.

Example 7   **Identifying Horizontal and Slant Asymptotes**

For the functions below, identify the horizontal or slant asymptote.

a. $g(x) = \dfrac{6x^3 - 10x}{2x^3 + 5x^2}$ **b.** $h(x) = \dfrac{x^2 - 4x + 1}{x + 2}$ **c.** $k(x) = \dfrac{x^2 + 4x}{x^3 - 8}$

Solution   For these solutions, we will use $f(x) = \dfrac{p(x)}{q(x)}$, $q(x) \neq 0$.

a. $g(x) = \dfrac{6x^3 - 10x}{2x^3 + 5x^2}$: The degree of p = degree of q = 3, so we can find the horizontal asymptote by taking the ratio of the leading terms. There is a horizontal asymptote at $y = \frac{6}{2}$ or $y = 3$.

b. $h(x) = \dfrac{x^2 - 4x + 1}{x + 2}$: The degree of p = 2 and degree of q = 1. Since $p > q$ by 1, there is a slant asymptote found

at $\dfrac{x^2 - 4x + 1}{x + 2}$.

$$\begin{array}{r|rrr} -2 & 1 & -4 & 1 \\ & & -2 & 12 \\ \hline & 1 & -6 & 13 \end{array}$$

The quotient is $x - 2$ and the remainder is 13. There is a slant asymptote at $y = x - 2$.

c. $k(x) = \dfrac{x^2 + 4x}{x^3 - 8}$: The degree of p = 2 < degree of q = 3, so there is a horizontal asymptote $y = 0$.

Example 8   **Identifying Horizontal Asymptotes**

In the sugar concentration problem earlier, we created the equation $C(t) = \dfrac{5 + t}{100 + 10t}$.

Find the horizontal asymptote and interpret it in context of the problem.

Solution   Both the numerator and denominator are linear (degree 1). Because the degrees are equal, there will be a horizontal asymptote at the ratio of the leading coefficients. In the numerator, the leading term is t, with coefficient 1. In the denominator, the leading term is $10t$, with coefficient 10. The horizontal asymptote will be at the ratio of these values:

$$t \to \infty,\ C(t) \to \dfrac{1}{10}$$

This function will have a horizontal asymptote at $y = \dfrac{1}{10}$.

This tells us that as the values of t increase, the values of C will approach $\dfrac{1}{10}$. In context, this means that, as more time goes by, the concentration of sugar in the tank will approach one-tenth of a pound of sugar per gallon of water or $\dfrac{1}{10}$ pounds per gallon.

Example 9   **Identifying Horizontal and Vertical Asymptotes**

Find the horizontal and vertical asymptotes of the function

$$f(x) = \dfrac{(x - 2)(x + 3)}{(x - 1)(x + 2)(x - 5)}$$

Solution   First, note that this function has no common factors, so there are no potential removable discontinuities.

The function will have vertical asymptotes when the denominator is zero, causing the function to be undefined. The denominator will be zero at $x = 1, -2$, and 5, indicating vertical asymptotes at these values.

The numerator has degree 2, while the denominator has degree 3. Since the degree of the denominator is greater than the degree of the numerator, the denominator will grow faster than the numerator, causing the outputs to tend towards zero as the inputs get large, and so as $x \to \pm\infty$, $f(x) \to 0$. This function will have a horizontal asymptote at $y = 0$. See **Figure 15**.

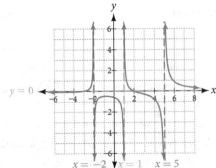

Figure 15

Try It #6

Find the vertical and horizontal asymptotes of the function:

$$f(x) = \frac{(2x-1)(2x+1)}{(x-2)(x+3)}$$

> ### *intercepts of rational functions*
>
> A rational function will have a *y*-intercept when the input is zero, if the function is defined at zero. A rational function will not have a *y*-intercept if the function is not defined at zero.
>
> Likewise, a rational function will have *x*-intercepts at the inputs that cause the output to be zero. Since a fraction is only equal to zero when the numerator is zero, *x*-intercepts can only occur when the numerator of the rational function is equal to zero.

Example 10   **Finding the Intercepts of a Rational Function**

Find the intercepts of $f(x) = \dfrac{(x-2)(x+3)}{(x-1)(x+2)(x-5)}$.

Solution   We can find the *y*-intercept by evaluating the function at zero

$$f(0) = \frac{(0-2)(0+3)}{(0-1)(0+2)(0-5)}$$

$$= \frac{-6}{10}$$

$$= -\frac{3}{5}$$

$$= -0.6$$

The *x*-intercepts will occur when the function is equal to zero:

$$0 = \frac{(x-2)(x+3)}{(x-1)(x+2)(x-5)} \qquad \text{This is zero when the numerator is zero.}$$

$$0 = (x-2)(x+3)$$

$$x = 2, -3$$

The *y*-intercept is $(0, -0.6)$, the *x*-intercepts are $(2, 0)$ and $(-3, 0)$. See **Figure 16**.

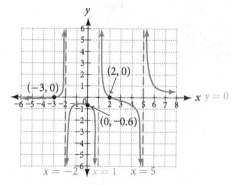

Figure 16

Try It #7

Given the reciprocal squared function that is shifted right 3 units and down 4 units, write this as a rational function. Then, find the *x*- and *y*-intercepts and the horizontal and vertical asymptotes.

Graphing Rational Functions

In **Example 9**, we see that the numerator of a rational function reveals the x-intercepts of the graph, whereas the denominator reveals the vertical asymptotes of the graph. As with polynomials, factors of the numerator may have integer powers greater than one. Fortunately, the effect on the shape of the graph at those intercepts is the same as we saw with polynomials.

The vertical asymptotes associated with the factors of the denominator will mirror one of the two toolkit reciprocal functions. When the degree of the factor in the denominator is odd, the distinguishing characteristic is that on one side of the vertical asymptote the graph heads towards positive infinity, and on the other side the graph heads towards negative infinity. See **Figure 17**.

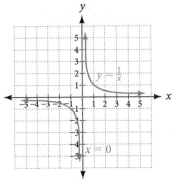

Figure 17

When the degree of the factor in the denominator is even, the distinguishing characteristic is that the graph either heads toward positive infinity on both sides of the vertical asymptote or heads toward negative infinity on both sides. See **Figure 18**.

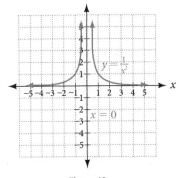

Figure 18

For example, the graph of $f(x) = \dfrac{(x+1)^2(x-3)}{(x+3)^2(x-2)}$ is shown in **Figure 19**.

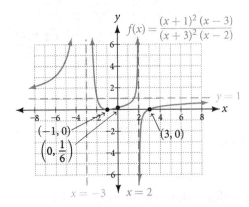

Figure 19

- At the x-intercept $x = -1$ corresponding to the $(x + 1)^2$ factor of the numerator, the graph bounces, consistent with the quadratic nature of the factor.

- At the x-intercept $x = 3$ corresponding to the $(x - 3)$ factor of the numerator, the graph passes through the axis as we would expect from a linear factor.

- At the vertical asymptote $x = -3$ corresponding to the $(x + 3)^2$ factor of the denominator, the graph heads towards positive infinity on both sides of the asymptote, consistent with the behavior of the function $f(x) = \dfrac{1}{x^2}$.

- At the vertical asymptote $x = 2$, corresponding to the $(x - 2)$ factor of the denominator, the graph heads towards positive infinity on the left side of the asymptote and towards negative infinity on the right side, consistent with the behavior of the function $f(x) = \dfrac{1}{x}$.

How To...

Given a rational function, sketch a graph.

1. Evaluate the function at 0 to find the y-intercept.
2. Factor the numerator and denominator.
3. For factors in the numerator not common to the denominator, determine where each factor of the numerator is zero to find the x-intercepts.
4. Find the multiplicities of the x-intercepts to determine the behavior of the graph at those points.
5. For factors in the denominator, note the multiplicities of the zeros to determine the local behavior. For those factors not common to the numerator, find the vertical asymptotes by setting those factors equal to zero and then solve.
6. For factors in the denominator common to factors in the numerator, find the removable discontinuities by setting those factors equal to 0 and then solve.
7. Compare the degrees of the numerator and the denominator to determine the horizontal or slant asymptotes.
8. Sketch the graph.

Example 11 **Graphing a Rational Function**

Sketch a graph of $f(x) = \dfrac{(x + 2)(x - 3)}{(x + 1)^2(x - 2)}$.

Solution We can start by noting that the function is already factored, saving us a step.

Next, we will find the intercepts. Evaluating the function at zero gives the y-intercept:

$$f(0) = \frac{(0 + 2)(0 - 3)}{(0 + 1)^2(0 - 2)}$$

$$= 3$$

To find the x-intercepts, we determine when the numerator of the function is zero. Setting each factor equal to zero, we find x-intercepts at $x = -2$ and $x = 3$. At each, the behavior will be linear (multiplicity 1), with the graph passing through the intercept.

We have a y-intercept at $(0, 3)$ and x-intercepts at $(-2, 0)$ and $(3, 0)$.

To find the vertical asymptotes, we determine when the denominator is equal to zero. This occurs when $x + 1 = 0$ and when $x - 2 = 0$, giving us vertical asymptotes at $x = -1$ and $x = 2$.

There are no common factors in the numerator and denominator. This means there are no removable discontinuities.

Finally, the degree of denominator is larger than the degree of the numerator, telling us this graph has a horizontal asymptote at $y = 0$.

To sketch the graph, we might start by plotting the three intercepts. Since the graph has no x-intercepts between the vertical asymptotes, and the y-intercept is positive, we know the function must remain positive between the asymptotes, letting us fill in the middle portion of the graph as shown in **Figure 20**.

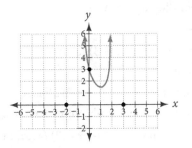

Figure 20

The factor associated with the vertical asymptote at $x = -1$ was squared, so we know the behavior will be the same on both sides of the asymptote. The graph heads toward positive infinity as the inputs approach the asymptote on the right, so the graph will head toward positive infinity on the left as well.

For the vertical asymptote at $x = 2$, the factor was not squared, so the graph will have opposite behavior on either side of the asymptote. See **Figure 21**. After passing through the x-intercepts, the graph will then level off toward an output of zero, as indicated by the horizontal asymptote.

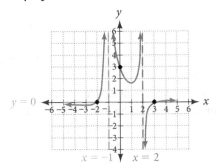

Figure 21

Try It #8

Given the function $f(x) = \dfrac{(x + 2)^2(x - 2)}{2(x - 1)^2(x - 3)}$, use the characteristics of polynomials and rational functions to describe its behavior and sketch the function.

Writing Rational Functions

Now that we have analyzed the equations for rational functions and how they relate to a graph of the function, we can use information given by a graph to write the function. A rational function written in factored form will have an x-intercept where each factor of the numerator is equal to zero. (An exception occurs in the case of a removable discontinuity.) As a result, we can form a numerator of a function whose graph will pass through a set of x-intercepts by introducing a corresponding set of factors. Likewise, because the function will have a vertical asymptote where each factor of the denominator is equal to zero, we can form a denominator that will produce the vertical asymptotes by introducing a corresponding set of factors.

---

writing rational functions from intercepts and asymptotes

If a rational function has x-intercepts at $x = x_1, x_2, \ldots, x_n$, vertical asymptotes at $x = v_1, v_2, \ldots, v_m$, and no $x_i =$ any v_j, then the function can be written in the form:

$$f(x) = a \frac{(x - x_1)^{p_1}(x - x_2)^{p_2} \ldots (x - x_n)^{p_n}}{(x - v_1)^{q_1}(x - v_2)^{q_2} \ldots (x - v_m)^{q_n}}$$

where the powers p_i or q_i on each factor can be determined by the behavior of the graph at the corresponding intercept or asymptote, and the stretch factor a can be determined given a value of the function other than the x-intercept or by the horizontal asymptote if it is nonzero.

How To...

Given a graph of a rational function, write the function.

1. Determine the factors of the numerator. Examine the behavior of the graph at the x-intercepts to determine the zeroes and their multiplicities. (This is easy to do when finding the "simplest" function with small multiplicities—such as 1 or 3—but may be difficult for larger multiplicities—such as 5 or 7, for example.)
2. Determine the factors of the denominator. Examine the behavior on both sides of each vertical asymptote to determine the factors and their powers.
3. Use any clear point on the graph to find the stretch factor.

Example 12 **Writing a Rational Function from Intercepts and Asymptotes**

Write an equation for the rational function shown in **Figure 22**.

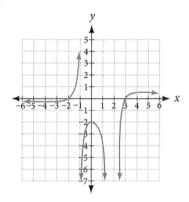

Figure 22

Solution The graph appears to have x-intercepts at $x = -2$ and $x = 3$. At both, the graph passes through the intercept, suggesting linear factors. The graph has two vertical asymptotes. The one at $x = -1$ seems to exhibit the basic behavior similar to $\frac{1}{x}$, with the graph heading toward positive infinity on one side and heading toward negative infinity on the other. The asymptote at $x = 2$ is exhibiting a behavior similar to $\frac{1}{x^2}$, with the graph heading toward negative infinity on both sides of the asymptote. See **Figure 23**.

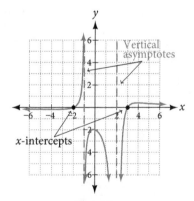

Figure 23

We can use this information to write a function of the form

$$f(x) = a\frac{(x+2)(x-3)}{(x+1)(x-2)^2}$$

To find the stretch factor, we can use another clear point on the graph, such as the y-intercept $(0, -2)$.

$$-2 = a\frac{(0 + 2)(0 - 3)}{(0 + 1)(0 - 2)^2}$$

$$-2 = a\frac{-6}{4}$$

$$a = \frac{-8}{-6} = \frac{4}{3}$$

This gives us a final function of $f(x) = \dfrac{4(x + 2)(x - 3)}{3(x + 1)(x - 2)^2}$.

Access these online resources for additional instruction and practice with rational functions.

- Graphing Rational Functions (http://openstaxcollege.org/l/graphrational)
- Find the Equation of a Rational Function (http://openstaxcollege.org/l/equatrational)
- Determining Vertical and Horizontal Asymptotes (http://openstaxcollege.org/l/asymptote)
- Find the Intercepts, Asymptotes, and Hole of a Rational Function (http://openstaxcollege.org/l/interasymptote)

3.7   SECTION EXERCISES

VERBAL

1. What is the fundamental difference in the algebraic representation of a polynomial function and a rational function?

2. What is the fundamental difference in the graphs of polynomial functions and rational functions?

3. If the graph of a rational function has a removable discontinuity, what must be true of the functional rule?

4. Can a graph of a rational function have no vertical asymptote? If so, how?

5. Can a graph of a rational function have no x-intercepts? If so, how?

ALGEBRAIC

For the following exercises, find the domain of the rational functions.

6. $f(x) = \dfrac{x-1}{x+2}$

7. $f(x) = \dfrac{x+1}{x^2-1}$

8. $f(x) = \dfrac{x^2+4}{x^2-2x-8}$

9. $f(x) = \dfrac{x^2+4x-3}{x^4-5x^2+4}$

For the following exercises, find the domain, vertical asymptotes, and horizontal asymptotes of the functions.

10. $f(x) = \dfrac{4}{x-1}$

11. $f(x) = \dfrac{2}{5x+2}$

12. $f(x) = \dfrac{x}{x^2-9}$

13. $f(x) = \dfrac{x}{x^2+5x-36}$

14. $f(x) = \dfrac{3+x}{x^3-27}$

15. $f(x) = \dfrac{3x-4}{x^3-16x}$

16. $f(x) = \dfrac{x^2-1}{x^3+9x^2+14x}$

17. $f(x) = \dfrac{x+5}{x^2-25}$

18. $f(x) = \dfrac{x-4}{x-6}$

19. $f(x) = \dfrac{4-2x}{3x-1}$

For the following exercises, find the x- and y-intercepts for the functions.

20. $f(x) = \dfrac{x+5}{x^2+4}$

21. $f(x) = \dfrac{x}{x^2-x}$

22. $f(x) = \dfrac{x^2+8x+7}{x^2+11x+30}$

23. $f(x) = \dfrac{x^2+x+6}{x^2-10x+24}$

24. $f(x) = \dfrac{94-2x^2}{3x^2-12}$

For the following exercises, describe the local and end behavior of the functions.

25. $f(x) = \dfrac{x}{2x+1}$

26. $f(x) = \dfrac{2x}{x-6}$

27. $f(x) = \dfrac{-2x}{x-6}$

28. $f(x) = \dfrac{x^2-4x+3}{x^2-4x-5}$

29. $f(x) = \dfrac{2x^2-32}{6x^2+13x-5}$

For the following exercises, find the slant asymptote of the functions.

30. $f(x) = \dfrac{24x^2+6x}{2x+1}$

31. $f(x) = \dfrac{4x^2-10}{2x-4}$

32. $f(x) = \dfrac{81x^2-18}{3x-2}$

33. $f(x) = \dfrac{6x^3-5x}{3x^2+4}$

34. $f(x) = \dfrac{x^2+5x+4}{x-1}$

GRAPHICAL

For the following exercises, use the given transformation to graph the function. Note the vertical and horizontal asymptotes.

35. The reciprocal function shifted up two units.

36. The reciprocal function shifted down one unit and left three units.

37. The reciprocal squared function shifted to the right 2 units.

38. The reciprocal squared function shifted down 2 units and right 1 unit.

For the following exercises, find the horizontal intercepts, the vertical intercept, the vertical asymptotes, and the horizontal or slant asymptote of the functions. Use that information to sketch a graph.

39. $p(x) = \dfrac{2x - 3}{x + 4}$

40. $q(x) = \dfrac{x - 5}{3x - 1}$

41. $s(x) = \dfrac{4}{(x - 2)^2}$

42. $r(x) = \dfrac{5}{(x + 1)^2}$

43. $f(x) = \dfrac{3x^2 - 14x - 5}{3x^2 + 8x - 16}$

44. $g(x) = \dfrac{2x^2 + 7x - 15}{3x^2 - 14 + 15}$

45. $a(x) = \dfrac{x^2 + 2x - 3}{x^2 - 1}$

46. $b(x) = \dfrac{x^2 - x - 6}{x^2 - 4}$

47. $h(x) = \dfrac{2x^2 + x - 1}{x - 4}$

48. $k(x) = \dfrac{2x^2 - 3x - 20}{x - 5}$

49. $w(x) = \dfrac{(x - 1)(x + 3)(x - 5)}{(x + 2)^2(x - 4)}$

50. $z(x) = \dfrac{(x + 2)^2(x - 5)}{(x - 3)(x + 1)(x + 4)}$

For the following exercises, write an equation for a rational function with the given characteristics.

51. Vertical asymptotes at $x = 5$ and $x = -5$, x-intercepts at $(2, 0)$ and $(-1, 0)$, y-intercept at $(0, 4)$

52. Vertical asymptotes at $x = -4$ and $x = -1$, x-intercepts at $(1, 0)$ and $(5, 0)$, y-intercept at $(0, 7)$

53. Vertical asymptotes at $x = -4$ and $x = -5$, x-intercepts at $(4, 0)$ and $(-6, 0)$, horizontal asymptote at $y = 7$

54. Vertical asymptotes at $x = -3$ and $x = 6$, x-intercepts at $(-2, 0)$ and $(1, 0)$, horizontal asymptote at $y = -2$

55. Vertical asymptote at $x = -1$, double zero at $x = 2$, y-intercept at $(0, 2)$

56. Vertical asymptote at $x = 3$, double zero at $x = 1$, y-intercept at $(0, 4)$

For the following exercises, use the graphs to write an equation for the function.

57.

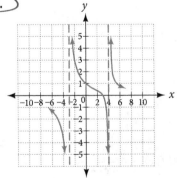

58.

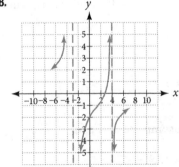

59.

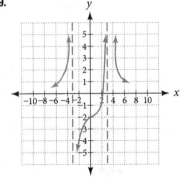

60.

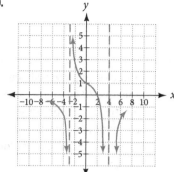

61.

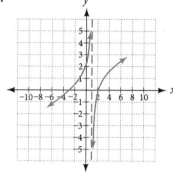

62.

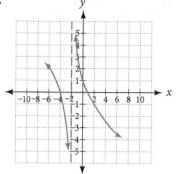

63.

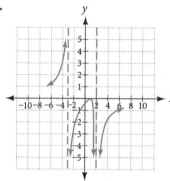

64.

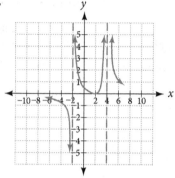

NUMERIC

For the following exercises, make tables to show the behavior of the function near the vertical asymptote and reflecting the horizontal asymptote.

65. $f(x) = \dfrac{1}{x-2}$

66. $f(x) = \dfrac{x}{x-3}$

67. $f(x) = \dfrac{2x}{x+4}$

68. $f(x) = \dfrac{2x}{(x-3)^2}$

69. $f(x) = \dfrac{x^2}{x^2+2x+1}$

TECHNOLOGY

For the following exercises, use a calculator to graph $f(x)$. Use the graph to solve $f(x) > 0$.

70. $f(x) = \dfrac{2}{x+1}$

71. $f(x) = \dfrac{4}{2x-3}$

72. $f(x) = \dfrac{2}{(x-1)(x+2)}$

73. $f(x) = \dfrac{x+2}{(x-1)(x-4)}$

74. $f(x) = \dfrac{(x+3)^2}{(x-1)^2(x+1)}$

EXTENSIONS

For the following exercises, identify the removable discontinuity.

75. $f(x) = \dfrac{x^2-4}{x-2}$

76. $f(x) = \dfrac{x^3+1}{x+1}$

77. $f(x) = \dfrac{x^2+x-6}{x-2}$

78. $f(x) = \dfrac{2x^2+5x-3}{x+3}$

79. $f(x) = \dfrac{x^3+x^2}{x+1}$

REAL-WORLD APPLICATIONS

For the following exercises, express a rational function that describes the situation.

80. A large mixing tank currently contains 200 gallons of water, into which 10 pounds of sugar have been mixed. A tap will open, pouring 10 gallons of water per minute into the tank at the same time sugar is poured into the tank at a rate of 3 pounds per minute. Find the concentration (pounds per gallon) of sugar in the tank after t minutes.

81. A large mixing tank currently contains 300 gallons of water, into which 8 pounds of sugar have been mixed. A tap will open, pouring 20 gallons of water per minute into the tank at the same time sugar is poured into the tank at a rate of 2 pounds per minute. Find the concentration (pounds per gallon) of sugar in the tank after t minutes.

For the following exercises, use the given rational function to answer the question.

82. The concentration C of a drug in a patient's bloodstream t hours after injection in given by $C(t) = \dfrac{2t}{3 + t^2}$. What happens to the concentration of the drug as t increases?

83. The concentration C of a drug in a patient's bloodstream t hours after injection is given by $C(t) = \dfrac{100t}{2t^2 + 75}$. Use a calculator to approximate the time when the concentration is highest.

For the following exercises, construct a rational function that will help solve the problem. Then, use a calculator to answer the question.

84. An open box with a square base is to have a volume of 108 cubic inches. Find the dimensions of the box that will have minimum surface area. Let x = length of the side of the base.

85. A rectangular box with a square base is to have a volume of 20 cubic feet. The material for the base costs 30 cents/square foot. The material for the sides costs 10 cents/square foot. The material for the top costs 20 cents/square foot. Determine the dimensions that will yield minimum cost. Let x = length of the side of the base.

86. A right circular cylinder has volume of 100 cubic inches. Find the radius and height that will yield minimum surface area. Let x = radius.

87. A right circular cylinder with no top has a volume of 50 cubic meters. Find the radius that will yield minimum surface area. Let x = radius.

88. A right circular cylinder is to have a volume of 40 cubic inches. It costs 4 cents/square inch to construct the top and bottom and 1 cent/square inch to construct the rest of the cylinder. Find the radius to yield minimum cost. Let x = radius.

LEARNING OBJECTIVES

In this section, you will:

- Find the inverse of a polynomial function.
- Restrict the domain to find the inverse of a polynomial function.

3.8   INVERSES AND RADICAL FUNCTIONS

A mound of gravel is in the shape of a cone with the height equal to twice the radius.

Figure 1

The volume is found using a formula from elementary geometry.

$$V = \frac{1}{3}\pi r^2 h$$

$$= \frac{1}{3}\pi r^2 (2r)$$

$$= \frac{2}{3}\pi r^3$$

We have written the volume V in terms of the radius r. However, in some cases, we may start out with the volume and want to find the radius. For example: A customer purchases 100 cubic feet of gravel to construct a cone shape mound with a height twice the radius. What are the radius and height of the new cone? To answer this question, we use the formula

$$r = \sqrt[3]{\frac{3V}{2\pi}}$$

This function is the inverse of the formula for V in terms of r.

In this section, we will explore the inverses of polynomial and rational functions and in particular the radical functions we encounter in the process.

Finding the Inverse of a Polynomial Function

Two functions f and g are inverse functions if for every coordinate pair in f, (a, b), there exists a corresponding coordinate pair in the inverse function, g, (b, a). In other words, the coordinate pairs of the inverse functions have the input and output interchanged.

For a function to have an inverse function the function to create a new function that is one-to-one and would have an inverse function.

For example, suppose a water runoff collector is built in the shape of a parabolic trough as shown in **Figure 2**. We can use the information in the figure to find the surface area of the water in the trough as a function of the depth of the water.

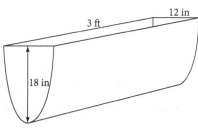

Figure 2

Because it will be helpful to have an equation for the parabolic cross-sectional shape, we will impose a coordinate system at the cross section, with x measured horizontally and y measured vertically, with the origin at the vertex of the parabola. See **Figure 3**.

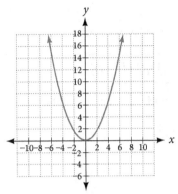

Figure 3

From this we find an equation for the parabolic shape. We placed the origin at the vertex of the parabola, so we know the equation will have form $y(x) = ax^2$. Our equation will need to pass through the point $(6, 18)$, from which we can solve for the stretch factor a.

$$18 = a6^2$$
$$a = \frac{18}{36}$$
$$= \frac{1}{2}$$

Our parabolic cross section has the equation

$$y(x) = \frac{1}{2}x^2$$

We are interested in the surface area of the water, so we must determine the width at the top of the water as a function of the water depth. For any depth y the width will be given by $2x$, so we need to solve the equation above for x and find the inverse function. However, notice that the original function is not one-to-one, and indeed, given any output there are two inputs that produce the same output, one positive and one negative.

To find an inverse, we can restrict our original function to a limited domain on which it *is* one-to-one. In this case, it makes sense to restrict ourselves to positive x values. On this domain, we can find an inverse by solving for the input variable:

$$y = \frac{1}{2}x^2$$
$$2y = x^2$$
$$x = \pm\sqrt{2y}$$

This is not a function as written. We are limiting ourselves to positive x values, so we eliminate the negative solution, giving us the inverse function we're looking for.

$$y = \frac{x^2}{2}, x > 0$$

Because x is the distance from the center of the parabola to either side, the entire width of the water at the top will be $2x$.

The trough is 3 feet (36 inches) long, so the surface area will then be:

$$\text{Area} = l \cdot w$$
$$= 36 \cdot 2x$$
$$= 72x$$
$$= 72\sqrt{2y}$$

This example illustrates two important points:

1. When finding the inverse of a quadratic, we have to limit ourselves to a domain on which the function is one-to-one.

2. The inverse of a quadratic function is a square root function. Both are toolkit functions and different types of power functions.

Functions involving roots are often called radical functions. While it is not possible to find an inverse of most polynomial functions, some basic polynomials do have inverses. Such functions are called **invertible functions**, and we use the notation $f^{-1}(x)$.

Warning: $f^{-1}(x)$ is not the same as the reciprocal of the function $f(x)$. This use of "−1" is reserved to denote inverse functions. To denote the reciprocal of a function $f(x)$, we would need to write $(f(x))^{-1} = \dfrac{1}{f(x)}$.

An important relationship between inverse functions is that they "undo" each other. If f^{-1} is the inverse of a function f, then f is the inverse of the function f^{-1}. In other words, whatever the function f does to x, f^{-1} undoes it—and viceversa. More formally, we write

$$f^{-1}(f(x)) = x, \text{ for all } x \text{ in the domain of } f$$

and

$$f(f^{-1}(x)) = x, \text{ for all } x \text{ in the domain of } f^{-1}$$

> ### *verifying two functions are inverses of one another*
> Two functions, f and g, are inverses of one another if for all x in the domain of f and g.
> $$g(f(x)) = f(g(x)) = x$$

How To...

Given a polynomial function, find the inverse of the function by restricting the domain in such a way that the new function is one-to-one.

1. Replace $f(x)$ with y.
2. Interchange x and y.
3. Solve for y, and rename the function $f^{-1}(x)$.

Example 1   **Verifying Inverse Functions**

Show that $f(x) = \dfrac{1}{x+1}$ and $f^{-1}(x) = \dfrac{1}{x} - 1$ are inverses, for $x \neq 0, -1$.

Solution   We must show that $f^{-1}(f(x)) = x$ and $f(f^{-1}(x)) = x$.

$$f^{-1}(f(x)) = f^{-1}\left(\frac{1}{x+1}\right)$$

$$= \frac{1}{\dfrac{1}{x+1}} - 1$$

$$= (x+1) - 1$$

$$= x$$

$$f(f^{-1}(x)) = f\left(\frac{1}{x} - 1\right)$$

$$= \frac{1}{\left(\dfrac{1}{x} - 1\right) + 1}$$

$$= \frac{1}{\dfrac{1}{x}}$$

$$= x$$

Therefore, $f(x) = \dfrac{1}{x+1}$ and $f^{-1}(x) = \dfrac{1}{x} - 1$ are inverses.

Try It #1

Show that $f(x) = \dfrac{x+5}{3}$ and $f^{-1}(x) = 3x - 5$ are inverses.

Example 2   **Finding the Inverse of a Cubic Function**

Find the inverse of the function $f(x) = 5x^3 + 1$.

Solution   This is a transformation of the basic cubic toolkit function, and based on our knowledge of that function, we know it is one-to-one. Solving for the inverse by solving for x.

$$y = 5x^3 + 1$$
$$x = 5y^3 + 1$$
$$x - 1 = 5y^3$$
$$\frac{x - 1}{5} = y^3$$
$$f^{-1}(x) = \sqrt[3]{\frac{x - 1}{5}}$$

Analysis   *Look at the graph of f and f^{-1}. Notice that the two graphs are symmetrical about the line $y = x$. This is always the case when graphing a function and its inverse function.*

Also, since the method involved interchanging x and y, notice corresponding points. If (a, b) is on the graph of f, then (b, a) is on the graph of f^{-1}. Since $(0, 1)$ is on the graph of f, then $(1, 0)$ is on the graph of f^{-1}. Similarly, since $(1, 6)$ is on the graph of f, then $(6, 1)$ is on the graph of f^{-1}. See Figure 4.

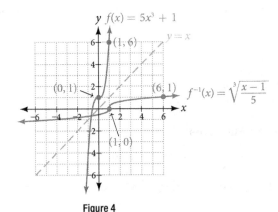

Figure 4

Try It #2

Find the inverse function of $f(x) = \sqrt[3]{x + 4}$

Restricting the Domain to Find the Inverse of a Polynomial Function

So far, we have been able to find the inverse functions of cubic functions without having to restrict their domains. However, as we know, not all cubic polynomials are one-to-one. Some functions that are not one-to-one may have their domain restricted so that they are one-to-one, but only over that domain. The function over the restricted domain would then have an inverse function. Since quadratic functions are not one-to-one, we must restrict their domain in order to find their inverses.

> **restricting the domain**
>
> If a function is not one-to-one, it cannot have an inverse. If we restrict the domain of the function so that it becomes one-to-one, thus creating a new function, this new function will have an inverse.

How To…

Given a polynomial function, restrict the domain of a function that is not one-to-one and then find the inverse.

1. Restrict the domain by determining a domain on which the original function is one-to-one.
2. Replace $f(x)$ with y.
3. Interchange x and y.
4. Solve for y, and rename the function or pair of functions $f^{-1}(x)$.
5. Revise the formula for $f^{-1}(x)$ by ensuring that the outputs of the inverse function correspond to the restricted domain of the original function.

Example 3   **Restricting the Domain to Find the Inverse of a Polynomial Function**

Find the inverse function of f:

    a. $f(x) = (x-4)^2, x \geq 4$ **b.** $f(x) = (x-4)^2, x \leq 4$

Solution   The original function $f(x) = (x-4)^2$ is not one-to-one, but the function is restricted to a domain of $x \geq 4$ or $x \leq 4$ on which it is one-to-one. See **Figure 5**.

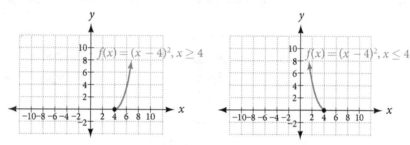

Figure 5

To find the inverse, start by replacing $f(x)$ with the simple variable y.

$$y = (x-4)^2 \quad \text{Interchange } x \text{ and } y.$$
$$x = (y-4)^2 \quad \text{Take the square root.}$$
$$\pm\sqrt{x} = y - 4 \quad \text{Add 4 to both sides.}$$
$$4 \pm \sqrt{x} = y$$

This is not a function as written. We need to examine the restrictions on the domain of the original function to determine the inverse. Since we reversed the roles of x and y for the original $f(x)$, we looked at the domain: the values x could assume. When we reversed the roles of x and y, this gave us the values y could assume. For this function, $x \geq 4$, so for the inverse, we should have $y \geq 4$, which is what our inverse function gives.

    a. The domain of the original function was restricted to $x \geq 4$, so the outputs of the inverse need to be the same, $f(x) \geq 4$, and we must use the $+$ case:

$$f^{-1}(x) = 4 + \sqrt{x}$$

    b. The domain of the original function was restricted to $x \leq 4$, so the outputs of the inverse need to be the same, $f(x) \leq 4$, and we must use the $-$ case:

$$f^{-1}(x) = 4 - \sqrt{x}$$

*Analysis   On the graphs in **Figure 6**, we see the original function graphed on the same set of axes as its inverse function. Notice that together the graphs show symmetry about the line $y = x$. The coordinate pair $(4, 0)$ is on the graph of f and the coordinate pair $(0, 4)$ is on the graph of f^{-1}. For any coordinate pair, if (a, b) is on the graph of f, then (b, a) is on the graph of f^{-1}. Finally, observe that the graph of f intersects the graph of f^{-1} on the line $y = x$. Points of intersection for the graphs of f and f^{-1} will always lie on the line $y = x$.*

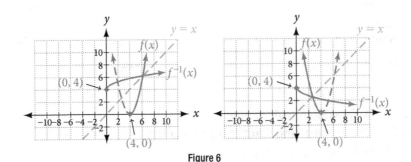

Figure 6

Example 4   **Finding the Inverse of a Quadratic Function When the Restriction Is Not Specified**

Restrict the domain and then find the inverse of

$$f(x) = (x - 2)^2 - 3.$$

Solution   We can see this is a parabola with vertex at $(2, -3)$ that opens upward. Because the graph will be decreasing on one side of the vertex and increasing on the other side, we can restrict this function to a domain on which it will be one-to-one by limiting the domain to $x \geq 2$.

To find the inverse, we will use the vertex form of the quadratic. We start by replacing $f(x)$ with a simple variable, y, then solve for x.

$y = (x - 2)^2 - 3$	Interchange x and y.
$x = (y - 2)^2 - 3$	Add 3 to both sides.
$x + 3 = (y - 2)^2$	Take the square root.
$\pm\sqrt{x + 3} = y - 2$	Add 2 to both sides.
$2 \pm \sqrt{x + 3} = y$	Rename the function.
$f^{-1}(x) = 2 \pm \sqrt{x + 3}$	

Now we need to determine which case to use. Because we restricted our original function to a domain of $x \geq 2$, the outputs of the inverse should be the same, telling us to utilize the $+$ case

$$f^{-1}(x) = 2 + \sqrt{x + 3}$$

If the quadratic had not been given in vertex form, rewriting it into vertex form would be the first step. This way we may easily observe the coordinates of the vertex to help us restrict the domain.

Analysis   *Notice that we arbitrarily decided to restrict the domain on $x \geq 2$. We could just have easily opted to restrict the domain on $x \leq 2$, in which case $f^{-1}(x) = 2 - \sqrt{x + 3}$. Observe the original function graphed on the same set of axes as its inverse function in* **Figure 7**. *Notice that both graphs show symmetry about the line $y = x$. The coordinate pair $(2, -3)$ is on the graph of f and the coordinate pair $(-3, 2)$ is on the graph of f^{-1}. Observe from the graph of both functions on the same set of axes that*

$$\text{domain of } f = \text{range of } f^{-1} = [2, \infty)$$

and

$$\text{domain of } f^{-1} = \text{range of } f = [-3, \infty)$$

Finally, observe that the graph of f intersects the graph of f^{-1} along the line $y = x$.

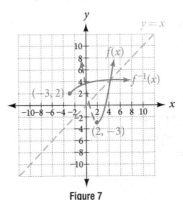

Figure 7

Try It #3

Find the inverse of the function $f(x) = x^2 + 1$, on the domain $x \geq 0$.

Solving Applications of Radical Functions

Notice that the functions from previous examples were all polynomials, and their inverses were radical functions. If we want to find the inverse of a radical function, we will need to restrict the domain of the answer because the range of the original function is limited.

How To...

Given a radical function, find the inverse.

1. Determine the range of the original function.
2. Replace $f(x)$ with y, then solve for x.
3. If necessary, restrict the domain of the inverse function to the range of the original function.

Example 5   **Finding the Inverse of a Radical Function**

Restrict the domain and then find the inverse of the function $f(x) = \sqrt{x - 4}$.

Solution   Note that the original function has range $f(x) \geq 0$. Replace $f(x)$ with y, then solve for x.

$$y = \sqrt{x - 4} \qquad \text{Replace } f(x) \text{ with } y.$$
$$x = \sqrt{y - 4} \qquad \text{Interchange } x \text{ and } y.$$
$$x = \sqrt{y - 4} \qquad \text{Square each side.}$$
$$x^2 = y - 4 \qquad \text{Add 4.}$$
$$x^2 + 4 = y \qquad \text{Rename the function } f^{-1}(x).$$
$$f^{-1}(x) = x^2 + 4$$

Recall that the domain of this function must be limited to the range of the original function.

$$f^{-1}(x) = x^2 + 4, \, x \geq 0$$

Analysis   Notice in **Figure 8** that the inverse is a reflection of the original function over the line $y = x$. Because the original function has only positive outputs, the inverse function has only positive inputs.

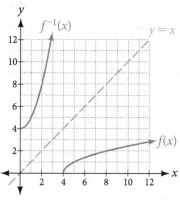

Figure 8

Try It #4

Restrict the domain and then find the inverse of the function $f(x) = \sqrt{2x + 3}$.

Solving Applications of Radical Functions

Radical functions are common in physical models, as we saw in the section opener. We now have enough tools to be able to solve the problem posed at the start of the section.

Example 6   **Solving an Application with a Cubic Function**

A mound of gravel is in the shape of a cone with the height equal to twice the radius. The volume of the cone in terms of the radius is given by

$$V = \frac{2}{3}\pi r^3$$

Find the inverse of the function $V = \frac{2}{3}\pi r^3$ that determines the volume V of a cone and is a function of the radius r. Then use the inverse function to calculate the radius of such a mound of gravel measuring 100 cubic feet. Use $\pi = 3.14$.

Solution   Start with the given function for V. Notice that the meaningful domain for the function is $r \geq 0$ since negative radii would not make sense in this context. Also note the range of the function (hence, the domain of the inverse function) is $V \geq 0$. Solve for r in terms of V, using the method outlined previously.

$$V = \frac{2}{3}\pi r^3$$

$$r^3 = \frac{3V}{2\pi} \qquad \text{Solve for } r^3.$$

$$r = \sqrt[3]{\frac{3V}{2\pi}} \qquad \text{Solve for } r.$$

This is the result stated in the section opener. Now evaluate this for $V = 100$ and $\pi = 3.14$.

$$r = \sqrt[3]{\frac{3V}{2\pi}}$$

$$= \sqrt[3]{\frac{3 \cdot 100}{2 \cdot 3.14}}$$

$$\approx \sqrt[3]{47.7707}$$

$$\approx 3.63$$

Therefore, the radius is about 3.63 ft.

Determining the Domain of a Radical Function Composed with Other Functions

When radical functions are composed with other functions, determining domain can become more complicated.

Example 7   **Finding the Domain of a Radical Function Composed with a Rational Function**

Find the domain of the function $f(x) = \sqrt{\dfrac{(x+2)(x-3)}{(x-1)}}$.

Solution   Because a square root is only defined when the quantity under the radical is non-negative, we need to determine where $\dfrac{(x+2)(x-3)}{(x-1)} \geq 0$. The output of a rational function can change signs (change from positive to negative or vice versa) at x-intercepts and at vertical asymptotes. For this equation, the graph could change signs at $x = -2$, 1, and 3.

To determine the intervals on which the rational expression is positive, we could test some values in the expression or sketch a graph. While both approaches work equally well, for this example we will use a graph as shown in **Figure 9**.

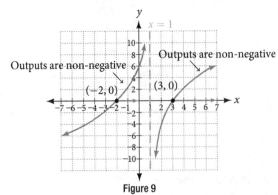

Figure 9

This function has two x-intercepts, both of which exhibit linear behavior near the x-intercepts. There is one vertical asymptote, corresponding to a linear factor; this behavior is similar to the basic reciprocal toolkit function, and there is no horizontal asymptote because the degree of the numerator is larger than the degree of the denominator. There is a y-intercept at $(0, \sqrt{6})$.

From the y-intercept and x-intercept at $x = -2$, we can sketch the left side of the graph. From the behavior at the asymptote, we can sketch the right side of the graph.

From the graph, we can now tell on which intervals the outputs will be non-negative, so that we can be sure that the original function $f(x)$ will be defined. $f(x)$ has domain $-2 \le x < 1$ or $x \ge 3$, or in interval notation, $[-2, 1) \cup [3, \infty)$.

Finding Inverses of Rational Functions

As with finding inverses of quadratic functions, it is sometimes desirable to find the inverse of a rational function, particularly of rational functions that are the ratio of linear functions, such as in concentration applications.

Example 8   **Finding the Inverse of a Rational Function**

The function $C = \dfrac{20 + 0.4n}{100 + n}$ represents the concentration C of an acid solution after n mL of 40% solution has been added to 100 mL of a 20% solution. First, find the inverse of the function; that is, find an expression for n in terms of C. Then use your result to determine how much of the 40% solution should be added so that the final mixture is a 35% solution.

Solution   We first want the inverse of the function. We will solve for n in terms of C.

$$C = \frac{20 + 0.4n}{100 + n}$$

$$C(100 + n) = 20 + 0.4n$$

$$100C + Cn = 20 + 0.4n$$

$$100C - 20 = 0.4n - Cn$$

$$100C - 20 = (0.4 - C)n$$

$$n = \frac{100C - 20}{0.4 - C}$$

Now evaluate this function for $C = 0.35$ (35%).

$$n = \frac{100(0.35) - 20}{0.4 - 0.35}$$

$$= \frac{15}{0.05}$$

$$= 300$$

We can conclude that 300 mL of the 40% solution should be added.

Try It #5

Find the inverse of the function $f(x) = \dfrac{x + 3}{x - 2}$.

Access these online resources for additional instruction and practice with inverses and radical functions.

- Graphing the Basic Square Root Function (http://openstaxcollege.org/l/graphsquareroot)
- Find the Inverse of a Square Root Function (http://openstaxcollege.org/l/inversesquare)
- Find the Inverse of a Rational Function (http://openstaxcollege.org/l/inverserational)
- Find the Inverse of a Rational Function and an Inverse Function Value (http://openstaxcollege.org/l/rationalinverse)
- Inverse Functions (http://openstaxcollege.org/l/inversefunction)

3.8   SECTION EXERCISES

VERBAL

1. Explain why we cannot find inverse functions for all polynomial functions.

2. Why must we restrict the domain of a quadratic function when finding its inverse?

3. When finding the inverse of a radical function, what restriction will we need to make?

4. The inverse of a quadratic function will always take what form?

ALGEBRAIC

For the following exercises, find the inverse of the function on the given domain.

5. $f(x) = (x - 4)^2$, $[4, \infty)$

6. $f(x) = (x + 2)^2$, $[-2, \infty)$

7. $f(x) = (x + 1)^2 - 3$, $[-1, \infty)$

8. $f(x) = 2 - \sqrt{3 + x}$

9. $f(x) = 3x^2 + 5$, $(-\infty, 0]$

10. $f(x) = 12 - x^2$, $[0, \infty)$

11. $f(x) = 9 - x^2$, $[0, \infty)$

12. $f(x) = 2x^2 + 4$, $[0, \infty)$

For the following exercises, find the inverse of the functions.

13. $f(x) = x^3 + 5$

14. $f(x) = 3x^3 + 1$

15. $f(x) = 4 - x^3$

16. $f(x) = 4 - 2x^3$

For the following exercises, find the inverse of the functions.

17. $f(x) = \sqrt{2x + 1}$

18. $f(x) = \sqrt{3 - 4x}$

19. $f(x) = 9 + \sqrt{4x - 4}$

20. $f(x) = \sqrt{6x - 8} + 5$

21. $f(x) = 9 + 2\sqrt[3]{x}$

22. $f(x) = 3 - \sqrt[3]{x}$

23. $f(x) = \dfrac{2}{x + 8}$

24. $f(x) = \dfrac{3}{x - 4}$

25. $f(x) = \dfrac{x + 3}{x + 7}$

26. $f(x) = \dfrac{x - 2}{x + 7}$

27. $f(x) = \dfrac{3x + 4}{5 - 4x}$

28. $f(x) = \dfrac{5x + 1}{2 - 5x}$

29. $f(x) = x^2 + 2x$, $[-1, \infty)$

30. $f(x) = x^2 + 4x + 1$, $[-2, \infty)$

31. $f(x) = x^2 - 6x + 3$, $[3, \infty)$

GRAPHICAL

For the following exercises, find the inverse of the function and graph both the function and its inverse.

32. $f(x) = x^2 + 2$, $x \geq 0$

33. $f(x) = 4 - x^2$, $x \geq 0$

34. $f(x) = (x + 3)^2$, $x \geq -3$

35. $f(x) = (x - 4)^2$, $x \geq 4$

36. $f(x) = x^3 + 3$

37. $f(x) = 1 - x^3$

38. $f(x) = x^2 + 4x$, $x \geq -2$

39. $f(x) = x^2 - 6x + 1$, $x \geq 3$

40. $f(x) = \dfrac{2}{x}$

41. $f(x) = \dfrac{1}{x^2}$, $x \geq 0$

For the following exercises, use a graph to help determine the domain of the functions.

42. $f(x) = \sqrt{\dfrac{(x + 1)(x - 1)}{x}}$

43. $f(x) = \sqrt{\dfrac{(x + 2)(x - 3)}{x - 1}}$

44. $f(x) = \sqrt{\dfrac{x(x + 3)}{x - 4}}$

45. $f(x) = \sqrt{\dfrac{x^2 - x - 20}{x - 2}}$

46. $f(x) = \sqrt{\dfrac{9 - x^2}{x + 4}}$

TECHNOLOGY

For the following exercises, use a calculator to graph the function. Then, using the graph, give three points on the graph of the inverse with y-coordinates given.

47. $f(x) = x^3 - x - 2, y = 1, 2, 3$ **48.** $f(x) = x^3 + x - 2, y = 0, 1, 2$ **49.** $f(x) = x^3 + 3x - 4, y = 0, 1, 2$

50. $f(x) = x^3 + 8x - 4, y = -1, 0, 1$ **51.** $f(x) = x^4 + 5x + 1, y = -1, 0, 1$

EXTENSIONS

For the following exercises, find the inverse of the functions with a, b, c positive real numbers.

52. $f(x) = ax^3 + b$ **53.** $f(x) = x^2 + bx$ **54.** $f(x) = \sqrt{ax^2 + b}$

55. $f(x) = \sqrt[3]{ax + b}$ **56.** $f(x) = \dfrac{ax + b}{x + c}$

REAL-WORLD APPLICATIONS

For the following exercises, determine the function described and then use it to answer the question.

57. An object dropped from a height of 200 meters has a height, $h(t)$, in meters after t seconds have lapsed, such that $h(t) = 200 - 4.9t^2$. Express t as a function of height, h, and find the time to reach a height of 50 meters.

58. An object dropped from a height of 600 feet has a height, $h(t)$, in feet after t seconds have elapsed, such that $h(t) = 600 - 16t^2$. Express t as a function of height h, and find the time to reach a height of 400 feet.

59. The volume, V, of a sphere in terms of its radius, r, is given by $V(r) = \dfrac{4}{3}\pi r^3$. Express r as a function of V, and find the radius of a sphere with volume of 200 cubic feet.

60. The surface area, A, of a sphere in terms of its radius, r, is given by $A(r) = 4\pi r^2$. Express r as a function of V, and find the radius of a sphere with a surface area of 1000 square inches.

61. A container holds 100 ml of a solution that is 25 ml acid. If n ml of a solution that is 60% acid is added, the function $C(n) = \dfrac{25 + 0.6n}{100 + n}$ gives the concentration, C, as a function of the number of ml added, n. Express n as a function of C and determine the number of mL that need to be added to have a solution that is 50% acid.

62. The period T, in seconds, of a simple pendulum as a function of its length l, in feet, is given by $T(l) = 2\pi \sqrt{\dfrac{l}{32.2}}$. Express l as a function of T and determine the length of a pendulum with period of 2 seconds.

63. The volume of a cylinder, V, in terms of radius, r, and height, h, is given by $V = \pi r^2 h$. If a cylinder has a height of 6 meters, express the radius as a function of V and find the radius of a cylinder with volume of 300 cubic meters.

64. The surface area, A, of a cylinder in terms of its radius, r, and height, h, is given by $A = 2\pi r^2 + 2\pi rh$. If the height of the cylinder is 4 feet, express the radius as a function of V and find the radius if the surface area is 200 square feet.

65. The volume of a right circular cone, V, in terms of its radius, r, and its height, h, is given by $V = \dfrac{1}{3}\pi r^2 h$. Express r in terms of h if the height of the cone is 12 feet and find the radius of a cone with volume of 50 cubic inches.

66. Consider a cone with height of 30 feet. Express the radius, r, in terms of the volume, V, and find the radius of a cone with volume of 1000 cubic feet.

LEARNING OBJECTIVES

In this section, you will:

- Solve direct variation problems.
- Solve inverse variation problems.
- Solve problems involving joint variation.

3.9   MODELING USING VARIATION

A used-car company has just offered their best candidate, Nicole, a position in sales. The position offers 16% commission on her sales. Her earnings depend on the amount of her sales. For instance, if she sells a vehicle for $4,600, she will earn $736. She wants to evaluate the offer, but she is not sure how. In this section, we will look at relationships, such as this one, between earnings, sales, and commission rate.

Solving Direct Variation Problems

In the example above, Nicole's earnings can be found by multiplying her sales by her commission. The formula $e = 0.16s$ tells us her earnings, e, come from the product of 0.16, her commission, and the sale price of the vehicle. If we create a table, we observe that as the sales price increases, the earnings increase as well, which should be intuitive. See **Table 1**.

s, sales prices	$e = 0.16s$	Interpretation
$4,600	$e = 0.16(4,600) = 736$	A sale of a $4,600 vehicle results in $736 earnings.
$9,200	$e = 0.16(9,200) = 1,472$	A sale of a $9,200 vehicle results in $1472 earnings.
$18,400	$e = 0.16(18,400) = 2,944$	A sale of a $18,400 vehicle results in $2944 earnings.

Table 1

Notice that earnings are a multiple of sales. As sales increase, earnings increase in a predictable way. Double the sales of the vehicle from $4,600 to $9,200, and we double the earnings from $736 to $1,472. As the input increases, the output increases as a multiple of the input. A relationship in which one quantity is a constant multiplied by another quantity is called **direct variation**. Each variable in this type of relationship **varies directly** with the other.

Figure 1 represents the data for Nicole's potential earnings. We say that earnings vary directly with the sales price of the car. The formula $y = kx^n$ is used for direct variation. The value k is a nonzero constant greater than zero and is called the **constant of variation**. In this case, $k = 0.16$ and $n = 1$.

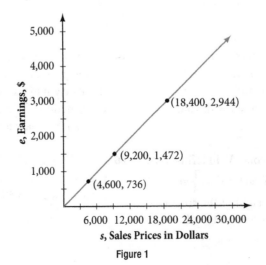

Figure 1

> ### direct variation
>
> If x and y are related by an equation of the form
>
> $$y = kx^n$$
>
> then we say that the relationship is **direct variation** and y **varies directly** with the nth power of x. In direct variation relationships, there is a nonzero constant ratio $k = \dfrac{y}{x^n}$, where k is called the **constant of variation**, which help defines the relationship between the variables.

How To...

Given a description of a direct variation problem, solve for an unknown.

1. Identify the input, x, and the output, y.
2. Determine the constant of variation. You may need to divide y by the specified power of x to determine the constant of variation.
3. Use the constant of variation to write an equation for the relationship.
4. Substitute known values into the equation to find the unknown.

Example 1   **Solving a Direct Variation Problem**

The quantity y varies directly with the cube of x. If $y = 25$ when $x = 2$, find y when x is 6.

Solution   The general formula for direct variation with a cube is $y = kx^3$. The constant can be found by dividing y by the cube of x.

$$k = \frac{y}{x^3}$$

$$= \frac{25}{2^3}$$

$$= \frac{25}{8}$$

Now use the constant to write an equation that represents this relationship.

$$y = \frac{25}{8}x^3$$

Substitute $x = 6$ and solve for y.

$$y = \frac{25}{8}(6)^3$$

$$= 675$$

Analysis   *The graph of this equation is a simple cubic, as shown in* **Figure 2**.

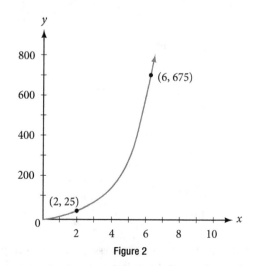

Figure 2

Q & A...

Do the graphs of all direct variation equations look like Example 1?

No. Direct variation equations are power functions—they may be linear, quadratic, cubic, quartic, radical, etc. But all of the graphs pass through (0,0).

Try It #1

The quantity y varies directly with the square of x. If $y = 24$ when $x = 3$, find y when x is 4.

Solving Inverse Variation Problems

Water temperature in an ocean varies inversely to the water's depth. Between the depths of 250 feet and 500 feet, the formula $T = \dfrac{14,000}{d}$ gives us the temperature in degrees Fahrenheit at a depth in feet below Earth's surface. Consider the Atlantic Ocean, which covers 22% of Earth's surface. At a certain location, at the depth of 500 feet, the temperature may be 28°F. If we create **Table 2**, we observe that, as the depth increases, the water temperature decreases.

d, depth	$T = \dfrac{14,000}{d}$	Interpretation
500 ft	$\dfrac{14,000}{500} = 28$	At a depth of 500 ft, the water temperature is 28° F.
350 ft	$\dfrac{14,000}{350} = 40$	At a depth of 350 ft, the water temperature is 40° F.
250 ft	$\dfrac{14,000}{250} = 56$	At a depth of 250 ft, the water temperature is 56° F.

Table 2

We notice in the relationship between these variables that, as one quantity increases, the other decreases. The two quantities are said to be **inversely proportional** and each term **varies inversely** with the other. Inversely proportional relationships are also called **inverse variations**.

For our example, **Figure 3** depicts the inverse variation. We say the water temperature varies inversely with the depth of the water because, as the depth increases, the temperature decreases. The formula $y = \dfrac{k}{x}$ for inverse variation in this case uses $k = 14,000$.

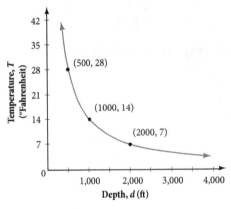

Figure 3

---

inverse variation

If x and y are related by an equation of the form

$$y = \frac{k}{x^n}$$

where k is a nonzero constant, then we say that y **varies inversely** with the nth power of x. In **inversely proportional** relationships, or **inverse variations**, there is a constant multiple $k = x^n y$.

Example 2 **Writing a Formula for an Inversely Proportional Relationship**

A tourist plans to drive 100 miles. Find a formula for the time the trip will take as a function of the speed the tourist drives.

Solution Recall that multiplying speed by time gives distance. If we let t represent the drive time in hours, and v represent the velocity (speed or rate) at which the tourist drives, then $vt =$ distance. Because the distance is fixed at 100 miles, $vt = 100$. Solving this relationship for the time gives us our function.

$$t(v) = \frac{100}{v}$$
$$= 100v^{-1}$$

We can see that the constant of variation is 100 and, although we can write the relationship using the negative exponent, it is more common to see it written as a fraction.

How To...

Given a description of an indirect variation problem, solve for an unknown.

1. Identify the input, x, and the output, y.
2. Determine the constant of variation. You may need to multiply y by the specified power of x to determine the constant of variation.
3. Use the constant of variation to write an equation for the relationship.
4. Substitute known values into the equation to find the unknown.

Example 3 **Solving an Inverse Variation Problem**

A quantity y varies inversely with the cube of x. If $y = 25$ when $x = 2$, find y when x is 6.

Solution The general formula for inverse variation with a cube is $y = \frac{k}{x^3}$. The constant can be found by multiplying y by the cube of x.

$$k = x^3 y$$
$$= 2^3 \cdot 25$$
$$= 200$$

Now we use the constant to write an equation that represents this relationship.

$$y = \frac{k}{x^3}, k = 200$$

$$y = \frac{200}{x^3}$$

Substitute $x = 6$ and solve for y.

$$y = \frac{200}{6^3}$$
$$= \frac{25}{27}$$

Analysis *The graph of this equation is a rational function, as shown in **Figure 4**.*

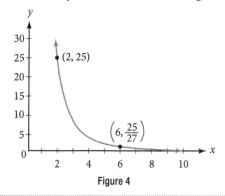

Figure 4

Try It #2

A quantity y varies inversely with the square of x. If $y = 8$ when $x = 3$, find y when x is 4.

Solving Problems Involving Joint Variation

Many situations are more complicated than a basic direct variation or inverse variation model. One variable often depends on multiple other variables. When a variable is dependent on the product or quotient of two or more variables, this is called **joint variation**. For example, the cost of busing students for each school trip varies with the number of students attending and the distance from the school. The variable c, cost, varies jointly with the number of students, n, and the distance, d.

---

joint variation

Joint variation occurs when a variable varies directly or inversely with multiple variables.

For instance, if x varies directly with both y and z, we have $x = kyz$. If x varies directly with y and inversely with z, we have $x = \dfrac{ky}{z}$. Notice that we only use one constant in a joint variation equation.

Example 4   **Solving Problems Involving Joint Variation**

A quantity x varies directly with the square of y and inversely with the cube root of z. If $x = 6$ when $y = 2$ and $z = 8$, find x when $y = 1$ and $z = 27$.

Solution   Begin by writing an equation to show the relationship between the variables.

$$x = \frac{ky^2}{\sqrt[3]{z}}$$

Substitute $x = 6$, $y = 2$, and $z = 8$ to find the value of the constant k.

$$6 = \frac{k2^2}{\sqrt[3]{8}}$$

$$6 = \frac{4k}{2}$$

$$3 = k$$

Now we can substitute the value of the constant into the equation for the relationship.

$$x = \frac{3y^2}{\sqrt[3]{z}}$$

To find x when $y = 1$ and $z = 27$, we will substitute values for y and z into our equation.

$$x = \frac{3(1)^2}{\sqrt[3]{27}}$$

$$= 1$$

Try It #3

x varies directly with the square of y and inversely with z. If $x = 40$ when $y = 4$ and $z = 2$, find x when $y = 10$ and $z = 25$.

Access these online resources for additional instruction and practice with direct and inverse variation.

- Direct Variation (http://openstaxcollege.org/l/directvariation)
- Inverse Variation (http://openstaxcollege.org/l/inversevariatio)
- Direct and Inverse Variation (http://openstaxcollege.org/l/directinverse)

3.9 SECTION EXERCISES

VERBAL

1. What is true of the appearance of graphs that reflect a direct variation between two variables?

2. If two variables vary inversely, what will an equation representing their relationship look like?

3. Is there a limit to the number of variables that can jointly vary? Explain.

ALGEBRAIC

For the following exercises, write an equation describing the relationship of the given variables.

4. y varies directly as x and when $x = 6$, $y = 12$.

5. y varies directly as the square of x and when $x = 4$, $y = 80$.

6. y varies directly as the square root of x and when $x = 36$, $y = 24$.

7. y varies directly as the cube of x and when $x = 36$, $y = 24$.

8. y varies directly as the cube root of x and when $x = 27$, $y = 15$.

9. y varies directly as the fourth power of x and when $x = 1$, $y = 6$.

10. y varies inversely as x and when $x = 4$, $y = 2$.

11. y varies inversely as the square of x and when $x = 3$, $y = 2$.

12. y varies inversely as the cube of x and when $x = 2$, $y = 5$.

13. y varies inversely as the fourth power of x and when $x = 3$, $y = 1$.

14. y varies inversely as the square root of x and when $x = 25$, $y = 3$.

15. y varies inversely as the cube root of x and when $x = 64$, $y = 5$.

16. y varies jointly with x and z and when $x = 2$ and $z = 3$, $y = 36$.

17. y varies jointly as x, z, and w and when $x = 1$, $z = 2$, $w = 5$, then $y = 100$.

18. y varies jointly as the square of x and the square of z and when $x = 3$ and $z = 4$, then $y = 72$.

19. y varies jointly as x and the square root of z and when $x = 2$ and $z = 25$, then $y = 100$.

20. y varies jointly as the square of x the cube of z and the square root of w. When $x = 1$, $z = 2$, and $w = 36$, then $y = 48$.

21. y varies jointly as x and z and inversely as w. When $x = 3$, $z = 5$, and $w = 6$, then $y = 10$.

22. y varies jointly as the square of x and the square root of z and inversely as the cube of w. When $x = 3$, $z = 4$, and $w = 3$, then $y = 6$.

23. y varies jointly as x and z and inversely as the square root of w and the square of t. When $x = 3$, $z = 1$, $w = 25$, and $t = 2$, then $y = 6$.

NUMERIC

For the following exercises, use the given information to find the unknown value.

24. y varies directly as x. When $x = 3$, then $y = 12$. Find y when $x = 20$.

25. y varies directly as the square of x. When $x = 2$, then $y = 16$. Find y when $x = 8$.

26. y varies directly as the cube of x. When $x = 3$, then $y = 5$. Find y when $x = 4$.

27. y varies directly as the square root of x. When $x = 16$, then $y = 4$. Find y when $x = 36$.

28. y varies directly as the cube root of x. When $x = 125$, then $y = 15$. Find y when $x = 1,000$.

29. y varies inversely with x. When $x = 3$, then $y = 2$. Find y when $x = 1$.

30. y varies inversely with the square of x. When $x = 4$, then $y = 3$. Find y when $x = 2$.

31. y varies inversely with the cube of x. When $x = 3$, then $y = 1$. Find y when $x = 1$.

32. y varies inversely with the square root of x. When $x = 64$, then $y = 12$. Find y when $x = 36$.

33. y varies inversely with the cube root of x. When $x = 27$, then $y = 5$. Find y when $x = 125$.

34. y varies jointly as x and z. When $x = 4$ and $z = 2$, then $y = 16$. Find y when $x = 3$ and $z = 3$.

35. y varies jointly as x, z, and w. When $x = 2$, $z = 1$, and $w = 12$, then $y = 72$. Find y when $x = 1$, $z = 2$, and $w = 3$.

36. y varies jointly as x and the square of z. When $x = 2$ and $z = 4$, then $y = 144$. Find y when $x = 4$ and $z = 5$.

37. y varies jointly as the square of x and the square root of z. When $x = 2$ and $z = 9$, then $y = 24$. Find y when $x = 3$ and $z = 25$.

38. y varies jointly as x and z and inversely as w. When $x = 5$, $z = 2$, and $w = 20$, then $y = 4$. Find y when $x = 3$ and $z = 8$, and $w = 48$.

39. y varies jointly as the square of x and the cube of z and inversely as the square root of w. When $x = 2$, $z = 2$, and $w = 64$, then $y = 12$. Find y when $x = 1$, $z = 3$, and $w = 4$.

40. y varies jointly as the square of x and of z and inversely as the square root of w and of t. When $x = 2$, $z = 3$, $w = 16$, and $t = 3$, then $y = 1$. Find y when $x = 3$, $z = 2$, $w = 36$, and $t = 5$.

TECHNOLOGY

For the following exercises, use a calculator to graph the equation implied by the given variation.

41. y varies directly with the square of x and when $x = 2$, $y = 3$.

42. y varies directly as the cube of x and when $x = 2$, $y = 4$.

43. y varies directly as the square root of x and when $x = 36$, $y = 2$.

44. y varies inversely with x and when $x = 6$, $y = 2$.

45. y varies inversely as the square of x and when $x = 1$, $y = 4$.

EXTENSIONS

For the following exercises, use Kepler's Law, which states that the square of the time, T, required for a planet to orbit the Sun varies directly with the cube of the mean distance, a, that the planet is from the Sun.

46. Using the Earth's time of 1 year and mean distance of 93 million miles, find the equation relating T and a.

47. Use the result from the previous exercise to determine the time required for Mars to orbit the Sun if its mean distance is 142 million miles.

48. Using Earth's distance of 150 million kilometers, find the equation relating T and a.

49. Use the result from the previous exercise to determine the time required for Venus to orbit the Sun if its mean distance is 108 million kilometers.

50. Using Earth's distance of 1 astronomical unit (A.U.), determine the time for Saturn to orbit the Sun if its mean distance is 9.54 A.U.

REAL-WORLD APPLICATIONS

For the following exercises, use the given information to answer the questions.

51. The distance s that an object falls varies directly with the square of the time, t, of the fall. If an object falls 16 feet in one second, how long for it to fall 144 feet?

52. The velocity v of a falling object varies directly to the time, t, of the fall. If after 2 seconds, the velocity of the object is 64 feet per second, what is the velocity after 5 seconds?

53. The rate of vibration of a string under constant tension varies inversely with the length of the string. If a string is 24 inches long and vibrates 128 times per second, what is the length of a string that vibrates 64 times per second?

54. The volume of a gas held at constant temperature varies indirectly as the pressure of the gas. If the volume of a gas is 1200 cubic centimeters when the pressure is 200 millimeters of mercury, what is the volume when the pressure is 300 millimeters of mercury?

55. The weight of an object above the surface of the Earth varies inversely with the square of the distance from the center of the Earth. If a body weighs 50 pounds when it is 3960 miles from Earth's center, what would it weigh it were 3970 miles from Earth's center?

56. The intensity of light measured in foot-candles varies inversely with the square of the distance from the light source. Suppose the intensity of a light bulb is 0.08 foot-candles at a distance of 3 meters. Find the intensity level at 8 meters.

57. The current in a circuit varies inversely with its resistance measured in ohms. When the current in a circuit is 40 amperes, the resistance is 10 ohms. Find the current if the resistance is 12 ohms.

58. The force exerted by the wind on a plane surface varies jointly with the square of the velocity of the wind and with the area of the plane surface. If the area of the surface is 40 square feet surface and the wind velocity is 20 miles per hour, the resulting force is 15 pounds. Find the force on a surface of 65 square feet with a velocity of 30 miles per hour.

59. The horsepower (hp) that a shaft can safely transmit varies jointly with its speed (in revolutions per minute (rpm)) and the cube of the diameter. If the shaft of a certain material 3 inches in diameter can transmit 45 hp at 100 rpm, what must the diameter be in order to transmit 60 hp at 150 rpm?

60. The kinetic energy K of a moving object varies jointly with its mass m and the square of its velocity v. If an object weighing 40 kilograms with a velocity of 15 meters per second has a kinetic energy of 1000 joules, find the kinetic energy if the velocity is increased to 20 meters per second.

CHAPTER 3 REVIEW

Key Terms

arrow notation a way to symbolically represent the local and end behavior of a function by using arrows to indicate that an input or output approaches a value

axis of symmetry a vertical line drawn through the vertex of a parabola around which the parabola is symmetric; it is defined by $x = -\dfrac{b}{2a}$.

coefficient a nonzero real number multiplied by a variable raised to an exponent

complex conjugate the complex number in which the sign of the imaginary part is changed and the real part of the number is left unchanged; when added to or multiplied by the original complex number, the result is a real number

complex number the sum of a real number and an imaginary number, written in the standard form $a + bi$, where a is the real part, and bi is the imaginary part

complex plane a coordinate system in which the horizontal axis is used to represent the real part of a complex number and the vertical axis is used to represent the imaginary part of a complex number

constant of variation the non-zero value k that helps define the relationship between variables in direct or inverse variation

continuous function a function whose graph can be drawn without lifting the pen from the paper because there are no breaks in the graph

degree the highest power of the variable that occurs in a polynomial

Descartes' Rule of Signs a rule that determines the maximum possible numbers of positive and negative real zeros based on the number of sign changes of $f(x)$ and $f(-x)$

direct variation the relationship between two variables that are a constant multiple of each other; as one quantity increases, so does the other

Division Algorithm given a polynomial dividend $f(x)$ and a non-zero polynomial divisor $d(x)$ where the degree of $d(x)$ is less than or equal to the degree of $f(x)$, there exist unique polynomials $q(x)$ and $r(x)$ such that $f(x) = d(x) q(x) + r(x)$ where $q(x)$ is the quotient and $r(x)$ is the remainder. The remainder is either equal to zero or has degree strictly less than $d(x)$.

end behavior the behavior of the graph of a function as the input decreases without bound and increases without bound

Factor Theorem k is a zero of polynomial function $f(x)$ if and only if $(x - k)$ is a factor of $f(x)$

Fundamental Theorem of Algebra a polynomial function with degree greater than 0 has at least one complex zero

general form of a quadratic function the function that describes a parabola, written in the form $f(x) = ax^2 + bx + c$, where a, b, and c are real numbers and $a \neq 0$.

global maximum highest turning point on a graph; $f(a)$ where $f(a) \geq f(x)$ for all x.

global minimum lowest turning point on a graph; $f(a)$ where $f(a) \leq f(x)$ for all x.

horizontal asymptote a horizontal line $y = b$ where the graph approaches the line as the inputs increase or decrease without bound.

Intermediate Value Theorem for two numbers a and b in the domain of f, if $a < b$ and $f(a) \neq f(b)$, then the function f takes on every value between $f(a)$ and $f(b)$; specifically, when a polynomial function changes from a negative value to a positive value, the function must cross the x-axis

inverse variation the relationship between two variables in which the product of the variables is a constant

inversely proportional a relationship where one quantity is a constant divided by the other quantity; as one quantity increases, the other decreases

invertible function any function that has an inverse function

imaginary number a number in the form bi where $i = \sqrt{-1}$

joint variation a relationship where a variable varies directly or inversely with multiple variables

leading coefficient the coefficient of the leading term

leading term the term containing the highest power of the variable

Linear Factorization Theorem allowing for multiplicities, a polynomial function will have the same number of factors as its degree, and each factor will be in the form $(x - c)$, where c is a complex number

multiplicity the number of times a given factor appears in the factored form of the equation of a polynomial; if a polynomial contains a factor of the form $(x - h)^p$, $x = h$ is a zero of multiplicity p.

polynomial function a function that consists of either zero or the sum of a finite number of non-zero terms, each of which is a product of a number, called the coefficient of the term, and a variable raised to a non-negative integer power.

power function a function that can be represented in the form $f(x) = kx^p$ where k is a constant, the base is a variable, and the exponent, p, is a constant

rational function a function that can be written as the ratio of two polynomials

Rational Zero Theorem the possible rational zeros of a polynomial function have the form $\frac{p}{q}$ where p is a factor of the constant term and q is a factor of the leading coefficient.

Remainder Theorem if a polynomial $f(x)$ is divided by $x - k$, then the remainder is equal to the value $f(k)$

removable discontinuity a single point at which a function is undefined that, if filled in, would make the function continuous; it appears as a hole on the graph of a function

smooth curve a graph with no sharp corners

standard form of a quadratic function the function that describes a parabola, written in the form $f(x) = a(x - h)^2 + k$, where (h, k) is the vertex.

synthetic division a shortcut method that can be used to divide a polynomial by a binomial of the form $x - k$

term of a polynomial function any $a_i x^i$ of a polynomial function in the form $f(x) = a_n x^n + ... + a_2 x^2 + a_1 x + a_0$

turning point the location at which the graph of a function changes direction

varies directly a relationship where one quantity is a constant multiplied by the other quantity

varies inversely a relationship where one quantity is a constant divided by the other quantity

vertex the point at which a parabola changes direction, corresponding to the minimum or maximum value of the quadratic function

vertex form of a quadratic function another name for the standard form of a quadratic function

vertical asymptote a vertical line $x = a$ where the graph tends toward positive or negative infinity as the inputs approach a

zeros in a given function, the values of x at which $y = 0$, also called roots

Key Equations

general form of a quadratic function	$f(x) = ax^2 + bx + c$
the quadratic formula	$x = \dfrac{-b \pm \sqrt{b^2 - 4ac}}{2a}$
standard form of a quadratic function	$f(x) = a(x - h)^2 + k$
general form of a polynomial function	$f(x) = a_n x^n + ... + a_2 x^2 + a_1 x + a_0$
Division Algorithm	$f(x) = d(x)q(x) + r(x)$ where $q(x) \neq 0$
Rational Function	$f(x) = \dfrac{P(x)}{Q(x)} = \dfrac{a_p x^p + a_{p-1} x^{p-1} + ... + a_1 x + a_0}{b_q x^q + b_{q-1} x^{q-1} + ... + b_1 x + b_0}, \; Q(x) \neq 0$
Direct variation	$y = kx^n$, k is a nonzero constant.
Inverse variation	$y = \dfrac{k}{x^n}$, k is a nonzero constant.

Key Concepts

3.1 Complex Numbers

- The square root of any negative number can be written as a multiple of i. See **Example 1**.
- To plot a complex number, we use two number lines, crossed to form the complex plane. The horizontal axis is the real axis, and the vertical axis is the imaginary axis. See **Example 2**.
- Complex numbers can be added and subtracted by combining the real parts and combining the imaginary parts. See **Example 3**.
- Complex numbers can be multiplied and divided.
- To multiply complex numbers, distribute just as with polynomials. See **Example 4**, **Example 5**, and **Example 8**.
- To divide complex numbers, multiply both the numerator and denominator by the complex conjugate of the denominator to eliminate the complex number from the denominator. See **Example 6**, **Example 7**, and **Example 9**.
- The powers of i are cyclic, repeating every fourth one. See **Example 10**.

3.2 Quadratic Functions

- A polynomial function of degree two is called a quadratic function.
- The graph of a quadratic function is a parabola. A parabola is a U-shaped curve that can open either up or down.
- The axis of symmetry is the vertical line passing through the vertex. The zeros, or x-intercepts, are the points at which the parabola crosses the x-axis. The y-intercept is the point at which the parabola crosses the y-axis. See **Example 1**, **Example 7**, and **Example 8**.
- Quadratic functions are often written in general form. Standard or vertex form is useful to easily identify the vertex of a parabola. Either form can be written from a graph. See **Example 2**.
- The vertex can be found from an equation representing a quadratic function. See **Example 3**.
- The domain of a quadratic function is all real numbers. The range varies with the function. See **Example 4**.
- A quadratic function's minimum or maximum value is given by the y-value of the vertex.
- The minimum or maximum value of a quadratic function can be used to determine the range of the function and to solve many kinds of real-world problems, including problems involving area and revenue. See **Example 5** and **Example 6**.
- Some quadratic equations must be solved by using the quadratic formula. See **Example 9**.
- The vertex and the intercepts can be identified and interpreted to solve real-world problems. See **Example 10**.

3.3 Power Functions and Polynomial Functions

- A power function is a variable base raised to a number power. See **Example 1**.
- The behavior of a graph as the input decreases beyond bound and increases beyond bound is called the end behavior.
- The end behavior depends on whether the power is even or odd. See **Example 2** and **Example 3**.
- A polynomial function is the sum of terms, each of which consists of a transformed power function with positive whole number power. See **Example 4**.
- The degree of a polynomial function is the highest power of the variable that occurs in a polynomial. The term containing the highest power of the variable is called the leading term. The coefficient of the leading term is called the leading coefficient. See **Example 5**.
- The end behavior of a polynomial function is the same as the end behavior of the power function represented by the leading term of the function. See **Example 6** and **Example 7**.
- A polynomial of degree n will have at most n x-intercepts and at most $n - 1$ turning points. See **Example 8**, **Example 9**, **Example 10**, **Example 11**, and **Example 12**.

3.4 Graphs of Polynomial Functions

- Polynomial functions of degree 2 or more are smooth, continuous functions. See **Example 1**.
- To find the zeros of a polynomial function, if it can be factored, factor the function and set each factor equal to zero. See **Example 2**, **Example 3**, and **Example 4**.
- Another way to find the x-intercepts of a polynomial function is to graph the function and identify the points at which the graph crosses the x-axis. See **Example 5**.
- The multiplicity of a zero determines how the graph behaves at the x-intercepts. See **Example 6**.
- The graph of a polynomial will cross the horizontal axis at a zero with odd multiplicity.
- The graph of a polynomial will touch the horizontal axis at a zero with even multiplicity.
- The end behavior of a polynomial function depends on the leading term.
- The graph of a polynomial function changes direction at its turning points.
- A polynomial function of degree n has at most $n - 1$ turning points. See **Example 7**.
- To graph polynomial functions, find the zeros and their multiplicities, determine the end behavior, and ensure that the final graph has at most $n - 1$ turning points. See **Example 8** and **Example 10**.
- Graphing a polynomial function helps to estimate local and global extremas. See **Example 11**.
- The Intermediate Value Theorem tells us that if $f(a)$ and $f(b)$ have opposite signs, then there exists at least one value c between a and b for which $f(c) = 0$. See **Example 9**.

3.5 Dividing Polynomials

- Polynomial long division can be used to divide a polynomial by any polynomial with equal or lower degree. See **Example 1** and **Example 2**.
- The Division Algorithm tells us that a polynomial dividend can be written as the product of the divisor and the quotient added to the remainder.
- Synthetic division is a shortcut that can be used to divide a polynomial by a binomial in the form $x - k$. See **Example 3**, **Example 4**, and **Example 5**.
- Polynomial division can be used to solve application problems, including area and volume. See **Example 6**.

3.6 Zeros of Polynomial Functions

- To find $f(k)$, determine the remainder of the polynomial $f(x)$ when it is divided by $x - k$. See **Example 1**.
- k is a zero of $f(x)$ if and only if $(x - k)$ is a factor of $f(x)$. See **Example 2**.
- Each rational zero of a polynomial function with integer coefficients will be equal to a factor of the constant term divided by a factor of the leading coefficient. See **Example 3** and **Example 4**.
- When the leading coefficient is 1, the possible rational zeros are the factors of the constant term.
- Synthetic division can be used to find the zeros of a polynomial function. See **Example 5**.
- According to the Fundamental Theorem, every polynomial function has at least one complex zero. See **Example 6**.
- Every polynomial function with degree greater than 0 has at least one complex zero.
- Allowing for multiplicities, a polynomial function will have the same number of factors as its degree. Each factor will be in the form $(x - c)$, where c is a complex number. See **Example 7**.
- The number of positive real zeros of a polynomial function is either the number of sign changes of the function or less than the number of sign changes by an even integer.
- The number of negative real zeros of a polynomial function is either the number of sign changes of $f(-x)$ or less than the number of sign changes by an even integer. See **Example 8**.
- Polynomial equations model many real-world scenarios. Solving the equations is easiest done by synthetic division. See **Example 9**.

3.7 Rational Functions

- We can use arrow notation to describe local behavior and end behavior of the toolkit functions $f(x) = \frac{1}{x}$ and $f(x) = \frac{1}{x^2}$. See **Example 1**.

- A function that levels off at a horizontal value has a horizontal asymptote. A function can have more than one vertical asymptote. See **Example 2**.

- Application problems involving rates and concentrations often involve rational functions. See **Example 3**.

- The domain of a rational function includes all real numbers except those that cause the denominator to equal zero. See **Example 4**.

- The vertical asymptotes of a rational function will occur where the denominator of the function is equal to zero and the numerator is not zero. See **Example 5**.

- A removable discontinuity might occur in the graph of a rational function if an input causes both numerator and denominator to be zero. See **Example 6**.

- A rational function's end behavior will mirror that of the ratio of the leading terms of the numerator and denominator functions. See **Example 7**, **Example 8**, **Example 9**, and **Example 10**.

- Graph rational functions by finding the intercepts, behavior at the intercepts and asymptotes, and end behavior. See **Example 11**.

- If a rational function has x-intercepts at $x = x_1, x_2, \ldots, x_n$, vertical asymptotes at $x = v_1, v_2, \ldots, v_m$, and no $x_i =$ any v_j, then the function can be written in the form

$$f(x) = a\frac{(x - x_1)^{p_1}(x - x_2)^{p_2}\ldots(x - x_n)^{p_n}}{(x - v_1)^{q_1}(x - v_2)^{q_2}\ldots(x - v_m)^{q_n}}$$

See **Example 12**.

3.8 Inverses and Radical Functions

- The inverse of a quadratic function is a square root function.

- If f^{-1} is the inverse of a function f, then f is the inverse of the function f^{-1}. See **Example 1**.

- While it is not possible to find an inverse of most polynomial functions, some basic polynomials are invertible. See **Example 2**.

- To find the inverse of certain functions, we must restrict the function to a domain on which it will be one-to-one. See **Example 3** and **Example 4**.

- When finding the inverse of a radical function, we need a restriction on the domain of the answer. See **Example 5** and **Example 7**.

- Inverse and radical and functions can be used to solve application problems. See **Example 6** and **Example 8**.

3.9 Modeling Using Variation

- A relationship where one quantity is a constant multiplied by another quantity is called direct variation. See **Example 1**.

- Two variables that are directly proportional to one another will have a constant ratio.

- A relationship where one quantity is a constant divided by another quantity is called inverse variation. See **Example 2**.

- Two variables that are inversely proportional to one another will have a constant multiple. See **Example 3**.

- In many problems, a variable varies directly or inversely with multiple variables. We call this type of relationship joint variation. See **Example 4**.

CHAPTER 3 REVIEW EXERCISES

You have reached the end of Chapter 3: Polynomial and Rational Functions. Let's review some of the Key Terms, Concepts and Equations you have learned.

COMPLEX NUMBERS

Perform the indicated operation with complex numbers.

1. $(4 + 3i) + (-2 - 5i)$

2. $(6 - 5i) - (10 + 3i)$

3. $(2 - 3i)(3 + 6i)$

4. $\dfrac{2 - i}{2 + i}$

Solve the following equations over the complex number system.

5. $x^2 - 4x + 5 = 0$

6. $x^2 + 2x + 10 = 0$

QUADRATIC FUNCTIONS

For the following exercises, write the quadratic function in standard form. Then, give the vertex and axes intercepts. Finally, graph the function.

7. $f(x) = x^2 - 4x - 5$

8. $f(x) = -2x^2 - 4x$

For the following problems, find the equation of the quadratic function using the given information.

9. The vertex is $(-2, 3)$ and a point on the graph is $(3, 6)$.

10. The vertex is $(-3, 6.5)$ and a point on the graph is $(2, 6)$.

Answer the following questions.

11. A rectangular plot of land is to be enclosed by fencing. One side is along a river and so needs no fence. If the total fencing available is 600 meters, find the dimensions of the plot to have maximum area.

12. An object projected from the ground at a 45 degree angle with initial velocity of 120 feet per second has height, h, in terms of horizontal distance traveled, x, given by $h(x) = \dfrac{-32}{(120)^2} x^2 + x$. Find the maximum height the object attains.

POWER FUNCTIONS AND POLYNOMIAL FUNCTIONS

For the following exercises, determine if the function is a polynomial function and, if so, give the degree and leading coefficient.

13. $f(x) = 4x^5 - 3x^3 + 2x - 1$

14. $f(x) = 5^{x+1} - x^2$

15. $f(x) = x^2(3 - 6x + x^2)$

For the following exercises, determine end behavior of the polynomial function.

16. $f(x) = 2x^4 + 3x^3 - 5x^2 + 7$

17. $f(x) = 4x^3 - 6x^2 + 2$

18. $f(x) = 2x^2(1 + 3x - x^2)$

GRAPHS OF POLYNOMIAL FUNCTIONS

For the following exercises, find all zeros of the polynomial function, noting multiplicities.

19. $f(x) = (x + 3)^2(2x - 1)(x + 1)^3$

20. $f(x) = x^5 + 4x^4 + 4x^3$

21. $f(x) = x^3 - 4x^2 + x - 4$

For the following exercises, based on the given graph, determine the zeros of the function and note multiplicity.

22.

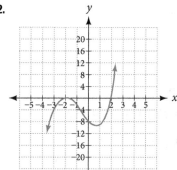

23.

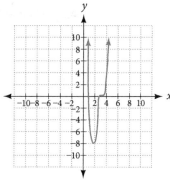

24. Use the Intermediate Value Theorem to show that at least one zero lies between 2 and 3 for the function
$f(x) = x^3 - 5x + 1$

DIVIDING POLYNOMIALS

For the following exercises, use long division to find the quotient and remainder.

25. $\dfrac{x^3 - 2x^2 + 4x + 4}{x - 2}$

26. $\dfrac{3x^4 - 4x^2 + 4x + 8}{x + 1}$

For the following exercises, use synthetic division to find the quotient. If the divisor is a factor, then write the factored form.

27. $\dfrac{x^3 - 2x^2 + 5x - 1}{x + 3}$

28. $\dfrac{x^3 + 4x + 10}{x - 3}$

29. $\dfrac{2x^3 + 6x^2 - 11x - 12}{x + 4}$

30. $\dfrac{3x^4 + 3x^3 + 2x + 2}{x + 1}$

ZEROS OF POLYNOMIAL FUNCTIONS

For the following exercises, use the Rational Zero Theorem to help you solve the polynomial equation.

31. $2x^3 - 3x^2 - 18x - 8 = 0$

32. $3x^3 + 11x^2 + 8x - 4 = 0$

33. $2x^4 - 17x^3 + 46x^2 - 43x + 12 = 0$

34. $4x^4 + 8x^3 + 19x^2 + 32x + 12 = 0$

For the following exercises, use Descartes' Rule of Signs to find the possible number of positive and negative solutions.

35. $x^3 - 3x^2 - 2x + 4 = 0$

36. $2x^4 - x^3 + 4x^2 - 5x + 1 = 0$

RATIONAL FUNCTIONS

For the following rational functions, find the intercepts and the vertical and horizontal asymptotes, and then use them to sketch a graph.

37. $f(x) = \dfrac{x + 2}{x - 5}$

38. $f(x) = \dfrac{x^2 + 1}{x^2 - 4}$

39. $f(x) = \dfrac{3x^2 - 27}{x^2 + x - 2}$

40. $f(x) = \dfrac{x + 2}{x^2 - 9}$

For the following exercises, find the slant asymptote.

41. $f(x) = \dfrac{x^2 - 1}{x + 2}$

42. $f(x) = \dfrac{2x^3 - x^2 + 4}{x^2 + 1}$

INVERSES AND RADICAL FUNCTIONS

For the following exercises, find the inverse of the function with the domain given.

43. $f(x) = (x - 2)^2, x \geq 2$

44. $f(x) = (x + 4)^2 - 3, x \geq -4$

45. $f(x) = x^2 + 6x - 2, x \geq -3$

46. $f(x) = 2x^3 - 3$

47. $f(x) = \sqrt{4x + 5} - 3$

48. $f(x) = \dfrac{x - 3}{2x + 1}$

MODELING USING VARIATION

For the following exercises, find the unknown value.

49. y varies directly as the square of x. If when $x = 3$, $y = 36$, find y if $x = 4$.

50. y varies inversely as the square root of x. If when $x = 25$, $y = 2$, find y if $x = 4$.

51. y varies jointly as the cube of x and as z. If when $x = 1$ and $z = 2$, $y = 6$, find y if $x = 2$ and $z = 3$.

52. y varies jointly as x and the square of z and inversely as the cube of w. If when $x = 3$, $z = 4$, and $w = 2$, $y = 48$, find y if $x = 4$, $z = 5$, and $w = 3$.

For the following exercises, solve the application problem.

53. The weight of an object above the surface of the earth varies inversely with the distance from the center of the earth.If a person weighs 150 pounds when he is on the surface of the earth (3,960 miles from center), find the weight of the person if he is 20 miles above the surface.

54. The volume V of an ideal gas varies directly with the temperature T and inversely with the pressure P. A cylinder contains oxygen at a temperature of 310 degrees K and a pressure of 18 atmospheres in a volume of 120 liters. Find the pressure if the volume is decreased to 100 liters and the temperature is increased to 320 degrees K.

CHAPTER 3 PRACTICE TEST

Perform the indicated operation or solve the equation.

1. $(3 - 4i)(4 + 2i)$

2. $\dfrac{1 - 4i}{3 + 4i}$

3. $x^2 - 4x + 13 = 0$

Give the degree and leading coefficient of the following polynomial function.

4. $f(x) = x^3(3 - 6x^2 - 2x^2)$

Determine the end behavior of the polynomial function.

5. $f(x) = 8x^3 - 3x^2 + 2x - 4$

6. $f(x) = -2x^2(4 - 3x - 5x^2)$

Write the quadratic function in standard form. Determine the vertex and axes intercepts and graph the function.

7. $f(x) = x^2 + 2x - 8$

Given information about the graph of a quadratic function, find its equation.

8. Vertex $(2, 0)$ and point on graph $(4, 12)$.

Solve the following application problem.

9. A rectangular field is to be enclosed by fencing. In addition to the enclosing fence, another fence is to divide the field into two parts, running parallel to two sides. If 1,200 feet of fencing is available, find the maximum area that can be enclosed.

Find all zeros of the following polynomial functions, noting multiplicities.

10. $f(x) = (x - 3)^3(3x - 1)(x - 1)^2$

11. $f(x) = 2x^6 - 12x^5 + 18x^4$

Based on the graph, determine the zeros of the function and multiplicities.

12.

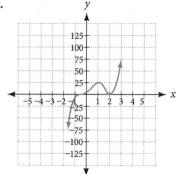

Use long division to find the quotient.

13. $\dfrac{2x^3 + 3x - 4}{x + 2}$

Use synthetic division to find the quotient. If the divisor is a factor, write the factored form.

14. $\dfrac{x^4 + 3x^2 - 4}{x - 2}$

15. $\dfrac{2x^3 + 5x^2 - 7x - 12}{x + 3}$

Use the Rational Zero Theorem to help you find the zeros of the polynomial functions.

16. $f(x) = 2x^3 + 5x^2 - 6x - 9$

17. $f(x) = 4x^4 + 8x^3 + 21x^2 + 17x + 4$

18. $f(x) = 4x^4 + 16x^3 + 13x^2 - 15x - 18$

19. $f(x) = x^5 + 6x^4 + 13x^3 + 14x^2 + 12x + 8$

Given the following information about a polynomial function, find the function.

20. It has a double zero at $x = 3$ and zeroes at $x = 1$ and $x = -2$. Its y-intercept is $(0, 12)$.

21. It has a zero of multiplicity 3 at $x = \frac{1}{2}$ and another zero at $x = -3$. It contains the point $(1, 8)$.

Use Descartes' Rule of Signs to determine the possible number of positive and negative solutions.

22. $8x^3 - 21x^2 + 6 = 0$

For the following rational functions, find the intercepts and horizontal and vertical asymptotes, and sketch a graph.

23. $f(x) = \dfrac{x + 4}{x^2 - 2x - 3}$

24. $f(x) = \dfrac{x^2 + 2x - 3}{x^2 - 4}$

Find the slant asymptote of the rational function.

25. $f(x) = \dfrac{x^2 + 3x - 3}{x - 1}$

Find the inverse of the function.

26. $f(x) = \sqrt{x - 2} + 4$

27. $f(x) = 3x^3 - 4$

28. $f(x) = \dfrac{2x + 3}{3x - 1}$

Find the unknown value.

29. y varies inversely as the square of x and when $x = 3$, $y = 2$. Find y if $x = 1$.

30. y varies jointly with x and the cube root of z. If when $x = 2$ and $z = 27$, $y = 12$, find y if $x = 5$ and $z = 8$.

Solve the following application problem.

31. The distance a body falls varies directly as the square of the time it falls. If an object falls 64 feet in 2 seconds, how long will it take to fall 256 feet?

Exponential and Logarithmic Functions

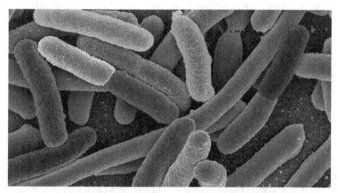

Figure 1 Electron micrograph of *E. Coli* bacteria (credit: "Mattosaurus," Wikimedia Commons)

CHAPTER OUTLINE

4.1 Exponential Functions

4.2 Graphs of Exponential Functions

4.3 Logarithmic Functions

4.4 Graphs of Logarithmic Functions

4.5 Logarithmic Properties

4.6 Exponential and Logarithmic Equations

4.7 Exponential and Logarithmic Models

4.8 Fitting Exponential Models to Data

Introduction

Focus in on a square centimeter of your skin. Look closer. Closer still. If you could look closely enough, you would see hundreds of thousands of microscopic organisms. They are bacteria, and they are not only on your skin, but in your mouth, nose, and even your intestines. In fact, the bacterial cells in your body at any given moment outnumber your own cells. But that is no reason to feel bad about yourself. While some bacteria can cause illness, many are healthy and even essential to the body.

Bacteria commonly reproduce through a process called binary fission, during which one bacterial cell splits into two. When conditions are right, bacteria can reproduce very quickly. Unlike humans and other complex organisms, the time required to form a new generation of bacteria is often a matter of minutes or hours, as opposed to days or years.[16]

For simplicity's sake, suppose we begin with a culture of one bacterial cell that can divide every hour. **Table 1** shows the number of bacterial cells at the end of each subsequent hour. We see that the single bacterial cell leads to over one thousand bacterial cells in just ten hours! And if we were to extrapolate the table to twenty-four hours, we would have over 16 million!

Hour	0	1	2	3	4	5	6	7	8	9	10
Bacteria	1	2	4	8	16	32	64	128	256	512	1024

Table 1

In this chapter, we will explore exponential functions, which can be used for, among other things, modeling growth patterns such as those found in bacteria. We will also investigate logarithmic functions, which are closely related to exponential functions. Both types of functions have numerous real-world applications when it comes to modeling and interpreting data.

16. Todar, PhD, Kenneth. Todar's Online Textbook of Bacteriology. http://textbookofbacteriology.net/growth_3.html.

In this section, you will:

- Evaluate exponential functions.
- Find the equation of an exponential function.
- Use compound interest formulas.
- Evaluate exponential functions with base e.

4.1 EXPONENTIAL FUNCTIONS

India is the second most populous country in the world with a population of about 1.25 billion people in 2013. The population is growing at a rate of about 1.2% each year[17]. If this rate continues, the population of India will exceed China's population by the year 2031. When populations grow rapidly, we often say that the growth is "exponential," meaning that something is growing very rapidly. To a mathematician, however, the term *exponential growth* has a very specific meaning. In this section, we will take a look at *exponential functions*, which model this kind of rapid growth.

Identifying Exponential Functions

When exploring linear growth, we observed a constant rate of change—a constant number by which the output increased for each unit increase in input. For example, in the equation $f(x) = 3x + 4$, the slope tells us the output increases by 3 each time the input increases by 1. The scenario in the India population example is different because we have a *percent* change per unit time (rather than a constant change) in the number of people.

Defining an Exponential Function

A study found that the percent of the population who are vegans in the United States doubled from 2009 to 2011. In 2011, 2.5% of the population was vegan, adhering to a diet that does not include any animal products—no meat, poultry, fish, dairy, or eggs. If this rate continues, vegans will make up 10% of the U.S. population in 2015, 40% in 2019, and 80% in 2021.

What exactly does it mean to *grow exponentially*? What does the word *double* have in common with *percent increase*? People toss these words around errantly. Are these words used correctly? The words certainly appear frequently in the media.

- **Percent change** refers to a *change* based on a *percent* of the original amount.
- **Exponential growth** refers to an *increase* based on a constant multiplicative rate of change over equal increments of time, that is, a *percent* increase of the original amount over time.
- **Exponential decay** refers to a *decrease* based on a constant multiplicative rate of change over equal increments of time, that is, a *percent* decrease of the original amount over time.

For us to gain a clear understanding of exponential growth, let us contrast exponential growth with linear growth. We will construct two functions. The first function is exponential. We will start with an input of 0, and increase each input by 1. We will double the corresponding consecutive outputs. The second function is linear. We will start with an input of 0, and increase each input by 1. We will add 2 to the corresponding consecutive outputs. See **Table 1**.

x	$f(x) = 2^x$	$g(x) = 2x$
0	1	0
1	2	2
2	4	4
3	8	6
4	16	8
5	32	10
6	64	12

Table 1

17. http://www.worldometers.info/world-population/. Accessed February 24, 2014.

From **Table 1** we can infer that for these two functions, exponential growth dwarfs linear growth.

- **Exponential growth** refers to the original value from the range increases by the *same percentage* over equal increments found in the domain.

- **Linear growth** refers to the original value from the range increases by the *same amount* over equal increments found in the domain.

Apparently, the difference between "the same percentage" and "the same amount" is quite significant. For exponential growth, over equal increments, the constant multiplicative rate of change resulted in doubling the output whenever the input increased by one. For linear growth, the constant additive rate of change over equal increments resulted in adding 2 to the output whenever the input was increased by one.

The general form of the exponential function is $f(x) = ab^x$, where a is any nonzero number, b is a positive real number not equal to 1.

- If $b > 1$, the function grows at a rate proportional to its size.

- If $0 < b < 1$, the function decays at a rate proportional to its size.

Let's look at the function $f(x) = 2^x$ from our example. We will create a table (**Table 2**) to determine the corresponding outputs over an interval in the domain from -3 to 3.

x	-3	-2	-1	0	1	2	3
$f(x) = 2^x$	$2^{-3} = \dfrac{1}{8}$	$2^{-2} = \dfrac{1}{4}$	$2^{-1} = \dfrac{1}{2}$	$2^0 = 1$	$2^1 = 2$	$2^2 = 4$	$2^3 = 8$

Table 2

Let us examine the graph of f by plotting the ordered pairs we observe on the table in **Figure 1**, and then make a few observations.

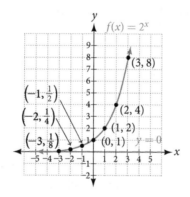

Figure 1

Let's define the behavior of the graph of the exponential function $f(x) = 2^x$ and highlight some its key characteristics.

- the domain is $(-\infty, \infty)$,

- the range is $(0, \infty)$,

- as $x \to \infty, f(x) \to \infty$,

- as $x \to -\infty, f(x) \to 0$,

- $f(x)$ is always increasing,

- the graph of $f(x)$ will never touch the x-axis because base two raised to any exponent never has the result of zero.

- $y = 0$ is the horizontal asymptote.

- the y-intercept is 1.

---

exponential function

For any real number x, an exponential function is a function with the form

$$f(x) = ab^x$$

where
- a is the a non-zero real number called the initial value and
- b is any positive real number such that $b \neq 1$.
- The domain of f is all real numbers.
- The range of f is all positive real numbers if $a > 0$.
- The range of f is all negative real numbers if $a < 0$.
- The y-intercept is $(0, a)$, and the horizontal asymptote is $y = 0$.

Example 1   **Identifying Exponential Functions**

Which of the following equations are *not* exponential functions?

$$f(x) = 4^{3(x-2)} \qquad g(x) = x^3 \qquad h(x) = \left(\frac{1}{3}\right)^x \qquad j(x) = (-2)^x$$

Solution   By definition, an exponential function has a constant as a base and an independent variable as an exponent. Thus, $g(x) = x^3$ does not represent an exponential function because the base is an independent variable. In fact, $g(x) = x^3$ is a power function.

Recall that the base b of an exponential function is always a positive constant, and $b \neq 1$. Thus, $j(x) = (-2)^x$ does not represent an exponential function because the base, -2, is less than 0.

Try It #1

Which of the following equations represent exponential functions?

- $f(x) = 2x^2 - 3x + 1$
- $g(x) = 0.875^x$
- $h(x) = 1.75x + 2$
- $j(x) = 1095.6^{-2x}$

Evaluating Exponential Functions

Recall that the base of an exponential function must be a positive real number other than 1. Why do we limit the base b to positive values? To ensure that the outputs will be real numbers. Observe what happens if the base is not positive:

- Let $b = -9$ and $x = \frac{1}{2}$. Then $f(x) = f\left(\frac{1}{2}\right) = (-9)^{\frac{1}{2}} = \sqrt{-9}$, which is not a real number.

Why do we limit the base to positive values other than 1? Because base 1 results in the constant function. Observe what happens if the base is 1:

- Let $b = 1$. Then $f(x) = 1^x = 1$ for any value of x.

To evaluate an exponential function with the form $f(x) = b^x$, we simply substitute x with the given value, and calculate the resulting power. For example:

Let $f(x) = 2^x$. What is $f(3)$?

$$f(x) = 2^x$$
$$f(3) = 2^3 \qquad \text{Substitute } x = 3.$$
$$= 8 \qquad \text{Evaluate the power.}$$

To evaluate an exponential function with a form other than the basic form, it is important to follow the order of operations.

For example:

Let $f(x) = 30(2)^x$. What is $f(3)$?

$$f(x) = 30(2)^x$$
$$f(3) = 30(2)^3 \qquad \text{Substitute } x = 3.$$
$$= 30(8) \qquad \text{Simplify the power first.}$$
$$= 240 \qquad \text{Multiply.}$$

Note that if the order of operations were not followed, the result would be incorrect:

$$f(3) = 30(2)^3 \neq 60^3 = 216{,}000$$

Example 2   Evaluating Exponential Functions

Let $f(x) = 5(3)^{x+1}$. Evaluate $f(2)$ without using a calculator.

Solution   Follow the order of operations. Be sure to pay attention to the parentheses.

$$f(x) = 5(3)^{x+1}$$
$$f(2) = 5(3)^{2+1} \qquad \text{Substitute } x = 2.$$
$$= 5(3)^3 \qquad \text{Add the exponents.}$$
$$= 5(27) \qquad \text{Simplify the power.}$$
$$= 135 \qquad \text{Multiply.}$$

Try It #2

Let $f(x) = 8(1.2)^{x-5}$. Evaluate $f(3)$ using a calculator. Round to four decimal places.

Defining Exponential Growth

Because the output of exponential functions increases very rapidly, the term "exponential growth" is often used in everyday language to describe anything that grows or increases rapidly. However, exponential growth can be defined more precisely in a mathematical sense. If the growth rate is proportional to the amount present, the function models exponential growth.

> ### *exponential growth*
>
> A function that models **exponential growth** grows by a rate proportional to the amount present. For any real number x and any positive real numbers a and b such that $b \neq 1$, an exponential growth function has the form
>
> $$f(x) = ab^x$$
>
> where
> - a is the initial or starting value of the function.
> - b is the growth factor or growth multiplier per unit x.

In more general terms, we have an *exponential function*, in which a constant base is raised to a variable exponent. To differentiate between linear and exponential functions, let's consider two companies, A and B. Company A has 100 stores and expands by opening 50 new stores a year, so its growth can be represented by the function $A(x) = 100 + 50x$. Company B has 100 stores and expands by increasing the number of stores by 50% each year, so its growth can be represented by the function $B(x) = 100(1 + 0.5)^x$.

A few years of growth for these companies are illustrated in **Table 3**.

Year, x	Stores, Company A	Stores, Company B
0	$100 + 50(0) = 100$	$100(1 + 0.5)^0 = 100$
1	$100 + 50(1) = 150$	$100(1 + 0.5)^1 = 150$
2	$100 + 50(2) = 200$	$100(1 + 0.5)^2 = 225$
3	$100 + 50(3) = 250$	$100(1 + 0.5)^3 = 337.5$
x	$A(x) = 100 + 50x$	$B(x) = 100(1 + 0.5)^x$

Table 3

The graphs comparing the number of stores for each company over a five-year period are shown in **Figure 2**. We can see that, with exponential growth, the number of stores increases much more rapidly than with linear growth.

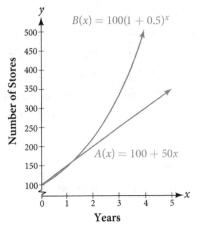

Figure 2 The graph shows the numbers of stores Companies A and B opened over a five-year period.

Notice that the domain for both functions is $[0, \infty)$, and the range for both functions is $[100, \infty)$. After year 1, Company B always has more stores than Company A.

Now we will turn our attention to the function representing the number of stores for Company B, $B(x) = 100(1 + 0.5)^x$. In this exponential function, 100 represents the initial number of stores, 0.50 represents the growth rate, and $1 + 0.5 = 1.5$ represents the growth factor. Generalizing further, we can write this function as $B(x) = 100(1.5)^x$, where 100 is the initial value, 1.5 is called the *base*, and x is called the *exponent*.

Example 3   **Evaluating a Real-World Exponential Model**

At the beginning of this section, we learned that the population of India was about 1.25 billion in the year 2013, with an annual growth rate of about 1.2%. This situation is represented by the growth function $P(t) = 1.25(1.012)^t$, where t is the number of years since 2013. To the nearest thousandth, what will the population of India be in 2031?

Solution   To estimate the population in 2031, we evaluate the models for $t = 18$, because 2031 is 18 years after 2013. Rounding to the nearest thousandth,

$$P(18) = 1.25(1.012)^{18} \approx 1.549$$

There will be about 1.549 billion people in India in the year 2031.

Try It #3

The population of China was about 1.39 billion in the year 2013, with an annual growth rate of about 0.6%. This situation is represented by the growth function $P(t) = 1.39(1.006)^t$, where t is the number of years since 2013. To the nearest thousandth, what will the population of China be for the year 2031? How does this compare to the population prediction we made for India in **Example 3**?

Finding Equations of Exponential Functions

In the previous examples, we were given an exponential function, which we then evaluated for a given input. Sometimes we are given information about an exponential function without knowing the function explicitly. We must use the information to first write the form of the function, then determine the constants a and b, and evaluate the function.

How To...

Given two data points, write an exponential model.

1. If one of the data points has the form $(0, a)$, then a is the initial value. Using a, substitute the second point into the equation $f(x) = a(b)^x$, and solve for b.
2. If neither of the data points have the form $(0, a)$, substitute both points into two equations with the form $f(x) = a(b)^x$. Solve the resulting system of two equations in two unknowns to find a and b.
3. Using the a and b found in the steps above, write the exponential function in the form $f(x) = a(b)^x$.

Example 4   **Writing an Exponential Model When the Initial Value Is Known**

In 2006, 80 deer were introduced into a wildlife refuge. By 2012, the population had grown to 180 deer. The population was growing exponentially. Write an algebraic function $N(t)$ representing the population (N) of deer over time t.

Solution   We let our independent variable t be the number of years after 2006. Thus, the information given in the problem can be written as input-output pairs: (0, 80) and (6, 180). Notice that by choosing our input variable to be measured as years after 2006, we have given ourselves the initial value for the function, $a = 80$. We can now substitute the second point into the equation $N(t) = 80b^t$ to find b:

$$N(t) = 80b^t$$

$$180 = 80b^6 \qquad \text{Substitute using point (6, 180).}$$

$$\frac{9}{4} = b^6 \qquad \text{Divide and write in lowest terms.}$$

$$b = \left(\frac{9}{4}\right)^{\frac{1}{6}} \qquad \text{Isolate } b \text{ using properties of exponents.}$$

$$b \approx 1.1447 \qquad \text{Round to 4 decimal places.}$$

NOTE: *Unless otherwise stated, do not round any intermediate calculations. Then round the final answer to four places for the remainder of this section.*

The exponential model for the population of deer is $N(t) = 80(1.1447)^t$. (Note that this exponential function models short-term growth. As the inputs gets large, the output will get increasingly larger, so much so that the model may not be useful in the long term.)

We can graph our model to observe the population growth of deer in the refuge over time. Notice that the graph in **Figure 3** passes through the initial points given in the problem, (0, 80) and (6, 180). We can also see that the domain for the function is $[0, \infty)$, and the range for the function is $[80, \infty)$.

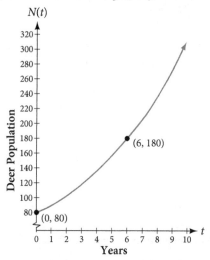

Figure 3 Graph showing the population of deer over time, $N(t) = 80(1.1447)^t$, t years after 2006.

Try It #4

A wolf population is growing exponentially. In 2011, 129 wolves were counted. By 2013, the population had reached 236 wolves. What two points can be used to derive an exponential equation modeling this situation? Write the equation representing the population N of wolves over time t.

Example 5   **Writing an Exponential Model When the Initial Value is Not Known**

Find an exponential function that passes through the points $(-2, 6)$ and $(2, 1)$.

Solution   Because we don't have the initial value, we substitute both points into an equation of the form $f(x) = ab^x$, and then solve the system for a and b.

- Substituting $(-2, 6)$ gives $6 = ab^{-2}$
- Substituting $(2, 1)$ gives $1 = ab^2$

Use the first equation to solve for a in terms of b:

$$6 = ab^{-2}$$

$$\frac{6}{b^{-2}} = a \qquad \text{Divide.}$$

$$a = 6b^2 \qquad \text{Use properties of exponents to rewrite the denominator.}$$

Substitute a in the second equation, and solve for b:

$$1 = ab^2$$

$$1 = 6b^2b^2 = 6b^4 \qquad \text{Substitute } a.$$

$$b = \left(\frac{1}{6}\right)^{\frac{1}{4}} \qquad \text{Use properties of exponents to isolate } b.$$

$$b \approx 0.6389 \qquad \text{Round 4 decimal places.}$$

Use the value of b in the first equation to solve for the value of a:

$$a = 6b^2 \approx 6(0.6389)^2 \approx 2.4492$$

Thus, the equation is $f(x) = 2.4492(0.6389)^x$.

We can graph our model to check our work. Notice that the graph in **Figure 4** passes through the initial points given in the problem, $(-2, 6)$ and $(2, 1)$. The graph is an example of an exponential decay function.

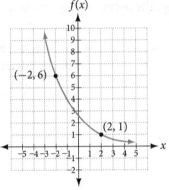

Figure 4 The graph of $f(x) = 2.4492(0.6389)^x$ models exponential decay.

Try It #5

Given the two points $(1, 3)$ and $(2, 4.5)$, find the equation of the exponential function that passes through these two points.

Q & A...

Do two points always determine a unique exponential function?

Yes, provided the two points are either both above the x-axis or both below the x-axis and have different x-coordinates. But keep in mind that we also need to know that the graph is, in fact, an exponential function. Not every graph that looks exponential really is exponential. We need to know the graph is based on a model that shows the same percent growth with each unit increase in x, which in many real world cases involves time.

How To...

Given the graph of an exponential function, write its equation.

1. First, identify two points on the graph. Choose the y-intercept as one of the two points whenever possible. Try to choose points that are as far apart as possible to reduce round-off error.
2. If one of the data points is the y-intercept $(0, a)$, then a is the initial value. Using a, substitute the second point into the equation $f(x) = a(b)^x$, and solve for b.
3. If neither of the data points have the form $(0, a)$, substitute both points into two equations with the form $f(x) = a(b)^x$. Solve the resulting system of two equations in two unknowns to find a and b.
4. Write the exponential function, $f(x) = a(b)^x$.

Example 6 **Writing an Exponential Function Given Its Graph**

Find an equation for the exponential function graphed in **Figure 5**.

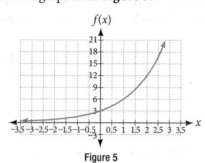

Figure 5

Solution We can choose the y-intercept of the graph, $(0, 3)$, as our first point. This gives us the initial value, $a = 3$. Next, choose a point on the curve some distance away from $(0, 3)$ that has integer coordinates. One such point is $(2, 12)$.

$y = ab^x$	Write the general form of an exponential equation.
$y = 3b^x$	Substitute the initial value 3 for a.
$12 = 3b^2$	Substitute in 12 for y and 2 for x.
$4 = b^2$	Divide by 3.
$b = \pm 2$	Take the square root.

Because we restrict ourselves to positive values of b, we will use $b = 2$. Substitute a and b into the standard form to yield the equation $f(x) = 3(2)^x$.

Try It #6

Find an equation for the exponential function graphed in **Figure 6**.

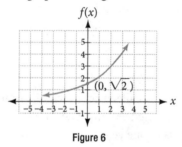

Figure 6

How To...

Given two points on the curve of an exponential function, use a graphing calculator to find the equation.
1. Press [STAT].
2. Clear any existing entries in columns **L1** or **L2**.
3. In **L1**, enter the x-coordinates given.
4. In **L2**, enter the corresponding y-coordinates.
5. Press [STAT] again. Cursor right to **CALC**, scroll down to **ExpReg (Exponential Regression)**, and press [ENTER].
6. The screen displays the values of a and b in the exponential equation $y = a \cdot b^x$

Example 7 **Using a Graphing Calculator to Find an Exponential Function**

Use a graphing calculator to find the exponential equation that includes the points $(2, 24.8)$ and $(5, 198.4)$.

Solution Follow the guidelines above. First press [STAT], [EDIT], [1: Edit...], and clear the lists **L1** and **L2**. Next, in the **L1** column, enter the x-coordinates, 2 and 5. Do the same in the **L2** column for the y-coordinates, 24.8 and 198.4. Now press [STAT], [CALC], [0: ExpReg] and press [ENTER]. The values $a = 6.2$ and $b = 2$ will be displayed. The exponential equation is $y = 6.2 \cdot 2^x$.

Try It #7

Use a graphing calculator to find the exponential equation that includes the points $(3, 75.98)$ and $(6, 481.07)$.

Applying the Compound-Interest Formula

Savings instruments in which earnings are continually reinvested, such as mutual funds and retirement accounts, use **compound interest**. The term *compounding* refers to interest earned not only on the original value, but on the accumulated value of the account.

The **annual percentage rate (APR)** of an account, also called the **nominal rate**, is the yearly interest rate earned by an investment account. The term *nominal* is used when the compounding occurs a number of times other than once per year. In fact, when interest is compounded more than once a year, the effective interest rate ends up being *greater* than the nominal rate! This is a powerful tool for investing.

We can calculate the compound interest using the compound interest formula, which is an exponential function of the variables time t, principal P, APR r, and number of compounding periods in a year n:

$$A(t) = P\left(1 + \frac{r}{n}\right)^{nt}$$

For example, observe **Table 4**, which shows the result of investing $1,000 at 10% for one year. Notice how the value of the account increases as the compounding frequency increases.

Frequency	Value after 1 year
Annually	$1100
Semiannually	$1102.50
Quarterly	$1103.81
Monthly	$1104.71
Daily	$1105.16

Table 4

---

the compound interest formula

Compound interest can be calculated using the formula

$$A(t) = P\left(1 + \frac{r}{n}\right)^{nt}$$

where

- $A(t)$ is the account value,
- t is measured in years,
- P is the starting amount of the account, often called the principal, or more generally present value,
- r is the annual percentage rate (APR) expressed as a decimal, and
- n is the number of compounding periods in one year.

Example 8   **Calculating Compound Interest**

If we invest $3,000 in an investment account paying 3% interest compounded quarterly, how much will the account be worth in 10 years?

Solution   Because we are starting with $3,000, $P = 3000$. Our interest rate is 3%, so $r = 0.03$. Because we are compounding quarterly, we are compounding 4 times per year, so $n = 4$. We want to know the value of the account in 10 years, so we are looking for $A(10)$, the value when $t = 10$.

$$A(t) = P\left(1 + \frac{r}{n}\right)^{nt} \qquad \text{Use the compound interest formula.}$$

$$A(10) = 3000\left(1 + \frac{0.03}{4}\right)^{4 \cdot 10} \qquad \text{Substitute using given values.}$$

$$\approx \$4{,}045.05 \qquad \text{Round to two decimal places.}$$

The account will be worth about $4,045.05 in 10 years.

Try It #8

An initial investment of $100,000 at 12% interest is compounded weekly (use 52 weeks in a year). What will the investment be worth in 30 years?

Example 9   **Using the Compound Interest Formula to Solve for the Principal**

A 529 Plan is a college-savings plan that allows relatives to invest money to pay for a child's future college tuition; the account grows tax-free. Lily wants to set up a 529 account for her new granddaughter and wants the account to grow to $40,000 over 18 years. She believes the account will earn 6% compounded semi-annually (twice a year). To the nearest dollar, how much will Lily need to invest in the account now?

Solution   The nominal interest rate is 6%, so $r = 0.06$. Interest is compounded twice a year, so $n = 2$.

We want to find the initial investment, P, needed so that the value of the account will be worth $40,000 in 18 years. Substitute the given values into the compound interest formula, and solve for P.

$$A(t) = P\left(1 + \frac{r}{n}\right)^{nt}$$ Use the compound interest formula.

$$40{,}000 = P\left(1 + \frac{0.06}{2}\right)^{2(18)}$$ Substitute using given values A, r, n, and t.

$$40{,}000 = P(1.03)^{36}$$ Simplify.

$$\frac{40{,}000}{(1.03)^{36}} = P$$ Isolate P.

$$P \approx \$13{,}801$$ Divide and round to the nearest dollar.

Lily will need to invest $13,801 to have $40,000 in 18 years.

Try It #9

Refer to **Example 9.** To the nearest dollar, how much would Lily need to invest if the account is compounded quarterly?

Evaluating Functions with Base *e*

As we saw earlier, the amount earned on an account increases as the compounding frequency increases. **Table 5** shows that the increase from annual to semi-annual compounding is larger than the increase from monthly to daily compounding. This might lead us to ask whether this pattern will continue.

Examine the value of $1 invested at 100% interest for 1 year, compounded at various frequencies, listed in **Table 5**.

Frequency	$A(t) = \left(1 + \frac{1}{n}\right)^n$	Value
Annually	$\left(1 + \frac{1}{1}\right)^1$	$2
Semiannually	$\left(1 + \frac{1}{2}\right)^2$	$2.25
Quarterly	$\left(1 + \frac{1}{4}\right)^4$	$2.441406
Monthly	$\left(1 + \frac{1}{12}\right)^{12}$	$2.613035
Daily	$\left(1 + \frac{1}{365}\right)^{365}$	$2.714567
Hourly	$\left(1 + \frac{1}{8760}\right)^{8760}$	$2.718127
Once per minute	$\left(1 + \frac{1}{525600}\right)^{525600}$	$2.718279
Once per second	$\left(1 + \frac{1}{31536000}\right)^{31536000}$	$2.718282

Table 5

These values appear to be approaching a limit as n increases without bound. In fact, as n gets larger and larger, the expression $\left(1 + \dfrac{1}{n}\right)^n$ approaches a number used so frequently in mathematics that it has its own name: the letter e. This value is an irrational number, which means that its decimal expansion goes on forever without repeating. Its approximation to six decimal places is shown below.

---

the number e

The letter e represents the irrational number

$$\left(1 + \frac{1}{n}\right)^n, \text{ as } n \text{ increases without bound}$$

The letter e is used as a base for many real-world exponential models. To work with base e, we use the approximation, $e \approx 2.718282$. The constant was named by the Swiss mathematician Leonhard Euler (1707–1783) who first investigated and discovered many of its properties.

Example 10   **Using a Calculator to Find Powers of e**

Calculate $e^{3.14}$. Round to five decimal places.

Solution   On a calculator, press the button labeled [e^x]. The window shows [$e^{\wedge}$(]. Type 3.14 and then close parenthesis, [)]. Press [**ENTER**]. Rounding to 5 decimal places, $e^{3.14} \approx 23.10387$. Caution: Many scientific calculators have an "**Exp**" button, which is used to enter numbers in scientific notation. It is not used to find powers of e.

Try It #10

Use a calculator to find $e^{-0.5}$. Round to five decimal places.

Investigating Continuous Growth

So far we have worked with rational bases for exponential functions. For most real-world phenomena, however, e is used as the base for exponential functions. Exponential models that use e as the base are called *continuous growth or decay models*. We see these models in finance, computer science, and most of the sciences, such as physics, toxicology, and fluid dynamics.

---

the continuous growth/decay formula

For all real numbers t, and all positive numbers a and r, continuous growth or decay is represented by the formula

$$A(t) = ae^{rt}$$

where

- a is the initial value,
- r is the continuous growth rate per unit time,
- and t is the elapsed time.

If $r > 0$, then the formula represents continuous growth. If $r < 0$, then the formula represents continuous decay.

For business applications, the continuous growth formula is called the continuous compounding formula and takes the form

$$A(t) = Pe^{rt}$$

where

- P is the principal or the initial invested,
- r is the growth or interest rate per unit time,
- and t is the period or term of the investment.

How To...

Given the initial value, rate of growth or decay, and time *t*, solve a continuous growth or decay function.

1. Use the information in the problem to determine *a*, the initial value of the function.
2. Use the information in the problem to determine the growth rate *r*.
   a. If the problem refers to continuous growth, then $r > 0$.
   b. If the problem refers to continuous decay, then $r < 0$.
3. Use the information in the problem to determine the time *t*.
4. Substitute the given information into the continuous growth formula and solve for *A(t)*.

Example 11 **Calculating Continuous Growth**

A person invested $1,000 in an account earning a nominal 10% per year compounded continuously. How much was in the account at the end of one year?

Solution   Since the account is growing in value, this is a continuous compounding problem with growth rate $r = 0.10$. The initial investment was $1,000, so $P = 1000$. We use the continuous compounding formula to find the value after $t = 1$ year:

$$A(t) = Pe^{rt} \qquad \text{Use the continuous compounding formula.}$$
$$= 1000(e)^{0.1} \qquad \text{Substitute known values for } P, r, \text{ and } t.$$
$$\approx 1105.17 \qquad \text{Use a calculator to approximate.}$$

The account is worth $1,105.17 after one year.

Try It #11

A person invests $100,000 at a nominal 12% interest per year compounded continuously. What will be the value of the investment in 30 years?

Example 12 **Calculating Continuous Decay**

Radon-222 decays at a continuous rate of 17.3% per day. How much will 100 mg of Radon-222 decay to in 3 days?

Solution   Since the substance is decaying, the rate, 17.3%, is negative. So, $r = -0.173$. The initial amount of radon-222 was 100 mg, so $a = 100$. We use the continuous decay formula to find the value after $t = 3$ days:

$$A(t) = ae^{rt} \qquad \text{Use the continuous growth formula.}$$
$$= 100e^{-0.173(3)} \qquad \text{Substitute known values for } a, r, \text{ and } t.$$
$$\approx 59.5115 \qquad \text{Use a calculator to approximate.}$$

So 59.5115 mg of radon-222 will remain.

Try It #12

Using the data in **Example 12**, how much radon-222 will remain after one year?

Access these online resources for additional instruction and practice with exponential functions.

- Exponential Growth Function (http://openstaxcollege.org/l/expgrowth)
- Compound Interest (http://openstaxcollege.org/l/compoundint)

4.1 SECTION EXERCISES

VERBAL

1. Explain why the values of an increasing exponential function will eventually overtake the values of an increasing linear function.

2. Given a formula for an exponential function, is it possible to determine whether the function grows or decays exponentially just by looking at the formula? Explain.

3. The Oxford Dictionary defines the word *nominal* as a value that is "stated or expressed but not necessarily corresponding exactly to the real value."[18] Develop a reasonable argument for why the term *nominal rate* is used to describe the annual percentage rate of an investment account that compounds interest.

ALGEBRAIC

For the following exercises, identify whether the statement represents an exponential function. Explain.

4. The average annual population increase of a pack of wolves is 25.

5. A population of bacteria decreases by a factor of $\frac{1}{8}$ every 24 hours.

6. The value of a coin collection has increased by 3.25% annually over the last 20 years.

7. For each training session, a personal trainer charges his clients $5 less than the previous training session.

8. The height of a projectile at time t is represented by the function $h(t) = -4.9t^2 + 18t + 40$.

For the following exercises, consider this scenario: For each year t, the population of a forest of trees is represented by the function $A(t) = 115(1.025)^t$. In a neighboring forest, the population of the same type of tree is represented by the function $B(t) = 82(1.029)^t$. (Round answers to the nearest whole number.)

9. Which forest's population is growing at a faster rate?

10. Which forest had a greater number of trees initially? By how many?

11. Assuming the population growth models continue to represent the growth of the forests, which forest will have a greater number of trees after 20 years? By how many?

12. Assuming the population growth models continue to represent the growth of the forests, which forest will have a greater number of trees after 100 years? By how many?

13. Discuss the above results from the previous four exercises. Assuming the population growth models continue to represent the growth of the forests, which forest will have the greater number of trees in the long run? Why? What are some factors that might influence the long-term validity of the exponential growth model?

For the following exercises, determine whether the equation represents exponential growth, exponential decay, or neither. Explain.

14. $y = 300(1 - t)^5$

15. $y = 220(1.06)^x$

16. $y = 16.5(1.025)^{\frac{1}{x}}$

17. $y = 11{,}701(0.97)^t$

For the following exercises, find the formula for an exponential function that passes through the two points given.

18. $(0, 6)$ and $(3, 750)$

19. $(0, 2000)$ and $(2, 20)$

20. $\left(-1, \frac{3}{2}\right)$ and $(3, 24)$

21. $(-2, 6)$ and $(3, 1)$

22. $(3, 1)$ and $(5, 4)$

18. Oxford Dictionary. http://oxforddictionaries.com/us/definition/american_english/nominal.

For the following exercises, determine whether the table could represent a function that is linear, exponential, or neither. If it appears to be exponential, find a function that passes through the points.

23.

x	1	2	3	4
f(x)	70	40	10	−20

24.

x	1	2	3	4
h(x)	70	49	34.3	24.01

25.

x	1	2	3	4
m(x)	80	61	42.9	25.61

26.

x	1	2	3	4
f(x)	10	20	40	80

27.

x	1	2	3	4
g(x)	−3.25	2	7.25	12.5

For the following exercises, use the compound interest formula, $A(t) = P\left(1 + \dfrac{r}{n}\right)^{nt}$.

28. After a certain number of years, the value of an investment account is represented by the equation $10,250\left(1 + \dfrac{0.04}{12}\right)^{120}$. What is the value of the account?

29. What was the initial deposit made to the account in the previous exercise?

30. How many years had the account from the previous exercise been accumulating interest?

31. An account is opened with an initial deposit of $6,500 and earns 3.6% interest compounded semi-annually. What will the account be worth in 20 years?

32. How much more would the account in the previous exercise have been worth if the interest were compounding weekly?

33. Solve the compound interest formula for the principal, P.

34. Use the formula found in Exercise #31 to calculate the initial deposit of an account that is worth $14,472.74 after earning 5.5% interest compounded monthly for 5 years. (Round to the nearest dollar.)

35. How much more would the account in Exercises #31 and #34 be worth if it were earning interest for 5 more years?

36. Use properties of rational exponents to solve the compound interest formula for the interest rate, r.

37. Use the formula found in the previous exercise to calculate the interest rate for an account that was compounded semi-annually, had an initial deposit of $9,000 and was worth $13,373.53 after 10 years.

38. Use the formula found in the previous exercise to calculate the interest rate for an account that was compounded monthly, had an initial deposit of $5,500, and was worth $38,455 after 30 years.

For the following exercises, determine whether the equation represents continuous growth, continuous decay, or neither. Explain.

39. $y = 3742(e)^{0.75t}$

40. $y = 150(e)^{\frac{3.25}{t}}$

41. $y = 2.25(e)^{-2t}$

42. Suppose an investment account is opened with an initial deposit of $12,000 earning 7.2% interest compounded continuously. How much will the account be worth after 30 years?

43. How much less would the account from Exercise 42 be worth after 30 years if it were compounded monthly instead?

NUMERIC

For the following exercises, evaluate each function. Round answers to four decimal places, if necessary.

44. $f(x) = 2(5)^x$, for $f(-3)$

45. $f(x) = -4^{2x+3}$, for $f(-1)$

46. $f(x) = e^x$, for $f(3)$

47. $f(x) = -2e^{x-1}$, for $f(-1)$

48. $f(x) = 2.7(4)^{-x+1} + 1.5$, for $f(-2)$

49. $f(x) = 1.2e^{2x} - 0.3$, for $f(3)$

50. $f(x) = -\dfrac{3}{2}(3)^{-x} + \dfrac{3}{2}$, for $f(2)$

TECHNOLOGY

For the following exercises, use a graphing calculator to find the equation of an exponential function given the points on the curve.

51. $(0, 3)$ and $(3, 375)$

52. $(3, 222.62)$ and $(10, 77.456)$

53. $(20, 29.495)$ and $(150, 730.89)$

54. $(5, 2.909)$ and $(13, 0.005)$

55. $(11,310.035)$ and $(25,356.3652)$

EXTENSIONS

56. The *annual percentage yield* (APY) of an investment account is a representation of the actual interest rate earned on a compounding account. It is based on a compounding period of one year. Show that the APY of an account that compounds monthly can be found with the formula $\text{APY} = \left(1 + \dfrac{r}{12}\right)^{12} - 1$.

57. Repeat the previous exercise to find the formula for the APY of an account that compounds daily. Use the results from this and the previous exercise to develop a function $I(n)$ for the APY of any account that compounds n times per year.

58. Recall that an exponential function is any equation written in the form $f(x) = a \cdot b^x$ such that a and b are positive numbers and $b \neq 1$. Any positive number b can be written as $b = e^n$ for some value of n. Use this fact to rewrite the formula for an exponential function that uses the number e as a base.

59. In an exponential decay function, the base of the exponent is a value between 0 and 1. Thus, for some number $b > 1$, the exponential decay function can be written as $f(x) = a \cdot \left(\dfrac{1}{b}\right)^x$. Use this formula, along with the fact that $b = e^n$, to show that an exponential decay function takes the form $f(x) = a(e)^{-nx}$ for some positive number n.

60. The formula for the amount A in an investment account with a nominal interest rate r at any time t is given by $A(t) = a(e)^{rt}$, where a is the amount of principal initially deposited into an account that compounds continuously. Prove that the percentage of interest earned to principal at any time t can be calculated with the formula $I(t) = e^{rt} - 1$.

REAL-WORLD APPLICATIONS

61. The fox population in a certain region has an annual growth rate of 9% per year. In the year 2012, there were 23,900 fox counted in the area. What is the fox population predicted to be in the year 2020?

62. A scientist begins with 100 milligrams of a radioactive substance that decays exponentially. After 35 hours, 50 mg of the substance remains. How many milligrams will remain after 54 hours?

63. In the year 1985, a house was valued at $110,000. By the year 2005, the value had appreciated to $145,000. What was the annual growth rate between 1985 and 2005? Assume that the value continued to grow by the same percentage. What was the value of the house in the year 2010?

64. A car was valued at $38,000 in the year 2007. By 2013, the value had depreciated to $11,000 If the car's value continues to drop by the same percentage, what will it be worth by 2017?

65. Jamal wants to save $54,000 for a down payment on a home. How much will he need to invest in an account with 8.2% APR, compounding daily, in order to reach his goal in 5 years?

66. Kyoko has $10,000 that she wants to invest. Her bank has several investment accounts to choose from, all compounding daily. Her goal is to have $15,000 by the time she finishes graduate school in 6 years. To the nearest hundredth of a percent, what should her minimum annual interest rate be in order to reach her goal? (*Hint*: solve the compound interest formula for the interest rate.)

67. Alyssa opened a retirement account with 7.25% APR in the year 2000. Her initial deposit was $13,500. How much will the account be worth in 2025 if interest compounds monthly? How much more would she make if interest compounded continuously?

68. An investment account with an annual interest rate of 7% was opened with an initial deposit of $4,000 Compare the values of the account after 9 years when the interest is compounded annually, quarterly, monthly, and continuously.

LEARNING OBJECTIVES

In this section, you will:

- Graph exponential functions.
- Graph exponential functions using transformations.

4.2   GRAPHS OF EXPONENTIAL FUNCTIONS

As we discussed in the previous section, exponential functions are used for many real-world applications such as finance, forensics, computer science, and most of the life sciences. Working with an equation that describes a real-world situation gives us a method for making predictions. Most of the time, however, the equation itself is not enough. We learn a lot about things by seeing their pictorial representations, and that is exactly why graphing exponential equations is a powerful tool. It gives us another layer of insight for predicting future events.

Graphing Exponential Functions

Before we begin graphing, it is helpful to review the behavior of exponential growth. Recall the table of values for a function of the form $f(x) = b^x$ whose base is greater than one. We'll use the function $f(x) = 2^x$. Observe how the output values in **Table 1** change as the input increases by 1.

x	-3	-2	-1	0	1	2	3
$f(x) = 2x$	$\frac{1}{8}$	$\frac{1}{4}$	$\frac{1}{2}$	1	2	4	8

Table 1

Each output value is the product of the previous output and the base, 2. We call the base 2 the *constant ratio*. In fact, for any exponential function with the form $f(x) = ab^x$, b is the constant ratio of the function. This means that as the input increases by 1, the output value will be the product of the base and the previous output, regardless of the value of a.

Notice from the table that

- the output values are positive for all values of x;
- as x increases, the output values increase without bound; and
- as x decreases, the output values grow smaller, approaching zero.

Figure 1 shows the exponential growth function $f(x) = 2^x$.

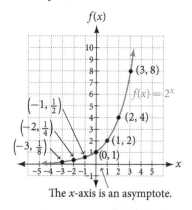

The x-axis is an asymptote.

Figure 1   Notice that the graph gets close to the x-axis, but never touches it.

The domain of $f(x) = 2^x$ is all real numbers, the range is $(0, \infty)$, and the horizontal asymptote is $y = 0$.

To get a sense of the behavior of exponential decay, we can create a table of values for a function of the form $f(x) = b^x$ whose base is between zero and one. We'll use the function $g(x) = \left(\frac{1}{2}\right)^x$. Observe how the output values in **Table 2** change as the input increases by 1.

x	-3	-2	-1	0	1	2	3
$g(x) = \left(\frac{1}{2}\right)^x$	8	4	2	1	$\frac{1}{2}$	$\frac{1}{4}$	$\frac{1}{8}$

Table 2

Again, because the input is increasing by 1, each output value is the product of the previous output and the base, or constant ratio $\frac{1}{2}$.

Notice from the table that

- the output values are positive for all values of x;
- as x increases, the output values grow smaller, approaching zero; and
- as x decreases, the output values grow without bound.

Figure 2 shows the exponential decay function, $g(x) = \left(\frac{1}{2}\right)^x$.

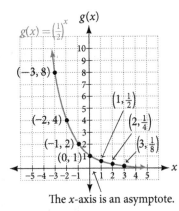

The x-axis is an asymptote.

Figure 2

The domain of $g(x) = \left(\frac{1}{2}\right)^x$ is all real numbers, the range is $(0, \infty)$, and the horizontal asymptote is $y = 0$.

---

characteristics of the graph of the parent function $f(x) = b^x$

An exponential function with the form $f(x) = b^x$, $b > 0$, $b \neq 1$, has these characteristics:

- one-to-one function
- horizontal asymptote: $y = 0$
- domain: $(-\infty, \infty)$
- range: $(0, \infty)$
- x-intercept: none
- y-intercept: $(0, 1)$
- increasing if $b > 1$
- decreasing if $b < 1$

Figure 3 compares the graphs of exponential growth and decay functions.

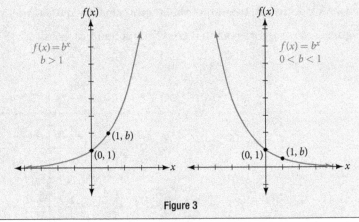

Figure 3

How To...

Given an exponential function of the form $f(x) = b^x$, graph the function.

1. Create a table of points.

2. Plot at least 3 point from the table, including the y-intercept $(0, 1)$.

3. Draw a smooth curve through the points.

4. State the domain, $(-\infty, \infty)$, the range, $(0, \infty)$, and the horizontal asymptote, $y = 0$.

Example 1   **Sketching the Graph of an Exponential Function of the Form $f(x) = b^x$**

Sketch a graph of $f(x) = 0.25^x$. State the domain, range, and asymptote.

Solution   Before graphing, identify the behavior and create a table of points for the graph.

- Since $b = 0.25$ is between zero and one, we know the function is decreasing. The left tail of the graph will increase without bound, and the right tail will approach the asymptote $y = 0$.

- Create a table of points as in **Table 3**.

x	-3	-2	-1	0	1	2	3
$f(x) = 0.25^x$	64	16	4	1	0.25	0.0625	0.015625

Table 3

- Plot the y-intercept, $(0, 1)$, along with two other points. We can use $(-1, 4)$ and $(1, 0.25)$.

Draw a smooth curve connecting the points as in **Figure 4**.

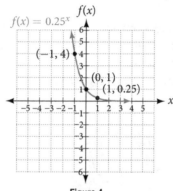

Figure 4

The domain is $(-\infty, \infty)$; the range is $(0, \infty)$; the horizontal asymptote is $y = 0$.

Try It #1

Sketch the graph of $f(x) = 4^x$. State the domain, range, and asymptote.

Graphing Transformations of Exponential Functions

Transformations of exponential graphs behave similarly to those of other functions. Just as with other parent functions, we can apply the four types of transformations—shifts, reflections, stretches, and compressions—to the parent function $f(x) = b^x$ without loss of shape. For instance, just as the quadratic function maintains its parabolic shape when shifted, reflected, stretched, or compressed, the exponential function also maintains its general shape regardless of the transformations applied.

Graphing a Vertical Shift

The first transformation occurs when we add a constant d to the parent function $f(x) = b^x$, giving us a vertical shift d units in the same direction as the sign. For example, if we begin by graphing a parent function, $f(x) = 2^x$, we can then graph two vertical shifts alongside it, using $d = 3$: the upward shift, $g(x) = 2^x + 3$ and the downward shift, $h(x) = 2^x - 3$. Both vertical shifts are shown in **Figure 5**.

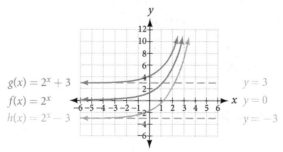

Figure 5

Observe the results of shifting $f(x) = 2^x$ vertically:

- The domain, $(-\infty, \infty)$ remains unchanged.
- When the function is shifted up 3 units to $g(x) = 2^x + 3$:
  - The y-intercept shifts up 3 units to $(0, 4)$.
  - The asymptote shifts up 3 units to $y = 3$.
  - The range becomes $(3, \infty)$.
- When the function is shifted down 3 units to $h(x) = 2^x - 3$:
  - The y-intercept shifts down 3 units to $(0, -2)$.
  - The asymptote also shifts down 3 units to $y = -3$.
  - The range becomes $(-3, \infty)$.

Graphing a Horizontal Shift

The next transformation occurs when we add a constant c to the input of the parent function $f(x) = b^x$, giving us a horizontal shift c units in the *opposite* direction of the sign. For example, if we begin by graphing the parent function $f(x) = 2^x$, we can then graph two horizontal shifts alongside it, using $c = 3$: the shift left, $g(x) = 2^{x+3}$, and the shift right, $h(x) = 2^{x-3}$. Both horizontal shifts are shown in **Figure 6**.

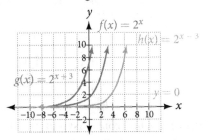

Figure 6

Observe the results of shifting $f(x) = 2^x$ horizontally:

- The domain, $(-\infty, \infty)$, remains unchanged.
- The asymptote, $y = 0$, remains unchanged.
- The y-intercept shifts such that:
  - When the function is shifted left 3 units to $g(x) = 2^{x+3}$, the y-intercept becomes $(0, 8)$. This is because $2^{x+3} = (8)2^x$, so the initial value of the function is 8.
  - When the function is shifted right 3 units to $h(x) = 2^{x-3}$, the y-intercept becomes $\left(0, \frac{1}{8}\right)$. Again, see that $2^{x-3} = \left(\frac{1}{8}\right)2^x$, so the initial value of the function is $\frac{1}{8}$.

---

shifts of the parent function $f(x) = b^x$

For any constants c and d, the function $f(x) = b^{x+c} + d$ shifts the parent function $f(x) = b^x$

- vertically d units, in the *same* direction of the sign of d.
- horizontally c units, in the *opposite* direction of the sign of c.
- The y-intercept becomes $(0, b^c + d)$.
- The horizontal asymptote becomes $y = d$.
- The range becomes (d, ∞).
- The domain, $(-\infty, \infty)$, remains unchanged.

How To...

Given an exponential function with the form $f(x) = b^{x+c} + d$, graph the translation.

1. Draw the horizontal asymptote $y = d$.

2. Identify the shift as $(-c, d)$. Shift the graph of $f(x) = b^x$ left c units if c is positive, and right c units if c is negative.

3. Shift the graph of $f(x) = b^x$ up d units if d is positive, and down d units if d is negative.

4. State the domain, $(-\infty, \infty)$, the range, (d, ∞), and the horizontal asymptote $y = d$.

Example 2   **Graphing a Shift of an Exponential Function**

Graph $f(x) = 2^{x+1} - 3$. State the domain, range, and asymptote.

Solution   We have an exponential equation of the form $f(x) = b^{x+c} + d$, with $b = 2$, $c = 1$, and $d = -3$.

Draw the horizontal asymptote $y = d$, so draw $y = -3$.

Identify the shift as $(-c, d)$, so the shift is $(-1, -3)$.

Shift the graph of $f(x) = b^x$ left 1 units and down 3 units.

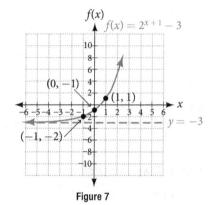

Figure 7

The domain is $(-\infty, \infty)$; the range is $(-3, \infty)$; the horizontal asymptote is $y = -3$.

Try It #2

Graph $f(x) = 2^{x-1} + 3$. State domain, range, and asymptote.

How To...

Given an equation of the form $f(x) = b^{x+c} + d$ for x, use a graphing calculator to approximate the solution.

1. Press **[Y=]**. Enter the given exponential equation in the line headed "**Y₁=**".

2. Enter the given value for $f(x)$ in the line headed "**Y₂=**".

3. Press **[WINDOW]**. Adjust the y-axis so that it includes the value entered for "**Y₂=**".

4. Press **[GRAPH]** to observe the graph of the exponential function along with the line for the specified value of $f(x)$.

5. To find the value of x, we compute the point of intersection. Press **[2ND]** then **[CALC]**. Select "intersect" and press **[ENTER]** three times. The point of intersection gives the value of x for the indicated value of the function.

Example 3   **Approximating the Solution of an Exponential Equation**

Solve $42 = 1.2(5)^x + 2.8$ graphically. Round to the nearest thousandth.

Solution   Press **[Y=]** and enter $1.2(5)^x + 2.8$ next to **Y₁=**. Then enter 42 next to **Y₂=**. For a window, use the values −3 to 3 for x and −5 to 55 for y. Press **[GRAPH]**. The graphs should intersect somewhere near $x = 2$.

For a better approximation, press **[2ND]** then **[CALC]**. Select **[5: intersect]** and press **[ENTER]** three times. The x-coordinate of the point of intersection is displayed as 2.1661943. (Your answer may be different if you use a different window or use a different value for **Guess?**) To the nearest thousandth, $x \approx 2.166$.

Try It #3

Solve $4 = 7.85(1.15)^x - 2.27$ graphically. Round to the nearest thousandth.

Graphing a Stretch or Compression

While horizontal and vertical shifts involve adding constants to the input or to the function itself, a stretch or compression occurs when we multiply the parent function $f(x) = b^x$ by a constant $|a| > 0$. For example, if we begin by graphing the parent function $f(x) = 2^x$, we can then graph the stretch, using $a = 3$, to get $g(x) = 3(2)^x$ as shown on the left in **Figure 8**, and the compression, using $a = \frac{1}{3}$, to get $h(x) = \frac{1}{3}(2)^x$ as shown on the right in **Figure 8**.

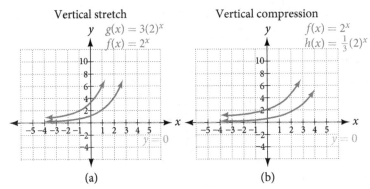

Vertical stretch

Vertical compression

(a)   (b)

Figure 8 (a) $g(x) = 3(2)^x$ stretches the graph of $f(x) = 2^x$ vertically by a factor of 3.

(b) $h(x) = \frac{1}{3}(2)^x$ compresses the graph of $f(x) = 2^x$ vertically by a factor of $\frac{1}{3}$.

---

stretches and compressions of the parent function $f(x) = b^x$

For any factor $a > 0$, the function $f(x) = a(b)^x$

- is stretched vertically by a factor of a if $|a| > 1$.
- is compressed vertically by a factor of a if $|a| < 1$.
- has a y-intercept of $(0, a)$.
- has a horizontal asymptote at $y = 0$, a range of $(0, \infty)$, and a domain of $(-\infty, \infty)$, which are unchanged from the parent function.

Example 4   **Graphing the Stretch of an Exponential Function**

Sketch a graph of $f(x) = 4\left(\frac{1}{2}\right)^x$. State the domain, range, and asymptote.

Solution   Before graphing, identify the behavior and key points on the graph.

- Since $b = \frac{1}{2}$ is between zero and one, the left tail of the graph will increase without bound as x decreases, and the right tail will approach the x-axis as x increases.

- Since $a = 4$, the graph of $f(x) = \left(\frac{1}{2}\right)^x$ will be stretched by a factor of 4.

- Create a table of points as shown in **Table 4**.

x	−3	−2	−1	0	1	2	3
$f(x) = 4\left(\frac{1}{2}\right)^x$	32	16	8	4	2	1	0.5

Table 4

- Plot the y-intercept, $(0, 4)$, along with two other points. We can use $(-1, 8)$ and $(1, 2)$.

Draw a smooth curve connecting the points, as shown in **Figure 9**.

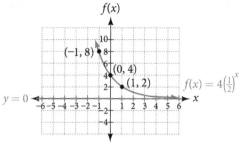

Figure 9

The domain is $(-\infty, \infty)$; the range is $(0, \infty)$; the horizontal asymptote is $y = 0$.

Try It #4

Sketch the graph of $f(x) = \dfrac{1}{2}(4)^x$. State the domain, range, and asymptote.

Graphing Reflections

In addition to shifting, compressing, and stretching a graph, we can also reflect it about the x-axis or the y-axis. When we multiply the parent function $f(x) = b^x$ by -1, we get a reflection about the x-axis. When we multiply the input by -1, we get a reflection about the y-axis. For example, if we begin by graphing the parent function $f(x) = 2^x$, we can then graph the two reflections alongside it. The reflection about the x-axis, $g(x) = -2^x$, is shown on the left side of **Figure 10**, and the reflection about the y-axis $h(x) = 2^{-x}$, is shown on the right side of **Figure 10**.

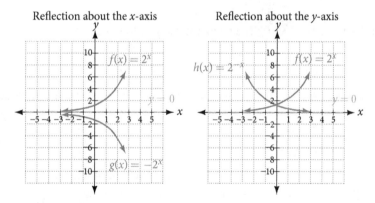

Figure 10 (a) $g(x) = -2^x$ reflects the graph of $f(x) = 2^x$ about the x-axis. (b) $g(x) = 2^{-x}$ reflects the graph of $f(x) = 2^x$ about the y-axis.

> ***reflections of the parent function $f(x) = b^x$***
>
> The function $f(x) = -b^x$
>
> - reflects the parent function $f(x) = b^x$ about the x-axis.
> - has a y-intercept of $(0, -1)$.
> - has a range of $(-\infty, 0)$.
> - has a horizontal asymptote at $y = 0$ and domain of $(-\infty, \infty)$, which are unchanged from the parent function.
>
> The function $f(x) = b^{-x}$
>
> - reflects the parent function $f(x) = b^x$ about the y-axis.
> - has a y-intercept of $(0, 1)$, a horizontal asymptote at $y = 0$, a range of $(0, \infty)$, and a domain of $(-\infty, \infty)$, which are unchanged from the parent function.

Example 5   **Writing and Graphing the Reflection of an Exponential Function**

Find and graph the equation for a function, $g(x)$, that reflects $f(x) = \left(\frac{1}{4}\right)^x$ about the x-axis. State its domain, range, and asymptote.

Solution   Since we want to reflect the parent function $f(x) = \left(\frac{1}{4}\right)^x$ about the x-axis, we multiply $f(x)$ by -1 to get, $g(x) = -\left(\frac{1}{4}\right)^x$. Next we create a table of points as in **Table 5**.

x	-3	-2	-1	0	1	2	3
$g(x) = -\left(\frac{1}{4}\right)^x$	-64	-16	-4	-1	-0.25	-0.0625	-0.0156

Table 5

Plot the y-intercept, $(0, -1)$, along with two other points. We can use $(-1, -4)$ and $(1, -0.25)$.

Draw a smooth curve connecting the points:

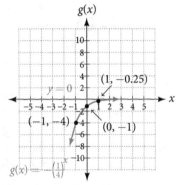

Figure 11

The domain is $(-\infty, \infty)$; the range is $(-\infty, 0)$; the horizontal asymptote is $y = 0$.

Try It #5

Find and graph the equation for a function, $g(x)$, that reflects $f(x) = 1.25^x$ about the y-axis. State its domain, range, and asymptote.

Summarizing Translations of the Exponential Function

Now that we have worked with each type of translation for the exponential function, we can summarize them in **Table 6** to arrive at the general equation for translating exponential functions.

Translations of the Parent Function $f(x) = b^x$	
Translation	**Form**
Shift • Horizontally c units to the left • Vertically d units up	$f(x) = b^{x+c} + d$
Stretch and Compress • Stretch if $\|a\| > 1$ • Compression if $0 < \|a\| < 1$	$f(x) = ab^x$
Reflect about the x-axis	$f(x) = -b^x$
Reflect about the y-axis	$f(x) = b^{-x} = \left(\frac{1}{b}\right)^x$
General equation for all translations	$f(x) = ab^{x+c} + d$

Table 6

> ### translations of exponential functions
>
> A translation of an exponential function has the form
>
> $$f(x) = ab^{x+c} + d$$
>
> Where the parent function, $y = b^x$, $b > 1$, is
>
> - shifted horizontally c units to the left.
> - stretched vertically by a factor of $|a|$ if $|a| > 0$.
> - compressed vertically by a factor of $|a|$ if $0 < |a| < 1$.
> - shifted vertically d units.
> - reflected about the x-axis when $a < 0$.
>
> Note the order of the shifts, transformations, and reflections follow the order of operations.

Example 6   **Writing a Function from a Description**

Write the equation for the function described below. Give the horizontal asymptote, the domain, and the range.

- $f(x) = e^x$ is vertically stretched by a factor of 2, reflected across the y-axis, and then shifted up 4 units.

Solution   We want to find an equation of the general form $f(x) = ab^{x+c} + d$. We use the description provided to find a, b, c, and d.

- We are given the parent function $f(x) = e^x$, so $b = e$.
- The function is stretched by a factor of 2, so $a = 2$.
- The function is reflected about the y-axis. We replace x with $-x$ to get: e^{-x}.
- The graph is shifted vertically 4 units, so $d = 4$.

Substituting in the general form we get,

$$
\begin{aligned}
f(x) &= ab^{x+c} + d \\
&= 2e^{-x+0} + 4 \\
&= 2e^{-x} + 4
\end{aligned}
$$

The domain is $(-\infty, \infty)$; the range is $(4, \infty)$; the horizontal asymptote is $y = 4$.

Try It #6

Write the equation for function described below. Give the horizontal asymptote, the domain, and the range.

- $f(x) = e^x$ is compressed vertically by a factor of $\frac{1}{3}$, reflected across the x-axis and then shifted down 2 units.

Access this online resource for additional instruction and practice with graphing exponential functions.

- Graph Exponential Functions (http://openstaxcollege.org/l/graphexpfunc)

4.2   SECTION EXERCISES

VERBAL

1. What role does the horizontal asymptote of an exponential function play in telling us about the end behavior of the graph?

2. What is the advantage of knowing how to recognize transformations of the graph of a parent function algebraically?

ALGEBRAIC

3. The graph of $f(x) = 3^x$ is reflected about the y-axis and stretched vertically by a factor of 4. What is the equation of the new function, $g(x)$? State its y-intercept, domain, and range.

4. The graph of $f(x) = \left(\frac{1}{2}\right)^{-x}$ is reflected about the y-axis and compressed vertically by a factor of $\frac{1}{5}$. What is the equation of the new function, $g(x)$? State its y-intercept, domain, and range.

5. The graph of $f(x) = 10^x$ is reflected about the x-axis and shifted upward 7 units. What is the equation of the new function, $g(x)$? State its y-intercept, domain, and range.

6. The graph of $f(x) = (1.68)^x$ is shifted right 3 units, stretched vertically by a factor of 2, reflected about the x-axis, and then shifted downward 3 units. What is the equation of the new function, $g(x)$? State its y-intercept (to the nearest thousandth), domain, and range.

7. The graph of $f(x) = -\frac{1}{2}\left(\frac{1}{4}\right)^{x-2} + 4$ is shifted downward 4 units, and then shifted left 2 units, stretched vertically by a factor of 4, and reflected about the x-axis. What is the equation of the new function, $g(x)$? State its y-intercept, domain, and range.

GRAPHICAL

For the following exercises, graph the function and its reflection about the y-axis on the same axes, and give the y-intercept.

8. $f(x) = 3\left(\frac{1}{2}\right)^x$

9. $g(x) = -2(0.25)^x$

10. $h(x) = 6(1.75)^{-x}$

For the following exercises, graph each set of functions on the same axes.

11. $f(x) = 3\left(\frac{1}{4}\right)^x$, $g(x) = 3(2)^x$, and $h(x) = 3(4)^x$

12. $f(x) = \frac{1}{4}(3)^x$, $g(x) = 2(3)^x$, and $h(x) = 4(3)^x$

For the following exercises, match each function with one of the graphs in **Figure 12**.

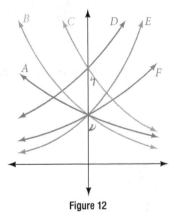

Figure 12

13. $f(x) = 2(0.69)^x$

14. $f(x) = 2(1.28)^x$

15. $f(x) = 2(0.81)^x$

16. $f(x) = 4(1.28)^x$

17. $f(x) = 2(1.59)^x$

18. $f(x) = 4(0.69)^x$

For the following exercises, use the graphs shown in **Figure 13**. All have the form $f(x) = ab^x$.

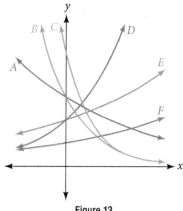

Figure 13

19. Which graph has the largest value for b?

20. Which graph has the smallest value for b?

21. Which graph has the largest value for a?

22. Which graph has the smallest value for a?

For the following exercises, graph the function and its reflection about the x-axis on the same axes.

23. $f(x) = \frac{1}{2}(4)^x$

24. $f(x) = 3(0.75)^x - 1$

25. $f(x) = -4(2)^x + 2$

For the following exercises, graph the transformation of $f(x) = 2^x$. Give the horizontal asymptote, the domain, and the range.

26. $f(x) = 2^{-x}$

27. $h(x) = 2^x + 3$

28. $f(x) = 2^{x-2}$

For the following exercises, describe the end behavior of the graphs of the functions.

29. $f(x) = -5(4)^x - 1$

30. $f(x) = 3\left(\frac{1}{2}\right)^x - 2$

31. $f(x) = 3(4)^{-x} + 2$

For the following exercises, start with the graph of $f(x) = 4^x$. Then write a function that results from the given transformation.

32. Shift $f(x)$ 4 units upward

33. Shift $f(x)$ 3 units downward

34. Shift $f(x)$ 2 units left

35. Shift $f(x)$ 5 units right

36. Reflect $f(x)$ about the x-axis

37. Reflect $f(x)$ about the y-axis

For the following exercises, each graph is a transformation of $y = 2^x$. Write an equation describing the transformation.

38.

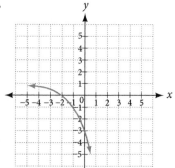

39.

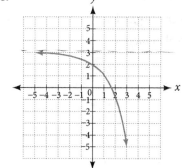

40.

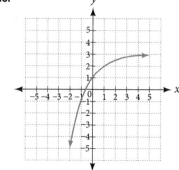

For the following exercises, find an exponential equation for the graph.

41.

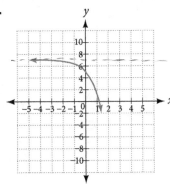

42.

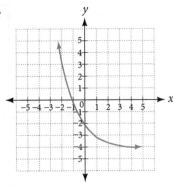

NUMERIC

For the following exercises, evaluate the exponential functions for the indicated value of x.

43. $g(x) = \frac{1}{3}(7)^{x-2}$ for $g(6)$.

44. $f(x) = 4(2)^{x-1} - 2$ for $f(5)$.

45. $h(x) = -\frac{1}{2}\left(\frac{1}{2}\right)^x + 6$ for $h(-7)$.

TECHNOLOGY

For the following exercises, use a graphing calculator to approximate the solutions of the equation. Round to the nearest thousandth. $f(x) = ab^x + d$.

46. $-50 = -\left(\frac{1}{2}\right)^{-x}$

47. $116 = \frac{1}{4}\left(\frac{1}{8}\right)^x$

48. $12 = 2(3)^x + 1$

49. $5 = 3\left(\frac{1}{2}\right)^{x-1} - 2$

50. $-30 = -4(2)^{x+2} + 2$

EXTENSIONS

51. Explore and discuss the graphs of $f(x) = (b)^x$ and $g(x) = \left(\frac{1}{b}\right)^x$. Then make a conjecture about the relationship between the graphs of the functions b^x and $\left(\frac{1}{b}\right)^x$ for any real number $b > 0$.

52. Prove the conjecture made in the previous exercise.

53. Explore and discuss the graphs of $f(x) = 4^x$, $g(x) = 4^{x-2}$, and $h(x) = \left(\frac{1}{16}\right)4^x$. Then make a conjecture about the relationship between the graphs of the functions b^x and $\left(\frac{1}{b^n}\right)b^x$ for any real number n and real number $b > 0$.

54. Prove the conjecture made in the previous exercise.

LEARNING OBJECTIVES

In this section, you will:

- Convert from logarithmic to exponential form.
- Convert from exponential to logarithmic form.
- Evaluate logarithms.
- Use common logarithms.
- Use natural logarithms.

4.3 LOGARITHMIC FUNCTIONS

Figure 1 Devastation of March 11, 2011 earthquake in Honshu, Japan. (credit: Daniel Pierce)

In 2010, a major earthquake struck Haiti, destroying or damaging over 285,000 homes[19]. One year later, another, stronger earthquake devastated Honshu, Japan, destroying or damaging over 332,000 buildings,[20] like those shown in **Figure 1**. Even though both caused substantial damage, the earthquake in 2011 was 100 times stronger than the earthquake in Haiti. How do we know? The magnitudes of earthquakes are measured on a scale known as the Richter Scale. The Haitian earthquake registered a 7.0 on the Richter Scale[21] whereas the Japanese earthquake registered a 9.0.[22]

The Richter Scale is a base-ten logarithmic scale. In other words, an earthquake of magnitude 8 is not twice as great as an earthquake of magnitude 4. It is $10^{8-4} = 10^4 = 10,000$ times as great! In this lesson, we will investigate the nature of the Richter Scale and the base-ten function upon which it depends.

Converting from Logarithmic to Exponential Form

In order to analyze the magnitude of earthquakes or compare the magnitudes of two different earthquakes, we need to be able to convert between logarithmic and exponential form. For example, suppose the amount of energy released from one earthquake were 500 times greater than the amount of energy released from another. We want to calculate the difference in magnitude. The equation that represents this problem is $10^x = 500$, where x represents the difference in magnitudes on the Richter Scale. How would we solve for x?

We have not yet learned a method for solving exponential equations. None of the algebraic tools discussed so far is sufficient to solve $10^x = 500$. We know that $10^2 = 100$ and $10^3 = 1000$, so it is clear that x must be some value between 2 and 3, since $y = 10^x$ is increasing. We can examine a graph, as in **Figure 2**, to better estimate the solution.

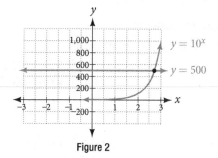

Figure 2

19 http://earthquake.usgs.gov/earthquakes/eqinthenews/2010/us2010rja6/#summary. Accessed 3/4/2013.
20 http://earthquake.usgs.gov/earthquakes/eqinthenews/2011/usc001xgp/#summary. Accessed 3/4/2013.
21 http://earthquake.usgs.gov/earthquakes/eqinthenews/2010/us2010rja6/. Accessed 3/4/2013.
22 http://earthquake.usgs.gov/earthquakes/eqinthenews/2011/usc001xgp/#details. Accessed 3/4/2013.

Estimating from a graph, however, is imprecise. To find an algebraic solution, we must introduce a new function. Observe that the graph in **Figure 2** passes the horizontal line test. The exponential function $y = b^x$ is one-to-one, so its inverse, $x = b^y$ is also a function. As is the case with all inverse functions, we simply interchange x and y and solve for y to find the inverse function. To represent y as a function of x, we use a logarithmic function of the form $y = \log_b(x)$. The base b **logarithm** of a number is the exponent by which we must raise b to get that number.

We read a logarithmic expression as, "The logarithm with base b of x is equal to y," or, simplified, "log base b of x is y." We can also say, "b raised to the power of y is x," because logs are exponents. For example, the base 2 logarithm of 32 is 5, because 5 is the exponent we must apply to 2 to get 32. Since $2^5 = 32$, we can write $\log_2 32 = 5$. We read this as "log base 2 of 32 is 5."

We can express the relationship between logarithmic form and its corresponding exponential form as follows:

$$\log_b(x) = y \Leftrightarrow b^y = x, b > 0, b \neq 1$$

Note that the base b is always positive.

$$\log_b(x) = y \qquad \text{Think} \atop \text{b to the $y = x$}$$

$$\text{to}$$

Because logarithm is a function, it is most correctly written as $\log_b(x)$, using parentheses to denote function evaluation, just as we would with $f(x)$. However, when the input is a single variable or number, it is common to see the parentheses dropped and the expression written without parentheses, as $\log_b x$. Note that many calculators require parentheses around the x.

We can illustrate the notation of logarithms as follows:

$$\log_b(c) = a \text{ means } b^a = c$$

$$\text{to}$$

Notice that, comparing the logarithm function and the exponential function, the input and the output are switched. This means $y = \log_b(x)$ and $y = b^x$ are inverse functions.

> ### *definition of the logarithmic function*
>
> A **logarithm** base b of a positive number x satisfies the following definition.
>
> For $x > 0, b > 0, b \neq 1$,
>
> $$y = \log_b(x) \text{ is equivalent to } b^y = x$$
>
> where,
> - we read $\log_b(x)$ as, "the logarithm with base b of x" or the "log base b of x."
> - the logarithm y is the exponent to which b must be raised to get x.
>
> Also, since the logarithmic and exponential functions switch the x and y values, the domain and range of the exponential function are interchanged for the logarithmic function. Therefore,
> - the domain of the logarithm function with base b is $(0, \infty)$.
> - the range of the logarithm function with base b is $(-\infty, \infty)$.

Q & A...

Can we take the logarithm of a negative number?

No. Because the base of an exponential function is always positive, no power of that base can ever be negative. We can never take the logarithm of a negative number. Also, we cannot take the logarithm of zero. Calculators may output a log of a negative number when in complex mode, but the log of a negative number is not a real number.

How To...

Given an equation in logarithmic form $\log_b(x) = y$, convert it to exponential form.

1. Examine the equation $y = \log_b(x)$ and identify b, y, and x.

2. Rewrite $\log_b(x) = y$ as $b^y = x$.

Example 1   **Converting from Logarithmic Form to Exponential Form**

Write the following logarithmic equations in exponential form.

     a. $\log_6\left(\sqrt{6}\right) = \frac{1}{2}$ **b.** $\log_3(9) = 2$

Solution   First, identify the values of b, y, and x. Then, write the equation in the form $b^y = x$.

     a. $\log_6\left(\sqrt{6}\right) = \frac{1}{2}$ Here, $b = 6$, $y = \frac{1}{2}$, and $x = \sqrt{6}$. Therefore, the equation $\log_6\left(\sqrt{6}\right) = \frac{1}{2}$ is equivalent to $6^{\frac{1}{2}} = \sqrt{6}$.

     b. $\log_3(9) = 2$ Here, $b = 3$, $y = 2$, and $x = 9$. Therefore, the equation $\log_3(9) = 2$ is equivalent to $3^2 = 9$.

Try It #1

Write the following logarithmic equations in exponential form.

     a. $\log_{10}(1,000,000) = 6$ **b.** $\log_5(25) = 2$

Converting From Exponential to Logarithmic Form

To convert from exponents to logarithms, we follow the same steps in reverse. We identify the base b, exponent x, and output y. Then we write $x = \log_b(y)$.

Example 2   **Converting from Exponential Form to Logarithmic Form**

Write the following exponential equations in logarithmic form.

     a. $2^3 = 8$ **b.** $5^2 = 25$ **c.** $10^{-4} = \frac{1}{10,000}$

Solution   First, identify the values of b, y, and x. Then, write the equation in the form $x = \log_b(y)$.

     a. $2^3 = 8$ Here, $b = 2$, $x = 3$, and $y = 8$. Therefore, the equation $2^3 = 8$ is equivalent to $\log_2(8) = 3$.

     b. $5^2 = 25$ Here, $b = 5$, $x = 2$, and $y = 25$. Therefore, the equation $5^2 = 25$ is equivalent to $\log_5(25) = 2$.

     c. $10^{-4} = \frac{1}{10,000}$ Here, $b = 10$, $x = -4$, and $y = \frac{1}{10,000}$. Therefore, the equation $10^{-4} = \frac{1}{10,000}$ is equivalent to $\log_{10}\left(\frac{1}{10,000}\right) = -4$.

Try It #2 O

Write the following exponential equations in logarithmic form.

     a. $3^2 = 9$ **b.** $5^3 = 125$ **c.** $2^{-1} = \frac{1}{2}$

Evaluating Logarithms

Knowing the squares, cubes, and roots of numbers allows us to evaluate many logarithms mentally. For example, consider $\log_2(8)$. We ask, "To what exponent must 2 be raised in order to get 8?" Because we already know $2^3 = 8$, it follows that $\log_2(8) = 3$.

Now consider solving $\log_7(49)$ and $\log_3(27)$ mentally.

- We ask, "To what exponent must 7 be raised in order to get 49?" We know $7^2 = 49$. Therefore, $\log_7(49) = 2$

- We ask, "To what exponent must 3 be raised in order to get 27?" We know $3^3 = 27$. Therefore, $\log_3(27) = 3$

Even some seemingly more complicated logarithms can be evaluated without a calculator. For example, let's evaluate $\log_{\frac{2}{3}}\left(\frac{4}{9}\right)$ mentally.

- We ask, "To what exponent must $\frac{2}{3}$ be raised in order to get $\frac{4}{9}$?" We know $2^2 = 4$ and $3^2 = 9$, so $\left(\frac{2}{3}\right)^2 = \frac{4}{9}$. Therefore, $\log_{\frac{2}{3}}\left(\frac{4}{9}\right) = 2$.

How To...

Given a logarithm of the form $y = \log_b(x)$, evaluate it mentally.

1. Rewrite the argument x as a power of b : $b^y = x$.
2. Use previous knowledge of powers of b identify y by asking, "To what exponent should b be raised in order to get x?"

Example 3   **Solving Logarithms Mentally**

Solve $y = \log_4(64)$ without using a calculator.

Solution   First we rewrite the logarithm in exponential form: $4^y = 64$. Next, we ask, "To what exponent must 4 be raised in order to get 64?"

We know $4^3 = 64$ therefore, $\log_4(64) = 3$.

Try It #3

Solve $y = \log_{121}(11)$ without using a calculator.

Example 4   **Evaluating the Logarithm of a Reciprocal**

Evaluate $y = \log_3\left(\dfrac{1}{27}\right)$ without using a calculator.

Solution   First we rewrite the logarithm in exponential form: $3^y = \dfrac{1}{27}$. Next, we ask, "To what exponent must 3 be raised in order to get $\dfrac{1}{27}$?"

We know $3^3 = 27$, but what must we do to get the reciprocal, $\dfrac{1}{27}$? Recall from working with exponents that $b^{-a} = \dfrac{1}{b^a}$. We use this information to write

$$3^{-3} = \frac{1}{3^3}$$
$$= \frac{1}{27}$$

Therefore, $\log_3\left(\dfrac{1}{27}\right) = -3$.

Try It #4

Evaluate $y = \log_2\left(\dfrac{1}{32}\right)$ without using a calculator.

Using Common Logarithms

Sometimes we may see a logarithm written without a base. In this case, we assume that the base is 10. In other words, the expression $\log(x)$ means $\log_{10}(x)$. We call a base-10 logarithm a **common logarithm**. Common logarithms are used to measure the Richter Scale mentioned at the beginning of the section. Scales for measuring the brightness of stars and the pH of acids and bases also use common logarithms.

> *definition of the common logarithm*
>
> A **common logarithm** is a logarithm with base 10. We write $\log_{10}(x)$ simply as $\log(x)$. The common logarithm of a positive number x satisfies the following definition.
>
> For $x > 0$,
>
> $$y = \log(x) \text{ is equivalent to } 10^y = x$$
>
> We read $\log(x)$ as, "the logarithm with base 10 of x" or "log base 10 of x."
>
> The logarithm y is the exponent to which 10 must be raised to get x.

How To...

Given a common logarithm of the form $y = \log(x)$, evaluate it mentally.

1. Rewrite the argument x as a power of 10: $10^y = x$.
2. Use previous knowledge of powers of 10 to identify y by asking, "To what exponent must 10 be raised in order to get x?"

Example 5   Finding the Value of a Common Logarithm Mentally

Evaluate $y = \log(1,000)$ without using a calculator.

Solution   First we rewrite the logarithm in exponential form: $10^y = 1,000$. Next, we ask, "To what exponent must 10 be raised in order to get 1,000?" We know $10^3 = 1,000$ therefore, $\log(1,000) = 3$.

Try It #5

Evaluate $y = \log(1,000,000)$.

How To...

Given a common logarithm with the form $y = \log(x)$, evaluate it using a calculator.

1. Press [**LOG**].
2. Enter the value given for x, followed by [ )].
3. Press [**ENTER**].

Example 6   Finding the Value of a Common Logarithm Using a Calculator

Evaluate $y = \log(321)$ to four decimal places using a calculator.

Solution

- Press [**LOG**].
- Enter 321, followed by [ )].
- Press [**ENTER**].

Rounding to four decimal places, $\log(321) \approx 2.5065$.

Analysis   *Note that $10^2 = 100$ and that $10^3 = 1000$. Since 321 is between 100 and 1000, we know that $\log(321)$ must be between $\log(100)$ and $\log(1000)$. This gives us the following:*

$$100 \; < \; 321 \; < \; 1000$$
$$2 \; < \; 2.5065 \; < \; 3$$

Try It #6

Evaluate $y = \log(123)$ to four decimal places using a calculator.

Example 7   Rewriting and Solving a Real-World Exponential Model

The amount of energy released from one earthquake was 500 times greater than the amount of energy released from another. The equation $10^x = 500$ represents this situation, where x is the difference in magnitudes on the Richter Scale. To the nearest thousandth, what was the difference in magnitudes?

Solution   We begin by rewriting the exponential equation in logarithmic form.

$$10^x = 500$$

$$\log(500) = x \qquad \qquad \text{Use the definition of the common log.}$$

Next we evaluate the logarithm using a calculator:

- Press [**LOG**].
- Enter 500, followed by [ )].
- Press [**ENTER**].
- To the nearest thousandth, $\log(500) \approx 2.699$.

The difference in magnitudes was about 2.699.

Try It #7

The amount of energy released from one earthquake was 8,500 times greater than the amount of energy released from another. The equation $10^x = 8500$ represents this situation, where x is the difference in magnitudes on the Richter Scale. To the nearest thousandth, what was the difference in magnitudes?

Using Natural Logarithms

The most frequently used base for logarithms is e. Base e logarithms are important in calculus and some scientific applications; they are called **natural logarithms**. The base e logarithm, $\log_e(x)$, has its own notation, $\ln(x)$.

Most values of $\ln(x)$ can be found only using a calculator. The major exception is that, because the logarithm of 1 is always 0 in any base, $\ln(1) = 0$. For other natural logarithms, we can use the $\ln$ key that can be found on most scientific calculators. We can also find the natural logarithm of any power of e using the inverse property of logarithms.

---

definition of the natural logarithm

A **natural logarithm** is a logarithm with base e. We write $\log_e(x)$ simply as $\ln(x)$. The natural logarithm of a positive number x satisfies the following definition.

For $x > 0$,
$$y = \ln(x) \text{ is equivalent to } e^y = x$$

We read $\ln(x)$ as, "the logarithm with base e of x" or "the natural logarithm of x."

The logarithm y is the exponent to which e must be raised to get x.

Since the functions $y = e$ and $y = \ln(x)$ are inverse functions, $\ln(e^x) = x$ for all x and $e = x$ for $x > 0$.

How To...

Given a natural logarithm with the form $y = \ln(x)$, evaluate it using a calculator.

1. Press [**LN**].
2. Enter the value given for x, followed by [ )].
3. Press [**ENTER**].

Example 8   **Evaluating a Natural Logarithm Using a Calculator**

Evaluate $y = \ln(500)$ to four decimal places using a calculator.

Solution

- Press [**LN**].
- Enter 500, followed by [ )].
- Press [**ENTER**].

Rounding to four decimal places, $\ln(500) \approx 6.2146$

Try It #8

Evaluate $\ln(-500)$.

Access this online resource for additional instruction and practice with logarithms.

- Introduction to Logarithms (http://openstaxcollege.org/l/intrologarithms)

4.3 SECTION EXERCISES

VERBAL

1. What is a base b logarithm? Discuss the meaning by interpreting each part of the equivalent equations $b^y = x$ and $\log_b(x) = y$ for $b > 0$, $b \neq 1$.

2. How is the logarithmic function $f(x) = \log_b(x)$ related to the exponential function $g(x) = b^x$? What is the result of composing these two functions?

3. How can the logarithmic equation $\log_b x = y$ be solved for x using the properties of exponents?

4. Discuss the meaning of the common logarithm. What is its relationship to a logarithm with base b, and how does the notation differ?

5. Discuss the meaning of the natural logarithm. What is its relationship to a logarithm with base b, and how does the notation differ?

ALGEBRAIC

For the following exercises, rewrite each equation in exponential form.

6. $\log_4(q) = m$ **7.** $\log_a(b) = c$ **8.** $\log_{16}(y) = x$ **9.** $\log_x(64) = y$

10. $\log_y(x) = -11$ **11.** $\log_{15}(a) = b$ **12.** $\log_y(137) = x$ **13.** $\log_{13}(142) = a$

14. $\log(v) = t$ **15.** $\ln(w) = n$

For the following exercises, rewrite each equation in logarithmic form.

16. $4^x = y$ **17.** $c^d = k$ **18.** $m^{-7} = n$ **19.** $19^x = y$

20. $x^{-\frac{10}{13}} = y$ **21.** $n^4 = 103$ **22.** $\left(\dfrac{7}{5}\right)^m = n$ **23.** $y^x = \dfrac{39}{100}$

24. $10^a = b$ **25.** $e^k = h$

For the following exercises, solve for x by converting the logarithmic equation to exponential form.

26. $\log_3(x) = 2$ **27.** $\log_2(x) = -3$ **28.** $\log_5(x) = 2$ **29.** $\log_3(x) = 3$

30. $\log_2(x) = 6$ **31.** $\log_9(x) = \dfrac{1}{2}$ **32.** $\log_{18}(x) = 2$ **33.** $\log_6(x) = -3$

34. $\log(x) = 3$ **35.** $\ln(x) = 2$

For the following exercises, use the definition of common and natural logarithms to simplify.

36. $\log(100^8)$ **37.** $10^{\log(32)}$ **38.** $2\log(0.0001)$ **39.** $e^{\ln(1.06)}$

40. $\ln(e^{-5.03})$ **41.** $e^{\ln(10.125)} + 4$

NUMERIC

For the following exercises, evaluate the base b logarithmic expression without using a calculator.

42. $\log_3\left(\dfrac{1}{27}\right)$ **43.** $\log_6(\sqrt{6})$ **44.** $\log_2\left(\dfrac{1}{8}\right) + 4$ **45.** $6\log_8(4)$

For the following exercises, evaluate the common logarithmic expression without using a calculator.

46. $\log(10,000)$ **47.** $\log(0.001)$ **48.** $\log(1) + 7$ **49.** $2\log(100^{-3})$

For the following exercises, evaluate the natural logarithmic expression without using a calculator.

50. $\ln\left(e^{\frac{1}{3}}\right)$　　　　　**51.** $\ln(1)$　　　　　**52.** $\ln(e^{-0.225}) - 3$　　　　　**53.** $25\ln\left(e^{\frac{2}{5}}\right)$

TECHNOLOGY

For the following exercises, evaluate each expression using a calculator. Round to the nearest thousandth.

54. $\log(0.04)$　　　**55.** $\ln(15)$　　　**56.** $\ln\left(\dfrac{4}{5}\right)$　　　**57.** $\log(\sqrt{2})$　　　**58.** $\ln(\sqrt{2})$

EXTENSIONS

59. Is $x = 0$ in the domain of the function $f(x) = \log(x)$? If so, what is the value of the function when $x = 0$? Verify the result.

60. Is $f(x) = 0$ in the range of the function $f(x) = \log(x)$? If so, for what value of x? Verify the result.

61. Is there a number x such that $\ln x = 2$? If so, what is that number? Verify the result.

62. Is the following true: $\dfrac{\log_3(27)}{\log_4\left(\dfrac{1}{64}\right)} = -1$? Verify the result.

63. Is the following true: $\dfrac{\ln(e^{1.725})}{\ln(1)} = 1.725$? Verify the result.

REAL-WORLD APPLICATIONS

64. The exposure index EI for a 35 millimeter camera is a measurement of the amount of light that hits the film. It is determined by the equation $EI = \log_2\left(\dfrac{f^2}{t}\right)$, where f is the "f-stop" setting on the camera, and t is the exposure time in seconds. Suppose the f-stop setting is 8 and the desired exposure time is 2 seconds. What will the resulting exposure index be?

65. Refer to the previous exercise. Suppose the light meter on a camera indicates an EI of -2, and the desired exposure time is 16 seconds. What should the f-stop setting be?

66. The intensity levels I of two earthquakes measured on a seismograph can be compared by the formula
$$\log\frac{I_1}{I_2} = M_1 - M_2$$
where M is the magnitude given by the Richter Scale. In August 2009, an earthquake of magnitude 6.1 hit Honshu, Japan. In March 2011, that same region experienced yet another, more devastating earthquake, this time with a magnitude of 9.0.[23] How many times greater was the intensity of the 2011 earthquake? Round to the nearest whole number.

23 http://earthquake.usgs.gov/earthquakes/world/historical.php. Accessed 3/4/2014.

LEARNING OBJECTIVES

In this section, you will:

- Identify the domain of a logarithmic function.
- Graph logarithmic functions.

4.4 GRAPHS OF LOGARITHMIC FUNCTIONS

In **Graphs of Exponential Functions**, we saw how creating a graphical representation of an exponential model gives us another layer of insight for predicting future events. How do logarithmic graphs give us insight into situations? Because every logarithmic function is the inverse function of an exponential function, we can think of every output on a logarithmic graph as the input for the corresponding inverse exponential equation. In other words, logarithms give the *cause* for an *effect*.

To illustrate, suppose we invest $2,500 in an account that offers an annual interest rate of 5%, compounded continuously.

We already know that the balance in our account for any year t can be found with the equation $A = 2500e^{0.05t}$.

But what if we wanted to know the year for any balance? We would need to create a corresponding new function by interchanging the input and the output; thus we would need to create a logarithmic model for this situation. By graphing the model, we can see the output (year) for any input (account balance). For instance, what if we wanted to know how many years it would take for our initial investment to double? **Figure 1** shows this point on the logarithmic graph.

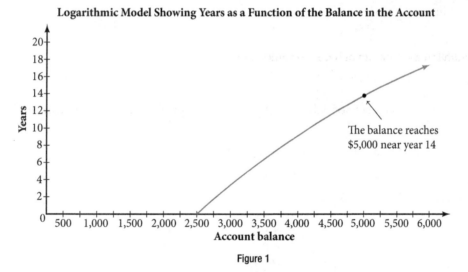

Logarithmic Model Showing Years as a Function of the Balance in the Account

The balance reaches $5,000 near year 14

Figure 1

In this section we will discuss the values for which a logarithmic function is defined, and then turn our attention to graphing the family of logarithmic functions.

Finding the Domain of a Logarithmic Function

Before working with graphs, we will take a look at the domain (the set of input values) for which the logarithmic function is defined.

Recall that the exponential function is defined as $y = b^x$ for any real number x and constant $b > 0$, $b \neq 1$, where

- The domain of y is $(-\infty, \infty)$.
- The range of y is $(0, \infty)$.

In the last section we learned that the logarithmic function $y = \log_b(x)$ is the inverse of the exponential function $y = b^x$. So, as inverse functions:

- The domain of $y = \log_b(x)$ is the range of $y = b^x : (0, \infty)$.
- The range of $y = \log_b(x)$ is the domain of $y = b^x : (-\infty, \infty)$.

Transformations of the parent function $y = \log_b(x)$ behave similarly to those of other functions. Just as with other parent functions, we can apply the four types of transformations—shifts, stretches, compressions, and reflections—to the parent function without loss of shape.

In **Graphs of Exponential Functions** we saw that certain transformations can change the *range* of $y = b^x$. Similarly, applying transformations to the parent function $y = \log_b(x)$ can change the *domain*. When finding the domain of a logarithmic function, therefore, it is important to remember that the domain consists *only of positive real numbers*. That is, the argument of the logarithmic function must be greater than zero.

For example, consider $f(x) = \log_4(2x - 3)$. This function is defined for any values of x such that the argument, in this case $2x - 3$, is greater than zero. To find the domain, we set up an inequality and solve for x:

$$2x - 3 > 0 \qquad \text{Show the argument greater than zero.}$$

$$2x > 3 \qquad \text{Add 3.}$$

$$x > 1.5 \qquad \text{Divide by 2.}$$

In interval notation, the domain of $f(x) = \log_4(2x - 3)$ is $(1.5, \infty)$.

How To...

Given a logarithmic function, identify the domain.

1. Set up an inequality showing the argument greater than zero.
2. Solve for x.
3. Write the domain in interval notation.

Example 1   **Identifying the Domain of a Logarithmic Shift**

What is the domain of $f(x) = \log_2(x + 3)$?

Solution   The logarithmic function is defined only when the input is positive, so this function is defined when $x + 3 > 0$.

Solving this inequality,

$$x + 3 > 0 \qquad \text{The input must be positive.}$$

$$x > -3 \qquad \text{Subtract 3.}$$

The domain of $f(x) = \log_2(x + 3)$ is $(-3, \infty)$.

Try It #1

What is the domain of $f(x) = \log_5(x - 2) + 1$?

Example 2   **Identifying the Domain of a Logarithmic Shift and Reflection**

What is the domain of $f(x) = \log(5 - 2x)$?

Solution   The logarithmic function is defined only when the input is positive, so this function is defined when $5 - 2x > 0$.

Solving this inequality,

$$5 - 2x > 0 \qquad \text{The input must be positive.}$$

$$-2x > -5 \qquad \text{Subtract 5.}$$

$$x < \frac{5}{2} \qquad \text{Divide by } -2 \text{ and switch the inequality.}$$

The domain of $f(x) = \log(5 - 2x)$ is $\left(-\infty, \dfrac{5}{2}\right)$.

Try It #2

What is the domain of $f(x) = \log(x - 5) + 2$?

Graphing Logarithmic Functions

Now that we have a feel for the set of values for which a logarithmic function is defined, we move on to graphing logarithmic functions. The family of logarithmic functions includes the parent function $y = \log_b(x)$ along with all its transformations: shifts, stretches, compressions, and reflections.

We begin with the parent function $y = \log_b(x)$. Because every logarithmic function of this form is the inverse of an exponential function with the form $y = b^x$, their graphs will be reflections of each other across the line $y = x$. To illustrate this, we can observe the relationship between the input and output values of $y = 2^x$ and its equivalent $x = \log_2(y)$ in **Table 1**.

x	-3	-2	-1	0	1	2	3
$2^x = y$	$\dfrac{1}{8}$	$\dfrac{1}{4}$	$\dfrac{1}{2}$	1	2	4	8
$\log_2(y) = x$	-3	-2	-1	0	1	2	3

Table 1

Using the inputs and outputs from **Table 1**, we can build another table to observe the relationship between points on the graphs of the inverse functions $f(x) = 2^x$ and $g(x) = \log_2(x)$. See **Table 2**.

$f(x) = 2^x$	$\left(-3, \dfrac{1}{8}\right)$	$\left(-2, \dfrac{1}{4}\right)$	$\left(-1, \dfrac{1}{2}\right)$	$(0, 1)$	$(1, 2)$	$(2, 4)$	$(3, 8)$
$g(x) = \log_2(x)$	$\left(\dfrac{1}{8}, -3\right)$	$\left(\dfrac{1}{4}, -2\right)$	$\left(\dfrac{1}{2}, -1\right)$	$(1, 0)$	$(2, 1)$	$(4, 2)$	$(8, 3)$

Table 2

As we'd expect, the x- and y-coordinates are reversed for the inverse functions. **Figure 2** shows the graph of f and g.

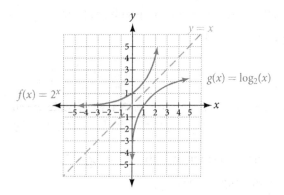

Figure 2 Notice that the graphs of $f(x) = 2^x$ and $g(x) = \log_2(x)$ are reflections about the line $y = x$.

Observe the following from the graph:

- $f(x) = 2^x$ has a y-intercept at $(0, 1)$ and $g(x) = \log_2(x)$ has an x-intercept at $(1, 0)$.
- The domain of $f(x) = 2^x$, $(-\infty, \infty)$, is the same as the range of $g(x) = \log_2(x)$.
- The range of $f(x) = 2^x$, $(0, \infty)$, is the same as the domain of $g(x) = \log_2(x)$.

characteristics of the graph of the parent function, $f(x) = \log_b(x)$

For any real number x and constant $b > 0$, $b \neq 1$, we can see the following characteristics in the graph of $f(x) = \log_b(x)$:

- one-to-one function
- vertical asymptote: $x = 0$
- domain: $(0, \infty)$
- range: $(-\infty, \infty)$
- x-intercept: $(1, 0)$
  and key point $(b, 1)$
- y-intercept: none
- increasing if $b > 1$
- decreasing if $0 < b < 1$

See **Figure 3**.

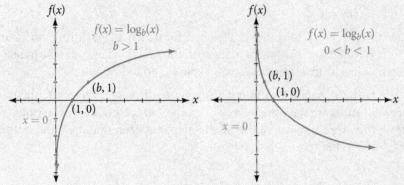

Figure 3

Figure 4 shows how changing the base b in $f(x) = \log_b(x)$ can affect the graphs. Observe that the graphs compress vertically as the value of the base increases. (*Note:* recall that the function $\ln(x)$ has base $e \approx 2.718$.)

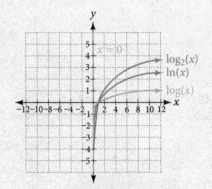

Figure 4 The graphs of three logarithmic functions with different bases, all greater than 1.

How To...

Given a logarithmic function with the form $f(x) = \log_b(x)$, graph the function.

1. Draw and label the vertical asymptote, $x = 0$.
2. Plot the x-intercept, $(1, 0)$.
3. Plot the key point $(b, 1)$.
4. Draw a smooth curve through the points.
5. State the domain, $(0, \infty)$, the range, $(-\infty, \infty)$, and the vertical asymptote, $x = 0$.

Example 3   **Graphing a Logarithmic Function with the Form $f(x) = \log_b(x)$.**

Graph $f(x) = \log_5(x)$. State the domain, range, and asymptote.

Solution   Before graphing, identify the behavior and key points for the graph.

- Since $b = 5$ is greater than one, we know the function is increasing. The left tail of the graph will approach the vertical asymptote $x = 0$, and the right tail will increase slowly without bound.
- The x-intercept is $(1, 0)$.
- The key point $(5, 1)$ is on the graph.
- We draw and label the asymptote, plot and label the points, and draw a smooth curve through the points (see **Figure 5**).

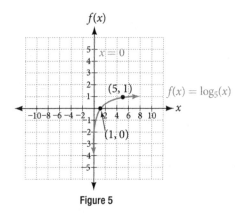

Figure 5

The domain is $(0, \infty)$, the range is $(-\infty, \infty)$, and the vertical asymptote is $x = 0$.

Try It #3

Graph $f(x) = \log_{\frac{1}{5}}(x)$. State the domain, range, and asymptote.

Graphing Transformations of Logarithmic Functions

As we mentioned in the beginning of the section, transformations of logarithmic graphs behave similarly to those of other parent functions. We can shift, stretch, compress, and reflect the parent function $y = \log_b(x)$ without loss of shape.

Graphing a Horizontal Shift of $f(x) = \log_b(x)$

When a constant c is added to the input of the parent function $f(x) = \log_b(x)$, the result is a horizontal shift c units in the *opposite* direction of the sign on c. To visualize horizontal shifts, we can observe the general graph of the parent function $f(x) = \log_b(x)$ and for $c > 0$ alongside the shift left, $g(x) = \log_b(x + c)$, and the shift right, $h(x) = \log_b(x - c)$. See **Figure 6**.

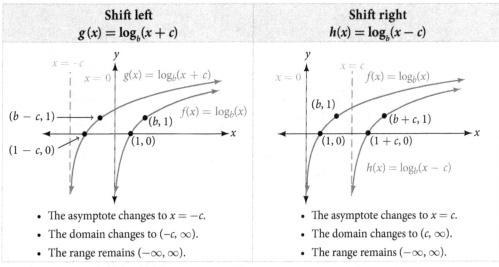

Figure 6

---

horizontal shifts of the parent function $y = \log_b(x)$

For any constant c, the function $f(x) = \log_b(x + c)$

- shifts the parent function $y = \log_b(x)$ left c units if $c > 0$.
- shifts the parent function $y = \log_b(x)$ right c units if $c < 0$.
- has the vertical asymptote $x = -c$.
- has domain $(-c, \infty)$.
- has range $(-\infty, \infty)$.

How To...

Given a logarithmic function with the form $f(x) = \log_b(x + c)$, graph the translation.

1. Identify the horizontal shift:

    a. If $c > 0$, shift the graph of $f(x) = \log_b(x)$ left c units.
    b. If $c < 0$, shift the graph of $f(x) = \log_b(x)$ right c units.

2. Draw the vertical asymptote $x = -c$.
3. Identify three key points from the parent function. Find new coordinates for the shifted functions by subtracting c from the x coordinate.
4. Label the three points.
5. The domain is $(-c, \infty)$, the range is $(-\infty, \infty)$, and the vertical asymptote is $x = -c$.

Example 4   **Graphing a Horizontal Shift of the Parent Function $y = \log_b(x)$**

Sketch the horizontal shift $f(x) = \log_3(x - 2)$ alongside its parent function. Include the key points and asymptotes on the graph. State the domain, range, and asymptote.

Solution   Since the function is $f(x) = \log_3(x - 2)$, we notice $x + (-2) = x - 2$.

Thus $c = -2$, so $c < 0$. This means we will shift the function $f(x) = \log_3(x)$ right 2 units.

The vertical asymptote is $x = -(-2)$ or $x = 2$.

Consider the three key points from the parent function, $\left(\frac{1}{3}, -1\right)$, $(1, 0)$, and $(3, 1)$.

The new coordinates are found by adding 2 to the x coordinates.

Label the points $\left(\frac{7}{3}, -1\right)$, $(3, 0)$, and $(5, 1)$.

The domain is $(2, \infty)$, the range is $(-\infty, \infty)$, and the vertical asymptote is $x = 2$.

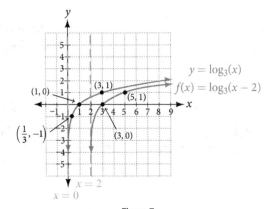

Figure 7

Try It #4

Sketch a graph of $f(x) = \log_3(x + 4)$ alongside its parent function. Include the key points and asymptotes on the graph. State the domain, range, and asymptote.

Graphing a Vertical Shift of $y = \log_b(x)$

When a constant d is added to the parent function $f(x) = \log_b(x)$, the result is a vertical shift d units in the direction of the sign on d. To visualize vertical shifts, we can observe the general graph of the parent function $f(x) = \log_b(x)$ alongside the shift up, $g(x) = \log_b(x) + d$ and the shift down, $h(x) = \log_b(x) - d$. See **Figure 8**.

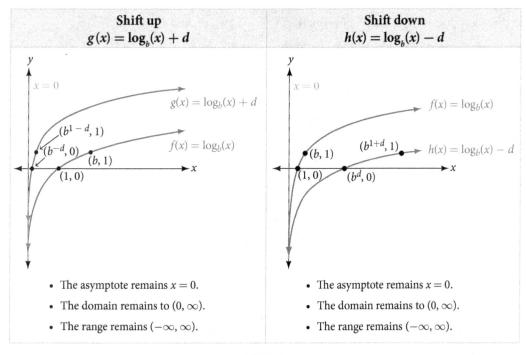

Shift up $g(x) = \log_b(x) + d$	Shift down $h(x) = \log_b(x) - d$
• The asymptote remains $x = 0$.	• The asymptote remains $x = 0$.
• The domain remains to $(0, \infty)$.	• The domain remains to $(0, \infty)$.
• The range remains $(-\infty, \infty)$.	• The range remains $(-\infty, \infty)$.

Figure 8

---

vertical shifts of the parent function $y = \log_b(x)$

For any constant d, the function $f(x) = \log_b(x) + d$

- shifts the parent function $y = \log_b(x)$ up d units if $d > 0$.
- shifts the parent function $y = \log_b(x)$ down d units if $d < 0$.
- has the vertical asymptote $x = 0$.
- has domain $(0, \infty)$.
- has range $(-\infty, \infty)$.

How To...

Given a logarithmic function with the form $f(x) = \log_b(x) + d$, graph the translation.

1. Identify the vertical shift:

    a. If $d > 0$, shift the graph of $f(x) = \log_b(x)$ up d units.
    b. If $d < 0$, shift the graph of $f(x) = \log_b(x)$ down d units.

2. Draw the vertical asymptote $x = 0$.
3. Identify three key points from the parent function. Find new coordinates for the shifted functions by adding d to the y coordinate.
4. Label the three points.
5. The domain is $(0, \infty)$, the range is $(-\infty, \infty)$, and the vertical asymptote is $x = 0$.

Example 5   **Graphing a Vertical Shift of the Parent Function $y = \log_b(x)$**

Sketch a graph of $f(x) = \log_3(x) - 2$ alongside its parent function. Include the key points and asymptote on the graph. State the domain, range, and asymptote.

Solution   Since the function is $f(x) = \log_3(x) - 2$, we will notice $d = -2$. Thus $d < 0$.

This means we will shift the function $f(x) = \log_3(x)$ down 2 units.

The vertical asymptote is $x = 0$.

Consider the three key points from the parent function, $\left(\frac{1}{3}, -1\right)$, $(1, 0)$, and $(3, 1)$.

The new coordinates are found by subtracting 2 from the y coordinates.

Label the points $\left(\frac{1}{3}, -3\right)$, $(1, -2)$, and $(3, -1)$.

The domain is $(0, \infty)$, the range is $(-\infty, \infty)$, and the vertical asymptote is $x = 0$.

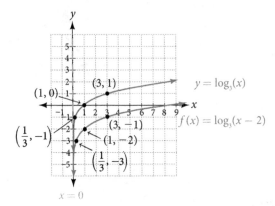

Figure 9

The domain is $(0, \infty)$, the range is $(-\infty, \infty)$, and the vertical asymptote is $x = 0$.

Try It #5

Sketch a graph of $f(x) = \log_2(x) + 2$ alongside its parent function. Include the key points and asymptote on the graph. State the domain, range, and asymptote.

Graphing Stretches and Compressions of $y = \log_b(x)$

When the parent function $f(x) = \log_b(x)$ is multiplied by a constant $a > 0$, the result is a vertical stretch or compression of the original graph. To visualize stretches and compressions, we set $a > 1$ and observe the general graph of the parent function $f(x) = \log_b(x)$ alongside the vertical stretch, $g(x) = a\log_b(x)$ and the vertical compression, $h(x) = \frac{1}{a}\log_b(x)$. See **Figure 10**.

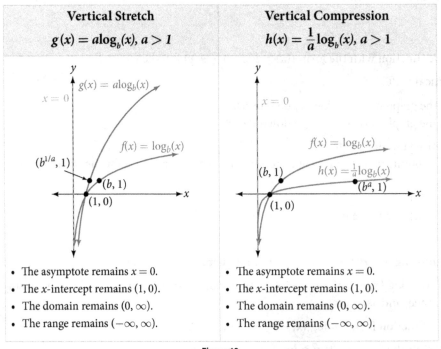

Vertical Stretch	**Vertical Compression**
$g(x) = a\log_b(x), a > 1$	$h(x) = \frac{1}{a}\log_b(x), a > 1$
• The asymptote remains $x = 0$.	• The asymptote remains $x = 0$.
• The x-intercept remains $(1, 0)$.	• The x-intercept remains $(1, 0)$.
• The domain remains $(0, \infty)$.	• The domain remains $(0, \infty)$.
• The range remains $(-\infty, \infty)$.	• The range remains $(-\infty, \infty)$.

Figure 10

vertical stretches and compressions of the parent function $y = \log_b(x)$

For any constant $a > 1$, the function

$$f(x) = a\log_b(x)$$

- stretches the parent function $y = \log_b(x)$ vertically by a factor of a if $a > 1$.
- compresses the parent function $y = \log_b(x)$ vertically by a factor of a if $0 < a < 1$.
- has the vertical asymptote $x = 0$.
- has the x-intercept $(1, 0)$.
- has domain $(0, \infty)$.
- has range $(-\infty, \infty)$.

How To...

Given a logarithmic function with the form $f(x) = a\log_b(x)$, $a > 0$, graph the translation.

1. Identify the vertical stretch or compressions:

   a. If $|a| > 1$, the graph of $f(x) = \log_b(x)$ is stretched by a factor of a units.

   b. If $|a| < 1$, the graph of $f(x) = \log_b(x)$ is compressed by a factor of a units.

2. Draw the vertical asymptote $x = 0$.
3. Identify three key points from the parent function. Find new coordinates for the shifted functions by multiplying the y coordinates by a.
4. Label the three points.
5. The domain is $(0, \infty)$, the range is $(-\infty, \infty)$, and the vertical asymptote is $x = 0$.

Example 6   **Graphing a Stretch or Compression of the Parent Function** $y = \log_b(x)$

Sketch a graph of $f(x) = 2\log_4(x)$ alongside its parent function. Include the key points and asymptote on the graph. State the domain, range, and asymptote.

Solution   Since the function is $f(x) = 2\log_4(x)$, we will notice $a = 2$.

This means we will stretch the function $f(x) = \log_4(x)$ by a factor of 2.

The vertical asymptote is $x = 0$.

Consider the three key points from the parent function, $\left(\dfrac{1}{4}, -1\right)$, $(1, 0)$, and $(4, 1)$.

The new coordinates are found by multiplying the y coordinates by 2.

Label the points $\left(\dfrac{1}{4}, -2\right)$, $(1, 0)$, and $(4, 2)$.

The domain is $(0, \infty)$, the range is $(-\infty, \infty)$, and the vertical asymptote is $x = 0$. See **Figure 11**.

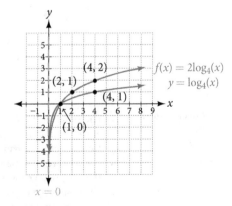

Figure 11

Try It #6

Sketch a graph of $f(x) = \frac{1}{2}\log_4(x)$ alongside its parent function. Include the key points and asymptote on the graph. State the domain, range, and asymptote.

Example 7   Combining a Shift and a Stretch

Sketch a graph of $f(x) = 5\log(x + 2)$. State the domain, range, and asymptote.

Solution   Remember: what happens inside parentheses happens first. First, we move the graph left 2 units, then stretch the function vertically by a factor of 5, as in **Figure 12**. The vertical asymptote will be shifted to $x = -2$. The x-intercept will be $(-1, 0)$. The domain will be $(-2, \infty)$. Two points will help give the shape of the graph: $(-1, 0)$ and $(8, 5)$. We chose $x = 8$ as the x-coordinate of one point to graph because when $x = 8$, $x + 2 = 10$, the base of the common logarithm.

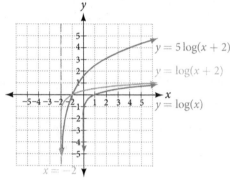

Figure 12

The domain is $(-2, \infty)$, the range is $(-\infty, \infty)$, and the vertical asymptote is $x = -2$.

Try It #7

Sketch a graph of the function $f(x) = 3\log(x - 2) + 1$. State the domain, range, and asymptote.

Graphing Reflections of $f(x) = \log b(x)$

When the parent function $f(x) = \log_b(x)$ is multiplied by -1, the result is a reflection about the x-axis. When the *input* is multiplied by -1, the result is a reflection about the y-axis. To visualize reflections, we restrict $b > 1$, and observe the general graph of the parent function $f(x) = \log_b(x)$ alongside the reflection about the x-axis, $g(x) = -\log_b(x)$ and the reflection about the y-axis, $h(x) = \log_b(-x)$.

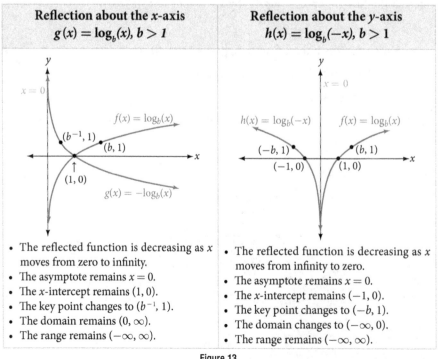

Reflection about the x-axis $g(x) = \log_b(x), b > 1$	Reflection about the y-axis $h(x) = \log_b(-x), b > 1$
• The reflected function is decreasing as x moves from zero to infinity. • The asymptote remains $x = 0$. • The x-intercept remains $(1, 0)$. • The key point changes to $(b^{-1}, 1)$. • The domain remains $(0, \infty)$. • The range remains $(-\infty, \infty)$.	• The reflected function is decreasing as x moves from infinity to zero. • The asymptote remains $x = 0$. • The x-intercept remains $(-1, 0)$. • The key point changes to $(-b, 1)$. • The domain changes to $(-\infty, 0)$. • The range remains $(-\infty, \infty)$.

Figure 13

> **reflections of the parent function $y = \log_b(x)$**
>
> The function $f(x) = -\log_b(x)$
> - reflects the parent function $y = \log_b(x)$ about the x-axis.
> - has domain, $(0, \infty)$, range, $(-\infty, \infty)$, and vertical asymptote, $x = 0$, which are unchanged from the parent function.
>
> The function $f(x) = \log_b(-x)$
> - reflects the parent function $y = \log_b(x)$ about the y-axis.
> - has domain $(-\infty, 0)$.
> - has range, $(-\infty, \infty)$, and vertical asymptote, $x = 0$, which are unchanged from the parent function.

How To...

Given a logarithmic function with the parent function $f(x) = \log_b(x)$, graph a translation.

If $f(x) = -\log_b(x)$	If $f(x) = \log_b(-x)$
1. Draw the vertical asymptote, $x = 0$.	1. Draw the vertical asymptote, $x = 0$.
2. Plot the x-intercept, $(1, 0)$.	2. Plot the x-intercept, $(1, 0)$.
3. Reflect the graph of the parent function $f(x) = \log_b(x)$ about the x-axis.	3. Reflect the graph of the parent function $f(x) = \log_b(x)$ about the y-axis.
4. Draw a smooth curve through the points.	4. Draw a smooth curve through the points.
5. State the domain, $(0, \infty)$, the range, $(-\infty, \infty)$, and the vertical asymptote $x = 0$.	5. State the domain, $(-\infty, 0)$, the range, $(-\infty, \infty)$, and the vertical asymptote $x = 0$.

Table 3

Example 8   **Graphing a Reflection of a Logarithmic Function**

Sketch a graph of $f(x) = \log(-x)$ alongside its parent function. Include the key points and asymptote on the graph. State the domain, range, and asymptote.

Solution   Before graphing $f(x) = \log(-x)$, identify the behavior and key points for the graph.

- Since $b = 10$ is greater than one, we know that the parent function is increasing. Since the *input* value is multiplied by -1, f is a reflection of the parent graph about the y-axis. Thus, $f(x) = \log(-x)$ will be decreasing as x moves from negative infinity to zero, and the right tail of the graph will approach the vertical asymptote $x = 0$.

- The x-intercept is $(-1, 0)$.

- We draw and label the asymptote, plot and label the points, and draw a smooth curve through the points.

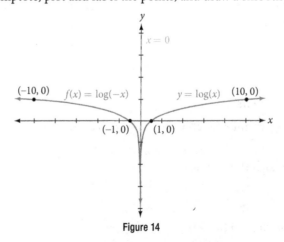

Figure 14

The domain is $(-\infty, 0)$, the range is $(-\infty, \infty)$, and the vertical asymptote is $x = 0$.

Try It #8

Graph $f(x) = -\log(-x)$. State the domain, range, and asymptote.

How To...

Given a logarithmic equation, use a graphing calculator to approximate solutions.

1. Press [Y=]. Enter the given logarithm equation or equations as Y_1= and, if needed, Y_2=.
2. Press [GRAPH] to observe the graphs of the curves and use [WINDOW] to find an appropriate view of the graphs, including their point(s) of intersection.
3. To find the value of x, we compute the point of intersection. Press [2ND] then [CALC]. Select "intersect" and press [ENTER] three times. The point of intersection gives the value of x, for the point(s) of intersection.

Example 9   **Approximating the Solution of a Logarithmic Equation**

Solve $4\ln(x) + 1 = -2\ln(x - 1)$ graphically. Round to the nearest thousandth.

Solution   Press [Y=] and enter $4\ln(x) + 1$ next to Y_1=. Then enter $-2\ln(x - 1)$ next to Y_2=. For a window, use the values 0 to 5 for x and -10 to 10 for y. Press [GRAPH]. The graphs should intersect somewhere a little to right of $x = 1$.

For a better approximation, press [2ND] then [CALC]. Select [5: intersect] and press [ENTER] three times. The x-coordinate of the point of intersection is displayed as 1.3385297. (Your answer may be different if you use a different window or use a different value for **Guess?**) So, to the nearest thousandth, $x \approx 1.339$.

Try It #9

Solve $5\log(x + 2) = 4 - \log(x)$ graphically. Round to the nearest thousandth.

Summarizing Translations of the Logarithmic Function

Now that we have worked with each type of translation for the logarithmic function, we can summarize each in **Table 4** to arrive at the general equation for translating exponential functions.

Translations of the Parent Function $y = \log_b(x)$	
Translation	**Form**
Shift • Horizontally c units to the left • Vertically d units up	$y = \log_b(x + c) + d$
Stretch and Compress • Stretch if $|a| > 1$ • Compression if $|a| < 1$	$y = a\log_b(x)$
Reflect about the x-axis	$y = -\log_b(x)$
Reflect about the y-axis	$y = \log_b(-x)$
General equation for all translations	$y = a\log_b(x + c) + d$

Table 4

---

translations of logarithmic functions

All translations of the parent logarithmic function, $y = \log_b(x)$, have the form

$$f(x) = a\log_b(x + c) + d$$

where the parent function, $y = \log_b(x)$, $b > 1$, is

• shifted vertically up d units.
• shifted horizontally to the left c units.
• stretched vertically by a factor of $|a|$ if $|a| > 0$.
• compressed vertically by a factor of $|a|$ if $0 < |a| < 1$.
• reflected about the x-axis when $a < 0$.

For $f(x) = \log(-x)$, the graph of the parent function is reflected about the y-axis.

Example 10 **Finding the Vertical Asymptote of a Logarithm Graph**

What is the vertical asymptote of $f(x) = -2\log_3(x + 4) + 5$?

Solution The vertical asymptote is at $x = -4$.

Analysis *The coefficient, the base, and the upward translation do not affect the asymptote. The shift of the curve 4 units to the left shifts the vertical asymptote to $x = -4$.*

Try It #10

What is the vertical asymptote of $f(x) = 3 + \ln(x - 1)$?

Example 11 **Finding the Equation from a Graph**

Find a possible equation for the common logarithmic function graphed in **Figure 15**.

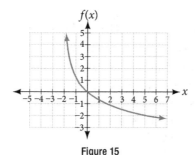

Figure 15

Solution This graph has a vertical asymptote at $x = -2$ and has been vertically reflected. We do not know yet the vertical shift or the vertical stretch. We know so far that the equation will have form:

$$f(x) = -a\log(x + 2) + k$$

It appears the graph passes through the points $(-1, 1)$ and $(2, -1)$. Substituting $(-1, 1)$,

$$1 = -a\log(-1 + 2) + k \quad \text{Substitute } (-1, 1).$$
$$1 = -a\log(1) + k \quad \text{Arithmetic.}$$
$$1 = k \quad \log(1) = 0.$$

Next, substituting in $(2, -1)$,

$$-1 = -a\log(2 + 2) + 1 \quad \text{Plug in } (2, -1).$$
$$-2 = -a\log(4) \quad \text{Arithmetic.}$$
$$a = \frac{2}{\log(4)} \quad \text{Solve for } a.$$

This gives us the equation $f(x) = -\dfrac{2}{\log(4)}\log(x + 2) + 1$.

Analysis *can verify this answer by comparing the function values in **Table 5** with the points on the graph in **Figure 15**.*

x	-1	0	1	2	3
$f(x)$	1	0	-0.58496	-1	-1.3219
x	4	5	6	7	8
$f(x)$	-1.5850	-1.8074	-2	-2.1699	-2.3219

Table 5

Try It #11

Give the equation of the natural logarithm graphed in **Figure 16**.

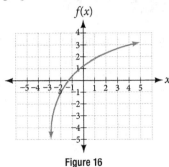

Figure 16

Q & A...

Is it possible to tell the domain and range and describe the end behavior of a function just by looking at the graph?

Yes, if we know the function is a general logarithmic function. For example, look at the graph in **Figure 16**. The graph approaches $x = -3$ (or thereabouts) more and more closely, so $x = -3$ is, or is very close to, the vertical asymptote. It approaches from the right, so the domain is all points to the right, $\{x \mid x > -3\}$. The range, as with all general logarithmic functions, is all real numbers. And we can see the end behavior because the graph goes down as it goes left and up as it goes right. The end behavior is that as $x \to -3^+$, $f(x) \to -\infty$ and as $x \to \infty$, $f(x) \to \infty$.

Access these online resources for additional instruction and practice with graphing logarithms.

- Graph an Exponential Function and Logarithmic Function (http://openstaxcollege.org/l/graphexplog)
- Match Graphs with Exponential and Logarithmic Functions (http://openstaxcollege.org/l/matchexplog)
- Find the Domain of Logarithmic Functions (http://openstaxcollege.org/l/domainlog)

4.4 SECTION EXERCISES

VERBAL

1. The inverse of every logarithmic function is an exponential function and vice-versa. What does this tell us about the relationship between the coordinates of the points on the graphs of each?

2. What type(s) of translation(s), if any, affect the range of a logarithmic function?

3. What type(s) of translation(s), if any, affect the domain of a logarithmic function?

4. Consider the general logarithmic function $f(x) = \log_b(x)$. Why can't x be zero?

5. Does the graph of a general logarithmic function have a horizontal asymptote? Explain.

ALGEBRAIC

For the following exercises, state the domain and range of the function.

6. $f(x) = \log_3(x + 4)$

7. $h(x) = \ln\left(\frac{1}{2} - x\right)$

8. $g(x) = \log_5(2x + 9) - 2$

9. $h(x) = \ln(4x + 17) - 5$

10. $f(x) = \log_2(12 - 3x) - 3$

For the following exercises, state the domain and the vertical asymptote of the function.

11. $f(x) = \log_b(x - 5)$

12. $g(x) = \ln(3 - x)$

13. $f(x) = \log(3x + 1)$

14. $f(x) = 3\log(-x) + 2$

15. $g(x) = -\ln(3x + 9) - 7$

For the following exercises, state the domain, vertical asymptote, and end behavior of the function.

16. $f(x) = \ln(2 - x)$

17. $f(x) = \log\left(x - \frac{3}{7}\right)$

18. $h(x) = -\log(3x - 4) + 3$

19. $g(x) = \ln(2x + 6) - 5$

20. $f(x) = \log_3(15 - 5x) + 6$

For the following exercises, state the domain, range, and x- and y-intercepts, if they exist. If they do not exist, write DNE.

21. $h(x) = \log_4(x - 1) + 1$

22. $f(x) = \log(5x + 10) + 3$

23. $g(x) = \ln(-x) - 2$

24. $f(x) = \log_2(x + 2) - 5$

25. $h(x) = 3\ln(x) - 9$

GRAPHICAL

For the following exercises, match each function in **Figure 17** with the letter corresponding to its graph.

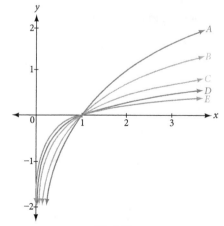

26. $d(x) = \log(x)$ D

27. $f(x) = \ln(x)$ B

28. $g(x) = \log_2(x)$ A

29. $h(x) = \log_5(x)$ C

30. $j(x) = \log_{25}(x)$ E

Figure 17

For the following exercises, match each function in **Figure 18** with the letter corresponding to its graph.

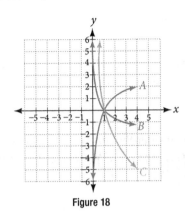

Figure 18

31. $f(x) = \log_{\frac{1}{3}}(x)$ B

32. $g(x) = \log_2(x)$ A

33. $h(x) = \log_{\frac{3}{4}}(x)$ c

For the following exercises, sketch the graphs of each pair of functions on the same axis.

34. $f(x) = \log(x)$ and $g(x) = 10^x$

35. $f(x) = \log(x)$ and $g(x) = \log_{\frac{1}{2}}(x)$

36. $f(x) = \log_4(x)$ and $g(x) = \ln(x)$

37. $f(x) = e^x$ and $g(x) = \ln(x)$

For the following exercises, match each function in **Figure 19** with the letter corresponding to its graph.

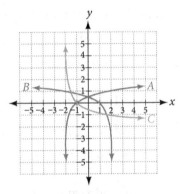

Figure 19

38. $f(x) = \log_4(-x + 2)$ B

39. $g(x) = -\log_4(x + 2)$

40. $h(x) = \log_4(x + 2)$

For the following exercises, sketch the graph of the indicated function.

41. $f(x) = \log_2(x + 2)$

42. $f(x) = 2\log(x)$

43. $f(x) = \ln(-x)$

44. $g(x) = \log(4x + 16) + 4$

45. $g(x) = \log(6 - 3x) + 1$

46. $h(x) = -\frac{1}{2} \ln(x + 1) - 3$

For the following exercises, write a logarithmic equation corresponding to the graph shown.

47. Use $y = \log_2(x)$ as the parent function.

48. Use $f(x) = \log_3(x)$ as the parent function.

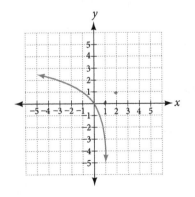

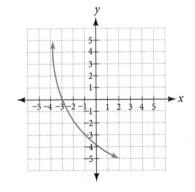

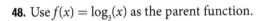

49. Use $f(x) = \log_4(x)$ as the parent function.

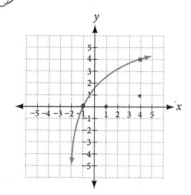

50. Use $f(x) = \log_5(x)$ as the parent function.

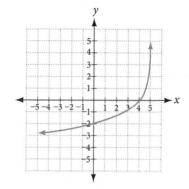

TECHNOLOGY

For the following exercises, use a graphing calculator to find approximate solutions to each equation.

51. $\log(x - 1) + 2 = \ln(x - 1) + 2$ **52.** $\log(2x - 3) + 2 = -\log(2x - 3) + 5$ **53.** $\ln(x - 2) = -\ln(x + 1)$

54. $2\ln(5x + 1) = \frac{1}{2}\ln(-5x) + 1$ **55.** $\frac{1}{3}\log(1 - x) = \log(x + 1) + \frac{1}{3}$

EXTENSIONS

56. Let b be any positive real number such that $b \neq 1$. What must $\log_b 1$ be equal to? Verify the result.

57. Explore and discuss the graphs of $f(x) = \log_{\frac{1}{2}}(x)$ and $g(x) = -\log_2(x)$. Make a conjecture based on the result.

58. Prove the conjecture made in the previous exercise.

59. What is the domain of the function $f(x) = \ln\left(\frac{x + 2}{x - 4}\right)$? Discuss the result.

60. Use properties of exponents to find the x-intercepts of the function $f(x) = \log(x^2 + 4x + 4)$ algebraically. Show the steps for solving, and then verify the result by graphing the function.

LEARNING OBJECTIVES

In this section, you will:

- Use the product rule for logarithms.
- Use the quotient rule for logarithms.
- Use the power rule for logarithms.
- Expand logarithmic expressions.
- Condense logarithmic expressions.
- Use the change-of-base formula for logarithms.

4.5   LOGARITHMIC PROPERTIES

Figure 1 The pH of hydrochloric acid is tested with litmus paper. (credit: David Berardan)

In chemistry, pH is used as a measure of the acidity or alkalinity of a substance. The pH scale runs from 0 to 14. Substances with a pH less than 7 are considered acidic, and substances with a pH greater than 7 are said to be alkaline. Our bodies, for instance, must maintain a pH close to 7.35 in order for enzymes to work properly. To get a feel for what is acidic and what is alkaline, consider the following pH levels of some common substances:

- Battery acid: 0.8
- Stomach acid: 2.7
- Orange juice: 3.3
- Pure water: 7 (at 25° C)

- Human blood: 7.35
- Fresh coconut: 7.8
- Sodium hydroxide (lye): 14

To determine whether a solution is acidic or alkaline, we find its pH, which is a measure of the number of active positive hydrogen ions in the solution. The pH is defined by the following formula, where a is the concentration of hydrogen ion in the solution

$$\text{pH} = -\log([H^+])$$

$$= \log\left(\frac{1}{([H^+])}\right)$$

The equivalence of $-\log([H^+])$ and $\log\left(\frac{1}{[H^+]}\right)$ is one of the logarithm properties we will examine in this section.

Using the Product Rule for Logarithms

Recall that the logarithmic and exponential functions "undo" each other. This means that logarithms have similar properties to exponents. Some important properties of logarithms are given here. First, the following properties are easy to prove.

$$\log_b(1) = 0$$

$$\log_b(b) = 1$$

For example, $\log_5 1 = 0$ since $5^0 = 1$. And $\log_5 5 = 1$ since $5^1 = 5$.

Next, we have the inverse property.

$$\log_b(b^x) = x$$
$$b^{\log_b(x)} = x, x > 0$$

For example, to evaluate $\log(100)$, we can rewrite the logarithm as $\log_{10}(10^2)$, and then apply the inverse property $\log_b(b^x) = x$ to get $\log_{10}(10^2) = 2$.

To evaluate $e^{\ln(7)}$, we can rewrite the logarithm as $e^{\log_e(7)}$, and then apply the inverse property $b^{\log_b(x)} = x$ to get $e^{\log_e(7)} = 7$.

Finally, we have the one-to-one property.

$$\log_b M = \log_b N \text{ if and only if } M = N$$

We can use the one-to-one property to solve the equation $\log_3(3x) = \log_3(2x + 5)$ for x. Since the bases are the same, we can apply the one-to-one property by setting the arguments equal and solving for x:

$$3x = 2x + 5 \qquad \text{Set the arguments equal.}$$
$$x = 5 \qquad \text{Subtract } 2x.$$

But what about the equation $\log_3(3x) + \log_3(2x + 5) = 2$? The one-to-one property does not help us in this instance. Before we can solve an equation like this, we need a method for combining terms on the left side of the equation.

Recall that we use the *product rule of exponents* to combine the product of exponents by adding: $x^a x^b = x^{a+b}$. We have a similar property for logarithms, called the **product rule for logarithms**, which says that the logarithm of a product is equal to a sum of logarithms. Because logs are exponents, and we multiply like bases, we can add the exponents. We will use the inverse property to derive the product rule below.

Given any real number x and positive real numbers M, N, and b, where $b \neq 1$, we will show

$$\log_b(MN) = \log_b(M) + \log_b(N).$$

Let $m = \log_b(M)$ and $n = \log_b(N)$. In exponential form, these equations are $b^m = M$ and $b^n = N$. It follows that

$$\log_b(MN) = \log_b(b^m b^n) \qquad \text{Substitute for } M \text{ and } N.$$
$$= \log_b(b^{m+n}) \qquad \text{Apply the product rule for exponents.}$$
$$= m + n \qquad \text{Apply the inverse property of logs.}$$
$$= \log_b(M) + \log_b(N) \qquad \text{Substitute for } m \text{ and } n.$$

Note that repeated applications of the product rule for logarithms allow us to simplify the logarithm of the product of any number of factors. For example, consider $\log_b(wxyz)$. Using the product rule for logarithms, we can rewrite this logarithm of a product as the sum of logarithms of its factors:

$$\log_b(wxyz) = \log_b(w) + \log_b(x) + \log_b(y) + \log_b(z)$$

---

the product rule for logarithms

The **product rule for logarithms** can be used to simplify a logarithm of a product by rewriting it as a sum of individual logarithms.

$$\log_b(MN) = \log_b(M) + \log_b(N) \text{ for } b > 0$$

How To...

Given the logarithm of a product, use the product rule of logarithms to write an equivalent sum of logarithms.

1. Factor the argument completely, expressing each whole number factor as a product of primes.
2. Write the equivalent expression by summing the logarithms of each factor.

Example 1   **Using the Product Rule for Logarithms**

Expand $\log_3(30x(3x + 4))$.

Solution   We begin by factoring the argument completely, expressing 30 as a product of primes.

$$\log_3(30x(3x + 4)) = \log_3(2 \cdot 3 \cdot 5 \cdot x \cdot (3x + 4))$$

Next we write the equivalent equation by summing the logarithms of each factor.

$$\log_3(30x(3x + 4)) = \log_3(2) + \log_3(3) + \log_3(5) + \log_3(x) + \log_3(3x + 4)$$

Try It #1

Expand $\log_b(8k)$.

Using the Quotient Rule for Logarithms

For quotients, we have a similar rule for logarithms. Recall that we use the *quotient rule of exponents* to combine the quotient of exponents by subtracting: $x^{\frac{a}{b}} = x^{a-b}$. The **quotient rule for logarithms** says that the logarithm of a quotient is equal to a difference of logarithms. Just as with the product rule, we can use the inverse property to derive the quotient rule.

Given any real number x and positive real numbers M, N, and b, where $b \neq 1$, we will show

$$\log_b\left(\frac{M}{N}\right) = \log_b(M) - \log_b(N).$$

Let $m = \log_b(M)$ and $n = \log_b(N)$. In exponential form, these equations are $b^m = M$ and $b^n = N$. It follows that

$$\log_b\left(\frac{M}{N}\right) = \log_b\left(\frac{b^m}{b^n}\right) \qquad \text{Substitute for } M \text{ and } N.$$

$$= \log_b(b^{m-n}) \qquad \text{Apply the quotient rule for exponents.}$$

$$= m - n \qquad \text{Apply the inverse property of logs.}$$

$$= \log_b(M) - \log_b(N) \qquad \text{Substitute for } m \text{ and } n.$$

For example, to expand $\log\left(\frac{2x^2 + 6x}{3x + 9}\right)$, we must first express the quotient in lowest terms. Factoring and canceling we get,

$$\log\left(\frac{2x^2 + 6x}{3x + 9}\right) = \log\left(\frac{2x(x + 3)}{3(x + 3)}\right) \qquad \text{Factor the numerator and denominator.}$$

$$= \log\left(\frac{2x}{3}\right) \qquad \text{Cancel the common factors.}$$

Next we apply the quotient rule by subtracting the logarithm of the denominator from the logarithm of the numerator. Then we apply the product rule.

$$\log\left(\frac{2x}{3}\right) = \log(2x) - \log(3)$$

$$= \log(2) + \log(x) - \log(3)$$

> ### the quotient rule for logarithms
>
> The **quotient rule for logarithms** can be used to simplify a logarithm or a quotient by rewriting it as the difference of individual logarithms.
>
> $$\log_b\left(\frac{M}{N}\right) = \log_b(M) - \log_b(N)$$

How To...

Given the logarithm of a quotient, use the quotient rule of logarithms to write an equivalent difference of logarithms.

1. Express the argument in lowest terms by factoring the numerator and denominator and canceling common terms.
2. Write the equivalent expression by subtracting the logarithm of the denominator from the logarithm of the numerator.
3. Check to see that each term is fully expanded. If not, apply the product rule for logarithms to expand completely.

Example 2   **Using the Quotient Rule for Logarithms**

Expand $\log_2\left(\dfrac{15x(x-1)}{(3x+4)(2-x)}\right)$.

Solution   First we note that the quotient is factored and in lowest terms, so we apply the quotient rule.

$$\log_2\left(\frac{15x(x-1)}{(3x+4)(2-x)}\right) = \log_2(15x(x-1)) - \log_2((3x+4)(2-x))$$

Notice that the resulting terms are logarithms of products. To expand completely, we apply the product rule, noting that the prime factors of the factor 15 are 3 and 5.

$$\log_2(15x(x-1)) - \log_2((3x+4)(2-x)) = [\log_2(3) + \log_2(5) + \log_2(x) + \log_2(x-1)] - [\log_2(3x+4) + \log_2(2-x)]$$

$$= \log_2(3) + \log_2(5) + \log_2(x) + \log_2(x-1) - \log_2(3x+4) - \log_2(2-x)$$

Analysis   *There are exceptions to consider in this and later examples. First, because denominators must never be zero, this expression is not defined for $x = -\dfrac{4}{3}$ and $x = 2$. Also, since the argument of a logarithm must be positive, we note as we observe the expanded logarithm, that $x > 0$, $x > 1$, $x > -\dfrac{4}{3}$, and $x < 2$. Combining these conditions is beyond the scope of this section, and we will not consider them here or in subsequent exercises.*

- - -

Try It #2

Expand $\log_3\left(\dfrac{7x^2 + 21x}{7x(x-1)(x-2)}\right)$.

- - -

Using the Power Rule for Logarithms

We've explored the product rule and the quotient rule, but how can we take the logarithm of a power, such as x^2? One method is as follows:

$$\log_b(x^2) = \log_b(x \cdot x)$$
$$= \log_b(x) + \log_b(x)$$
$$= 2\log_b(x)$$

Notice that we used the product rule for logarithms to find a solution for the example above. By doing so, we have derived the **power rule for logarithms**, which says that the log of a power is equal to the exponent times the log of the base. Keep in mind that, although the input to a logarithm may not be written as a power, we may be able to change it to a power. For example,

$$100 = 10^2 \qquad \sqrt{3} = 3^{\frac{1}{2}} \qquad \frac{1}{e} = e^{-1}$$

> **the power rule for logarithms**
>
> The **power rule for logarithms** can be used to simplify the logarithm of a power by rewriting it as the product of the exponent times the logarithm of the base.
>
> $$\log_b(M^n) = n\log_b(M)$$

- - -

How To...

Given the logarithm of a power, use the power rule of logarithms to write an equivalent product of a factor and a logarithm.

1. Express the argument as a power, if needed.

2. Write the equivalent expression by multiplying the exponent times the logarithm of the base.

Example 3   **Expanding a Logarithm with Powers**

Expand $\log_2(x^5)$.

Solution   The argument is already written as a power, so we identify the exponent, 5, and the base, x, and rewrite the equivalent expression by multiplying the exponent times the logarithm of the base.

$$\log_2(x^5) = 5\log_2(x)$$

Try It #3

Expand $\ln(x^2)$.

Example 4   **Rewriting an Expression as a Power before Using the Power Rule**

Expand $\log_3(25)$ using the power rule for logs.

Solution   Expressing the argument as a power, we get $\log_3(25) = \log_3(5^2)$.

Next we identify the exponent, 2, and the base, 5, and rewrite the equivalent expression by multiplying the exponent times the logarithm of the base.

$$\log_3(5^2) = 2\log_3(5)$$

Try It #4

Expand $\ln\left(\dfrac{1}{x^2}\right)$.

Example 5   **Using the Power Rule in Reverse**

Rewrite $4\ln(x)$ using the power rule for logs to a single logarithm with a leading coefficient of 1.

Solution   Because the logarithm of a power is the product of the exponent times the logarithm of the base, it follows that the product of a number and a logarithm can be written as a power. For the expression $4\ln(x)$, we identify the factor, 4, as the exponent and the argument, x, as the base, and rewrite the product as a logarithm of a power: $4\ln(x) = \ln(x^4)$.

Try It #5

Rewrite $2\log_3(4)$ using the power rule for logs to a single logarithm with a leading coefficient of 1.

Expanding Logarithmic Expressions

Taken together, the product rule, quotient rule, and power rule are often called "laws of logs." Sometimes we apply more than one rule in order to simplify an expression. For example:

$$\log_b\left(\frac{6x}{y}\right) = \log_b(6x) - \log_b(y)$$
$$= \log_b(6) + \log_b(x) - \log_b(y)$$

We can use the power rule to expand logarithmic expressions involving negative and fractional exponents. Here is an alternate proof of the quotient rule for logarithms using the fact that a reciprocal is a negative power:

$$\log_b\left(\frac{A}{C}\right) = \log_b(AC^{-1})$$
$$= \log_b(A) + \log_b(C^{-1})$$
$$= \log_b(A) + (-1)\log_b(C)$$
$$= \log_b(A) - \log_b(C)$$

We can also apply the product rule to express a sum or difference of logarithms as the logarithm of a product. With practice, we can look at a logarithmic expression and expand it mentally, writing the final answer. Remember, however, that we can only do this with products, quotients, powers, and roots—never with addition or subtraction inside the argument of the logarithm.

___Example 6___ **Expanding Logarithms Using Product, Quotient, and Power Rules**

Rewrite $\ln\left(\dfrac{x^4 y}{7}\right)$ as a sum or difference of logs.

Solution   First, because we have a quotient of two expressions, we can use the quotient rule:

$$\ln\left(\frac{x^4 y}{7}\right) = \ln(x^4 y) - \ln(7)$$

Then seeing the product in the first term, we use the product rule:

$$\ln(x^4 y) - \ln(7) = \ln(x^4) + \ln(y) - \ln(7)$$

Finally, we use the power rule on the first term:

$$\ln(x^4) + \ln(y) - \ln(7) = 4\ln(x) + \ln(y) - \ln(7)$$

___Try It #6___

Expand $\log\left(\dfrac{x^2 y^3}{z^4}\right)$.

___Example 7___   **Using the Power Rule for Logarithms to Simplify the Logarithm of a Radical Expression**

Expand $\log(\sqrt{x})$.

Solution

$$\log(\sqrt{x}) = \log(x)^{\frac{1}{2}}$$

$$= \frac{1}{2}\log(x)$$

___Try It #7___

Expand $\ln(\sqrt[3]{x^2})$.

___Q & A...___

Can we expand $\ln(x^2 + y^2)$?

No. There is no way to expand the logarithm of a sum or difference inside the argument of the logarithm.

___Example 8___   **Expanding Complex Logarithmic Expressions**

Expand $\log_6\left(\dfrac{64 x^3 (4x + 1)}{(2x - 1)}\right)$.

Solution   We can expand by applying the Product and Quotient Rules.

$$\log_6\left(\frac{64 x^3(4x + 1)}{(2x - 1)}\right) = \log_6(64) + \log_6(x^3) + \log_6(4x + 1) - \log_6(2x - 1) \qquad \text{Apply the Quotient Rule.}$$

$$= \log_6(2^6) + \log_6(x^3) + \log_6(4x + 1) - \log_6(2x - 1) \qquad \text{Simplify by writing 64 as } 2^6.$$

$$= 6\log_6(2) + 3\log_6(x) + \log_6(4x + 1) - \log_6(2x - 1) \qquad \text{Apply the Power Rule.}$$

___Try It #8___

Expand $\ln\left(\dfrac{\sqrt{(x - 1)(2x + 1)^2}}{x^2 - 9}\right)$.

Condensing Logarithmic Expressions

We can use the rules of logarithms we just learned to condense sums, differences, and products with the same base as a single logarithm. It is important to remember that the logarithms must have the same base to be combined. We will learn later how to change the base of any logarithm before condensing.

How To...

Given a sum, difference, or product of logarithms with the same base, write an equivalent expression as a single logarithm.

1. Apply the power property first. Identify terms that are products of factors and a logarithm, and rewrite each as the logarithm of a power.
2. Next apply the product property. Rewrite sums of logarithms as the logarithm of a product.
3. Apply the quotient property last. Rewrite differences of logarithms as the logarithm of a quotient.

Example 9   Using the Product and Quotient Rules to Combine Logarithms

Write $\log_3(5) + \log_3(8) - \log_3(2)$ as a single logarithm.

Solution   Using the product and quotient rules

$$\log_3(5) + \log_3(8) = \log_3(5 \cdot 8) = \log_3(40)$$

This reduces our original expression to

$$\log_3(40) - \log_3(2)$$

Then, using the quotient rule

$$\log_3(40) - \log_3(2) = \log_3\left(\frac{40}{2}\right) = \log_3(20)$$

Try It #9

Condense $\log(3) - \log(4) + \log(5) - \log(6)$.

Example 10   Condensing Complex Logarithmic Expressions

Condense $\log_2(x^2) + \frac{1}{2}\log_2(x - 1) - 3\log_2((x + 3)^2)$.

Solution   We apply the power rule first:

$$\log_2(x^2) + \frac{1}{2}\log_2(x - 1) - 3\log_2((x + 3)^2) = \log_2(x^2) + \log_2\left(\sqrt{x - 1}\right) - \log_2((x + 3)^6)$$

Next we apply the product rule to the sum:

$$\log_2(x^2) + \log_2\left(\sqrt{x - 1}\right) - \log_2((x + 3)^6) = \log_2\left(x^2\sqrt{x - 1}\right) - \log_2((x + 3)^6)$$

Finally, we apply the quotient rule to the difference:

$$\log_2\left(x^2\sqrt{x - 1}\right) - \log_2((x + 3)^6) = \log_2\left(\frac{x^2\sqrt{x - 1}}{(x + 3)^6}\right)$$

Try It #10

Rewrite $\log(5) + 0.5\log(x) - \log(7x - 1) + 3\log(x - 1)$ as a single logarithm.

Example 11   Rewriting as a Single Logarithm

Rewrite $2\log(x) - 4\log(x + 5) + \frac{1}{x}\log(3x + 5)$ as a single logarithm.

Solution   We apply the power rule first:

$$2\log(x) - 4\log(x + 5) + \frac{1}{x}\log(3x + 5) = \log(x^2) - \log((x + 5)^4) + \log\left((3x + 5)^{x^{-1}}\right)$$

Next we apply the product rule to the sum:

$$\log(x^2) - \log((x + 5)^4) + \log\left((3x + 5)^{x^{-1}}\right) = \log(x^2) - \log\left((x + 5)^4(3x + 5)^{x^{-1}}\right)$$

Finally, we apply the quotient rule to the difference:

$$\log(x^2) - \log\left((x + 5)^4(3x + 5)^{x^{-1}}\right) = \log\left(\frac{x^2}{(x + 5)^4(3x + 5)^{x^{-1}}}\right)$$

Try It #11

Condense $4(3\log(x) + \log(x + 5) - \log(2x + 3))$.

Example 12   **Applying of the Laws of Logs**

Recall that, in chemistry, $\text{pH} = -\log[H^+]$. If the concentration of hydrogen ions in a liquid is doubled, what is the effect on pH?

Solution   Suppose C is the original concentration of hydrogen ions, and P is the original pH of the liquid. Then $P = -\log(C)$. If the concentration is doubled, the new concentration is $2C$. Then the pH of the new liquid is

$$\text{pH} = -\log(2C)$$

Using the product rule of logs

$$\text{pH} = -\log(2C) = -(\log(2) + \log(C)) = -\log(2) - \log(C)$$

Since $P = -\log(C)$, the new pH is

$$\text{pH} = P - \log(2) \approx P - 0.301$$

When the concentration of hydrogen ions is doubled, the pH decreases by about 0.301.

Try It #12

How does the pH change when the concentration of positive hydrogen ions is decreased by half?

Using the Change-of-Base Formula for Logarithms

Most calculators can evaluate only common and natural logs. In order to evaluate logarithms with a base other than 10 or e, we use the **change-of-base formula** to rewrite the logarithm as the quotient of logarithms of any other base; when using a calculator, we would change them to common or natural logs.

To derive the change-of-base formula, we use the one-to-one property and **power rule for logarithms**.

Given any positive real numbers M, b, and n, where $n \neq 1$ and $b \neq 1$, we show

$$\log_b(M) = \frac{\log_n(M)}{\log_n(b)}$$

Let $y = \log_b(M)$. By taking the log base n of both sides of the equation, we arrive at an exponential form, namely $b^y = M$. It follows that

$$\log_n(b^y) = \log_n(M) \qquad \text{Apply the one-to-one property.}$$

$$y\log_n(b) = \log_n(M) \qquad \text{Apply the power rule for logarithms.}$$

$$y = \frac{\log_n(M)}{\log_n(b)} \qquad \text{Isolate } y.$$

$$\log_b(M) = \frac{\log_n(M)}{\log_n(b)} \qquad \text{Substitute for } y.$$

For example, to evaluate $\log_5(36)$ using a calculator, we must first rewrite the expression as a quotient of common or natural logs. We will use the common log.

$$\log_5(36) = \frac{\log(36)}{\log(5)} \qquad \text{Apply the change of base formula using base 10.}$$

$$\approx 2.2266 \qquad \text{Use a calculator to evaluate to 4 decimal places.}$$

> ### the change-of-base formula
>
> The **change-of-base formula** can be used to evaluate a logarithm with any base.
> For any positive real numbers M, b, and n, where $n \neq 1$ and $b \neq 1$,
>
> $$\log_b(M) = \frac{\log_n(M)}{\log_n(b)}.$$
>
> It follows that the change-of-base formula can be used to rewrite a logarithm with any base as the quotient of common or natural logs.
>
> $$\log_b(M) = \frac{\ln(M)}{\ln(b)} \quad \text{and} \quad \log_b(M) = \frac{\log_n(M)}{\log_n(b)}$$

How To...

Given a logarithm with the form $\log_b(M)$, use the change-of-base formula to rewrite it as a quotient of logs with any positive base n, where $n \neq 1$.

1. Determine the new base n, remembering that the common log, $\log(x)$, has base 10, and the natural log, $\ln(x)$, has base e.
2. Rewrite the log as a quotient using the change-of-base formula
   a. The numerator of the quotient will be a logarithm with base n and argument M.
   b. The denominator of the quotient will be a logarithm with base n and argument b.

Example 13   **Changing Logarithmic Expressions to Expressions Involving Only Natural Logs**

Change $\log_5(3)$ to a quotient of natural logarithms.

Solution   Because we will be expressing $\log_5(3)$ as a quotient of natural logarithms, the new base, $n = e$.
We rewrite the log as a quotient using the change-of-base formula. The numerator of the quotient will be the natural log with argument 3. The denominator of the quotient will be the natural log with argument 5.

$$\log_b(M) = \frac{\ln(M)}{\ln(b)} \qquad \log_5(3) = \frac{\ln(3)}{\ln(5)}$$

Try It #13

Change $\log_{0.5}(8)$ to a quotient of natural logarithms.

Q & A...

Can we change common logarithms to natural logarithms?

Yes. Remember that $\log(9)$ means $\log_{10}(9)$. So, $\log(9) = \dfrac{\ln(9)}{\ln(10)}$.

Example 14   **Using the Change-of-Base Formula with a Calculator**

Evaluate $\log_2(10)$ using the change-of-base formula with a calculator.

Solution   According to the change-of-base formula, we can rewrite the log base 2 as a logarithm of any other base. Since our calculators can evaluate the natural log, we might choose to use the natural logarithm, which is the log base e.

$$\log_2(10) = \frac{\ln(10)}{\ln(2)} \qquad \text{Apply the change of base formula using base } e.$$
$$\approx 3.3219 \qquad \text{Use a calculator to evaluate to 4 decimal places.}$$

Try It #14

Evaluate $\log_5(100)$ using the change-of-base formula.

Access this online resource for additional instruction and practice with laws of logarithms.

- The Properties of Logarithms (http://openstaxcollege.org/l/proplog)
- Expand Logarithmic Expressions (http://openstaxcollege.org/l/expandlog)
- Evaluate a Natural Logarithmic Expression (http://openstaxcollege.org/l/evaluatelog)

4.5 SECTION EXERCISES

VERBAL

1. How does the power rule for logarithms help when solving logarithms with the form $\log_b(\sqrt[n]{x})$?

2. What does the change-of-base formula do? Why is it useful when using a calculator?

ALGEBRAIC

For the following exercises, expand each logarithm as much as possible. Rewrite each expression as a sum, difference, or product of logs.

3. $\log_b(7x \cdot 2y)$

4. $\ln(3ab \cdot 5c)$

5. $\log_b\left(\dfrac{13}{17}\right)$

6. $\log_4\left(\dfrac{\frac{x}{z}}{w}\right)$

7. $\ln\left(\dfrac{1}{4^k}\right)$

8. $\log_2(y^x)$

For the following exercises, condense to a single logarithm if possible.

9. $\ln(7) + \ln(x) + \ln(y)$

10. $\log_3(2) + \log_3(a) + \log_3(11) + \log_3(b)$

11. $\log_b(28) - \log_b(7)$

12. $\ln(a) - \ln(d) - \ln(c)$

13. $-\log_b\left(\dfrac{1}{7}\right)$

14. $\dfrac{1}{3}\ln(8)$

For the following exercises, use the properties of logarithms to expand each logarithm as much as possible. Rewrite each expression as a sum, difference, or product of logs.

15. $\log\left(\dfrac{x^{15}y^{13}}{z^{19}}\right)$

16. $\ln\left(\dfrac{a^{-2}}{b^{-4}c^5}\right)$

17. $\log\left(\sqrt{x^3y^{-4}}\right)$

18. $\ln\left(y\sqrt{\dfrac{y}{1-y}}\right)$

19. $\log\left(x^2y^3\sqrt[3]{x^2y^5}\right)$

For the following exercises, condense each expression to a single logarithm using the properties of logarithms.

20. $\log(2x^4) + \log(3x^5)$

21. $\ln(6x^9) - \ln(3x^2)$

22. $2\log(x) + 3\log(x+1)$

23. $\log(x) - \dfrac{1}{2}\log(y) + 3\log(z)$

24. $4\log_7(c) + \dfrac{\log_7(a)}{3} + \dfrac{\log_7(b)}{3}$

For the following exercises, rewrite each expression as an equivalent ratio of logs using the indicated base.

25. $\log_7(15)$ to base e

26. $\log_{14}(55.875)$ to base 10

For the following exercises, suppose $\log_5(6) = a$ and $\log_5(11) = b$. Use the change-of-base formula along with properties of logarithms to rewrite each expression in terms of a and b. Show the steps for solving.

27. $\log_{11}(5)$

28. $\log_6(55)$

29. $\log_{11}\left(\dfrac{6}{11}\right)$

NUMERIC

For the following exercises, use properties of logarithms to evaluate without using a calculator.

30. $\log_3\left(\dfrac{1}{9}\right) - 3\log_3(3)$

31. $6\log_8(2) + \dfrac{\log_8(64)}{3\log_8(4)}$

32. $2\log_9(3) - 4\log_9(3) + \log_9\left(\dfrac{1}{729}\right)$

For the following exercises, use the change-of-base formula to evaluate each expression as a quotient of natural logs. Use a calculator to approximate each to five decimal places.

33. $\log_3(22)$

34. $\log_8(65)$

35. $\log_6(5.38)$

36. $\log_4\left(\dfrac{15}{2}\right)$

37. $\log_{\frac{1}{2}}(4.7)$

EXTENSIONS

38. Use the product rule for logarithms to find all x values such that $\log_{12}(2x+6) + \log_{12}(x+2) = 2$. Show the steps for solving.

39. Use the quotient rule for logarithms to find all x values such that $\log_6(x+2) - \log_6(x-3) = 1$. Show the steps for solving.

40. Can the power property of logarithms be derived from the power property of exponents using the equation $b^x = m$? If not, explain why. If so, show the derivation.

41. Prove that $\log_b(n) = \dfrac{1}{\log_n(b)}$ for any positive integers $b > 1$ and $n > 1$.

42. Does $\log_{81}(2401) = \log_3(7)$? Verify the claim algebraically.

LEARNING OBJECTIVES

In this section, you will:

- Use like bases to solve exponential equations.
- Use logarithms to solve exponential equations.
- Use the definition of a logarithm to solve logarithmic equations.
- Use the one-to-one property of logarithms to solve logarithmic equations.
- Solve applied problems involving exponential and logarithmic equations.

4.6   EXPONENTIAL AND LOGARITHMIC EQUATIONS

Figure 1 Wild rabbits in Australia. The rabbit population grew so quickly in Australia that the event became known as the "rabbit plague." (credit: Richard Taylor, Flickr)

In 1859, an Australian landowner named Thomas Austin released 24 rabbits into the wild for hunting. Because Australia had few predators and ample food, the rabbit population exploded. In fewer than ten years, the rabbit population numbered in the millions.

Uncontrolled population growth, as in the wild rabbits in Australia, can be modeled with exponential functions. Equations resulting from those exponential functions can be solved to analyze and make predictions about exponential growth. In this section, we will learn techniques for solving exponential functions.

Using Like Bases to Solve Exponential Equations

The first technique involves two functions with like bases. Recall that the one-to-one property of exponential functions tells us that, for any real numbers b, S, and T, where $b > 0$, $b \neq 1$, $b^S = b^T$ if and only if $S = T$.

In other words, when an exponential equation has the same base on each side, the exponents must be equal. This also applies when the exponents are algebraic expressions. Therefore, we can solve many exponential equations by using the rules of exponents to rewrite each side as a power with the same base. Then, we use the fact that exponential functions are one-to-one to set the exponents equal to one another, and solve for the unknown.

For example, consider the equation $3^{4x-7} = \dfrac{3^{2x}}{3}$. To solve for x, we use the division property of exponents to rewrite the right side so that both sides have the common base, 3. Then we apply the one-to-one property of exponents by setting the exponents equal to one another and solving for x:

$$3^{4x-7} = \frac{3^{2x}}{3}$$

$$3^{4x-7} = \frac{3^{2x}}{3^1} \qquad \text{Rewrite 3 as } 3^1.$$

$$3^{4x-7} = 3^{2x-1} \qquad \text{Use the division property of exponents.}$$

$$4x - 7 = 2x - 1 \qquad \text{Apply the one-to-one property of exponents.}$$

$$2x = 6 \qquad \text{Subtract } 2x \text{ and add 7 to both sides.}$$

$$x = 3 \qquad \text{Divide by 3.}$$

---

using the one-to-one property of exponential functions to solve exponential equations

For any algebraic expressions S and T, and any positive real number $b \neq 1$,

$$b^S = b^T \text{ if and only if } S = T$$

How To...

Given an exponential equation with the form $b^S = b^T$, where S and T are algebraic expressions with an unknown, solve for the unknown.

1. Use the rules of exponents to simplify, if necessary, so that the resulting equation has the form $b^S = b^T$.
2. Use the one-to-one property to set the exponents equal.
3. Solve the resulting equation, $S = T$, for the unknown.

Example 1   **Solving an Exponential Equation with a Common Base**

Solve $2^{x-1} = 2^{2x-4}$.

Solution

$2^{x-1} = 2^{2x-4}$	The common base is 2.
$x - 1 = 2x - 4$	By the one-to-one property the exponents must be equal.
$x = 3$	Solve for x.

Try It #1

Solve $5^{2x} = 5^{3x+2}$.

Rewriting Equations So All Powers Have the Same Base

Sometimes the common base for an exponential equation is not explicitly shown. In these cases, we simply rewrite the terms in the equation as powers with a common base, and solve using the one-to-one property.

For example, consider the equation $256 = 4^{x-5}$. We can rewrite both sides of this equation as a power of 2. Then we apply the rules of exponents, along with the one-to-one property, to solve for x :

$256 = 4^{x-5}$	
$2^8 = (2^2)^{x-5}$	Rewrite each side as a power with base 2.
$2^8 = 2^{2x-10}$	Use the one-to-one property of exponents.
$8 = 2x - 10$	Apply the one-to-one property of exponents.
$18 = 2x$	Add 10 to both sides.
$x = 9$	Divide by 2.

How To...

Given an exponential equation with unlike bases, use the one-to-one property to solve it.

1. Rewrite each side in the equation as a power with a common base.
2. Use the rules of exponents to simplify, if necessary, so that the resulting equation has the form $b^S = b^T$.
3. Use the one-to-one property to set the exponents equal.
4. Solve the resulting equation, $S = T$, for the unknown.

Example 2   **Solving Equations by Rewriting Them to Have a Common Base**

Solve $8^{x+2} = 16^{x+1}$.

Solution

$8^{x+2} = 16^{x+1}$	
$(2^3)^{x+2} = (2^4)^{x+1}$	Write 8 and 16 as powers of 2.
$2^{3x+6} = 2^{4x+4}$	To take a power of a power, multiply exponents .
$3x + 6 = 4x + 4$	Use the one-to-one property to set the exponents equal.
$x = 2$	Solve for x.

Try It #2

Solve $5^{2x} = 25^{3x+2}$.

Example 3   **Solving Equations by Rewriting Roots with Fractional Exponents to Have a Common Base**

Solve $2^{5x} = \sqrt{2}$.

Solution

$$2^{5x} = 2^{\frac{1}{2}}$$ Write the square root of 2 as a power of 2.

$$5x = \frac{1}{2}$$ Use the one-to-one property.

$$x = \frac{1}{10}$$ Solve for x.

Try It #3

Solve $5^{x} = \sqrt{5}$.

Q & A...

Do all exponential equations have a solution? If not, how can we tell if there is a solution during the problem-solving process?

No. Recall that the range of an exponential function is always positive. While solving the equation, we may obtain an expression that is undefined.

Example 4   **Solving an Equation with Positive and Negative Powers**

Solve $3^{x+1} = -2$.

Solution   This equation has no solution. There is no real value of x that will make the equation a true statement because any power of a positive number is positive.

Analysis **Figure 2** *shows that the two graphs do not cross so the left side is never equal to the right side. Thus the equation has no solution.*

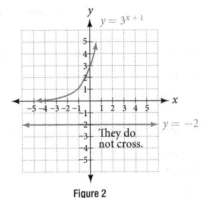

Figure 2

Try It #4

Solve $2^{x} = -100$.

Solving Exponential Equations Using Logarithms

Sometimes the terms of an exponential equation cannot be rewritten with a common base. In these cases, we solve by taking the logarithm of each side. Recall, since $\log(a) = \log(b)$ is equivalent to $a = b$, we may apply logarithms with the same base on both sides of an exponential equation.

How To...

Given an exponential equation in which a common base cannot be found, solve for the unknown.

1. Apply the logarithm of both sides of the equation.

   a. If one of the terms in the equation has base 10, use the common logarithm.

   b. If none of the terms in the equation has base 10, use the natural logarithm.

2. Use the rules of logarithms to solve for the unknown.

Example 5   **Solving an Equation Containing Powers of Different Bases**

Solve $5^{x+2} = 4^x$.

Solution

$$5^{x+2} = 4^x$$ There is no easy way to get the powers to have the same base .

$$\ln(5^{x+2}) = \ln(4^x)$$ Take ln of both sides.

$$(x+2)\ln(5) = x\ln(4)$$ Use laws of logs.

$$x\ln(5) + 2\ln(5) = x\ln(4)$$ Use the distributive law.

$$x\ln(5) - x\ln(4) = -2\ln(5)$$ Get terms containing x on one side, terms without x on the other.

$$x(\ln(5) - \ln(4)) = -2\ln(5)$$ On the left hand side, factor out an x.

$$x\ln\left(\frac{5}{4}\right) = \ln\left(\frac{1}{25}\right)$$ Use the laws of logs.

$$x = \frac{\ln\left(\dfrac{1}{25}\right)}{\ln\left(\dfrac{5}{4}\right)}$$ Divide by the coefficient of x.

Try It #5

Solve $2^x = 3^{x+1}$.

Q & A...

Is there any way to solve $2^x = 3^x$?

Yes. The solution is 0.

Equations Containing e

One common type of exponential equations are those with base e. This constant occurs again and again in nature, in mathematics, in science, in engineering, and in finance. When we have an equation with a base e on either side, we can use the natural logarithm to solve it.

How To...

Given an equation of the form $y = Ae^{kt}$, solve for t.

1. Divide both sides of the equation by A.

2. Apply the natural logarithm of both sides of the equation.

3. Divide both sides of the equation by k.

Example 6   **Solve an Equation of the Form $y = Ae^{kt}$**

Solve $100 = 20e^{2t}$.

Solution

$$100 = 20e^{2t}$$

$$5 = e^{2t}$$ Divide by the coefficient of the power .

$$\ln(5) = 2t$$ Take ln of both sides. Use the fact that $\ln(x)$ and e^x are inverse functions.

$$t = \frac{\ln(5)}{2}$$ Divide by the coefficient of t.

Analysis   Using laws of logs, we can also write this answer in the form $t = \ln\sqrt{5}$. If we want a decimal approximation of the answer, we use a calculator.

Try It #6

Solve $3e^{0.5t} = 11$.

Q & A...

Does every equation of the form $y = Ae^{kt}$ have a solution?

No. There is a solution when $k \neq 0$, and when y and A are either both 0 or neither 0, and they have the same sign. An example of an equation with this form that has no solution is $2 = -3e^t$.

Example 7   Solving an Equation That Can Be Simplified to the Form $y = Ae^{kt}$

Solve $4e^{2x} + 5 = 12$.

Solution

$$4e^{2x} + 5 = 12$$

$$4e^{2x} = 7 \qquad \text{Combine like terms.}$$

$$e^{2x} = \frac{7}{4} \qquad \text{Divide by the coefficient of the power.}$$

$$2x = \ln\left(\frac{7}{4}\right) \qquad \text{Take ln of both sides.}$$

$$x = \frac{1}{2}\ln\left(\frac{7}{4}\right) \qquad \text{Solve for } x.$$

Try It #7

Solve $3 + e^{2t} = 7e^{2t}$.

Extraneous Solutions

Sometimes the methods used to solve an equation introduce an **extraneous solution**, which is a solution that is correct algebraically but does not satisfy the conditions of the original equation. One such situation arises in solving when the logarithm is taken on both sides of the equation. In such cases, remember that the argument of the logarithm must be positive. If the number we are evaluating in a logarithm function is negative, there is no output.

Example 8   Solving Exponential Functions in Quadratic Form

Solve $e^{2x} - e^x = 56$.

Solution

$$e^{2x} - e^x = 56$$

$$e^{2x} - e^x - 56 = 0 \qquad \text{Get one side of the equation equal to zero.}$$

$$(e^x + 7)(e^x - 8) = 0 \qquad \text{Factor by the FOIL method.}$$

$$e^x + 7 = 0 \text{ or } e^x - 8 = 0 \qquad \text{If a product is zero, then one factor must be zero.}$$

$$e^x = -7 \text{ or } e^x = 8 \qquad \text{Isolate the exponentials.}$$

$$e^x = 8 \qquad \text{Reject the equation in which the power equals a negative number.}$$

$$x = \ln(8) \qquad \text{Solve the equation in which the power equals a positive number.}$$

Analysis   When we plan to use factoring to solve a problem, we always get zero on one side of the equation, because zero has the unique property that when a product is zero, one or both of the factors must be zero. We reject the equation $e^x = -7$ because a positive number never equals a negative number. The solution $\ln(-7)$ is not a real number, and in the real number system this solution is rejected as an extraneous solution.

Try It #8

Solve $e^{2x} = e^x + 2$.

Q & A...

Does every logarithmic equation have a solution?

No. Keep in mind that we can only apply the logarithm to a positive number. Always check for extraneous solutions.

Using the Definition of a Logarithm to Solve Logarithmic Equations

We have already seen that every logarithmic equation $\log_b(x) = y$ is equivalent to the exponential equation $b^y = x$. We can use this fact, along with the rules of logarithms, to solve logarithmic equations where the argument is an algebraic expression.

For example, consider the equation $\log_2(2) + \log_2(3x - 5) = 3$. To solve this equation, we can use rules of logarithms to rewrite the left side in compact form and then apply the definition of logs to solve for x:

$$\log_2(2) + \log_2(3x - 5) = 3$$
$$\log_2(2(3x - 5)) = 3 \qquad \text{Apply the product rule of logarithms.}$$
$$\log_2(6x - 10) = 3 \qquad \text{Distribute.}$$
$$2^3 = 6x - 10 \qquad \text{Apply the definition of a logarithm.}$$
$$8 = 6x - 10 \qquad \text{Calculate } 2^3.$$
$$18 = 6x \qquad \text{Add 10 to both sides.}$$
$$x = 3 \qquad \text{Divide by 6.}$$

---

using the definition of a logarithm to solve logarithmic equations

For any algebraic expression S and real numbers b and c, where $b > 0$, $b \neq 1$,
$$\log_b(S) = c \text{ if and only if } b^c = S$$

Example 9 **Using Algebra to Solve a Logarithmic Equation**

Solve $2\ln(x) + 3 = 7$.

Solution
$$2\ln(x) + 3 = 7$$
$$2\ln(x) = 4 \qquad \text{Subtract 3.}$$
$$\ln(x) = 2 \qquad \text{Divide by 2.}$$
$$x = e^2 \qquad \text{Rewrite in exponential form.}$$

Try It #9

Solve $6 + \ln(x) = 10$.

Example 10 **Using Algebra Before and After Using the Definition of the Natural Logarithm**

Solve $2\ln(6x) = 7$.

Solution
$$2\ln(6x) = 7$$
$$\ln(6x) = \frac{7}{2} \qquad \text{Divide by 2.}$$
$$6x = e^{\frac{7}{2}} \qquad \text{Use the definition of ln.}$$
$$x = \frac{1}{6}e^{\frac{7}{2}} \qquad \text{Divide by 6.}$$

Try It #10

Solve $2\ln(x+1) = 10$.

Example 11 **Using a Graph to Understand the Solution to a Logarithmic Equation**

Solve $\ln(x) = 3$.

Solution
$$\ln(x) = 3$$
$$x = e^3 \qquad \text{Use the definition of the natural logarithm.}$$

Figure 3 represents the graph of the equation. On the graph, the x-coordinate of the point at which the two graphs intersect is close to 20. In other words $e^3 \approx 20$. A calculator gives a better approximation: $e^3 \approx 20.0855$.

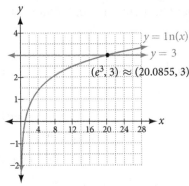

Figure 3 The graphs of $y = \ln(x)$ and $y = 3$ cross at the point $(e^3, 3)$, which is approximately (20.0855, 3).

Try It #11

Use a graphing calculator to estimate the approximate solution to the logarithmic equation $2^x = 1000$ to 2 decimal places.

Using the One-to-One Property of Logarithms to Solve Logarithmic Equations

As with exponential equations, we can use the one-to-one property to solve logarithmic equations. The one-to-one property of logarithmic functions tells us that, for any real numbers $x > 0$, $S > 0$, $T > 0$ and any positive real number b, where $b \neq 1$,

$$\log_b(S) = \log_b(T) \text{ if and only if } S = T.$$

For example,

$$\text{If } \log_2(x - 1) = \log_2(8), \text{ then } x - 1 = 8.$$

So, if $x - 1 = 8$, then we can solve for x, and we get $x = 9$. To check, we can substitute $x = 9$ into the original equation: $\log_2(9 - 1) = \log_2(8) = 3$. In other words, when a logarithmic equation has the same base on each side, the arguments must be equal. This also applies when the arguments are algebraic expressions. Therefore, when given an equation with logs of the same base on each side, we can use rules of logarithms to rewrite each side as a single logarithm. Then we use the fact that logarithmic functions are one-to-one to set the arguments equal to one another and solve for the unknown.

For example, consider the equation $\log(3x - 2) - \log(2) = \log(x + 4)$. To solve this equation, we can use the rules of logarithms to rewrite the left side as a single logarithm, and then apply the one-to-one property to solve for x:

$$\log(3x - 2) - \log(2) = \log(x + 4)$$

$$\log\left(\frac{3x - 2}{2}\right) = \log(x + 4) \qquad \text{Apply the quotient rule of logarithms.}$$

$$\frac{3x - 2}{2} = x + 4 \qquad \text{Apply the one to one property of a logarithm.}$$

$$3x - 2 = 2x + 8 \qquad \text{Multiply both sides of the equation by 2.}$$

$$x = 10 \qquad \text{Subtract } 2x \text{ and add 2.}$$

To check the result, substitute $x = 10$ into $\log(3x - 2) - \log(2) = \log(x + 4)$.

$$\log(3(10) - 2) - \log(2) = \log((10) + 4)$$

$$\log(28) - \log(2) = \log(14)$$

$$\log\left(\frac{28}{2}\right) = \log(14) \qquad \text{The solution checks.}$$

> ***using the one-to-one property of logarithms to solve logarithmic equations***
>
> For any algebraic expressions S and T and any positive real number b, where $b \neq 1$,
>
> $$\log_b(S) = \log_b(T) \text{ if and only if } S = T$$
>
> Note, when solving an equation involving logarithms, always check to see if the answer is correct or if it is an extraneous solution.

How To...

Given an equation containing logarithms, solve it using the one-to-one property.

1. Use the rules of logarithms to combine like terms, if necessary, so that the resulting equation has the form $\log_b S = \log_b T$.
2. Use the one-to-one property to set the arguments equal.
3. Solve the resulting equation, $S = T$, for the unknown.

Example 12 **Solving an Equation Using the One-to-One Property of Logarithms**

Solve $\ln(x^2) = \ln(2x + 3)$.

Solution

$$\ln(x^2) = \ln(2x + 3)$$

$$x^2 = 2x + 3 \qquad \text{Use the one-to-one property of the logarithm.}$$

$$x^2 - 2x - 3 = 0 \qquad \text{Get zero on one side before factoring.}$$

$$(x - 3)(x + 1) = 0 \qquad \text{Factor using FOIL.}$$

$$x - 3 = 0 \text{ or } x + 1 = 0 \qquad \text{If a product is zero, one of the factors must be zero.}$$

$$x = 3 \text{ or } x = -1 \qquad \text{Solve for } x.$$

Analysis *There are two solutions: 3 or −1. The solution −1 is negative, but it checks when substituted into the original equation because the argument of the logarithm functions is still positive.*

Try It #12

Solve $\ln(x^2) = \ln(1)$.

Solving Applied Problems Using Exponential and Logarithmic Equations

In previous sections, we learned the properties and rules for both exponential and logarithmic functions. We have seen that any exponential function can be written as a logarithmic function and vice versa. We have used exponents to solve logarithmic equations and logarithms to solve exponential equations. We are now ready to combine our skills to solve equations that model real-world situations, whether the unknown is in an exponent or in the argument of a logarithm.

One such application is in science, in calculating the time it takes for half of the unstable material in a sample of a radioactive substance to decay, called its half-life. **Table 1** lists the half-life for several of the more common radioactive substances.

Substance	Use	Half-life
gallium-67	nuclear medicine	80 hours
cobalt-60	manufacturing	5.3 years
technetium-99m	nuclear medicine	6 hours
americium-241	construction	432 years
carbon-14	archeological dating	5,715 years
uranium-235	atomic power	703,800,000 years

Table 1

We can see how widely the half-lives for these substances vary. Knowing the half-life of a substance allows us to calculate the amount remaining after a specified time. We can use the formula for radioactive decay:

$$A(t) = A_0 e^{\frac{\ln(0.5)}{T}t}$$
$$A(t) = A_0 e^{\ln(0.5)\frac{t}{T}}$$
$$A(t) = A_0 (e^{\ln(0.5)})^{\frac{t}{T}}$$
$$A(t) = A_0 \left(\frac{1}{2}\right)^{\frac{t}{T}}$$

where
- A_0 is the amount initially present
- T is the half-life of the substance
- t is the time period over which the substance is studied
- y is the amount of the substance present after time t

Example 13   Using the Formula for Radioactive Decay to Find the Quantity of a Substance

How long will it take for ten percent of a 1,000-gram sample of uranium-235 to decay?

Solution

$$y = 1000e^{\frac{\ln(0.5)}{703,800,000}t}$$

$$900 = 1000e^{\frac{\ln(0.5)}{703,800,000}t} \qquad \text{After 10\% decays, 900 grams are left.}$$

$$0.9 = e^{\frac{\ln(0.5)}{703,800,000}t} \qquad \text{Divide by 1000.}$$

$$\ln(0.9) = \ln\left(e^{\frac{\ln(0.5)}{703,800,000}t}\right) \qquad \text{Take ln of both sides.}$$

$$\ln(0.9) = \frac{\ln(0.5)}{703,800,000}t \qquad \ln(e^M) = M$$

$$t = 703,800,000 \times \frac{\ln(0.9)}{\ln(0.5)} \text{ years} \qquad \text{Solve for } t.$$

$$t \approx 106,979,777 \text{ years}$$

Analysis   *Ten percent of 1,000 grams is 100 grams. If 100 grams decay, the amount of uranium-235 remaining is 900 grams.*

Try It #13

How long will it take before twenty percent of our 1,000-gram sample of uranium-235 has decayed?

Access these online resources for additional instruction and practice with exponential and logarithmic equations.

- Solving Logarithmic Equations (http://openstaxcollege.org/l/solvelogeq)
- Solving Exponential Equations with Logarithms (http://openstaxcollege.org/l/solveexplog)

4.6 SECTION EXERCISES

VERBAL

1. How can an exponential equation be solved?

2. When does an extraneous solution occur? How can an extraneous solution be recognized?

3. When can the one-to-one property of logarithms be used to solve an equation? When can it not be used?

ALGEBRAIC

For the following exercises, use like bases to solve the exponential equation.

4. $4^{-3v-2} = 4^{-v}$

5. $64 \cdot 4^{3x} = 16$

6. $3^{2x+1} \cdot 3^x = 243$

7. $2^{-3n} \cdot \dfrac{1}{4} = 2^{n+2}$

8. $625 \cdot 5^{3x+3} = 125$

9. $\dfrac{36^{3b}}{36^{2b}} = 216^{2-b}$

10. $\left(\dfrac{1}{64}\right)^{3n} \cdot 8 = 2^6$

For the following exercises, use logarithms to solve.

11. $9^{x-10} = 1$

12. $2e^{6x} = 13$

13. $e^{r+10} - 10 = -42$

14. $2 \cdot 10^{9a} = 29$

15. $-8 \cdot 10^{p+7} - 7 = -24$

16. $7e^{3n-5} + 5 = -89$

17. $e^{-3k} + 6 = 44$

18. $-5e^{9x-8} - 8 = -62$

19. $-6e^{9x+8} + 2 = -74$

20. $2^{x+1} = 5^{2x-1}$

21. $e^{2x} - e^x - 132 = 0$

22. $7e^{8x+8} - 5 = -95$

23. $10e^{8x+3} + 2 = 8$

24. $4e^{3x+3} - 7 = 53$

25. $8e^{-5x-2} - 4 = -90$

26. $3^{2x+1} = 7^{x-2}$

27. $e^{2x} - e^x - 6 = 0$

28. $3e^{3-3x} + 6 = -31$

For the following exercises, use the definition of a logarithm to rewrite the equation as an exponential equation.

29. $\log\left(\dfrac{1}{100}\right) = -2$

30. $\log_{324}(18) = \dfrac{1}{2}$

For the following exercises, use the definition of a logarithm to solve the equation.

31. $5\log_7(n) = 10$

32. $-8\log_9(x) = 16$

33. $4 + \log_2(9k) = 2$

34. $2\log(8n + 4) + 6 = 10$

35. $10 - 4\ln(9 - 8x) = 6$

For the following exercises, use the one-to-one property of logarithms to solve.

36. $\ln(10 - 3x) = \ln(-4x)$

37. $\log_{13}(5n - 2) = \log_{13}(8 - 5n)$

38. $\log(x + 3) - \log(x) = \log(74)$

39. $\ln(-3x) = \ln(x^2 - 6x)$

40. $\log_4(6 - m) = \log_4 3(m)$

41. $\ln(x - 2) - \ln(x) = \ln(54)$

42. $\log_9(2n^2 - 14n) = \log_9(-45 + n^2)$

43. $\ln(x^2 - 10) + \ln(9) = \ln(10)$

For the following exercises, solve each equation for x.

44. $\log(x + 12) = \log(x) + \log(12)$

45. $\ln(x) + \ln(x - 3) = \ln(7x)$

46. $\log_2(7x + 6) = 3$

47. $\ln(7) + \ln(2 - 4x^2) = \ln(14)$

48. $\log_8(x + 6) - \log_8(x) = \log_8(58)$

49. $\ln(3) - \ln(3 - 3x) = \ln(4)$

50. $\log_3(3x) - \log_3(6) = \log_3(77)$

GRAPHICAL

For the following exercises, solve the equation for x, if there is a solution. Then graph both sides of the equation, and observe the point of intersection (if it exists) to verify the solution.

51. $\log_9(x) - 5 = -4$

52. $\log_3(x) + 3 = 2$

53. $\ln(3x) = 2$

54. $\ln(x - 5) = 1$

55. $\log(4) + \log(-5x) = 2$

56. $-7 + \log_3(4 - x) = -6$

57. $\ln(4x - 10) - 6 = -5$

58. $\log(4 - 2x) = \log(-4x)$

59. $\log_{11}(-2x^2 - 7x) = \log_{11}(x - 2)$

60. $\ln(2x + 9) = \ln(-5x)$

61. $\log_9(3 - x) = \log_9(4x - 8)$

62. $\log(x^2 + 13) = \log(7x + 3)$

63. $\dfrac{3}{\log_2(10)} - \log(x - 9) = \log(44)$

64. $\ln(x) - \ln(x + 3) = \ln(6)$

For the following exercises, solve for the indicated value, and graph the situation showing the solution point.

65. An account with an initial deposit of $6,500 earns 7.25% annual interest, compounded continuously. How much will the account be worth after 20 years?

66. The formula for measuring sound intensity in decibels D is defined by the equation $D = 10 \log\left(\frac{I}{I_0}\right)$, where I is the intensity of the sound in watts per square meter and $I_0 = 10^{-12}$ is the lowest level of sound that the average person can hear. How many decibels are emitted from a jet plane with a sound intensity of $8.3 \cdot 10^2$ watts per square meter?

67. The population of a small town is modeled by the equation $P = 1650e^{0.5t}$ where t is measured in years. In approximately how many years will the town's population reach 20,000?

TECHNOLOGY

For the following exercises, solve each equation by rewriting the exponential expression using the indicated logarithm. Then use a calculator to approximate the variable to 3 decimal places.

68. $1000(1.03)^t = 5000$ using the common log.

69. $e^{5x} = 17$ using the natural log

70. $3(1.04)^{3t} = 8$ using the common log

71. $3^{4x - 5} = 38$ using the common log

72. $50e^{-0.12t} = 10$ using the natural log

For the following exercises, use a calculator to solve the equation. Unless indicated otherwise, round all answers to the nearest ten-thousandth.

73. $7e^{3x - 5} + 7.9 = 47$

74. $\ln(3) + \ln(4.4x + 6.8) = 2$

75. $\log(-0.7x - 9) = 1 + 5\log(5)$

76. Atmospheric pressure P in pounds per square inch is represented by the formula $P = 14.7e^{-0.21x}$, where x is the number of miles above sea level. To the nearest foot, how high is the peak of a mountain with an atmospheric pressure of 8.369 pounds per square inch? (*Hint*: there are 5,280 feet in a mile)

77. The magnitude M of an earthquake is represented by the equation $M = \frac{2}{3} \log\left(\frac{E}{E_0}\right)$ where E is the amount of energy released by the earthquake in joules and $E_0 = 10^{4.4}$ is the assigned minimal measure released by an earthquake. To the nearest hundredth, what would the magnitude be of an earthquake releasing $1.4 \cdot 10^{13}$ joules of energy?

EXTENSIONS

78. Use the definition of a logarithm along with the one-to-one property of logarithms to prove that $b^{\log_b x} = x$.

79. Recall the formula for continually compounding interest, $y = Ae^{kt}$. Use the definition of a logarithm along with properties of logarithms to solve the formula for time t such that t is equal to a single logarithm.

80. Recall the compound interest formula $A = a\left(1 + \frac{r}{k}\right)^{kt}$. Use the definition of a logarithm along with properties of logarithms to solve the formula for time t.

81. Newton's Law of Cooling states that the temperature T of an object at any time t can be described by the equation $T = T_s + (T_0 - T_s)e^{-kt}$, where T_s is the temperature of the surrounding environment, T_0 is the initial temperature of the object, and k is the cooling rate. Use the definition of a logarithm along with properties of logarithms to solve the formula for time t such that t is equal to a single logarithm.

LEARNING OBJECTIVES

In this section, you will:

- Model exponential growth and decay.
- Use Newton's Law of Cooling.
- Use logistic-growth models.
- Choose an appropriate model for data.
- Express an exponential model in base *e*.

4.7   EXPONENTIAL AND LOGARITHMIC MODELS

Figure 1 A nuclear research reactor inside the Neely Nuclear Research Center on the Georgia Institute of Technology campus. (credit: Georgia Tech Research Institute)

We have already explored some basic applications of exponential and logarithmic functions. In this section, we explore some important applications in more depth, including radioactive isotopes and Newton's Law of Cooling.

Modeling Exponential Growth and Decay

In real-world applications, we need to model the behavior of a function. In mathematical modeling, we choose a familiar general function with properties that suggest that it will model the real-world phenomenon we wish to analyze. In the case of rapid growth, we may choose the exponential growth function:

$$y = A_0 e^{kt}$$

where A_0 is equal to the value at time zero, *e* is Euler's constant, and *k* is a positive constant that determines the rate (percentage) of growth. We may use the exponential growth function in applications involving **doubling time**, the time it takes for a quantity to double. Such phenomena as wildlife populations, financial investments, biological samples, and natural resources may exhibit growth based on a doubling time. In some applications, however, as we will see when we discuss the logistic equation, the logistic model sometimes fits the data better than the exponential model.

On the other hand, if a quantity is falling rapidly toward zero, without ever reaching zero, then we should probably choose the exponential decay model. Again, we have the form $y = A_0 e^{kt}$ where A_0 is the starting value, and *e* is Euler's constant. Now *k* is a negative constant that determines the rate of decay. We may use the exponential decay model when we are calculating **half-life**, or the time it takes for a substance to exponentially decay to half of its original quantity. We use half-life in applications involving radioactive isotopes.

In our choice of a function to serve as a mathematical model, we often use data points gathered by careful observation and measurement to construct points on a graph and hope we can recognize the shape of the graph. Exponential growth and decay graphs have a distinctive shape, as we can see in **Figure 2** and **Figure 3**. It is important to remember that, although parts of each of the two graphs seem to lie on the *x*-axis, they are really a tiny distance above the *x*-axis.

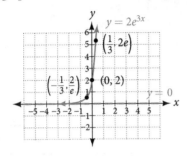

Figure 2 A graph showing exponential growth. The equation is $y = 2e^{3x}$.

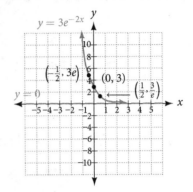

Figure 3 A graph showing exponential decay. The equation is $y = 3e^{-2x}$.

Exponential growth and decay often involve very large or very small numbers. To describe these numbers, we often use orders of magnitude. The **order of magnitude** is the power of ten, when the number is expressed in scientific notation, with one digit to the left of the decimal. For example, the distance to the nearest star, Proxima Centauri, measured in kilometers, is 40,113,497,200,000 kilometers. Expressed in scientific notation, this is $4.01134972 \times 10^{13}$. So, we could describe this number as having order of magnitude 10^{13}.

---

characteristics of the exponential function, $y = A_0 e^{kt}$

An exponential function with the form $y = A_0 e^{kt}$ has the following characteristics:

- one-to-one function
- horizontal asymptote: $y = 0$
- domain: $(-\infty, \infty)$
- range: $(0, \infty)$
- *x*-intercept: none
- *y*-intercept: $(0, A_0)$
- increasing if $k > 0$ (see **Figure 4**)
- decreasing if $k < 0$ (see **Figure 4**)

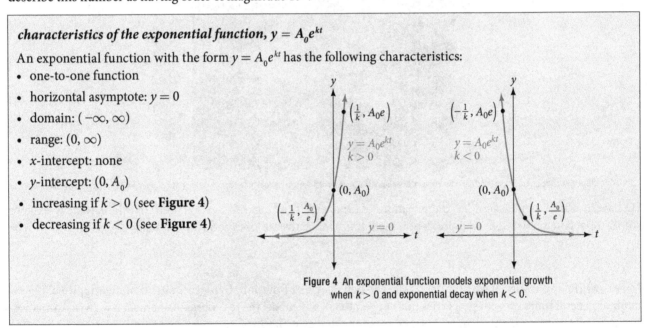

Figure 4 An exponential function models exponential growth when $k > 0$ and exponential decay when $k < 0$.

Example 1   Graphing Exponential Growth

A population of bacteria doubles every hour. If the culture started with 10 bacteria, graph the population as a function of time.

Solution   When an amount grows at a fixed percent per unit time, the growth is exponential. To find A_0 we use the fact that A_0 is the amount at time zero, so $A_0 = 10$. To find k, use the fact that after one hour ($t = 1$) the population doubles from 10 to 20. The formula is derived as follows

$$20 = 10e^{k \cdot 1}$$

$$2 = e^k \qquad \text{Divide by 10}$$

$$\ln 2 = k \qquad \text{Take the natural logarithm}$$

so $k = \ln(2)$. Thus the equation we want to graph is $y = 10e^{(\ln 2)t} = 10(e^{\ln 2})^t = 10 \cdot 2^t$. The graph is shown in **Figure 5**.

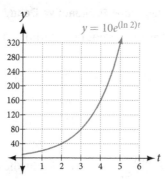

Figure 5 The graph of $y = 10e^{(\ln 2)t}$.

Analysis *The population of bacteria after ten hours is 10,240. We could describe this amount is being of the order of magnitude 10^4. The population of bacteria after twenty hours is 10,485,760 which is of the order of magnitude 10^7, so we could say that the population has increased by three orders of magnitude in ten hours.*

Half-Life

We now turn to exponential decay. One of the common terms associated with exponential decay, as stated above, is **half-life**, the length of time it takes an exponentially decaying quantity to decrease to half its original amount. Every radioactive isotope has a half-life, and the process describing the exponential decay of an isotope is called radioactive decay.

To find the half-life of a function describing exponential decay, solve the following equation:

$$\frac{1}{2} A_0 = A_0 e^{kt}$$

We find that the half-life depends only on the constant k and not on the starting quantity A_0.

The formula is derived as follows

$$\frac{1}{2} A_0 = A_0 e^{kt}$$

$$\frac{1}{2} = e^{kt} \qquad \text{Divide by } A_0.$$

$$\ln\left(\frac{1}{2}\right) = kt \qquad \text{Take the natural log.}$$

$$-\ln(2) = kt \qquad \text{Apply laws of logarithms.}$$

$$-\frac{\ln(2)}{k} = t \qquad \text{Divide by } k.$$

Since t, the time, is positive, k must, as expected, be negative. This gives us the half-life formula

$$t = -\frac{\ln(2)}{k}$$

How To...

Given the half-life, find the decay rate.

1. Write $A = A_0 e^{kt}$.

2. Replace A by $\frac{1}{2} A_0$ and replace t by the given half-life.

3. Solve to find k. Express k as an exact value (do not round).

Note: It is also possible to find the decay rate using $k = -\dfrac{\ln(2)}{t}$.

Example 2   **Finding the Function that Describes Radioactive Decay**

The half-life of carbon-14 is 5,730 years. Express the amount of carbon-14 remaining as a function of time, t.

Solution   This formula is derived as follows.

$$A = A_0 e^{kt}$$ 　　　　　The continuous growth formula.

$$0.5A_0 = A_0 e^{k \cdot 5730}$$ 　　Substitute the half-life for t and $0.5A_0$ for $f(t)$.

$$0.5 = e^{5730k}$$ 　　　　Divide by A_0.

$$\ln(0.5) = 5730k$$ 　　　Take the natural log of both sides.

$$k = \frac{\ln(0.5)}{5730}$$ 　　　　Divide by the coefficient of k.

$$A = A_0 e^{\left(\frac{\ln(0.5)}{5730}\right)t}$$ 　　Substitute for k in the continuous growth formula.

The function that describes this continuous decay is $f(t) = A_0 e^{\left(\frac{\ln(0.5)}{5730}\right)t}$. We observe that the coefficient of t, $\frac{\ln(0.5)}{5730} \approx -1.2097$ is negative, as expected in the case of exponential decay.

Try It #14

The half-life of plutonium-244 is 80,000,000 years. Find function gives the amount of carbon-14 remaining as a function of time, measured in years.

Radiocarbon Dating

The formula for radioactive decay is important in radiocarbon dating, which is used to calculate the approximate date a plant or animal died. Radiocarbon dating was discovered in 1949 by Willard Libby, who won a Nobel Prize for his discovery. It compares the difference between the ratio of two isotopes of carbon in an organic artifact or fossil to the ratio of those two isotopes in the air. It is believed to be accurate to within about 1% error for plants or animals that died within the last 60,000 years.

Carbon-14 is a radioactive isotope of carbon that has a half-life of 5,730 years. It occurs in small quantities in the carbon dioxide in the air we breathe. Most of the carbon on earth is carbon-12, which has an atomic weight of 12 and is not radioactive. Scientists have determined the ratio of carbon-14 to carbon-12 in the air for the last 60,000 years, using tree rings and other organic samples of known dates—although the ratio has changed slightly over the centuries.

As long as a plant or animal is alive, the ratio of the two isotopes of carbon in its body is close to the ratio in the atmosphere. When it dies, the carbon-14 in its body decays and is not replaced. By comparing the ratio of carbon-14 to carbon-12 in a decaying sample to the known ratio in the atmosphere, the date the plant or animal died can be approximated.

Since the half-life of carbon-14 is 5,730 years, the formula for the amount of carbon-14 remaining after t years is

$$A \approx A_0 e^{\left(\frac{\ln(0.5)}{5730}\right)t}$$

where

- A is the amount of carbon-14 remaining
- A_0 is the amount of carbon-14 when the plant or animal began decaying.

This formula is derived as follows:

$$A = A_0 e^{kt}$$ 　　　　　The continuous growth formula.

$$0.5A_0 = A_0 e^{k \cdot 5730}$$ 　　Substitute the half-life for t and $0.5A_0$ for $f(t)$.

$$0.5 = e^{5730k}$$ 　　　　Divide by A_0.

$$\ln(0.5) = 5730k$$ 　　　Take the natural log of both sides.

$$k = \frac{\ln(0.5)}{5730}$$ 　　　　Divide by the coefficient of k.

$$A = A_0 e^{\left(\frac{\ln(0.5)}{5730}\right)t}$$ 　　Substitute for r in the continuous growth formula.

To find the age of an object, we solve this equation for t:

$$t = \frac{\ln\left(\frac{A}{A_0}\right)}{-0.000121}$$

Out of necessity, we neglect here the many details that a scientist takes into consideration when doing carbon-14 dating, and we only look at the basic formula. The ratio of carbon-14 to carbon-12 in the atmosphere is approximately 0.0000000001%. Let r be the ratio of carbon-14 to carbon-12 in the organic artifact or fossil to be dated, determined by a method called liquid scintillation. From the equation $A \approx A_0 e^{-0.000121t}$ we know the ratio of the percentage of carbon-14 in the object we are dating to the percentage of carbon-14 in the atmosphere is $r = \dfrac{A}{A_0} \approx e^{-0.000121t}$. We solve this equation for t, to get

$$t = \frac{\ln(r)}{-0.000121}$$

How To...

Given the percentage of carbon-14 in an object, determine its age.

1. Express the given percentage of carbon-14 as an equivalent decimal, k.
2. Substitute for k in the equation $t = \dfrac{\ln(r)}{-0.000121}$ and solve for the age, t.

Example 3   **Finding the Age of a Bone**

A bone fragment is found that contains 20% of its original carbon-14. To the nearest year, how old is the bone?

Solution   We substitute $20\% = 0.20$ for k in the equation and solve for t:

$$t = \frac{\ln(r)}{-0.000121}$$ Use the general form of the equation.

$$= \frac{\ln(0.20)}{-0.000121}$$ Substitute for r.

$$\approx 13301$$ Round to the nearest year.

The bone fragment is about 13,301 years old.

Analysis   The instruments that measure the percentage of carbon-14 are extremely sensitive and, as we mention above, a scientist will need to do much more work than we did in order to be satisfied. Even so, carbon dating is only accurate to about 1%, so this age should be given as 13,301 years ± 1% or 13,301 years ± 133 years.

Try It #15

Cesium-137 has a half-life of about 30 years. If we begin with 200 mg of cesium-137, will it take more or less than 230 years until only 1 milligram remains?

Calculating Doubling Time

For decaying quantities, we determined how long it took for half of a substance to decay. For growing quantities, we might want to find out how long it takes for a quantity to double. As we mentioned above, the time it takes for a quantity to double is called the **doubling time**.

Given the basic exponential growth equation $A = A_0 e^{kt}$, doubling time can be found by solving for when the original quantity has doubled, that is, by solving $2A_0 = A_0 e^{kt}$.

The formula is derived as follows:

$$2A_0 = A_0 e^{kt}$$

$$2 = e^{kt}$$ Divide by A_0.

$$\ln(2) = kt$$ Take the natural logarithm.

$$t = \frac{\ln(2)}{k}$$ Divide by the coefficient of t.

Thus the doubling time is

$$t = \frac{\ln(2)}{k}$$

Example 4   **Finding a Function That Describes Exponential Growth**

According to Moore's Law, the doubling time for the number of transistors that can be put on a computer chip is approximately two years. Give a function that describes this behavior.

Solution   The formula is derived as follows:

$$t = \frac{\ln(2)}{k}$$ The doubling time formula.

$$2 = \frac{\ln(2)}{k}$$ Use a doubling time of two years.

$$k = \frac{\ln(2)}{2}$$ Multiply by k and divide by 2.

$$A = A_0 e^{\frac{\ln(2)}{2} t}$$ Substitute k into the continuous growth formula.

The function is $A_0 e^{\frac{\ln(2)}{2} t}$.

Try It #16

Recent data suggests that, as of 2013, the rate of growth predicted by Moore's Law no longer holds. Growth has slowed to a doubling time of approximately three years. Find the new function that takes that longer doubling time into account.

Using Newton's Law of Cooling

Exponential decay can also be applied to temperature. When a hot object is left in surrounding air that is at a lower temperature, the object's temperature will decrease exponentially, leveling off as it approaches the surrounding air temperature. On a graph of the temperature function, the leveling off will correspond to a horizontal asymptote at the temperature of the surrounding air. Unless the room temperature is zero, this will correspond to a vertical shift of the generic exponential decay function. This translation leads to **Newton's Law of Cooling**, the scientific formula for temperature as a function of time as an object's temperature is equalized with the ambient temperature

$$T(t) = A e^{kt} + T_s$$

This formula is derived as follows:

$$T(t) = A b^{ct} + T_s$$

$$T(t) = A e^{\ln(b^{ct})} + T_s$$ Laws of logarithms.

$$T(t) = A e^{ct \ln(b)} + T_s$$ Laws of logarithms.

$$T(t) = A e^{kt} + T_s$$ Rename the constant $c\ln(b)$, calling it k.

Newton's law of cooling

The temperature of an object, T, in surrounding air with temperature T_s will behave according to the formula

$$T(t) = A e^{kt} + T_s$$

where

- t is time
- A is the difference between the initial temperature of the object and the surroundings
- k is a constant, the continuous rate of cooling of the object

---

How To...

Given a set of conditions, apply Newton's Law of Cooling.

1. Set T_s equal to the y-coordinate of the horizontal asymptote (usually the ambient temperature).
2. Substitute the given values into the continuous growth formula $T(t) = A e^{kt} + T_s$ to find the parameters A and k.
3. Substitute in the desired time to find the temperature or the desired temperature to find the time.

Example 5   **Using Newton's Law of Cooling**

A cheesecake is taken out of the oven with an ideal internal temperature of 165°F, and is placed into a 35°F refrigerator. After 10 minutes, the cheesecake has cooled to 150°F. If we must wait until the cheesecake has cooled to 70°F before we eat it, how long will we have to wait?

Solution   Because the surrounding air temperature in the refrigerator is 35 degrees, the cheesecake's temperature will decay exponentially toward 35, following the equation

$$T(t) = Ae^{kt} + 35$$

We know the initial temperature was 165, so $T(0) = 165$.

$$165 = Ae^{k0} + 35 \qquad \text{Substitute (0, 165).}$$

$$A = 130 \qquad \text{Solve for } A.$$

We were given another data point, $T(10) = 150$, which we can use to solve for k.

$$150 = 130e^{k10} + 35 \qquad \text{Substitute (10, 150).}$$

$$115 = 130e^{k10} \qquad \text{Subtract 35.}$$

$$\frac{115}{130} = e^{10k} \qquad \text{Divide by 130.}$$

$$\ln\left(\frac{115}{130}\right) = 10k \qquad \text{Take the natural log of both sides.}$$

$$k = \frac{\ln\left(\dfrac{115}{130}\right)}{10} \approx -0.0123 \text{ Divide by the coefficient of } k.$$

This gives us the equation for the cooling of the cheesecake: $T(t) = 130e^{-0.0123t} + 35$.

Now we can solve for the time it will take for the temperature to cool to 70 degrees.

$$70 = 130e^{-0.0123t} + 35 \qquad \text{Substitute in 70 for } T(t).$$

$$35 = 130e^{-0.0123t} \qquad \text{Subtract 35.}$$

$$\frac{35}{130} = e^{-0.0123t} \qquad \text{Divide by 130.}$$

$$\ln\left(\frac{35}{130}\right) = -0.0123t \qquad \text{Take the natural log of both sides}$$

$$t = \frac{\ln\left(\dfrac{35}{130}\right)}{-0.0123} \approx 106.68 \qquad \text{Divide by the coefficient of } t.$$

It will take about 107 minutes, or one hour and 47 minutes, for the cheesecake to cool to 70°F.

Try It #17

A pitcher of water at 40 degrees Fahrenheit is placed into a 70 degree room. One hour later, the temperature has risen to 45 degrees. How long will it take for the temperature to rise to 60 degrees?

Using Logistic Growth Models

Exponential growth cannot continue forever. Exponential models, while they may be useful in the short term, tend to fall apart the longer they continue. Consider an aspiring writer who writes a single line on day one and plans to double the number of lines she writes each day for a month. By the end of the month, she must write over 17 billion lines, or one-half-billion pages. It is impractical, if not impossible, for anyone to write that much in such a short period of time. Eventually, an exponential model must begin to approach some limiting value, and then the growth is forced to slow. For this reason, it is often better to use a model with an upper bound instead of an exponential growth model, though the exponential growth model is still useful over a short term, before approaching the limiting value.

The **logistic growth model** is approximately exponential at first, but it has a reduced rate of growth as the output approaches the model's upper bound, called the **carrying capacity**. For constants a, b, and c, the logistic growth of a population over time x is represented by the model

$$f(x) = \frac{c}{1 + ae^{-bx}}$$

The graph in **Figure 6** shows how the growth rate changes over time. The graph increases from left to right, but the growth rate only increases until it reaches its point of maximum growth rate, at which point the rate of increase decreases.

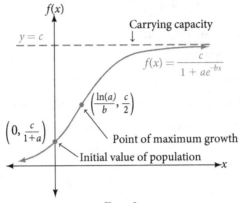

Figure 6

---

logistic growth

The logistic growth model is

$$f(x) = \frac{c}{1 + ae^{-bx}}$$

where

- $\dfrac{c}{1 + a}$ is the initial value
- c is the *carrying capacity, or limiting value*
- b is a constant determined by the rate of growth.

Example 6   **Using the Logistic-Growth Model**

An influenza epidemic spreads through a population rapidly, at a rate that depends on two factors: The more people who have the flu, the more rapidly it spreads, and also the more uninfected people there are, the more rapidly it spreads. These two factors make the logistic model a good one to study the spread of communicable diseases. And, clearly, there is a maximum value for the number of people infected: the entire population.

For example, at time $t = 0$ there is one person in a community of 1,000 people who has the flu. So, in that community, at most 1,000 people can have the flu. Researchers find that for this particular strain of the flu, the logistic growth constant is $b = 0.6030$. Estimate the number of people in this community who will have had this flu after ten days. Predict how many people in this community will have had this flu after a long period of time has passed.

Solution   We substitute the given data into the logistic growth model

$$f(x) = \frac{c}{1 + ae^{-bx}}$$

Because at most 1,000 people, the entire population of the community, can get the flu, we know the limiting value is $c = 1000$. To find a, we use the formula that the number of cases at time $t = 0$ is $\dfrac{c}{1 + a} = 1$, from which it follows that $a = 999$. This model predicts that, after ten days, the number of people who have had the flu is $f(x) = \dfrac{1000}{1 + 999e^{-0.6030x}} \approx 293.8$. Because the actual number must be a whole number (a person has either had the flu or not) we round to 294. In the long term, the number of people who will contract the flu is the limiting value, $c = 1000$.

Analysis   Remember that, because we are dealing with a virus, we cannot predict with certainty the number of people infected. The model only approximates the number of people infected and will not give us exact or actual values. The graph in Figure 7 gives a good picture of how this model fits the data.

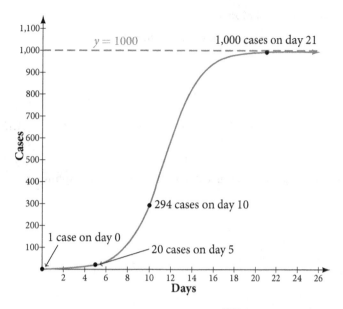

Figure 7 The graph of $f(x) = \dfrac{1000}{1 + 999e^{-0.6030x}}$

Try It #18

Using the model in **Example 6**, estimate the number of cases of flu on day 15.

Choosing an Appropriate Model for Data

Now that we have discussed various mathematical models, we need to learn how to choose the appropriate model for the raw data we have. Many factors influence the choice of a mathematical model, among which are experience, scientific laws, and patterns in the data itself. Not all data can be described by elementary functions. Sometimes, a function is chosen that approximates the data over a given interval. For instance, suppose data were gathered on the number of homes bought in the United States from the years 1960 to 2013. After plotting these data in a scatter plot, we notice that the shape of the data from the years 2000 to 2013 follow a logarithmic curve. We could restrict the interval from 2000 to 2010, apply regression analysis using a logarithmic model, and use it to predict the number of home buyers for the year 2015.

Three kinds of functions that are often useful in mathematical models are linear functions, exponential functions, and logarithmic functions. If the data lies on a straight line, or seems to lie approximately along a straight line, a linear model may be best. If the data is non-linear, we often consider an exponential or logarithmic model, though other models, such as quadratic models, may also be considered.

In choosing between an exponential model and a logarithmic model, we look at the way the data curves. This is called the concavity. If we draw a line between two data points, and all (or most) of the data between those two points lies above that line, we say the curve is concave down. We can think of it as a bowl that bends downward and therefore cannot hold water. If all (or most) of the data between those two points lies below the line, we say the curve is concave up. In this case, we can think of a bowl that bends upward and can therefore hold water. An exponential curve, whether rising or falling, whether representing growth or decay, is always concave up away from its horizontal asymptote. A logarithmic curve is always concave away from its vertical asymptote. In the case of positive data, which is the most common case, an exponential curve is always concave up, and a logarithmic curve always concave down.

A logistic curve changes concavity. It starts out concave up and then changes to concave down beyond a certain point, called a point of inflection.

After using the graph to help us choose a type of function to use as a model, we substitute points, and solve to find the parameters. We reduce round-off error by choosing points as far apart as possible.

<u>Example 7</u>   **Choosing a Mathematical Model**

Does a linear, exponential, logarithmic, or logistic model best fit the values listed in **Table 1**? Find the model, and use a graph to check your choice.

x	1	2	3	4	5	6	7	8	9
y	0	1.386	2.197	2.773	3.219	3.584	3.892	4.159	4.394

Table 1

Solution   First, plot the data on a graph as in **Figure 8**. For the purpose of graphing, round the data to two significant digits.

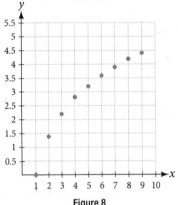

Figure 8

Clearly, the points do not lie on a straight line, so we reject a linear model. If we draw a line between any two of the points, most or all of the points between those two points lie above the line, so the graph is concave down, suggesting a logarithmic model. We can try $y = a\ln(bx)$. Plugging in the first point, $(1,0)$, gives $0 = a\ln b$.

We reject the case that $a = 0$ (if it were, all outputs would be 0), so we know $\ln(b) = 0$. Thus $b = 1$ and $y = a\ln(x)$. Next we can use the point $(9, 4.394)$ to solve for a:

$$y = a\ln(x)$$

$$4.394 = a\ln(9)$$

$$a = \frac{4.394}{\ln(9)}$$

Because $a = \dfrac{4.394}{\ln(9)} \approx 2$, an appropriate model for the data is $y = 2\ln(x)$.

To check the accuracy of the model, we graph the function together with the given points as in **Figure 9**.

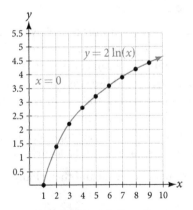

Figure 9   The graph of $y = 2\ln x$.

We can conclude that the model is a good fit to the data.

Compare **Figure 9** to the graph of $y = \ln(x^2)$ shown in **Figure 10**.

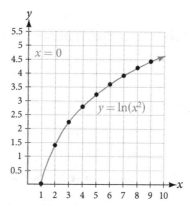

Figure 10 The graph of $y = \ln(x^2)$

The graphs appear to be identical when $x > 0$. A quick check confirms this conclusion: $y = \ln(x^2) = 2\ln(x)$ for $x > 0$.

However, if $x < 0$, the graph of $y = \ln(x^2)$ includes a "extra" branch, as shown in **Figure 11**. This occurs because, while $y = 2\ln(x)$ cannot have negative values in the domain (as such values would force the argument to be negative), the function $y = \ln(x^2)$ can have negative domain values.

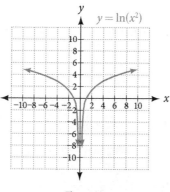

Figure 11

Try It #19

Does a linear, exponential, or logarithmic model best fit the data in **Table 2**? Find the model.

x	1	2	3	4	5	6	7	8	9
y	3.297	5.437	8.963	14.778	24.365	40.172	66.231	109.196	180.034

Table 2

Expressing an Exponential Model in Base *e*

While powers and logarithms of any base can be used in modeling, the two most common bases are 10 and *e*. In science and mathematics, the base *e* is often preferred. We can use laws of exponents and laws of logarithms to change any base to base *e*.

How To...

Given a model with the form $y = ab^x$, change it to the form $y = A_0 e^{kx}$.

1. Rewrite $y = ab^x$ as $y = ae^{\ln(b^x)}$.

2. Use the power rule of logarithms to rewrite y as $y = ae^{x\ln(b)} = ae^{\ln(b)x}$.

3. Note that $a = A_0$ and $k = \ln(b)$ in the equation $y = A_0 e^{kx}$.

Example 8   **Changing to base e**

Change the function $y = 2.5(3.1)^x$ so that this same function is written in the form $y = A_0 e^{kx}$.

Solution

The formula is derived as follows

$$y = 2.5(3.1)^x$$

$\quad = 2.5e^{\ln(3.1^x)}$ Insert exponential and its inverse.

$\quad = 2.5e^{x\ln 3.1}$ Laws of logs.

$\quad = 2.5e^{(\ln 3.1)x}$ Commutative law of multiplication

Try It #20

Change the function $y = 3(0.5)^x$ to one having e as the base.

Access these online resources for additional instruction and practice with exponential and logarithmic models.

- Logarithm Application – pH (http://openstaxcollege.org/l/logph)
- Exponential Model – Age Using Half-Life (http://openstaxcollege.org/l/expmodelhalf)
- Newton's Law of Cooling (http://openstaxcollege.org/l/newtoncooling)
- Exponential Growth Given Doubling Time (http://openstaxcollege.org/l/expgrowthdbl)
- Exponential Growth – Find Initial Amount Given Doubling Time (http://openstaxcollege.org/l/initialdouble)

4.7 SECTION EXERCISES

VERBAL

1. With what kind of exponential model would *half-life* be associated? What role does half-life play in these models?

2. What is carbon dating? Why does it work? Give an example in which carbon dating would be useful.

3. With what kind of exponential model would *doubling time* be associated? What role does doubling time play in these models?

4. Define Newton's Law of Cooling. Then name at least three real-world situations where Newton's Law of Cooling would be applied.

5. What is an order of magnitude? Why are orders of magnitude useful? Give an example to explain.

NUMERIC

6. The temperature of an object in degrees Fahrenheit after t minutes is represented by the equation $T(t) = 68e^{-0.0174t} + 72$. To the nearest degree, what is the temperature of the object after one and a half hours?

For the following exercises, use the logistic growth model $f(x) = \dfrac{150}{1 + 8e^{-2x}}$.

7. Find and interpret $f(0)$. Round to the nearest tenth.

8. Find and interpret $f(4)$. Round to the nearest tenth.

9. Find the carrying capacity.

10. Graph the model.

11. Determine whether the data from the table could best be represented as a function that is linear, exponential, or logarithmic. Then write a formula for a model that represents the data.

x	−2	−1	0	1	2	3	4	5
$f(x)$	0.694	0.833	1	1.2	1.44	1.728	2.074	2.488

12. Rewrite $f(x) = 1.68(0.65)^x$ as an exponential equation with base e to five significant digits.

TECHNOLOGY

For the following exercises, enter the data from each table into a graphing calculator and graph the resulting scatter plots. Determine whether the data from the table could represent a function that is linear, exponential, or logarithmic.

13.

x	1	2	3	4	5	6	7	8	9	10
$f(x)$	2	4.079	5.296	6.159	6.828	7.375	7.838	8.238	8.592	8.908

14.

x	1	2	3	4	5	6	7	8	9	10
$f(x)$	2.4	2.88	3.456	4.147	4.977	5.972	7.166	8.6	10.32	12.383

15.

x	4	5	6	7	8	9	10	11	12	13
$f(x)$	9.429	9.972	10.415	10.79	11.115	11.401	11.657	11.889	12.101	12.295

16.

x	1.25	2.25	3.56	4.2	5.65	6.75	7.25	8.6	9.25	10.5
$f(x)$	5.75	8.75	12.68	14.6	18.95	22.25	23.75	27.8	29.75	33.5

For the following exercises, use a graphing calculator and this scenario: the population of a fish farm in t years is modeled by the equation $P(t) = \dfrac{1000}{1 + 9e^{-0.6t}}$.

17. Graph the function.

18. What is the initial population of fish?

19. To the nearest tenth, what is the doubling time for the fish population?

20. To the nearest whole number, what will the fish population be after 2 years?

21. To the nearest tenth, how long will it take for the population to reach 900?

22. What is the carrying capacity for the fish population? Justify your answer using the graph of P.

EXTENSIONS

23. A substance has a half-life of 2.045 minutes. If the initial amount of the substance was 132.8 grams, how many half-lives will have passed before the substance decays to 8.3 grams? What is the total time of decay?

24. The formula for an increasing population is given by $P(t) = P_0 e^{rt}$ where P_0 is the initial population and $r > 0$. Derive a general formula for the time t it takes for the population to increase by a factor of M.

25. Recall the formula for calculating the magnitude of an earthquake, $M = \frac{2}{3}\log\left(\frac{S}{S_0}\right)$. Show each step for solving this equation algebraically for the seismic moment S.

26. What is the y-intercept of the logistic growth model $y = \frac{c}{1 + ae^{-rx}}$? Show the steps for calculation. What does this point tell us about the population?

27. Prove that $b^x = e^{x\ln(b)}$ for positive $b \neq 1$.

REAL-WORLD APPLICATIONS

For the following exercises, use this scenario: A doctor prescribes 125 milligrams of a therapeutic drug that decays by about 30% each hour.

28. To the nearest hour, what is the half-life of the drug?

29. Write an exponential model representing the amount of the drug remaining in the patient's system after t hours. Then use the formula to find the amount of the drug that would remain in the patient's system after 3 hours. Round to the nearest milligram.

30. Using the model found in the previous exercise, find $f(10)$ and interpret the result. Round to the nearest hundredth.

For the following exercises, use this scenario: A tumor is injected with 0.5 grams of Iodine-125, which has a decay rate of 1.15% per day.

31. To the nearest day, how long will it take for half of the Iodine-125 to decay?

32. Write an exponential model representing the amount of Iodine-125 remaining in the tumor after t days. Then use the formula to find the amount of Iodine-125 that would remain in the tumor after 60 days. Round to the nearest tenth of a gram.

33. A scientist begins with 250 grams of a radioactive substance. After 250 minutes, the sample has decayed to 32 grams. Rounding to five significant digits, write an exponential equation representing this situation. To the nearest minute, what is the half-life of this substance?

34. The half-life of Radium-226 is 1590 years. What is the annual decay rate? Express the decimal result to four significant digits and the percentage to two significant digits.

35. The half-life of Erbium-165 is 10.4 hours. What is the hourly decay rate? Express the decimal result to four significant digits and the percentage to two significant digits.

36. A wooden artifact from an archeological dig contains 60 percent of the carbon-14 that is present in living trees. To the nearest year, about how many years old is the artifact? (The half-life of carbon-14 is 5730 years.)

37. A research student is working with a culture of bacteria that doubles in size every twenty minutes. The initial population count was 1350 bacteria. Rounding to five significant digits, write an exponential equation representing this situation. To the nearest whole number, what is the population size after 3 hours?

For the following exercises, use this scenario: A biologist recorded a count of 360 bacteria present in a culture after 5 minutes and 1,000 bacteria present after 20 minutes.

38. To the nearest whole number, what was the initial population in the culture?

39. Rounding to six significant digits, write an exponential equation representing this situation. To the nearest minute, how long did it take the population to double?

For the following exercises, use this scenario: A pot of boiling soup with an internal temperature of 100° Fahrenheit was taken off the stove to cool in a 69° F room. After fifteen minutes, the internal temperature of the soup was 95° F.

40. Use Newton's Law of Cooling to write a formula that models this situation.

41. To the nearest minute, how long will it take the soup to cool to 80° F?

42. To the nearest degree, what will the temperature be after 2 and a half hours?

For the following exercises, use this scenario: A turkey is taken out of the oven with an internal temperature of 165° Fahrenheit and is allowed to cool in a 75° F room. After half an hour, the internal temperature of the turkey is 145° F.

43. Write a formula that models this situation.

44. To the nearest degree, what will the temperature be after 50 minutes?

45. To the nearest minute, how long will it take the turkey to cool to 110° F?

For the following exercises, find the value of the number shown on each logarithmic scale. Round all answers to the nearest thousandth.

46.

$\log(x)$

47.

$\log(x)$

48. Plot each set of approximate values of intensity of sounds on a logarithmic scale: Whisper: $10^{-10}\dfrac{W}{m^2}$, Vacuum: $10^{-4}\dfrac{W}{m^2}$, Jet: $10^2\dfrac{W}{m^2}$

49. Recall the formula for calculating the magnitude of an earthquake, $M = \dfrac{2}{3}\log\left(\dfrac{S}{S_0}\right)$. One earthquake has magnitude 3.9 on the MMS scale. If a second earthquake has 750 times as much energy as the first, find the magnitude of the second quake. Round to the nearest hundredth.

For the following exercises, use this scenario: The equation $N(t) = \dfrac{500}{1 + 49e^{-0.7t}}$ models the number of people in a town who have heard a rumor after t days.

50. How many people started the rumor?

51. To the nearest whole number, how many people will have heard the rumor after 3 days?

52. As t increases without bound, what value does $N(t)$ approach? Interpret your answer.

For the following exercise, choose the correct answer choice.

53. A doctor and injects a patient with 13 milligrams of radioactive dye that decays exponentially. After 12 minutes, there are 4.75 milligrams of dye remaining in the patient's system. Which is an appropriate model for this situation?

    a. $f(t) = 13(0.0805)^t$ **b.** $f(t) = 13e^{0.9195t}$ **c.** $f(t) = 13e^{(-0.0839t)}$ **d.** $f(t) = \dfrac{4.75}{1 + 13e^{-0.83925t}}$

LEARNING OBJECTIVES

In this section, you will:

- Build an exponential model from data.
- Build a logarithmic model from data.
- Build a logistic model from data.

4.8   FITTING EXPONENTIAL MODELS TO DATA

In previous sections of this chapter, we were either given a function explicitly to graph or evaluate, or we were given a set of points that were guaranteed to lie on the curve. Then we used algebra to find the equation that fit the points exactly. In this section, we use a modeling technique called *regression analysis* to find a curve that models data collected from real-world observations. With regression analysis, we don't expect all the points to lie perfectly on the curve. The idea is to find a model that best fits the data. Then we use the model to make predictions about future events.

Do not be confused by the word *model*. In mathematics, we often use the terms *function*, *equation*, and *model* interchangeably, even though they each have their own formal definition. The term *model* is typically used to indicate that the equation or function approximates a real-world situation.

We will concentrate on three types of regression models in this section: exponential, logarithmic, and logistic. Having already worked with each of these functions gives us an advantage. Knowing their formal definitions, the behavior of their graphs, and some of their real-world applications gives us the opportunity to deepen our understanding. As each regression model is presented, key features and definitions of its associated function are included for review. Take a moment to rethink each of these functions, reflect on the work we've done so far, and then explore the ways regression is used to model real-world phenomena.

Building an Exponential Model from Data

As we've learned, there are a multitude of situations that can be modeled by exponential functions, such as investment growth, radioactive decay, atmospheric pressure changes, and temperatures of a cooling object. What do these phenomena have in common? For one thing, all the models either increase or decrease as time moves forward. But that's not the whole story. It's the *way* data increase or decrease that helps us determine whether it is best modeled by an exponential equation. Knowing the behavior of exponential functions in general allows us to recognize when to use exponential regression, so let's review exponential growth and decay.

Recall that exponential functions have the form $y = ab^x$ or $y = A_0 e^{kx}$. When performing regression analysis, we use the form most commonly used on graphing utilities, $y = ab^x$. Take a moment to reflect on the characteristics we've already learned about the exponential function $y = ab^x$ (assume $a > 0$):

- b must be greater than zero and not equal to one.
- The initial value of the model is $y = a$.
  - If $b > 1$, the function models exponential growth. As x increases, the outputs of the model increase slowly at first, but then increase more and more rapidly, without bound.
  - If $0 < b < 1$, the function models exponential decay. As x increases, the outputs for the model decrease rapidly at first and then level off to become asymptotic to the x-axis. In other words, the outputs never become equal to or less than zero.

As part of the results, your calculator will display a number known as the *correlation coefficient*, labeled by the variable r, or r^2. (You may have to change the calculator's settings for these to be shown.) The values are an indication of the "goodness of fit" of the regression equation to the data. We more commonly use the value of r^2 instead of r, but the closer either value is to 1, the better the regression equation approximates the data.

exponential regression

Exponential regression is used to model situations in which growth begins slowly and then accelerates rapidly without bound, or where decay begins rapidly and then slows down to get closer and closer to zero. We use the command "**ExpReg**" on a graphing utility to fit an exponential function to a set of data points. This returns an equation of the form, $y = ab^x$

Note that:

- b must be non-negative.
- when $b > 1$, we have an exponential growth model.
- when $0 < b < 1$, we have an exponential decay model.

How To...

Given a set of data, perform exponential regression using a graphing utility.

1. Use the **STAT** then **EDIT** menu to enter given data.

   a. Clear any existing data from the lists.
   b. List the input values in the L1 column.
   c. List the output values in the L2 column.

2. Graph and observe a scatter plot of the data using the **STATPLOT** feature.

   a. Use **ZOOM** [9] to adjust axes to fit the data.
   b. Verify the data follow an exponential pattern.

3. Find the equation that models the data.

   a. Select "**ExpReg**" from the **STAT** then **CALC** menu.
   b. Use the values returned for a and b to record the model, $y = ab^x$.

4. Graph the model in the same window as the scatterplot to verify it is a good fit for the data.

Example 1   **Using Exponential Regression to Fit a Model to Data**

In 2007, a university study was published investigating the crash risk of alcohol impaired driving. Data from 2,871 crashes were used to measure the association of a person's blood alcohol level (BAC) with the risk of being in an accident.

Table 1 shows results from the study[24]. The *relative risk* is a measure of how many times more likely a person is to crash. So, for example, a person with a BAC of 0.09 is 3.54 times as likely to crash as a person who has not been drinking alcohol.

BAC	0	0.01	0.03	0.05	0.07	0.09
Relative Risk of Crashing	1	1.03	1.06	1.38	2.09	3.54
BAC	0.11	0.13	0.15	0.17	0.19	0.21
Relative Risk of Crashing	6.41	12.6	22.1	39.05	65.32	99.78

Table 1

a. Let x represent the BAC level, and let y represent the corresponding relative risk. Use exponential regression to fit a model to these data.

b. After 6 drinks, a person weighing 160 pounds will have a BAC of about 0.16. How many times more likely is a person with this weight to crash if they drive after having a 6-pack of beer? Round to the nearest hundredth.

24 Source: *Indiana University Center for Studies of Law in Action*, 2007

Solution

a. Using the **STAT** then **EDIT** menu on a graphing utility, list the **BAC** values in L1 and the relative risk values in L2. Then use the **STATPLOT** feature to verify that the scatterplot follows the exponential pattern shown in **Figure 1**:

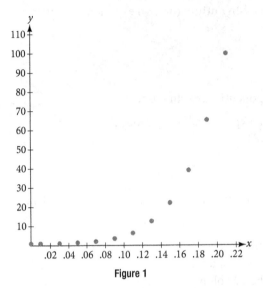

Figure 1

Use the "**ExpReg**" command from the **STAT** then **CALC** menu to obtain the exponential model,

$$y = 0.58304829(2.20720213\text{E}10)^x$$

Converting from scientific notation, we have:

$$y = 0.58304829(22,072,021,300)^x$$

Notice that $r^2 \approx 0.97$ which indicates the model is a good fit to the data. To see this, graph the model in the same window as the scatterplot to verify it is a good fit as shown in **Figure 2**:

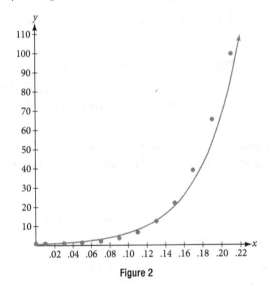

Figure 2

b. Use the model to estimate the risk associated with a BAC of 0.16. Substitute 0.16 for x in the model and solve for y.

$$y = 0.58304829(22,072,021,300)^x \qquad \text{Use the regression model found in part (a).}$$

$$= 0.58304829(22,072,021,300)^{0.16} \qquad \text{Substitute 0.16 for } x.$$

$$\approx 26.35 \qquad\qquad\qquad\qquad\qquad\qquad \text{Round to the nearest hundredth.}$$

If a 160-pound person drives after having 6 drinks, he or she is about 26.35 times more likely to crash than if driving while sober.

Try It #1

Table 2 shows a recent graduate's credit card balance each month after graduation.

Month	1	2	3	4	5	6	7	8
Debt ($)	620.00	761.88	899.80	1039.93	1270.63	1589.04	1851.31	2154.92

Table 2

a. Use exponential regression to fit a model to these data.

b. If spending continues at this rate, what will the graduate's credit card debt be one year after graduating?

Q & A...

Is it reasonable to assume that an exponential regression model will represent a situation indefinitely?

No. Remember that models are formed by real-world data gathered for regression. It is usually reasonable to make estimates within the interval of original observation (interpolation). However, when a model is used to make predictions, it is important to use reasoning skills to determine whether the model makes sense for inputs far beyond the original observation interval (extrapolation).

Building a Logarithmic Model from Data

Just as with exponential functions, there are many real-world applications for logarithmic functions: intensity of sound, pH levels of solutions, yields of chemical reactions, production of goods, and growth of infants. As with exponential models, data modeled by logarithmic functions are either always increasing or always decreasing as time moves forward. Again, it is the *way* they increase or decrease that helps us determine whether a logarithmic model is best.

Recall that logarithmic functions increase or decrease rapidly at first, but then steadily slow as time moves on. By reflecting on the characteristics we've already learned about this function, we can better analyze real world situations that reflect this type of growth or decay. When performing logarithmic regression analysis, we use the form of the logarithmic function most commonly used on graphing utilities, $y = a + b\ln(x)$. For this function

- All input values, x, must be greater than zero.
- The point $(1, a)$ is on the graph of the model.
- If $b > 0$, the model is increasing. Growth increases rapidly at first and then steadily slows over time.
- If $b < 0$, the model is decreasing. Decay occurs rapidly at first and then steadily slows over time.

---

logarithmic regression

Logarithmic regression is used to model situations where growth or decay accelerates rapidly at first and then slows over time. We use the command "LnReg" on a graphing utility to fit a logarithmic function to a set of data points. This returns an equation of the form,

$$y = a + b\ln(x)$$

Note that:

- all input values, x, must be non-negative.
- when $b > 0$, the model is increasing.
- when $b < 0$, the model is decreasing.

How To...

Given a set of data, perform logarithmic regression using a graphing utility.

1. Use the **STAT** then **EDIT** menu to enter given data.

    a. Clear any existing data from the lists.

    b. List the input values in the L1 column.

c. List the output values in the L2 column.

2. Graph and observe a scatter plot of the data using the **STATPLOT** feature.
   a. Use **ZOOM** [9] to adjust axes to fit the data.
   b. Verify the data follow a logarithmic pattern.

3. Find the equation that models the data.
   a. Select "**LnReg**" from the **STAT** then **CALC** menu.
   b. Use the values returned for a and b to record the model, $y = a + b\ln(x)$.

4. Graph the model in the same window as the scatterplot to verify it is a good fit for the data.

Example 2   **Using Logarithmic Regression to Fit a Model to Data**

Due to advances in medicine and higher standards of living, life expectancy has been increasing in most developed countries since the beginning of the 20th century.

Table 3 shows the average life expectancies, in years, of Americans from 1900–2010[25].

Year	1900	1910	1920	1930	1940	1950
Life Expectancy (Years)	47.3	50.0	54.1	59.7	62.9	68.2

Year	1960	1970	1980	1990	2000	2010
Life Expectancy (Years)	69.7	70.8	73.7	75.4	76.8	78.7

Table 3

a. Let x represent time in decades starting with $x = 1$ for the year 1900, $x = 2$ for the year 1910, and so on. Let y represent the corresponding life expectancy. Use logarithmic regression to fit a model to these data.

b. Use the model to predict the average American life expectancy for the year 2030.

Solution

a. Using the **STAT** then **EDIT** menu on a graphing utility, list the years using values 1–12 in L1 and the corresponding life expectancy in L2. Then use the **STATPLOT** feature to verify that the scatterplot follows a logarithmic pattern as shown in **Figure 3**:

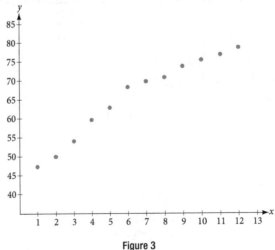

Figure 3

Use the "**LnReg**" command from the **STAT** then **CALC** menu to obtain the logarithmic model,

$$y = 42.52722583 + 13.85752327\ln(x)$$

Next, graph the model in the same window as the scatterplot to verify it is a good fit as shown in **Figure 4**:

25 Source: *Center for Disease Control and Prevention*, 2013

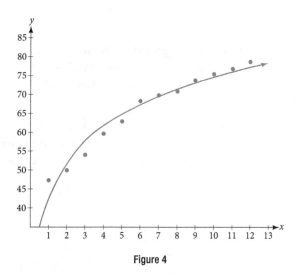

Figure 4

b. To predict the life expectancy of an American in the year 2030, substitute $x = 14$ for the in the model and solve for y:

$$y = 42.52722583 + 13.85752327\ln(x) \quad \text{Use the regression model found in part (a).}$$

$$= 42.52722583 + 13.85752327\ln(14) \quad \text{Substitute 14 for } x.$$

$$\approx 79.1 \quad \text{Round to the nearest tenth}$$

If life expectancy continues to increase at this pace, the average life expectancy of an American will be 79.1 by the year 2030.

Try It #2

Sales of a video game released in the year 2000 took off at first, but then steadily slowed as time moved on. **Table 4** shows the number of games sold, in thousands, from the years 2000–2010.

Year	Number Sold (Thousands)
2000	142
2001	149
2002	154
2003	155
2004	159
2005	161
2006	163
2007	164
2008	164
2009	166
2010	167

Table 4

a. Let x represent time in years starting with $x = 1$ for the year 2000. Let y represent the number of games sold in thousands. Use logarithmic regression to fit a model to these data.

b. If games continue to sell at this rate, how fmany games will sell in 2015? Round to the nearest thousand.

Building a Logistic Model from Data

Like exponential and logarithmic growth, logistic growth increases over time. One of the most notable differences with logistic growth models is that, at a certain point, growth steadily slows and the function approaches an upper bound, or *limiting value*. Because of this, logistic regression is best for modeling phenomena where there are limits in expansion, such as availability of living space or nutrients.

It is worth pointing out that logistic functions actually model resource-limited exponential growth. There are many examples of this type of growth in real-world situations, including population growth and spread of disease, rumors, and even stains in fabric. When performing logistic regression analysis, we use the form most commonly used on graphing utilities:

$$y = \frac{c}{1 + ae^{-bx}}$$

Recall that:

- $\dfrac{c}{1+a}$ is the initial value of the model.
- when $b > 0$, the model increases rapidly at first until it reaches its point of maximum growth rate, $\left(\dfrac{\ln(a)}{b}, \dfrac{c}{2} \right)$. At that point, growth steadily slows and the function becomes asymptotic to the upper bound $y = c$.
- c is the limiting value, sometimes called the *carrying capacity*, of the model.

---

logistic regression

Logistic regression is used to model situations where growth accelerates rapidly at first and then steadily slows to an upper limit. We use the command "Logistic" on a graphing utility to fit a logistic function to a set of data points. This returns an equation of the form

$$y = \frac{c}{1 + ae^{-bx}}$$

Note that

- The initial value of the model is $\dfrac{c}{1+a}$.
- Output values for the model grow closer and closer to $y = c$ as time increases.

How To...

Given a set of data, perform logistic regression using a graphing utility.

1. Use the **STAT** then **EDIT** menu to enter given data.

   a. Clear any existing data from the lists.
   b. List the input values in the L1 column.
   c. List the output values in the L2 column.

2. Graph and observe a scatter plot of the data using the **STATPLOT** feature.

   a. Use **ZOOM** [9] to adjust axes to fit the data.
   b. Verify the data follow a logistic pattern.

3. Find the equation that models the data.

   a. Select "**Logistic**" from the **STAT** then **CALC** menu.
   b. Use the values returned for a, b, and c to record the model, $y = \dfrac{c}{1 + ae^{-bx}}$.

4. Graph the model in the same window as the scatterplot to verify it is a good fit for the data.

Example 3   **Using Logistic Regression to Fit a Model to Data**

Mobile telephone service has increased rapidly in America since the mid 1990s. Today, almost all residents have cellular service. **Table 5** shows the percentage of Americans with cellular service between the years 1995 and 2012[26].

26 Source: *The World Bankn*, 2013

Year	Americans with Cellular Service (%)	Year	Americans with Cellular Service (%)
1995	12.69	2004	62.852
1996	16.35	2005	68.63
1997	20.29	2006	76.64
1998	25.08	2007	82.47
1999	30.81	2008	85.68
2000	38.75	2009	89.14
2001	45.00	2010	91.86
2002	49.16	2011	95.28
2003	55.15	2012	98.17

Table 5

a. Let x represent time in years starting with $x = 0$ for the year 1995. Let y represent the corresponding percentage of residents with cellular service. Use logistic regression to fit a model to these data.

b. Use the model to calculate the percentage of Americans with cell service in the year 2013. Round to the nearest tenth of a percent.

c. Discuss the value returned for the upper limit c. What does this tell you about the model? What would the limiting value be if the model were exact?

Solution

a. Using the **STAT** then **EDIT** menu on a graphing utility, list the years using values 0–15 in L1 and the corresponding percentage in L2. Then use the **STATPLOT** feature to verify that the scatterplot follows a logistic pattern as shown in **Figure 5**:

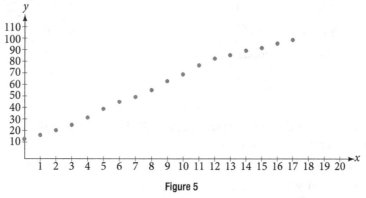

Figure 5

Use the "**Logistic**" command from the **STAT** then **CALC** menu to obtain the logistic model,

$$y = \frac{105.7379526}{1 + 6.88328979e^{-0.2595440013x}}$$

Next, graph the model in the same window as shown in **Figure 6** the scatterplot to verify it is a good fit:

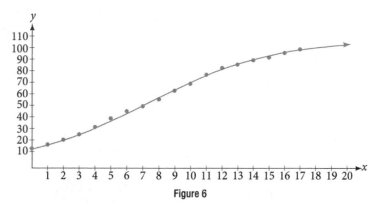

Figure 6

b. To approximate the percentage of Americans with cellular service in the year 2013, substitute $x = 18$ for the in the model and solve for y:

$$y = \frac{105.7379526}{1 + 6.88328979e^{-0.2595440013x}} \qquad \text{Use the regression model found in part (a).}$$

$$= \frac{105.7379526}{1 + 6.88328979e^{-0.2595440013(18)}} \qquad \text{Substitute 18 for } x.$$

$$\approx 99.3\% \qquad \text{Round to the nearest tenth}$$

According to the model, about 99.3% of Americans had cellular service in 2013.

c. The model gives a limiting value of about 105. This means that the maximum possible percentage of Americans with cellular service would be 105%, which is impossible. (How could over 100% of a population have cellular service?) If the model were exact, the limiting value would be $c = 100$ and the model's outputs would get very close to, but never actually reach 100%. After all, there will always be someone out there without cellular service!

Try It #3

Table 6 shows the population, in thousands, of harbor seals in the Wadden Sea over the years 1997 to 2012.

Year	Seal Population (Thousands)	Year	Seal Population (Thousands)
1997	3.493	2005	19.590
1998	5.282	2006	21.955
1999	6.357	2007	22.862
2000	9.201	2008	23.869
2001	11.224	2009	24.243
2002	12.964	2010	24.344
2003	16.226	2011	24.919
2004	18.137	2012	25.108

Table 6

a. Let x represent time in years starting with $x = 0$ for the year 1997. Let y represent the number of seals in thousands. Use logistic regression to fit a model to these data.

b. Use the model to predict the seal population for the year 2020.

c. To the nearest whole number, what is the limiting value of this model?

Access this online resource for additional instruction and practice with exponential function models.

- Exponential Regression on a Calculator (http://openstaxcollege.org/l/pregresscalc)

4.8 SECTION EXERCISES

VERBAL

1. What situations are best modeled by a logistic equation? Give an example, and state a case for why the example is a good fit.

2. What is a carrying capacity? What kind of model has a carrying capacity built into its formula? Why does this make sense?

3. What is regression analysis? Describe the process of performing regression analysis on a graphing utility.

4. What might a scatterplot of data points look like if it were best described by a logarithmic model?

5. What does the *y*-intercept on the graph of a logistic equation correspond to for a population modeled by that equation?

GRAPHICAL

For the following exercises, match the given function of best fit with the appropriate scatterplot in **Figure 7** through **Figure 11**. Answer using the letter beneath the matching graph.

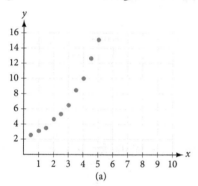

(a)

Figure 7

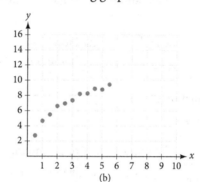

(b)

Figure 8

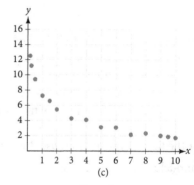

(c)

Figure 9

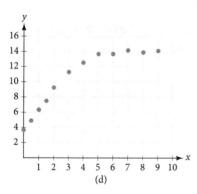

(d)

Figure 10

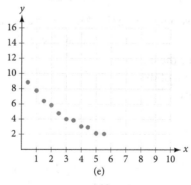

(e)

Figure 11

6. $y = 10.209e^{-0.294x}$

7. $y = 5.598 - 1.912\ln(x)$

8. $y = 2.104(1.479)^x$

9. $y = 4.607 + 2.733\ln(x)$

10. $y = \dfrac{14.005}{1 + 2.79e^{-0.812x}}$

NUMERIC

11. To the nearest whole number, what is the initial value of a population modeled by the logistic equation
$$P(t) = \frac{175}{1 + 6.995e^{-0.68t}}?$$ What is the carrying capacity?

12. Rewrite the exponential model $A(t) = 1550(1.085)^x$ as an equivalent model with base e. Express the exponent to four significant digits.

13. A logarithmic model is given by the equation $h(p) = 67.682 - 5.792\ln(p)$. To the nearest hundredth, for what value of p does $h(p) = 62$?

14. A logistic model is given by the equation $P(t) = \frac{90}{1 + 5e^{-0.42t}}$. To the nearest hundredth, for what value of t does $P(t) = 45$?

15. What is the y-intercept on the graph of the logistic model given in the previous exercise?

TECHNOLOGY

For the following exercises, use this scenario: The population P of a koi pond over x months is modeled by the function $P(x) = \frac{68}{1 + 16e^{-0.28x}}$.

16. Graph the population model to show the population over a span of 3 years.

17. What was the initial population of koi?

18. How many koi will the pond have after one and a half years?

19. How many months will it take before there are 20 koi in the pond?

20. Use the intersect feature to approximate the number of months it will take before the population of the pond reaches half its carrying capacity.

For the following exercises, use this scenario: The population P of an endangered species habitat for wolves is modeled by the function $P(x) = \frac{558}{1 + 54.8e^{-0.462x}}$, where x is given in years.

21. Graph the population model to show the population over a span of 10 years.

22. What was the initial population of wolves transported to the habitat?

23. How many wolves will the habitat have after 3 years?

24. How many years will it take before there are 100 wolves in the habitat?

25. Use the intersect feature to approximate the number of years it will take before the population of the habitat reaches half its carrying capacity.

For the following exercises, refer to **Table 7**.

x	1	2	3	4	5	6
$f(x)$	1125	1495	2310	3294	4650	6361

Table 7

26. Use a graphing calculator to create a scatter diagram of the data.

27. Use the regression feature to find an exponential function that best fits the data in the table.

28. Write the exponential function as an exponential equation with base e.

29. Graph the exponential equation on the scatter diagram.

30. Use the intersect feature to find the value of x for which $f(x) = 4000$.

For the following exercises, refer to **Table 8**.

x	1	2	3	4	5	6
f(x)	555	383	307	210	158	122

Table 8

31. Use a graphing calculator to create a scatter diagram of the data.

32. Use the regression feature to find an exponential function that best fits the data in the table.

33. Write the exponential function as an exponential equation with base e.

34. Graph the exponential equation on the scatter diagram.

35. Use the intersect feature to find the value of x for which $f(x) = 250$.

For the following exercises, refer to **Table 9**.

x	1	2	3	4	5	6
f(x)	5.1	6.3	7.3	7.7	8.1	8.6

Table 9

36. Use a graphing calculator to create a scatter diagram of the data.

37. Use the **LOG**arithm option of the **REG**ression feature to find a logarithmic function of the form $y = a + b\ln(x)$ that best fits the data in the table.

38. Use the logarithmic function to find the value of the function when $x = 10$.

39. Graph the logarithmic equation on the scatter diagram.

40. Use the intersect feature to find the value of x for which $f(x) = 7$.

For the following exercises, refer to **Table 10**.

x	1	2	3	4	5	6	7	8
f(x)	7.5	6	5.2	4.3	3.9	3.4	3.1	2.9

Table 10

41. Use a graphing calculator to create a scatter diagram of the data.

42. Use the **LOG**arithm option of the **REG**ression feature to find a logarithmic function of the form $y = a + b\ln(x)$ that best fits the data in the table.

43. Use the logarithmic function to find the value of the function when $x = 10$.

44. Graph the logarithmic equation on the scatter diagram.

45. Use the intersect feature to find the value of x for which $f(x) = 8$.

For the following exercises, refer to **Table 11**.

x	1	2	3	4	5	6	7	8	9	10
f(x)	8.7	12.3	15.4	18.5	20.7	22.5	23.3	24	24.6	24.8

Table 11

46. Use a graphing calculator to create a scatter diagram of the data.

47. Use the **LOGISTIC** regression option to find a logistic growth model of the form $y = \dfrac{c}{1 + ae^{-bx}}$ that best fits the data in the table.

48. Graph the logistic equation on the scatter diagram.

49. To the nearest whole number, what is the predicted carrying capacity of the model?

50. Use the intersect feature to find the value of x for which the model reaches half its carrying capacity.

For the following exercises, refer to **Table 12**.

x	0	2	4	5	7	8	10	11	15	17
$f(x)$	12	28.6	52.8	70.3	99.9	112.5	125.8	127.9	135.1	135.9

Table 12

51. Use a graphing calculator to create a scatter diagram of the data.

52. Use the **LOGISTIC** regression option to find a logistic growth model of the form $y = \dfrac{c}{1 + ae^{-bx}}$ that best fits the data in the table.

53. Graph the logistic equation on the scatter diagram.

54. To the nearest whole number, what is the predicted carrying capacity of the model?

55. Use the intersect feature to find the value of x for which the model reaches half its carrying capacity.

EXTENSIONS

56. Recall that the general form of a logistic equation for a population is given by $P(t) = \dfrac{c}{1 + ae^{-bt}}$, such that the initial population at time $t = 0$ is $P(0) = P_0$. Show algebraically that
$$\frac{c - P(t)}{P(t)} = \frac{c - P_0}{P_0} e^{-bt}.$$

57. Use a graphing utility to find an exponential regression formula $f(x)$ and a logarithmic regression formula $g(x)$ for the points $(1.5, 1.5)$ and $(8.5, 8.5)$. Round all numbers to 6 decimal places. Graph the points and both formulas along with the line $y = x$ on the same axis. Make a conjecture about the relationship of the regression formulas.

58. Verify the conjecture made in the previous exercise. Round all numbers to six decimal places when necessary.

59. Find the inverse function $f^{-1}(x)$ for the logistic function $f(x) = \dfrac{c}{1 + ae^{-bx}}$. Show all steps.

60. Use the result from the previous exercise to graph the logistic model $P(t) = \dfrac{20}{1 + 4e^{-0.5t}}$ along with its inverse on the same axis. What are the intercepts and asymptotes of each function?

CHAPTER 4 REVIEW

Key Terms

annual percentage rate (APR) the yearly interest rate earned by an investment account, also called *nominal rate*

carrying capacity in a logistic model, the limiting value of the output

change-of-base formula a formula for converting a logarithm with any base to a quotient of logarithms with any other base.

common logarithm the exponent to which 10 must be raised to get x; $\log_{10}(x)$ is written simply as $\log(x)$.

compound interest interest earned on the total balance, not just the principal

doubling time the time it takes for a quantity to double

exponential growth a model that grows by a rate proportional to the amount present

extraneous solution a solution introduced while solving an equation that does not satisfy the conditions of the original equation

half-life the length of time it takes for a substance to exponentially decay to half of its original quantity

logarithm the exponent to which b must be raised to get x; written $y = \log_b(x)$

logistic growth model a function of the form $f(x) = \dfrac{c}{1 + ae^{-bx}}$ where $\dfrac{c}{1 + a}$ is the initial value, c is the carrying capacity, or limiting value, and b is a constant determined by the rate of growth

natural logarithm the exponent to which the number e must be raised to get x; $\log_e(x)$ is written as $\ln(x)$.

Newton's Law of Cooling the scientific formula for temperature as a function of time as an object's temperature is equalized with the ambient temperature

nominal rate the yearly interest rate earned by an investment account, also called *annual percentage rate*

order of magnitude the power of ten, when a number is expressed in scientific notation, with one non-zero digit to the left of the decimal

power rule for logarithms a rule of logarithms that states that the log of a power is equal to the product of the exponent and the log of its base

product rule for logarithms a rule of logarithms that states that the log of a product is equal to a sum of logarithms

quotient rule for logarithms a rule of logarithms that states that the log of a quotient is equal to a difference of logarithms

Key Equations

definition of the exponential function	$f(x) = b^x$, where $b > 0$, $b \neq 1$
definition of exponential growth	$f(x) = ab^x$, where $a > 0$, $b > 0$, $b \neq 1$
compound interest formula	$A(t) = P\left(1 + \dfrac{r}{n}\right)^{nt}$, where $A(t)$ is the account value at time t t is the number of years P is the initial investment, often called the principal r is the annual percentage rate (APR), or nominal rate n is the number of compounding periods in one year
continuous growth formula	$A(t) = ae^{rt}$, where t is the number of unit time periods of growth a is the starting amount (in the continuous compounding formula a is replaced with P, the principal) e is the mathematical constant, $e \approx 2.718282$
General Form for the Translation of the Parent Function $f(x) = b^x$	$f(x) = ab^{x+c} + d$
Definition of the logarithmic function	For $x > 0$, $b > 0$, $b \neq 1$, $y = \log_b(x)$ if and only if $b^y = x$.
Definition of the common logarithm	For $x > 0$, $y = \log(x)$ if and only if $10^y = x$.

Definition of the natural logarithm	For $x > 0$, $y = \ln(x)$ if and only if $e^y = x$.
General Form for the Translation of the Parent Logarithmic Function $f(x) = \log_b(x)$	$f(x) = a\log_b(x + c) + d$
The Product Rule for Logarithms	$\log_b(MN) = \log_b(M) + \log_b(N)$
The Quotient Rule for Logarithms	$\log_b\left(\dfrac{M}{N}\right) = \log_b M - \log_b N$
The Power Rule for Logarithms	$\log_b(M^n) = n\log_b M$
The Change-of-Base Formula	$\log_b M = \dfrac{\log_n M}{\log_n b}$ $n > 0$, $n \neq 1$, $b \neq 1$
One-to-one property for exponential functions	For any algebraic expressions S and T and any positive real number b, where $b^S = b^T$ if and only if $S = T$.
Definition of a logarithm	For any algebraic expression S and positive real numbers b and c, where $b \neq 1$, $\log_b(S) = c$ if and only if $b^c = S$.
One-to-one property for logarithmic functions	For any algebraic expressions S and T and any positive real number b, where $b \neq 1$, $\log_b S = \log_b T$ if and only if $S = T$.
Half-life formula	If $A = A_0 e^{kt}$, $k < 0$, the half-life is $t = -\dfrac{\ln(2)}{k}$. $t = \dfrac{\ln\left(\dfrac{A}{A_0}\right)}{-0.000121}$
Carbon-14 dating	A_0 is the amount of carbon-14 when the plant or animal died, A is the amount of carbon-14 remaining today, t is the age of the fossil in years
Doubling time formula	If $A = A_0 e^{kt}$, $k > 0$, the doubling time is $t = \dfrac{\ln(2)}{k}$
Newton's Law of Cooling	$T(t) = Ae^{kt} + T_s$, where T_s is the ambient temperature, $A = T(0) - T_s$, and k is the continuous rate of cooling.

Key Concepts

4.1 Exponential Functions

- An exponential function is defined as a function with a positive constant other than 1 raised to a variable exponent. See **Example 1**.
- A function is evaluated by solving at a specific value. See **Example 2** and **Example 3**.
- An exponential model can be found when the growth rate and initial value are known. See **Example 4**.
- An exponential model can be found when the two data points from the model are known. See **Example 5**.
- An exponential model can be found using two data points from the graph of the model. See **Example 6**.
- An exponential model can be found using two data points from the graph and a calculator. See **Example 7**.
- The value of an account at any time t can be calculated using the compound interest formula when the principal, annual interest rate, and compounding periods are known. See **Example 8**.
- The initial investment of an account can be found using the compound interest formula when the value of the account, annual interest rate, compounding periods, and life span of the account are known. See **Example 9**.
- The number e is a mathematical constant often used as the base of real world exponential growth and decay models. Its decimal approximation is $e \approx 2.718282$.
- Scientific and graphing calculators have the key $[e^x]$ or $[\exp(x)]$ for calculating powers of e. See **Example 10**.
- Continuous growth or decay models are exponential models that use e as the base. Continuous growth and decay models can be found when the initial value and growth or decay rate are known. See **Example 11** and **Example 12**.

4.2 Graphs of Exponential Functions

- The graph of the function $f(x) = b^x$ has a y-intercept at $(0, 1)$, domain $(-\infty, \infty)$, range $(0, \infty)$, and horizontal asymptote $y = 0$. See **Example 1**.
- If $b > 1$, the function is increasing. The left tail of the graph will approach the asymptote $y = 0$, and the right tail will increase without bound.
- If $0 < b < 1$, the function is decreasing. The left tail of the graph will increase without bound, and the right tail will approach the asymptote $y = 0$.
- The equation $f(x) = b^x + d$ represents a vertical shift of the parent function $f(x) = b^x$.
- The equation $f(x) = b^{x+c}$ represents a horizontal shift of the parent function $f(x) = b^x$. See **Example 2**.
- Approximate solutions of the equation $f(x) = b^{x+c} + d$ can be found using a graphing calculator. See **Example 3**.
- The equation $f(x) = ab^x$, where $a > 0$, represents a vertical stretch if $|a| > 1$ or compression if $0 < |a| < 1$ of the parent function $f(x) = b^x$. See **Example 4**.
- When the parent function $f(x) = b^x$ is multiplied by -1, the result, $f(x) = -b^x$, is a reflection about the x-axis. When the input is multiplied by -1, the result, $f(x) = b^{-x}$, is a reflection about the y-axis. See **Example 5**.
- All translations of the exponential function can be summarized by the general equation $f(x) = ab^{x+c} + d$. See **Table 3**.
- Using the general equation $f(x) = ab^{x+c} + d$, we can write the equation of a function given its description. See **Example 6**.

4.3 Logarithmic Functions

- The inverse of an exponential function is a logarithmic function, and the inverse of a logarithmic function is an exponential function.
- Logarithmic equations can be written in an equivalent exponential form, using the definition of a logarithm. See **Example 1**.
- Exponential equations can be written in their equivalent logarithmic form using the definition of a logarithm See **Example 2**.
- Logarithmic functions with base b can be evaluated mentally using previous knowledge of powers of b. See **Example 3** and **Example 4**.
- Common logarithms can be evaluated mentally using previous knowledge of powers of 10. See **Example 5**.
- When common logarithms cannot be evaluated mentally, a calculator can be used. See **Example 6**.
- Real-world exponential problems with base 10 can be rewritten as a common logarithm and then evaluated using a calculator. See **Example 7**.
- Natural logarithms can be evaluated using a calculator **Example 8**.

4.4 Graphs of Logarithmic Functions

- To find the domain of a logarithmic function, set up an inequality showing the argument greater than zero, and solve for x. See **Example 1** and **Example 2**
- The graph of the parent function $f(x) = \log_b(x)$ has an x-intercept at $(1, 0)$, domain $(0, \infty)$, range $(-\infty, \infty)$, vertical asymptote $x = 0$, and
  - if $b > 1$, the function is increasing.
  - if $0 < b < 1$, the function is decreasing.

  See **Example 3**.
- The equation $f(x) = \log_b(x + c)$ shifts the parent function $y = \log_b(x)$ horizontally
  - left c units if $c > 0$.
  - right c units if $c < 0$.

  See **Example 4**.
- The equation $f(x) = \log_b(x) + d$ shifts the parent function $y = \log_b(x)$ vertically
  - up d units if $d > 0$.
  - down d units if $d < 0$.

  See **Example 5**.

- For any constant $a > 0$, the equation $f(x) = a\log_b(x)$
  - stretches the parent function $y = \log_b(x)$ vertically by a factor of a if $|a| > 1$.
  - compresses the parent function $y = \log_b(x)$ vertically by a factor of a if $|a| < 1$.

  See **Example 6** and **Example 7**.

- When the parent function $y = \log_b(x)$ is multiplied by -1, the result is a reflection about the x-axis. When the input is multiplied by -1, the result is a reflection about the y-axis.
  - The equation $f(x) = -\log_b(x)$ represents a reflection of the parent function about the x-axis.
- The equation $f(x) = \log_b(-x)$ represents a reflection of the parent function about the y-axis.

  See **Example 8**.

  - A graphing calculator may be used to approximate solutions to some logarithmic equations See **Example 9**.

- All translations of the logarithmic function can be summarized by the general equation $f(x) = a\log_b(x + c) + d$. See **Table 4**.

- Given an equation with the general form $f(x) = a\log_b(x + c) + d$, we can identify the vertical asymptote $x = -c$ for the transformation. See **Example 10**.

- Using the general equation $f(x) = a\log_b(x + c) + d$, we can write the equation of a logarithmic function given its graph. See **Example 11**.

4.5 Logarithmic Properties

- We can use the product rule of logarithms to rewrite the log of a product as a sum of logarithms. See **Example 1**.

- We can use the quotient rule of logarithms to rewrite the log of a quotient as a difference of logarithms. See **Example 2**.

- We can use the power rule for logarithms to rewrite the log of a power as the product of the exponent and the log of its base. See **Example 3**, **Example 4**, and **Example 5**.

- We can use the product rule, the quotient rule, and the power rule together to combine or expand a logarithm with a complex input. See **Example 6**, **Example 7**, and **Example 8**.

- The rules of logarithms can also be used to condense sums, differences, and products with the same base as a single logarithm. See **Example 9**, **Example 10**, **Example 11**, and **Example 12**.

- We can convert a logarithm with any base to a quotient of logarithms with any other base using the change-of-base formula. See **Example 13**.

- The change-of-base formula is often used to rewrite a logarithm with a base other than 10 and e as the quotient of natural or common logs. That way a calculator can be used to evaluate. See **Example 14**.

4.6 Exponential and Logarithmic Equations

- We can solve many exponential equations by using the rules of exponents to rewrite each side as a power with the same base. Then we use the fact that exponential functions are one-to-one to set the exponents equal to one another and solve for the unknown.

- When we are given an exponential equation where the bases are explicitly shown as being equal, set the exponents equal to one another and solve for the unknown. See **Example 1**.

- When we are given an exponential equation where the bases are *not* explicitly shown as being equal, rewrite each side of the equation as powers of the same base, then set the exponents equal to one another and solve for the unknown. See **Example 2**, **Example 3**, and **Example 4**.

- When an exponential equation cannot be rewritten with a common base, solve by taking the logarithm of each side. See **Example 5**.

- We can solve exponential equations with base e, by applying the natural logarithm of both sides because exponential and logarithmic functions are inverses of each other. See **Example 6** and **Example 7**.

- After solving an exponential equation, check each solution in the original equation to find and eliminate any extraneous solutions. See **Example 8**.

- When given an equation of the form $\log_b(S) = c$, where S is an algebraic expression, we can use the definition of a logarithm to rewrite the equation as the equivalent exponential equation $b^c = S$, and solve for the unknown. See **Example 9** and **Example 10**.

- We can also use graphing to solve equations with the form $\log_b(S) = c$. We graph both equations $y = \log_b(S)$ and $y = c$ on the same coordinate plane and identify the solution as the x-value of the intersecting point. See **Example 11**.

- When given an equation of the form $\log_b S = \log_b T$, where S and T are algebraic expressions, we can use the one-to-one property of logarithms to solve the equation $S = T$ for the unknown. See **Example 12**.

- Combining the skills learned in this and previous sections, we can solve equations that model real world situations, whether the unknown is in an exponent or in the argument of a logarithm. See **Example 13**.

4.7 Exponential and Logarithmic Models

- The basic exponential function is $f(x) = ab^x$. If $b > 1$, we have exponential growth; if $0 < b < 1$, we have exponential decay.

- We can also write this formula in terms of continuous growth as $A = A_0 e^{kx}$, where A_0 is the starting value. If A_0 is positive, then we have exponential growth when $k > 0$ and exponential decay when $k < 0$. See **Example 1**.

- In general, we solve problems involving exponential growth or decay in two steps. First, we set up a model and use the model to find the parameters. Then we use the formula with these parameters to predict growth and decay. See **Example 2**.

- We can find the age, t, of an organic artifact by measuring the amount, k, of carbon-14 remaining in the artifact and using the formula $t = \dfrac{\ln(k)}{-0.000121}$ to solve for t. See **Example 3**.

- Given a substance's doubling time or half-life we can find a function that represents its exponential growth or decay. See **Example 4**.

- We can use Newton's Law of Cooling to find how long it will take for a cooling object to reach a desired temperature, or to find what temperature an object will be after a given time. See **Example 5**.

- We can use logistic growth functions to model real-world situations where the rate of growth changes over time, such as population growth, spread of disease, and spread of rumors. See **Example 6**.

- We can use real-world data gathered over time to observe trends. Knowledge of linear, exponential, logarithmic, and logistic graphs help us to develop models that best fit our data. See **Example 7**.

- Any exponential function with the form $y = ab^x$ can be rewritten as an equivalent exponential function with the form $y = A_0 e^{kx}$ where $k = \ln b$. See **Example 8**.

4.8 Fitting Exponential Models to Data

- Exponential regression is used to model situations where growth begins slowly and then accelerates rapidly without bound, or where decay begins rapidly and then slows down to get closer and closer to zero.

- We use the command "ExpReg" on a graphing utility to fit function of the form $y = ab^x$ to a set of data points. See **Example 1**.

- Logarithmic regression is used to model situations where growth or decay accelerates rapidly at first and then slows over time.

- We use the command "LnReg" on a graphing utility to fit a function of the form $y = a + b\ln(x)$ to a set of data points. See **Example 2**.

- Logistic regression is used to model situations where growth accelerates rapidly at first and then steadily slows as the function approaches an upper limit.

- We use the command "Logistic" on a graphing utility to fit a function of the form $y = \dfrac{c}{1 + ae^{-bx}}$ to a set of data points. See **Example 3**.

CHAPTER 4 REVIEW EXERCISES

EXPONENTIAL FUNCTIONS

1. Determine whether the function $y = 156(0.825)^t$ represents exponential growth, exponential decay, or neither. Explain

2. The population of a herd of deer is represented by the function $A(t) = 205(1.13)^t$, where t is given in years. To the nearest whole number, what will the herd population be after 6 years?

3. Find an exponential equation that passes through the points $(2, 2.25)$ and $(5, 60.75)$.

4. Determine whether **Table 1** could represent a function that is linear, exponential, or neither. If it appears to be exponential, find a function that passes through the points.

x	1	2	3	4
$f(x)$	3	0.9	0.27	0.081

Table 1

5. A retirement account is opened with an initial deposit of $8,500 and earns 8.12% interest compounded monthly. What will the account be worth in 20 years?

6. Hsu-Mei wants to save $5,000 for a down payment on a car. To the nearest dollar, how much will she need to invest in an account now with 7.5% APR, compounded daily, in order to reach her goal in 3 years?

7. Does the equation $y = 2.294e^{-0.654t}$ represent continuous growth, continuous decay, or neither? Explain.

8. Suppose an investment account is opened with an initial deposit of $10,500 earning 6.25% interest, compounded continuously. How much will the account be worth after 25 years?

GRAPHS OF EXPONENTIAL FUNCTIONS

9. Graph the function $f(x) = 3.5(2)^x$. State the domain and range and give the y-intercept.

10. Graph the function $f(x) = 4\left(\dfrac{1}{8}\right)^x$ and its reflection about the y-axis on the same axes, and give the y-intercept.

11. The graph of $f(x) = 6.5^x$ is reflected about the y-axis and stretched vertically by a factor of 7. What is the equation of the new function, $g(x)$? State its y-intercept, domain, and range.

12. The graph here shows transformations of the graph of $f(x) = 2^x$. What is the equation for the transformation?

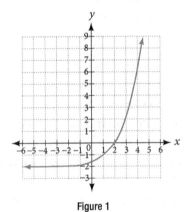

Figure 1

LOGARITHMIC FUNCTIONS

13. Rewrite $\log_{17}(4913) = x$ as an equivalent exponential equation.

14. Rewrite $\ln(s) = t$ as an equivalent exponential equation.

15. Rewrite $a^{-\frac{2}{5}} = b$ as an equivalent logarithmic equation.

16. Rewrite $e^{-3.5} = h$ as an equivalent logarithmic equation.

17. Solve for $x \log_{64}(x) = \left(\dfrac{1}{3}\right)$ to exponential form.

18. Evaluate $\log_5\left(\dfrac{1}{125}\right)$ without using a calculator.

19. Evaluate $\log(0.000001)$ without using a calculator.

20. Evaluate $\log(4.005)$ using a calculator. Round to the nearest thousandth.

21. Evaluate $\ln(e^{-0.8648})$ without using a calculator.

22. Evaluate $\ln(\sqrt[3]{18})$ using a calculator. Round to the nearest thousandth.

GRAPHS OF LOGARITHMIC FUNCTIONS

23. Graph the function $g(x) = \log(7x + 21) - 4$.

24. Graph the function $h(x) = 2\ln(9 - 3x) + 1$.

25. State the domain, vertical asymptote, and end behavior of the function $g(x) = \ln(4x + 20) - 17$.

LOGARITHMIC PROPERTIES

26. Rewrite $\ln(7r \cdot 11st)$ in expanded form.

27. Rewrite $\log_8(x) + \log_8(5) + \log_8(y) + \log_8(13)$ in compact form.

28. Rewrite $\log_m\left(\dfrac{67}{83}\right)$ in expanded form.

29. Rewrite $\ln(z) - \ln(x) - \ln(y)$ in compact form.

30. Rewrite $\ln\left(\dfrac{1}{x^5}\right)$ as a product.

31. Rewrite $-\log_y\left(\dfrac{1}{12}\right)$ as a single logarithm.

32. Use properties of logarithms to expand $\log\left(\dfrac{r^2 s^{11}}{t^{14}}\right)$.

33. Use properties of logarithms to expand
$$\ln\left(2b\sqrt{\dfrac{b+1}{b-1}}\right).$$

34. Condense the expression $5\ln(b) + \ln(c) + \dfrac{\ln(4-a)}{2}$ to a single logarithm.

35. Condense the expression $3\log_7 v + 6\log_7 w - \dfrac{\log_7 u}{3}$ to a single logarithm.

36. Rewrite $\log_3(12.75)$ to base e.

37. Rewrite $5^{12x-17} = 125$ as a logarithm. Then apply the change of base formula to solve for x using the common log. Round to the nearest thousandth.

EXPONENTIAL AND LOGARITHMIC EQUATIONS

38. Solve $216^{3x} \cdot 216^x = 36^{3x+2}$ by rewriting each side with a common base.

39. Solve $\dfrac{125}{\left(\dfrac{1}{625}\right)^{-x-3}} = 5^3$ by rewriting each side with a common base.

40. Use logarithms to find the exact solution for $7 \cdot 17^{-9x} - 7 = 49$. If there is no solution, write *no solution*.

41. Use logarithms to find the exact solution for $3e^{6n-2} + 1 = -60$. If there is no solution, write *no solution*.

42. Find the exact solution for $5e^{3x} - 4 = 6$. If there is no solution, write *no solution*.

43. Find the exact solution for $2e^{5x-2} - 9 = -56$. If there is no solution, write *no solution*.

44. Find the exact solution for $5^{2x-3} = 7^{x+1}$. If there is no solution, write *no solution*.

45. Find the exact solution for $e^{2x} - e^x - 110 = 0$. If there is no solution, write *no solution*.

46. Use the definition of a logarithm to solve. $-5\log_7(10n) = 5$.

47. Use the definition of a logarithm to find the exact solution for $9 + 6\ln(a + 3) = 33$.

48. Use the one-to-one property of logarithms to find an exact solution for $\log_8(7) + \log_8(-4x) = \log_8(5)$. If there is no solution, write *no solution*.

49. Use the one-to-one property of logarithms to find an exact solution for $\ln(5) + \ln(5x^2 - 5) = \ln(56)$. If there is no solution, write *no solution*.

50. The formula for measuring sound intensity in decibels D is defined by the equation $D = 10\log\left(\dfrac{I}{I_0}\right)$, where I is the intensity of the sound in watts per square meter and $I_0 = 10^{-12}$ is the lowest level of sound that the average person can hear. How many decibels are emitted from a large orchestra with a sound intensity of $6.3 \cdot 10^{-3}$ watts per square meter?

51. The population of a city is modeled by the equation $P(t) = 256,114e^{0.25t}$ where t is measured in years. If the city continues to grow at this rate, how many years will it take for the population to reach one million?

52. Find the inverse function f^{-1} for the exponential function $f(x) = 2 \cdot e^{x+1} - 5$.

53. Find the inverse function f^{-1} for the logarithmic function $f(x) = 0.25 \cdot \log_2(x^3 + 1)$.

EXPONENTIAL AND LOGARITHMIC MODELS

For the following exercises, use this scenario: A doctor prescribes 300 milligrams of a therapeutic drug that decays by about 17% each hour.

54. To the nearest minute, what is the half-life of the drug?

55. Write an exponential model representing the amount of the drug remaining in the patient's system after t hours. Then use the formula to find the amount of the drug that would remain in the patient's system after 24 hours. Round to the nearest hundredth of a gram.

For the following exercises, use this scenario: A soup with an internal temperature of 350° Fahrenheit was taken off the stove to cool in a 71°F room. After fifteen minutes, the internal temperature of the soup was 175°F.

56. Use Newton's Law of Cooling to write a formula that models this situation.

57. How many minutes will it take the soup to cool to 85°F?

For the following exercises, use this scenario: The equation $N(t) = \dfrac{1200}{1 + 199e^{-0.625t}}$ models the number of people in a school who have heard a rumor after t days.

58. How many people started the rumor?

59. To the nearest tenth, how many days will it be before the rumor spreads to half the carrying capacity?

60. What is the carrying capacity?

For the following exercises, enter the data from each table into a graphing calculator and graph the resulting scatter plots. Determine whether the data from the table would likely represent a function that is linear, exponential, or logarithmic.

61.

x	1	2	3	4	5	6	7	8	9	10
$f(x)$	3.05	4.42	6.4	9.28	13.46	19.52	28.3	41.04	59.5	86.28

62.

x	0.5	1	3	5	7	10	12	13	15	17	20
$f(x)$	18.05	17	15.33	14.55	14.04	13.5	13.22	13.1	12.88	12.69	12.45

63. Find a formula for an exponential equation that goes through the points $(-2, 100)$ and $(0, 4)$. Then express the formula as an equivalent equation with base e.

FITTING EXPONENTIAL MODELS TO DATA

64. What is the carrying capacity for a population modeled by the logistic equation $P(t) = \dfrac{250,000}{1 + 499e^{-0.45t}}$? What is the initial population for the model?

65. The population of a culture of bacteria is modeled by the logistic equation $P(t) = \dfrac{14,250}{1 + 29e^{-0.62t}}$, where t is in days. To the nearest tenth, how many days will it take the culture to reach 75% of its carrying capacity?

For the following exercises, use a graphing utility to create a scatter diagram of the data given in the table. Observe the shape of the scatter diagram to determine whether the data is best described by an exponential, logarithmic, or logistic model. Then use the appropriate regression feature to find an equation that models the data. When necessary, round values to five decimal places.

66.

x	1	2	3	4	5	6	7	8	9	10
$f(x)$	409.4	260.7	170.4	110.6	74	44.7	32.4	19.5	12.7	8.1

67.

x	0.15	0.25	0.5	0.75	1	1.5	2	2.25	2.75	3	3.5
$f(x)$	36.21	28.88	24.39	18.28	16.5	12.99	9.91	8.57	7.23	5.99	4.81

68.

x	0	2	4	5	7	8	10	11	15	17
$f(x)$	9	22.6	44.2	62.1	96.9	113.4	133.4	137.6	148.4	149.3

CHAPTER 4 PRACTICE TEST

1. The population of a pod of bottlenose dolphins is modeled by the function $A(t) = 8(1.17)^t$, where t is given in years. To the nearest whole number, what will the pod population be after 3 years?

2. Find an exponential equation that passes through the points $(0, 4)$ and $(2, 9)$.

3. Drew wants to save \$2,500 to go to the next World Cup. To the nearest dollar, how much will he need to invest in an account now with 6.25% APR, compounding daily, in order to reach his goal in 4 years?

4. An investment account was opened with an initial deposit of \$9,600 and earns 7.4% interest, compounded continuously. How much will the account be worth after 15 years?

5. Graph the function $f(x) = 5(0.5)^{-x}$ and its reflection across the y-axis on the same axes, and give the y-intercept.

6. The graph below shows transformations of the graph of $f(x) = \left(\dfrac{1}{2}\right)^x$. What is the equation for the transformation?

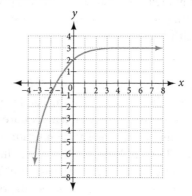

7. Rewrite $\log_{8.5}(614.125) = a$ as an equivalent exponential equation.

8. Rewrite $e^{\frac{1}{2}} = m$ as an equivalent logarithmic equation.

9. Solve for x by converting the logarithmic equation $\log_{\frac{1}{7}}(x) = 2$ to exponential form.

10. Evaluate $\log(10,000,000)$ without using a calculator.

11. Evaluate $\ln(0.716)$ using a calculator. Round to the nearest thousandth.

12. Graph the function $g(x) = \log(12 - 6x) + 3$.

13. State the domain, vertical asymptote, and end behavior of the function $f(x) = \log_5(39 - 13x) + 7$.

14. Rewrite $\log(17a \cdot 2b)$ as a sum.

15. Rewrite $\log_t(96) - \log_t(8)$ in compact form.

16. Rewrite $\log_8\left(a^{\frac{1}{b}}\right)$ as a product.

17. Use properties of logarithm to expand $\ln\left(y^3 z^2 \cdot \sqrt[3]{x - 4}\right)$.

18. Condense the expression
$4\ln(c) + \ln(d) + \dfrac{\ln(a)}{3} + \dfrac{\ln(b + 3)}{3}$ to a single logarithm.

19. Rewrite $16^{3x - 5} = 1000$ as a logarithm. Then apply the change of base formula to solve for x using the natural log. Round to the nearest thousandth.

20. Solve $\left(\dfrac{1}{81}\right)^x \cdot \dfrac{1}{243} = \left(\dfrac{1}{9}\right)^{-3x - 1}$ by rewriting each side with a common base.

21. Use logarithms to find the exact solution for $-9e^{10a - 8} - 5 = -41$. If there is no solution, write *no solution*.

22. Find the exact solution for $10e^{4x + 2} + 5 = 56$. If there is no solution, write *no solution*.

23. Find the exact solution for $-5e^{-4x - 1} - 4 = 64$. If there is no solution, write *no solution*.

24. Find the exact solution for $2^{x - 3} = 6^{2x - 1}$. If there is no solution, write *no solution*.

25. Find the exact solution for $e^{2x} - e^x - 72 = 0$. If there is no solution, write *no solution*.

26. Use the definition of a logarithm to find the exact solution for $4\log(2n) - 7 = -11$.

27. Use the one-to-one property of logarithms to find an exact solution for $\log(4x^2 - 10) + \log(3) = \log(51)$ If there is no solution, write *no solution*.

28. The formula for measuring sound intensity in decibels D is defined by the equation

$$D = 10\log\left(\frac{I}{I_0}\right)$$

where I is the intensity of the sound in watts per square meter and $I_0 = 10^{-12}$ is the lowest level of sound that the average person can hear. How many decibels are emitted from a rock concert with a sound intensity of $4.7 \cdot 10^{-1}$ watts per square meter?

29. A radiation safety officer is working with 112 grams of a radioactive substance. After 17 days, the sample has decayed to 80 grams. Rounding to five significant digits, write an exponential equation representing this situation. To the nearest day, what is the half-life of this substance?

30. Write the formula found in the previous exercise as an equivalent equation with base e. Express the exponent to five significant digits.

31. A bottle of soda with a temperature of 71° Fahrenheit was taken off a shelf and placed in a refrigerator with an internal temperature of 35° F. After ten minutes, the internal temperature of the soda was 63° F. Use Newton's Law of Cooling to write a formula that models this situation. To the nearest degree, what will the temperature of the soda be after one hour?

32. The population of a wildlife habitat is modeled by the equation $P(t) = \dfrac{360}{1 + 6.2e^{-0.35t}}$, where t is given in years. How many animals were originally transported to the habitat? How many years will it take before the habitat reaches half its capacity?

33. Enter the data from **Table 2** into a graphing calculator and graph the resulting scatter plot. Determine whether the data from the table would likely represent a function that is linear, exponential, or logarithmic.

x	1	2	3	4	5	6	7	8	9	10
$f(x)$	3	8.55	11.79	14.09	15.88	17.33	18.57	19.64	20.58	21.42

Table 2

34. The population of a lake of fish is modeled by the logistic equation $P(t) = \dfrac{16,120}{1 + 25e^{-0.75t}}$, where t is time in years. To the nearest hundredth, how many years will it take the lake to reach 80% of its carrying capacity?

For the following exercises, use a graphing utility to create a scatter diagram of the data given in the table. Observe the shape of the scatter diagram to determine whether the data is best described by an exponential, logarithmic, or logistic model. Then use the appropriate regression feature to find an equation that models the data. When necessary, round values to five decimal places.

35.

x	1	2	3	4	5	6	7	8	9	10
$f(x)$	20	21.6	29.2	36.4	46.6	55.7	72.6	87.1	107.2	138.1

36.

x	3	4	5	6	7	8	9	10	11	12	13
$f(x)$	13.98	17.84	20.01	22.7	24.1	26.15	27.37	28.38	29.97	31.07	31.43

37.

x	0	0.5	1	1.5	2	3	4	5	6	7	8
$f(x)$	2.2	2.9	3.9	4.8	6.4	9.3	12.3	15	16.2	17.3	17.9

5

Trigonometric Functions

Figure 1 The tide rises and falls at regular, predictable intervals. (credit: Andrea Schaffer, Flickr)

CHAPTER OUTLINE

Introduction

Life is dense with phenomena that repeat in regular intervals. Each day, for example, the tides rise and fall in response to the gravitational pull of the moon. Similarly, the progression from day to night occurs as a result of Earth's rotation, and the pattern of the seasons repeats in response to Earth's revolution around the sun. Outside of nature, many stocks that mirror a company's profits are influenced by changes in the economic business cycle.

In mathematics, a function that repeats its values in regular intervals is known as a periodic function. The graphs of such functions show a general shape reflective of a pattern that keeps repeating. This means the graph of the function has the same output at exactly the same place in every cycle. And this translates to all the cycles of the function having exactly the same length. So, if we know all the details of one full cycle of a true periodic function, then we know the state of the function's outputs at all times, future and past. In this chapter, we will investigate various examples of periodic functions.

LEARNING OBJECTIVES

In this section, you will:

- Draw angles in standard position.
- Convert between degrees and radians.
- Find coterminal angles.
- Find the length of a circular arc.
- Use linear and angular speed to describe motion on a circular path.

5.1   ANGLES

A golfer swings to hit a ball over a sand trap and onto the green. An airline pilot maneuvers a plane toward a narrow runway. A dress designer creates the latest fashion. What do they all have in common? They all work with angles, and so do all of us at one time or another. Sometimes we need to measure angles exactly with instruments. Other times we estimate them or judge them by eye. Either way, the proper angle can make the difference between success and failure in many undertakings. In this section, we will examine properties of angles.

Drawing Angles in Standard Position

Properly defining an angle first requires that we define a ray. A **ray** consists of one point on a line and all points extending in one direction from that point. The first point is called the endpoint of the ray. We can refer to a specific ray by stating its endpoint and any other point on it. The ray in **Figure 1** can be named as ray EF, or in symbol form $\overrightarrow{EF}$.

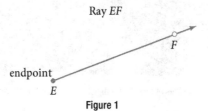

Ray *EF*

Figure 1

An **angle** is the union of two rays having a common endpoint. The endpoint is called the **vertex** of the angle, and the two rays are the sides of the angle. The angle in **Figure 2** is formed from $\overrightarrow{ED}$ and $\overrightarrow{EF}$. Angles can be named using a point on each ray and the vertex, such as angle *DEF*, or in symbol form $\angle DEF$.

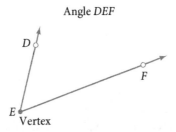

Angle *DEF*

Figure 2

Greek letters are often used as variables for the measure of an angle. **Table 1** is a list of Greek letters commonly used to represent angles, and a sample angle is shown in **Figure 3**.

θ	φ or ϕ	α	β	γ
theta	phi	alpha	beta	gamma

Table 1

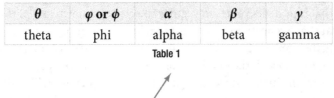

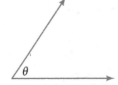

Figure 3 Angle theta, shown as $\angle \theta$

Angle creation is a dynamic process. We start with two rays lying on top of one another. We leave one fixed in place, and rotate the other. The fixed ray is the **initial side,** and the rotated ray is the **terminal side**. In order to identify the different sides, we indicate the rotation with a small arc and arrow close to the vertex as in **Figure 4**.

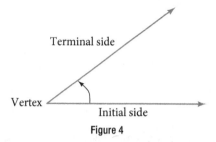

Figure 4

As we discussed at the beginning of the section, there are many applications for angles, but in order to use them correctly, we must be able to measure them. The **measure of an angle** is the amount of rotation from the initial side to the terminal side. Probably the most familiar unit of angle measurement is the degree. One **degree** is $\frac{1}{360}$ of a circular rotation, so a complete circular rotation contains 360 degrees. An angle measured in degrees should always include the unit "degrees" after the number, or include the degree symbol °. For example, 90 degrees = 90°.

To formalize our work, we will begin by drawing angles on an *x-y* coordinate plane. Angles can occur in any position on the coordinate plane, but for the purpose of comparison, the convention is to illustrate them in the same position whenever possible. An angle is in **standard position** if its vertex is located at the origin, and its initial side extends along the positive *x*-axis. See **Figure 5**.

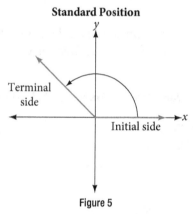

Figure 5

If the angle is measured in a counterclockwise direction from the initial side to the terminal side, the angle is said to be a **positive angle**. If the angle is measured in a clockwise direction, the angle is said to be a **negative angle**.

Drawing an angle in standard position always starts the same way—draw the initial side along the positive *x*-axis. To place the terminal side of the angle, we must calculate the fraction of a full rotation the angle represents. We do that by dividing the angle measure in degrees by 360°. For example, to draw a 90° angle, we calculate that $\frac{90°}{360°} = \frac{1}{4}$. So, the terminal side will be one-fourth of the way around the circle, moving counterclockwise from the positive *x*-axis. To draw a 360° angle, we calculate that $\frac{360°}{360°} = 1$. So the terminal side will be 1 complete rotation around the circle, moving counterclockwise from the positive *x*-axis. In this case, the initial side and the terminal side overlap. See **Figure 6**.

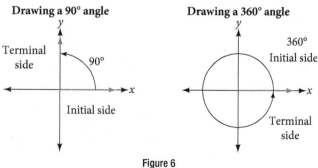

Figure 6

Since we define an angle in standard position by its initial side, we have a special type of angle whose terminal side lies on an axis, a **quadrantal angle**. This type of angle can have a measure of 0°, 90°, 180°, 270° or 360°. See **Figure 7**.

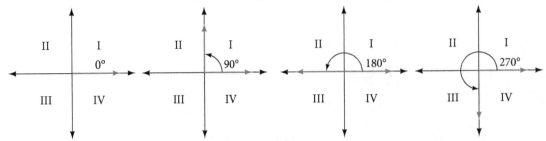

Figure 7 Quadrantal angles have a terminal side that lies along an axis. Examples are shown.

---

quadrantal angles

Quadrantal angles are angles in standard position whose terminal side lies on an axis, including 0°, 90°, 180°, 270°, or 360°.

How To...

Given an angle measure in degrees, draw the angle in standard position.

1. Express the angle measure as a fraction of 360°.
2. Reduce the fraction to simplest form.
3. Draw an angle that contains that same fraction of the circle, beginning on the positive *x*-axis and moving counterclockwise for positive angles and clockwise for negative angles.

Example 1   **Drawing an Angle in Standard Position Measured in Degrees**

a. Sketch an angle of 30° in standard position.

b. Sketch an angle of −135° in standard position.

Solution

a. Divide the angle measure by 360°.

$$\frac{30°}{360°} = \frac{1}{12}$$

To rewrite the fraction in a more familiar fraction, we can recognize that

$$\frac{1}{12} = \frac{1}{3}\left(\frac{1}{4}\right)$$

One-twelfth equals one-third of a quarter, so by dividing a quarter rotation into thirds, we can sketch a line at 30° as in **Figure 8**.

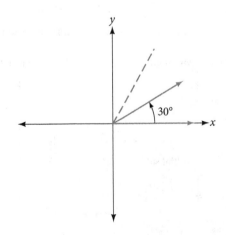

Figure 8

b. Divide the angle measure by 360°.

$$\frac{-135°}{360°} = -\frac{3}{8}$$

In this case, we can recognize that

$$-\frac{3}{8} = -\frac{3}{2}\left(\frac{1}{4}\right)$$

Negative three-eighths is one and one-half times a quarter, so we place a line by moving clockwise one full quarter and one-half of another quarter, as in **Figure 9**.

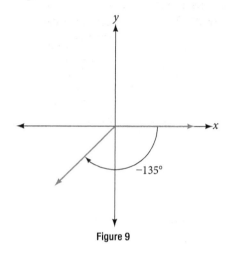

Figure 9

Try It #1

Show an angle of 240° on a circle in standard position.

Converting Between Degrees and Radians

Dividing a circle into 360 parts is an arbitrary choice, although it creates the familiar degree measurement. We may choose other ways to divide a circle. To find another unit, think of the process of drawing a circle. Imagine that you stop before the circle is completed. The portion that you drew is referred to as an arc. An arc may be a portion of a full circle, a full circle, or more than a full circle, represented by more than one full rotation. The length of the arc around an entire circle is called the circumference of that circle.

The circumference of a circle is $C = 2\pi r$. If we divide both sides of this equation by r, we create the ratio of the circumference to the radius, which is always 2π regardless of the length of the radius. So the circumference of any circle is $2\pi \approx 6.28$ times the length of the radius. That means that if we took a string as long as the radius and used it to measure consecutive lengths around the circumference, there would be room for six full string-lengths and a little more than a quarter of a seventh, as shown in **Figure 10**.

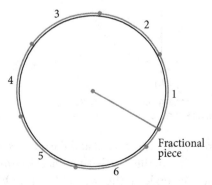

Figure 10

This brings us to our new angle measure. One **radian** is the measure of a central angle of a circle that intercepts an arc equal in length to the radius of that circle. A central angle is an angle formed at the center of a circle by two radii. Because the total circumference equals 2π times the radius, a full circular rotation is 2π radians. So

$$2\pi \text{ radians} = 360°$$

$$\pi \text{ radians} = \frac{360°}{2} = 180°$$

$$1 \text{ radian} = \frac{180°}{\pi} \approx 57.3°$$

See **Figure 11**. Note that when an angle is described without a specific unit, it refers to radian measure. For example, an angle measure of 3 indicates 3 radians. In fact, radian measure is dimensionless, since it is the quotient of a length (circumference) divided by a length (radius) and the length units cancel out.

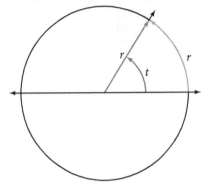

Figure 11 The angle t sweeps out a measure of one radian. Note that the length of the intercepted arc is the same as the length of the radius of the circle.

Relating Arc Lengths to Radius

An **arc length** s is the length of the curve along the arc. Just as the full circumference of a circle always has a constant ratio to the radius, the arc length produced by any given angle also has a constant relation to the radius, regardless of the length of the radius.

This ratio, called the radian measure, is the same regardless of the radius of the circle—it depends only on the angle. This property allows us to define a measure of any angle as the ratio of the arc length s to the radius r. See **Figure 12**.

$$s = r\theta$$

$$\theta = \frac{s}{r}$$

If $s = r$, then $\theta = \frac{r}{r} = 1$ radian.

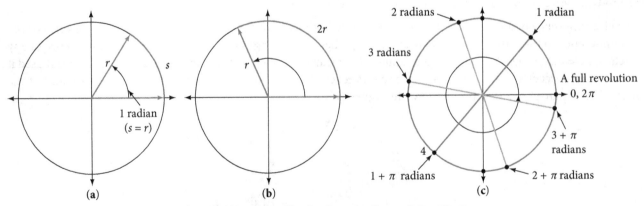

Figure 12 (a) In an angle of 1 radian, the arc length s equals the radius r.
(b) An angle of 2 radians has an arc length $s = 2r$. (c) A full revolution is 2π or about 6.28 radians.

To elaborate on this idea, consider two circles, one with radius 2 and the other with radius 3. Recall the circumference of a circle is $C = 2\pi r$, where r is the radius. The smaller circle then has circumference $2\pi(2) = 4\pi$ and the larger has circumference $2\pi(3) = 6\pi$. Now we draw a 45°angle on the two circles, as in **Figure 13**.

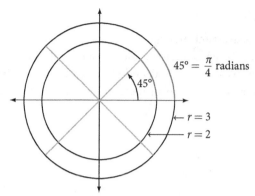

Figure 13 A 45° angle contains one-eighth of the circumference of a circle, regardless of the radius.

Notice what happens if we find the ratio of the arc length divided by the radius of the circle.

$$\text{Smaller circle:} \quad \frac{\frac{1}{2}\pi}{2} = \frac{1}{4}\pi$$

$$\text{Larger circle:} \quad \frac{\frac{3}{4}\pi}{3} = \frac{1}{4}\pi$$

Since both ratios are $\frac{1}{4}\pi$, the angle measures of both circles are the same, even though the arc length and radius differ.

---

radians

One **radian** is the measure of the central angle of a circle such that the length of the arc between the initial side and the terminal side is equal to the radius of the circle. A full revolution (360°) equals 2π radians. A half revolution (180°) is equivalent to π radians.

The **radian measure** of an angle is the ratio of the length of the arc subtended by the angle to the radius of the circle. In other words, if s is the length of an arc of a circle, and r is the radius of the circle, then the central angle containing that arc measures $\frac{s}{r}$ radians. In a circle of radius 1, the radian measure corresponds to the length of the arc.

Q & A...

A measure of 1 radian looks to be about 60°. Is that correct?

Yes. It is approximately 57.3°. Because 2π radians equals 360°, 1 radian equals $\frac{360°}{2\pi} \approx 57.3°$.

Using Radians

Because radian measure is the ratio of two lengths, it is a unitless measure. For example, in **Figure 12**, suppose the radius was 2 inches and the distance along the arc was also 2 inches. When we calculate the radian measure of the angle, the "inches" cancel, and we have a result without units. Therefore, it is not necessary to write the label "radians" after a radian measure, and if we see an angle that is not labeled with "degrees" or the degree symbol, we can assume that it is a radian measure.

Considering the most basic case, the unit circle (a circle with radius 1), we know that 1 rotation equals 360 degrees, 360°. We can also track one rotation around a circle by finding the circumference, $C = 2\pi r$, and for the unit circle $C = 2\pi$. These two different ways to rotate around a circle give us a way to convert from degrees to radians.

$$1 \text{ rotation} = 360° = 2\pi \text{ radians}$$

$$\frac{1}{2} \text{ rotation} = 180° = \pi \text{ radians}$$

$$\frac{1}{4} \text{ rotation} = 90° = \frac{\pi}{2} \text{ radians}$$

Identifying Special Angles Measured in Radians

In addition to knowing the measurements in degrees and radians of a quarter revolution, a half revolution, and a full revolution, there are other frequently encountered angles in one revolution of a circle with which we should be familiar. It is common to encounter multiples of 30, 45, 60, and 90 degrees. These values are shown in **Figure 14**. Memorizing these angles will be very useful as we study the properties associated with angles.

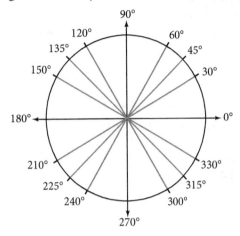

Figure 14 Commonly encountered angles measured in degrees

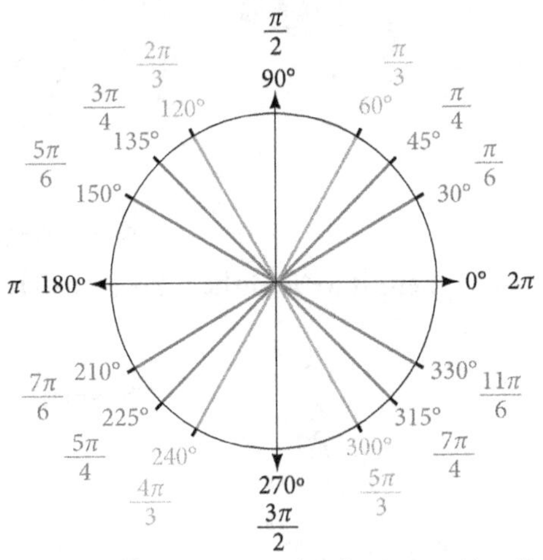

Figure 15 Commonly encountered angles measured in radians

Now, we can list the corresponding radian values for the common measures of a circle corresponding to those listed in **Figure 14**, which are shown in **Figure 15**. Be sure you can verify each of these measures.

Example 2   **Finding a Radian Measure**

Find the radian measure of one-third of a full rotation.

Solution   For any circle, the arc length along such a rotation would be one-third of the circumference. We know that

$$1 \text{ rotation} = 2\pi r$$

So,

$$s = \frac{1}{3}(2\pi r)$$

$$= \frac{2\pi r}{3}$$

The radian measure would be the arc length divided by the radius.

$$\text{radian measure} = \frac{\frac{2\pi r}{3}}{r}$$

$$= \frac{2\pi r}{3r}$$

$$= \frac{2\pi}{3}$$

Try It #2

Find the radian measure of three-fourths of a full rotation.

Converting Between Radians and Degrees

Because degrees and radians both measure angles, we need to be able to convert between them. We can easily do so using a proportion.

$$\frac{\theta}{180} = \frac{\theta^R}{\pi}$$

This proportion shows that the measure of angle θ in degrees divided by 180 equals the measure of angle θ in radians divided by π. Or, phrased another way, degrees is to 180 as radians is to π.

$$\frac{\text{Degrees}}{180} = \frac{\text{Radians}}{\pi}$$

> **converting between radians and degrees**
>
> To convert between degrees and radians, use the proportion
>
> $$\frac{\theta}{180} = \frac{\theta^R}{\pi}$$

Example 3   **Converting Radians to Degrees**

Convert each radian measure to degrees.

    a. $\dfrac{\pi}{6}$ **b.** 3

Solution   Because we are given radians and we want degrees, we should set up a proportion and solve it.

  a. We use the proportion, substituting the given information.

$$\frac{\theta}{180} = \frac{\theta^R}{\pi}$$

$$\frac{\theta}{180} = \frac{\frac{\pi}{6}}{\pi}$$

$$\theta = \frac{180}{6}$$

$$\theta = 30°$$

  b. We use the proportion, substituting the given information.

$$\frac{\theta}{180} = \frac{\theta^R}{\pi}$$

$$\frac{\theta}{180} = \frac{3}{\pi}$$

$$\theta = \frac{3(180)}{\pi}$$

$$\theta \approx 172°$$

Try It #3

Convert $-\dfrac{3\pi}{4}$ radians to degrees.

Example 4   **Converting Degrees to Radians**

Convert 15 degrees to radians.

Solution   In this example, we start with degrees and want radians, so we again set up a proportion and solve it, but we substitute the given information into a different part of the proportion.

$$\frac{\theta}{180} = \frac{\theta^R}{\pi}$$

$$\frac{15}{180} = \frac{\theta^R}{\pi}$$

$$\frac{15\pi}{180} = \theta^R$$

$$\frac{\pi}{12} = \theta^R$$

Analysis   *Another way to think about this problem is by remembering that $30° = \dfrac{\pi}{6}$. Because $15° = \dfrac{1}{2}(30°)$, we can find that $\dfrac{1}{2}\left(\dfrac{\pi}{6}\right)$ is $\dfrac{\pi}{12}$.*

Try It #4

Convert 126° to radians.

Finding Coterminal Angles

Converting between degrees and radians can make working with angles easier in some applications. For other applications, we may need another type of conversion. Negative angles and angles greater than a full revolution are more awkward to work with than those in the range of 0° to 360°, or 0 to 2π. It would be convenient to replace those out-of-range angles with a corresponding angle within the range of a single revolution.

It is possible for more than one angle to have the same terminal side. Look at **Figure 16**. The angle of 140° is a positive angle, measured counterclockwise. The angle of −220° is a negative angle, measured clockwise. But both angles have the same terminal side. If two angles in standard position have the same terminal side, they are coterminal angles. Every angle greater than 360° or less than 0° is coterminal with an angle between 0° and 360°, and it is often more convenient to find the coterminal angle within the range of 0° to 360° than to work with an angle that is outside that range.

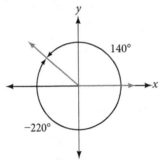

Figure 16 An angle of 140° and an angle of −220° are coterminal angles.

Any angle has infinitely many coterminal angles because each time we add 360° to that angle—or subtract 360° from it—the resulting value has a terminal side in the same location. For example, 100° and 460° are coterminal for this reason, as is −260°. Recognizing that any angle has infinitely many coterminal angles explains the repetitive shape in the graphs of trigonometric functions.

An angle's reference angle is the measure of the smallest, positive, acute angle *t* formed by the terminal side of the angle *t* and the horizontal axis. Thus positive reference angles have terminal sides that lie in the first quadrant and can be used as models for angles in other quadrants. See **Figure 17** for examples of reference angles for angles in different quadrants.

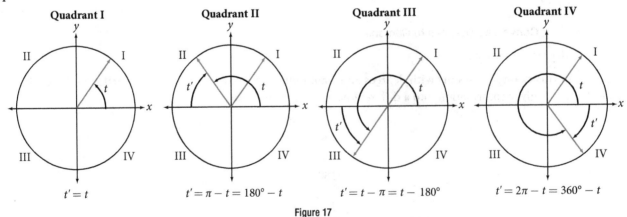

Figure 17

---

coterminal and reference angles

Coterminal angles are two angles in standard position that have the same terminal side.

An angle's **reference angle** is the size of the smallest acute angle, *t′*, formed by the terminal side of the angle *t* and the horizontal axis.

How To...

Given an angle greater than 360°, find a coterminal angle between 0° and 360°.

1. Subtract 360° from the given angle.
2. If the result is still greater than 360°, subtract 360° again till the result is between 0° and 360°.
3. The resulting angle is coterminal with the original angle.

Example 5   **Finding an Angle Coterminal with an Angle of Measure Greater Than 360°**

Find the least positive angle θ that is coterminal with an angle measuring 800°, where $0° \leq \theta < 360°$.

Solution   An angle with measure 800° is coterminal with an angle with measure $800 - 360 = 440°$, but 440° is still greater than 360°, so we subtract 360° again to find another coterminal angle: $440 - 360 = 80°$.

The angle $\theta = 80°$ is coterminal with 800°. To put it another way, 800° equals 80° plus two full rotations, as shown in **Figure 18**.

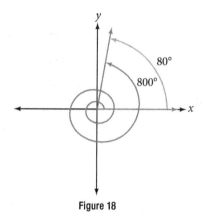

Figure 18

Try It #5

Find an angle α that is coterminal with an angle measuring 870°, where $0° \leq \alpha < 360°$.

How To...

Given an angle with measure less than 0°, find a coterminal angle having a measure between 0° and 360°.

1. Add 360° to the given angle.
2. If the result is still less than 0°, add 360° again until the result is between 0° and 360°.
3. The resulting angle is coterminal with the original angle.

Example 6   **Finding an Angle Coterminal with an Angle Measuring Less Than 0°**

Show the angle with measure −45° on a circle and find a positive coterminal angle α such that $0° \leq \alpha < 360°$.

Solution   Since 45° is half of 90°, we can start at the positive horizontal axis and measure clockwise half of a 90° angle.

Because we can find coterminal angles by adding or subtracting a full rotation of 360°, we can find a positive coterminal angle here by adding 360°:

$$-45° + 360° = 315°$$

We can then show the angle on a circle, as in **Figure 19**.

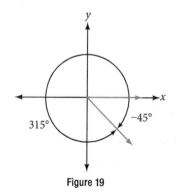

Figure 19

Try It #6

Find an angle β that is coterminal with an angle measuring −300° such that $0° \leq \beta < 360°$.

Finding Coterminal Angles Measured in Radians

We can find coterminal angles measured in radians in much the same way as we have found them using degrees. In both cases, we find coterminal angles by adding or subtracting one or more full rotations.

How To…

Given an angle greater than 2π, find a coterminal angle between 0 and 2π.

1. Subtract 2π from the given angle.
2. If the result is still greater than 2π, subtract 2π again until the result is between 0 and 2π.
3. The resulting angle is coterminal with the original angle.

Example 7   **Finding Coterminal Angles Using Radians**

Find an angle β that is coterminal with $\dfrac{19\pi}{4}$, where $0 \leq \beta < 2\pi$.

Solution   When working in degrees, we found coterminal angles by adding or subtracting 360 degrees, a full rotation. Likewise, in radians, we can find coterminal angles by adding or subtracting full rotations of 2π radians:

$$\frac{19\pi}{4} - 2\pi = \frac{19\pi}{4} - \frac{8\pi}{4}$$

$$= \frac{11\pi}{4}$$

The angle $\dfrac{11\pi}{4}$ is coterminal, but not less than 2π, so we subtract another rotation:

$$\frac{11\pi}{4} - 2\pi = \frac{11\pi}{4} - \frac{8\pi}{4}$$

$$= \frac{3\pi}{4}$$

The angle $\dfrac{3\pi}{4}$ is coterminal with $\dfrac{19\pi}{4}$, as shown in **Figure 20**.

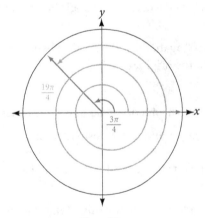

Figure 20

Try It #7

Find an angle of measure θ that is coterminal with an angle of measure $-\dfrac{17\pi}{6}$ where $0 \leq \theta < 2\pi$.

Determining the Length of an Arc

Recall that the radian measure θ of an angle was defined as the ratio of the arc length s of a circular arc to the radius r of the circle, $\theta = \frac{s}{r}$. From this relationship, we can find arc length along a circle, given an angle.

arc length on a circle

In a circle of radius *r*, the length of an arc *s* subtended by an angle with measure θ in radians, shown in **Figure 21**, is

$$s = r\theta$$

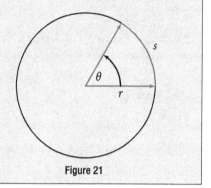

Figure 21

How To...

Given a circle of radius *r*, calculate the length *s* of the arc subtended by a given angle of measure θ.

1. If necessary, convert θ to radians.

2. Multiply the radius *r* by the radian measure of $\theta : s = r\theta$.

Example 8   **Finding the Length of an Arc**

Assume the orbit of Mercury around the sun is a perfect circle. Mercury is approximately 36 million miles from the sun.

a. In one Earth day, Mercury completes 0.0114 of its total revolution. How many miles does it travel in one day?

b. Use your answer from part (a) to determine the radian measure for Mercury's movement in one Earth day.

Solution

a. Let's begin by finding the circumference of Mercury's orbit.

$$C = 2\pi r$$
$$= 2\pi(36 \text{ million miles})$$
$$\approx 226 \text{ million miles}$$

Since Mercury completes 0.0114 of its total revolution in one Earth day, we can now find the distance traveled:

$$(0.0114)226 \text{ million miles} = 2.58 \text{ million miles}$$

b. Now, we convert to radians:

$$\text{radian} = \frac{\text{arclength}}{\text{radius}}$$
$$= \frac{2.58 \text{ million miles}}{36 \text{ million miles}}$$
$$= 0.0717$$

Try It #8

Find the arc length along a circle of radius 10 units subtended by an angle of 215°.

Finding the Area of a Sector of a Circle

In addition to arc length, we can also use angles to find the area of a sector of a circle. A sector is a region of a circle bounded by two radii and the intercepted arc, like a slice of pizza or pie. Recall that the area of a circle with radius *r* can be found using the formula $A = \pi r^2$. If the two radii form an angle of θ, measured in radians, then $\frac{\theta}{2\pi}$ is the ratio of the angle measure to the measure of a full rotation and is also, therefore, the ratio of the area of the sector to the area of the circle. Thus, the **area of a sector** is the fraction $\frac{\theta}{2\pi}$ multiplied by the entire area. (Always remember that this formula only applies if θ is in radians.)

$$\text{Area of sector} = \left(\frac{\theta}{2\pi}\right)\pi r^2$$
$$= \frac{\theta\pi r^2}{2\pi}$$
$$= \frac{1}{2}\theta r^2$$

> ### area of a sector
>
> The **area of a sector** of a circle with radius r subtended by an angle θ, measured in radians, is
>
> $$A = \frac{1}{2}\theta r^2$$
>
> See **Figure 22**.

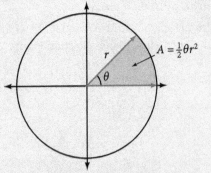

Figure 22 The area of the sector equals half the square of the radius times the central angle measured in radians.

How To...

Given a circle of radius r, find the area of a sector defined by a given angle θ.

1. If necessary, convert θ to radians.
2. Multiply half the radian measure of θ by the square of the radius r: $A = \frac{1}{2}\theta r^2$.

Example 9   **Finding the Area of a Sector**

An automatic lawn sprinkler sprays a distance of 20 feet while rotating 30 degrees, as shown in **Figure 23**. What is the area of the sector of grass the sprinkler waters?

Solution   First, we need to convert the angle measure into radians. Because 30 degrees is one of our special angles, we already know the equivalent radian measure, but we can also convert:

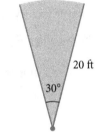

Figure 23 The sprinkler sprays 20 ft within an arc of 30°.

$$30 \text{ degrees} = 30 \cdot \frac{\pi}{180}$$

$$= \frac{\pi}{6} \text{ radians}$$

The area of the sector is then

$$\text{Area} = \frac{1}{2}\left(\frac{\pi}{6}\right)(20)^2$$

$$\approx 104.72$$

So the area is about 104.72 ft².

Try It #9

In central pivot irrigation, a large irrigation pipe on wheels rotates around a center point. A farmer has a central pivot system with a radius of 400 meters. If water restrictions only allow her to water 150 thousand square meters a day, what angle should she set the system to cover? Write the answer in radian measure to two decimal places.

Use Linear and Angular Speed to Describe Motion on a Circular Path

In addition to finding the area of a sector, we can use angles to describe the speed of a moving object. An object traveling in a circular path has two types of speed. **Linear speed** is speed along a straight path and can be determined by the distance it moves along (its **displacement**) in a given time interval. For instance, if a wheel with radius 5 inches rotates once a second, a point on the edge of the wheel moves a distance equal to the circumference, or 10π inches, every second. So the linear speed of the point is 10π in./s. The equation for linear speed is as follows where v is linear speed, s is displacement, and t is time.

$$v = \frac{s}{t}$$

Angular speed results from circular motion and can be determined by the angle through which a point rotates in a given time interval. In other words, angular speed is angular rotation per unit time. So, for instance, if a gear makes a full rotation every 4 seconds, we can calculate its angular speed as $\dfrac{360 \text{ degrees}}{4 \text{ seconds}} = 90$ degrees per second. Angular speed can be given in radians per second, rotations per minute, or degrees per hour for example. The equation for angular speed is as follows, where ω (read as omega) is angular speed, θ is the angle traversed, and t is time.

$$\omega = \frac{\theta}{t}$$

Combining the definition of angular speed with the arc length equation, $s = r\theta$, we can find a relationship between angular and linear speeds. The angular speed equation can be solved for θ, giving $\theta = \omega t$. Substituting this into the arc length equation gives:

$$s = r\theta$$
$$= r\omega t$$

Substituting this into the linear speed equation gives:

$$v = \frac{s}{t}$$
$$= \frac{r\omega t}{t}$$
$$= r\omega$$

---

angular and linear speed

As a point moves along a circle of radius r, its **angular speed**, ω, is the angular rotation θ per unit time, t.

$$\omega = \frac{\theta}{t}$$

The **linear speed**, v, of the point can be found as the distance traveled, arc length s, per unit time, t.

$$v = \frac{s}{t}$$

When the angular speed is measured in radians per unit time, linear speed and angular speed are related by the equation

$$v = r\omega$$

This equation states that the angular speed in radians, ω, representing the amount of rotation occurring in a unit of time, can be multiplied by the radius r to calculate the total arc length traveled in a unit of time, which is the definition of linear speed.

How To...

Given the amount of angle rotation and the time elapsed, calculate the angular speed.

1. If necessary, convert the angle measure to radians.
2. Divide the angle in radians by the number of time units elapsed: $\omega = \dfrac{\theta}{t}$.
3. The resulting speed will be in radians per time unit.

Example 10 **Finding Angular Speed**

A water wheel, shown in **Figure 24**, completes 1 rotation every 5 seconds. Find the angular speed in radians per second.

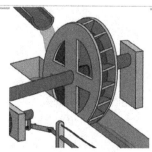

Solution   The wheel completes 1 rotation, or passes through an angle of 2π radians in 5 seconds, so the angular speed would be $\omega = \dfrac{2\pi}{5} \approx 1.257$ radians per second.

Figure 24

Try It #10

An old vinyl record is played on a turntable rotating clockwise at a rate of 45 rotations per minute. Find the angular speed in radians per second.

How To...

Given the radius of a circle, an angle of rotation, and a length of elapsed time, determine the linear speed.

1. Convert the total rotation to radians if necessary.
2. Divide the total rotation in radians by the elapsed time to find the angular speed: apply $\omega = \dfrac{\theta}{t}$.
3. Multiply the angular speed by the length of the radius to find the linear speed, expressed in terms of the length unit used for the radius and the time unit used for the elapsed time: apply $v = r\omega$.

Example 11   Finding a Linear Speed

A bicycle has wheels 28 inches in diameter. A tachometer determines the wheels are rotating at 180 RPM (revolutions per minute). Find the speed the bicycle is traveling down the road.

Solution   Here, we have an angular speed and need to find the corresponding linear speed, since the linear speed of the outside of the tires is the speed at which the bicycle travels down the road.

We begin by converting from rotations per minute to radians per minute. It can be helpful to utilize the units to make this conversion:

$$180 \ \frac{\text{rotations}}{\text{minute}} \cdot \frac{2\pi \ \text{radians}}{\text{rotation}} = 360\pi \ \frac{\text{radians}}{\text{minute}}$$

Using the formula from above along with the radius of the wheels, we can find the linear speed:

$$v = (14 \ \text{inches})\left(360\pi \ \frac{\text{radians}}{\text{minute}}\right)$$
$$= 5040\pi \ \frac{\text{inches}}{\text{minute}}$$

Remember that radians are a unitless measure, so it is not necessary to include them.

Finally, we may wish to convert this linear speed into a more familiar measurement, like miles per hour.

$$5040\pi \ \frac{\text{inches}}{\text{minute}} \cdot \frac{1 \ \text{feet}}{12 \ \text{inches}} \cdot \frac{1 \ \text{mile}}{5280 \ \text{feet}} \cdot \frac{60 \ \text{minutes}}{1 \ \text{hour}} \approx 14.99 \ \text{miles per hour (mph)}$$

Try It #11

A satellite is rotating around Earth at 0.25 radians per hour at an altitude of 242 km above Earth. If the radius of Earth is 6378 kilometers, find the linear speed of the satellite in kilometers per hour.

Access these online resources for additional instruction and practice with angles, arc length, and areas of sectors.

- Angles in Standard Position (http://openstaxcollege.org/l/standardpos)
- Angle of Rotation (http://openstaxcollege.org/l/angleofrotation)
- Coterminal Angles (http://openstaxcollege.org/l/coterminal)
- Determining Coterminal Angles (http://openstaxcollege.org/l/detcoterm)
- Positive and Negative Coterminal Angles (http://openstaxcollege.org/l/posnegcoterm)
- Radian Measure (http://openstaxcollege.org/l/radianmeas)
- Coterminal Angles in Radians (http://openstaxcollege.org/l/cotermrad)
- Arc Length and Area of a Sector (http://openstaxcollege.org/l/arclength)

5.1 SECTION EXERCISES

VERBAL

1. Draw an angle in standard position. Label the vertex, initial side, and terminal side.

2. Explain why there are an infinite number of angles that are coterminal to a certain angle.

3. State what a positive or negative angle signifies, and explain how to draw each.

4. How does radian measure of an angle compare to the degree measure? Include an explanation of 1 radian in your paragraph.

5. Explain the differences between linear speed and angular speed when describing motion along a circular path.

For the following exercises, draw an angle in standard position with the given measure.

6. 30°   **7.** 300°   **8.** −80°   **9.** 135°   **10.** −150°   **11.** $\frac{2\pi}{3}$

12. $\frac{7\pi}{4}$ **13.** $\frac{5\pi}{6}$ **14.** $\frac{\pi}{2}$ **15.** $-\frac{\pi}{10}$ **16.** 415°   **17.** −120°

18. −315°   **19.** $\frac{22\pi}{3}$ **20.** $-\frac{\pi}{6}$ **21.** $-\frac{4\pi}{3}$

For the following exercises, refer to **Figure 25**. Round to two decimal places.

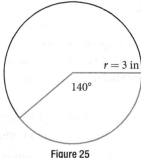

Figure 25

For the following exercises, refer to **Figure 26**. Round to two decimal places.

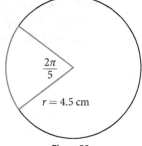

Figure 26

22. Find the arc length.

23. Find the area of the sector.

24. Find the arc length.

25. Find the area of the sector.

ALGEBRAIC

For the following exercises, convert angles in radians to degrees.

26. $\frac{3\pi}{4}$ radians   **27.** $\frac{\pi}{9}$ radians   **28.** $-\frac{5\pi}{4}$ radians   **29.** $\frac{\pi}{3}$ radians

30. $-\frac{7\pi}{3}$ radians   **31.** $-\frac{5\pi}{12}$ radians   **32.** $\frac{11\pi}{6}$ radians

For the following exercises, convert angles in degrees to radians.

33. 90°   **34.** 100°   **35.** −540°   **36.** −120°

37. 180°   **38.** −315°   **39.** 150°

For the following exercises, use to given information to find the length of a circular arc. Round to two decimal places.

40. Find the length of the arc of a circle of radius 12 inches subtended by a central angle of $\frac{\pi}{4}$ radians.

41. Find the length of the arc of a circle of radius 5.02 miles subtended by the central angle of $\frac{\pi}{3}$.

42. Find the length of the arc of a circle of diameter 14 meters subtended by the central angle of $\frac{5\pi}{6}$.

43. Find the length of the arc of a circle of radius 10 centimeters subtended by the central angle of 50°.

44. Find the length of the arc of a circle of radius 5 inches subtended by the central angle of 220°.

45. Find the length of the arc of a circle of diameter 12 meters subtended by the central angle is 63°.

For the following exercises, use the given information to find the area of the sector. Round to four decimal places.

46. A sector of a circle has a central angle of 45° and a radius 6 cm.

47. A sector of a circle has a central angle of 30° and a radius of 20 cm.

48. A sector of a circle with diameter 10 feet and an angle of $\frac{\pi}{2}$ radians.

49. A sector of a circle with radius of 0.7 inches and an angle of π radians.

For the following exercises, find the angle between 0° and 360° that is coterminal to the given angle.

50. −40°

51. −110°

52. 700°

53. 1400°

For the following exercises, find the angle between 0 and 2π in radians that is coterminal to the given angle.

54. $-\frac{\pi}{9}$

55. $\frac{10\pi}{3}$

56. $\frac{13\pi}{6}$

57. $\frac{44\pi}{9}$

REAL-WORLD APPLICATIONS

58. A truck with 32-inch diameter wheels is traveling at 60 mi/h. Find the angular speed of the wheels in rad/min. How many revolutions per minute do the wheels make?

59. A bicycle with 24-inch diameter wheels is traveling at 15 mi/h. Find the angular speed of the wheels in rad/min. How many revolutions per minute do the wheels make?

60. A wheel of radius 8 inches is rotating 15°/s. What is the linear speed v, the angular speed in RPM, and the angular speed in rad/s?

61. A wheel of radius 14 inches is rotating 0.5 rad/s. What is the linear speed v, the angular speed in RPM, and the angular speed in deg/s?

62. A CD has diameter of 120 millimeters. When playing audio, the angular speed varies to keep the linear speed constant where the disc is being read. When reading along the outer edge of the disc, the angular speed is about 200 RPM (revolutions per minute). Find the linear speed.

63. When being burned in a writable CD-R drive, the angular speed of a CD varies to keep the linear speed constant where the disc is being written. When writing along the outer edge of the disc, the angular speed of one drive is about 4,800 RPM (revolutions per minute). Find the linear speed if the CD has diameter of 120 millimeters.

64. A person is standing on the equator of Earth (radius 3960 miles). What are his linear and angular speeds?

65. Find the distance along an arc on the surface of Earth that subtends a central angle of 5 minutes $\left(1 \text{ minute} = \frac{1}{60} \text{ degree}\right)$. The radius of Earth is 3,960 mi.

66. Find the distance along an arc on the surface of Earth that subtends a central angle of 7 minutes $\left(1 \text{ minute} = \frac{1}{60} \text{ degree}\right)$. The radius of Earth is 3,960 miles.

67. Consider a clock with an hour hand and minute hand. What is the measure of the angle the minute hand traces in 20 minutes?

EXTENSIONS

68. Two cities have the same longitude. The latitude of city A is 9.00 degrees north and the latitude of city B is 30.00 degree north. Assume the radius of the earth is 3960 miles. Find the distance between the two cities.

69. A city is located at 40 degrees north latitude. Assume the radius of the earth is 3960 miles and the earth rotates once every 24 hours. Find the linear speed of a person who resides in this city.

70. A city is located at 75 degrees north latitude. Assume the radius of the earth is 3960 miles and the earth rotates once every 24 hours. Find the linear speed of a person who resides in this city.

71. Find the linear speed of the moon if the average distance between the earth and moon is 239,000 miles, assuming the orbit of the moon is circular and requires about 28 days. Express answer in miles per hour.

72. A bicycle has wheels 28 inches in diameter. A tachometer determines that the wheels are rotating at 180 RPM (revolutions per minute). Find the speed the bicycle is travelling down the road.

73. A car travels 3 miles. Its tires make 2640 revolutions. What is the radius of a tire in inches?

74. A wheel on a tractor has a 24-inch diameter. How many revolutions does the wheel make if the tractor travels 4 miles?

LEARNING OBJECTIVES

In this section, you will:

- Find function values for the sine and cosine of 30° or $\left(\dfrac{\pi}{6}\right)$, 45° or $\left(\dfrac{\pi}{4}\right)$ and 60° or $\left(\dfrac{\pi}{3}\right)$.
- Identify the domain and range of sine and cosine functions.
- Use reference angles to evaluate trigonometric functions.

5.2 UNIT CIRCLE: SINE AND COSINE FUNCTIONS

Figure 1 The Singapore Flyer is the world's tallest Ferris wheel. (credit: "Vibin JK"/Flickr)

Looking for a thrill? Then consider a ride on the Singapore Flyer, the world's tallest Ferris wheel. Located in Singapore, the Ferris wheel soars to a height of 541 feet—a little more than a tenth of a mile! Described as an observation wheel, riders enjoy spectacular views as they travel from the ground to the peak and down again in a repeating pattern. In this section, we will examine this type of revolving motion around a circle. To do so, we need to define the type of circle first, and then place that circle on a coordinate system. Then we can discuss circular motion in terms of the coordinate pairs.

Finding Function Values for the Sine and Cosine

To define our trigonometric functions, we begin by drawing a unit circle, a circle centered at the origin with radius 1, as shown in **Figure 2**. The angle (in radians) that t intercepts forms an arc of length s. Using the formula $s = rt$, and knowing that $r = 1$, we see that for a unit circle, $s = t$.

Recall that the x- and y-axes divide the coordinate plane into four quarters called quadrants. We label these quadrants to mimic the direction a positive angle would sweep. The four quadrants are labeled I, II, III, and IV.

For any angle t, we can label the intersection of the terminal side and the unit circle as by its coordinates, (x, y). The coordinates x and y will be the outputs of the trigonometric functions $f(t) = \cos t$ and $f(t) = \sin t$, respectively. This means $x = \cos t$ and $y = \sin t$.

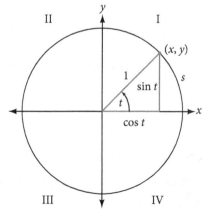

Figure 2 Unit circle where the central angle is t radians

> ### unit circle
>
> A **unit circle** has a center at $(0, 0)$ and radius 1. In a unit circle, the length of the intercepted arc is equal to the radian measure of the central angle t.
>
> Let (x, y) be the endpoint on the unit circle of an arc of arc length s. The (x, y) coordinates of this point can be described as functions of the angle.

Defining Sine and Cosine Functions

Now that we have our unit circle labeled, we can learn how the (x, y) coordinates relate to the arc length and angle. The **sine function** relates a real number t to the y-coordinate of the point where the corresponding angle intercepts the unit circle. More precisely, the sine of an angle t equals the y-value of the endpoint on the unit circle of an arc of length t. In **Figure 2**, the sine is equal to y. Like all functions, the sine function has an input and an output. Its input is the measure of the angle; its output is the y-coordinate of the corresponding point on the unit circle.

The **cosine function** of an angle t equals the x-value of the endpoint on the unit circle of an arc of length t. In **Figure 3**, the cosine is equal to x.

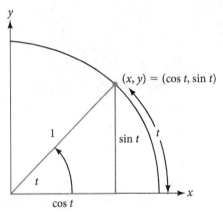

Figure 3

Because it is understood that sine and cosine are functions, we do not always need to write them with parentheses: $\sin t$ is the same as $\sin(t)$ and $\cos t$ is the same as $\cos(t)$. Likewise, $\cos^2 t$ is a commonly used shorthand notation for $(\cos(t))^2$. Be aware that many calculators and computers do not recognize the shorthand notation. When in doubt, use the extra parentheses when entering calculations into a calculator or computer.

> ### sine and cosine functions
>
> If t is a real number and a point (x, y) on the unit circle corresponds to an angle of t, then
>
> $$\cos t = x$$
> $$\sin t = y$$

How To…

Given a point $P(x, y)$ on the unit circle corresponding to an angle of t, find the sine and cosine.

1. The sine of t is equal to the y-coordinate of point P: $\sin t = y$.
2. The cosine of t is equal to the x-coordinate of point P: $\cos t = x$.

Example 1   **Finding Function Values for Sine and Cosine**

Point P is a point on the unit circle corresponding to an angle of t, as shown in **Figure 4**. Find $\cos(t)$ and $\sin(t)$.

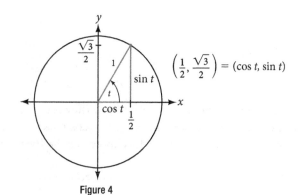

Figure 4

Solution We know that cos t is the x-coordinate of the corresponding point on the unit circle and sin t is the y-coordinate of the corresponding point on the unit circle. So:

$$x = \cos t = \frac{1}{2}$$

$$y = \sin t = \frac{\sqrt{3}}{2}$$

Try It #1

A certain angle t corresponds to a point on the unit circle at $\left(-\frac{\sqrt{2}}{2}, \frac{\sqrt{2}}{2} \right)$ as shown in **Figure 5**. Find cos t and sin t.

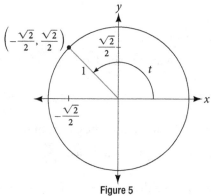

Figure 5

Finding Sines and Cosines of Angles on an Axis

For quadrantral angles, the corresponding point on the unit circle falls on the x- or y-axis. In that case, we can easily calculate cosine and sine from the values of x and y.

Example 2   **Calculating Sines and Cosines along an Axis**

Find cos(90°) and sin(90°).

Solution Moving 90° counterclockwise around the unit circle from the positive x-axis brings us to the top of the circle, where the (x, y) coordinates are (0, 1), as shown in **Figure 6**.

Using our definitions of cosine and sine,

$$x = \cos t = \cos(90°) = 0$$

$$y = \sin t = \sin(90°) = 1$$

The cosine of 90° is 0; the sine of 90° is 1.

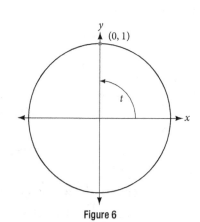

Figure 6

Try It #2

Find cosine and sine of the angle π.

The Pythagorean Identity

Now that we can define sine and cosine, we will learn how they relate to each other and the unit circle. Recall that the equation for the unit circle is $x^2 + y^2 = 1$. Because $x = \cos t$ and $y = \sin t$, we can substitute for x and y to get $\cos^2 t + \sin^2 t = 1$. This equation, $\cos^2 t + \sin^2 t = 1$, is known as the **Pythagorean Identity**. See **Figure 7**.

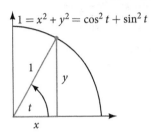

Figure 7

We can use the Pythagorean Identity to find the cosine of an angle if we know the sine, or vice versa. However, because the equation yields two solutions, we need additional knowledge of the angle to choose the solution with the correct sign. If we know the quadrant where the angle is, we can easily choose the correct solution.

> **Pythagorean Identity**
>
> The **Pythagorean Identity** states that, for any real number t,
>
> $$\cos^2 t + \sin^2 t = 1$$

How To…

Given the sine of some angle t and its quadrant location, find the cosine of t.

1. Substitute the known value of $\sin(t)$ into the Pythagorean Identity.
2. Solve for $\cos(t)$.
3. Choose the solution with the appropriate sign for the x-values in the quadrant where t is located.

Example 3   **Finding a Cosine from a Sine or a Sine from a Cosine**

If $\sin(t) = \dfrac{3}{7}$ and t is in the second quadrant, find $\cos(t)$.

Solution   If we drop a vertical line from the point on the unit circle corresponding to t, we create a right triangle, from which we can see that the Pythagorean Identity is simply one case of the Pythagorean Theorem. See **Figure 8**.

Substituting the known value for sine into the Pythagorean Identity,

$$\cos^2(t) + \sin^2(t) = 1$$

$$\cos^2(t) + \frac{9}{49} = 1$$

$$\cos^2(t) = \frac{40}{49}$$

$$\cos(t) = \pm\sqrt{\frac{40}{49}} = \pm\frac{\sqrt{40}}{7} = \pm\frac{2\sqrt{10}}{7}$$

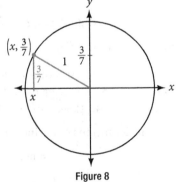

Figure 8

Because the angle is in the second quadrant, we know the x-value is a negative real number, so the cosine is also negative. So $\cos(t) = -\dfrac{2\sqrt{10}}{7}$

Try It #3

If $\cos(t) = \dfrac{24}{25}$ and t is in the fourth quadrant, find $\sin(t)$.

Finding Sines and Cosines of Special Angles

We have already learned some properties of the special angles, such as the conversion from radians to degrees. We can also calculate sines and cosines of the special angles using the Pythagorean Identity and our knowledge of triangles.

Finding Sines and Cosines of 45° Angles

First, we will look at angles of 45° or $\dfrac{\pi}{4}$, as shown in **Figure 9**. A 45° − 45° − 90° triangle is an isosceles triangle, so the x- and y-coordinates of the corresponding point on the circle are the same. Because the x- and y-values are the same, the sine and cosine values will also be equal.

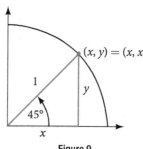

Figure 9

At $t = \dfrac{\pi}{4}$, which is 45 degrees, the radius of the unit circle bisects the first quadrantal angle. This means the radius lies along the line $y = x$. A unit circle has a radius equal to 1. So, the right triangle formed below the line $y = x$ has sides x and y $(y = x)$, and a radius = 1. See **Figure 10**.

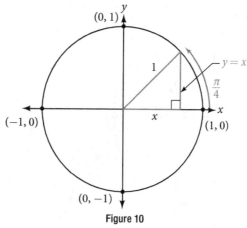

Figure 10

From the Pythagorean Theorem we get

$$x^2 + y^2 = 1$$

Substituting $y = x$, we get

$$x^2 + x^2 = 1$$

Combining like terms we get

$$2x^2 = 1$$

And solving for x, we get

$$x^2 = \frac{1}{2}$$

$$x = \pm\frac{1}{\sqrt{2}}$$

In quadrant I, $x = \dfrac{1}{\sqrt{2}}$.

At $t = \dfrac{\pi}{4}$ or 45 degrees,

$$(x, y) = (x, x) = \left(\dfrac{1}{\sqrt{2}}, \dfrac{1}{\sqrt{2}} \right)$$

$$x = \dfrac{1}{\sqrt{2}}, \ y = \dfrac{1}{\sqrt{2}}$$

$$\cos t = \dfrac{1}{\sqrt{2}}, \ \sin t = \dfrac{1}{\sqrt{2}}$$

If we then rationalize the denominators, we get

$$\cos t = \dfrac{1}{\sqrt{2}} \cdot \dfrac{\sqrt{2}}{\sqrt{2}}$$

$$= \dfrac{\sqrt{2}}{2}$$

$$\sin t = \dfrac{1}{\sqrt{2}} \cdot \dfrac{\sqrt{2}}{\sqrt{2}}$$

$$= \dfrac{\sqrt{2}}{2}$$

Therefore, the (x, y) coordinates of a point on a circle of radius 1 at an angle of 45° are $\left(\dfrac{\sqrt{2}}{2}, \dfrac{\sqrt{2}}{2} \right)$.

Finding Sines and Cosines of 30° and 60° Angles

Next, we will find the cosine and sine at an angle of 30°, or $\dfrac{\pi}{6}$. First, we will draw a triangle inside a circle with one side at an angle of 30°, and another at an angle of −30°, as shown in **Figure 11**. If the resulting two right triangles are combined into one large triangle, notice that all three angles of this larger triangle will be 60°, as shown in **Figure 12**.

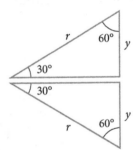

Figure 12

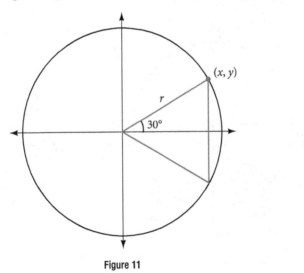

Figure 11

Because all the angles are equal, the sides are also equal. The vertical line has length $2y$, and since the sides are all equal, we can also conclude that $r = 2y$ or $y = \dfrac{1}{2}r$. Since $\sin t = y$,

$$\sin\left(\dfrac{\pi}{6} \right) = \dfrac{1}{2}r$$

And since $r = 1$ in our unit circle,

$$\sin\left(\dfrac{\pi}{6} \right) = \dfrac{1}{2}(1)$$

$$= \dfrac{1}{2}$$

Using the Pythagorean Identity, we can find the cosine value.

$$\cos^2 \frac{\pi}{6} + \sin^2\left(\frac{\pi}{6}\right) = 1$$

$$\cos^2\left(\frac{\pi}{6}\right) + \left(\frac{1}{2}\right)^2 = 1$$

$$\cos^2\left(\frac{\pi}{6}\right) = \frac{3}{4} \qquad \text{Use the square root property.}$$

$$\cos\left(\frac{\pi}{6}\right) = \frac{\pm\sqrt{3}}{\pm\sqrt{4}} = \frac{\sqrt{3}}{2} \qquad \text{Since } y \text{ is positive, choose the positive root.}$$

The (x, y) coordinates for the point on a circle of radius 1 at an angle of 30° are $\left(\frac{\sqrt{3}}{2}, \frac{1}{2}\right)$. At $t = \frac{\pi}{3}$ (60°), the radius of the unit circle, 1, serves as the hypotenuse of a 30-60-90 degree right triangle, BAD, as shown in **Figure 13**. Angle A has measure 60°. At point B, we draw an angle ABC with measure of 60°. We know the angles in a triangle sum to 180°, so the measure of angle C is also 60°. Now we have an equilateral triangle. Because each side of the equilateral triangle ABC is the same length, and we know one side is the radius of the unit circle, all sides must be of length 1.

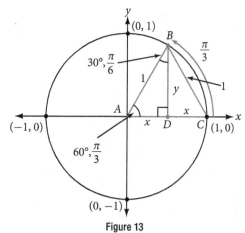

Figure 13

The measure of angle ABD is 30°. So, if double, angle ABC is 60°. BD is the perpendicular bisector of AC, so it cuts AC in half. This means that AD is $\frac{1}{2}$ the radius, or $\frac{1}{2}$. Notice that AD is the x-coordinate of point B, which is at the intersection of the 60° angle and the unit circle. This gives us a triangle BAD with hypotenuse of 1 and side x of length $\frac{1}{2}$.

From the Pythagorean Theorem, we get

$$x^2 + y^2 = 1$$

Substituting $x = \frac{1}{2}$, we get

$$\left(\frac{1}{2}\right)^2 + y^2 = 1$$

Solving for y, we get

$$\frac{1}{4} + y^2 = 1$$

$$y^2 = 1 - \frac{1}{4}$$

$$y^2 = \frac{3}{4}$$

$$y = \pm\frac{\sqrt{3}}{2}$$

Since $t = \frac{\pi}{3}$ has the terminal side in quadrant I where the y-coordinate is positive, we choose $y = \frac{\sqrt{3}}{2}$, the positive value.

At $t = \frac{\pi}{3}$ (60°), the (x, y) coordinates for the point on a circle of radius 1 at an angle of 60° are $\left(\frac{1}{2}, \frac{\sqrt{3}}{2} \right)$, so we can find the sine and cosine.

$$(x, y) = \left(\frac{1}{2}, \frac{\sqrt{3}}{2} \right)$$

$$x = \frac{1}{2}, y = \frac{\sqrt{3}}{2}$$

$$\cos t = \frac{1}{2}, \sin t = \frac{\sqrt{3}}{2}$$

We have now found the cosine and sine values for all of the most commonly encountered angles in the first quadrant of the unit circle. **Table 1** summarizes these values.

Angle	0	$\frac{\pi}{6}$, or 30°	$\frac{\pi}{4}$, or 45°	$\frac{\pi}{3}$, or 60°	$\frac{\pi}{2}$, or 90°
Cosine	1	$\frac{\sqrt{3}}{2}$	$\frac{\sqrt{2}}{2}$	$\frac{1}{2}$	0
Sine	0	$\frac{1}{2}$	$\frac{\sqrt{2}}{2}$	$\frac{\sqrt{3}}{2}$	1

Table 1

Figure 14 shows the common angles in the first quadrant of the unit circle.

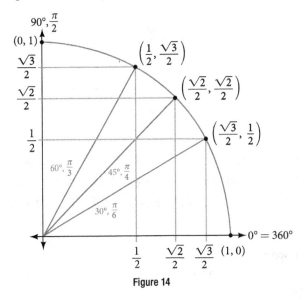

Figure 14

Using a Calculator to Find Sine and Cosine

To find the cosine and sine of angles other than the special angles, we turn to a computer or calculator. **Be aware**: Most calculators can be set into "degree" or "radian" mode, which tells the calculator the units for the input value. When we evaluate cos(30) on our calculator, it will evaluate it as the cosine of 30 degrees if the calculator is in degree mode, or the cosine of 30 radians if the calculator is in radian mode.

How To...

Given an angle in radians, use a graphing calculator to find the cosine.

1. If the calculator has degree mode and radian mode, set it to radian mode.
2. Press the **COS** key.
3. Enter the radian value of the angle and press the close-parentheses key ")".
4. Press **ENTER**.

Example 4   **Using a Graphing Calculator to Find Sine and Cosine**

Evaluate $\cos\left(\dfrac{5\pi}{3}\right)$ using a graphing calculator or computer.

Solution   Enter the following keystrokes:

$$\text{COS}(5 \times \pi \div 3)\ \text{ENTER}$$

$$\cos\left(\frac{5\pi}{3}\right) = 0.5$$

Analysis   We can find the cosine or sine of an angle in degrees directly on a calculator with degree mode. For calculators or software that use only radian mode, we can find the sign of 20°, for example, by including the conversion factor to radians as part of the input:

$$\text{SIN}(20 \times \pi \div 180)\ \text{ENTER}$$

Try It #4

Evaluate $\sin\left(\dfrac{\pi}{3}\right)$.

Identifying the Domain and Range of Sine and Cosine Functions

Now that we can find the sine and cosine of an angle, we need to discuss their domains and ranges. What are the domains of the sine and cosine functions? That is, what are the smallest and largest numbers that can be inputs of the functions? Because angles smaller than 0 and angles larger than 2π can still be graphed on the unit circle and have real values of x, y, and r, there is no lower or upper limit to the angles that can be inputs to the sine and cosine functions. The input to the sine and cosine functions is the rotation from the positive x-axis, and that may be any real number.

What are the ranges of the sine and cosine functions? What are the least and greatest possible values for their output? We can see the answers by examining the unit circle, as shown in **Figure 15**. The bounds of the x-coordinate are $[-1, 1]$.

The bounds of the y-coordinate are also $[-1, 1]$. Therefore, the range of both the sine and cosine functions is $[-1, 1]$.

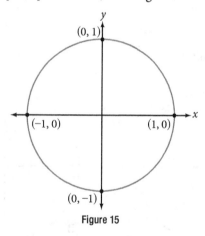

Figure 15

Finding Reference Angles

We have discussed finding the sine and cosine for angles in the first quadrant, but what if our angle is in another quadrant? For any given angle in the first quadrant, there is an angle in the second quadrant with the same sine value. Because the sine value is the y-coordinate on the unit circle, the other angle with the same sine will share the same y-value, but have the opposite x-value. Therefore, its cosine value will be the opposite of the first angle's cosine value.

Likewise, there will be an angle in the fourth quadrant with the same cosine as the original angle. The angle with the same cosine will share the same x-value but will have the opposite y-value. Therefore, its sine value will be the opposite of the original angle's sine value.

As shown in **Figure 16**, angle α has the same sine value as angle t; the cosine values are opposites. Angle β has the same cosine value as angle t; the sine values are opposites.

$$\sin(t) = \sin(\alpha) \quad \text{and} \cos(t) = -\cos(\alpha)$$

$$\sin(t) = -\sin(\beta) \text{ and } \cos(t) = \cos(\beta)$$

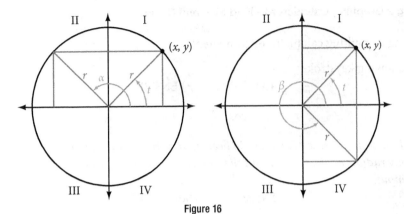

Figure 16

Recall that an angle's reference angle is the acute angle, t, formed by the terminal side of the angle t and the horizontal axis. A reference angle is always an angle between 0 and 90°, or 0 and $\frac{\pi}{2}$ radians. As we can see from **Figure 17**, for any angle in quadrants II, III, or IV, there is a reference angle in quadrant I.

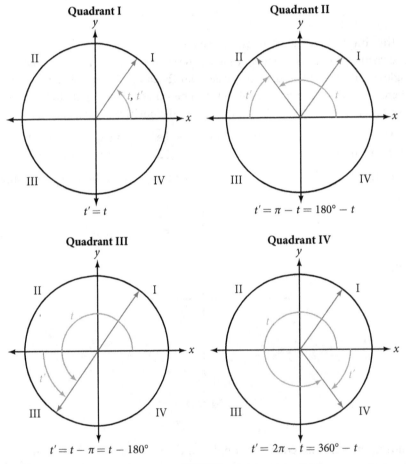

Figure 17

How To...

Given an angle between 0 and 2π, find its reference angle.

1. An angle in the first quadrant is its own reference angle.
2. For an angle in the second or third quadrant, the reference angle is $|\pi - t|$ or $|180° - t|$.
3. For an angle in the fourth quadrant, the reference angle is $2\pi - t$ or $360° - t$.
4. If an angle is less than 0 or greater than 2π, add or subtract 2π as many times as needed to find an equivalent angle between 0 and 2π.

Example 5   **Finding a Reference Angle**

Find the reference angle of 225° as shown in **Figure 18**.

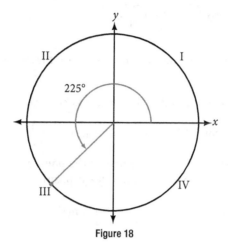

Figure 18

Solution   Because 225° is in the third quadrant, the reference angle is

$$|(180° − 225°)| = |−45°| = 45°$$

Try It #5

Find the reference angle of $\dfrac{5\pi}{3}$.

Using Reference Angles

Now let's take a moment to reconsider the Ferris wheel introduced at the beginning of this section. Suppose a rider snaps a photograph while stopped twenty feet above ground level. The rider then rotates three-quarters of the way around the circle. What is the rider's new elevation? To answer questions such as this one, we need to evaluate the sine or cosine functions at angles that are greater than 90 degrees or at a negative angle. Reference angles make it possible to evaluate trigonometric functions for angles outside the first quadrant. They can also be used to find (x, y) coordinates for those angles. We will use the reference angle of the angle of rotation combined with the quadrant in which the terminal side of the angle lies.

Using Reference Angles to Evaluate Trigonometric Functions

We can find the cosine and sine of any angle in any quadrant if we know the cosine or sine of its reference angle. The absolute values of the cosine and sine of an angle are the same as those of the reference angle. The sign depends on the quadrant of the original angle. The cosine will be positive or negative depending on the sign of the x-values in that quadrant. The sine will be positive or negative depending on the sign of the y-values in that quadrant.

> **using reference angles to find cosine and sine**
>
> Angles have cosines and sines with the same absolute value as cosines and sines of their reference angles. The sign (positive or negative) can be determined from the quadrant of the angle.

How To...

Given an angle in standard position, find the reference angle, and the cosine and sine of the original angle.

1. Measure the angle between the terminal side of the given angle and the horizontal axis. That is the reference angle.
2. Determine the values of the cosine and sine of the reference angle.
3. Give the cosine the same sign as the x-values in the quadrant of the original angle.
4. Give the sine the same sign as the y-values in the quadrant of the original angle.

Example 6   **Using Reference Angles to Find Sine and Cosine**

    a. Using a reference angle, find the exact value of $\cos(150°)$ and $\sin(150°)$.

    b. Using the reference angle, find $\cos\dfrac{5\pi}{4}$ and $\sin\dfrac{5\pi}{4}$.

Solution

    a. $150°$ is located in the second quadrant. The angle it makes with the x-axis is $180° - 150° = 30°$, so the reference angle is $30°$.

    This tells us that $150°$ has the same sine and cosine values as $30°$, except for the sign. We know that

$$\cos(30°) = \frac{\sqrt{3}}{2} \text{ and } \sin(30°) = \frac{1}{2}.$$

    Since $150°$ is in the second quadrant, the x-coordinate of the point on the circle is negative, so the cosine value is negative. The y-coordinate is positive, so the sine value is positive.

$$\cos(150°) = -\frac{\sqrt{3}}{2} \text{ and } \sin(150°) = \frac{1}{2}$$

    b. $\dfrac{5\pi}{4}$ is in the third quadrant. Its reference angle is $\dfrac{5\pi}{4} - \pi = \dfrac{\pi}{4}$. The cosine and sine of $\dfrac{\pi}{4}$ are both $\dfrac{\sqrt{2}}{2}$. In the third quadrant, both x and y are negative, so:

$$\cos\frac{5\pi}{4} = -\frac{\sqrt{2}}{2} \text{ and } \sin\frac{5\pi}{4} = -\frac{\sqrt{2}}{2}$$

Try It #6

a. Use the reference angle of $315°$ to find $\cos(315°)$ and $\sin(315°)$.

b. Use the reference angle of $-\dfrac{\pi}{6}$ to find $\cos\left(-\dfrac{\pi}{6}\right)$ and $\sin\left(-\dfrac{\pi}{6}\right)$.

Using Reference Angles to Find Coordinates

Now that we have learned how to find the cosine and sine values for special angles in the first quadrant, we can use symmetry and reference angles to fill in cosine and sine values for the rest of the special angles on the unit circle. They are shown in **Figure 19**. Take time to learn the (x, y) coordinates of all of the major angles in the first quadrant.

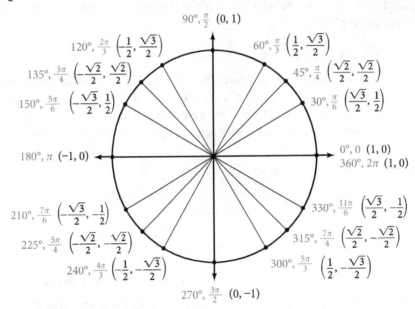

Figure 19 Special angles and coordinates of corresponding points on the unit circle

In addition to learning the values for special angles, we can use reference angles to find (x, y) coordinates of any point on the unit circle, using what we know of reference angles along with the identities

$$x = \cos t \qquad\qquad y = \sin t$$

First we find the reference angle corresponding to the given angle. Then we take the sine and cosine values of the reference angle, and give them the signs corresponding to the y- and x-values of the quadrant.

How To...

Given the angle of a point on a circle and the radius of the circle, find the (x, y) coordinates of the point.

1. Find the reference angle by measuring the smallest angle to the x-axis.
2. Find the cosine and sine of the reference angle.
3. Determine the appropriate signs for x and y in the given quadrant.

Example 7   **Using the Unit Circle to Find Coordinates**

Find the coordinates of the point on the unit circle at an angle of $\dfrac{7\pi}{6}$.

Solution   We know that the angle $\dfrac{7\pi}{6}$ is in the third quadrant.

First, let's find the reference angle by measuring the angle to the x-axis. To find the reference angle of an angle whose terminal side is in quadrant III, we find the difference of the angle and π.

$$\frac{7\pi}{6} - \pi = \frac{\pi}{6}$$

Next, we will find the cosine and sine of the reference angle:

$$\cos\left(\frac{\pi}{6}\right) = \frac{\sqrt{3}}{2} \text{ and } \sin\left(\frac{\pi}{6}\right) = \frac{1}{2}$$

We must determine the appropriate signs for x and y in the given quadrant. Because our original angle is in the third quadrant, where both x and y are negative, both cosine and sine are negative.

$$\cos\left(\frac{7\pi}{6}\right) = -\frac{\sqrt{3}}{2}$$

$$\sin\left(\frac{7\pi}{6}\right) = -\frac{1}{2}$$

Now we can calculate the (x, y) coordinates using the identities $x = \cos\theta$ and $y = \sin\theta$.

The coordinates of the point are $\left(-\dfrac{\sqrt{3}}{2}, -\dfrac{1}{2}\right)$ on the unit circle.

Try It #7

Find the coordinates of the point on the unit circle at an angle of $\dfrac{5\pi}{3}$.

Access these online resources for additional instruction and practice with sine and cosine functions.

- Trigonometric Functions Using the Unit Circle (http://openstaxcollege.org/l/trigunitcir)
- Sine and Cosine from the Unit Circle (http://openstaxcollege.org/l/sincosuc)
- Sine and Cosine from the Unit Circle and Multiples of Pi Divided by Six (http://openstaxcollege.org/l/sincosmult)
- Sine and Cosine from the Unit Circle and Multiples of Pi Divided by Four (http://openstaxcollege.org/l/sincosmult4)
- Trigonometric Functions Using Reference Angles (http://openstaxcollege.org/l/trigrefang)

5.2   SECTION EXERCISES

VERBAL

1. Describe the unit circle.

2. What do the x- and y-coordinates of the points on the unit circle represent?

3. Discuss the difference between a coterminal angle and a reference angle.

4. Explain how the cosine of an angle in the second quadrant differs from the cosine of its reference angle in the unit circle.

5. Explain how the sine of an angle in the second quadrant differs from the sine of its reference angle in the unit circle.

ALGEBRAIC

For the following exercises, use the given sign of the sine and cosine functions to find the quadrant in which the terminal point determined by t lies.

6. $\sin(t) < 0$ and $\cos(t) < 0$

7. $\sin(t) > 0$ and $\cos(t) > 0$

8. $\sin(t) > 0$ and $\cos(t) < 0$

9. $\sin(t) < 0$ and $\cos(t) > 0$

For the following exercises, find the exact value of each trigonometric function.

10. $\sin \dfrac{\pi}{2}$

11. $\sin \dfrac{\pi}{3}$

12. $\cos \dfrac{\pi}{2}$

13. $\cos \dfrac{\pi}{3}$

14. $\sin \dfrac{\pi}{4}$

15. $\cos \dfrac{\pi}{4}$

16. $\sin \dfrac{\pi}{6}$

17. $\sin \pi$

18. $\sin \dfrac{3\pi}{2}$

19. $\cos \pi$

20. $\cos 0$

21. $\cos \dfrac{\pi}{6}$

22. $\sin 0$

NUMERIC

For the following exercises, state the reference angle for the given angle.

23. $240°$

24. $-170°$

25. $100°$

26. $-315°$

27. $135°$

28. $\dfrac{5\pi}{4}$

29. $\dfrac{2\pi}{3}$

30. $\dfrac{5\pi}{6}$

31. $\dfrac{-11\pi}{3}$

32. $\dfrac{-7\pi}{4}$

33. $\dfrac{-\pi}{8}$

For the following exercises, find the reference angle, the quadrant of the terminal side, and the sine and cosine of each angle. If the angle is not one of the angles on the unit circle, use a calculator and round to three decimal places.

34. $225°$

35. $300°$

36. $320°$

37. $135°$

38. $210°$

39. $120°$

40. $250°$

41. $150°$

42. $\dfrac{5\pi}{4}$

43. $\dfrac{7\pi}{6}$

44. $\dfrac{5\pi}{3}$

45. $\dfrac{3\pi}{4}$

46. $\dfrac{4\pi}{3}$

47. $\dfrac{2\pi}{3}$

48. $\dfrac{5\pi}{6}$

49. $\dfrac{7\pi}{4}$

For the following exercises, find the requested value.

50. If $\cos(t) = \dfrac{1}{7}$ and t is in the 4th quadrant, find $\sin(t)$.

51. If $\cos(t) = \dfrac{2}{9}$ and t is in the 1st quadrant, find $\sin(t)$.

52. If $\sin(t) = \dfrac{3}{8}$ and t is in the 2nd quadrant, find $\cos(t)$.

53. If $\sin(t) = -\dfrac{1}{4}$ and t is in the 3rd quadrant, find $\cos(t)$.

54. Find the coordinates of the point on a circle with radius 15 corresponding to an angle of $220°$.

55. Find the coordinates of the point on a circle with radius 20 corresponding to an angle of $120°$.

56. Find the coordinates of the point on a circle with radius 8 corresponding to an angle of $\frac{7\pi}{4}$.

57. Find the coordinates of the point on a circle with radius 16 corresponding to an angle of $\frac{5\pi}{9}$.

58. State the domain of the sine and cosine functions.

59. State the range of the sine and cosine functions.

GRAPHICAL

For the following exercises, use the given point on the unit circle to find the value of the sine and cosine of t.

60.

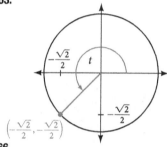

61.

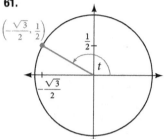

62.

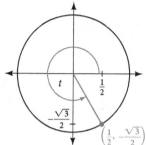

63.

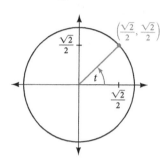

64.

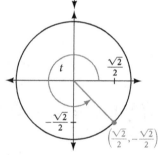

65.

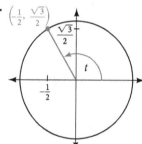

66.

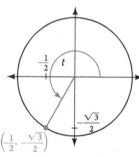

67.

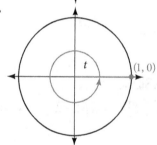

68.

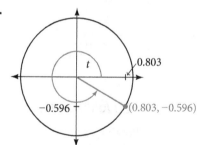

69.

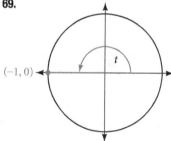

70.

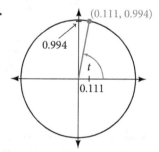

71.

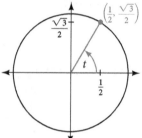

72.

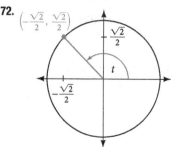

73.

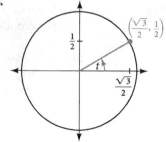

74.

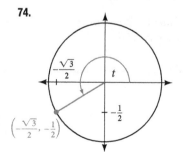

75.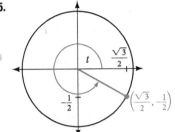

76.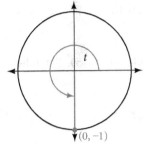

77.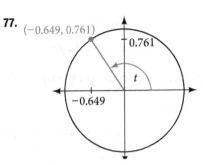

78.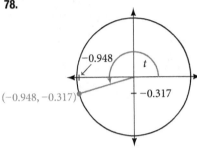

79.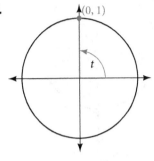

TECHNOLOGY

For the following exercises, use a graphing calculator to evaluate.

80. $\sin \dfrac{5\pi}{9}$

81. $\cos \dfrac{5\pi}{9}$

82. $\sin \dfrac{\pi}{10}$

83. $\cos \dfrac{\pi}{10}$

84. $\sin \dfrac{3\pi}{4}$

85. $\cos \dfrac{3\pi}{4}$

86. $\sin 98°$

87. $\cos 98°$

88. $\cos 310°$

89. $\sin 310°$

EXTENSIONS

90. $\sin\left(\dfrac{11\pi}{3}\right)\cos\left(\dfrac{-5\pi}{6}\right)$

91. $\sin\left(\dfrac{3\pi}{4}\right)\cos\left(\dfrac{5\pi}{3}\right)$

92. $\sin\left(-\dfrac{4\pi}{3}\right)\cos\left(\dfrac{\pi}{2}\right)$

93. $\sin\left(\dfrac{-9\pi}{4}\right)\cos\left(\dfrac{-\pi}{6}\right)$

94. $\sin\left(\dfrac{\pi}{6}\right)\cos\left(\dfrac{-\pi}{3}\right)$

95. $\sin\left(\dfrac{7\pi}{4}\right)\cos\left(\dfrac{-2\pi}{3}\right)$

96. $\cos\left(\dfrac{5\pi}{6}\right)\cos\left(\dfrac{2\pi}{3}\right)$

97. $\cos\left(\dfrac{-\pi}{3}\right)\cos\left(\dfrac{\pi}{4}\right)$

98. $\sin\left(\dfrac{-5\pi}{4}\right)\sin\left(\dfrac{11\pi}{6}\right)$

99. $\sin(\pi)\sin\left(\dfrac{\pi}{6}\right)$

REAL-WORLD APPLICATIONS

For the following exercises, use this scenario: A child enters a carousel that takes one minute to revolve once around. The child enters at the point (0, 1), that is, on the due north position. Assume the carousel revolves counter clockwise.

100. What are the coordinates of the child after 45 seconds?

101. What are the coordinates of the child after 90 seconds?

102. What is the coordinates of the child after 125 seconds?

103. When will the child have coordinates (0.707, −0.707) if the ride lasts 6 minutes? (There are multiple answers.)

104. When will the child have coordinates (−0.866, −0.5) if the ride last 6 minutes?

LEARNING OBJECTIVES

In this section, you will:

- Find exact values of the trigonometric functions secant, cosecant, tangent, and cotangent of $\frac{\pi}{3}$, $\frac{\pi}{4}$, and $\frac{\pi}{6}$.
- Use reference angles to evaluate the trigonometric functions secant, cosecant, tangent, and cotangent.
- Use properties of even and odd trigonometric functions.
- Recognize and use fundamental identities.
- Evaluate trigonometric functions with a calculator.

5.3   THE OTHER TRIGONOMETRIC FUNCTIONS

A wheelchair ramp that meets the standards of the Americans with Disabilities Act must make an angle with the ground whose tangent is $\frac{1}{12}$ or less, regardless of its length. A tangent represents a ratio, so this means that for every 1 inch of rise, the ramp must have 12 inches of run. Trigonometric functions allow us to specify the shapes and proportions of objects independent of exact dimensions. We have already defined the sine and cosine functions of an angle. Though sine and cosine are the trigonometric functions most often used, there are four others. Together they make up the set of six trigonometric functions. In this section, we will investigate the remaining functions.

Finding Exact Values of the Trigonometric Functions Secant, Cosecant, Tangent, and Cotangent

To define the remaining functions, we will once again draw a unit circle with a point (x, y) corresponding to an angle of t, as shown in **Figure 1**. As with the sine and cosine, we can use the (x, y) coordinates to find the other functions.

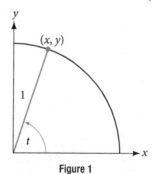

Figure 1

The first function we will define is the tangent. The **tangent** of an angle is the ratio of the y-value to the x-value of the corresponding point on the unit circle. In **Figure 1**, the tangent of angle t is equal to $\frac{y}{x}$, $x \neq 0$. Because the y-value is equal to the sine of t, and the x-value is equal to the cosine of t, the tangent of angle t can also be defined as $\frac{\sin t}{\cos t}$, $\cos t \neq 0$. The tangent function is abbreviated as tan. The remaining three functions can all be expressed as reciprocals of functions we have already defined.

- The **secant** function is the reciprocal of the cosine function. In **Figure 1**, the secant of angle t is equal to $\frac{1}{\cos t} = \frac{1}{x}$, $x \neq 0$. The secant function is abbreviated as sec.
- The **cotangent** function is the reciprocal of the tangent function. In **Figure 1**, the cotangent of angle t is equal to $\frac{\cos t}{\sin t} = \frac{x}{y}$, $y \neq 0$. The cotangent function is abbreviated as cot.
- The **cosecant** function is the reciprocal of the sine function. In **Figure 1**, the cosecant of angle t is equal to $\frac{1}{\sin t} = \frac{1}{y}$, $y \neq 0$. The cosecant function is abbreviated as csc.

tangent, secant, cosecant, and cotangent functions
If t is a real number and (x, y) is a point where the terminal side of an angle of t radians intercepts the unit circle, then

$$\tan t = \frac{y}{x}, x \neq 0 \qquad \sec t = \frac{1}{x}, x \neq 0$$

$$\csc t = \frac{1}{y}, y \neq 0 \qquad \cot t = \frac{x}{y}, y \neq 0$$

Example 1   Finding Trigonometric Functions from a Point on the Unit Circle

The point $\left(-\dfrac{\sqrt{3}}{2}, \dfrac{1}{2}\right)$ is on the unit circle, as shown in **Figure 2**. Find $\sin t$, $\cos t$, $\tan t$, $\sec t$, $\csc t$, and $\cot t$.

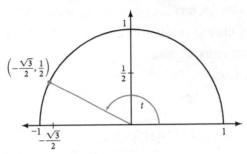

Figure 2

Solution   Because we know the (x, y) coordinates of the point on the unit circle indicated by angle t, we can use those coordinates to find the six functions:

$$\sin t = y = \frac{1}{2}$$

$$\cos t = x = -\frac{\sqrt{3}}{2}$$

$$\tan t = \frac{y}{x} = \frac{\frac{1}{2}}{-\frac{\sqrt{3}}{2}} = \frac{1}{2}\left(-\frac{2}{\sqrt{3}}\right) = -\frac{1}{\sqrt{3}} = -\frac{\sqrt{3}}{3}$$

$$\sec t = \frac{1}{x} = \frac{1}{-\frac{\sqrt{3}}{2}} = -\frac{2}{\sqrt{3}} = -\frac{2\sqrt{3}}{3}$$

$$\csc t = \frac{1}{y} = \frac{1}{\frac{1}{2}} = 2$$

$$\cot t = \frac{x}{y} = \frac{-\frac{\sqrt{3}}{2}}{\frac{1}{2}} = -\frac{\sqrt{3}}{2}\left(\frac{2}{1}\right) = -\sqrt{3}$$

Try It #1

The point $\left(\dfrac{\sqrt{2}}{2}, -\dfrac{\sqrt{2}}{2}\right)$ is on the unit circle, as shown in **Figure 3**. Find $\sin t$, $\cos t$, $\tan t$, $\sec t$, $\csc t$, and $\cot t$.

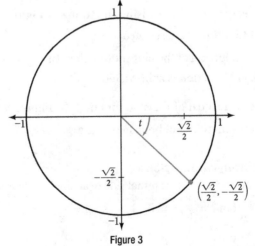

Figure 3

Example 2   **Finding the Trigonometric Functions of an Angle**

Find $\sin t$, $\cos t$, $\tan t$, $\sec t$, $\csc t$, and $\cot t$ when $t = \dfrac{\pi}{6}$.

Solution   We have previously used the properties of equilateral triangles to demonstrate that $\sin \dfrac{\pi}{6} = \dfrac{1}{2}$ and $\cos \dfrac{\pi}{6} = \dfrac{\sqrt{3}}{2}$.

We can use these values and the definitions of tangent, secant, cosecant, and cotangent as functions of sine and cosine to find the remaining function values.

$$\tan \frac{\pi}{6} = \frac{\sin \dfrac{\pi}{6}}{\cos \dfrac{\pi}{6}}$$

$$= \frac{\dfrac{1}{2}}{\dfrac{\sqrt{3}}{2}} = \frac{1}{\sqrt{3}} = \frac{\sqrt{3}}{3}$$

$$\sec \frac{\pi}{6} = \frac{1}{\cos \dfrac{\pi}{6}}$$

$$= \frac{1}{\dfrac{\sqrt{3}}{2}} = \frac{2}{\sqrt{3}} = \frac{2\sqrt{3}}{3}$$

$$\csc \frac{\pi}{6} = \frac{1}{\sin \dfrac{\pi}{6}} = \frac{1}{\dfrac{1}{2}} = 2$$

$$\cot \frac{\pi}{6} = \frac{\cos \dfrac{\pi}{6}}{\sin \dfrac{\pi}{6}}$$

$$= \frac{\dfrac{\sqrt{3}}{2}}{\dfrac{1}{2}} = \sqrt{3}$$

Try It #2

Find $\sin t$, $\cos t$, $\tan t$, $\sec t$, $\csc t$, and $\cot t$ when $t = \dfrac{\pi}{3}$.

Because we know the sine and cosine values for the common first-quadrant angles, we can find the other function values for those angles as well by setting x equal to the cosine and y equal to the sine and then using the definitions of tangent, secant, cosecant, and cotangent. The results are shown in **Table 1**.

Angle	0	$\dfrac{\pi}{6}$, or 30°	$\dfrac{\pi}{4}$, or 45°	$\dfrac{\pi}{3}$, or 60°	$\dfrac{\pi}{2}$, or 90°
Cosine	1	$\dfrac{\sqrt{3}}{2}$	$\dfrac{\sqrt{2}}{2}$	$\dfrac{1}{2}$	0
Sine	0	$\dfrac{1}{2}$	$\dfrac{\sqrt{2}}{2}$	$\dfrac{\sqrt{3}}{2}$	1
Tangent	0	$\dfrac{\sqrt{3}}{3}$	1	$\sqrt{3}$	Undefined
Secant	1	$\dfrac{2\sqrt{3}}{3}$	$\sqrt{2}$	2	Undefined
Cosecant	Undefined	2	$\sqrt{2}$	$\dfrac{2\sqrt{3}}{3}$	1
Cotangent	Undefined	$\sqrt{3}$	1	$\dfrac{\sqrt{3}}{3}$	0

Table 1

Using Reference Angles to Evaluate Tangent, Secant, Cosecant, and Cotangent

We can evaluate trigonometric functions of angles outside the first quadrant using reference angles as we have already done with the sine and cosine functions. The procedure is the same: Find the reference angle formed by the terminal side of the given angle with the horizontal axis. The trigonometric function values for the original angle will be the same as those for the reference angle, except for the positive or negative sign, which is determined by *x*- and *y*-values in the original quadrant. **Figure 4** shows which functions are positive in which quadrant.

To help us remember which of the six trigonometric functions are positive in each quadrant, we can use the mnemonic phrase "A Smart Trig Class." Each of the four words in the phrase corresponds to one of the four quadrants, starting with quadrant I and rotating counterclockwise. In quadrant I, which is "**A**," **a**ll of the six trigonometric functions are positive. In quadrant II, "**S**mart," only **s**ine and its reciprocal function, cosecant, are positive. In quadrant III, "**T**rig," only **t**angent and its reciprocal function, cotangent, are positive. Finally, in quadrant IV, "**C**lass," only **c**osine and its reciprocal function, secant, are positive.

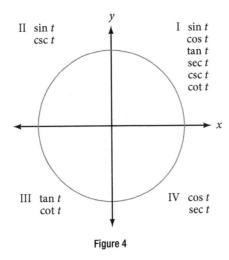

Figure 4

How To...

Given an angle not in the first quadrant, use reference angles to find all six trigonometric functions.

1. Measure the angle formed by the terminal side of the given angle and the horizontal axis. This is the reference angle.
2. Evaluate the function at the reference angle.
3. Observe the quadrant where the terminal side of the original angle is located. Based on the quadrant, determine whether the output is positive or negative.

Example 3   **Using Reference Angles to Find Trigonometric Functions**

Use reference angles to find all six trigonometric functions of $-\dfrac{5\pi}{6}$.

Solution   The angle between this angle's terminal side and the *x*-axis is $\dfrac{\pi}{6}$, so that is the reference angle. Since $-\dfrac{5\pi}{6}$ is in the third quadrant, where both *x* and *y* are negative, cosine, sine, secant, and cosecant will be negative, while tangent and cotangent will be positive.

$$\cos\left(-\frac{5\pi}{6}\right)=-\frac{\sqrt{3}}{2}, \quad \sin\left(-\frac{5\pi}{6}\right)=-\frac{1}{2}, \quad \tan\left(-\frac{5\pi}{6}\right)=\frac{\sqrt{3}}{3}$$

$$\sec\left(-\frac{5\pi}{6}\right)=-\frac{2\sqrt{3}}{3}, \quad \csc\left(-\frac{5\pi}{6}\right)=-2, \quad \cot\left(-\frac{5\pi}{6}\right)=\sqrt{3}$$

Try It #3

Use reference angles to find all six trigonometric functions of $-\dfrac{7\pi}{4}$.

Using Even and Odd Trigonometric Functions

To be able to use our six trigonometric functions freely with both positive and negative angle inputs, we should examine how each function treats a negative input. As it turns out, there is an important difference among the functions in this regard. Consider the function $f(x) = x^2$, shown in **Figure 5**. The graph of the function is symmetrical about the y-axis. All along the curve, any two points with opposite x-values have the same function value. This matches the result of calculation: $(4)^2 = (-4)^2$, $(-5)^2 = (5)^2$, and so on. So $f(x) = x^2$ is an even function, a function such that two inputs that are opposites have the same output. That means $f(-x) = f(x)$.

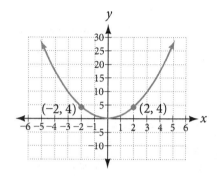

Figure 5 The function $f(x) = x^2$ is an even function.

Now consider the function $f(x) = x^3$, shown in **Figure 6**. The graph is not symmetrical about the y-axis. All along the graph, any two points with opposite x-values also have opposite y-values. So $f(x) = x^3$ is an odd function, one such that two inputs that are opposites have outputs that are also opposites. That means $f(-x) = -f(x)$.

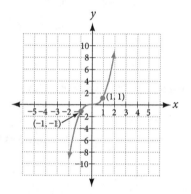

Figure 6 The function $f(x) = x^3$ is an odd function.

We can test whether a trigonometric function is even or odd by drawing a unit circle with a positive and a negative angle, as in **Figure 7**. The sine of the positive angle is y. The sine of the negative angle is $-y$. The sine function, then, is an odd function. We can test each of the six trigonometric functions in this fashion. The results are shown in **Table 2**.

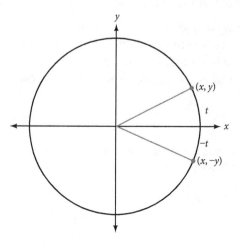

Figure 7

$\sin t = y$	$\cos t = x$	$\tan(t) = \dfrac{y}{x}$
$\sin(-t) = -y$	$\cos(-t) = x$	$\tan(-t) = -\dfrac{y}{x}$
$\sin t \neq \sin(-t)$	$\cos t = \cos(-t)$	$\tan t \neq \tan(-t)$
$\sec t = \dfrac{1}{x}$	$\csc t = \dfrac{1}{y}$	$\cot t = \dfrac{x}{y}$
$\sec(-t) = \dfrac{1}{x}$	$\csc(-t) = \dfrac{1}{-y}$	$\cot(-t) = \dfrac{x}{-y}$
$\sec t = \sec(-t)$	$\csc t \neq \csc(-t)$	$\cot t \neq \cot(-t)$

Table 2

even and odd trigonometric functions

An even function is one in which $f(-x) = f(x)$. An odd function is one in which $f(-x) = -f(x)$.
Cosine and secant are even:

$$\cos(-t) = \cos t$$
$$\sec(-t) = \sec t$$

Sine, tangent, cosecant, and cotangent are odd:

$$\sin(-t) = -\sin t$$
$$\tan(-t) = -\tan t$$
$$\csc(-t) = -\csc t$$
$$\cot(-t) = -\cot t$$

Example 4   Using Even and Odd Properties of Trigonometric Functions

If the secant of angle t is 2, what is the secant of $-t$?

Solution   Secant is an even function. The secant of an angle is the same as the secant of its opposite. So if the secant of angle t is 2, the secant of $-t$ is also 2.

Try It #4

If the cotangent of angle t is $\sqrt{3}$, what is the cotangent of $-t$?

Recognizing and Using Fundamental Identities

We have explored a number of properties of trigonometric functions. Now, we can take the relationships a step further, and derive some fundamental identities. Identities are statements that are true for all values of the input on which they are defined. Usually, identities can be derived from definitions and relationships we already know. For example, the Pythagorean Identity we learned earlier was derived from the Pythagorean Theorem and the definitions of sine and cosine.

fundamental identities

We can derive some useful identities from the six trigonometric functions. The other four trigonometric functions can be related back to the sine and cosine functions using these basic relationships:

$$\tan t = \frac{\sin t}{\cos t} \qquad \sec t = \frac{1}{\cos t}$$

$$\csc t = \frac{1}{\sin t} \qquad \cot t = \frac{1}{\tan t} = \frac{\cos t}{\sin t}$$

Example 5   **Using Identities to Evaluate Trigonometric Functions**

a. Given $\sin(45°) = \dfrac{\sqrt{2}}{2,}$, $\cos(45°) = \dfrac{\sqrt{2}}{2}$, evaluate $\tan(45°)$.

b. Given $\sin\left(\dfrac{5\pi}{6}\right) = \dfrac{1}{2}$, $\cos\left(\dfrac{5\pi}{6}\right) = -\dfrac{\sqrt{3}}{2}$, evaluate $\sec\left(\dfrac{5\pi}{6}\right)$.

Solution   Because we know the sine and cosine values for these angles, we can use identities to evaluate the other functions.

a.
$$\tan(45°) = \frac{\sin(45°)}{\cos(45°)}$$

$$= \frac{\dfrac{\sqrt{2}}{2}}{\dfrac{\sqrt{2}}{2}}$$

$$= 1$$

b.
$$\sec\left(\frac{5\pi}{6}\right) = \frac{1}{\left(\cos\dfrac{5\pi}{6}\right)}$$

$$= \frac{1}{-\dfrac{\sqrt{3}}{2}}$$

$$= \frac{-2}{\sqrt{3}}$$

$$= -\frac{2\sqrt{3}}{3}$$

Try It #5

Evaluate $\csc\left(\dfrac{7\pi}{6}\right)$.

Example 6   **Using Identities to Simplify Trigonometric Expressions**

Simplify $\dfrac{\sec t}{\tan t}$.

Solution   We can simplify this by rewriting both functions in terms of sine and cosine.

$$\frac{\sec t}{\tan t} = \frac{\dfrac{1}{\cos t}}{\dfrac{\sin t}{\cos t}} \qquad \text{To divide the functions, we multiply by the reciprocal.}$$

$$= \frac{1}{\cos t}\ \frac{\cos t}{\sin t} \qquad \text{Divide out the cosines.}$$

$$= \frac{1}{\sin t} \qquad \text{Simplify and use the identity.}$$

$$= \csc t$$

By showing that $\dfrac{\sec t}{\tan t}$ can be simplified to $\csc t$, we have, in fact, established a new identity.

$$\frac{\sec t}{\tan t} = \csc t$$

Try It #6

Simplify $(\tan t)(\cos t)$.

Alternate Forms of the Pythagorean Identity

We can use these fundamental identities to derive alternative forms of the Pythagorean Identity, $\cos^2 t + \sin^2 t = 1$. One form is obtained by dividing both sides by $\cos^2 t$:

$$\frac{\cos^2 t}{\cos^2 t} + \frac{\sin^2 t}{\cos^2 t} = \frac{1}{\cos^2 t}$$

$$1 + \tan^2 t = \sec^2 t$$

The other form is obtained by dividing both sides by $\sin^2 t$:

$$\frac{\cos^2 t}{\sin^2 t} + \frac{\sin^2 t}{\sin^2 t} = \frac{1}{\sin^2 t}$$

$$\cot^2 t + 1 = \csc^2 t$$

---

alternate forms of the pythagorean identity

$$1 + \tan^2 t = \sec^2 t$$

$$\cot^2 t + 1 = \csc^2 t$$

Example 7   **Using Identities to Relate Trigonometric Functions**

If $\cos(t) = \dfrac{12}{13}$ and t is in quadrant IV, as shown in **Figure 8**, find the values of the other five trigonometric functions.

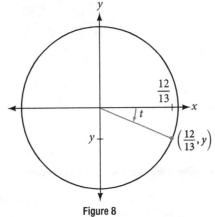

Figure 8

Solution   We can find the sine using the Pythagorean Identity, $\cos^2 t + \sin^2 t = 1$, and the remaining functions by relating them to sine and cosine.

$$\left(\frac{12}{13}\right)^2 + \sin^2 t = 1$$

$$\sin^2 t = 1 - \left(\frac{12}{13}\right)^2$$

$$\sin^2 t = 1 - \frac{144}{169}$$

$$\sin^2 t = \frac{25}{169}$$

$$\sin t = \pm\sqrt{\frac{25}{169}}$$

$$\sin t = \pm\frac{\sqrt{25}}{\sqrt{169}}$$

$$\sin t = \pm\frac{5}{13}$$

The sign of the sine depends on the y-values in the quadrant where the angle is located. Since the angle is in quadrant IV, where the y-values are negative, its sine is negative, $-\dfrac{5}{13}$.

The remaining functions can be calculated using identities relating them to sine and cosine.

$$\tan t = \frac{\sin t}{\cos t} = \frac{-\dfrac{5}{13}}{\dfrac{12}{13}} = -\frac{5}{12}$$

$$\sec t = \frac{1}{\cos t} = \frac{1}{\dfrac{12}{13}} = \frac{13}{12}$$

$$\csc t = \frac{1}{\sin t} = \frac{1}{-\dfrac{5}{13}} = -\frac{13}{5}$$

$$\cot t = \frac{1}{\tan t} = \frac{1}{-\dfrac{5}{12}} = -\frac{12}{5}$$

Try It #7

If $\sec(t) = -\dfrac{17}{8}$ and $0 < t < \pi$, find the values of the other five functions.

As we discussed in the chapter opening, a function that repeats its values in regular intervals is known as a periodic function. The trigonometric functions are periodic. For the four trigonometric functions, sine, cosine, cosecant and secant, a revolution of one circle, or 2π, will result in the same outputs for these functions. And for tangent and cotangent, only a half a revolution will result in the same outputs.

Other functions can also be periodic. For example, the lengths of months repeat every four years. If x represents the length time, measured in years, and $f(x)$ represents the number of days in February, then $f(x + 4) = f(x)$. This pattern repeats over and over through time. In other words, every four years, February is guaranteed to have the same number of days as it did 4 years earlier. The positive number 4 is the smallest positive number that satisfies this condition and is called the period. A **period** is the shortest interval over which a function completes one full cycle—in this example, the period is 4 and represents the time it takes for us to be certain February has the same number of days.

> *period of a function*
>
> The **period** P of a repeating function f is the number representing the interval such that $f(x + P) = f(x)$ for any value of x.
> The period of the cosine, sine, secant, and cosecant functions is 2π.
> The period of the tangent and cotangent functions is π.

Example 8   **Finding the Values of Trigonometric Functions**

Find the values of the six trigonometric functions of angle t based on **Figure 9**.

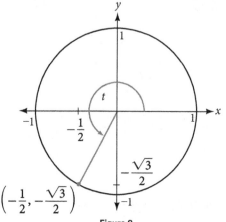

Figure 9

Solution

$$\sin t = y = -\frac{\sqrt{3}}{2}$$

$$\cos t = x = -\frac{1}{2}$$

$$\tan t = \frac{\sin t}{\cos t} = \frac{-\dfrac{\sqrt{3}}{2}}{-\dfrac{1}{2}} = \sqrt{3}$$

$$\sec t = \frac{1}{\cos t} = \frac{1}{-\dfrac{1}{2}} = -2$$

$$\csc t = \frac{1}{\sin t} = \frac{1}{-\dfrac{\sqrt{3}}{2}} = -\frac{2\sqrt{3}}{3}$$

$$\cot t = \frac{1}{\tan t} = \frac{1}{\sqrt{3}} = \frac{\sqrt{3}}{3}$$

Try It #8

Find the values of the six trigonometric functions of angle t based on **Figure 10**.

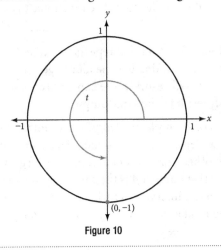

Figure 10

Example 9   **Finding the Value of Trigonometric Functions**

If $\sin(t) = -\dfrac{\sqrt{3}}{2}$ and $\cos(t) = \dfrac{1}{2}$, find $\sec(t)$, $\csc(t)$, $\tan(t)$, $\cot(t)$.

Solution

$$\sec t = \frac{1}{\cos t} = \frac{1}{\dfrac{1}{2}} = 2$$

$$\csc t = \frac{1}{\sin t} = \frac{1}{-\dfrac{\sqrt{3}}{2}} = -\frac{2\sqrt{3}}{3}$$

$$\tan t = \frac{\sin t}{\cos t} = \frac{-\dfrac{\sqrt{3}}{2}}{\dfrac{1}{2}} = -\sqrt{3}$$

$$\cot t = \frac{1}{\tan t} = \frac{1}{-\sqrt{3}} = -\frac{\sqrt{3}}{3}$$

Try It #9

If $\sin(t) = \dfrac{\sqrt{2}}{2}$ and $\cos(t) = \dfrac{\sqrt{2}}{2}$, find $\sec(t)$, $\csc(t)$, $\tan(t)$, and $\cot(t)$.

Evaluating Trigonometric Functions with a Calculator

We have learned how to evaluate the six trigonometric functions for the common first-quadrant angles and to use them as reference angles for angles in other quadrants. To evaluate trigonometric functions of other angles, we use a scientific or graphing calculator or computer software. If the calculator has a degree mode and a radian mode, confirm the correct mode is chosen before making a calculation.

Evaluating a tangent function with a scientific calculator as opposed to a graphing calculator or computer algebra system is like evaluating a sine or cosine: Enter the value and press the **TAN** key. For the reciprocal functions, there may not be any dedicated keys that say **CSC**, **SEC**, or **COT**. In that case, the function must be evaluated as the reciprocal of a sine, cosine, or tangent.

If we need to work with degrees and our calculator or software does not have a degree mode, we can enter the degrees multiplied by the conversion factor $\dfrac{\pi}{180}$ to convert the degrees to radians. To find the secant of 30°, we could press

$$(\text{for a scientific calculator}): \frac{1}{30 \times \dfrac{\pi}{180}} \text{COS} \qquad \text{or} \qquad (\text{for a graphing calculator}): \frac{1}{\cos\left(\dfrac{30\pi}{180}\right)}$$

How To...

Given an angle measure in radians, use a scientific calculator to find the cosecant.

1. If the calculator has degree mode and radian mode, set it to radian mode.
2. Enter: **1 /**
3. Enter the value of the angle inside parentheses.
4. Press the **SIN** key.
5. Press the = key.

How To...

Given an angle measure in radians, use a graphing utility/calculator to find the cosecant.

1. If the graphing utility has degree mode and radian mode, set it to radian mode.
2. Enter: **1 /**
3. Press the **SIN** key.
4. Enter the value of the angle inside parentheses.
5. Press the **ENTER** key.

Example 10 **Evaluating the Secant Using Technology**

Evaluate the cosecant of $\dfrac{5\pi}{7}$.

Solution

For a scientific calculator, enter information as follows:

$$1 / (5 \times \pi / 7) \text{SIN} =$$

$$\csc\left(\frac{5\pi}{7}\right) \approx 1.279$$

Try It #10

Evaluate the cotangent of $-\dfrac{\pi}{8}$.

Access these online resources for additional instruction and practice with other trigonometric functions.

- Determining Trig Function Values (http://openstaxcollege.org/l/trigfuncval)
- More Examples of Determining Trig Functions (http://openstaxcollege.org/l/moretrigfun)
- Pythagorean Identities (http://openstaxcollege.org/l/pythagiden)
- Trig Functions on a Calculator (http://openstaxcollege.org/l/trigcalc)

5.3　SECTION EXERCISES

VERBAL

1. On an interval of $[0, 2\pi)$, can the sine and cosine values of a radian measure ever be equal? If so, where?

2. What would you estimate the cosine of π degrees to be? Explain your reasoning.

3. For any angle in quadrant II, if you knew the sine of the angle, how could you determine the cosine of the angle?

4. Describe the secant function.

5. Tangent and cotangent have a period of π. What does this tell us about the output of these functions?

ALGEBRAIC

For the following exercises, find the exact value of each expression.

6. $\tan \dfrac{\pi}{6}$

7. $\sec \dfrac{\pi}{6}$

8. $\csc \dfrac{\pi}{6}$

9. $\cot \dfrac{\pi}{6}$

10. $\tan \dfrac{\pi}{4}$

11. $\sec \dfrac{\pi}{4}$

12. $\csc \dfrac{\pi}{4}$

13. $\cot \dfrac{\pi}{4}$

14. $\tan \dfrac{\pi}{3}$

15. $\sec \dfrac{\pi}{3}$

16. $\csc \dfrac{\pi}{3}$

17. $\cot \dfrac{\pi}{3}$

For the following exercises, use reference angles to evaluate the expression.

18. $\tan \dfrac{5\pi}{6}$

19. $\sec \dfrac{7\pi}{6}$

20. $\csc \dfrac{11\pi}{6}$

21. $\cot \dfrac{13\pi}{6}$

22. $\tan \dfrac{7\pi}{4}$

23. $\sec \dfrac{3\pi}{4}$

24. $\csc \dfrac{5\pi}{4}$

25. $\cot \dfrac{11\pi}{4}$

26. $\tan \dfrac{8\pi}{3}$

27. $\sec \dfrac{4\pi}{3}$

28. $\csc \dfrac{2\pi}{3}$

29. $\cot \dfrac{5\pi}{3}$

30. $\tan 225°$

31. $\sec 300°$

32. $\csc 150°$

33. $\cot 240°$

34. $\tan 330°$

35. $\sec 120°$

36. $\csc 210°$

37. $\cot 315°$

38. If $\sin t = \dfrac{3}{4}$, and t is in quadrant II, find $\cos t$, $\sec t$, $\csc t$, $\tan t$, $\cot t$.

39. If $\cos t = -\dfrac{1}{3}$, and t is in quadrant III, find $\sin t$, $\sec t$, $\csc t$, $\tan t$, $\cot t$.

40. If $\tan t = \dfrac{12}{5}$, and $0 \le t < \dfrac{\pi}{2}$, find $\sin t$, $\cos t$, $\sec t$, $\csc t$, and $\cot t$.

41. If $\sin t = \dfrac{\sqrt{3}}{2}$ and $\cos t = \dfrac{1}{2}$, find $\sec t$, $\csc t$, $\tan t$, and $\cot t$.

42. If $\sin 40° \approx 0.643$ and $\cos 40° \approx 0.766$, find $\sec 40°$, $\csc 40°$, $\tan 40°$, and $\cot 40°$.

43. If $\sin t = \dfrac{\sqrt{2}}{2}$, what is the $\sin(-t)$?

44. If $\cos t = \dfrac{1}{2}$, what is the $\cos(-t)$?

45. If $\sec t = 3.1$, what is the $\sec(-t)$?

46. If $\csc t = 0.34$, what is the $\csc(-t)$?

47. If $\tan t = -1.4$, what is the $\tan(-t)$?

48. If $\cot t = 9.23$, what is the $\cot(-t)$?

GRAPHICAL

For the following exercises, use the angle in the unit circle to find the value of the each of the six trigonometric functions.

49.

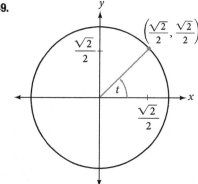

50.

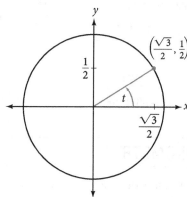

51.

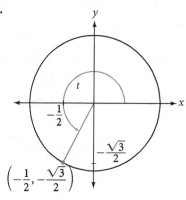

TECHNOLOGY

For the following exercises, use a graphing calculator to evaluate.

52. $\csc \dfrac{5\pi}{9}$

53. $\cot \dfrac{4\pi}{7}$

54. $\sec \dfrac{\pi}{10}$

55. $\tan \dfrac{5\pi}{8}$

56. $\sec \dfrac{3\pi}{4}$

57. $\csc \dfrac{\pi}{4}$

58. $\tan 98°$

59. $\cot 33°$

60. $\cot 140°$

61. $\sec 310°$

EXTENSIONS

For the following exercises, use identities to evaluate the expression.

62. If $\tan(t) \approx 2.7$, and $\sin(t) \approx 0.94$, find $\cos(t)$.

63. If $\tan(t) \approx 1.3$, and $\cos(t) \approx 0.61$, find $\sin(t)$.

64. If $\csc(t) \approx 3.2$, and $\cos(t) \approx 0.95$, find $\tan(t)$.

65. If $\cot(t) \approx 0.58$, and $\cos(t) \approx 0.5$, find $\csc(t)$.

66. Determine whether the function $f(x) = 2\sin x \cos x$ is even, odd, or neither.

67. Determine whether the function $f(x) = 3\sin^2 x \cos x + \sec x$ is even, odd, or neither.

68. Determine whether the function $f(x) = \sin x - 2\cos^2 x$ is even, odd, or neither.

69. Determine whether the function $f(x) = \csc^2 x + \sec x$ is even, odd, or neither.

For the following exercises, use identities to simplify the expression.

70. $\csc t \tan t$

71. $\dfrac{\sec t}{\csc t}$

REAL-WORLD APPLICATIONS

72. The amount of sunlight in a certain city can be modeled by the function $h = 15 \cos\left(\dfrac{1}{600}d\right)$, where h represents the hours of sunlight, and d is the day of the year. Use the equation to find how many hours of sunlight there are on February 10, the 42nd day of the year. State the period of the function.

73. The amount of sunlight in a certain city can be modeled by the function $h = 16\cos\left(\dfrac{1}{500}d\right)$, where h represents the hours of sunlight, and d is the day of the year. Use the equation to find how many hours of sunlight there are on September 24, the 267th day of the year. State the period of the function.

74. The equation $P = 20\sin(2\pi t) + 100$ models the blood pressure, P, where t represents time in seconds. **a.** Find the blood pressure after 15 seconds. **b.** What are the maximum and minimum blood pressures?

75. The height of a piston, h, in inches, can be modeled by the equation $y = 2\cos x + 6$, where x represents the crank angle. Find the height of the piston when the crank angle is 55°.

76. The height of a piston, h, in inches, can be modeled by the equation $y = 2\cos x + 5$, where x represents the crank angle. Find the height of the piston when the crank angle is 55°.

LEARNING OBJECTIVES

In this section, you will:

- Use right triangles to evaluate trigonometric functions.
- Find function values for $30°\left(\dfrac{\pi}{6}\right)$, $45°\left(\dfrac{\pi}{4}\right)$, and $60°\left(\dfrac{\pi}{3}\right)$.
- Use cofunctions of complementary angles.
- Use the definitions of trigonometric functions of any angle.
- Use right triangle trigonometry to solve applied problems.

5.4 RIGHT TRIANGLE TRIGONOMETRY

We have previously defined the sine and cosine of an angle in terms of the coordinates of a point on the unit circle intersected by the terminal side of the angle:

$$\cos t = x$$

$$\sin t = y$$

In this section, we will see another way to define trigonometric functions using properties of right triangles.

Using Right Triangles to Evaluate Trigonometric Functions

In earlier sections, we used a unit circle to define the trigonometric functions. In this section, we will extend those definitions so that we can apply them to right triangles. The value of the sine or cosine function of t is its value at t radians. First, we need to create our right triangle. **Figure 1** shows a point on a unit circle of radius 1. If we drop a vertical line segment from the point (x, y) to the x-axis, we have a right triangle whose vertical side has length y and whose horizontal side has length x. We can use this right triangle to redefine sine, cosine, and the other trigonometric functions as ratios of the sides of a right triangle.

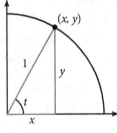

Figure 1

We know

$$\cos t = \frac{x}{1} = x$$

Likewise, we know

$$\sin t = \frac{y}{1} = y$$

These ratios still apply to the sides of a right triangle when no unit circle is involved and when the triangle is not in standard position and is not being graphed using (x, y) coordinates. To be able to use these ratios freely, we will give the sides more general names: Instead of x, we will call the side between the given angle and the right angle the **adjacent side** to angle t. (Adjacent means "next to.") Instead of y, we will call the side most distant from the given angle the **opposite side** from angle t. And instead of 1, we will call the side of a right triangle opposite the right angle the **hypotenuse**. These sides are labeled in **Figure 2**.

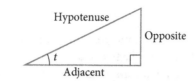

Figure 2 The sides of a right triangle in relation to angle *t*.

Understanding Right Triangle Relationships

Given a right triangle with an acute angle of *t*,

$$\sin(t) = \frac{\text{opposite}}{\text{hypotenuse}}$$

$$\cos(t) = \frac{\text{adjacent}}{\text{hypotenuse}}$$

$$\tan(t) = \frac{\text{opposite}}{\text{adjacent}}$$

A common mnemonic for remembering these relationships is SohCahToa, formed from the first letters of "Sine is opposite over hypotenuse, Cosine is adjacent over hypotenuse, Tangent is opposite over adjacent."

How To...

Given the side lengths of a right triangle and one of the acute angles, find the sine, cosine, and tangent of that angle.

1. Find the sine as the ratio of the opposite side to the hypotenuse.
2. Find the cosine as the ratio of the adjacent side to the hypotenuse.
3. Find the tangent as the ratio of the opposite side to the adjacent side.

Example 1   **Evaluating a Trigonometric Function of a Right Triangle**

Given the triangle shown in **Figure 3**, find the value of cos α.

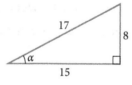

Figure 3

Solution   The side adjacent to the angle is 15, and the hypotenuse of the triangle is 17, so:

$$\cos(\alpha) = \frac{\text{adjacent}}{\text{hypotenuse}}$$

$$= \frac{15}{17}$$

Try It #1

Given the triangle shown in **Figure 4**, find the value of sin *t*.

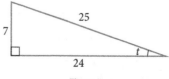

Figure 4

Relating Angles and Their Functions

When working with right triangles, the same rules apply regardless of the orientation of the triangle. In fact, we can evaluate the six trigonometric functions of either of the two acute angles in the triangle in **Figure 5**. The side opposite one acute angle is the side adjacent to the other acute angle, and vice versa.

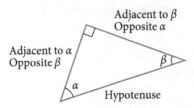

Figure 5 The side adjacent to one angle is opposite the other

We will be asked to find all six trigonometric functions for a given angle in a triangle. Our strategy is to find the sine, cosine, and tangent of the angles first. Then, we can find the other trigonometric functions easily because we know that the reciprocal of sine is cosecant, the reciprocal of cosine is secant, and the reciprocal of tangent is cotangent.

How To...

Given the side lengths of a right triangle, evaluate the six trigonometric functions of one of the acute angles.

1. If needed, draw the right triangle and label the angle provided.
2. Identify the angle, the adjacent side, the side opposite the angle, and the hypotenuse of the right triangle.
3. Find the required function:

   - sine as the ratio of the opposite side to the hypotenuse
   - cosine as the ratio of the adjacent side to the hypotenuse
   - tangent as the ratio of the opposite side to the adjacent side
   - secant as the ratio of the hypotenuse to the adjacent side
   - cosecant as the ratio of the hypotenuse to the opposite side
   - cotangent as the ratio of the adjacent side to the opposite side

---

Example 2   **Evaluating Trigonometric Functions of Angles Not in Standard Position**

Using the triangle shown in **Figure 6**, evaluate sin α, cos α, tan α, sec α, csc α, and cot α.

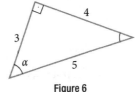

Figure 6

Solution

$$\sin \alpha = \frac{\text{opposite } \alpha}{\text{hypotenuse}} = \frac{4}{5}$$

$$\cos \alpha = \frac{\text{adjacent to } \alpha}{\text{hypotenuse}} = \frac{3}{5}$$

$$\tan \alpha = \frac{\text{opposite } \alpha}{\text{adjacent to } \alpha} = \frac{4}{3}$$

$$\sec \alpha = \frac{\text{hypotenuse}}{\text{adjacent to } \alpha} = \frac{5}{3}$$

$$\csc \alpha = \frac{\text{hypotenuse}}{\text{opposite } \alpha} = \frac{5}{4}$$

$$\cot \alpha = \frac{\text{adjacent to } \alpha}{\text{opposite } \alpha} = \frac{3}{4}$$

Try It #2

Using the triangle shown in **Figure 7**, evaluate sin t, cos t, tan t, sec t, csc t, and cot t.

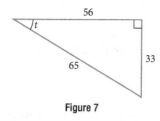

Figure 7

Finding Trigonometric Functions of Special Angles Using Side Lengths

We have already discussed the trigonometric functions as they relate to the special angles on the unit circle. Now, we can use those relationships to evaluate triangles that contain those special angles. We do this because when we evaluate the special angles in trigonometric functions, they have relatively friendly values, values that contain either no or just one square root in the ratio. Therefore, these are the angles often used in math and science problems. We will use multiples of 30°, 60°, and 45°, however, remember that when dealing with right triangles, we are limited to angles between 0° and 90°.

Suppose we have a 30°, 60°, 90° triangle, which can also be described as a $\frac{\pi}{6}, \frac{\pi}{3}, \frac{\pi}{2}$ triangle. The sides have lengths in the relation s, $\sqrt{3}s$, $2s$. The sides of a 45°, 45°, 90° triangle, which can also be described as a $\frac{\pi}{4}, \frac{\pi}{4}, \frac{\pi}{2}$ triangle, have lengths in the relation s, s, $\sqrt{2}s$. These relations are shown in **Figure 8**.

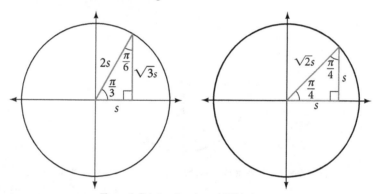

Figure 8 Side lengths of special triangles

We can then use the ratios of the side lengths to evaluate trigonometric functions of special angles.

How To...

Given trigonometric functions of a special angle, evaluate using side lengths.

1. Use the side lengths shown in **Figure 8** for the special angle you wish to evaluate.
2. Use the ratio of side lengths appropriate to the function you wish to evaluate.

Example 3   **Evaluating Trigonometric Functions of Special Angles Using Side Lengths**

Find the exact value of the trigonometric functions of $\frac{\pi}{3}$, using side lengths.

Solution

$$\sin\left(\frac{\pi}{3}\right) = \frac{\text{opp}}{\text{hyp}} = \frac{\sqrt{3}s}{2s} = \frac{\sqrt{3}}{2}$$

$$\cos\left(\frac{\pi}{3}\right) = \frac{\text{adj}}{\text{hyp}} = \frac{s}{2s} = \frac{1}{2}$$

$$\tan\left(\frac{\pi}{3}\right) = \frac{\text{opp}}{\text{adj}} = \frac{\sqrt{3}s}{s} = \sqrt{3}$$

$$\sec\left(\frac{\pi}{3}\right) = \frac{\text{hyp}}{\text{adj}} = \frac{2s}{s} = 2$$

$$\csc\left(\frac{\pi}{3}\right) = \frac{\text{hyp}}{\text{opp}} = \frac{2s}{\sqrt{3}s} = \frac{2}{\sqrt{3}} = \frac{2\sqrt{3}}{3}$$

$$\cot\left(\frac{\pi}{3}\right) = \frac{\text{adj}}{\text{opp}} = \frac{s}{\sqrt{3}s} = \frac{1}{\sqrt{3}} = \frac{\sqrt{3}}{3}$$

Try It #3

Find the exact value of the trigonometric functions of $\frac{\pi}{4}$, using side lengths.

Using Equal Cofunction of Complements

If we look more closely at the relationship between the sine and cosine of the special angles relative to the unit circle, we will notice a pattern. In a right triangle with angles of $\frac{\pi}{6}$ and $\frac{\pi}{3}$, we see that the sine of $\frac{\pi}{3}$ namely $\frac{\sqrt{3}}{2}$, is also the cosine of $\frac{\pi}{6}$, while the sine of $\frac{\pi}{6}$, namely $\frac{1}{2}$, is also the cosine of $\frac{\pi}{3}$.

$$\sin\frac{\pi}{3} = \cos\frac{\pi}{6} = \frac{\sqrt{3}s}{2s} = \frac{\sqrt{3}}{2}$$

$$\sin\frac{\pi}{6} = \cos\frac{\pi}{3} = \frac{s}{2s} = \frac{1}{2}$$

See **Figure 9.**

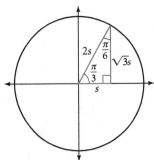

Figure 9 The sine of $\frac{\pi}{3}$ equals the cosine of $\frac{\pi}{6}$ and vice versa

This result should not be surprising because, as we see from **Figure 9**, the side opposite the angle of $\frac{\pi}{3}$ is also the side adjacent to $\frac{\pi}{6}$, so $\sin\left(\frac{\pi}{3}\right)$ and $\cos\left(\frac{\pi}{6}\right)$ are exactly the same ratio of the same two sides, $\sqrt{3}s$ and $2s$. Similarly, $\cos\left(\frac{\pi}{3}\right)$ and $\sin\left(\frac{\pi}{6}\right)$ are also the same ratio using the same two sides, s and $2s$.

The interrelationship between the sines and cosines of $\frac{\pi}{6}$ and $\frac{\pi}{3}$ also holds for the two acute angles in any right triangle, since in every case, the ratio of the same two sides would constitute the sine of one angle and the cosine of the other. Since the three angles of a triangle add to π, and the right angle is $\frac{\pi}{2}$, the remaining two angles must also add up to $\frac{\pi}{2}$. That means that a right triangle can be formed with any two angles that add to $\frac{\pi}{2}$—in other words, any two complementary angles. So we may state a *cofunction identity*: If any two angles are complementary, the sine of one is the cosine of the other, and vice versa. This identity is illustrated in **Figure 10.**

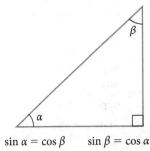

$$\sin\alpha = \cos\beta \qquad \sin\beta = \cos\alpha$$

Figure 10 Cofunction identity of sine and cosine of complementary angles

Using this identity, we can state without calculating, for instance, that the sine of $\frac{\pi}{12}$ equals the cosine of $\frac{5\pi}{12}$, and that the sine of $\frac{5\pi}{12}$ equals the cosine of $\frac{\pi}{12}$. We can also state that if, for a certain angle t, $\cos t = \frac{5}{13}$, then $\sin\left(\frac{\pi}{2} - t\right) = \frac{5}{13}$ as well.

---

cofunction identities

The cofunction identities in radians are listed in **Table 1.**

$\cos t = \sin\left(\frac{\pi}{2} - t\right)$	$\sin t = \cos\left(\frac{\pi}{2} - t\right)$
$\tan t = \cot\left(\frac{\pi}{2} - t\right)$	$\cot t = \tan\left(\frac{\pi}{2} - t\right)$
$\sec t = \csc\left(\frac{\pi}{2} - t\right)$	$\csc t = \sec\left(\frac{\pi}{2} - t\right)$

Table 1

How To...

Given the sine and cosine of an angle, find the sine or cosine of its complement.

1. To find the sine of the complementary angle, find the cosine of the original angle.
2. To find the cosine of the complementary angle, find the sine of the original angle.

Example 4 **Using Cofunction Identities**

If $\sin t = \frac{5}{12}$, find $\cos\left(\frac{\pi}{2} - t\right)$.

Solution According to the cofunction identities for sine and cosine,

$$\sin t = \cos\left(\frac{\pi}{2} - t\right).$$

So

$$\cos\left(\frac{\pi}{2} - t\right) = \frac{5}{12}.$$

Try It #4

If $\csc\left(\frac{\pi}{6}\right) = 2$, find $\sec\left(\frac{\pi}{3}\right)$.

Using Trigonometric Functions

In previous examples, we evaluated the sine and cosine in triangles where we knew all three sides. But the real power of right-triangle trigonometry emerges when we look at triangles in which we know an angle but do not know all the sides.

How To...

Given a right triangle, the length of one side, and the measure of one acute angle, find the remaining sides.

1. For each side, select the trigonometric function that has the unknown side as either the numerator or the denominator. The known side will in turn be the denominator or the numerator.
2. Write an equation setting the function value of the known angle equal to the ratio of the corresponding sides.
3. Using the value of the trigonometric function and the known side length, solve for the missing side length.

Example 5   **Finding Missing Side Lengths Using Trigonometric Ratios**

Find the unknown sides of the triangle in **Figure 11**.

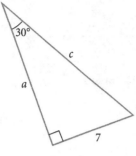

Figure 11

Solution We know the angle and the opposite side, so we can use the tangent to find the adjacent side.

$$\tan(30°) = \frac{7}{a}$$

We rearrange to solve for a.

$$a = \frac{7}{\tan(30°)}$$

$$\approx 12.1$$

We can use the sine to find the hypotenuse.

$$\sin(30°) = \frac{7}{c}$$

Again, we rearrange to solve for c.

$$c = \frac{7}{\sin(30°)}$$

$$\approx 14$$

Try It #5

A right triangle has one angle of $\frac{\pi}{3}$ and a hypotenuse of 20. Find the unknown sides and angle of the triangle.

Using Right Triangle Trigonometry to Solve Applied Problems

Right-triangle trigonometry has many practical applications. For example, the ability to compute the lengths of sides of a triangle makes it possible to find the height of a tall object without climbing to the top or having to extend a tape measure along its height. We do so by measuring a distance from the base of the object to a point on the ground some distance away, where we can look up to the top of the tall object at an angle. The **angle of elevation** of an object above an observer relative to the observer is the angle between the horizontal and the line from the object to the observer's eye. The right triangle this position creates has sides that represent the unknown height, the measured distance from the base, and the angled line of sight from the ground to the top of the object. Knowing the measured distance to the base of the object and the angle of the line of sight, we can use trigonometric functions to calculate the unknown height. Similarly, we can form a triangle from the top of a tall object by looking downward. The **angle of depression** of an object below an observer relative to the observer is the angle between the horizontal and the line from the object to the observer's eye. See **Figure 12**.

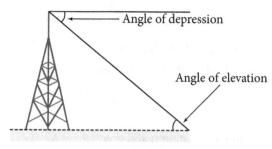

Figure 12

How To...

Given a tall object, measure its height indirectly.

1. Make a sketch of the problem situation to keep track of known and unknown information.
2. Lay out a measured distance from the base of the object to a point where the top of the object is clearly visible.
3. At the other end of the measured distance, look up to the top of the object. Measure the angle the line of sight makes with the horizontal.
4. Write an equation relating the unknown height, the measured distance, and the tangent of the angle of the line of sight.
5. Solve the equation for the unknown height.

Example 6 **Measuring a Distance Indirectly**

To find the height of a tree, a person walks to a point 30 feet from the base of the tree. She measures an angle of 57° between a line of sight to the top of the tree and the ground, as shown in **Figure 13**. Find the height of the tree.

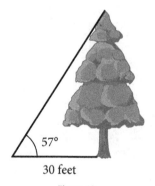

57°

30 feet

Figure 13

Solution We know that the angle of elevation is 57° and the adjacent side is 30 ft long. The opposite side is the unknown height.

The trigonometric function relating the side opposite to an angle and the side adjacent to the angle is the tangent. So we will state our information in terms of the tangent of 57°, letting h be the unknown height.

$$\tan \theta = \frac{\text{opposite}}{\text{adjacent}}$$

$$\tan(57°) = \frac{h}{30} \qquad \text{Solve for } h.$$

$$h = 30\tan(57°) \quad \text{Multiply.}$$

$$h \approx 46.2 \qquad \text{Use a calculator.}$$

The tree is approximately 46 feet tall.

Try It #6

How long a ladder is needed to reach a windowsill 50 feet above the ground if the ladder rests against the building making an angle of $\dfrac{5\pi}{12}$ with the ground? Round to the nearest foot.

Access these online resources for additional instruction and practice with right triangle trigonometry.

- Finding Trig Functions on Calculator (http://openstaxcollege.org/l/findtrigcal)
- Finding Trig Functions Using a Right Triangle (http://openstaxcollege.org/l/trigrttri)
- Relate Trig Functions to Sides of a Right Triangle (http://openstaxcollege.org/l/reltrigtri)
- Determine Six Trig Functions from a Triangle (http://openstaxcollege.org/l/sixtrigfunc)
- Determine Length of Right Triangle Side (http://openstaxcollege.org/l/rttriside)

5.4   SECTION EXERCISES

VERBAL

1. For the given right triangle, label the adjacent side, opposite side, and hypotenuse for the indicated angle.

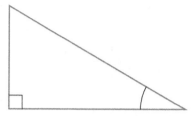

2. When a right triangle with a hypotenuse of 1 is placed in the unit circle, which sides of the triangle correspond to the x- and y-coordinates?

3. The tangent of an angle compares which sides of the right triangle?

4. What is the relationship between the two acute angles in a right triangle?

5. Explain the cofunction identity.

ALGEBRAIC

For the following exercises, use cofunctions of complementary angles.

6. $\cos(34°) = \sin(\underline{\hspace{0.5cm}}°)$

7. $\cos\left(\dfrac{\pi}{3}\right) = \sin(\underline{\hspace{0.8cm}})$

8. $\csc(21°) = \sec(\underline{\hspace{0.5cm}}°)$

9. $\tan\left(\dfrac{\pi}{4}\right) = \cot(\underline{\hspace{0.6cm}})$

For the following exercises, find the lengths of the missing sides if side a is opposite angle A, side b is opposite angle B, and side c is the hypotenuse.

10. $\cos B = \dfrac{4}{5}, a = 10$

11. $\sin B = \dfrac{1}{2}, a = 20$

12. $\tan A = \dfrac{5}{12}, b = 6$

13. $\tan A = 100, b = 100$

14. $\sin B = \dfrac{1}{\sqrt{3}}, a = 2$

15. $a = 5, \angle A = 60°$

16. $c = 12, \angle A = 45°$

GRAPHICAL

For the following exercises, use **Figure 14** to evaluate each trigonometric function of angle A.

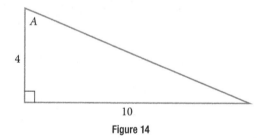

Figure 14

17. $\sin A$

18. $\cos A$

19. $\tan A$

20. $\csc A$

21. $\sec A$

22. $\cot A$

For the following exercises, use **Figure 15** to evaluate each trigonometric function of angle A.

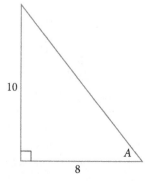

Figure 15

23. $\sin A$

24. $\cos A$

25. $\tan A$

26. $\csc A$

27. $\sec A$

28. $\cot A$

For the following exercises, solve for the unknown sides of the given triangle.

29.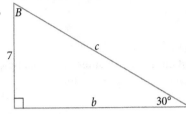

30.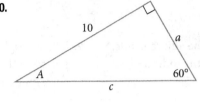

31.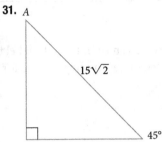

TECHNOLOGY

For the following exercises, use a calculator to find the length of each side to four decimal places.

32.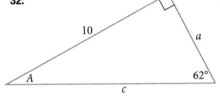

33.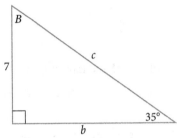

34.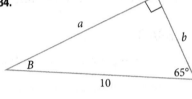

35.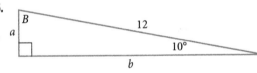

36.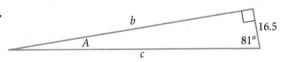

37. $b = 15, \measuredangle B = 15°$

38. $c = 200, \measuredangle B = 5°$

39. $c = 50, \measuredangle B = 21°$

40. $a = 30, \measuredangle A = 27°$

41. $b = 3.5, \measuredangle A = 78°$

EXTENSIONS

42. Find x.

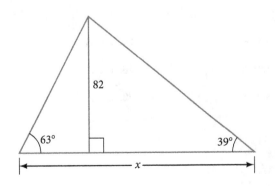

43. Find x.

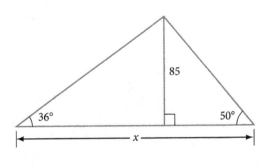

44. Find *x*.

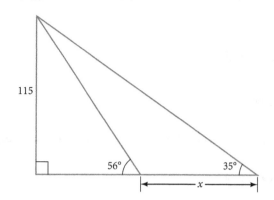

45. Find *x*.

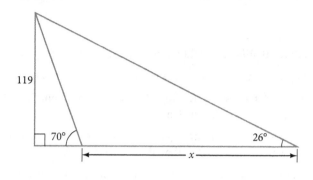

46. A radio tower is located 400 feet from a building. From a window in the building, a person determines that the angle of elevation to the top of the tower is 36°, and that the angle of depression to the bottom of the tower is 23°. How tall is the tower?

47. A radio tower is located 325 feet from a building. From a window in the building, a person determines that the angle of elevation to the top of the tower is 43°, and that the angle of depression to the bottom of the tower is 31°. How tall is the tower?

48. A 200-foot tall monument is located in the distance. From a window in a building, a person determines that the angle of elevation to the top of the monument is 15°, and that the angle of depression to the bottom of the tower is 2°. How far is the person from the monument?

49. A 400-foot tall monument is located in the distance. From a window in a building, a person determines that the angle of elevation to the top of the monument is 18°, and that the angle of depression to the bottom of the monument is 3°. How far is the person from the monument?

50. There is an antenna on the top of a building. From a location 300 feet from the base of the building, the angle of elevation to the top of the building is measured to be 40°. From the same location, the angle of elevation to the top of the antenna is measured to be 43°. Find the height of the antenna.

51. There is lightning rod on the top of a building. From a location 500 feet from the base of the building, the angle of elevation to the top of the building is measured to be 36°. From the same location, the angle of elevation to the top of the lightning rod is measured to be 38°. Find the height of the lightning rod.

REAL-WORLD APPLICATIONS

52. A 33-ft ladder leans against a building so that the angle between the ground and the ladder is 80°. How high does the ladder reach up the side of the building?

53. A 23-ft ladder leans against a building so that the angle between the ground and the ladder is 80°. How high does the ladder reach up the side of the building?

54. The angle of elevation to the top of a building in New York is found to be 9 degrees from the ground at a distance of 1 mile from the base of the building. Using this information, find the height of the building.

55. The angle of elevation to the top of a building in Seattle is found to be 2 degrees from the ground at a distance of 2 miles from the base of the building. Using this information, find the height of the building.

56. Assuming that a 370-foot tall giant redwood grows vertically, if I walk a certain distance from the tree and measure the angle of elevation to the top of the tree to be 60°, how far from the base of the tree am I?

CHAPTER 5 REVIEW

Key Terms

adjacent side in a right triangle, the side between a given angle and the right angle

angle the union of two rays having a common endpoint

angle of depression the angle between the horizontal and the line from the object to the observer's eye, assuming the object is positioned lower than the observer

angle of elevation the angle between the horizontal and the line from the object to the observer's eye, assuming the object is positioned higher than the observer

angular speed the angle through which a rotating object travels in a unit of time

arc length the length of the curve formed by an arc

area of a sector area of a portion of a circle bordered by two radii and the intercepted arc; the fraction $\frac{\theta}{2\pi}$ multiplied by the area of the entire circle

cosecant the reciprocal of the sine function: on the unit circle, $\csc t = \frac{1}{y}, y \neq 0$

cosine function the x-value of the point on a unit circle corresponding to a given angle

cotangent the reciprocal of the tangent function: on the unit circle, $\cot t = \frac{x}{y}, y \neq 0$

coterminal angles description of positive and negative angles in standard position sharing the same terminal side

degree a unit of measure describing the size of an angle as one-360th of a full revolution of a circle

hypotenuse the side of a right triangle opposite the right angle

identities statements that are true for all values of the input on which they are defined

initial side the side of an angle from which rotation begins

linear speed the distance along a straight path a rotating object travels in a unit of time; determined by the arc length

measure of an angle the amount of rotation from the initial side to the terminal side

negative angle description of an angle measured clockwise from the positive x-axis

opposite side in a right triangle, the side most distant from a given angle

period the smallest interval P of a repeating function f such that $f(x + P) = f(x)$

positive angle description of an angle measured counterclockwise from the positive x-axis

Pythagorean Identity a corollary of the Pythagorean Theorem stating that the square of the cosine of a given angle plus the square of the sine of that angle equals 1

quadrantal angle an angle whose terminal side lies on an axis

radian the measure of a central angle of a circle that intercepts an arc equal in length to the radius of that circle

radian measure the ratio of the arc length formed by an angle divided by the radius of the circle

ray one point on a line and all points extending in one direction from that point; one side of an angle

reference angle the measure of the acute angle formed by the terminal side of the angle and the horizontal axis

secant the reciprocal of the cosine function: on the unit circle, $\sec t = \frac{1}{x}, x \neq 0$

sine function the y-value of the point on a unit circle corresponding to a given angle

standard position the position of an angle having the vertex at the origin and the initial side along the positive x-axis

tangent the quotient of the sine and cosine: on the unit circle, $\tan t = \frac{y}{x}, x \neq 0$

terminal side the side of an angle at which rotation ends

unit circle a circle with a center at $(0, 0)$ and radius 1.

vertex the common endpoint of two rays that form an angle

Key Equations

arc length	$s = r\theta$
area of a sector	$A = \dfrac{1}{2}\theta r^2$
angular speed	$\omega = \dfrac{\theta}{t}$
linear speed	$v = \dfrac{s}{t}$
linear speed related to angular speed	$v = r\omega$
cosine	$\cos t = x$
sine	$\sin t = y$
Pythagorean Identity	$\cos^2 t + \sin^2 t = 1$
tangent function	$\tan t = \dfrac{\sin t}{\cos t}$
secant function	$\sec t = \dfrac{1}{\cos t}$
cosecant function	$\csc t = \dfrac{1}{\sin t}$
cotangent function	$\cot t = \dfrac{1}{\tan t} = \dfrac{\cos t}{\sin t}$
cofunction identities	$\cos t = \sin\left(\dfrac{\pi}{2} - t\right)$
	$\sin t = \cos\left(\dfrac{\pi}{2} - t\right)$
	$\tan t = \cot\left(\dfrac{\pi}{2} - t\right)$
	$\cot t = \tan\left(\dfrac{\pi}{2} - t\right)$
	$\sec t = \csc\left(\dfrac{\pi}{2} - t\right)$
	$\csc t = \sec\left(\dfrac{\pi}{2} - t\right)$

Key Concepts

5.1 Angles

- An angle is formed from the union of two rays, by keeping the initial side fixed and rotating the terminal side. The amount of rotation determines the measure of the angle.

- An angle is in standard position if its vertex is at the origin and its initial side lies along the positive x-axis. A positive angle is measured counterclockwise from the initial side and a negative angle is measured clockwise.

- To draw an angle in standard position, draw the initial side along the positive x-axis and then place the terminal side according to the fraction of a full rotation the angle represents. See **Example 1**.

- In addition to degrees, the measure of an angle can be described in radians. See **Example 2**.

- To convert between degrees and radians, use the proportion $\dfrac{\theta}{180} = \dfrac{\theta^R}{\pi}$. See **Example 3** and **Example 4**.

- Two angles that have the same terminal side are called coterminal angles.

- We can find coterminal angles by adding or subtracting 360° or 2π. See **Example 5** and **Example 6**.

- Coterminal angles can be found using radians just as they are for degrees. See **Example 7**.

- The length of a circular arc is a fraction of the circumference of the entire circle. See **Example 8**.

- The area of sector is a fraction of the area of the entire circle. See **Example 9**.

- An object moving in a circular path has both linear and angular speed.

- The angular speed of an object traveling in a circular path is the measure of the angle through which it turns in a unit of time. See **Example 10**.

- The linear speed of an object traveling along a circular path is the distance it travels in a unit of time. See **Example 11**.

5.2 Unit Circle: Sine and Cosine Functions

- Finding the function values for the sine and cosine begins with drawing a unit circle, which is centered at the origin and has a radius of 1 unit.

- Using the unit circle, the sine of an angle t equals the y-value of the endpoint on the unit circle of an arc of length t whereas the cosine of an angle t equals the x-value of the endpoint. See **Example 1**.

- The sine and cosine values are most directly determined when the corresponding point on the unit circle falls on an axis. See **Example 2**.

- When the sine or cosine is known, we can use the Pythagorean Identity to find the other. The Pythagorean Identity is also useful for determining the sines and cosines of special angles. See **Example 3**.

- Calculators and graphing software are helpful for finding sines and cosines if the proper procedure for entering information is known. See **Example 4**.

- The domain of the sine and cosine functions is all real numbers.

- The range of both the sine and cosine functions is $[-1, 1]$.

- The sine and cosine of an angle have the same absolute value as the sine and cosine of its reference angle.

- The signs of the sine and cosine are determined from the x- and y-values in the quadrant of the original angle.

- An angle's reference angle is the size angle, t, formed by the terminal side of the angle t and the horizontal axis. See **Example 5**.

- Reference angles can be used to find the sine and cosine of the original angle. See **Example 6**.

- Reference angles can also be used to find the coordinates of a point on a circle. See **Example 7**.

5.3 The Other Trigonometric Functions

- The tangent of an angle is the ratio of the y-value to the x-value of the corresponding point on the unit circle.

- The secant, cotangent, and cosecant are all reciprocals of other functions. The secant is the reciprocal of the cosine function, the cotangent is the reciprocal of the tangent function, and the cosecant is the reciprocal of the sine function.

- The six trigonometric functions can be found from a point on the unit circle. See **Example 1**.

- Trigonometric functions can also be found from an angle. See **Example 2**.

- Trigonometric functions of angles outside the first quadrant can be determined using reference angles. See **Example 3**.

- A function is said to be even if $f(-x) = f(x)$ and odd if $f(-x) = -f(x)$.

- Cosine and secant are even; sine, tangent, cosecant, and cotangent are odd.

- Even and odd properties can be used to evaluate trigonometric functions. See **Example 4**.

- The Pythagorean Identity makes it possible to find a cosine from a sine or a sine from a cosine.

- Identities can be used to evaluate trigonometric functions. See **Example 5** and **Example 6**.

- Fundamental identities such as the Pythagorean Identity can be manipulated algebraically to produce new identities. See **Example 7**.

- The trigonometric functions repeat at regular intervals.

- The period P of a repeating function f is the smallest interval such that $f(x + P) = f(x)$ for any value of x.

- The values of trigonometric functions of special angles can be found by mathematical analysis.

- To evaluate trigonometric functions of other angles, we can use a calculator or computer software. See **Example 8**.

5.4 Right Triangle Trigonometry

- We can define trigonometric functions as ratios of the side lengths of a right triangle. See **Example 1**.

- The same side lengths can be used to evaluate the trigonometric functions of either acute angle in a right triangle. See **Example 2**.

- We can evaluate the trigonometric functions of special angles, knowing the side lengths of the triangles in which they occur. See **Example 3**.

- Any two complementary angles could be the two acute angles of a right triangle.

- If two angles are complementary, the cofunction identities state that the sine of one equals the cosine of the other and vice versa. See **Example 4**.

- We can use trigonometric functions of an angle to find unknown side lengths.

- Select the trigonometric function representing the ratio of the unknown side to the known side. See **Example 5**.

- Right-triangle trigonometry permits the measurement of inaccessible heights and distances.

- The unknown height or distance can be found by creating a right triangle in which the unknown height or distance is one of the sides, and another side and angle are known. See **Example 6**.

CHAPTER 5 REVIEW EXERCISES

ANGLES

For the following exercises, convert the angle measures to degrees.

1. $\dfrac{\pi}{4}$

2. $-\dfrac{5\pi}{3}$

For the following exercises, convert the angle measures to radians.

3. $-210°$

4. $180°$

5. Find the length of an arc in a circle of radius 7 meters subtended by the central angle of $85°$.

6. Find the area of the sector of a circle with diameter 32 feet and an angle of $\dfrac{3\pi}{5}$ radians.

For the following exercises, find the angle between $0°$ and $360°$ that is coterminal with the given angle.

7. $420°$

8. $-80°$

For the following exercises, find the angle between 0 and 2π in radians that is coterminal with the given angle.

9. $-\dfrac{20\pi}{11}$

10. $\dfrac{14\pi}{5}$

For the following exercises, draw the angle provided in standard position on the Cartesian plane.

11. $-210°$

12. $75°$

13. $\dfrac{5\pi}{4}$

14. $-\dfrac{\pi}{3}$

15. Find the linear speed of a point on the equator of the earth if the earth has a radius of 3,960 miles and the earth rotates on its axis every 24 hours. Express answer in miles per hour.

16. A car wheel with a diameter of 18 inches spins at the rate of 10 revolutions per second. What is the car's speed in miles per hour?

UNIT CIRCLE: SINE AND COSINE FUNCTIONS

17. Find the exact value of $\sin\dfrac{\pi}{3}$.

18. Find the exact value of $\cos\dfrac{\pi}{4}$.

19. Find the exact value of $\cos\pi$.

20. State the reference angle for $300°$.

21. State the reference angle for $\dfrac{3\pi}{4}$.

22. Compute cosine of $330°$.

23. Compute sine of $\dfrac{5\pi}{4}$.

24. State the domain of the sine and cosine functions.

25. State the range of the sine and cosine functions.

THE OTHER TRIGONOMETRIC FUNCTIONS

For the following exercises, find the exact value of the given expression.

26. $\cos\dfrac{\pi}{6}$

27. $\tan\dfrac{\pi}{4}$

28. $\csc\dfrac{\pi}{3}$

29. $\sec\dfrac{\pi}{4}$

For the following exercises, use reference angles to evaluate the given expression.

30. $\sec\dfrac{11\pi}{3}$

31. $\sec 315°$

32. If $\sec(t) = -2.5$, what is the $\sec(-t)$?

33. If $\tan(t) = -0.6$, what is the $\tan(-t)$?

34. If $\tan(t) = \dfrac{1}{3}$, find $\tan(t - \pi)$.

35. If $\cos(t) = \dfrac{\sqrt{2}}{2}$, find $\sin(t + 2\pi)$.

36. Which trigonometric functions are even?

37. Which trigonometric functions are odd?

RIGHT TRIANGLE TRIGONOMETRY

For the following exercises, use side lengths to evaluate.

38. $\cos \dfrac{\pi}{4}$

39. $\cot \dfrac{\pi}{3}$

40. $\tan \dfrac{\pi}{6}$

41. $\cos\left(\dfrac{\pi}{2}\right) = \sin(\underline{}°)$

42. $\csc(18°) = \sec(\underline{}°)$

For the following exercises, use the given information to find the lengths of the other two sides of the right triangle.

43. $\cos B = \dfrac{3}{5}, a = 6$

44. $\tan A = \dfrac{5}{9}, b = 6$

For the following exercises, use **Figure 1** to evaluate each trigonometric function.

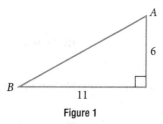

Figure 1

45. $\sin A$

46. $\tan B$

For the following exercises, solve for the unknown sides of the given triangle.

47.

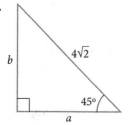

48.

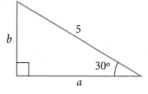

49. A 15-ft ladder leans against a building so that the angle between the ground and the ladder is 70°. How high does the ladder reach up the side of the building?

50. The angle of elevation to the top of a building in Baltimore is found to be 4 degrees from the ground at a distance of 1 mile from the base of the building. Using this information, find the height of the building.

CHAPTER 5 PRACTICE TEST

1. Convert $\dfrac{5\pi}{6}$ radians to degrees.

2. Convert $-620°$ to radians.

3. Find the length of a circular arc with a radius 12 centimeters subtended by the central angle of $30°$.

4. Find the area of the sector with radius of 8 feet and an angle of $\dfrac{5\pi}{4}$ radians.

5. Find the angle between $0°$ and $360°$ that is coterminal with $375°$.

6. Find the angle between 0 and 2π in radians that is coterminal with $-\dfrac{4\pi}{7}$.

7. Draw the angle $315°$ in standard position on the Cartesian plane.

8. Draw the angle $-\dfrac{\pi}{6}$ in standard position on the Cartesian plane.

9. A carnival has a Ferris wheel with a diameter of 80 feet. The time for the Ferris wheel to make one revolution is 75 seconds. What is the linear speed in feet per second of a point on the Ferris wheel? What is the angular speed in radians per second?

10. Find the exact value of $\sin\dfrac{\pi}{6}$.

11. Compute sine of $240°$.

12. State the domain of the sine and cosine functions.

13. State the range of the sine and cosine functions.

14. Find the exact value of $\cot\dfrac{\pi}{4}$.

15. Find the exact value of $\tan\dfrac{\pi}{3}$.

16. Use reference angles to evaluate $\csc\dfrac{7\pi}{4}$.

17. Use reference angles to evaluate $\tan 210°$.

18. If $\csc t = 0.68$, what is the $\csc(-t)$?

19. If $\cos t = \dfrac{\sqrt{3}}{2}$, find $\cos(t - 2\pi)$.

20. Which trigonometric functions are even?

21. Find the missing angle: $\cos\left(\dfrac{\pi}{6}\right) = \sin(\underline{\quad})$

22. Find the missing sides of the triangle ABC:
$\sin B = \dfrac{3}{4}, c = 12$

23. Find the missing sides of the triangle.

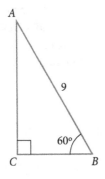

24. The angle of elevation to the top of a building in Chicago is found to be 9 degrees from the ground at a distance of 2,000 feet from the base of the building. Using this information, find the height of the building.

6

Periodic Functions

Figure 1 (credit: "Maxxer_", Flickr)

CHAPTER OUTLINE

Introduction

Each day, the sun rises in an easterly direction, approaches some maximum height relative to the celestial equator, and sets in a westerly direction. The celestial equator is an imaginary line that divides the visible universe into two halves in much the same way Earth's equator is an imaginary line that divides the planet into two halves. The exact path the sun appears to follow depends on the exact location on Earth, but each location observes a predictable pattern over time.

The pattern of the sun's motion throughout the course of a year is a periodic function. Creating a visual representation of a periodic function in the form of a graph can help us analyze the properties of the function. In this chapter, we will investigate graphs of sine, cosine, and other trigonometric functions.

LEARNING OBJECTIVES

In this section, you will:

- Graph variations of $y = \sin(x)$ and $y = \cos(x)$.
- Use phase shifts of sine and cosine curves.

6.1   GRAPHS OF THE SINE AND COSINE FUNCTIONS

Figure 1 Light can be separated into colors because of its wavelike properties. (credit: "wonderferret"/ Flickr)

White light, such as the light from the sun, is not actually white at all. Instead, it is a composition of all the colors of the rainbow in the form of waves. The individual colors can be seen only when white light passes through an optical prism that separates the waves according to their wavelengths to form a rainbow.

Light waves can be represented graphically by the sine function. In the chapter on **Trigonometric Functions**, we examined trigonometric functions such as the sine function. In this section, we will interpret and create graphs of sine and cosine functions.

Graphing Sine and Cosine Functions

Recall that the sine and cosine functions relate real number values to the x- and y-coordinates of a point on the unit circle. So what do they look like on a graph on a coordinate plane? Let's start with the sine function. We can create a table of values and use them to sketch a graph. **Table 1** lists some of the values for the sine function on a unit circle.

x	0	$\frac{\pi}{6}$	$\frac{\pi}{4}$	$\frac{\pi}{3}$	$\frac{\pi}{2}$	$\frac{2\pi}{3}$	$\frac{3\pi}{4}$	$\frac{5\pi}{6}$	π
$\sin(x)$	0	$\frac{1}{2}$	$\frac{\sqrt{2}}{2}$	$\frac{\sqrt{3}}{2}$	1	$\frac{\sqrt{3}}{2}$	$\frac{\sqrt{2}}{2}$	$\frac{1}{2}$	0

Table 1

Plotting the points from the table and continuing along the x-axis gives the shape of the sine function. See **Figure 2**.

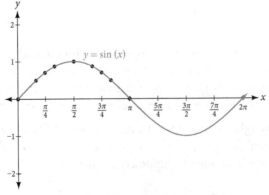

Figure 2 The sine function

Notice how the sine values are positive between 0 and π, which correspond to the values of the sine function in quadrants I and II on the unit circle, and the sine values are negative between π and 2π, which correspond to the values of the sine function in quadrants III and IV on the unit circle. See **Figure 3**.

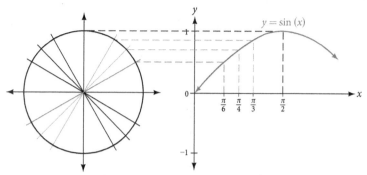

Figure 3 Plotting values of the sine function

Now let's take a similar look at the cosine function. Again, we can create a table of values and use them to sketch a graph. **Table 2** lists some of the values for the cosine function on a unit circle.

x	0	$\dfrac{\pi}{6}$	$\dfrac{\pi}{4}$	$\dfrac{\pi}{3}$	$\dfrac{\pi}{2}$	$\dfrac{2\pi}{3}$	$\dfrac{3\pi}{4}$	$\dfrac{5\pi}{6}$	π
$\cos(x)$	1	$\dfrac{\sqrt{3}}{2}$	$\dfrac{\sqrt{2}}{2}$	$\dfrac{1}{2}$	0	$-\dfrac{1}{2}$	$-\dfrac{\sqrt{2}}{2}$	$-\dfrac{\sqrt{3}}{2}$	-1

Table 2

As with the sine function, we can plots points to create a graph of the cosine function as in **Figure 4**.

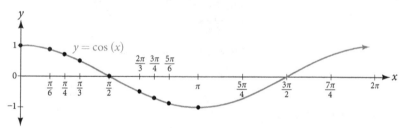

Figure 4 The cosine function

Because we can evaluate the sine and cosine of any real number, both of these functions are defined for all real numbers. By thinking of the sine and cosine values as coordinates of points on a unit circle, it becomes clear that the range of both functions must be the interval $[-1, 1]$.

In both graphs, the shape of the graph repeats after 2π, which means the functions are periodic with a period of 2π. A **periodic function** is a function for which a specific horizontal shift, P, results in a function equal to the original function: $f(x + P) = f(x)$ for all values of x in the domain of f. When this occurs, we call the smallest such horizontal shift with $P > 0$ the period of the function. **Figure 5** shows several periods of the sine and cosine functions.

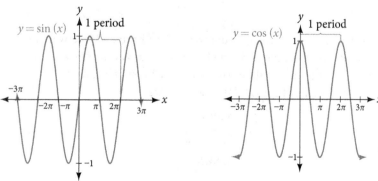

Figure 5

Looking again at the sine and cosine functions on a domain centered at the y-axis helps reveal symmetries. As we can see in **Figure 6**, the sine function is symmetric about the origin. Recall from **The Other Trigonometric Functions** that we determined from the unit circle that the sine function is an odd function because $\sin(-x) = -\sin x$. Now we can clearly see this property from the graph.

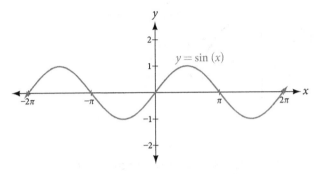

Figure 6 Odd symmetry of the sine function

Figure 7 shows that the cosine function is symmetric about the y-axis. Again, we determined that the cosine function is an even function. Now we can see from the graph that $\cos(-x) = \cos x$.

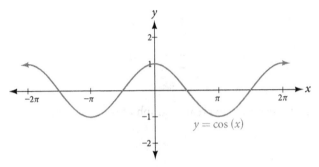

Figure 7 Even symmetry of the cosine function

---

characteristics of sine and cosine functions

The sine and cosine functions have several distinct characteristics:

- They are periodic functions with a period of 2π.
- The domain of each function is $(-\infty, \infty)$ and the range is $[-1, 1]$.
- The graph of $y = \sin x$ is symmetric about the origin, because it is an odd function.
- The graph of $y = \cos x$ is symmetric about the y- axis, because it is an even function.

Investigating Sinusoidal Functions

As we can see, sine and cosine functions have a regular period and range. If we watch ocean waves or ripples on a pond, we will see that they resemble the sine or cosine functions. However, they are not necessarily identical. Some are taller or longer than others. A function that has the same general shape as a sine or cosine function is known as a **sinusoidal function**. The general forms of sinusoidal functions are

$$y = A\sin(Bx - C) + D$$

and

$$y = A\cos(Bx - C) + D$$

Determining the Period of Sinusoidal Functions

Looking at the forms of sinusoidal functions, we can see that they are transformations of the sine and cosine functions. We can use what we know about transformations to determine the period.

In the general formula, B is related to the period by $P = \dfrac{2\pi}{|B|}$. If $|B| > 1$, then the period is less than 2π and the function undergoes a horizontal compression, whereas if $|B| < 1$, then the period is greater than 2π and the function undergoes a horizontal stretch. For example, $f(x) = \sin(x)$, $B = 1$, so the period is 2π, which we knew. If $f(x) = \sin(2x)$, then $B = 2$, so the period is π and the graph is compressed. If $f(x) = \sin\left(\dfrac{x}{2}\right)$, then $B = \dfrac{1}{2}$, so the period is 4π and the graph is stretched. Notice in **Figure 8** how the period is indirectly related to $|B|$.

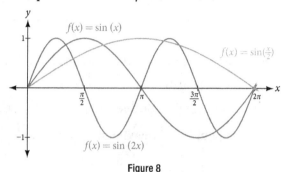

Figure 8

---

period of sinusoidal functions

If we let $C = 0$ and $D = 0$ in the general form equations of the sine and cosine functions, we obtain the forms

$$y = A\sin(Bx) \qquad y = A\cos(Bx)$$

The period is $\dfrac{2\pi}{|B|}$.

Example 1   **Identifying the Period of a Sine or Cosine Function**

Determine the period of the function $f(x) = \sin\left(\dfrac{\pi}{6}x\right)$.

Solution   Let's begin by comparing the equation to the general form $y = A\sin(Bx)$.

In the given equation, $B = \dfrac{\pi}{6}$, so the period will be

$$
\begin{aligned}
P &= \frac{2\pi}{|B|} \\
&= \frac{2\pi}{\frac{\pi}{6}} \\
&= 2\pi \cdot \frac{6}{\pi} \\
&= 12
\end{aligned}
$$

Try It #1

Determine the period of the function $g(x) = \left(\cos\dfrac{x}{3}\right)$.

Determining Amplitude

Returning to the general formula for a sinusoidal function, we have analyzed how the variable B relates to the period. Now let's turn to the variable A so we can analyze how it is related to the **amplitude**, or greatest distance from rest. A represents the vertical stretch factor, and its absolute value $|A|$ is the amplitude. The local maxima will be a distance $|A|$ above the vertical **midline** of the graph, which is the line $x = D$; because $D = 0$ in this case, the midline is the x-axis. The local minima will be the same distance below the midline. If $|A| > 1$, the function is stretched. For example, the amplitude of $f(x) = 4\sin x$ is twice the amplitude of $f(x) = 2\sin x$. If $|A| < 1$, the function is compressed. **Figure 9** compares several sine functions with different amplitudes.

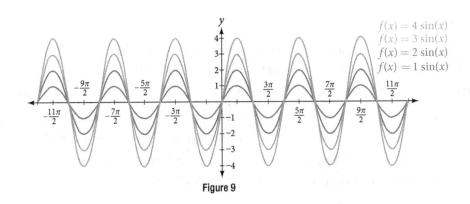

Figure 9

---

amplitude of sinusoidal functions

If we let $C = 0$ and $D = 0$ in the general form equations of the sine and cosine functions, we obtain the forms

$$y = A\sin(Bx) \text{ and } y = A\cos(Bx)$$

The **amplitude** is A, and the vertical height from the **midline** is $|A|$. In addition, notice in the example that

$$|A| = \text{amplitude} = \frac{1}{2}|\text{maximum} - \text{minimum}|$$

Example 2   **Identifying the Amplitude of a Sine or Cosine Function**

What is the amplitude of the sinusoidal function $f(x) = -4\sin(x)$? Is the function stretched or compressed vertically?

Solution   Let's begin by comparing the function to the simplified form $y = A\sin(Bx)$.

In the given function, $A = -4$, so the amplitude is $|A| = |-4| = 4$. The function is stretched.

Analysis   *The negative value of A results in a reflection across the x-axis of the sine function, as shown in* **Figure 10**.

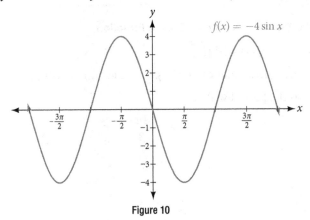

Figure 10

Try It #2

What is the amplitude of the sinusoidal function $f(x) = \frac{1}{2}\sin(x)$? Is the function stretched or compressed vertically?

Analyzing Graphs of Variations of $y = \sin x$ and $y = \cos x$

Now that we understand how A and B relate to the general form equation for the sine and cosine functions, we will explore the variables C and D. Recall the general form:

$$y = A\sin(Bx - C) + D \text{ and } y = A\cos(Bx - C) + D$$

or

$$y = A\sin\left(B\left(x - \frac{C}{B}\right)\right) + D \text{ and } y = A\cos\left(B\left(x - \frac{C}{B}\right)\right) + D$$

The value $\dfrac{C}{B}$ for a sinusoidal function is called the **phase shift**, or the horizontal displacement of the basic sine or cosine function. If $C > 0$, the graph shifts to the right. If $C < 0$, the graph shifts to the left. The greater the value of $|C|$, the more the graph is shifted. **Figure 11** shows that the graph of $f(x) = \sin(x - \pi)$ shifts to the right by π units, which is more than we see in the graph of $f(x) = \sin\left(x - \dfrac{\pi}{4}\right)$, which shifts to the right by $\dfrac{\pi}{4}$ units.

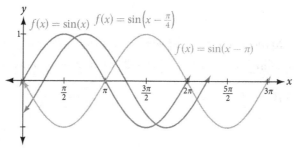

Figure 11

While C relates to the horizontal shift, D indicates the vertical shift from the midline in the general formula for a sinusoidal function. See **Figure 12**. The function $y = \cos(x) + D$ has its midline at $y = D$.

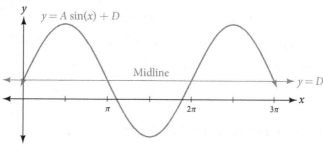

Figure 12

Any value of D other than zero shifts the graph up or down. **Figure 13** compares $f(x) = \sin x$ with $f(x) = \sin x + 2$, which is shifted 2 units up on a graph.

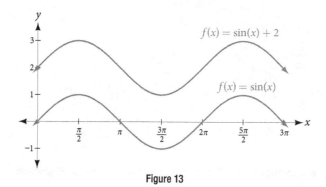

Figure 13

---

variations of sine and cosine functions

Given an equation in the form $f(x) = A\sin(Bx - C) + D$ or $f(x) = A\cos(Bx - C) + D$, $\dfrac{C}{B}$ is the **phase shift** and D is the vertical shift.

Example 3   **Identifying the Phase Shift of a Function**

Determine the direction and magnitude of the phase shift for $f(x) = \sin\left(x + \dfrac{\pi}{6}\right) - 2$.

Solution   Let's begin by comparing the equation to the general form $y = A\sin(Bx - C) + D$.

In the given equation, notice that $B = 1$ and $C = -\frac{\pi}{6}$. So the phase shift is

$$\frac{C}{B} = -\frac{\frac{\pi}{6}}{1}$$

$$= -\frac{\pi}{6}$$

or $\frac{\pi}{6}$ units to the left.

Analysis   We must pay attention to the sign in the equation for the general form of a sinusoidal function. The equation shows a minus sign before C. Therefore $f(x) = \sin\left(x + \frac{\pi}{6}\right) - 2$ can be rewritten as $f(x) = \sin\left(x - \left(-\frac{\pi}{6}\right)\right) - 2$.

If the value of C is negative, the shift is to the left.

Try It #3

Determine the direction and magnitude of the phase shift for $f(x) = 3\cos\left(x - \frac{\pi}{2}\right)$.

Example 4   Identifying the Vertical Shift of a Function

Determine the direction and magnitude of the vertical shift for $f(x) = \cos(x) - 3$.

Solution   Let's begin by comparing the equation to the general form $y = A\cos(Bx - C) + D$.

In the given equation, $D = -3$ so the shift is 3 units downward.

Try It #4

Determine the direction and magnitude of the vertical shift for $f(x) = 3\sin(x) + 2$.

How To...

Given a sinusoidal function in the form $f(x) = A\sin(Bx - C) + D$, identify the midline, amplitude, period, and phase shift.

1. Determine the amplitude as $|A|$.
2. Determine the period as $P = \frac{2\pi}{|B|}$.
3. Determine the phase shift as $\frac{C}{B}$.
4. Determine the midline as $y = D$.

Example 5   Identifying the Variations of a Sinusoidal Function from an Equation

Determine the midline, amplitude, period, and phase shift of the function $y = 3\sin(2x) + 1$.

Solution   Let's begin by comparing the equation to the general form $y = A\sin(Bx - C) + D$.

$A = 3$, so the amplitude is $|A| = 3$.

Next, $B = 2$, so the period is $P = \frac{2\pi}{|B|} = \frac{2\pi}{2} = \pi$.

There is no added constant inside the parentheses, so $C = 0$ and the phase shift is $\frac{C}{B} = \frac{0}{2} = 0$.

Finally, $D = 1$, so the midline is $y = 1$.

Analysis   Inspecting the graph, we can determine that the period is π, the midline is $y = 1$, and the amplitude is 3. See **Figure 14**.

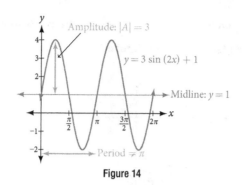

Figure 14

Try It #5

Determine the midline, amplitude, period, and phase shift of the function $y = \dfrac{1}{2}\cos\left(\dfrac{x}{3} - \dfrac{\pi}{3}\right)$.

Example 6   **Identifying the Equation for a Sinusoidal Function from a Graph**

Determine the formula for the cosine function in **Figure 15**.

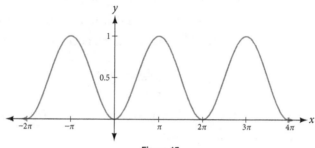

Figure 15

Solution   To determine the equation, we need to identify each value in the general form of a sinusoidal function.

$$y = A\sin(Bx - C) + D \qquad\qquad y = A\cos(Bx - C) + D$$

The graph could represent either a sine or a cosine function that is shifted and/or reflected. When $x = 0$, the graph has an extreme point, $(0, 0)$. Since the cosine function has an extreme point for $x = 0$, let us write our equation in terms of a cosine function.

Let's start with the midline. We can see that the graph rises and falls an equal distance above and below $y = 0.5$. This value, which is the midline, is D in the equation, so $D = 0.5$.

The greatest distance above and below the midline is the amplitude. The maxima are 0.5 units above the midline and the minima are 0.5 units below the midline. So $|A| = 0.5$. Another way we could have determined the amplitude is by recognizing that the difference between the height of local maxima and minima is 1, so $|A| = \dfrac{1}{2} = 0.5$. Also, the graph is reflected about the x-axis so that $A = -0.5$.

The graph is not horizontally stretched or compressed, so $B = 1$; and the graph is not shifted horizontally, so $C = 0$.

Putting this all together,

$$g(x) = -0.5\cos(x) + 0.5$$

Try It #6

Determine the formula for the sine function in **Figure 16**.

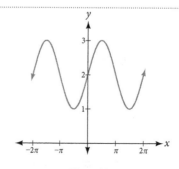

Figure 16

Example 7   **Identifying the Equation for a Sinusoidal Function from a Graph**

Determine the equation for the sinusoidal function in **Figure 17**.

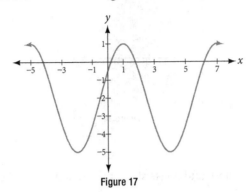

Figure 17

Solution   With the highest value at 1 and the lowest value at -5, the midline will be halfway between at -2. So $D = -2$.

The distance from the midline to the highest or lowest value gives an amplitude of $|A| = 3$.

The period of the graph is 6, which can be measured from the peak at $x = 1$ to the next peak at $x = 7$, or from the distance between the lowest points. Therefore, $P = \dfrac{2\pi}{|B|} = 6$. Using the positive value for B, we find that

$$B = \frac{2\pi}{P} = \frac{2\pi}{6} = \frac{\pi}{3}$$

So far, our equation is either $y = 3\sin\left(\dfrac{\pi}{3}x - C\right) - 2$ or $y = 3\cos\left(\dfrac{\pi}{3}x - C\right) - 2$. For the shape and shift, we have more than one option. We could write this as any one of the following:

- a cosine shifted to the right
- a negative cosine shifted to the left
- a sine shifted to the left
- a negative sine shifted to the right

While any of these would be correct, the cosine shifts are easier to work with than the sine shifts in this case because they involve integer values. So our function becomes

$$y = 3\cos\left(\frac{\pi}{3}x - \frac{\pi}{3}\right) - 2 \text{ or } y = -3\cos\left(\frac{\pi}{3}x + \frac{2\pi}{3}\right) - 2$$

Again, these functions are equivalent, so both yield the same graph.

Try It #7

Write a formula for the function graphed in **Figure 18**.

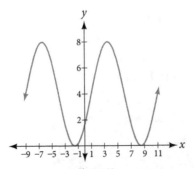

Figure 18

Graphing Variations of $y = \sin x$ and $y = \cos x$

Throughout this section, we have learned about types of variations of sine and cosine functions and used that information to write equations from graphs. Now we can use the same information to create graphs from equations.

Instead of focusing on the general form equations

$$y = A\sin(Bx - C) + D \text{ and } y = A\cos(Bx - C) + D,$$

we will let $C = 0$ and $D = 0$ and work with a simplified form of the equations in the following examples.

How To...

Given the function $y = A\sin(Bx)$, sketch its graph.

1. Identify the amplitude, $|A|$.

2. Identify the period, $P = \dfrac{2\pi}{|B|}$.

3. Start at the origin, with the function increasing to the right if A is positive or decreasing if A is negative.

4. At $x = \dfrac{\pi}{2|B|}$ there is a local maximum for $A > 0$ or a minimum for $A < 0$, with $y = A$.

5. The curve returns to the x-axis at $x = \dfrac{\pi}{|B|}$.

6. There is a local minimum for $A > 0$ (maximum for $A < 0$) at $x = \dfrac{3\pi}{2|B|}$ with $y = -A$.

7. The curve returns again to the x-axis at $x = \dfrac{\pi}{2|B|}$.

Example 8   **Graphing a Function and Identifying the Amplitude and Period**

Sketch a graph of $f(x) = -2\sin\left(\dfrac{\pi x}{2}\right)$.

Solution   Let's begin by comparing the equation to the form $y = A\sin(Bx)$.

Step 1. We can see from the equation that $A = -2$, so the amplitude is 2.

$$|A| = 2$$

Step 2. The equation shows that $B = \dfrac{\pi}{2}$, so the period is

$$P = \dfrac{2\pi}{\dfrac{\pi}{2}}$$
$$= 2\pi \cdot \dfrac{2}{\pi}$$
$$= 4$$

Step 3. Because A is negative, the graph descends as we move to the right of the origin.

Step 4–7. The x-intercepts are at the beginning of one period, $x = 0$, the horizontal midpoints are at $x = 2$ and at the end of one period at $x = 4$.

The quarter points include the minimum at $x = 1$ and the maximum at $x = 3$. A local minimum will occur 2 units below the midline, at $x = 1$, and a local maximum will occur at 2 units above the midline, at $x = 3$. **Figure 19** shows the graph of the function.

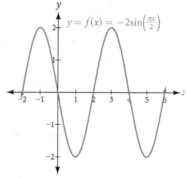

Figure 19

Try It #8

Sketch a graph of $g(x) = -0.8\cos(2x)$. Determine the midline, amplitude, period, and phase shift.

How To...

Given a sinusoidal function with a phase shift and a vertical shift, sketch its graph.

1. Express the function in the general form $y = A\sin(Bx - C) + D$ or $y = A\cos(Bx - C) + D$.

2. Identify the amplitude, $|A|$.

3. Identify the period, $P = \dfrac{2\pi}{|B|}$.

4. Identify the phase shift, $\dfrac{C}{B}$.

5. Draw the graph of $f(x) = A\sin(Bx)$ shifted to the right or left by $\dfrac{C}{B}$ and up or down by D.

Example 9   **Graphing a Transformed Sinusoid**

Sketch a graph of $f(x) = 3\sin\left(\dfrac{\pi}{4}x - \dfrac{\pi}{4}\right)$.

Solution

Step 1. The function is already written in general form: $f(x) = 3\sin\left(\dfrac{\pi}{4}x - \dfrac{\pi}{4}\right)$. This graph will have the shape of a sine function, starting at the midline and increasing to the right.

Step 2. $|A| = |3| = 3$. The amplitude is 3.

Step 3. Since $|B| = \left|\dfrac{\pi}{4}\right| = \dfrac{\pi}{4}$, we determine the period as follows.

$$P = \frac{2\pi}{|B|} = \frac{2\pi}{\dfrac{\pi}{4}} = 2\pi \cdot \frac{4}{\pi} = 8$$

The period is 8.

Step 4. Since $C = \dfrac{\pi}{4}$, the phase shift is

$$\frac{C}{B} = \frac{\dfrac{\pi}{4}}{\dfrac{\pi}{4}} = 1.$$

The phase shift is 1 unit.

Step 5. **Figure 20** shows the graph of the function.

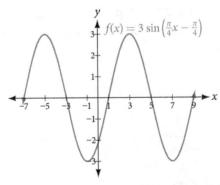

Figure 20 A horizontally compressed, vertically stretched, and horizontally shifted sinusoid

Try It #9

Draw a graph of $g(x) = -2\cos\left(\dfrac{\pi}{3}x + \dfrac{\pi}{6}\right)$. Determine the midline, amplitude, period, and phase shift.

Example 10 Identifying the Properties of a Sinusoidal Function

Given $y = -2\cos\left(\dfrac{\pi}{2}x + \pi\right) + 3$, determine the amplitude, period, phase shift, and horizontal shift. Then graph the function.

Solution Begin by comparing the equation to the general form and use the steps outlined in **Example 9**.

$$y = A\cos(Bx - C) + D$$

Step 1. The function is already written in general form.

Step 2. Since $A = -2$, the amplitude is $|A| = 2$.

Step 3. $|B| = \dfrac{\pi}{2}$, so the period is $P = \dfrac{2\pi}{|B|} = \dfrac{2\pi}{\dfrac{\pi}{2}} = 2\pi \cdot \dfrac{2}{\pi} = 4$. The period is 4.

Step 4. $C = -\pi$, so we calculate the phase shift as $\dfrac{C}{B} = \dfrac{-\pi}{\dfrac{\pi}{2}} = -\pi \cdot \dfrac{2}{\pi} = -2$. The phase shift is -2.

Step 5. $D = 3$, so the midline is $y = 3$, and the vertical shift is up 3.

Since A is negative, the graph of the cosine function has been reflected about the x-axis. **Figure 21** shows one cycle of the graph of the function.

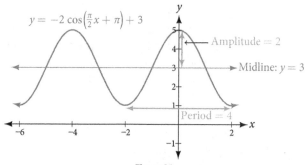

Figure 21

Using Transformations of Sine and Cosine Functions

We can use the transformations of sine and cosine functions in numerous applications. As mentioned at the beginning of the chapter, circular motion can be modeled using either the sine or cosine function.

Example 11 Finding the Vertical Component of Circular Motion

A point rotates around a circle of radius 3 centered at the origin. Sketch a graph of the y-coordinate of the point as a function of the angle of rotation.

Solution Recall that, for a point on a circle of radius r, the y-coordinate of the point is $y = r\sin(x)$, so in this case, we get the equation $y(x) = 3\sin(x)$. The constant 3 causes a vertical stretch of the y-values of the function by a factor of 3, which we can see in the graph in **Figure 22**.

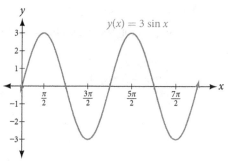

Figure 22

Analysis   Notice that the period of the function is still 2π; as we travel around the circle, we return to the point (3, 0) for x = 2π, 4π, 6π, ... Because the outputs of the graph will now oscillate between –3 and 3, the amplitude of the sine wave is 3.

Try It #10

What is the amplitude of the function $f(x) = 7\cos(x)$? Sketch a graph of this function.

Example 12   **Finding the Vertical Component of Circular Motion**

A circle with radius 3 ft is mounted with its center 4 ft off the ground. The point closest to the ground is labeled P, as shown in **Figure 23**. Sketch a graph of the height above the ground of the point P as the circle is rotated; then find a function that gives the height in terms of the angle of rotation.

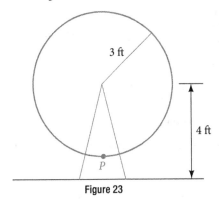

3 ft

4 ft

P

Figure 23

Solution   Sketching the height, we note that it will start 1 ft above the ground, then increase up to 7 ft above the ground, and continue to oscillate 3 ft above and below the center value of 4 ft, as shown in **Figure 24**.

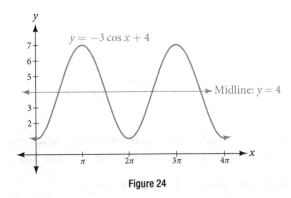

$y = -3\cos x + 4$

Midline: $y = 4$

Figure 24

Although we could use a transformation of either the sine or cosine function, we start by looking for characteristics that would make one function easier to use than the other. Let's use a cosine function because it starts at the highest or lowest value, while a sine function starts at the middle value. A standard cosine starts at the highest value, and this graph starts at the lowest value, so we need to incorporate a vertical reflection.

Second, we see that the graph oscillates 3 above and below the center, while a basic cosine has an amplitude of 1, so this graph has been vertically stretched by 3, as in the last example.

Finally, to move the center of the circle up to a height of 4, the graph has been vertically shifted up by 4. Putting these transformations together, we find that

$$y = -3\cos(x) + 4$$

Try It #11

A weight is attached to a spring that is then hung from a board, as shown in **Figure 25**. As the spring oscillates up and down, the position *y* of the weight relative to the board ranges from −1 in. (at time *x* = 0) to −7 in. (at time *x* = π) below the board. Assume the position of *y* is given as a sinusoidal function of *x*. Sketch a graph of the function, and then find a cosine function that gives the position *y* in terms of *x*.

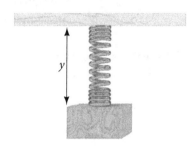

Figure 25

Example 13 Determining a Rider's Height on a Ferris Wheel

The London Eye is a huge Ferris wheel with a diameter of 135 meters (443 feet). It completes one rotation every 30 minutes. Riders board from a platform 2 meters above the ground. Express a rider's height above ground as a function of time in minutes.

Solution   With a diameter of 135 m, the wheel has a radius of 67.5 m. The height will oscillate with amplitude 67.5 m above and below the center.

Passengers board 2 m above ground level, so the center of the wheel must be located 67.5 + 2 = 69.5 m above ground level. The midline of the oscillation will be at 69.5 m.

The wheel takes 30 minutes to complete 1 revolution, so the height will oscillate with a period of 30 minutes.

Lastly, because the rider boards at the lowest point, the height will start at the smallest value and increase, following the shape of a vertically reflected cosine curve.

- Amplitude: 67.5, so $A = 67.5$
- Midline: 69.5, so $D = 69.5$
- Period: 30, so $B = \dfrac{2\pi}{30} = \dfrac{\pi}{15}$
- Shape: $-\cos(t)$

An equation for the rider's height would be

$$y = -\,67.5\cos\!\left(\frac{\pi}{15}t\right) + 69.5$$

where *t* is in minutes and *y* is measured in meters.

Access these online resources for additional instruction and practice with graphs of sine and cosine functions.

- Amplitude and Period of Sine and Cosine (http://openstaxcollege.org/l/ampperiod)
- Translations of Sine and Cosine (http://openstaxcollege.org/l/translasincos)
- Graphing Sine and Cosine Transformations (http://openstaxcollege.org/l/transformsincos)
- Graphing the Sine Function (http://openstaxcollege.org/l/graphsinefunc)

6.1   SECTION EXERCISES

VERBAL

1. Why are the sine and cosine functions called periodic functions?

2. How does the graph of $y = \sin x$ compare with the graph of $y = \cos x$? Explain how you could horizontally translate the graph of $y = \sin x$ to obtain $y = \cos x$.

3. For the equation $A\cos(Bx + C) + D$, what constants affect the range of the function and how do they affect the range?

4. How does the range of a translated sine function relate to the equation $y = A\sin(Bx + C) + D$?

5. How can the unit circle be used to construct the graph of $f(t) = \sin t$?

GRAPHICAL

For the following exercises, graph two full periods of each function and state the amplitude, period, and midline. State the maximum and minimum y-values and their corresponding x-values on one period for $x > 0$. Round answers to two decimal places if necessary.

6. $f(x) = 2\sin x$

7. $f(x) = \dfrac{2}{3}\cos x$

8. $f(x) = -3\sin x$

9. $f(x) = 4\sin x$

10. $f(x) = 2\cos x$

11. $f(x) = \cos(2x)$

12. $f(x) = 2\sin\left(\dfrac{1}{2}x\right)$

13. $f(x) = 4\cos(\pi x)$

14. $f(x) = 3\cos\left(\dfrac{6}{5}x\right)$

15. $y = 3\sin(8(x + 4)) + 5$

16. $y = 2\sin(3x - 21) + 4$

17. $y = 5\sin(5x + 20) - 2$

For the following exercises, graph one full period of each function, starting at $x = 0$. For each function, state the amplitude, period, and midline. State the maximum and minimum y-values and their corresponding x-values on one period for $x > 0$. State the phase shift and vertical translation, if applicable. Round answers to two decimal places if necessary.

18. $f(t) = 2\sin\left(t - \dfrac{5\pi}{6}\right)$

19. $f(t) = -\cos\left(t + \dfrac{\pi}{3}\right) + 1$

20. $f(t) = 4\cos\left(2\left(t + \dfrac{\pi}{4}\right)\right) - 3$

21. $f(t) = -\sin\left(\dfrac{1}{2}t + \dfrac{5\pi}{3}\right)$

22. $f(x) = 4\sin\left(\dfrac{\pi}{2}(x - 3)\right) + 7$

23. Determine the amplitude, midline, period, and an equation involving the sine function for the graph shown in **Figure 26**.

24. Determine the amplitude, period, midline, and an equation involving cosine for the graph shown in **Figure 27**.

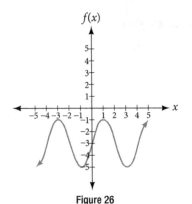

Figure 26

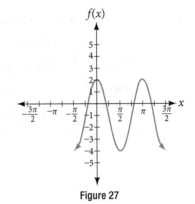

Figure 27

25. Determine the amplitude, period, midline, and an equation involving cosine for the graph shown in **Figure 28**.

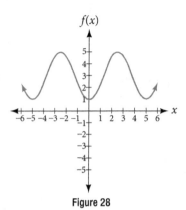

Figure 28

26. Determine the amplitude, period, midline, and an equation involving sine for the graph shown in **Figure 29**.

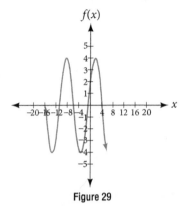

Figure 29

27. Determine the amplitude, period, midline, and an equation involving cosine for the graph shown in **Figure 30**.

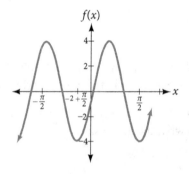

Figure 30

28. Determine the amplitude, period, midline, and an equation involving sine for the graph shown in **Figure 31**.

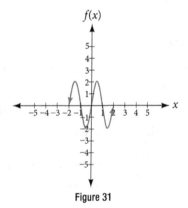

Figure 31

29. Determine the amplitude, period, midline, and an equation involving cosine for the graph shown in **Figure 32**.

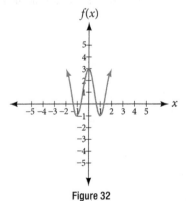

Figure 32

30. Determine the amplitude, period, midline, and an equation involving sine for the graph shown in **Figure 33**.

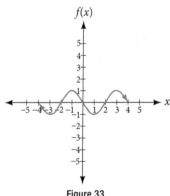

Figure 33

ALGEBRAIC

For the following exercises, let $f(x) = \sin x$.

31. On $[0, 2\pi)$, solve $f(x) = 0$.

32. On $[0, 2\pi)$, solve $f(x) = \dfrac{1}{2}$.

33. Evaluate $f\left(\dfrac{\pi}{2}\right)$.

34. On $[0, 2\pi)$, $f(x) = \dfrac{\sqrt{2}}{2}$. Find all values of x.

35. On $[0, 2\pi)$, the maximum value(s) of the function occur(s) at what x-value(s)?

36. On $[0, 2\pi)$, the minimum value(s) of the function occur(s) at what x-value(s)?

37. Show that $f(-x) = -f(x)$. This means that $f(x) = \sin x$ is an odd function and possesses symmetry with respect to _____.

For the following exercises, let $f(x) = \cos x$.

38. On $[0, 2\pi)$, solve the equation $f(x) = \cos x = 0$.

39. On $[0, 2\pi)$, solve $f(x) = \dfrac{1}{2}$.

40. On $[0, 2\pi)$, find the x-intercepts of $f(x) = \cos x$.

41. On $[0, 2\pi)$, find the x-values at which the function has a maximum or minimum value.

42. On $[0, 2\pi)$, solve the equation $f(x) = \dfrac{\sqrt{3}}{2}$.

TECHNOLOGY

43. Graph $h(x) = x + \sin x$ on $[0, 2\pi]$. Explain why the graph appears as it does.

44. Graph $h(x) = x + \sin x$ on $[-100, 100]$. Did the graph appear as predicted in the previous exercise?

45. Graph $f(x) = x \sin x$ on $[0, 2\pi]$ and verbalize how the graph varies from the graph of $f(x) = \sin x$.

46. Graph $f(x) = x \sin x$ on the window $[-10, 10]$ and explain what the graph shows.

47. Graph $f(x) = \dfrac{\sin x}{x}$ on the window $[-5\pi, 5\pi]$ and explain what the graph shows.

REAL-WORLD APPLICATIONS

48. A Ferris wheel is 25 meters in diameter and boarded from a platform that is 1 meter above the ground. The six o'clock position on the Ferris wheel is level with the loading platform. The wheel completes 1 full revolution in 10 minutes. The function $h(t)$ gives a person's height in meters above the ground t minutes after the wheel begins to turn.
    a. Find the amplitude, midline, and period of $h(t)$.
    b. Find a formula for the height function $h(t)$.
    c. How high off the ground is a person after 5 minutes?

LEARNING OBJECTIVES

In this section, you will:

- Analyze the graph of $y = \tan x$.
- Graph variations of $y = \tan x$.
- Analyze the graphs of $y = \sec x$ and $y = \csc x$.
- Graph variations of $y = \sec x$ and $y = \csc x$.
- Analyze the graph of $y = \cot x$.
- Graph variations of $y = \cot x$.

6.2 GRAPHS OF THE OTHER TRIGONOMETRIC FUNCTIONS

We know the tangent function can be used to find distances, such as the height of a building, mountain, or flagpole. But what if we want to measure repeated occurrences of distance? Imagine, for example, a police car parked next to a warehouse. The rotating light from the police car would travel across the wall of the warehouse in regular intervals. If the input is time, the output would be the distance the beam of light travels. The beam of light would repeat the distance at regular intervals. The tangent function can be used to approximate this distance. Asymptotes would be needed to illustrate the repeated cycles when the beam runs parallel to the wall because, seemingly, the beam of light could appear to extend forever. The graph of the tangent function would clearly illustrate the repeated intervals. In this section, we will explore the graphs of the tangent and other trigonometric functions.

Analyzing the Graph of $y = \tan x$

We will begin with the graph of the tangent function, plotting points as we did for the sine and cosine functions. Recall that

$$\tan x = \frac{\sin x}{\cos x}$$

The period of the tangent function is π because the graph repeats itself on intervals of $k\pi$ where k is a constant. If we graph the tangent function on $-\frac{\pi}{2}$ to $\frac{\pi}{2}$, we can see the behavior of the graph on one complete cycle. If we look at any larger interval, we will see that the characteristics of the graph repeat.

We can determine whether tangent is an odd or even function by using the definition of tangent.

$$\tan(-x) = \frac{\sin(-x)}{\cos(-x)} \qquad \text{Definition of tangent.}$$

$$= \frac{-\sin x}{\cos x} \qquad \text{Sine is an odd function, cosine is even.}$$

$$= -\frac{\sin x}{\cos x} \qquad \text{The quotient of an odd and an even function is odd.}$$

$$= -\tan x \qquad \text{Definition of tangent.}$$

Therefore, tangent is an odd function. We can further analyze the graphical behavior of the tangent function by looking at values for some of the special angles, as listed in **Table 1**.

x	$-\frac{\pi}{2}$	$-\frac{\pi}{3}$	$-\frac{\pi}{4}$	$-\frac{\pi}{6}$	0	$\frac{\pi}{6}$	$\frac{\pi}{4}$	$\frac{\pi}{3}$	$\frac{\pi}{2}$
$\tan(x)$	undefined	$-\sqrt{3}$	-1	$-\frac{\sqrt{3}}{3}$	0	$\frac{\sqrt{3}}{3}$	1	$\sqrt{3}$	undefined

Table 1

These points will help us draw our graph, but we need to determine how the graph behaves where it is undefined. If we look more closely at values when $\frac{\pi}{3} < x < \frac{\pi}{2}$, we can use a table to look for a trend. Because $\frac{\pi}{3} \approx 1.05$ and $\frac{\pi}{2} \approx 1.57$, we will evaluate x at radian measures $1.05 < x < 1.57$ as shown in **Table 2**.

x	1.3	1.5	1.55	1.56
tan x	3.6	14.1	48.1	92.6

Table 2

As x approaches $\frac{\pi}{2}$, the outputs of the function get larger and larger. Because $y = \tan x$ is an odd function, we see the corresponding table of negative values in **Table 3**.

x	−1.3	−1.5	−1.55	−1.56
tan x	−3.6	−14.1	−48.1	−92.6

Table 3

We can see that, as x approaches $-\frac{\pi}{2}$, the outputs get smaller and smaller. Remember that there are some values of x for which $\cos x = 0$. For example, $\cos\left(\frac{\pi}{2}\right) = 0$ and $\cos\left(\frac{3\pi}{2}\right) = 0$. At these values, the tangent function is undefined, so the graph of $y = \tan x$ has discontinuities at $x = \frac{\pi}{2}$ and $\frac{3\pi}{2}$. At these values, the graph of the tangent has vertical asymptotes. **Figure 1** represents the graph of $y = \tan x$. The tangent is positive from 0 to $\frac{\pi}{2}$ and from π to $\frac{3\pi}{2}$, corresponding to quadrants I and III of the unit circle.

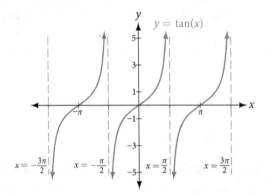

Figure 1 Graph of the tangent function

Graphing Variations of $y = \tan x$

As with the sine and cosine functions, the tangent function can be described by a general equation.

$$y = A\tan(Bx)$$

We can identify horizontal and vertical stretches and compressions using values of A and B. The horizontal stretch can typically be determined from the period of the graph. With tangent graphs, it is often necessary to determine a vertical stretch using a point on the graph.

Because there are no maximum or minimum values of a tangent function, the term *amplitude* cannot be interpreted as it is for the sine and cosine functions. Instead, we will use the phrase *stretching/compressing factor* when referring to the constant A.

---

features of the graph of $y = A\tan(Bx)$

- The stretching factor is $|A|$.
- The period is $P = \frac{\pi}{|B|}$.
- The domain is all real numbers x, where $x \neq \frac{\pi}{2|B|} + \frac{\pi}{|B|}k$ such that k is an integer.
- The range is $(-\infty, \infty)$.
- The asymptotes occur at $x = \frac{\pi}{2|B|} + \frac{\pi}{|B|}k$, where k is an integer.
- $y = A\tan(Bx)$ is an odd function.

Graphing One Period of a Stretched or Compressed Tangent Function

We can use what we know about the properties of the tangent function to quickly sketch a graph of any stretched and/or compressed tangent function of the form $f(x) = A\tan(Bx)$. We focus on a single period of the function including the origin, because the periodic property enables us to extend the graph to the rest of the function's domain if we wish. Our limited domain is then the interval $\left(-\dfrac{P}{2}, \dfrac{P}{2}\right)$ and the graph has vertical asymptotes at $\pm\dfrac{P}{2}$ where $P = \dfrac{\pi}{B}$. On $\left(-\dfrac{\pi}{2}, \dfrac{\pi}{2}\right)$, the graph will come up from the left asymptote at $x = -\dfrac{\pi}{2}$, cross through the origin, and continue to increase as it approaches the right asymptote at $x = \dfrac{\pi}{2}$. To make the function approach the asymptotes at the correct rate, we also need to set the vertical scale by actually evaluating the function for at least one point that the graph will pass through. For example, we can use

$$f\left(\frac{P}{4}\right) = A\tan\left(B\frac{P}{4}\right) = A\tan\left(B\frac{\pi}{4B}\right) = A$$

because $\tan\left(\dfrac{\pi}{4}\right) = 1$.

How To...

Given the function $f(x) = A\tan(Bx)$, graph one period.

1. Identify the stretching factor, $|A|$.
2. Identify B and determine the period, $P = \dfrac{\pi}{|B|}$.
3. Draw vertical asymptotes at $x = -\dfrac{P}{2}$ and $x = \dfrac{P}{2}$.
4. For $A > 0$, the graph approaches the left asymptote at negative output values and the right asymptote at positive output values (reverse for $A < 0$).
5. Plot reference points at $\left(\dfrac{P}{4}, A\right)$, $(0, 0)$, and $\left(-\dfrac{P}{4}, -A\right)$, and draw the graph through these points.

Example 1   **Sketching a Compressed Tangent**

Sketch a graph of one period of the function $y = 0.5\tan\left(\dfrac{\pi}{2}x\right)$.

Solution   First, we identify A and B.

$$y = 0.5\,\tan\left(\frac{\pi}{2}x\right)$$
$$\uparrow \qquad \nearrow$$
$$y = A\tan(Bx)$$

Because $A = 0.5$ and $B = \dfrac{\pi}{2}$, we can find the stretching/compressing factor and period. The period is $\dfrac{\pi}{\frac{\pi}{2}} = 2$, so the asymptotes are at $x = \pm 1$. At a quarter period from the origin, we have

$$f(0.5) = 0.5\tan\left(\frac{0.5\pi}{2}\right)$$

$$= 0.5\tan\left(\frac{\pi}{4}\right)$$

$$= 0.5$$

This means the curve must pass through the points $(0.5, 0.5)$, $(0, 0)$, and $(-0.5, -0.5)$. The only inflection point is at the origin. **Figure 2** shows the graph of one period of the function.

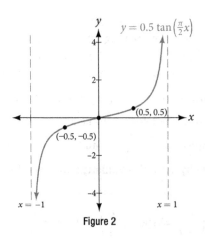

Figure 2

Try It #1

Sketch a graph of $f(x) = 3\tan\left(\dfrac{\pi}{6}x\right)$.

Graphing One Period of a Shifted Tangent Function

Now that we can graph a tangent function that is stretched or compressed, we will add a vertical and/or horizontal (or phase) shift. In this case, we add C and D to the general form of the tangent function.

$$f(x) = A\tan(Bx - C) + D$$

The graph of a transformed tangent function is different from the basic tangent function $\tan x$ in several ways:

---

features of the graph of $y = A\tan(Bx - C) + D$

- The stretching factor is $|A|$.
- The period is $\dfrac{\pi}{|B|}$.
- The domain is $x \neq \dfrac{C}{B} + \dfrac{\pi}{2|B|}k$, where k is an odd integer.
- The range is $(-\infty, \infty)$.
- The vertical asymptotes occur at $x = \dfrac{C}{B} + \dfrac{\pi}{2|B|}k$, where k is an odd integer.
- There is no amplitude.
- $y = A\tan(Bx)$ is an odd function because it is the quotient of odd and even functions (sine and cosine respectively).

How To...

Given the function $y = A\tan(Bx - C) + D$, sketch the graph of one period.

1. Express the function given in the form $y = A\tan(Bx - C) + D$.

2. Identify the stretching/compressing factor, $|A|$.

3. Identify B and determine the period, $P = \dfrac{\pi}{|B|}$.

4. Identify C and determine the phase shift, $\dfrac{C}{B}$.

5. Draw the graph of $y = A\tan(Bx)$ shifted to the right by $\dfrac{C}{B}$ and up by D.

6. Sketch the vertical asymptotes, which occur at $x = \dfrac{C}{B} + \dfrac{\pi}{2|B|}k$, where k is an odd integer.

7. Plot any three reference points and draw the graph through these points.

Example 2 **Graphing One Period of a Shifted Tangent Function**

Graph one period of the function $y = -2\tan(\pi x + \pi) - 1$.

Solution

Step 1. The function is already written in the form $y = A\tan(Bx - C) + D$.

Step 2. $A = -2$, so the stretching factor is $|A| = 2$.

Step 3. $B = \pi$, so the period is $P = \dfrac{\pi}{|B|} = \dfrac{\pi}{\pi} = 1$.

Step 4. $C = -\pi$, so the phase shift is $\dfrac{C}{B} = \dfrac{-\pi}{\pi} = -1$.

Step 5-7. The asymptotes are at $x = -\dfrac{3}{2}$ and $x = -\dfrac{1}{2}$ and the three recommended reference points are $(-1.25, 1)$, $(-1, -1)$, and $(-0.75, -3)$. The graph is shown in **Figure 3**.

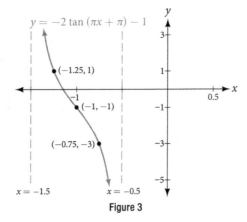

Figure 3

Analysis Note that this is a decreasing function because $A < 0$.

Try It #2

How would the graph in **Example 2** look different if we made $A = 2$ instead of -2?

How To...

Given the graph of a tangent function, identify horizontal and vertical stretches.

1. Find the period P from the spacing between successive vertical asymptotes or x-intercepts.

2. Write $f(x) = A\tan\left(\dfrac{\pi}{P}x\right)$.

3. Determine a convenient point $(x, f(x))$ on the given graph and use it to determine A.

Example 3 **Identifying the Graph of a Stretched Tangent**

Find a formula for the function graphed in **Figure 4**.

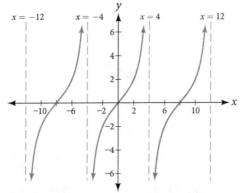

Figure 4 A stretched tangent function

Solution   The graph has the shape of a tangent function.

Step 1. One cycle extends from −4 to 4, so the period is $P = 8$. Since $P = \dfrac{\pi}{|B|}$, we have $B = \dfrac{\pi}{P} = \dfrac{\pi}{8}$.

Step 2. The equation must have the form $f(x) = A\tan\left(\dfrac{\pi}{8}x\right)$.

Step 3. To find the vertical stretch A, we can use the point $(2, 2)$.

$$2 = A\tan\left(\frac{\pi}{8} \cdot 2\right) = A\tan\left(\frac{\pi}{4}\right)$$

Because $\tan\left(\dfrac{\pi}{4}\right) = 1$, $A = 2$.

This function would have a formula $f(x) = 2\tan\left(\dfrac{\pi}{8}x\right)$.

Try It #3

Find a formula for the function in **Figure 5**.

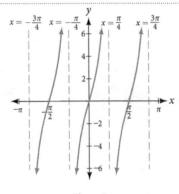

Figure 5

Analyzing the Graphs of $y = \sec x$ and $y = \csc x$

The secant was defined by the reciprocal identity $\sec x = \dfrac{1}{\cos x}$. Notice that the function is undefined when the cosine is 0, leading to vertical asymptotes at $\dfrac{\pi}{2}, \dfrac{3\pi}{2}$, etc. Because the cosine is never more than 1 in absolute value, the secant, being the reciprocal, will never be less than 1 in absolute value.

We can graph $y = \sec x$ by observing the graph of the cosine function because these two functions are reciprocals of one another. See **Figure 6**. The graph of the cosine is shown as a blue wave so we can see the relationship. Where the graph of the cosine function decreases, the graph of the secant function increases. Where the graph of the cosine function increases, the graph of the secant function decreases. When the cosine function is zero, the secant is undefined.

The secant graph has vertical asymptotes at each value of x where the cosine graph crosses the x-axis; we show these in the graph below with dashed vertical lines, but will not show all the asymptotes explicitly on all later graphs involving the secant and cosecant.

Note that, because cosine is an even function, secant is also an even function. That is, $\sec(-x) = \sec x$.

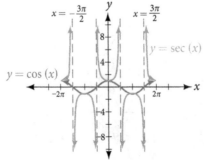

Figure 6 Graph of the secant function, $f(x) = \sec x = \dfrac{1}{\cos x}$

As we did for the tangent function, we will again refer to the constant $|A|$ as the stretching factor, not the amplitude.

---

features of the graph of $y = A\sec(Bx)$

- The stretching factor is $|A|$.
- The period is $\dfrac{2\pi}{|B|}$.
- The domain is $x \neq \dfrac{\pi}{2|B|}k$, where k is an odd integer.
- The range is $(-\infty, -|A|] \cup [|A|, \infty)$.
- The vertical asymptotes occur at $x = \dfrac{\pi}{2|B|}k$, where k is an odd integer.
- There is no amplitude.
- $y = A\sec(Bx)$ is an even function because cosine is an even function.

Similar to the secant, the cosecant is defined by the reciprocal identity $\csc x = \dfrac{1}{\sin x}$. Notice that the function is undefined when the sine is 0, leading to a vertical asymptote in the graph at 0, π, etc. Since the sine is never more than 1 in absolute value, the cosecant, being the reciprocal, will never be less than 1 in absolute value.

We can graph $y = \csc x$ by observing the graph of the sine function because these two functions are reciprocals of one another. See **Figure 7**. The graph of sine is shown as a blue wave so we can see the relationship. Where the graph of the sine function decreases, the graph of the cosecant function increases. Where the graph of the sine function increases, the graph of the cosecant function decreases.

The cosecant graph has vertical asymptotes at each value of x where the sine graph crosses the x-axis; we show these in the graph below with dashed vertical lines.

Note that, since sine is an odd function, the cosecant function is also an odd function. That is, $\csc(-x) = -\csc x$.

The graph of cosecant, which is shown in **Figure 7**, is similar to the graph of secant.

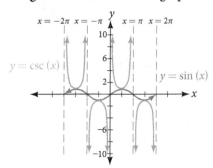

Figure 7 The graph of the cosecant function, $f(x) = \csc x = \dfrac{1}{\sin x}$

---

features of the graph of $y = A\csc(Bx)$

- The stretching factor is $|A|$.
- The period is $\dfrac{2\pi}{|B|}$.
- The domain is $x \neq \dfrac{\pi}{|B|}k$, where k is an integer.
- The range is $(-\infty, -|A|] \cup [|A|, \infty)$.
- The asymptotes occur at $x = \dfrac{\pi}{|B|}k$, where k is an integer.
- $y = A\csc(Bx)$ is an odd function because sine is an odd function.

Graphing Variations of $y = \sec x$ and $y = \csc x$

For shifted, compressed, and/or stretched versions of the secant and cosecant functions, we can follow similar methods to those we used for tangent and cotangent. That is, we locate the vertical asymptotes and also evaluate the functions for a few points (specifically the local extrema). If we want to graph only a single period, we can choose the interval for the period in more than one way. The procedure for secant is very similar, because the cofunction identity means that the secant graph is the same as the cosecant graph shifted half a period to the left. Vertical and phase shifts may be applied to the cosecant function in the same way as for the secant and other functions. The equations become the following.

$$y = A\sec(Bx - C) + D \qquad y = A\csc(Bx - C) + D$$

---

features of the graph of $y = A\sec(Bx - C) + D$

- The stretching factor is $|A|$.
- The period is $\dfrac{2\pi}{|B|}$.
- The domain is $x \neq \dfrac{C}{B} + \dfrac{\pi}{2|B|}k$, where k is an odd integer.
- The range is $(-\infty, -|A| + D] \cup [|A| + D, \infty)$.
- The vertical asymptotes occur at $x = \dfrac{C}{B} + \dfrac{\pi}{2|B|}k$, where k is an odd integer.
- There is no amplitude.
- $y = A\sec(Bx)$ is an even function because cosine is an even function.

---

features of the graph of $y = A\csc(Bx - C) + D$

- The stretching factor is $|A|$.
- The period is $\dfrac{2\pi}{|B|}$.
- The domain is $x \neq \dfrac{C}{B} + \dfrac{\pi}{|B|}k$, where k is an integer.
- The range is $(-\infty, -|A| + D] \cup [|A| + D, \infty)$.
- The vertical asymptotes occur at $x = \dfrac{C}{B} + \dfrac{\pi}{|B|}k$, where k is an integer.
- There is no amplitude.
- $y = A\csc(Bx)$ is an odd function because sine is an odd function.

How To...

Given a function of the form $y = A\sec(Bx)$, graph one period.

1. Express the function given in the form $y = A\sec(Bx)$.
2. Identify the stretching/compressing factor, $|A|$.
3. Identify B and determine the period, $P = \dfrac{2\pi}{|B|}$.
4. Sketch the graph of $y = A\cos(Bx)$.
5. Use the reciprocal relationship between $y = \cos x$ and $y = \sec x$ to draw the graph of $y = A\sec(Bx)$.
6. Sketch the asymptotes.
7. Plot any two reference points and draw the graph through these points.

Example 4   **Graphing a Variation of the Secant Function**

Graph one period of $f(x) = 2.5\sec(0.4x)$.

Solution

Step 1. The given function is already written in the general form, $y = A\sec(Bx)$.

Step 2. $A = 2.5$ so the stretching factor is 2.5.

Step 3. $B = 0.4$ so $P = \dfrac{2\pi}{0.4} = 5\pi$. The period is 5π units.

Step 4. Sketch the graph of the function $g(x) = 2.5\cos(0.4x)$.

Step 5. Use the reciprocal relationship of the cosine and secant functions to draw the cosecant function.

Steps 6–7. Sketch two asymptotes at $x = 1.25\pi$ and $x = 3.75\pi$. We can use two reference points, the local minimum at $(0, 2.5)$ and the local maximum at $(2.5\pi, -2.5)$. **Figure 8** shows the graph.

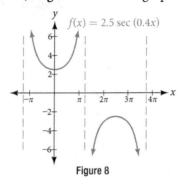

Figure 8

Try It #4

Graph one period of $f(x) = -2.5\sec(0.4x)$.

Q & A...

Do the vertical shift and stretch/compression affect the secant's range?

Yes. The range of $f(x) = A\sec(Bx - C) + D$ is $(-\infty, -|A| + D] \cup [|A| + D, \infty)$.

How To...

Given a function of the form $f(x) = A\sec(Bx - C) + D$, graph one period.

1. Express the function given in the form $y = A\sec(Bx - C) + D$.
2. Identify the stretching/compressing factor, $|A|$.
3. Identify B and determine the period, $\dfrac{2\pi}{|B|}$.
4. Identify C and determine the phase shift, $\dfrac{C}{B}$.
5. Draw the graph of $y = A\sec(Bx)$ but shift it to the right by $\dfrac{C}{B}$ and up by D.
6. Sketch the vertical asymptotes, which occur at $x = \dfrac{C}{B} + \dfrac{\pi}{2|B|}k$, where k is an odd integer.

Example 5   **Graphing a Variation of the Secant Function**

Graph one period of $y = 4\sec\left(\dfrac{\pi}{3}x - \dfrac{\pi}{2}\right) + 1$.

Solution

Step 1. Express the function given in the form $y = 4\sec\left(\dfrac{\pi}{3}x - \dfrac{\pi}{2}\right) + 1$.

Step 2. The stretching/compressing factor is $|A| = 4$.

Step 3. The period is

$$\frac{2\pi}{|B|} = \frac{2\pi}{\dfrac{\pi}{3}}$$

$$= \frac{2\pi}{1} \cdot \frac{3}{\pi}$$

$$= 6$$

Step 4. The phase shift is

$$\frac{C}{B} = \frac{\dfrac{\pi}{2}}{\dfrac{\pi}{3}}$$

$$= \frac{\pi}{2} \cdot \frac{3}{\pi}$$

$$= 1.5$$

Step 5. Draw the graph of $y = A\sec(Bx)$, but shift it to the right by $\dfrac{C}{B} = 1.5$ and up by $D = 6$.

Step 6. Sketch the vertical asymptotes, which occur at $x = 0$, $x = 3$, and $x = 6$. There is a local minimum at $(1.5, 5)$ and a local maximum at $(4.5, -3)$. **Figure 9** shows the graph.

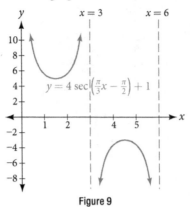

Figure 9

Try It #5

Graph one period of $f(x) = -6\sec(4x + 2) - 8$.

Q & A...

The domain of csc x was given to be all x such that $x \neq k\pi$ for any integer k. Would the domain of $y = A\csc(Bx - C) + D$ be $x \neq \dfrac{C + k\pi}{B}$?

Yes. The excluded points of the domain follow the vertical asymptotes. Their locations show the horizontal shift and compression or expansion implied by the transformation to the original function's input.

How To...

Given a function of the form $y = A\csc(Bx)$, graph one period.

1. Express the function given in the form $y = A\csc(Bx)$.
2. Identify the stretching/compressing factor, $|A|$.
3. Identify B and determine the period, $P = \dfrac{2\pi}{|B|}$.
4. Draw the graph of $y = A\sin(Bx)$.
5. Use the reciprocal relationship between $y = \sin x$ and $y = \csc x$ to draw the graph of $y = A\csc(Bx)$.
6. Sketch the asymptotes.
7. Plot any two reference points and draw the graph through these points.

Example 6   **Graphing a Variation of the Cosecant Function**

Graph one period of $f(x) = -3\csc(4x)$.

Solution

Step 1. The given function is already written in the general form, $y = A\csc(Bx)$.

Step 2. $|A| = |-3| = 3$, so the stretching factor is 3.

Step 3. $B = 4$, so $P = \dfrac{2\pi}{4} = \dfrac{\pi}{2}$. The period is $\dfrac{\pi}{2}$ units.

Step 4. Sketch the graph of the function $g(x) = -3\sin(4x)$.

Step 5. Use the reciprocal relationship of the sine and cosecant functions to draw the cosecant function.

Steps 6–7. Sketch three asymptotes at $x = 0$, $x = \dfrac{\pi}{4}$, and $x = \dfrac{\pi}{2}$. We can use two reference points, the local maximum at $\left(\dfrac{\pi}{8}, -3\right)$ and the local minimum at $\left(\dfrac{3\pi}{8}, 3\right)$. **Figure 10** shows the graph.

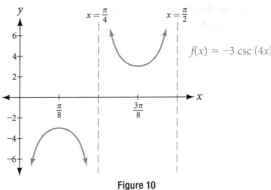

Figure 10

Try It #6

Graph one period of $f(x) = 0.5\csc(2x)$.

How To...

Given a function of the form $f(x) = A\csc(Bx - C) + D$, graph one period.

1. Express the function given in the form $y = A\csc(Bx - C) + D$.
2. Identify the stretching/compressing factor, $|A|$.
3. Identify B and determine the period, $\dfrac{2\pi}{|B|}$.
4. Identify C and determine the phase shift, $\dfrac{C}{B}$.
5. Draw the graph of $y = A\csc(Bx)$ but shift it to the right by $\dfrac{C}{B}$ and up by D.
6. Sketch the vertical asymptotes, which occur at $x = \dfrac{C}{B} + \dfrac{\pi}{|B|}k$, where k is an integer.

Example 7   **Graphing a Vertically Stretched, Horizontally Compressed, and Vertically Shifted Cosecant**

Sketch a graph of $y = 2\csc\left(\dfrac{\pi}{2}x\right) + 1$. What are the domain and range of this function?

Solution

Step 1. Express the function given in the form $y = 2\csc\left(\dfrac{\pi}{2}x\right) + 1$.

Step 2. Identify the stretching/compressing factor, $|A| = 2$.

Step 3. The period is $\dfrac{2\pi}{|B|} = \dfrac{2\pi}{\dfrac{\pi}{2}} = \dfrac{2\pi}{1} \cdot \dfrac{2}{\pi} = 4$.

Step 4. The phase shift is $\dfrac{0}{\dfrac{\pi}{2}} = 0$.

Step 5. Draw the graph of $y = A\csc(Bx)$ but shift it up $D = 1$.

Step 6. Sketch the vertical asymptotes, which occur at $x = 0, x = 2, x = 4$.

The graph for this function is shown in **Figure 11**.

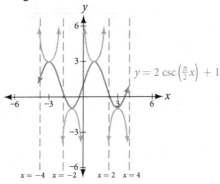

Figure 11 A transformed cosecant function

Analysis The vertical asymptotes shown on the graph mark off one period of the function, and the local extrema in this interval are shown by dots. Notice how the graph of the transformed cosecant relates to the graph of $f(x) = 2\sin\left(\frac{\pi}{2}x\right) + 1$, shown as the blue wave.

Try It #7

Given the graph of $f(x) = 2\cos\left(\frac{\pi}{2}x\right) + 1$ shown in **Figure 12**, sketch the graph of $g(x) = 2\sec\left(\frac{\pi}{2}x\right) + 1$ on the same axes.

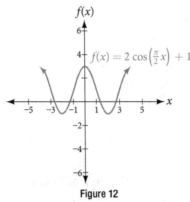

Figure 12

Analyzing the Graph of $y = \cot x$

The last trigonometric function we need to explore is cotangent. The cotangent is defined by the reciprocal identity $\cot x = \frac{1}{\tan x}$. Notice that the function is undefined when the tangent function is 0, leading to a vertical asymptote in the graph at 0, π, etc. Since the output of the tangent function is all real numbers, the output of the cotangent function is also all real numbers.

We can graph $y = \cot x$ by observing the graph of the tangent function because these two functions are reciprocals of one another. See **Figure 13**. Where the graph of the tangent function decreases, the graph of the cotangent function increases. Where the graph of the tangent function increases, the graph of the cotangent function decreases.

The cotangent graph has vertical asymptotes at each value of x where $\tan x = 0$; we show these in the graph below with dashed lines. Since the cotangent is the reciprocal of the tangent, $\cot x$ has vertical asymptotes at all values of x where $\tan x = 0$, and $\cot x = 0$ at all values of x where $\tan x$ has its vertical asymptotes.

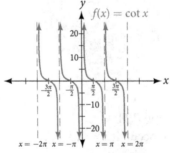

Figure 13 The cotangent function

---

features of the graph of $y = A\cot(Bx)$

- The stretching factor is $|A|$.
- The period is $P = \dfrac{\pi}{|B|}$.
- The domain is $x \neq \dfrac{\pi}{|B|}k$, where k is an integer.
- The range is $(-\infty, \infty)$.
- The asymptotes occur at $x = \dfrac{\pi}{|B|}k$, where k is an integer.
- $y = A\cot(Bx)$ is an odd function.

Graphing Variations of $y = \cot x$

We can transform the graph of the cotangent in much the same way as we did for the tangent. The equation becomes the following.

$$y = A\cot(Bx - C) + D$$

> **features of the graph of $y = A\cot(Bx - C) + D$**
>
> - The stretching factor is $|A|$.
> - The period is $\dfrac{\pi}{|B|}$.
> - The domain is $x \neq \dfrac{C}{B} + \dfrac{\pi}{|B|}k$, where k is an integer.
> - The range is $(-\infty, \infty)$.
> - The vertical asymptotes occur at $x = \dfrac{C}{B} + \dfrac{\pi}{|B|}k$, where k is an integer.
> - There is no amplitude.
> - $y = A\cot(Bx)$ is an odd function because it is the quotient of even and odd functions (cosine and sine, respectively)

How To...

Given a modified cotangent function of the form $f(x) = A\cot(Bx)$, graph one period.

1. Express the function in the form $f(x) = A\cot(Bx)$.
2. Identify the stretching factor, $|A|$.
3. Identify the period, $P = \dfrac{\pi}{|B|}$.
4. Draw the graph of $y = A\tan(Bx)$.
5. Plot any two reference points.
6. Use the reciprocal relationship between tangent and cotangent to draw the graph of $y = A\cot(Bx)$.
7. Sketch the asymptotes.

Example 8   **Graphing Variations of the Cotangent Function**

Determine the stretching factor, period, and phase shift of $y = 3\cot(4x)$, and then sketch a graph.

Solution

Step 1. Expressing the function in the form $f(x) = A\cot(Bx)$ gives $f(x) = 3\cot(4x)$.

Step 2. The stretching factor is $|A| = 3$.

Step 3. The period is $P = \dfrac{\pi}{4}$.

Step 4. Sketch the graph of $y = 3\tan(4x)$.

Step 5. Plot two reference points. Two such points are $\left(\dfrac{\pi}{16}, 3\right)$ and $\left(\dfrac{3\pi}{16}, -3\right)$.

Step 6. Use the reciprocal relationship to draw $y = 3\cot(4x)$.

Step 7. Sketch the asymptotes, $x = 0$, $x = \dfrac{\pi}{4}$.

The blue graph in **Figure 14** shows $y = 3\tan(4x)$ and the red graph shows $y = 3\cot(4x)$.

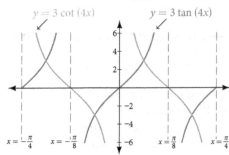

Figure 14

How To...

Given a modified cotangent function of the form $f(x) = A\cot(Bx - C) + D$, graph one period.

1. Express the function in the form $f(x) = A\cot(Bx - C) + D$.
2. Identify the stretching factor, $|A|$.
3. Identify the period, $P = \dfrac{\pi}{|B|}$.
4. Identify the phase shift, $\dfrac{C}{B}$.
5. Draw the graph of $y = A\tan(Bx)$ shifted to the right by $\dfrac{C}{B}$ and up by D.
6. Sketch the asymptotes $x = \dfrac{C}{B} + \dfrac{\pi}{|B|}k$, where k is an integer.
7. Plot any three reference points and draw the graph through these points.

Example 9   **Graphing a Modified Cotangent**

Sketch a graph of one period of the function $f(x) = 4\cot\left(\dfrac{\pi}{8}x - \dfrac{\pi}{2}\right) - 2$.

Solution

Step 1. The function is already written in the general form $f(x) = A\cot(Bx - C) + D$.

Step 2. $A = 4$, so the stretching factor is 4.

Step 3. $B = \dfrac{\pi}{8}$, so the period is $P = \dfrac{\pi}{|B|} = \dfrac{\pi}{\dfrac{\pi}{8}} = 8$.

Step 4. $C = \dfrac{\pi}{2}$, so the phase shift is $\dfrac{C}{B} = \dfrac{\dfrac{\pi}{2}}{\dfrac{\pi}{8}} = 4$.

Step 5. We draw $f(x) = 4\tan\left(\dfrac{\pi}{8}x - \dfrac{\pi}{2}\right) - 2$.

Step 6-7. Three points we can use to guide the graph are $(6, 2)$, $(8, -2)$, and $(10, -6)$. We use the reciprocal relationship of tangent and cotangent to draw $f(x) = 4\cot\left(\dfrac{\pi}{8}x - \dfrac{\pi}{2}\right) - 2$.

Step 8. The vertical asymptotes are $x = 4$ and $x = 12$.

The graph is shown in **Figure 15**.

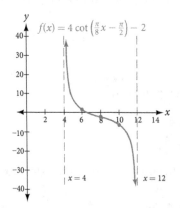

Figure 15 One period of a modified cotangent function

Using the Graphs of Trigonometric Functions to Solve Real-World Problems

Many real-world scenarios represent periodic functions and may be modeled by trigonometric functions. As an example, let's return to the scenario from the section opener. Have you ever observed the beam formed by the rotating light on a police car and wondered about the movement of the light beam itself across the wall? The periodic behavior of the distance the light shines as a function of time is obvious, but how do we determine the distance? We can use the tangent function.

Example 10   **Using Trigonometric Functions to Solve Real-World Scenarios**

Suppose the function $y = 5\tan\left(\frac{\pi}{4}t\right)$ marks the distance in the movement of a light beam from the top of a police car across a wall where t is the time in seconds and y is the distance in feet from a point on the wall directly across from the police car.

    a. Find and interpret the stretching factor and period.

    b. Graph on the interval $[0, 5]$.

    c. Evaluate $f(1)$ and discuss the function's value at that input.

Solution

    a. We know from the general form of $y = A\tan(Bt)$ that $|A|$ is the stretching factor and $\frac{\pi}{B}$ is the period.

$$y = 5\,\tan\left(\frac{\pi}{4}t\right)$$
$$\uparrow \qquad \uparrow$$
$$A \qquad B$$

Figure 16

    We see that the stretching factor is 5. This means that the beam of light will have moved 5 ft after half the period.

    The period is $\dfrac{\pi}{\frac{\pi}{4}} = \dfrac{\pi}{1} \cdot \dfrac{4}{\pi} = 4$. This means that every 4 seconds, the beam of light sweeps the wall. The distance from the spot across from the police car grows larger as the police car approaches.

    b. To graph the function, we draw an asymptote at $t = 2$ and use the stretching factor and period. See **Figure 17**

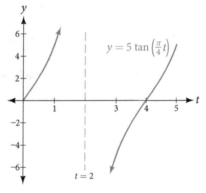

Figure 17

    c. Period: $f(1) = 5\tan\left(\frac{\pi}{4}(1)\right) = 5(1) = 5$; after 1 second, the beam of light has moved 5 ft from the spot across from the police car.

Access these online resources for additional instruction and practice with graphs of other trigonometric functions.

- Graphing the Tangent Function (http://openstaxcollege.org/l/graphtangent)
- Graphing Cosecant and Secant Functions (http://openstaxcollege.org/l/graphcscsec)
- Graphing the Cotangent Function (http://openstaxcollege.org/l/graphcot)

6.2 SECTION EXERCISES

VERBAL

1. Explain how the graph of the sine function can be used to graph $y = \csc x$.

2. How can the graph of $y = \cos x$ be used to construct the graph of $y = \sec x$?

3. Explain why the period of $\tan x$ is equal to π.

4. Why are there no intercepts on the graph of $y = \csc x$?

5. How does the period of $y = \csc x$ compare with the period of $y = \sin x$?

ALGEBRAIC

For the following exercises, match each trigonometric function with one of the graphs in **Figure 18**.

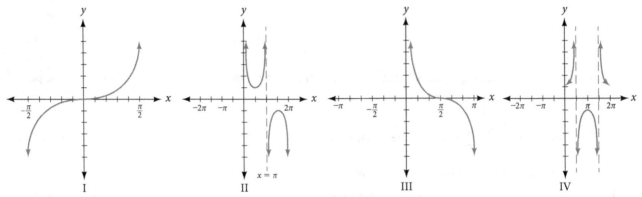

Figure 18

6. $f(x) = \tan x$

7. $f(x) = \sec x$

8. $f(x) = \csc x$

9. $f(x) = \cot x$

For the following exercises, find the period and horizontal shift of each of the functions.

10. $f(x) = 2\tan(4x - 32)$

11. $h(x) = 2\sec\left(\frac{\pi}{4}(x + 1)\right)$

12. $m(x) = 6\csc\left(\frac{\pi}{3}x + \pi\right)$

13. If $\tan x = -1.5$, find $\tan(-x)$.

14. If $\sec x = 2$, find $\sec(-x)$.

15. If $\csc x = -5$, find $\csc(-x)$.

16. If $x\sin x = 2$, find $(-x)\sin(-x)$.

For the following exercises, rewrite each expression such that the argument x is positive.

17. $\cot(-x)\cos(-x) + \sin(-x)$

18. $\cos(-x) + \tan(-x)\sin(-x)$

GRAPHICAL

For the following exercises, sketch two periods of the graph for each of the following functions. Identify the stretching factor, period, and asymptotes.

19. $f(x) = 2\tan(4x - 32)$

20. $h(x) = 2\sec\left(\frac{\pi}{4}(x + 1)\right)$

21. $m(x) = 6\csc\left(\frac{\pi}{3}x + \pi\right)$

22. $j(x) = \tan\left(\frac{\pi}{2}x\right)$

23. $p(x) = \tan\left(x - \frac{\pi}{2}\right)$

24. $f(x) = 4\tan(x)$

25. $f(x) = \tan\left(x + \frac{\pi}{4}\right)$

26. $f(x) = \pi\tan(\pi x - \pi) - \pi$

27. $f(x) = 2\csc(x)$

28. $f(x) = -\frac{1}{4}\csc(x)$

29. $f(x) = 4\sec(3x)$

30. $f(x) = -3\cot(2x)$

31. $f(x) = 7\sec(5x)$

32. $f(x) = \frac{9}{10}\csc(\pi x)$

33. $f(x) = 2\csc\left(x + \frac{\pi}{4}\right) - 1$

34. $f(x) = -\sec\left(x - \frac{\pi}{3}\right) - 2$

35. $f(x) = \frac{7}{5}\csc\left(x - \frac{\pi}{4}\right)$

36. $f(x) = 5\left(\cot\left(x + \frac{\pi}{2}\right) - 3\right)$

For the following exercises, find and graph two periods of the periodic function with the given stretching factor, $|A|$, period, and phase shift.

37. A tangent curve, $A = 1$, period of $\frac{\pi}{3}$; and phase shift $(h, k) = \left(\frac{\pi}{4}, 2\right)$

38. A tangent curve, $A = -2$, period of $\frac{\pi}{4}$, and phase shift $(h, k) = \left(-\frac{\pi}{4}, -2\right)$

For the following exercises, find an equation for the graph of each function.

39.

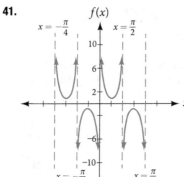

40.

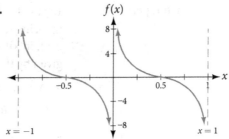

41.

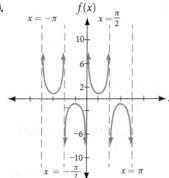

42.

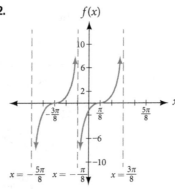

43.

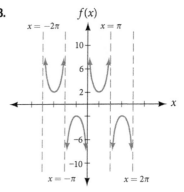

44.

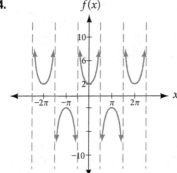

45.

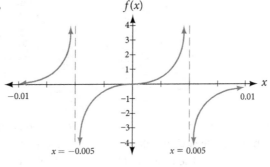

TECHNOLOGY

For the following exercises, use a graphing calculator to graph two periods of the given function. Note: most graphing calculators do not have a cosecant button; therefore, you will need to input csc x as $\frac{1}{\sin x}$.

46. $f(x) = |\csc(x)|$

47. $f(x) = |\cot(x)|$

48. $f(x) = 2^{\csc(x)}$

49. $f(x) = \dfrac{\csc(x)}{\sec(x)}$

50. Graph $f(x) = 1 + \sec^2(x) - \tan^2(x)$. What is the function shown in the graph?

51. $f(x) = \sec(0.001x)$

52. $f(x) = \cot(100\pi x)$

53. $f(x) = \sin^2 x + \cos^2 x$

REAL-WORLD APPLICATIONS

54. The function $f(x) = 20\tan\left(\dfrac{\pi}{10}x\right)$ marks the distance in the movement of a light beam from a police car across a wall for time x, in seconds, and distance $f(x)$, in feet.

     a. Graph on the interval $[0, 5]$.

     b. Find and interpret the stretching factor, period, and asymptote.

     c. Evaluate $f(1)$ and $f(2.5)$ and discuss the function's values at those inputs.

55. Standing on the shore of a lake, a fisherman sights a boat far in the distance to his left. Let x, measured in radians, be the angle formed by the line of sight to the ship and a line due north from his position. Assume due north is 0 and x is measured negative to the left and positive to the right. (See **Figure 19**.) The boat travels from due west to due east and, ignoring the curvature of the Earth, the distance $d(x)$, in kilometers, from the fisherman to the boat is given by the function $d(x) = 1.5\sec(x)$.

     a. What is a reasonable domain for $d(x)$?

     b. Graph $d(x)$ on this domain.

     c. Find and discuss the meaning of any vertical asymptotes on the graph of $d(x)$.

     d. Calculate and interpret $d\left(-\dfrac{\pi}{3}\right)$. Round to the second decimal place.

     e. Calculate and interpret $d\left(\dfrac{\pi}{6}\right)$. Round to the second decimal place.

     f. What is the minimum distance between the fisherman and the boat? When does this occur?

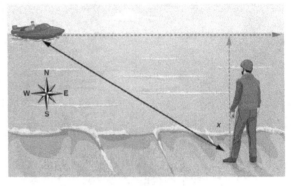

Figure 19

56. A laser rangefinder is locked on a comet approaching Earth. The distance $g(x)$, in kilometers, of the comet after x days, for x in the interval 0 to 30 days, is given by $g(x) = 250{,}000\csc\left(\dfrac{\pi}{30}x\right)$.

     a. Graph $g(x)$ on the interval $[0, 35]$.

     b. Evaluate $g(5)$ and interpret the information.

     c. What is the minimum distance between the comet and Earth? When does this occur? To which constant in the equation does this correspond?

     d. Find and discuss the meaning of any vertical asymptotes.

57. A video camera is focused on a rocket on a launching pad 2 miles from the camera. The angle of elevation from the ground to the rocket after x seconds is $\dfrac{\pi}{120}x$.

     a. Write a function expressing the altitude $h(x)$, in miles, of the rocket above the ground after x seconds. Ignore the curvature of the Earth.

     b. Graph $h(x)$ on the interval $(0, 60)$.

     c. Evaluate and interpret the values $h(0)$ and $h(30)$.

     d. What happens to the values of $h(x)$ as x approaches 60 seconds? Interpret the meaning of this in terms of the problem.

LEARNING OBJECTIVES

In this section, you will:

- Understand and use the inverse sine, cosine, and tangent functions.
- Find the exact value of expressions involving the inverse sine, cosine, and tangent functions.
- Use a calculator to evaluate inverse trigonometric functions.
- Find exact values of composite functions with inverse trigonometric functions.

6.3 INVERSE TRIGONOMETRIC FUNCTIONS

For any right triangle, given one other angle and the length of one side, we can figure out what the other angles and sides are. But what if we are given only two sides of a right triangle? We need a procedure that leads us from a ratio of sides to an angle. This is where the notion of an inverse to a trigonometric function comes into play. In this section, we will explore the inverse trigonometric functions.

Understanding and Using the Inverse Sine, Cosine, and Tangent Functions

In order to use inverse trigonometric functions, we need to understand that an inverse trigonometric function "undoes" what the original trigonometric function "does," as is the case with any other function and its inverse. In other words, the domain of the inverse function is the range of the original function, and vice versa, as summarized in **Figure 1**.

Trig Functions	Inverse Trig Functions
Domain: Measure of an angle	Domain: Ratio
Range: Ratio	Range: Measure of an angle

Figure 1

For example, if $f(x) = \sin x$, then we would write $f^{-1}(x) = \sin^{-1}x$. Be aware that $\sin^{-1}x$ does not mean $\dfrac{1}{\sin x}$. The following examples illustrate the inverse trigonometric functions:

- Since $\sin\left(\dfrac{\pi}{6}\right) = \dfrac{1}{2}$, then $\dfrac{\pi}{6} = \sin^{-1}\left(\dfrac{1}{2}\right)$.
- Since $\cos(\pi) = -1$, then $\pi = \cos^{-1}(-1)$.
- Since $\tan\left(\dfrac{\pi}{4}\right) = 1$, then $\dfrac{\pi}{4} = \tan^{-1}(1)$.

In previous sections, we evaluated the trigonometric functions at various angles, but at times we need to know what angle would yield a specific sine, cosine, or tangent value. For this, we need inverse functions. Recall that, for a one-to-one function, if $f(a) = b$, then an inverse function would satisfy $f^{-1}(b) = a$.

Bear in mind that the sine, cosine, and tangent functions are not one-to-one functions. The graph of each function would fail the horizontal line test. In fact, no periodic function can be one-to-one because each output in its range corresponds to at least one input in every period, and there are an infinite number of periods. As with other functions that are not one-to-one, we will need to restrict the domain of each function to yield a new function that is one-to-one. We choose a domain for each function that includes the number 0. **Figure 2** shows the graph of the sine function limited to $\left[-\dfrac{\pi}{2}, \dfrac{\pi}{2}\right]$ and the graph of the cosine function limited to $[0, \pi]$.

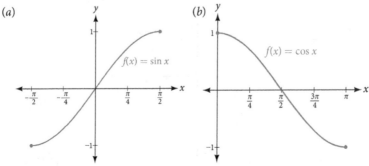

Figure 2 (a) Sine function on a restricted domain of $\left[-\dfrac{\pi}{2}, \dfrac{\pi}{2}\right]$; (b) Cosine function on a restricted domain of $[0, \pi]$

Figure 3 shows the graph of the tangent function limited to $\left(-\dfrac{\pi}{2}, \dfrac{\pi}{2} \right)$.

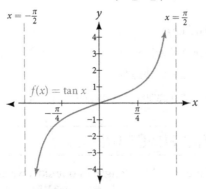

Figure 3 Tangent function on a restricted domain of $\left(-\dfrac{\pi}{2}, \dfrac{\pi}{2} \right)$

These conventional choices for the restricted domain are somewhat arbitrary, but they have important, helpful characteristics. Each domain includes the origin and some positive values, and most importantly, each results in a one-to-one function that is invertible. The conventional choice for the restricted domain of the tangent function also has the useful property that it extends from one vertical asymptote to the next instead of being divided into two parts by an asymptote.

On these restricted domains, we can define the inverse trigonometric functions.

- The **inverse sine function** $y = \sin^{-1} x$ means $x = \sin y$. The inverse sine function is sometimes called the **arcsine function**, and notated arcsin$x$.

$$y = \sin^{-1} x \text{ has domain } [-1, 1] \text{ and range } \left[-\frac{\pi}{2}, \frac{\pi}{2} \right]$$

- The **inverse cosine function** $y = \cos^{-1} x$ means $x = \cos y$. The inverse cosine function is sometimes called the **arccosine** function, and notated arccos x.

$$y = \cos^{-1} x \text{ has domain } [-1, 1] \text{ and range } [0, \pi]$$

- The **inverse tangent function** $y = \tan^{-1} x$ means $x = \tan y$. The inverse tangent function is sometimes called the **arctangent** function, and notated arctan x.

$$y = \tan^{-1} x \text{ has domain } (-\infty, \infty) \text{ and range } \left(-\frac{\pi}{2}, \frac{\pi}{2} \right)$$

The graphs of the inverse functions are shown in **Figure 4**, **Figure 5**, and **Figure 6**. Notice that the output of each of these inverse functions is a number, an angle in radian measure. We see that $\sin^{-1} x$ has domain $[-1, 1]$ and range $\left[-\frac{\pi}{2}, \frac{\pi}{2} \right]$, $\cos^{-1} x$ has domain $[-1, 1]$ and range $[0, \pi]$, and $\tan^{-1} x$ has domain of all real numbers and range $\left(-\frac{\pi}{2}, \frac{\pi}{2} \right)$. To find the domain and range of inverse trigonometric functions, switch the domain and range of the original functions. Each graph of the inverse trigonometric function is a reflection of the graph of the original function about the line $y = x$.

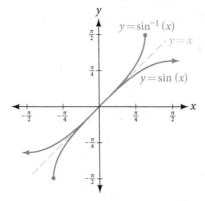

Figure 4 The sine function and inverse sine (or arcsine) function

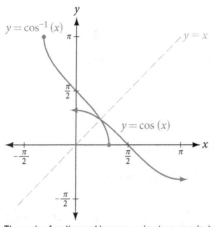

Figure 5 The cosine function and inverse cosine (or arccosine) function   **Figure 6** The tangent function and inverse tangent (or arctangent) function

---

relations for inverse sine, cosine, and tangent functions

For angles in the interval $\left[-\dfrac{\pi}{2}, \dfrac{\pi}{2}\right]$, if $\sin y = x$, then $\sin^{-1} x = y$.

For angles in the interval $[0, \pi]$, if $\cos y = x$, then $\cos^{-1} x = y$.

For angles in the interval $\left(-\dfrac{\pi}{2}, \dfrac{\pi}{2}\right)$, if $\tan y = x$, then $\tan^{-1} x = y$.

Example 1   **Writing a Relation for an Inverse Function**

Given $\sin\left(\dfrac{5\pi}{12}\right) \approx 0.96593$, write a relation involving the inverse sine.

Solution   Use the relation for the inverse sine. If $\sin y = x$, then $\sin^{-1} x = y$.

In this problem, $x = 0.96593$, and $y = \dfrac{5\pi}{12}$.

$$\sin^{-1}(0.96593) \approx \dfrac{5\pi}{12}$$

Try It #1

Given $\cos(0.5) \approx 0.8776$, write a relation involving the inverse cosine.

Finding the Exact Value of Expressions Involving the Inverse Sine, Cosine, and Tangent Functions

Now that we can identify inverse functions, we will learn to evaluate them. For most values in their domains, we must evaluate the inverse trigonometric functions by using a calculator, interpolating from a table, or using some other numerical technique. Just as we did with the original trigonometric functions, we can give exact values for the inverse functions when we are using the special angles, specifically $\dfrac{\pi}{6}$ (30°), $\dfrac{\pi}{4}$ (45°), and $\dfrac{\pi}{3}$ (60°), and their reflections into other quadrants.

How To...

Given a "special" input value, evaluate an inverse trigonometric function.

1. Find angle x for which the original trigonometric function has an output equal to the given input for the inverse trigonometric function.

2. If x is not in the defined range of the inverse, find another angle y that is in the defined range and has the same sine, cosine, or tangent as x, depending on which corresponds to the given inverse function.

Example 2   **Evaluating Inverse Trigonometric Functions for Special Input Values**

Evaluate each of the following.

    a. $\sin^{-1}\left(\dfrac{1}{2}\right)$ **b.** $\sin^{-1}\left(-\dfrac{\sqrt{2}}{2}\right)$ **c.** $\cos^{-1}\left(-\dfrac{\sqrt{3}}{2}\right)$ **d.** $\tan^{-1}(1)$

Solution

a. Evaluating $\sin^{-1}\left(\frac{1}{2}\right)$ is the same as determining the angle that would have a sine value of $\frac{1}{2}$. In other words, what angle x would satisfy $\sin(x) = \frac{1}{2}$? There are multiple values that would satisfy this relationship, such as $\frac{\pi}{6}$ and $\frac{5\pi}{6}$, but we know we need the angle in the interval $\left[-\frac{\pi}{2}, \frac{\pi}{2}\right]$, so the answer will be $\sin^{-1}\left(\frac{1}{2}\right) = \frac{\pi}{6}$. Remember that the inverse is a function, so for each input, we will get exactly one output.

b. To evaluate $\sin^{-1}\left(-\frac{\sqrt{2}}{2}\right)$, we know that $\frac{5\pi}{4}$ and $\frac{7\pi}{4}$ both have a sine value of $-\frac{\sqrt{2}}{2}$, but neither is in the interval $\left[-\frac{\pi}{2}, \frac{\pi}{2}\right]$. For that, we need the negative angle coterminal with $\frac{7\pi}{4}$: $\sin^{-1}\left(-\frac{\sqrt{2}}{2}\right) = -\frac{\pi}{4}$.

c. To evaluate $\cos^{-1}\left(-\frac{\sqrt{3}}{2}\right)$, we are looking for an angle in the interval $[0, \pi]$ with a cosine value of $-\frac{\sqrt{3}}{2}$. The angle that satisfies this is $\cos^{-1}\left(-\frac{\sqrt{3}}{2}\right) = \frac{5\pi}{6}$.

d. Evaluating $\tan^{-1}(1)$, we are looking for an angle in the interval $\left(-\frac{\pi}{2}, \frac{\pi}{2}\right)$ with a tangent value of 1. The correct angle is $\tan^{-1}(1) = \frac{\pi}{4}$.

Try It #2

Evaluate each of the following.

a. $\sin^{-1}(-1)$ b. $\tan^{-1}(-1)$ c. $\cos^{-1}(-1)$ d. $\cos^{-1}\left(\frac{1}{2}\right)$

Using a Calculator to Evaluate Inverse Trigonometric Functions

To evaluate inverse trigonometric functions that do not involve the special angles discussed previously, we will need to use a calculator or other type of technology. Most scientific calculators and calculator-emulating applications have specific keys or buttons for the inverse sine, cosine, and tangent functions. These may be labeled, for example, **SIN-1**, **ARCSIN**, or **ASIN**.

In the previous chapter, we worked with trigonometry on a right triangle to solve for the sides of a triangle given one side and an additional angle. Using the inverse trigonometric functions, we can solve for the angles of a right triangle given two sides, and we can use a calculator to find the values to several decimal places.

In these examples and exercises, the answers will be interpreted as angles and we will use θ as the independent variable. The value displayed on the calculator may be in degrees or radians, so be sure to set the mode appropriate to the application.

Example 3   **Evaluating the Inverse Sine on a Calculator**

Evaluate $\sin^{-1}(0.97)$ using a calculator.

Solution   Because the output of the inverse function is an angle, the calculator will give us a degree value if in degree mode and a radian value if in radian mode. Calculators also use the same domain restrictions on the angles as we are using.

In radian mode, $\sin^{-1}(0.97) \approx 1.3252$. In degree mode, $\sin^{-1}(0.97) \approx 75.93°$. Note that in calculus and beyond we will use radians in almost all cases.

Try It #3

Evaluate $\cos^{-1}(-0.4)$ using a calculator.

Given two sides of a right triangle like the one shown in **Figure 7**, find an angle.

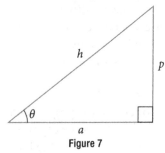

Figure 7

1. If one given side is the hypotenuse of length h and the side of length a adjacent to the desired angle is given, use the equation $\theta = \cos^{-1}\left(\dfrac{a}{h}\right)$.

2. If one given side is the hypotenuse of length h and the side of length p opposite to the desired angle is given, use the equation $\theta = \sin^{-1}\left(\dfrac{p}{h}\right)$

3. If the two legs (the sides adjacent to the right angle) are given, then use the equation $\theta = \tan^{-1}\left(\dfrac{p}{a}\right)$.

Example 4   **Applying the Inverse Cosine to a Right Triangle**

Solve the triangle in **Figure 8** for the angle θ.

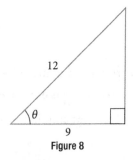

Figure 8

Solution   Because we know the hypotenuse and the side adjacent to the angle, it makes sense for us to use the cosine function.

$$\cos \theta = \frac{9}{12}$$

$$\theta = \cos^{-1}\left(\frac{9}{12}\right)$$ Apply definition of the inverse.

$$\theta \approx 0.7227 \text{ or about } 41.4096°$$ Evaluate.

Try It #4

Solve the triangle in **Figure 9** for the angle θ.

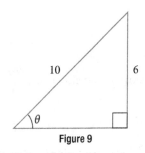

Figure 9

Finding Exact Values of Composite Functions with Inverse Trigonometric Functions

There are times when we need to compose a trigonometric function with an inverse trigonometric function. In these cases, we can usually find exact values for the resulting expressions without resorting to a calculator. Even when the input to the composite function is a variable or an expression, we can often find an expression for the output. To help sort out different cases, let $f(x)$ and $g(x)$ be two different trigonometric functions belonging to the set $\{\sin(x), \cos(x), \tan(x)\}$ and let $f^{-1}(y)$ and $g^{-1}(y)$ be their inverses.

Evaluating Compositions of the Form $f(f^{-1}(y))$ and $f^{-1}(f(x))$

For any trigonometric function, $f(f^{-1}(y)) = y$ for all y in the proper domain for the given function. This follows from the definition of the inverse and from the fact that the range of f was defined to be identical to the domain of f^{-1}. However, we have to be a little more careful with expressions of the form $f^{-1}(f(x))$.

---

compositions of a trigonometric function and its inverse

$$\sin(\sin^{-1} x) = x \text{ for } -1 \leq x \leq 1$$

$$\cos(\cos^{-1} x) = x \text{ for } -1 \leq x \leq 1$$

$$\tan(\tan^{-1} x) = x \text{ for } -\infty < x < \infty$$

$$\sin^{-1}(\sin x) = x \text{ only for } -\frac{\pi}{2} \leq x \leq \frac{\pi}{2}$$

$$\cos^{-1}(\cos x) = x \text{ only for } 0 \leq x \leq \pi$$

$$\tan^{-1}(\tan x) = x \text{ only for } -\frac{\pi}{2} < x < \frac{\pi}{2}$$

Q & A...

Is it correct that $\sin^{-1}(\sin x) = x$?

No. This equation is correct if x belongs to the restricted domain $\left[-\frac{\pi}{2}, \frac{\pi}{2} \right]$, but sine is defined for all real input values, and for x outside the restricted interval, the equation is not correct because its inverse always returns a value in $\left[-\frac{\pi}{2}, \frac{\pi}{2} \right]$. The situation is similar for cosine and tangent and their inverses. For example, $\sin^{-1}\left(\sin\left(\frac{3\pi}{4} \right) \right) = \frac{\pi}{4}$.

How To...

Given an expression of the form $f^{-1}(f(\theta))$ where $f(\theta) = \sin \theta$, $\cos \theta$, or $\tan \theta$, evaluate.

1. If θ is in the restricted domain of f, then $f^{-1}(f(\theta)) = \theta$.
2. If not, then find an angle ϕ within the restricted domain of f such that $f(\phi) = f(\theta)$. Then $f^{-1}(f(\theta)) = \phi$.

Example 5   **Using Inverse Trigonometric Functions**

Evaluate the following:

   a. $\sin^{-1}\left(\sin\left(\frac{\pi}{3} \right) \right)$ **b.** $\sin^{-1}\left(\sin\left(\frac{2\pi}{3} \right) \right)$ **c.** $\cos^{-1}\left(\cos\left(\frac{2\pi}{3} \right) \right)$ **d.** $\cos^{-1}\left(\cos\left(-\frac{\pi}{3} \right) \right)$

Solution

   a. $\frac{\pi}{3}$ is in $\left[-\frac{\pi}{2}, \frac{\pi}{2} \right]$, so $\sin^{-1}\left(\sin\left(\frac{\pi}{3} \right) \right) = \frac{\pi}{3}$.

   b. $\frac{2\pi}{3}$ is not in $\left[-\frac{\pi}{2}, \frac{\pi}{2} \right]$, but $\sin\left(\frac{2\pi}{3} \right) = \sin\left(\frac{\pi}{3} \right)$, so $\sin^{-1}\left(\sin\left(\frac{2\pi}{3} \right) \right) = \frac{\pi}{3}$.

   c. $\frac{2\pi}{3}$ is in $[0, \pi]$, so $\cos^{-1}\left(\cos\left(\frac{2\pi}{3} \right) \right) = \frac{2\pi}{3}$.

   d. $-\frac{\pi}{3}$ is not in $[0, \pi]$, but $\cos\left(-\frac{\pi}{3} \right) = \cos\left(\frac{\pi}{3} \right)$ because cosine is an even function. $\frac{\pi}{3}$ is in $[0, \pi]$, so $\cos^{-1}\left(\cos\left(-\frac{\pi}{3} \right) \right) = \frac{\pi}{3}$.

Try It #5

Evaluate $\tan^{-1}\left(\tan\left(\frac{\pi}{8}\right)\right)$ and $\tan^{-1}\left(\tan\left(\frac{11\pi}{9}\right)\right)$.

Evaluating Compositions of the Form $f^{-1}(g(x))$

Now that we can compose a trigonometric function with its inverse, we can explore how to evaluate a composition of a trigonometric function and the inverse of another trigonometric function. We will begin with compositions of the form $f^{-1}(g(x))$. For special values of x, we can exactly evaluate the inner function and then the outer, inverse function. However, we can find a more general approach by considering the relation between the two acute angles of a right triangle where one is θ, making the other $\frac{\pi}{2} - \theta$. Consider the sine and cosine of each angle of the right triangle in **Figure 10**.

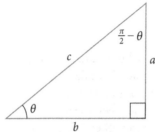

Figure 10 Right triangle illustrating the cofunction relationships

Because $\cos\theta = \frac{b}{c} = \sin\left(\frac{\pi}{2} - \theta\right)$, we have $\sin^{-1}(\cos\theta) = \frac{\pi}{2} - \theta$ if $0 \leq \theta \leq \pi$. If θ is not in this domain, then we need to find another angle that has the same cosine as θ and does belong to the restricted domain; we then subtract this angle from $\frac{\pi}{2}$. Similarly, $\sin\theta = \frac{a}{c} = \cos\left(\frac{\pi}{2} - \theta\right)$, so $\cos^{-1}(\sin\theta) = \frac{\pi}{2} - \theta$ if $-\frac{\pi}{2} \leq \theta \leq \frac{\pi}{2}$. These are just the function-cofunction relationships presented in another way.

How To...

Given functions of the form $\sin^{-1}(\cos x)$ and $\cos^{-1}(\sin x)$, evaluate them.

1. If x is in $[0, \pi]$, then $\sin^{-1}(\cos x) = \frac{\pi}{2} - x$.
2. If x is not in $[0, \pi]$, then find another angle y in $[0, \pi]$ such that $\cos y = \cos x$.
$$\sin^{-1}(\cos x) = \frac{\pi}{2} - y$$
3. If x is in $\left[-\frac{\pi}{2}, \frac{\pi}{2}\right]$, then $\cos^{-1}(\sin x) = \frac{\pi}{2} - x$.
4. If x is not in $\left[-\frac{\pi}{2}, \frac{\pi}{2}\right]$, then find another angle y in $\left[-\frac{\pi}{2}, \frac{\pi}{2}\right]$ such that $\sin y = \sin x$.
$$\cos^{-1}(\sin x) = \frac{\pi}{2} - y$$

Example 6   **Evaluating the Composition of an Inverse Sine with a Cosine**

Evaluate $\sin^{-1}\left(\cos\left(\frac{13\pi}{6}\right)\right)$

 a. by direct evaluation.   b. by the method described previously.

Solution

 a. Here, we can directly evaluate the inside of the composition.

$$\cos\left(\frac{13\pi}{6}\right) = \cos\left(\frac{\pi}{6} + 2\pi\right)$$

$$= \cos\left(\frac{\pi}{6}\right)$$

$$= \frac{\sqrt{3}}{2}$$

Now, we can evaluate the inverse function as we did earlier.

$$\sin^{-1}\left(\frac{\sqrt{3}}{2}\right) = \frac{\pi}{3}$$

b. We have $x = \frac{13\pi}{6}$, $y = \frac{\pi}{6}$, and

$$\sin^{-1}\left(\cos\left(\frac{13\pi}{6}\right)\right) = \frac{\pi}{2} - \frac{\pi}{6}$$

$$= \frac{\pi}{3}$$

Try It #6

Evaluate $\cos^{-1}\left(\sin\left(-\frac{11\pi}{4}\right)\right)$.

Evaluating Compositions of the Form $f(g^{-1}(x))$

To evaluate compositions of the form $f(g^{-1}(x))$, where f and g are any two of the functions sine, cosine, or tangent and x is any input in the domain of g^{-1}, we have exact formulas, such as $\sin(\cos^{-1} x) = \sqrt{1 - x^2}$. When we need to use them, we can derive these formulas by using the trigonometric relations between the angles and sides of a right triangle, together with the use of Pythagorean's relation between the lengths of the sides. We can use the Pythagorean identity, $\sin^2 x + \cos^2 x = 1$, to solve for one when given the other. We can also use the inverse trigonometric functions to find compositions involving algebraic expressions.

Example 7   **Evaluating the Composition of a Sine with an Inverse Cosine**

Find an exact value for $\sin\left(\cos^{-1}\left(\frac{4}{5}\right)\right)$.

Solution   Beginning with the inside, we can say there is some angle such that $\theta = \cos^{-1}\left(\frac{4}{5}\right)$, which means $\cos\theta = \frac{4}{5}$, and we are looking for $\sin\theta$. We can use the Pythagorean identity to do this.

$$\sin^2\theta + \cos^2\theta = 1 \qquad \text{Use our known value for cosine.}$$

$$\sin^2\theta + \left(\frac{4}{5}\right)^2 = 1 \qquad \text{Solve for sine.}$$

$$\sin^2\theta = 1 - \frac{16}{25}$$

$$\sin\theta = \pm\sqrt{\frac{9}{25}} = \pm\frac{3}{5}$$

Since $\theta = \cos^{-1}\left(\frac{4}{5}\right)$ is in quadrant I, $\sin\theta$ must be positive, so the solution is $\frac{3}{5}$. See **Figure 11**.

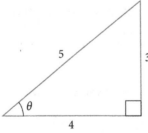

Figure 11   Right triangle illustrating that if $\cos\theta = \frac{4}{5}$, then $\sin\theta = \frac{3}{5}$

We know that the inverse cosine always gives an angle on the interval $[0, \pi]$, so we know that the sine of that angle must be positive; therefore $\sin\left(\cos^{-1}\left(\frac{4}{5}\right)\right) = \sin\theta = \frac{3}{5}$.

Try It #7

Evaluate $\cos\left(\tan^{-1}\left(\frac{5}{12}\right)\right)$.

Example 8   **Evaluating the Composition of a Sine with an Inverse Tangent**

Find an exact value for $\sin\left(\tan^{-1}\left(\frac{7}{4}\right)\right)$.

Solution   While we could use a similar technique as in **Example 6**, we will demonstrate a different technique here.

From the inside, we know there is an angle such that $\tan\theta = \frac{7}{4}$. We can envision this as the opposite and adjacent sides on a right triangle, as shown in **Figure 12**.

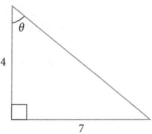

Figure 12 A right triangle with two sides known

Using the Pythagorean Theorem, we can find the hypotenuse of this triangle.

$$4^2 + 7^2 = \text{hypotenuse}^2$$
$$\text{hypotenuse} = \sqrt{65}$$

Now, we can evaluate the sine of the angle as the opposite side divided by the hypotenuse.

$$\sin\theta = \frac{7}{\sqrt{65}}$$

This gives us our desired composition.

$$\sin\left(\tan^{-1}\left(\frac{7}{4}\right)\right) = \sin\theta$$
$$= \frac{7}{\sqrt{65}}$$
$$= \frac{7\sqrt{65}}{65}$$

Try It #8

Evaluate $\cos\left(\sin^{-1}\left(\frac{7}{9}\right)\right)$.

Example 9   **Finding the Cosine of the Inverse Sine of an Algebraic Expression**

Find a simplified expression for $\cos\left(\sin^{-1}\left(\frac{x}{3}\right)\right)$ for $-3 \le x \le 3$.

Solution   We know there is an angle θ such that $\sin\theta = \frac{x}{3}$.

$$\sin^2\theta + \cos^2\theta = 1 \qquad \text{Use the Pythagorean Theorem.}$$
$$\left(\frac{x}{3}\right)^2 + \cos^2\theta = 1 \qquad \text{Solve for cosine.}$$
$$\cos^2\theta = 1 - \frac{x^2}{9}$$
$$\cos\theta = \pm\sqrt{\frac{9-x^2}{9}} = \pm\frac{\sqrt{9-x^2}}{3}$$

Because we know that the inverse sine must give an angle on the interval $\left[-\frac{\pi}{2}, \frac{\pi}{2}\right]$, we can deduce that the cosine of that angle must be positive.

$$\cos\left(\sin^{-1}\left(\frac{x}{3}\right)\right) = \frac{\sqrt{9-x^2}}{3}$$

Try It #9

Find a simplified expression for $\sin(\tan^{-1}(4x))$ for $-\frac{1}{4} \le x \le \frac{1}{4}$.

Access this online resource for additional instruction and practice with inverse trigonometric functions.

• Evaluate Expressions Involving Inverse Trigonometric Functions (http://openstaxcollege.org/l/evalinverstrig)

6.3   SECTION EXERCISES

VERBAL

1. Why do the functions $f(x) = \sin^{-1} x$ and $g(x) = \cos^{-1} x$ have different ranges?

2. Since the functions $y = \cos x$ and $y = \cos^{-1} x$ are inverse functions, why is $\cos^{-1}\left(\cos\left(-\dfrac{\pi}{6}\right)\right)$ not equal to $-\dfrac{\pi}{6}$?

3. Explain the meaning of $\dfrac{\pi}{6} = \arcsin(0.5)$.

4. Most calculators do not have a key to evaluate $\sec^{-1}(2)$. Explain how this can be done using the cosine function or the inverse cosine function.

5. Why must the domain of the sine function, $\sin x$, be restricted to $\left[-\dfrac{\pi}{2}, \dfrac{\pi}{2}\right]$ for the inverse sine function to exist?

6. Discuss why this statement is incorrect: $\arccos(\cos x) = x$ for all x.

7. Determine whether the following statement is true or false and explain your answer: $\arccos(-x) = \pi - \arccos x$.

ALGEBRAIC

For the following exercises, evaluate the expressions.

8. $\sin^{-1}\left(\dfrac{\sqrt{2}}{2}\right)$

9. $\sin^{-1}\left(-\dfrac{1}{2}\right)$

10. $\cos^{-1}\left(\dfrac{1}{2}\right)$

11. $\cos^{-1}\left(-\dfrac{\sqrt{2}}{2}\right)$

12. $\tan^{-1}(1)$

13. $\tan^{-1}(-\sqrt{3})$

14. $\tan^{-1}(-1)$

15. $\tan^{-1}(\sqrt{3})$

16. $\tan^{-1}\left(\dfrac{-1}{\sqrt{3}}\right)$

For the following exercises, use a calculator to evaluate each expression. Express answers to the nearest hundredth.

17. $\cos^{-1}(-0.4)$

18. $\arcsin(0.23)$

19. $\arccos\left(\dfrac{3}{5}\right)$

20. $\cos^{-1}(0.8)$

21. $\tan^{-1}(6)$

For the following exercises, find the angle θ in the given right triangle. Round answers to the nearest hundredth.

22.

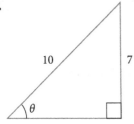

23.

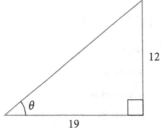

For the following exercises, find the exact value, if possible, without a calculator. If it is not possible, explain why.

24. $\sin^{-1}(\cos(\pi))$

25. $\tan^{-1}(\sin(\pi))$

26. $\cos^{-1}\left(\sin\left(\dfrac{\pi}{3}\right)\right)$

27. $\tan^{-1}\left(\sin\left(\dfrac{\pi}{3}\right)\right)$

28. $\sin^{-1}\left(\cos\left(\dfrac{-\pi}{2}\right)\right)$

29. $\tan^{-1}\left(\sin\left(\dfrac{4\pi}{3}\right)\right)$

30. $\sin^{-1}\left(\sin\left(\dfrac{5\pi}{6}\right)\right)$

31. $\tan^{-1}\left(\sin\left(\dfrac{-5\pi}{2}\right)\right)$

32. $\cos\left(\sin^{-1}\left(\dfrac{4}{5}\right)\right)$

33. $\sin\left(\cos^{-1}\left(\dfrac{3}{5}\right)\right)$

34. $\sin\left(\tan^{-1}\left(\dfrac{4}{3}\right)\right)$

35. $\cos\left(\tan^{-1}\left(\dfrac{12}{5}\right)\right)$

36. $\cos\left(\sin^{-1}\left(\dfrac{1}{2}\right)\right)$

For the following exercises, find the exact value of the expression in terms of x with the help of a reference triangle.

37. $\tan(\sin^{-1}(x-1))$

38. $\sin(\cos^{-1}(1-x))$

39. $\cos\left(\sin^{-1}\left(\dfrac{1}{x}\right)\right)$

40. $\cos(\tan^{-1}(3x-1))$

41. $\tan\left(\sin^{-1}\left(x+\dfrac{1}{2}\right)\right)$

EXTENSIONS

For the following exercise, evaluate the expression without using a calculator. Give the exact value.

42. $\dfrac{\sin^{-1}\left(\dfrac{1}{2}\right)-\cos^{-1}\left(\dfrac{\sqrt{2}}{2}\right)+\sin^{-1}\left(\dfrac{\sqrt{3}}{2}\right)-\cos^{-1}(1)}{\cos^{-1}\left(\dfrac{\sqrt{3}}{2}\right)-\sin^{-1}\left(\dfrac{\sqrt{2}}{2}\right)+\cos^{-1}\left(\dfrac{1}{2}\right)-\sin^{-1}(0)}$

For the following exercises, find the function if $\sin t = \dfrac{x}{x+1}$.

43. $\cos t$

44. $\sec t$

45. $\cot t$

46. $\cos\left(\sin^{-1}\left(\dfrac{x}{x+1}\right)\right)$

47. $\tan^{-1}\left(\dfrac{x}{\sqrt{2x+1}}\right)$

GRAPHICAL

48. Graph $y = \sin^{-1} x$ and state the domain and range of the function.

49. Graph $y = \arccos x$ and state the domain and range of the function.

50. Graph one cycle of $y = \tan^{-1} x$ and state the domain and range of the function.

51. For what value of x does $\sin x = \sin^{-1} x$? Use a graphing calculator to approximate the answer.

52. For what value of x does $\cos x = \cos^{-1} x$? Use a graphing calculator to approximate the answer.

REAL-WORLD APPLICATIONS

53. Suppose a 13-foot ladder is leaning against a building, reaching to the bottom of a second-floor window 12 feet above the ground. What angle, in radians, does the ladder make with the building?

54. Suppose you drive 0.6 miles on a road so that the vertical distance changes from 0 to 150 feet. What is the angle of elevation of the road?

55. An isosceles triangle has two congruent sides of length 9 inches. The remaining side has a length of 8 inches. Find the angle that a side of 9 inches makes with the 8-inch side.

56. Without using a calculator, approximate the value of arctan(10,000). Explain why your answer is reasonable.

57. A truss for the roof of a house is constructed from two identical right triangles. Each has a base of 12 feet and height of 4 feet. Find the measure of the acute angle adjacent to the 4-foot side.

58. The line $y = \dfrac{3}{5}x$ passes through the origin in the x,y-plane. What is the measure of the angle that the line makes with the positive x-axis?

59. The line $y = -\dfrac{3}{7}x$ passes through the origin in the x,y-plane. What is the measure of the angle that the line makes with the negative x-axis?

60. What percentage grade should a road have if the angle of elevation of the road is 4 degrees? (The percentage grade is defined as the change in the altitude of the road over a 100-foot horizontal distance. For example a 5% grade means that the road rises 5 feet for every 100 feet of horizontal distance.)

61. A 20-foot ladder leans up against the side of a building so that the foot of the ladder is 10 feet from the base of the building. If specifications call for the ladder's angle of elevation to be between 35 and 45 degrees, does the placement of this ladder satisfy safety specifications?

62. Suppose a 15-foot ladder leans against the side of a house so that the angle of elevation of the ladder is 42 degrees. How far is the foot of the ladder from the side of the house?

CHAPTER 6 REVIEW

Key Terms

amplitude the vertical height of a function; the constant A appearing in the definition of a sinusoidal function

arccosine another name for the inverse cosine; $\arccos x = \cos^{-1} x$

arcsine another name for the inverse sine; $\arcsin x = \sin^{-1} x$

arctangent another name for the inverse tangent; $\arctan x = \tan^{-1} x$

inverse cosine function the function $\cos^{-1} x$, which is the inverse of the cosine function and the angle that has a cosine equal to a given number

inverse sine function the function $\sin^{-1} x$, which is the inverse of the sine function and the angle that has a sine equal to a given number

inverse tangent function the function $\tan^{-1} x$, which is the inverse of the tangent function and the angle that has a tangent equal to a given number

midline the horizontal line $y = D$, where D appears in the general form of a sinusoidal function

periodic function a function $f(x)$ that satisfies $f(x + P) = f(x)$ for a specific constant P and any value of x

phase shift the horizontal displacement of the basic sine or cosine function; the constant $\dfrac{C}{B}$

sinusoidal function any function that can be expressed in the form $f(x) = A\sin(Bx - C) + D$ or $f(x) = A\cos(Bx - C) + D$

Key Equations

Sinusoidal functions	$f(x) = A\sin(Bx - C) + D$
	$f(x) = A\cos(Bx - C) + D$
Shifted, compressed, and/or stretched tangent function	$y = A\tan(Bx - C) + D$
Shifted, compressed, and/or stretched secant function	$y = A\sec(Bx - C) + D$
Shifted, compressed, and/or stretched cosecant function	$y = A\csc(Bx - C) + D$
Shifted, compressed, and/or stretched cotangent function	$y = A\cot(Bx - C) + D$

Key Concepts

6.1 Graphs of the Sine and Cosine Functions

- Periodic functions repeat after a given value. The smallest such value is the period. The basic sine and cosine functions have a period of 2π.

- The function $\sin x$ is odd, so its graph is symmetric about the origin. The function $\cos x$ is even, so its graph is symmetric about the y-axis.

- The graph of a sinusoidal function has the same general shape as a sine or cosine function.

- In the general formula for a sinusoidal function, the period is $P = \dfrac{2\pi}{|B|}$ See **Example 1**.

- In the general formula for a sinusoidal function, $|A|$ represents amplitude. If $|A| > 1$, the function is stretched, whereas if $|A| < 1$, the function is compressed. See **Example 2**.

- The value $\dfrac{C}{B}$ in the general formula for a sinusoidal function indicates the phase shift. See **Example 3**.

- The value D in the general formula for a sinusoidal function indicates the vertical shift from the midline. See **Example 4**.

- Combinations of variations of sinusoidal functions can be detected from an equation. See **Example 5**.

- The equation for a sinusoidal function can be determined from a graph. See **Example 6** and **Example 7**.

- A function can be graphed by identifying its amplitude and period. See **Example 8** and **Example 9**.

- A function can also be graphed by identifying its amplitude, period, phase shift, and horizontal shift. See **Example 10**.

- Sinusoidal functions can be used to solve real-world problems. See **Example 11**, **Example 12**, and **Example 13**.

6.2 Graphs of the Other Trigonometric Functions

- The tangent function has period π.

- $f(x) = A\tan(Bx - C) + D$ is a tangent with vertical and/or horizontal stretch/compression and shift. See **Example 1**, **Example 2**, and **Example 3**.

- The secant and cosecant are both periodic functions with a period of 2π. $f(x) = A\sec(Bx - C) + D$ gives a shifted, compressed, and/or stretched secant function graph. See **Example 4** and **Example 5**.

- $f(x) = A\csc(Bx - C) + D$ gives a shifted, compressed, and/or stretched cosecant function graph. See **Example 6** and **Example 7**.

- The cotangent function has period π and vertical asymptotes at $0, \pm\pi, \pm 2\pi, \ldots$

- The range of cotangent is $(-\infty, \infty)$, and the function is decreasing at each point in its range.

- The cotangent is zero at $\pm\dfrac{\pi}{2}, \pm\dfrac{3\pi}{2}, \ldots$

- $f(x) = A\cot(Bx - C) + D$ is a cotangent with vertical and/or horizontal stretch/compression and shift. See **Example 8** and **Example 9**.

- Real-world scenarios can be solved using graphs of trigonometric functions. See **Example 10**.

6.3 Inverse Trigonometric Functions

- An inverse function is one that "undoes" another function. The domain of an inverse function is the range of the original function and the range of an inverse function is the domain of the original function.

- Because the trigonometric functions are not one-to-one on their natural domains, inverse trigonometric functions are defined for restricted domains.

- For any trigonometric function $f(x)$, if $x = f^{-1}(y)$, then $f(x) = y$. However, $f(x) = y$ only implies $x = f^{-1}(y)$ if x is in the restricted domain of f. See **Example 1**.

- Special angles are the outputs of inverse trigonometric functions for special input values; for example, $\dfrac{\pi}{4} = \tan^{-1}(1)$ and $\dfrac{\pi}{6} = \sin^{-1}\left(\dfrac{1}{2}\right)$. See **Example 2**.

- A calculator will return an angle within the restricted domain of the original trigonometric function. See **Example 3**.

- Inverse functions allow us to find an angle when given two sides of a right triangle. See **Example 4**.

- In function composition, if the inside function is an inverse trigonometric function, then there are exact expressions; for example, $\sin(\cos^{-1}(x)) = \sqrt{1 - x^2}$. See **Example 5**.

- If the inside function is a trigonometric function, then the only possible combinations are $\sin^{-1}(\cos x) = \dfrac{\pi}{2} - x$ if $0 \le x \le \pi$ and $\cos^{-1}(\sin x) = \dfrac{\pi}{2} - x$ if $-\dfrac{\pi}{2} \le x \le \dfrac{\pi}{2}$. See **Example 6** and **Example 7**.

- When evaluating the composition of a trigonometric function with an inverse trigonometric function, draw a reference triangle to assist in determining the ratio of sides that represents the output of the trigonometric function. See **Example 8**.

- When evaluating the composition of a trigonometric function with an inverse trigonometric function, you may use trig identities to assist in determining the ratio of sides. See **Example 9**.

CHAPTER 6 REVIEW EXERCISES

GRAPHS OF THE SINE AND COSINE FUNCTIONS

For the following exercises, graph the functions for two periods and determine the amplitude or stretching factor, period, midline equation, and asymptotes.

1. $f(x) = -3\cos x + 3$

2. $f(x) = \frac{1}{4}\sin x$

3. $f(x) = 3\cos\left(x + \frac{\pi}{6}\right)$

4. $f(x) = -2\sin\left(x - \frac{2\pi}{3}\right)$

5. $f(x) = 3\sin\left(x - \frac{\pi}{4}\right) - 4$

6. $f(x) = 2\left(\cos\left(x - \frac{4\pi}{3}\right) + 1\right)$

7. $f(x) = 6\sin\left(3x - \frac{\pi}{6}\right) - 1$

8. $f(x) = -100\sin(50x - 20)$

GRAPHS OF THE OTHER TRIGONOMETRIC FUNCTIONS

For the following exercises, graph the functions for two periods and determine the amplitude or stretching factor, period, midline equation, and asymptotes.

9. $f(x) = \tan x - 4$

10. $f(x) = 2\tan\left(x - \frac{\pi}{6}\right)$

11. $f(x) = -3\tan(4x) - 2$

12. $f(x) = 0.2\cos(0.1x) + 0.3$

For the following exercises, graph two full periods. Identify the period, the phase shift, the amplitude, and asymptotes.

13. $f(x) = \frac{1}{3}\sec x$

14. $f(x) = 3\cot x$

15. $f(x) = 4\csc(5x)$

16. $f(x) = 8\sec\left(\frac{1}{4}x\right)$

17. $f(x) = \frac{2}{3}\csc\left(\frac{1}{2}x\right)$

18. $f(x) = -\csc(2x + \pi)$

For the following exercises, use this scenario: The population of a city has risen and fallen over a 20-year interval. Its population may be modeled by the following function: $y = 12{,}000 + 8{,}000\sin(0.628x)$, where the domain is the years since 1980 and the range is the population of the city.

19. What is the largest and smallest population the city may have?

20. Graph the function on the domain of $[0, 40]$.

21. What are the amplitude, period, and phase shift for the function?

22. Over this domain, when does the population reach 18,000? 13,000?

23. What is the predicted population in 2007? 2010?

For the following exercises, suppose a weight is attached to a spring and bobs up and down, exhibiting symmetry.

24. Suppose the graph of the displacement function is shown in **Figure 1**, where the values on the x-axis represent the time in seconds and the y-axis represents the displacement in inches. Give the equation that models the vertical displacement of the weight on the spring.

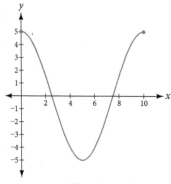

Figure 1

25. At time $= 0$, what is the displacement of the weight?

26. At what time does the displacement from the equilibrium point equal zero?

27. What is the time required for the weight to return to its initial height of 5 inches? In other words, what is the period for the displacement function?

INVERSE TRIGONOMETRIC FUNCTIONS

For the following exercises, find the exact value without the aid of a calculator.

28. $\sin^{-1}(1)$

29. $\cos^{-1}\left(\dfrac{\sqrt{3}}{2}\right)$

30. $\tan^{-1}(-1)$

31. $\cos^{-1}\left(\dfrac{1}{\sqrt{2}}\right)$

32. $\sin^{-1}\left(\dfrac{-\sqrt{3}}{2}\right)$

33. $\sin^{-1}\left(\cos\left(\dfrac{\pi}{6}\right)\right)$

34. $\cos^{-1}\left(\tan\left(\dfrac{3\pi}{4}\right)\right)$

35. $\sin\left(\sec^{-1}\left(\dfrac{3}{5}\right)\right)$

36. $\cot\left(\sin^{-1}\left(\dfrac{3}{5}\right)\right)$

37. $\tan\left(\cos^{-1}\left(\dfrac{5}{13}\right)\right)$

38. $\sin\left(\cos^{-1}\left(\dfrac{x}{x+1}\right)\right)$

39. Graph $f(x) = \cos x$ and $f(x) = \sec x$ on the interval $[0, 2\pi)$ and explain any observations.

40. Graph $f(x) = \sin x$ and $f(x) = \csc x$ and explain any observations.

41. Graph the function $f(x) = \dfrac{x}{1} - \dfrac{x^3}{3!} + \dfrac{x^5}{5!} - \dfrac{x^7}{7!}$ on the interval $[-1, 1]$ and compare the graph to the graph of $f(x) = \sin x$ on the same interval. Describe any observations.

CHAPTER 6 PRACTICE TEST

For the following exercises, sketch the graph of each function for two full periods. Determine the amplitude, the period, and the equation for the midline.

1. $f(x) = 0.5\sin x$

2. $f(x) = 5\cos x$

3. $f(x) = 5\sin x$

4. $f(x) = \sin(3x)$

5. $f(x) = -\cos\left(x + \dfrac{\pi}{3}\right) + 1$

6. $f(x) = 5\sin\left(3\left(x - \dfrac{\pi}{6}\right)\right) + 4$

7. $f(x) = 3\cos\left(\dfrac{1}{3}x - \dfrac{5\pi}{6}\right)$

8. $f(x) = \tan(4x)$

9. $f(x) = -2\tan\left(x - \dfrac{7\pi}{6}\right) + 2$

10. $f(x) = \pi\cos(3x + \pi)$

11. $f(x) = 5\csc(3x)$

12. $f(x) = \pi\sec\left(\dfrac{\pi}{2}x\right)$

13. $f(x) = 2\csc\left(x + \dfrac{\pi}{4}\right) - 3$

For the following exercises, determine the amplitude, period, and midline of the graph, and then find a formula for the function.

14. Give in terms of a sine function.   **15.** Give in terms of a sine function.   **16.** Give in terms of a tangent function.

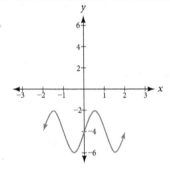 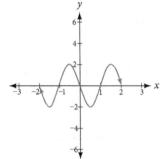 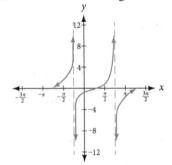

For the following exercises, find the amplitude, period, phase shift, and midline.

17. $y = \sin\left(\dfrac{\pi}{6}x + \pi\right) - 3$

18. $y = 8\sin\left(\dfrac{7\pi}{6}x + \dfrac{7\pi}{2}\right) + 6$

19. The outside temperature over the course of a day can be modeled as a sinusoidal function. Suppose you know the temperature is 68°F at midnight and the high and low temperatures during the day are 80°F and 56°F, respectively. Assuming t is the number of hours since midnight, find a function for the temperature, D, in terms of t.

20. Water is pumped into a storage bin and empties according to a periodic rate. The depth of the water is 3 feet at its lowest at 2:00 a.m. and 71 feet at its highest, which occurs every 5 hours. Write a cosine function that models the depth of the water as a function of time, and then graph the function for one period.

For the following exercises, find the period and horizontal shift of each function.

21. $g(x) = 3\tan(6x + 42)$

22. $n(x) = 4\csc\left(\dfrac{5\pi}{3}x - \dfrac{20\pi}{3}\right)$

23. Write the equation for the graph in **Figure 1** in terms of the secant function and give the period and phase shift.

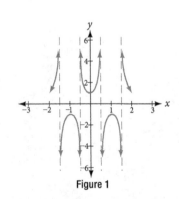

Figure 1

24. If $\tan x = 3$, find $\tan(-x)$.

25. If $\sec x = 4$, find $\sec(-x)$.

For the following exercises, graph the functions on the specified window and answer the questions.

26. Graph $m(x) = \sin(2x) + \cos(3x)$ on the viewing window $[-10, 10]$ by $[-3, 3]$. Approximate the graph's period.

27. Graph $n(x) = 0.02\sin(50\pi x)$ on the following domains in x: $[0, 1]$ and $[0, 3]$. Suppose this function models sound waves. Why would these views look so different?

28. Graph $f(x) = \dfrac{\sin x}{x}$ on $[-0.5, 0.5]$ and explain any observations.

For the following exercises, let $f(x) = \dfrac{3}{5}\cos(6x)$.

29. What is the largest possible value for $f(x)$?

30. What is the smallest possible value for $f(x)$?

31. Where is the function increasing on the interval $[0, 2\pi]$?

For the following exercises, find and graph one period of the periodic function with the given amplitude, period, and phase shift.

32. Sine curve with amplitude 3, period $\dfrac{\pi}{3}$, and phase shift $(h, k) = \left(\dfrac{\pi}{4}, 2\right)$

33. Cosine curve with amplitude 2, period $\dfrac{\pi}{6}$, and phase shift $(h, k) = \left(-\dfrac{\pi}{4}, 3\right)$

For the following exercises, graph the function. Describe the graph and, wherever applicable, any periodic behavior, amplitude, asymptotes, or undefined points.

34. $f(x) = 5\cos(3x) + 4\sin(2x)$

35. $f(x) = e^{\sin t}$

For the following exercises, find the exact value.

36. $\sin^{-1}\left(\dfrac{\sqrt{3}}{2}\right)$

37. $\tan^{-1}\left(\sqrt{3}\right)$

38. $\cos^{-1}\left(-\dfrac{\sqrt{3}}{2}\right)$

39. $\cos^{-1}(\sin(\pi))$

40. $\cos^{-1}\left(\tan\left(\dfrac{7\pi}{4}\right)\right)$

41. $\cos(\sin^{-1}(1 - 2x))$

42. $\cos^{-1}(-0.4)$

43. $\cos(\tan^{-1}(x^2))$

For the following exercises, suppose $\sin t = \dfrac{x}{x + 1}$.

44. $\tan t$

45. $\csc t$

46. Given **Figure 2**, find the measure of angle θ to three decimal places. Answer in radians.

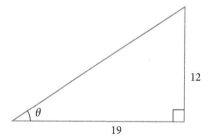

For the following exercises, determine whether the equation is true or false.

47. $\arcsin\left(\sin\left(\dfrac{5\pi}{6}\right)\right) = \dfrac{5\pi}{6}$

48. $\arccos\left(\cos\left(\dfrac{5\pi}{6}\right)\right) = \dfrac{5\pi}{6}$

49. The grade of a road is 7%. This means that for every horizontal distance of 100 feet on the road, the vertical rise is 7 feet. Find the angle the road makes with the horizontal in radians.

Basic Functions and Identities

A1 Graphs of the Parent Functions

Identity

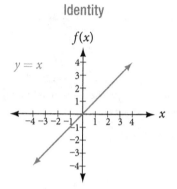

$y = x$

Domain: $(-\infty, \infty)$
Range: $(-\infty, \infty)$

Square

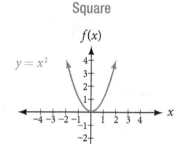

$y = x^2$

Domain: $(-\infty, \infty)$
Range: $[0, \infty)$

Square Root

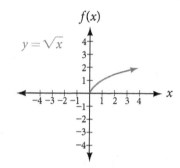

$y = \sqrt{x}$

Domain: $[0, \infty)$
Range: $[0, \infty)$

Figure A1

Cubic

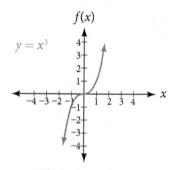

$y = x^3$

Domain: $(-\infty, \infty)$
Range: $(-\infty, \infty)$

Cube Root

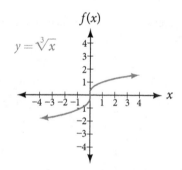

$y = \sqrt[3]{x}$

Domain: $(-\infty, \infty)$
Range: $(-\infty, \infty)$

Reciprocal

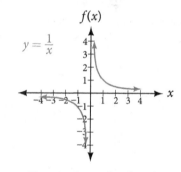

$y = \dfrac{1}{x}$

Domain: $(-\infty, 0) \cup (0, \infty)$
Range: $(-\infty, 0) \cup (0, \infty)$

Figure A2

Absolute Value

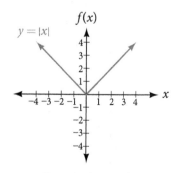

$y = |x|$

Domain: $(-\infty, \infty)$
Range: $[0, \infty)$

Exponential

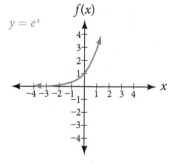

$y = e^x$

Domain: $(-\infty, \infty)$
Range: $[0, \infty)$

Natural Logarithm

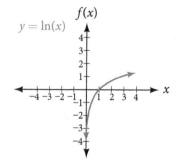

$y = \ln(x)$

Domain: $(0, \infty)$
Range: $(-\infty, \infty)$

Figure A3

A2 Graphs of the Trigonometric Functions

Sine

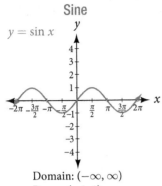

$y = \sin x$

Domain: $(-\infty, \infty)$
Range: $(-1, 1)$

Cosine

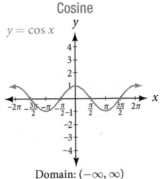

$y = \cos x$

Domain: $(-\infty, \infty)$
Range: $(-1, 1)$

Figure A4

Tangent

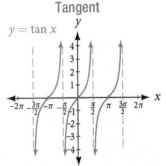

$y = \tan x$

Domain: $x \neq \frac{\pi}{2}k$ where k is an odd integer
Range: $(-\infty, -1] \cup [1, \infty)$

Cosecant

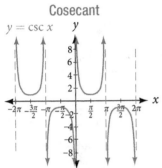

$y = \csc x$

Domain: $x \neq \pi k$ where k is an integer
Range: $(-\infty, -1] \cup [1, \infty)$

Secant

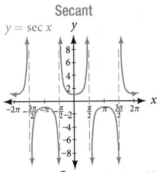

$y = \sec x$

Domain: $x \neq \frac{\pi}{2}k$ where k is an odd integer
Range: $(-\infty, -1] \cup [1, \infty)$

Figure A5

Cotangent

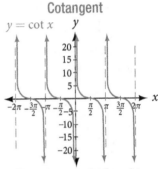

$y = \cot x$

Domain: $x \neq \pi k$ where k is an integer
Range: $(-\infty, \infty)$

Inverse Sine

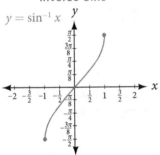

$y = \sin^{-1} x$

Domain: $[-1, 1]$
Range: $\left[-\frac{\pi}{2}, \frac{\pi}{2}\right]$

Inverse Cosine

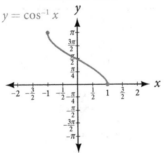

$y = \cos^{-1} x$

Domain: $[-1, 1]$
Range: $[0, \pi)$

Figure A6

Inverse Tangent

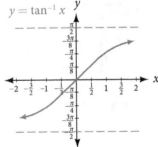

$y = \tan^{-1} x$

Domain: $(-\infty, \infty)$
Range: $\left(-\frac{\pi}{2}, \frac{\pi}{2}\right)$

Inverse Cosecant

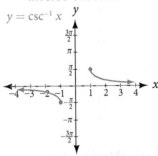

$y = \csc^{-1} x$

Domain: $(-\infty, -1] \cup [1, \infty)$
Range: $\left[-\frac{\pi}{2}, 0\right) \cup \left(0, \frac{\pi}{2}\right]$

Inverse Secant

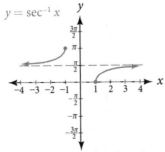

$y = \sec^{-1} x$

Domain: $(-\infty, -1] \cup [1, \infty)$
Range: $\left[0, \frac{\pi}{2}\right) \cup \left(\frac{\pi}{2}, \pi\right]$

Figure A7

Inverse Cotangent

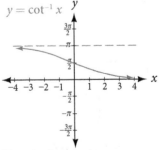

$y = \cot^{-1} x$

Domain: $(-\infty, \infty)$
Range: $\left[-\frac{\pi}{2}, 0\right) \cup \left(0, \frac{\pi}{2}\right]$

A3 Trigonometric Identities

Identities	Equations
Pythagorean Identities	$\sin^2\theta + \cos^2\theta = 1$ $1 + \tan^2\theta = \sec^2\theta$ $1 + \cot^2\theta = \csc^2\theta$
Even-odd Identities	$\cos(-\theta) = \cos\theta$ $\sec(-\theta) = \sec\theta$ $\sin(-\theta) = -\sin\theta$ $\tan(-\theta) = -\tan\theta$ $\csc(-\theta) = -\csc\theta$ $\cot(-\theta) = -\cot\theta$
Cofunction identities	$\sin\theta = \cos\left(\dfrac{\pi}{2} - \theta\right)$ $\cos\theta = \sin\left(\dfrac{\pi}{2} - \theta\right)$ $\tan\theta = \cot\left(\dfrac{\pi}{2} - \theta\right)$ $\cot\theta = \tan\left(\dfrac{\pi}{2} - \theta\right)$ $\sec\theta = \csc\left(\dfrac{\pi}{2} - \theta\right)$ $\csc\theta = \sec\left(\dfrac{\pi}{2} - \theta\right)$
Fundamental Identities	$\tan\theta = \dfrac{\sin\theta}{\cos\theta}$ $\sec\theta = \dfrac{1}{\cos\theta}$ $\csc\theta = \dfrac{1}{\sin\theta}$ $\cot\theta = \dfrac{1}{\tan\theta} = \dfrac{\cos\theta}{\sin\theta}$
Sum and Difference Identities	$\cos(\alpha + \beta) = \cos\alpha\cos\beta - \sin\alpha\sin\beta$ $\cos(\alpha - \beta) = \cos\alpha\cos\beta + \sin\alpha\sin\beta$ $\sin(\alpha + \beta) = \sin\alpha\cos\beta + \cos\alpha\sin\beta$ $\sin(\alpha - \beta) = \sin\alpha\cos\beta - \cos\alpha\sin\beta$ $\tan(\alpha + \beta) = \dfrac{\tan\alpha + \tan\beta}{1 - \tan\alpha\tan\beta}$ $\tan(\alpha - \beta) = \dfrac{\tan\alpha - \tan\beta}{1 + \tan\alpha\tan\beta}$
Double-Angle Formulas	$\sin(2\theta) = 2\sin\theta\cos\theta$ $\cos(2\theta) = \cos^2\theta - \sin^2\theta$ $\cos(2\theta) = 1 - 2\sin^2\theta$ $\cos(2\theta) = 2\cos^2\theta - 1$ $\tan(2\theta) = \dfrac{2\tan\theta}{1 - \tan^2\theta}$

Table A1

Identities	Equations
Half-Angle formulas	$\sin\dfrac{\alpha}{2} = \pm\sqrt{\dfrac{1-\cos\alpha}{2}}$ $\cos\dfrac{\alpha}{2} = \pm\sqrt{\dfrac{1+\cos\alpha}{2}}$ $\tan\dfrac{\alpha}{2} = \pm\sqrt{\dfrac{1-\cos\alpha}{1+\cos\alpha}}$ $= \dfrac{\sin\alpha}{1-\cos\alpha}$ $= \dfrac{1-\cos\alpha}{\sin\alpha}$
Reduction Formulas	$\sin^2\theta = \dfrac{1-\cos(2\theta)}{2}$ $\cos^2\theta = \dfrac{1+\cos(2\theta)}{2}$ $\tan^2\theta = \dfrac{1-\cos(2\theta)}{1+\cos(2\theta)}$
Product-to-Sum Formulas	$\cos\alpha\cos\beta = \dfrac{1}{2}\left[\cos(\alpha-\beta) + \cos(\alpha+\beta)\right]$ $\sin\alpha\cos\beta = \dfrac{1}{2}\left[\sin(\alpha+\beta) + \sin(\alpha-\beta)\right]$ $\sin\alpha\sin\beta = \dfrac{1}{2}\left[\cos(\alpha-\beta) - \cos(\alpha+\beta)\right]$ $\cos\alpha\sin\beta = \dfrac{1}{2}\left[\sin(\alpha+\beta) - \sin(\alpha-\beta)\right]$
Sum-to-Product Formulas	$\sin\alpha + \sin\beta = 2\sin\left(\dfrac{\alpha+\beta}{2}\right)\cos\left(\dfrac{\alpha-\beta}{2}\right)$ $\sin\alpha - \sin\beta = 2\sin\left(\dfrac{\alpha-\beta}{2}\right)\cos\left(\dfrac{\alpha+\beta}{2}\right)$ $\cos\alpha - \cos\beta = -2\sin\left(\dfrac{\alpha+\beta}{2}\right)\sin\left(\dfrac{\alpha-\beta}{2}\right)$ $\cos\alpha + \cos\beta = 2\cos\left(\dfrac{\alpha+\beta}{2}\right)\cos\left(\dfrac{\alpha-\beta}{2}\right)$
Law of Sines	$\dfrac{\sin\alpha}{a} = \dfrac{\sin\beta}{b} = \dfrac{\sin\gamma}{c}$ $\dfrac{\sin a}{\alpha} = \dfrac{\sin b}{\beta} = \dfrac{\sin c}{\gamma}$
Law of Cosines	$a^2 = b^2 + c^2 - 2bc\cos\alpha$ $b^2 = a^2 + c^2 - 2ac\cos\beta$ $c^2 = a^2 + b^2 - 2aa\cos\gamma$

Table A1

Try It Answers for Chapters 1–6

Chapter 1

Section 1.1

1. a. Yes **b.** Yes   (Note: If two players had been tied for, say, 4th place, then the name would not have been a function of rank.)
2. $w = f(d)$ **3.** Yes   **4.** $g(5) = 1$ **5.** $m = 8$
6. $y = f(x) = \frac{\sqrt[3]{x}}{2}$ **7.** $g(1) = 8$ **8.** $x = 0$ or $x = 2$
9. a. Yes, because each bank account has a single balance at any given time. **b.** No, because several bank account numbers may have the same balance. **c.** No, because the same output may correspond to more than one input.   **10. a.** Yes, letter grade is a function of percent grade. **b.** No, it is not one-to-one. There are 100 different percent numbers we could get but only about five possible letter grades, so there cannot be only one percent number that corresponds to each letter grade.   **11.** Yes
12. No, because it does not pass the horizontal line test.

Section 1.2

1. $\{-5, 0, 5, 10, 15\}$ **2.** $(-\infty, \infty)$ **3.** $\left(-\infty, \frac{1}{2}\right) \cup \left(\frac{1}{2}, \infty\right)$
4. $\left[-\frac{5}{2}, \infty\right)$ **5. a.** Values that are less than or equal to –2, or values that are greater than or equal to –1 and less than 3;
b. $\{x \mid x \leq -2 \text{ or } -1 \leq x < 3\}$ **c.** $(-\infty, -2] \cup [-1, 3)$
6. Domain = $[1950, 2002]$; Range = $[47{,}000{,}000, 89{,}000{,}000]$
7. Domain: $(-\infty, 2]$; Range: $(-\infty, 0]$
8.

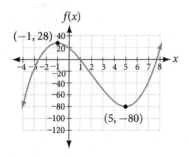

Section 1.3

1. $\dfrac{\$2.84 - \$2.31}{5 \text{ years}} = \dfrac{\$0.53}{5 \text{ years}} = \$0.106$ per year.   **2.** $\dfrac{1}{2}$
3. $a + 7$ **4.** The local maximum appears to occur at $(-1, 28)$, and the local minimum occurs at $(5, -80)$. The function is increasing on $(-\infty, -1) \cup (5, \infty)$ and decreasing on $(-1, 5)$.

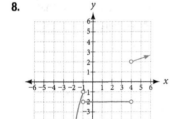

Section 1.4

1. a. $(fg)(x) = f(x)g(x) = (x - 1)(x^2 - 1) = x^3 - x^2 - x + 1$
$(f - g)(x) = f(x) - g(x) = (x - 1) - (x^2 - 1) = x - x^2$
b. No, the functions are not the same.
2. A gravitational force is still a force, so $a(G(r))$ makes sense as the acceleration of a planet at a distance r from the Sun (due to gravity), but $G(a(F))$ does not make sense.
3. $f(g(1)) = f(3) = 3$ and $g(f(4)) = g(1) = 3$ **4.** $g(f(2)) = g(5) = 3$
5. a. 8; **b.** 20   **6.** $[-4, 0) \cup (0, \infty)$
7. Possible answer: $g(x) = \sqrt{4 + x^2}$; $h(x) = \dfrac{4}{3 - x}$; $f = h \circ g$

Section 1.5

1. $b(t) = h(t) + 10 = -4.9t^2 + 30t + 10$
2.

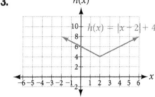

The graphs of $f(x)$ and $g(x)$ are shown here. The transformation is a horizontal shift. The function is shifted to the left by 2 units.

3.

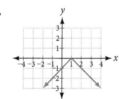

4. $g(x) = \dfrac{1}{x - 1} + 1$

5. a.

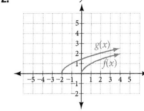

b.

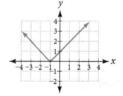

6. a. $g(x) = -f(x)$ **b.** $h(x) = f(-x)$

x	-2	0	2	4
$g(x)$	-5	-10	-15	-20

x	-2	0	2	4
$h(x)$	15	10	5	unknown

7.

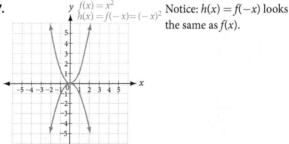

Notice: $h(x) = f(-x)$ looks the same as $f(x)$.

8. even   **9.**

x	2	4	6	8
$g(x)$	9	12	15	0

10. $g(x) = 3x - 2$

11. $g(x) = f\left(\dfrac{1}{3}x\right)$ so using the square root function we get
$g(x) = \sqrt{\dfrac{1}{3}x}$

Section 1.6

1. $|x - 2| \leq 3$ **2.** Using the variable p for passing, $|p - 80| \leq 20$
3. $f(x) = -|x + 2| + 3$ **4.** $x = -1$ or $x = 2$
5. $f(0) = 1$, so the graph intersects the vertical axis at $(0, 1)$.
$f(x) = 0$ when $x = -5$ and $x = 1$ so the graph intersects the
horizontal axis at $(-5, 0)$ and $(1, 0)$.   **6.** $4 \leq x \leq 8$
7. $k \leq 1$ or $k \geq 7$; in interval notation, this would be
$(-\infty, 1] \cup [7, \infty)$.

Section 1.7

1. $h(2) = 6$ **2.** Yes   **3.** Yes   **4.** The domain of function
f^{-1} is $(-\infty, -2)$ and the range of function f^{-1} is $(1, \infty)$.
5. a. $f(60) = 50$. In 60 minutes, 50 miles are traveled.
b. $f^{-1}(60) = 70$. To travel 60 miles, it will take 70 minutes.
6. a. 3 **b.** 5.6   **7.** $x = 3y + 5$ **8.** $f^{-1}(x) = (2 - x)^2$;
domain of f: $[0, \infty)$; domain of f^{-1}: $(-\infty, 2]$
9.

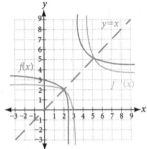

Chapter 2

Section 2.1

1. $m = \dfrac{4 - 3}{0 - 2} = \dfrac{1}{-2} = -\dfrac{1}{2}$; decreasing because $m < 0$.

2. $m = \dfrac{1{,}868 - 1{,}442}{2{,}012 - 2{,}009} = \dfrac{426}{3} = 142$ people per year

3. $y - 2 = -2(x + 2)$; $y = -2x - 2$
4. $y - 0 = -3(x - 0)$; $y = -3x$ **5.** $y = -7x + 3$
6. $H(x) = 0.5x + 12.5$

Section 2.2

1.

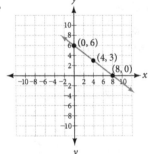

2. Possible answers include $(-3, 7)$, $(-6, 9)$, or $(-9, 11)$

3.

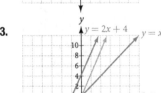

4. $(16, 0)$

5. a. $f(x) = 2x$;

    b. $g(x) = -\dfrac{1}{2}x$

6. $y = -\dfrac{1}{3}x + 6$

7. a. $(0, 5)$ **b.** $(5, 0)$ **c.** Slope -1 **d.** Neither parallel nor
perpendicular   **e.** Decreasing function   **f.** Given the identity
function, perform a vertical flip (over the t-axis) and shift up 5 units.

Section 2.3

1. $C(x) = 0.25x + 25{,}000$; The y-intercept is $(0, 25{,}000)$. If the
company does not produce a single doughnut, they still incur a
cost of $25,000.   **2. a.** 41,100 **b.** 2020   **3.** 21.15 miles

Section 2.4

1. 54° F   **2.** 150.871 billion gallons; extrapolation

Chapter 3

Section 3.1

1. $\sqrt{-24} = 0 + 2i\sqrt{6}$ **2.**
3. $(3 - 4i) - (2 - 5i) = 1 - 9i$
4. $-8 - 24i$ **5.** $18 + i$
6. $102 - 29i$ **7.** $-\dfrac{3}{17} + \dfrac{5}{17}i$

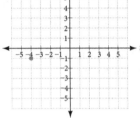

Section 3.2

1. The path passes through the origin and has vertex at $(-4, 7)$,
so $(h)x = -\dfrac{7}{16}(x + 4)^2 + 7$. To make the shot, $h(-7.5)$ would
need to be about 4 but $h(-7.5) \approx 1.64$; he doesn't make it.
2. $g(x) = x^2 - 6x + 13$ in general form; $g(x) = (x - 3)^2 + 4$
in standard form   **3.** The domain is all real numbers. The
range is $f(x) \geq \dfrac{8}{11}$, or $\left[\dfrac{8}{11}, \infty\right)$.   **4.** y-intercept at $(0, 13)$, No
x-intercepts   **5.** 3 seconds; 256 feet; 7 seconds

Section 3.3

1. $f(x)$ is a power function because it can be written as $f(x) = 8x^5$.
The other functions are not power functions.
2. As x approaches positive or negative infinity, $f(x)$ decreases
without bound: as $x \to \pm\infty$, $f(x) \to -\infty$ because of the negative
coefficient.   **3.** The degree is 6. The leading term is $-x^6$.
The leading coefficient is -1.   **4.** As $x \to \infty$, $f(x) \to -\infty$; as
$x \to -\infty$, $f(x) \to -\infty$. It has the shape of an even degree power
function with a negative coefficient.   **5.** The leading term is
$0.2x^3$, so it is a degree 3 polynomial. As x approaches positive
infinity, $f(x)$ increases without bound; as x approaches negative
infinity, $f(x)$ decreases without bound.   **6.** y-intercept $(0, 0)$;
x-intercepts $(0, 0)$, $(-2, 0)$, and $(5, 0)$ **7.** There are at most
12 x-intercepts and at most 11 turning points.   **8.** The end
behavior indicates an odd-degree polynomial function; there
are 3 x-intercepts and 2 turning points, so the degree is odd and
at least 3. Because of the end behavior, we know that the lead
coefficient must be negative.   **9.** The x-intercepts are $(2, 0)$,
$(-1, 0)$, and $(5, 0)$, the y-intercept is $(0, 2)$, and the graph has at
most 2 turning points.

Section 3.4

1. y-intercept $(0, 0)$; x-intercepts $(0, 0)$, $(-5, 0)$, $(2, 0)$, and $(3, 0)$
2. The graph has a zero of -5 with multiplicity 3, a zero of -1 with
multiplicity 2, and a zero of 3 with multiplicity 4.

3.

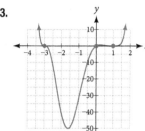

4. Because f is a polynomial function and since $f(1)$ is negative and $f(2)$ is positive, there is at least one real zero between $x = 1$ and $x = 2$.

5. $f(x) = -\dfrac{1}{8}(x-2)^3(x+1)^2(x-4)$ **6.** The minimum occurs at approximately the point $(0, -6.5)$, and the maximum occurs at approximately the point $(3.5, 7)$.

Section 3.5

1. $4x^2 - 8x + 15 - \dfrac{78}{4x+5}$ **2.** $3x^3 - 3x^2 + 21x - 150 + \dfrac{1,090}{x+7}$

3. $3x^2 - 4x + 1$

Section 3.6

1. $f(-3) = -412$ **2.** The zeros are 2, -2, and -4.

3. There are no rational zeros.   **4.** The zeros are -4, $\dfrac{1}{2}$, and 1.

5. $f(x) = -\dfrac{1}{2}x^3 + \dfrac{5}{2}x^2 - 2x + 10$ **6.** There must be 4, 2, or 0 positive real roots and 0 negative real roots. The graph shows that there are 2 positive real zeros and 0 negative real zeros.

7. 3 meters by 4 meters by 7 meters

Section 3.7

1. End behavior: as $x \to \pm\infty$, $f(x) \to 0$; Local behavior: as $x \to 0$, $f(x) \to \infty$ (there are no x- or y-intercepts).

2.

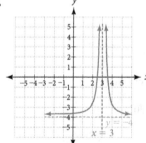

The function and the asymptotes are shifted 3 units right and 4 units down. As $x \to 3, f(x) \to \infty$, and as $x \to \pm\infty$, $f(x) \to -4$. The function is $f(x) = \dfrac{1}{(x-3)^2} - 4$.

3. $\dfrac{12}{11}$ **4.** The domain is all real numbers except $x = 1$ and $x = 5$.

5. Removable discontinuity at $x = 5$. Vertical asymptotes: $x = 0$, $x = 1$.   **6.** Vertical asymptotes at $x = 2$ and $x = -3$; horizontal asymptote at $y = 4$.   **7.** For the transformed reciprocal squared function, we find the rational form.

$f(x) = \dfrac{1}{(x-3)^2} - 4$

$= \dfrac{1 - 4(x-3)^2}{(x-3)^2}$

$= \dfrac{1 - 4(x^2 - 6x + 9)}{(x-3)(x-3)}$

$= \dfrac{-4x^2 + 24x - 35}{x^2 - 6x + 9}$

Because the numerator is the same degree as the denominator we know that as $x \to \pm\infty$, $f(x) \to -4$; so $y = -4$ is the horizontal asymptote. Next, we set the denominator equal to zero, and find that the vertical asymptote is $x = 3$, because as $x \to 3$, $f(x) \to \infty$. We then set the numerator equal to 0 and find the x-intercepts are at $(2.5, 0)$ and $(3.5, 0)$. Finally, we evaluate the function at 0 and find the y-intercept to be at $\left(0, \dfrac{-35}{9}\right)$.

8.

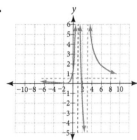

Horizontal asymptote at $y = \dfrac{1}{2}$. Vertical asymptotes at $x = 1$ and $x = 3$. y-intercept at $\left(0, \dfrac{4}{3}\right)$. x-intercepts at $(2, 0)$ and $(-2, 0)$. $(-2, 0)$ is a zero with multiplicity 2, and the graph bounces off the x-axis at this point. $(2, 0)$ is a single zero and the graph crosses the axis at this point.

Section 3.8

1. $f^{-1}(f(x)) = f^{-1}\left(\dfrac{x+5}{3}\right) = 3\left(\dfrac{x+5}{3}\right) - 5 = (x-5) + 5 = x$ and $f(f^{-1}(x)) = f(3x - 5) = \dfrac{(3x-5)+5}{3} = \dfrac{3x}{3} = x$

2. $f^{-1}(x) = x^3 - 4$ **3.** $f^{-1}(x) = \sqrt{x-1}$

4. $f^{-1}(x) = \dfrac{x^2 - 3}{2}$, $x \geq 0$ **5.** $f^{-1}(x) = \dfrac{2x+3}{x-1}$

Section 3.9

1. $\dfrac{128}{3}$ **2.** $\dfrac{9}{2}$ **3.** $x = 20$

Chapter 4

Section 4.1

1. $g(x) = 0.875^x$ and $j(x) = 1095.6^{-2x}$ represent exponential functions.
2. 5.5556   **3.** About 1.548 billion people; by the year 2031, India's population will exceed China's by about 0.001 billion, or 1 million people.   **4.** $(0, 129)$ and $(2, 236)$; $N(t) = 129(1.3526)^t$
5. $f(x) = 2(1.5)^x$ **6.** $f(x) = \sqrt{2}(\sqrt{2})^x$; Answers may vary due to round-off error. the answer should be very close to $1.4142(1.4142)^x$.
7. $y \approx 12 \cdot 1.85^x$ **8.** About $3,644,675.88   **9.** $13,693
10. $e^{-0.5} \approx 0.60653$ **11.** $3,659,823.44   **12.** 3.77E-26(This is calculator notation for the number written as 3.77×10^{-26} in scientific notation. While the output of an exponential function is never zero, this number is so close to zero that for all practical purposes we can accept zero as the answer.)

Section 4.2

1.

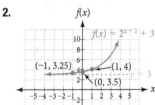

The domain is $(-\infty, \infty)$; the range is $(0, \infty)$; the horizontal asymptote is $y = 0$.

2.

The domain is $(-\infty, \infty)$; the range is $(3, \infty)$; the horizontal asymptote is $y = 3$.

3. $x \approx -1.608$

4.

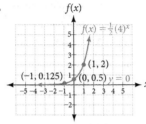

The domain is $(-\infty, \infty)$; the range is $(0, \infty)$; the horizontal asymptote is $y = 0$.

5.

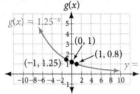

The domain is $(-\infty, \infty)$; the range is $(0, \infty)$; the horizontal asymptote is $y = 0$.

6. $f(x) = -\dfrac{1}{3}e^x - 2$; the domain is $(-\infty, \infty)$; the range is $(-\infty, 2)$; the horizontal asymptote is $y = 2$.

Section 4.3

1. a. $\log_{10}(1{,}000{,}000) = 6$ is equivalent to $10^6 = 1{,}000{,}000$
b. $\log_5(25) = 2$ is equivalent to $5^2 = 25$ **2. a.** $3^2 = 9$ is equivalent to $\log_3(9) = 2$ **b.** $5^3 = 125$ is equivalent to $\log_5(125) = 3$
c. $2^{-1} = \dfrac{1}{2}$ is equivalent to $\log_2\!\left(\dfrac{1}{2}\right) = -1$

3. $\log_{121}(11) = \dfrac{1}{2}$ (recalling that $\sqrt{121} = 121^{\frac{1}{2}} = 11$)

4. $\log_2\!\left(\dfrac{1}{32}\right) = -5$ **5.** $\log(1{,}000{,}000) = 6$ **6.** $\log(123) \approx 2.0899$

7. The difference in magnitudes was about 3.929.   **8.** It is not possible to take the logarithm of a negative number in the set of real numbers.

Section 4.4

1. $(2, \infty)$ **2.** $(5, \infty)$
3.

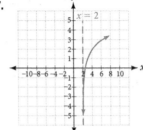

The domain is $(0, \infty)$, the range is $(-\infty, \infty)$, and the vertical asymptote is $x = 0$.

4.

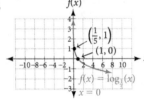

The domain is $(-4, \infty)$, the range $(-\infty, \infty)$, and the asymptote $x = -4$.

5.

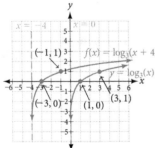

The domain is $(0, \infty)$, the range is $(-\infty, \infty)$, and the vertical asymptote is $x = 0$.

6.

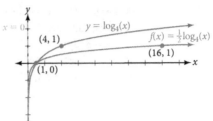

The domain is $(0, \infty)$, the range is $(-\infty, \infty)$, and the vertical asymptote is $x = 0$.

7.

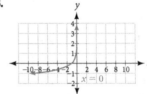

The domain is $(2, \infty)$, the range is $(-\infty, \infty)$, and the vertical asymptote is $x = 2$.

8.

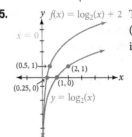

The domain is $(-\infty, 0)$, the range is $(-\infty, \infty)$, and the vertical asymptote is $x = 0$.
9. $x \approx 3.049$ **10.** $x = 1$
11. $f(x) = 2\ln(x + 3) - 1$

Section 4.5

1. $\log_b(2) + \log_b(2) + \log_b(2) + \log_b(k) = 3\log_b(2) + \log_b(k)$
2. $\log_3(x + 3) - \log_3(x - 1) - \log_3(x - 2)$ **3.** $2\ln(x)$
4. $-2\ln(x)$ **5.** $\log_3(16)$ **6.** $2\log(x) + 3\log(y) - 4\log(z)$
7. $\dfrac{2}{3}\ln(x)$ **8.** $\dfrac{1}{2}\ln(x - 1) + \ln(2x + 1) - \ln(x + 3) - \ln(x - 3)$
9. $\log\!\left(\dfrac{3 \cdot 5}{4 \cdot 6}\right)$; can also be written $\log\!\left(\dfrac{5}{8}\right)$ by reducing the fraction to lowest terms.   **10.** $\log\!\left(\dfrac{5(x-1)^3\sqrt{x}}{(7x-1)}\right)$
11. $\log\dfrac{x^{12}(x+5)^4}{(2x+3)^4}$; this answer could also be written $\log\!\left(\dfrac{x^3(x+5)}{(2x+3)}\right)^4$.
12. The pH increases by about 0.301.   **13.** $\dfrac{\ln(8)}{\ln(0.5)}$
14. $\dfrac{\ln(100)}{\ln(5)} \approx \dfrac{4.6051}{1.6094} = 2.861$

Section 4.6

1. $x = -2$ **2.** $x = -1$ **3.** $x = \dfrac{1}{2}$
4. The equation has no solution.   **5.** $x = \dfrac{\ln(3)}{\ln\!\left(\dfrac{2}{3}\right)}$
6. $t = 2\ln\!\left(\dfrac{11}{3}\right)$ or $\ln\!\left(\dfrac{11}{3}\right)^2$
7. $t = \ln\!\left(\dfrac{1}{\sqrt{2}}\right) = -\dfrac{1}{2}\ln(2)$ **8.** $x = \ln(2)$ **9.** $x = e^4$
10. $x = e^5 - 1$ **11.** $x \approx 9.97$ **12.** $x = 1$ or $x = -1$
13. $t = 703{,}800{,}000 \times \dfrac{\ln(0.8)}{\ln(0.5)}$ years $\approx 226{,}572{,}993$ years.

Section 4.7

1. $f(t) = A_0 e^{-0.0000000087t}$ **2.** Less than 230 years; 229.3157 to be exact
3. $f(t) = A_0 e^{\left(\frac{\ln(2)}{3}\right)t}$ **4.** 6.026 hours   **5.** 895 cases on day 15
6. Exponential. $y = 2e^{0.5x}$ **7.** $y = 3e^{(\ln 0.5)x}$

Section 4.8

1. a. The exponential regression model that fits these data is $y = 522.88585984(1.19645256)^x$. **b.** If spending continues at this rate, the graduate's credit card debt will be \$4,499.38 after one year.
2. a. The logarithmic regression model that fits these data is $y = 141.91242949 + 10.45366573\ln(x)$ **b.** If sales continue at this rate, about 171,000 games will be sold in the year 2015.
3. a. The logistic regression model that fits these data is
$$y = \frac{25.65665979}{1 + 6.113686306e^{-0.3852149008x}}.$$ **b.** If the population continues to grow at this rate, there will be about 25,634 seals in 2020. **c.** To the nearest whole number, the carrying capacity is 25,657.

Chapter 5

Section 5.1

1.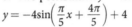

240°

2. $\frac{3\pi}{2}$ **3.** $-135°$ **4.** $\frac{7\pi}{10}$
5. $\alpha = 150°$ **6.** $\beta = 60°$ **7.** $\frac{7\pi}{6}$
8. $\frac{215\pi}{18} = 37.525$ units **9.** 1.88
10. $-\frac{3\pi}{2}$ rad/s
11. 1,655 kilometers per hour

Section 5.2

1. $\cos(t) = -\frac{\sqrt{2}}{2}$, $\sin(t) = \frac{\sqrt{2}}{2}$ **2.** $\cos(\pi) = -1$, $\sin(\pi) = 0$
3. $\sin(t) = -\frac{7}{25}$ **4.** Approximately 0.866025403 **5.** $\frac{\pi}{3}$
6. a. $\cos(315°) = \frac{\sqrt{2}}{2}$, $\sin(315°) = -\frac{\sqrt{2}}{2}$ **b.** $\cos\left(-\frac{\pi}{6}\right) = \frac{\sqrt{3}}{2}$, $\sin\left(-\frac{\pi}{6}\right) = -\frac{1}{2}$ **7.** $\left(\frac{1}{2}, -\frac{\sqrt{3}}{2}\right)$

Section 5.3

1. $\sin t = -\frac{\sqrt{2}}{2}$ $\cos t = \frac{\sqrt{2}}{2}$ $\tan t = -1$
  $\sec t = \sqrt{2}$, $\csc t = -\sqrt{2}$ $\cot t = -1$
2. $\sin\frac{\pi}{3} = \frac{\sqrt{3}}{2}$ $\cos\frac{\pi}{3} = \frac{1}{2}$ $\tan\frac{\pi}{3} = \sqrt{3}$
  $\sec\frac{\pi}{3} = 2$ $\csc\frac{\pi}{3} = \frac{2\sqrt{3}}{3}$ $\cot\frac{\pi}{3} = \frac{\sqrt{3}}{3}$
3. $\sin\left(-\frac{7\pi}{4}\right) = \frac{\sqrt{2}}{2}$ $\cos\left(-\frac{7\pi}{4}\right) = \frac{\sqrt{2}}{2}$ $\tan\left(-\frac{7\pi}{4}\right) = 1$
  $\sec\left(-\frac{7\pi}{4}\right) = \sqrt{2}$ $\csc\left(-\frac{7\pi}{4}\right) = \sqrt{2}$ $\cot\left(-\frac{7\pi}{4}\right) = 1$
4. $-\sqrt{3}$ **5.** -2 **6.** $\sin t$
7. $\cot t = -\frac{8}{17}$ $\sin t = \frac{15}{17}$ $\tan t = -\frac{15}{8}$
  $\csc t = \frac{17}{15}$ $\cot t = -\frac{8}{15}$
8. $\sin t = -1$ $\cos t = 0$ $\tan t = $ Undefined
  $\sec t = $ Undefined $\csc t = -1$ $\cot t = 0$
9. $\sec t = \sqrt{2}$ $\csc t = \sqrt{2}$ $\tan t = 1$
  $\cot t = 1$
10. ≈ -2.414

Section 5.4

1. $\frac{7}{25}$
2. $\sin(t) = \frac{33}{65}$ $\cos(t) = \frac{56}{65}$ $\tan(t) = \frac{33}{56}$
  $\sec(t) = \frac{65}{56}$ $\csc(t) = \frac{65}{33}$ $\cot(t) = \frac{56}{33}$
3. $\sin\left(\frac{\pi}{4}\right) = \frac{\sqrt{2}}{2}$ $\cos\left(\frac{\pi}{4}\right) = \frac{\sqrt{2}}{2}$ $\tan\left(\frac{\pi}{4}\right) = 1$
  $\sec\left(\frac{\pi}{4}\right) = \sqrt{2}$ $\csc\left(\frac{\pi}{4}\right) = \sqrt{2}$ $\cot\left(\frac{\pi}{4}\right) = 1$
4. 2 **5.** Adjacent = 10; opposite = $10\sqrt{3}$; missing angle is $\frac{\pi}{6}$.
6. About 52 ft.

Chapter 6

Section 6.1

1. 6π **2.** $\frac{1}{2}$ compressed **3.** $\frac{\pi}{2}$; right
4. 2 units up **5.** Midline: $y = 0$; Amplitude: $|A| = \frac{1}{2}$;
Period: $P = \frac{2\pi}{|B|} = 6\pi$; Phase shift: $\frac{C}{B} = \pi$ **6.** $f(x) = \sin(x) + 2$
7. Two possibilities: $y = 4\sin\left(\frac{\pi}{5}x - \frac{\pi}{5}\right) + 4$ or
$y = -4\sin\left(\frac{\pi}{5}x + \frac{4\pi}{5}\right) + 4$
8.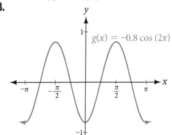

Midline: $y = 0$;
Amplitude: $|A| = 0.8$;
Period: $P = \frac{2\pi}{|B|} = \pi$;
Phase shift: $\frac{C}{B} = 0$ or none

9.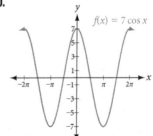

Midline: $y = 0$;
Amplitude: $|A| = 2$;
Period: $P = \frac{2\pi}{|B|} = 6$;
Phase shift: $\frac{C}{B} = -\frac{1}{2}$

10.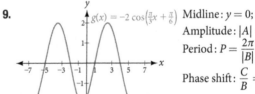

7

11.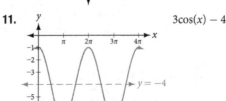

$3\cos(x) - 4$

Section 6.2

1.

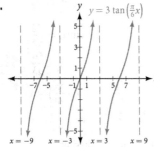

$y = 3 \tan\left(\frac{\pi}{6}x\right)$

$x = -9$ $x = -3$ $x = 3$ $x = 9$

2. It would be reflected across the line $y = -1$, becoming an increasing function.

3. $g(x) = 4\tan(2x)$

4.

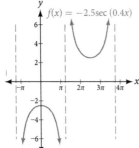

$f(x) = -2.5\sec(0.4x)$

This is a vertical reflection of the preceding graph because A is negative.

5.

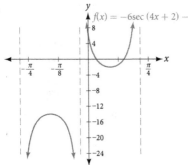

$f(x) = -6\sec(4x + 2) - 8$

6.

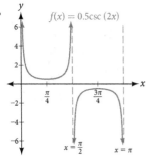

$f(x) = 0.5\csc(2x)$

$x = \frac{\pi}{2}$ $x = \pi$

7.

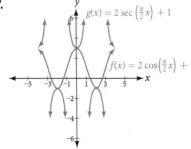

$g(x) = 2\sec\left(\frac{\pi}{2}x\right) + 1$

$f(x) = 2\cos\left(\frac{\pi}{2}x\right) + 1$

Section 6.3

1. $\arccos(0.8776) \approx 0.5$ **2. a.** $-\frac{\pi}{2}$ **b.** $-\frac{\pi}{4}$ **c.** π **d.** $\frac{\pi}{3}$

3. 1.9823 or 113.578°   **4.** $\sin^{-1}(0.6) = 36.87° = 0.6435$ radians

5. $\frac{\pi}{8}; \frac{2\pi}{9}$ **6.** $\frac{3\pi}{4}$ **7.** $\frac{12}{13}$ **8.** $\frac{4\sqrt{2}}{9}$ **9.** $\frac{4x}{\sqrt{16x^2 + 1}}$

Odd Answers for Chapters 1–6

CHAPTER 1

Section 1.1

1. A relation is a set of ordered pairs. A function is a special kind of relation in which no two ordered pairs have the same first coordinate.   **3.** When a vertical line intersects the graph of a relation more than once, that indicates that for that input there is more than one output. At any particular input value, there can be only one output if the relation is to be a function.   **5.** When a horizontal line intersects the graph of a function more than once, that indicates that for that output there is more than one input. A function is one-to-one if each output corresponds to only one input.

7. Function   **9.** Function   **11.** Function   **13.** Function
15. Function   **17.** Function   **19.** Function
21. Function   **23.** Function   **25.** Not a function
27. $f(-3) = -11, f(2) = -1, f(-a) = -2a - 5, -f(a) = -2a + 5,$ $f(a + h) = 2a + 2h - 5$ **29.** $f(-3) = \sqrt{5} + 5, f(2) = 5,$ $f(-a) = \sqrt{2 + a} + 5, -f(a) = -\sqrt{2 - a} - 5, f(a + h) =$ $\sqrt{2 - a - h} + 5$ **31.** $f(-3) = 2, f(2) = -2,$ $f(-a) = |-a - 1| - |-a + 1|, -f(a) = -|a - 1| + |a + 1|,$ $f(a + h) = |a + h - 1| - |a + h + 1|$

33. $\dfrac{g(x) - g(a)}{x - a} = x + a + 2, x \neq a$ **35. a.** $f(-2) = 14$ **b.** $x = 3$

37. a. $f(5) = 10$ **b.** $x = 4 \text{ or } -1$ **39. a.** $r = 6 - \dfrac{2}{3}t$

b. $f(-3) = 8$ **c.** $t = 6$ **41.** Not a function   **43.** Function
45. Function   **47.** Function   **49.** Function
51. Function   **53. a.** $f(0) = 1$ **b.** $f(x) = -3, x = -2 \text{ or } 2$
55. Not a function, not one-to-one   **57.** One-to-one function
59. Function, not one-to-one   **61.** Function   **63.** Function
65. Not a function   **67.** $f(x) = 1, x = 2$
69. $f(-2) = 14; f(-1) = 11; f(0) = 8; f(1) = 5; f(2) = 2$
71. $f(-2) = 4; f(-1) = 4.414; f(0) = 4.732; f(1) = 5; f(2) = 5.236$
73. $f(-2) = \dfrac{1}{9}; f(-1) = \dfrac{1}{3}; f(0) = 1; f(1) = 3; f(2) = 9$ **75.** 20

77. The range for this viewing window is [0, 100].

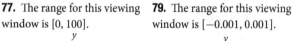
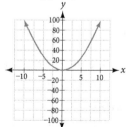

79. The range for this viewing window is [−0.001, 0.001].

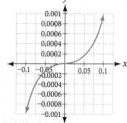

81. The range for this viewing window is [−1,000,000, 1,000,000].

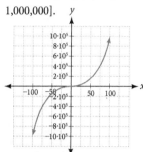

83. The range for this viewing window is [0, 10].

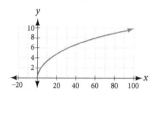

85. The range for this viewing window is [−0.1, 0.1].

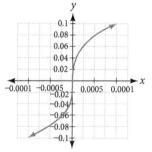

87. The range for this viewing window is [−100, 100].

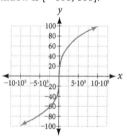

89. a. $g(5000) = 50$ **b.** The number of cubic yards of dirt required for a garden of 100 square feet is 1.   **91. a.** The height of the rocket above ground after 1 second is 200 ft.
b. The height of the rocket above ground after 2 seconds is 350 ft.

Section 1.2

1. The domain of a function depends upon what values of the independent variable make the function undefined or imaginary.
3. There is no restriction on x for $f(x) = \sqrt[3]{x}$ because you can take the cube root of any real number. So the domain is all real numbers, $(-\infty, \infty)$. When dealing with the set of real numbers, you cannot take the square root of negative numbers. So x-values are restricted for $f(x) = \sqrt{x}$ to nonnegative numbers and the domain is $[0, \infty)$.   **5.** Graph each formula of the piecewise function over its corresponding domain. Use the same scale for the x-axis and y-axis for each graph. Indicate included endpoints with a solid circle and excluded endpoints with an open circle. Use an arrow to indicate $-\infty$ or ∞. Combine the graphs to find the graph of the piecewise function.   **7.** $(-\infty, \infty)$ **9.** $(-\infty, 3]$
11. $(-\infty, \infty)$ **13.** $(-\infty, \infty)$ **15.** $\left(-\infty, -\dfrac{1}{2}\right) \cup \left(-\dfrac{1}{2}, \infty\right)$
17. $(-\infty, -11) \cup (-11, 2) \cup (2, \infty)$ **19.** $(-\infty, -3) \cup (-3, 5) \cup (5, \infty)$
21. $(-\infty, 5)$ **23.** $[6, \infty)$ **25.** $(-\infty, -9) \cup (-9, 9) \cup (9, \infty)$
27. domain: $(2, 8]$, range: $[6, 8)$ **29.** domain: $[-4, 4]$, range: $[0, 2]$
31. domain: $[-5, 3)$, range: $[0, 2]$ **33.** domain: $(-\infty, 1]$, range: $[0, \infty)$

35. domain: $\left[-6, -\frac{1}{6}\right] \cup \left[\frac{1}{6}, 6\right]$, range: $\left[-6, -\frac{1}{6}\right] \cup \left[\frac{1}{6}, 6\right]$

37. domain: $[-3, \infty)$, range is $[0, \infty)$

39. domain: $(-\infty, \infty)$ **41.** domain: $(-\infty, \infty)$

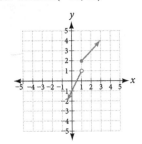   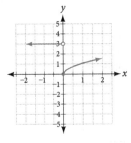

43. domain: $(-\infty, \infty)$ **45.** domain: $(-\infty, \infty)$

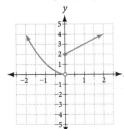   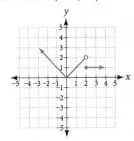

47. $f(-3) = 1; f(-2) = 0; f(-1) = 0; f(0) = 0$

49. $f(-1) = -4; f(0) = 6; f(2) = 20; f(4) = 34$

51. $f(-1) = -5; f(0) = 3; f(2) = 3; f(4) = 16$

53. $(-\infty, 1) \cup (1, \infty)$

55.

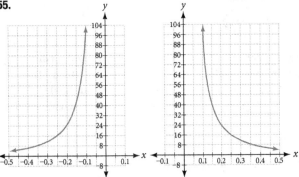

The viewing window: $[-0.5, -0.1]$ The viewing window: $[0.1, 0.5]$
has a range: $[4, 100]$.   has a range: $[4, 100]$.

57. $[0, 8]$ **59.** Many answers; one function is $f(x) = \frac{1}{\sqrt{x-2}}$.

61. a. The fixed cost is $500.   **b.** The cost of making 25 items is $750.   **c.** The domain is $[0, 100]$ and the range is $[500, 1500]$.

Section 1.3

1. Yes, the average rate of change of all linear functions is constant.

3. The absolute maximum and minimum relate to the entire graph, whereas the local extrema relate only to a specific region in an open interval.   **5.** $4(b + 1)$ **7.** 3   **9.** $4x + 2h$

11. $\frac{-1}{13(13 + h)}$ **13.** $3h^2 + 9h + 9$ **15.** $4x + 2h - 3$

7. $\frac{4}{3}$ **19.** Increasing on $(-\infty, -2.5) \cup (1, \infty)$ and decreasing on $(-2.5, 1)$ **21.** Increasing on $(-\infty, 1) \cup (3, 4)$ and decreasing on $(1, 3) \cup (4, \infty)$ **23.** Local maximum: $(-3, 50)$ and local minimum: $(3, 50)$

25. absolute maximum at approximately $(7, 150)$ and absolute minimum at approximately $(-7.5, -220)$

27. a. $-3,000$ people per year   **b.** $-1,250$ people per year

29. -4 **31.** 27   **33.** ≈ -0.167 **35.** local minimum: $(3, -22)$, decreasing on $(-\infty, 3)$, increasing on $(3, \infty)$

37. local minimum: $(-2, -2)$, decreasing on $(-3, -2)$, increasing on $(-2, \infty)$ **39.** local maximum: $(-0.5, 6)$, local minima: $(-3.25, -47)$ and $(2.1, -32)$, decreasing on $(-\infty, -3.25)$ and $(-0.5, 2.1)$, increasing on $(-3.25, -0.5)$ and $(2.1, \infty)$

41. A   **43.** $b = 5$ **45.** ≈ 2.7 gallons per minute

47. ≈ -0.6 milligrams per day

Section 1.4

1. Find the numbers that make the function in the denominator g equal to zero, and check for any other domain restrictions on f and g, such as an even-indexed root or zeros in the denominator.

3. Yes, sample answer: Let $f(x) = x + 1$ and $g(x) = x - 1$. Then $f(g(x)) = f(x - 1) = (x - 1) + 1 = x$ and $g(f(x)) = g(x + 1) = (x + 1) - 1 = x$ so $f \circ g = g \circ f$.

5. $(f + g)(x) = 2x + 6$; domain: $(-\infty, \infty)$
$(f - g)(x) = 2x^2 + 2x - 6$; domain: $(-\infty, \infty)$
$(fg)(x) = -x^4 - 2x^3 + 6x^2 + 12x$; domain: $(-\infty, \infty)$
$\left(\frac{f}{g}\right)(x) = \frac{x^2 + 2x}{6 - x^2}$; domain: $(-\infty, -\sqrt{6}) \cup (-\sqrt{6}, \sqrt{6}) \cup (\sqrt{6}, \infty)$

7. $(f + g)(x) = \frac{4x^3 + 8x^2 + 1}{2x}$; domain: $(-\infty, 0) \cup (0, \infty)$
$(f - g)(x) = \frac{4x^3 + 8x^2 - 1}{2x}$; domain: $(-\infty, 0) \cup (0, \infty)$
$(fg)(x) = x + 2$; domain: $(-\infty, 0) \cup (0, \infty)$
$\left(\frac{f}{g}\right)(x) = 4x^3 + 8x^2$; domain: $(-\infty, 0) \cup (0, \infty)$

9. $(f + g)(x) = 3x^2 + \sqrt{x - 5}$; domain: $[5, \infty)$
$(f - g)(x) = 3x^2 - \sqrt{x - 5}$; domain: $[5, \infty)$
$(fg)(x) = 3x^2\sqrt{x - 5}$; domain: $[5, \infty)$
$\left(\frac{f}{g}\right)(x) = \frac{3x^2}{\sqrt{x - 5}}$; domain: $(5, \infty)$ **11. a.** $f(g(2)) = 3$

b. $f(g(x)) = 18x^2 - 60x + 51$ **c.** $g(f(x)) = 6x^2 - 2$

d. $(g \circ g)(x) = 9x - 20$ **e.** $(f \circ f)(-2) = 163$

13. $f(g(x)) = \sqrt{x^2 + 3} + 2$; $g(f(x)) = x + 4\sqrt{x} + 7$

15. $f(g(x)) = \frac{\sqrt[3]{x + 1}}{x}$; $g(f(x)) = \frac{\sqrt[3]{x} + 1}{x}$

17. $f(g(x)) = \frac{x}{2}, x \neq 0$; $g(f(x)) = 2x - 4, x \neq 4$

19. $f(g(h(x))) = \frac{1}{(x + 3)^2} + 1$

21. a. $(g \circ f)(x) = -\frac{3}{\sqrt{2 - 4x}}$ **b.** $\left(-\infty, \frac{1}{2}\right)$

23. a. $(0, 2) \cup (2, \infty)$ except $x = -2$ **b.** $(0, \infty)$ **c.** $(0, \infty)$ **25.** $(1, \infty)$

27. Many solutions; one possible answer: $f(x) = x^3; g(x) = x - 5$

29. Many solutions; one possible answer: $f(x) = \frac{4}{x}; g(x) = (x + 2)^2$

31. Many solutions; one possible answer: $f(x) = \sqrt[3]{x}; g(x) = \frac{1}{2x - 3}$

33. Many solutions; one possible answer: $f(x) = \sqrt[4]{x}; g(x) = \frac{3x - 2}{x + 5}$

35. Many solutions; one possible answer: $f(x) = \sqrt{x}; g(x) = 2x + 6$

37. Many solutions; one possible answer: $f(x) = \sqrt[3]{x}; g(x) = x - 1$

39. Many solutions; one possible answer: $f(x) = x^3; g(x) = \frac{1}{x - 2}$

41. Many solutions; one possible answer: $f(x) = \sqrt{x}$; $g(x) = \dfrac{2x-1}{3x+4}$

43. 2   **45.** 5   **47.** 4   **49.** 0   **51.** 2   **53.** 1

55. 4   **57.** 4   **59.** 9   **61.** 4   **63.** 2   **65.** 3

67. 11   **69.** 0   **71.** 7   **73.** $f(g(0)) = 27, g(f(0)) = -94$

75. $f(g(0)) = \dfrac{1}{5}, g(f(0)) = 5$ **77.** $f(g(x)) = 18x^2 + 60x + 51$

79. $g \circ g(x) = 9x + 20$ **81.** $(f \circ g)(x) = 2, (g \circ f)(x) = 2$

83. $(-\infty, \infty)$ **85.** False   **87.** $(f \circ g)(6) = 6; (g \circ f)(6) = 6$

89. $(f \circ g)(11) = 11; (g \circ f)(11) = 11$ **91.** C

93. $A(t) = \pi(25\sqrt{t+2})^2$ and $A(2) = \pi(25\sqrt{4})^2 = 2{,}500\pi$ square inches   **95.** $A(5) = 121\pi$ square units

97. a. $N(T(t)) = 575t^2 + 65t - 31.25$ **b.** ≈ 3.38 hours

Section 1.5

1. A horizontal shift results when a constant is added to or subtracted from the input. A vertical shift results when a constant is added to or subtracted from the output.   **3.** A horizontal compression results when a constant greater than 1 multiplies the input. A vertical compression results when a constant between 0 and 1 multiplies the output.   **5.** For a function f, substitute $(-x)$ for (x) in $f(x)$ and simplify. If the resulting function is the same as the original function, $f(-x) = f(x)$, then the function is even. If the resulting function is the opposite of the original function, $f(-x) = -f(x)$, then the original function is odd. If the function is not the same or the opposite, then the function is neither odd nor even.   **7.** $g(x) = |x - 1| - 3$

9. $g(x) = \dfrac{1}{(x+4)^2} + 2$ **11.** The graph of $f(x + 43)$ is a horizontal shift to the left 43 units of the graph of f.

13. The graph of $f(x - 4)$ is a horizontal shift to the right 4 units of the graph of f.   **15.** The graph of $f(x) + 8$ is a vertical shift up 8 units of the graph of f.   **17.** The graph of $f(x) - 7$ is a vertical shift down 7 units of the graph of f.   **19.** The graph of $f(x + 4) - 1$ is a horizontal shift to the left 4 units and a vertical shift down 1 unit of the graph of f.   **21.** Decreasing on $(-\infty, -3)$ and increasing on $(-3, \infty)$ **23.** Decreasing on $(0, \infty)$

25.

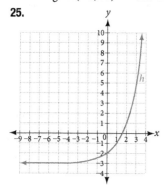

27.

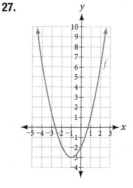

29.

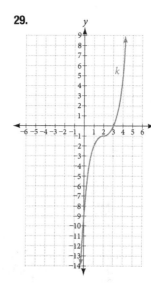

31. $g(x) = f(x - 1)$, $h(x) = f(x) + 1$

33. $f(x) = |x - 3| - 2$

35. $f(x) = \sqrt{x + 3} - 1$

37. $f(x) = (x - 2)^2$

39. $f(x) = |x + 3| - 2$

41. $f(x) = -\sqrt{x}$

43. $f(x) = -(x + 1)^2 + 2$

45. $f(x) = \sqrt{-x} + 1$

47. Even   **49.** Odd

51. Even   **53.** The graph of g is a vertical reflection (across the x-axis) of the graph of f.   **55.** The graph of g is a vertical stretch by a factor of 4 of the graph of f.

57. The graph of g is a horizontal compression by a factor of $\dfrac{1}{5}$ of the graph of f.   **59.** The graph of g is a horizontal stretch by a factor of 3 of the graph of f.   **61.** The graph of g is a horizontal reflection across the y-axis and a vertical stretch by a factor of 3 of the graph of f.   **63.** $g(x) = |-4x|$

65. $g(x) = \dfrac{1}{3(x+2)^2} - 3$ **67.** $g(x) = \dfrac{1}{2}(x - 5)^2 + 1$

69. This is a parabola shifted to the left 1 unit, stretched vertically by a factor of 4, and shifted down 5 units.

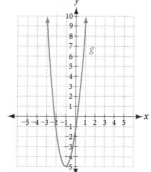

71. This is an absolute value function stretched vertically by a factor of 2, shifted 4 units to the right, reflected across the horizontal axis, and then shifted 3 units up.

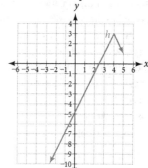

73. This is a cubic function compressed vertically by a factor of $\dfrac{1}{2}$.

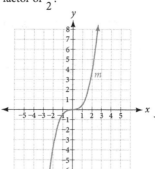

75. The graph of the function is stretched horizontally by a factor of 3 and then shifted downward by 3 units.

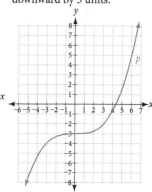

77. The graph of $f(x) = \sqrt{x}$ is shifted right 4 units and then reflected across the y-axis.

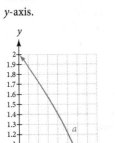

79.

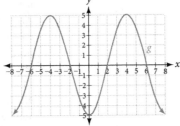

81.

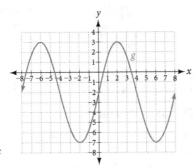

41.

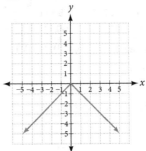

43.

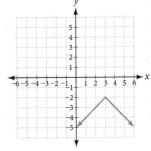

45.

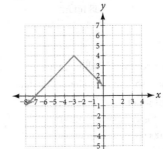

47.

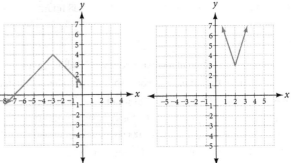

49.

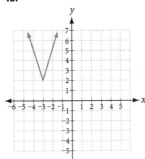

51.

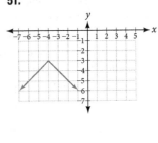

Section 1.6

1. Isolate the absolute value term so that the equation is of the form $|A| = B$. Form one equation by setting the expression inside the absolute value symbol, A, equal to the expression on the other side of the equation, B. Form a second equation by setting A equal to the opposite of the expression on the other side of the equation, $-B$. Solve each equation for the variable.   **3.** The graph of the absolute value function does not cross the x-axis, so the graph is either completely above or completely below the x-axis.   **5.** First determine the boundary points by finding the solution(s) of the equation. Use the boundary points to form possible solution intervals. Choose a test value in each interval to determine which values satisfy the inequality.   **7.** $|x + 4| = \dfrac{1}{2}$

9. $|f(x) - 8| < 0.03$ **11.** $\{1, 11\}$ **13.** $\left\{-\dfrac{9}{4}, \dfrac{13}{4}\right\}$

15. $\left\{\dfrac{10}{3}, \dfrac{20}{3}\right\}$ **17.** $\left\{\dfrac{11}{5}, \dfrac{29}{5}\right\}$ **19.** $\left\{\dfrac{5}{2}, \dfrac{7}{2}\right\}$

21. No solution   **23.** $\{-57, 27\}$ **25.** $(0, -8); (-6, 0)$ and $(4, 0)$

27. $(0, -7)$; no x-intercepts.   **29.** $(-\infty, -8) \cup (12, \infty)$

31. $\left[-\dfrac{4}{3}, 4\right]$ **33.** $\left(-\infty, -\dfrac{8}{3}\right] \cup [6, \infty)$ **35.** $\left(-\infty, -\dfrac{8}{3}\right] \cup [16, \infty)$

37.

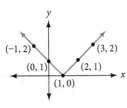

39.

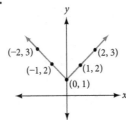

53. range: $[0, 20]$

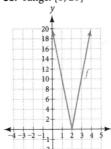

55.

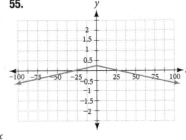

57. $(-\infty, \infty)$ **59.** There is no value for a that will keep the function from having a y-intercept. The absolute value function always crosses the y-intercept when $x = 0$.

61. $|p - 0.08| \leq 0.015$ **63.** $|x - 5.0| \leq 0.01$

SECTION 1.7

1. Each output of a function must have exactly one input for the function to be one-to-one. If any horizontal line crosses the graph of a function more than once, that means that y-values repeat and the function is not one-to-one. If no horizontal line crosses the graph of the function more than once, then no y-values repeat and the function is one-to-one.

3. Yes. For example, $f(x) = \frac{1}{x}$ is its own inverse.   **5.** $y = f^{-1}(x)$

7. $f^{-1}(x) = x - 3$ **9.** $f^{-1}(x) = 2 - x$ **11.** $f^{-1}(x) = -\frac{2x}{x-1}$

13. Domain of $f(x)$: $[-7, \infty)$; $f^{-1}(x) = \sqrt{x} - 7$

15. Domain of $f(x)$: $[0, \infty)$; $f^{-1}(x) = \sqrt{x+5}$

17. $f(g(x)) = x$ and $g(f(x)) = x$ **19.** One-to-one

21. One-to-one   **23.** Not one-to-one   **25.** 3   **27.** 2

29.

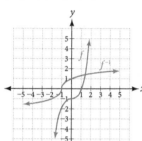

31. $[2, 10]$ **33.** 6

35. -4 **37.** 0   **39.** 1

41.

x	1	4	7	12	16
$f^{-1}(x)$	3	6	9	13	14

43. $f^{-1}(x) = (1 + x)^{\frac{1}{3}}$ **45.** $f^{-1}(x) = \frac{5}{9}(x - 32)$

47. $t(d) = \frac{d}{50}$; $t(180) = \frac{180}{50}$. The time for the car to travel 180 miles is 3.6 hours.

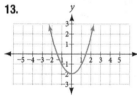

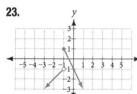

41. $(f \circ g)(x) = \frac{1}{\sqrt{x}}$; Domain: $(0, \infty)$

43. Many solutions; one possible answer: $g(x) = \frac{2x - 1}{3x + 4}$ and $f(x) = \sqrt{x}$.

45.

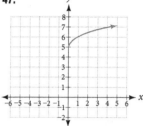

47.

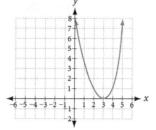

49.

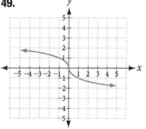

51.

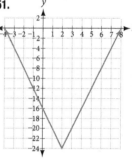

53.

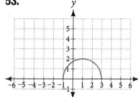

55. $f(x) = |x - 3|$

57. Even   **59.** Odd

61. Even

63. $f(x) = \frac{1}{2}|x + 2| + 1$

65. $f(x) = -3|x - 3| + 3$

67.

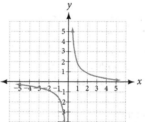

69. $\{-22, 14\}$

71. $\left(-\frac{5}{3}, 3\right)$

73. $f^{-1}(x) = \frac{x - 9}{10}$

75. $f^{-1}(x) = \sqrt{x - 1}$

Chapter 1 Review Exercises

1. Function   **3.** Not a function   **5.** $f(-3) = -27$; $f(2) = -2$;
$f(-a) = -2a^2 - 3a$; $-f(a) = 2a^2 - 3a$;
$f(a + h) = -2a^2 - 4ah - 2h^2 + 3a + 3h$

7. One-to-one   **9.** Function   **11.** Function

13.

15. 2   **17.** -1.8 or 1.8

19. $\dfrac{-64 + 80a - 16a^2}{-1 + a}$
$= -16a + 64$; $a \neq 1$

21. $(-\infty, -2) \cup (-2, 6) \cup (6, \infty)$

23.

25. 31

27. Increasing on $(2, \infty)$, decreasing on $(-\infty, 2)$

29. Increasing on $(-3, 1)$, constant on $(-\infty, -3)$ and $(1, \infty)$

31. Local minimum: $(-2, -3)$; local maximum: $(1, 3)$

33. Absolute maximum: 10

35. $(f \circ g)(x) = 17 - 18x$, $(g \circ f)(x) = -7 - 18x$

37. $(f \circ g)(x) = \sqrt{\frac{1}{x} + 2}$; $(g \circ f)(x) = \frac{1}{\sqrt{x+2}}$

39. $(f \circ g)(x) = \dfrac{\frac{1}{\frac{1}{x}+1}}{\frac{1}{\frac{1}{x}+4}} = \dfrac{1+x}{1+4x}$; Domain: $\left(-\infty, -\frac{1}{4}\right) \cup \left(-\frac{1}{4}, 0\right) \cup (0, \infty)$

77. The function is one-to-one.   **79.** 5

Chapter 1 Practice Test

1. Relation is a function   **3.** -16 **5.** The graph is a parabola and the graph fails the horizontal line test.

7. $2a^2 - a$ **9.** $-2(a + b) + 1$; $b \neq a$ **11.** $\sqrt{2}$

13.

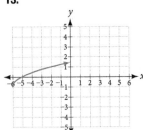

15. Even　　**17.** Odd

19. $\{-7, 10\}$

21. $f^{-1}(x) = \dfrac{x+5}{3}$

23. $(-\infty, -1.1)$ and $(1.1, \infty)$

25. $(1.1, -0.9)$　　**27.** $f(2) = 2$

29. $f(x) = \begin{cases} |x| & \text{if } x \le 2 \\ 3 & \text{if } x > 2 \end{cases}$

31. $x = 2$　　**33.** Yes

35. $f^{-1}(x) = -\dfrac{x-11}{2}$ or $\dfrac{11-x}{2}$

CHAPTER 2

Section 2.1

1. Terry starts at an elevation of 3,000 feet and descends 70 feet per second　　**3.** 3 miles per hour　　**5.** $d(t) = 100 - 10t$

7. Yes　　**9.** No　　**11.** No　　**13.** No　　**15.** Increasing

17. Decreasing　　**19.** Decreasing　　**21.** Increasing

23. Decreasing　　**25.** 3　　**27.** $-\dfrac{1}{3}$　　**29.** $\dfrac{4}{5}$

31. $y = -\dfrac{1}{2}x + \dfrac{7}{2}$　　**33.** $y = 2x + 3$　　**35.** $y = -\dfrac{1}{3}x + \dfrac{22}{3}$

37. $y = \dfrac{4}{5}x + 4$　　**39.** $-\dfrac{5}{4}$　　**41.** $y = \dfrac{2}{3}x + 1$　　**43.** $y = -2x + 3$

45. $y = 3$　　**47.** Linear, $g(x) = -3x + 5$

49. Linear, $f(x) = 5x - 5$　　**51.** Linear, $g(x) = -\dfrac{25}{2}x + 6$

53. Linear, $f(x) = 10x - 24$　　**55.** $f(x) = -58x + 17.3$

59. a. $a = 11,900, b = 1001.1$

b. $q(p) = 1000p - 100$

57.

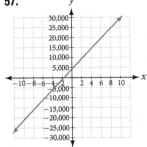

61.

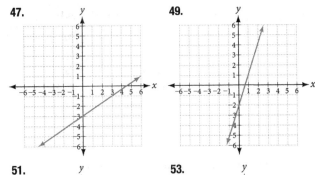

63. $x = -\dfrac{16}{3}$　　**65.** $x = a$

67. $y = \dfrac{d}{c-a}x - \dfrac{ad}{c-a}$

69. $45 per training session

71. The rate of change is 0.1. For every additional minute talked, the monthly charge increases by $0.1 or 10 cents. The initial value is 24. When there are no minutes talked, initially the charge is $24.

73. The slope is -400. this means for every year between 1960 and 1989, the population dropped by 400 per year in the city.

75. C

Section 2.2

1. The slopes are equal; y-intercepts are not equal.　　**3.** The point of intersection is (a, a). This is because for the horizontal line, all of the y-coordinates are a and for the vertical line, all of the x coordinates are a. The point of intersection is on both lines and therefore will have these two characteristics.

5. First, find the slope of the linear function. Then take the negative reciprocal of the slope; this is the slope of the perpendicular line. Substitute the slope of the perpendicular line and the coordinate of the given point into the equation $y = mx + b$ and solve for b. Then write the equation of the line in the form $y = mx + b$ by substituting in m and b.　　**7.** Neither

9. Perpendicular　　**11.** Parallel　　**13.** $(-2, 0), (0, 4)$

15. $\left(\dfrac{1}{5}, 0\right), (0, 1)$　　**17.** $(8, 0), (0, 28)$

19. Line 1: $m = 8$, Line 2: $m = -6$, neither

21. Line 1: $m = -\dfrac{1}{2}$, Line 2: $m = 2$, perpendicular

23. Line 1: $m = -2$, Line 2: $m = -2$, parallel

25. $g(x) = 3x - 3$　　**27.** $p(t) = -\dfrac{1}{3}t + 2$　　**29.** $(-2, 1)$

31. $\left(-\dfrac{17}{5}, \dfrac{5}{3}\right)$　　**33.** F　　**35.** C　　**37.** A

39.　　**41.**

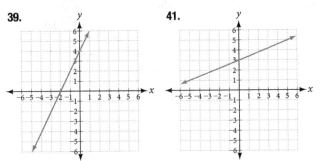

43.　　**45.**

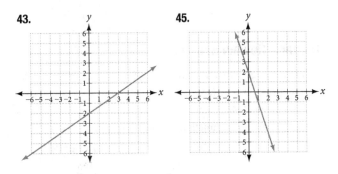

47.　　**49.**

51.　　**53.**

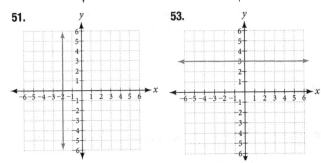

55. **57.**

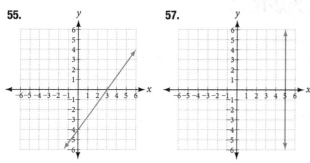

59. a. $g(x) = 0.75x - 5.5$ **b.** 0.75 **c.** $(0, -5.5)$

61. $y = 3$ **63.** $x = -3$ **65.** no point of intersection

67. $(2, 7)$ **69.** $(-10, -5)$ **71.** $y = 100x - 98$

73. $x < \dfrac{1999}{201}, x > \dfrac{1999}{201}$ **75.** Greater than 3,000 texts

Section 2.3

1. Determine the independent variable. This is the variable upon which the output depends. **3.** To determine the initial value, find the output when the input is equal to zero. **5.** 6 square units. **7.** 20.012 square units **9.** 2,300 **11.** 64,170 **13.** $P(t) = 2500t + 75,000$ **15.** $(-30, 0)$ 30 years before the start of this model, the town has no citizens. $(0, 75,000)$ Initially, the town had a population of 75,000. **17.** Ten years after the model began. **19.** $W(t) = 0.5t + 7.5$ **21.** $(-15, 0)$ The x-intercept is not a plausible set of data for this model because it means the baby weighed 0 pounds 15 months prior to birth. $(0, 7.5)$ the baby weighed 7.5 pounds at birth. **23.** At age 5.8 months **25.** $C(t) = 12,025 - 205t$ **27.** $(58.7, 0)$ In 58.7 years, the number of people afflicted with the common cold would be zero $(0, 12,025)$ Initially, 12,025 people were afflicted with the common cold **29.** 2063 **31.** $y = -2t + 180$ **33.** In 2070, the company's profits will be zero **35.** $y = 30t - 300$ **37.** $(10, 0)$ In the year 1990, the company's profits were zero **39.** Hawaii **41.** During the year 1933 **43.** $105,620 **45. a.** 696 people **b.** 4 years **c.** 174 people per year **d.** 305 people **e.** $P(t) = 305 + 174t$ **f.** 2,219 people **47. a.** $C(x) = 0.15x + 10$ **b.** The flat monthly fee is $10 and there is a $0.15 fee for each additional minute used **c.** $113.05 **49. a.** $P(t) = 190t + 4,360$ **b.** 6,640 moose **51. a.** $R(t) = -2.1t + 16$ **b.** 5.5 billion cubic feet **c.** During the year 2017 **53.** More than 133 minutes **55.** More than $42,857.14 worth of jewelry **57.** More than $66,666.67 in sales

Section 2.4

1. When our model no longer applies, after some value in the domain, the model itself doesn't hold. **3.** We predict a value outside the domain and range of the data. **5.** The closer the number is to 1, the less scattered the data, the closer the number is to 0, the more scattered the data. **7.** 61.966 years

9. No

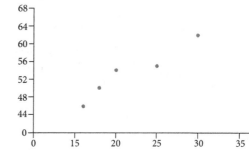

11. No

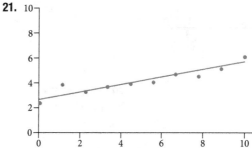

13. Interpolation, about 60° F **15.** C **17.** B

19.

21.

23. Yes, trend appears linear; during 2016
25. $y = 1.640x + 13.800, r = 0.987$ **27.** $y = -0.962x + 26.86, r = -0.965$ **29.** $y = -1.981x + 60.197; r = -0.998$
31. $y = 0.121x - 38.841, r = 0.998$ **33.** $(-2, -6), (1, -12), (5, -20), (6, -22), (9, -28)$ **35.** $(189.8, 0)$ If the company sells 18,980 units, its profits will be zero dollars
37. $y = 0.00587x + 1985.41$ **39.** $y = 20.25x - 671.5$
41. $y = -10.75x + 742.50$

Chapter 2 Review Exercises

1. Yes   **3.** Increasing   **5.** $y = -3x + 26$ **7.** 3
9. $y = 2x - 2$ **11.** Not linear   **13.** Parallel   **15.** $(-9, 0); (0, -7)$
17. Line 1: $m -2$, Line 2: $m = -2$, parallel   **19.** $y = -0.2x + 21$

21.

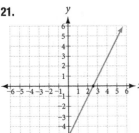

23. More than 250
25. 118,000
27. $y = -300x + 11,500$
29. a. 800   **b.** 100 students per year   **c.** $P(t) = 100t + 1700$
31. 18,500   **33.** $y = \$91,625$

35. Extrapolation

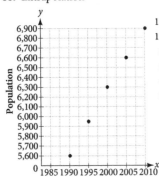

37.

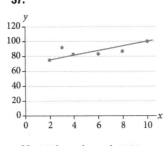

39. Midway through 2023
41. $y = -1.294x + 49.412$; $r = -0.974$
43. Early in 2027
45. 7,660

Chapter 2 Practice Test

1. Yes   **3.** Increasing   **5.** $y = -1.5x - 6$ **7.** $y = -2x - 1$
9. No   **11.** perpendicular   **13.** $(-7, 0); (0, -2)$
15. $y = -0.25x + 12$

17. Slope $= -1$ and y-intercept $= 6$

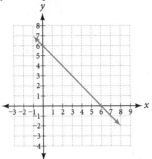

19. 150   **21.** 165,000
23. $y = 875x + 10,625$
25. a. 375   **b.** dropped an average of 46.875, or about 47 people per year
c. $y = -46.875t + 1250$

27.

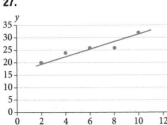

29. Early in 2018
31. $y = 0.00455x + 1979.5$
33. $r = 0.999$

CHAPTER 3

Section 3.1

1. Add the real parts together and the imaginary parts together.
3. i times i equals -1, which is not imaginary. (answers vary)
5. $-8 + 2i$ **7.** $14 + 7i$ **9.** $-\dfrac{23}{29} + \dfrac{15}{29}i$ **11.** 2 real and 0 nonreal

13.

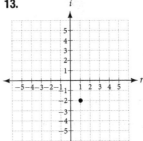

15.

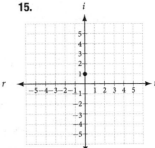

17. $8 - i$ **19.** $-11 + 4i$ **21.** $2 - 5i$ **23.** $6 + 15i$
25. $-16 + 32i$ **27.** $-4 - 7i$ **29.** 25   **31.** $2 - \dfrac{2}{3}i$
33. $4 - 6i$ **35.** $\dfrac{2}{5} + \dfrac{11}{5}i$ **37.** $15i$ **39.** $1 + i\sqrt{3}$
41. 1   **43.** -1 **45.** $128i$ **47.** $\left(\dfrac{\sqrt{3}}{2} + \dfrac{1}{2}i\right)^6 = -1$
49. $3i$ **51.** 0   **53.** $5 - 5i$ **55.** $-2i$ **57.** $\dfrac{9}{2} - \dfrac{9}{2}i$

Section 3.2

1. When written in that form, the vertex can be easily identified.
3. If $a = 0$ then the function becomes a linear function.
5. If possible, we can use factoring. Otherwise, we can use the quadratic formula.   **7.** $g(x) = (x + 1)^2 - 4$; vertex: $(-1, -4)$
9. $f(x) = \left(x + \dfrac{5}{2}\right)^2 - \dfrac{33}{4}$; vertex: $\left(-\dfrac{5}{2}, -\dfrac{33}{4}\right)$
11. $k(x) = 3(x - 1)^2 - 12$; vertex: $(1, -12)$
13. $f(x) = 3\left(x - \dfrac{5}{6}\right)^2 - \dfrac{37}{12}$; vertex: $\left(\dfrac{5}{6}, -\dfrac{37}{12}\right)$
15. Minimum is $-\dfrac{17}{2}$ and occurs at $\dfrac{5}{2}$; axis of symmetry: $x = \dfrac{5}{2}$
17. Minimum is $-\dfrac{17}{16}$ and occurs at $-\dfrac{1}{8}$; axis of symmetry: $x = -\dfrac{1}{8}$
19. Minimum is $-\dfrac{7}{2}$ and occurs at -3; axis of symmetry: $x = -3$
21. Domain: $(-\infty, \infty)$; range: $[2, \infty)$ **23.** Domain: $(-\infty, \infty)$; range: $[-5, \infty)$ **25.** Domain: $(-\infty, \infty)$; range: $[-12, \infty)$
27. $\left\{2i\sqrt{2}, -2i\sqrt{2}\right\}$ **29.** $\left\{3i\sqrt{3}, -3i\sqrt{3}\right\}$
31. $\{2 + i, 2 - i\}$ **33.** $\{2 + 3i, 2 - 3i\}$ **35.** $\{5 + i, 5 - i\}$
37. $\left\{2 + 2\sqrt{6}, 2 - 2\sqrt{6}\right\}$ **39.** $\left\{-\dfrac{1}{2} + \dfrac{3}{2}i, -\dfrac{1}{2} - \dfrac{3}{2}i\right\}$
41. $\left\{-\dfrac{3}{5} + \dfrac{1}{5}i, -\dfrac{3}{5} - \dfrac{1}{5}i\right\}$ **43.** $\left\{-\dfrac{1}{2} + \dfrac{1}{2}i\sqrt{7}, -\dfrac{1}{2} - \dfrac{1}{2}i\sqrt{7}\right\}$
45. $f(x) = x^2 - 4x + 4$ **47.** $f(x) = x^2 + 1$
49. $f(x) = \dfrac{6}{49}x^2 + \dfrac{60}{49}x + \dfrac{297}{49}$ **51.** $f(x) = -x^2 + 1$

53. Vertex: $(1, -1)$, axis of symmetry: $x = 1$, intercepts: $(0, 0)$, $(2, 0)$

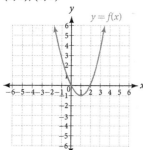

55. Vertex: $\left(\dfrac{5}{2}, -\dfrac{49}{4}\right)$, axis of symmetry: $x = \dfrac{5}{2}$, intercepts: $(6, 0)$, $(-1, 0)$

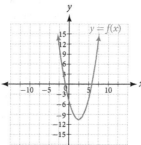

51. y-intercept: $(0, 0)$; x-intercepts: $(0, 0)$ and $(2, 0)$; as $x \to -\infty, f(x) \to \infty$, as $x \to \infty, f(x) \to \infty$

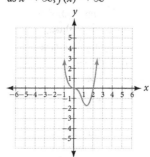

53. y-intercept: $(0, 0)$; x-intercepts: $(0, 0)$, $(5, 0)$, $(7, 0)$; as $x \to -\infty, f(x) \to -\infty$, as $x \to \infty, f(x) \to \infty$

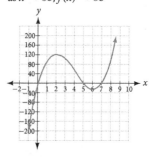

57. Vertex: $\left(\dfrac{5}{4}, -\dfrac{39}{8}\right)$, axis of symmetry: $x = \dfrac{5}{4}$, intercept: $(0, -8)$

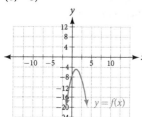

59. $f(x) = x^2 - 4x + 1$
61. $f(x) = -2x^2 + 8x - 1$
63. $f(x) = \dfrac{1}{2}x^2 - 3x + \dfrac{7}{2}$
65. $f(x) = x^2 + 1$
67. $f(x) = 2 - x^2$
69. $f(x) = 2x^2$
71. The graph is shifted up or down (a vertical shift).
73. 50 feet

55. y-intercept: $(0, 0)$; x-intercepts: $(-4, 0)$, $(0, 0)$, $(4, 0)$; as $x \to -\infty, f(x) \to -\infty$, as $x \to \infty, f(x) \to \infty$

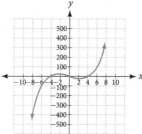

57. y-intercept: $(0, -81)$; x-intercepts: $(-3, 0)$, and $(3, 0)$; as $x \to -\infty, f(x) \to \infty$, as $x \to \infty, f(x) \to \infty$

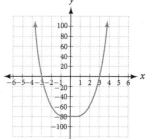

75. Domain: $(-\infty, \infty)$; range: $[-2, \infty)$
77. Domain: $(-\infty, \infty)$; range: $(-\infty, 11]$　　**79.** $f(x) = 2x^2 - 1$
81. $f(x) = 3x^2 - 9$　　**83.** $f(x) = 5x^2 - 77$
85. 50 feet by 50 feet　　**87.** 125 feet by 62.5 feet
89. 6 and -6; product is -36　　**91.** 2909.56 meters　　**93.** \$10.70

Section 3.3

1. The coefficient of the power function is the real number that is multiplied by the variable raised to a power. The degree is the highest power appearing in the function.　　**3.** As x decreases without bound, so does $f(x)$. As x increases without bound, so does $f(x)$.　　**5.** The polynomial function is of even degree and leading coefficient is negative.　　**7.** Power function　　**9.** Neither
11. Neither　　**13.** Degree: 2, coefficient: -2　　**15.** Degree: 4, coefficient: -2　　**17.** As $x \to \infty, f(x) \to \infty$, as $x \to -\infty, f(x) \to \infty$
19. As $x \to -\infty, f(x) \to -\infty$, as $x \to \infty, f(x) \to -\infty$
21. As $x \to -\infty, f(x) \to -\infty$, as $x \to \infty, f(x) \to -\infty$
23. As $x \to \infty, f(x) \to \infty$, as $x \to -\infty, f(x) \to -\infty$
25. y-intercept is $(0, 12)$, t-intercepts are $(1, 0)$, $(-2, 0)$, and $(3, 0)$
27. y-intercept is $(0, -16)$, x-intercepts are $(2, 0)$, and $(-2, 0)$
29. y-intercept is $(0, 0)$, x-intercepts are $(0, 0)$, $(4, 0)$, and $(-2, 0)$
31. 3　　**33.** 5　　**35.** 3　　**37.** 5　　**39.** Yes, 2 turning points, least possible degree: 3　　**41.** Yes, 1 turning point, least possible degree: 2　　**43.** Yes, 0 turning points, least possible degree: 1
45. Yes, 0 turning points, least possible degree: 1

47. As $x \to -\infty, f(x) \to \infty$, as $x \to \infty, f(x) \to \infty$

x	$f(x)$
10	9,500
100	99,950,000
-10	9,500
-100	99,950,000

49. As $x \to -\infty, f(x) \to \infty$, as $x \to \infty, f(x) \to -\infty$

x	$f(x)$
10	-504
100	$-941,094$
-10	1,716
-100	1,061,106

59. y-intercept: $(0, 0)$; x-intercepts: $(-3, 0)$, $(0, 0)$, $(5, 0)$; as $x \to -\infty, f(x) \to -\infty$, as $x \to \infty, f(x) \to \infty$

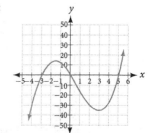

61. $f(x) = x^2 - 4$
63. $f(x) = x^3 - 4x^2 + 4x$
65. $f(x) = x^4 + 1$
67. $V(m) = 8m^3 + 36m^2 + 54m + 27$
69. $V(x) = 4x^3 - 32x^2 + 64x$

Section 3.4

1. The x-intercept is where the graph of the function crosses the x-axis, and the zero of the function is the input value for which $f(x) = 0$.　　**3.** If we evaluate the function at a and at b and the sign of the function value changes, then we know a zero exists between a and b.　　**5.** There will be a factor raised to an even power.　　**7.** $(-2, 0)$, $(3, 0)$, $(-5, 0)$　　**9.** $(3, 0)$, $(-1, 0)$, $(0, 0)$
11. $(0, 0)$, $(-5, 0)$, $(2, 0)$　　**13.** $(0, 0)$, $(-5, 0)$, $(4, 0)$
15. $(2, 0)$, $(-2, 0)$, $(-1, 0)$　　**17.** $(-2, 0)$, $(2, 0)$, $\left(\dfrac{1}{2}, 0\right)$
19. $(1, 0)$, $(-1, 0)$　　**21.** $(0, 0)$, $\left(\sqrt{3}, 0\right)$, $\left(-\sqrt{3}, 0\right)$
23. $(0, 0)$, $(1, 0)$, $(-1, 0)$, $(2, 0)$, $(-2, 0)$
25. $f(2) = -10, f(4) = 28$; sign change confirms
27. $f(1) = 3, f(3) = -77$; sign change confirms
29. $f(0.01) = 1.000001, f(0.1) = -7.999$; sign change confirms
31. 0 with multiplicity 2, $-\dfrac{3}{2}$ multiplicity 5, 4 multiplicity 2
33. 0 with multiplicity 2, -2 with multiplicity 2
35. $-\dfrac{2}{3}$ with multiplicity 5, 5 with multiplicity 2

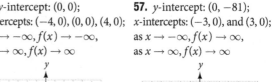

37. 0 with multiplicity 4, 2 with multiplicity 1, −1 with multiplicity 1

39. $\frac{3}{2}$ with multiplicity 2, 0 with multiplicity 3   **41.** 0 with multiplicity 6, $\frac{2}{3}$ with multiplicity 2

43. x-intercept: $(1, 0)$ with multiplicity 2, $(−4, 0)$ with multiplicity 1; y-intercept: $(0, 4)$; as $x \to −\infty$, $g(x) \to −\infty$, as $x \to \infty$, $g(x) \to \infty$

45. x-intercept: $(3, 0)$ with multiplicity 3, $(2, 0)$ with multiplicity 2; y-intercept: $(0, −108)$; as $x \to −\infty$, $k(x) \to −\infty$, as $x \to \infty$, $k(x) \to \infty$

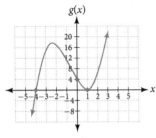

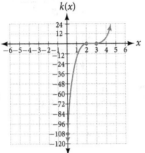

47. x-intercepts: $(0, 0)$, $(−2, 0)$, $(4, 0)$ with multiplicity 1; y-intercept: $(0, 0)$; as $x \to −\infty$, $n(x) \to \infty$, as $x \to \infty$, $n(x) \to −\infty$

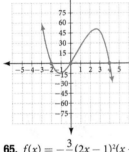

49. $f(x) = −\frac{2}{9}(x − 3)(x + 1)(x + 3)$

51. $f(x) = \frac{1}{4}(x + 2)^2(x − 3)$

53. $−4, −2, 1, 3$ with multiplicity 1

55. $−2, 3$ each with multiplicity 2

57. $f(x) = −\frac{2}{3}(x + 2)(x − 1)(x − 3)$

59. $f(x) = \frac{1}{3}(x − 3)^2(x − 1)^2(x + 3)$

61. $f(x) = −15(x − 1)^2(x − 3)^3$

63. $f(x) = −2(x + 3)(x + 2)(x − 1)$

65. $f(x) = −\frac{3}{2}(2x − 1)^2(x − 6)(x + 2)$

67. Local max: $(−0.58, −0.62)$; local min: $(0.58, −1.38)$

69. Global min: $(−0.63, −0.47)$ **71.** Global min: $(0.75, −1.11)$

73. $f(x) = (x − 500)^2(x + 200)$ **75.** $f(x) = 4x^3 − 36x^2 + 80x$

77. $f(x) = 4x^3 − 36x^2 + 60x + 100$

79. $f(x) = \frac{1}{\pi}(9x^3 + 45x^2 + 72x + 36)$

Section 3.5

1. The binomial is a factor of the polynomial.

3. $x + 6 + \dfrac{5}{x − 1}$, quotient: $x + 6$, remainder: 5

5. $3x + 2$, quotient: $3x + 2$, remainder: 0   **7.** $x − 5$, quotient: $x − 5$, remainder: 0   **9.** $2x − 7 + \dfrac{16}{x + 2}$, quotient: $2x − 7$, remainder 16   **11.** $x − 2 + \dfrac{6}{3x + 1}$, quotient: $x − 2$, remainder: 6

13. $2x^2 − 3x + 5$, quotient: $2x^2 − 3x + 5$, remainder: 0

15. $2x^2 + 2x + 1 + \dfrac{10}{x − 4}$ **17.** $2x^2 − 7x + 1 − \dfrac{2}{2x + 1}$

19. $3x^2 − 11x + 34 − \dfrac{106}{x + 3}$ **21.** $x^2 + 5x + 1$

23. $4x^2 − 21x + 84 − \dfrac{323}{x + 4}$ **25.** $x^2 − 14x + 49$

27. $3x^2 + x + \dfrac{2}{3x − 1}$ **29.** $x^3 − 3x + 1$ **31.** $x^3 − x^2 + 2$

33. $x^3 − 6x^2 + 12x − 8$ **35.** $x^3 − 9x^2 + 27x − 27$

37. $2x^3 − 2x + 2$ **39.** Yes, $(x − 2)(3x^3 − 5)$ **41.** Yes, $(x − 2)(4x^3 + 8x^2 + x + 2)$ **43.** No

45. $(x − 1)(x^2 + 2x + 4)$ **47.** $(x − 5)(x^2 + x + 1)$

49. Quotient: $4x^2 + 8x + 16$, remainder: $−1$ **51.** Quotient is $3x^2 + 3x + 5$, remainder: 0   **53.** Quotient is $x^3 − 2x^2 + 4x − 8$, remainder: $−6$ **55.** $x^6 − x^5 + x^4 − x^3 + x^2 − x + 1$

57. $x^3 − x^2 + x − 1 + \dfrac{1}{x + 1}$ **59.** $1 + \dfrac{1 + i}{x − i}$ **61.** $1 + \dfrac{1 − i}{x + i}$

63. $x^2 + ix − 1 + \dfrac{1 − i}{x − i}$ **65.** $2x^2 + 3$ **67.** $2x + 3$

69. $x + 2$ **71.** $x − 3$ **73.** $3x^2 − 2$

Section 3.6

1. The theorem can be used to evaluate a polynomial.
3. Rational zeros can be expressed as fractions whereas real zeros include irrational numbers.   **5.** Polynomial functions can have repeated zeros, so the fact that number is a zero doesn't preclude it being a zero again.   **7.** $−106$ **9.** 0   **11.** 255

13. $−1$ **15.** $−2, 1, \frac{1}{2}$ **17.** $−2$ **19.** $−3$

21. $−\frac{5}{2}, \sqrt{6}, −\sqrt{6}$ **23.** $2, −4, −\frac{3}{2}$ **25.** $4, −4, −5$

27. $5, −3, −\frac{1}{2}$ **29.** $\frac{1}{2}, \dfrac{1 + \sqrt{5}}{2}, \dfrac{1 − \sqrt{5}}{2}$

31. $\frac{3}{2}$ **33.** $2, 3, −1, −2$ **35.** $\frac{1}{2}, −\frac{1}{2}, 2, −3$

37. $−1, −1, \sqrt{5}, −\sqrt{5}$ **39.** $−\frac{3}{4}, −\frac{1}{2}$ **41.** $2, 3 + 2i, 3 − 2i$

43. $−\frac{2}{3}, 1 + 2i, 1 − 2i$ **45.** $−\frac{1}{2}, 1 + 4i, 1 − 4i$

47. 1 positive, 1 negative   **49.** 1 positive, 0 negative

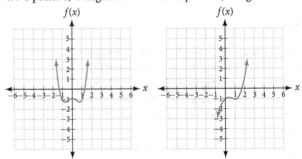

51. 0 positive, 3 negative   **53.** 2 positive, 2 negative

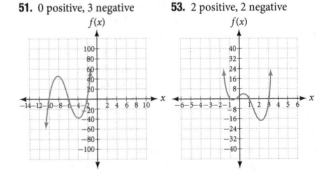

55. 2 positive, 2 negative

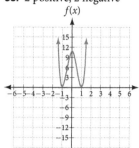
f(x)

57. $\pm\frac{1}{2}, \pm 1, \pm 5, \pm\frac{5}{2}$

59. $\pm 1, \pm\frac{1}{2}, \pm\frac{1}{3}, \pm\frac{1}{6}$

61. $1, \frac{1}{2}, -\frac{1}{3}$

63. $2, \frac{1}{4}, -\frac{3}{2}$ **65.** $\frac{5}{4}$

67. $f(x) = \frac{4}{9}(x^3 + x^2 - x - 1)$

69. $f(x) = -\frac{1}{5}(4x^3 - x)$

71. 8 by 4 by 6 inches

73. 5.5 by 4.5 by 3.5 inches **75.** 8 by 5 by 3 inches
77. Radius: 6 meters; height: 2 meters **79.** Radius: 2.5 meters, height: 4.5 meters

Section 3.7

1. The rational function will be represented by a quotient of polynomial functions. **3.** The numerator and denominator must have a common factor. **5.** Yes. The numerator of the formula of the functions would have only complex roots and/or factors common to both the numerator and denominator.
7. All reals except $x = -1, 1$ **9.** All reals except $x = -1, 1, -2, 2$
11. Vertical asymptote: $x = -\frac{2}{5}$; horizontal asymptote: $y = 0$;

domain: all reals except $x = -\frac{2}{5}$ **13.** Vertical asymptotes:

$x = 4, -9$; horizontal asymptote: $y = 0$; domain: all reals except
$x = 4, -9$ **15.** Vertical asymptotes: $x = 0, 4, -4$; horizontal
asymptote: $y = 0$; domain: all reals except $x = 0, 4, -4$
17. Vertical asymptotes: $x = -5$; horizontal asymptote: $y = 0$;
domain: all reals except $x = 5, -5$

19. Vertical asymptote: $x = \frac{1}{3}$; horizontal asymptote: $y = -\frac{2}{3}$;

domain: all reals except $x = \frac{1}{3}$ **21.** None

23. x-intercepts: none, y-intercept: $\left(0, \frac{1}{4}\right)$

25. Local behavior: $x \to -\frac{1}{2}^+, f(x) \to -\infty, x \to -\frac{1}{2}^-, f(x) \to \infty$

End behavior: $x \to \pm\infty, f(x) \to \frac{1}{2}$

27. Local behavior: $x \to 6^+, f(x) \to -\infty, x \to 6^-, f(x) \to \infty$
End behavior: $x \to \pm\infty, f(x) \to -2$

29. Local behavior: $x \to -\frac{1}{3}^+, f(x) \to \infty, x \to -\frac{1}{3}^-, f(x) \to -\infty$,

$x \to -\frac{5}{2}^-, f(x) \to \infty, x \to -\frac{5}{2}^+, f(x) \to -\infty$

End behavior: $x \to \pm\infty, f(x) \to \frac{1}{3}$

31. $y = 2x + 4$ **33.** $y = 2x$

35. Vertical asymptote at $x = 0$, horizontal asymptote at $y = 2$

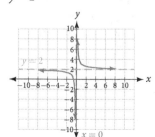

37. Vertical asymptote at $x = 2$, horizontal asymptote at $y = 0$

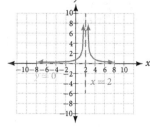

39. Vertical asymptote at $x = -4$; horizontal asymptote at $y = 2$; $\left(\frac{3}{2}, 0\right), \left(0, -\frac{3}{4}\right)$

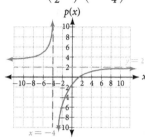
p(x)

41. Vertical asymptote at $x = 2$; horizontal asymptote at $y = 0$; $(0, 1)$

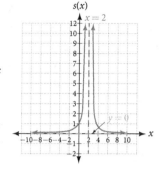
s(x)

43. Vertical asymptote at $x = -4, \frac{4}{3}$; horizontal asymptote at $y = 1$; $(5, 0)$, $\left(-\frac{1}{3}, 0\right), \left(0, \frac{5}{16}\right)$

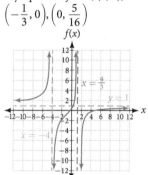
f(x)

45. Vertical asymptote at $x = -1$; horizontal asymptote at $y = 1$; $(-3, 0), (0, 3)$

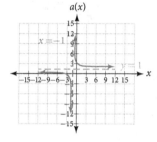
a(x)

47. Vertical asymptote at $x = 4$; slant asymptote at $y = 2x + 9$; $(-1, 0), \left(\frac{1}{2}, 0\right), \left(0, \frac{1}{4}\right)$

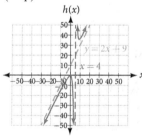
h(x)

49. Vertical asymptote at $x = -2$, 4; horizontal asymptote at $y = 1$; $(1, 0), (5, 0), (-3, 0), \left(0, -\frac{15}{16}\right)$

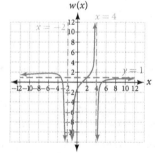
w(x)

51. $f(x) = 50\dfrac{x^2 - x - 2}{x^2 - 25}$ **53.** $f(x) = 7\dfrac{x^2 + 2x - 24}{x^2 + 9x + 20}$

55. $f(x) = \dfrac{1}{2} \cdot \dfrac{x^2 - 4x + 4}{x + 1}$ **57.** $f(x) = 4\dfrac{x - 3}{x^2 - x - 12}$

59. $f(x) = -9\dfrac{x - 2}{x^2 - 9}$ **61.** $f(x) = \dfrac{1}{3} \cdot \dfrac{x^2 + x - 6}{x - 1}$

63. $f(x) = -6\dfrac{(x - 1)^2}{(x + 3)(x - 2)^2}$

65. Vertical asymptote at $x = 2$; horizontal asymptote at $y = 0$

x	2.01	2.001	2.0001	1.99	1.999
y	100	1,000	10,000	−100	−1,000

x	10	100	1,000	10,000	100,000
y	0.125	0.0102	0.001	0.0001	0.00001

67. Vertical asymptote at $x = -4$; horizontal asymptote at $y = 2$

x	-4.1	-4.01	-4.001	-3.99	-3.999
y	82	802	8,002	-798	-7998

x	10	100	1,000	10,000	100,000
y	1.4286	1.9331	1.992	1.9992	1.999992

69. Vertical asymptote at $x = -1$; horizontal asymptote at $y = 1$

x	-0.9	-0.99	-0.999	-1.1	-1.01
y	81	9,801	998,001	121	10,201

x	10	100	1,000	10,000	100,000
y	0.82645	0.9803	0.998	0.9998	

71. $\left(\dfrac{3}{2}, \infty\right)$ **73.** $(-\infty, 1) \cup (4, \infty)$

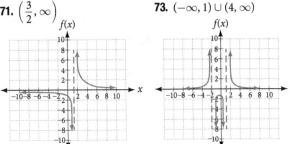

75. $(2, 4)$ **77.** $(2, 5)$ **79.** $(-1, 1)$ **81.** $C(t) = \dfrac{8 + 2t}{300 + 20t}$

83. After about 6.12 hours   **85.** 2 by 2 by 5 feet

87. radius 2.52 meters

Section 3.8

1. It can be too difficult or impossible to solve for x in terms of y.

3. We will need a restriction on the domain of the answer.   **5.** $f^{-1}(x) = \sqrt{x} + 4$ **7.** $f^{-1}(x) = \sqrt{x+3} - 1$

9. $f^{-1}(x) = -\sqrt{\dfrac{x-5}{3}}$ **11.** $f^{-1}(x) = \sqrt{9 - x}$

13. $f^{-1}(x) = \sqrt[3]{x} - 5$ **15.** $f^{-1}(x) = \sqrt[3]{4 - x}$

17. $f^{-1}(x) = \dfrac{x^2 - 1}{2}, [0, \infty)$ **19.** $f^{-1}(x) = \dfrac{(x-9)^2 + 4}{4}, [9, \infty)$

21. $f^{-1}(x) = \left(\dfrac{x-9}{2}\right)^3$ **23.** $f^{-1}(x) = \dfrac{2 - 8x}{x}$

25. $f^{-1}(x) = \dfrac{7x - 3}{1 - x}$ **27.** $f^{-1}(x) = \dfrac{5x - 4}{4x + 3}$

29. $f^{-1}(x) = \sqrt{1 + x} - 1$ **31.** $f^{-1}(x) = \sqrt{x + 6} + 3$

33. $f^{-1}(x) = \sqrt{4 - x}$ **35.** $f^{-1}(x) = \sqrt{x} + 4$

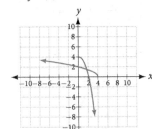 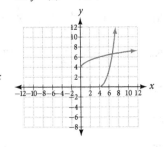

37. $f^{-1}(x) = \sqrt[3]{1 - x}$ **39.** $f^{-1}(x) = \sqrt{x + 8} + 3$

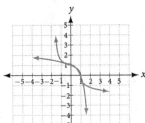 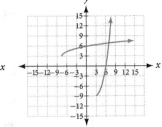

41. $f^{-1}(x) = \sqrt{\dfrac{1}{x}}$ **43.** $[-2, 1) \cup [3, \infty)$

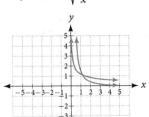 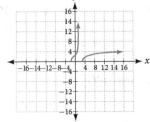

45. $[-4, 2) \cup [5, \infty)$ **47.** $(-2, 0), (4, 2), (22, 3)$

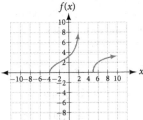 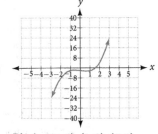

49. $(-4, 0), (0, 1), (10, 2)$ **51.** $(-3, -1), (1, 0), (7, 1)$

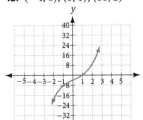 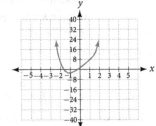

53. $f^{-1}(x) = -\dfrac{b}{2} + \dfrac{\sqrt{b^2 + 4x}}{2}$ **55.** $f^{-1}(x) = \dfrac{x^3 - b}{a}$

57. $t(h) = \sqrt{\dfrac{200 - h}{4.9}}$, 5.53 seconds

59. $r(V) = \sqrt[3]{\dfrac{3V}{4\pi}}, \approx 3.63$ feet   **61.** $n(C) = \dfrac{100C - 25}{0.6 - C}, 250\,\text{mL}$

63. $r(V) = \sqrt{\dfrac{V}{6\pi}}, \approx 3.99\,\text{m}$ **65.** $r(V) = \sqrt{\dfrac{V}{4\pi}}, \approx 1.99$ inches

Section 3.9

1. The graph will have the appearance of a power function.

3. No. Multiple variables may jointly vary.   **5.** $y = 5x^2$

7. $y = 10x^3$ **9.** $y = 6x^4$ **11.** $y = \dfrac{18}{x^2}$ **13.** $y = \dfrac{81}{x^4}$

15. $y = \dfrac{20}{\sqrt[3]{x}}$ **17.** $y = 10xzw$ **19.** $y = 10x\sqrt{z}$

21. $y = 4\dfrac{xz}{w}$ **23.** $y = 40\dfrac{xz}{\sqrt{wt^2}}$ **25.** $y = 256$

27. $y = 6$ **29.** $y = 6$ **31.** $y = 27$ **33.** $y = 3$

35. $y = 18$ **37.** $y = 90$ **39.** $y = \dfrac{81}{2}$

41. $y = \dfrac{3}{4}x^2$ **43.** $y = \dfrac{1}{3}\sqrt{x}$

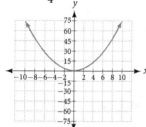

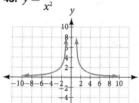

45. $y = \dfrac{4}{x^2}$

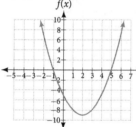

47. ≈ 1.89 years
49. ≈ 0.61 years
51. 3 seconds
53. 48 inches
55. ≈ 49.75 pounds
57. ≈ 33.33 amperes
59. ≈ 2.88

Chapter 3 Review Exercises

1. $2 - 2i$ **3.** $24 + 3i$ **5.** $\{2 + i, 2 - i\}$

7. $f(x) = (x - 2)^2 - 9$;
vertex: $(2, -9)$;
intercepts: $(-1, 0), (5, 0), (0, -5)$

9. $f(x) = \dfrac{3}{25}(x + 2)^2 + 3$

11. 300 meters by 150 meters, the longer side parallel to the river

13. Yes; degree: 5, leading coefficient: 4

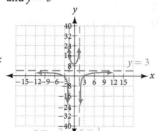

15. Yes; degree: 4; leading coefficient: 1

17. As $x \to -\infty, f(x) \to -\infty$, as $x \to \infty, f(x) \to \infty$

19. -3 with multiplicity 2, $-\dfrac{1}{2}$ with multiplicity 1, -1 with multiplicity 3   **21.** 4 with multiplicity 1   **23.** $\dfrac{1}{2}$ with multiplicity 1, 3 with multiplicity 3

25. $x^2 + 4$ with remainder 12   **27.** $x^2 - 5x + 20 - \dfrac{61}{x + 3}$

29. $2x^2 - 2x - 3$, so factored form is $(x + 4)(2x^2 - 2x - 3)$

31. $\left\{-2, 4, -\dfrac{1}{2}\right\}$ **33.** $\left\{1, 3, 4, \dfrac{1}{2}\right\}$

35. 2 or 0 positive, 1 negative

37. Intercepts: $(-2, 0), \left(0, -\dfrac{2}{5}\right)$, asymptotes: $x = 5$ and $y = 1$

39. Intercepts: $(3, 0), (-3, 0)$, $\left(0, \dfrac{27}{2}\right)$; asymptotes: $x = 1, -2$ and $y = 3$

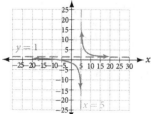

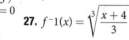

41. $y = x - 2$ **43.** $f^{-1}(x) = \sqrt{x} + 2$ **45.** $f^{-1}(x) = \sqrt{x + 11} - 3$

47. $f^{-1}(x) = \dfrac{(x + 3)^2 - 5}{4}, x \geq -3$ **49.** $y = 64$ **51.** $y = 72$

53. ≈ 148.5 pounds

Chapter 3 Practice Test

1. $20 - 10i$ **3.** $\{2 + 3i, 2 - 3i\}$

5. As $x \to -\infty, f(x) \to -\infty$, as $x \to \infty, f(x) \to \infty$

7. $f(x) = (x + 1)^2 - 9$, vertex: $(-1, -9)$, intercepts: $(2, 0)$, $(-4, 0)(0, -8)$

9. 60,000 square feet

11. 0 with multiplicity 4, 3 with multiplicity 2

13. $2x^2 - 4x + 11 - \dfrac{26}{x + 2}$

15. $2x^2 - x - 4$, so factored form is $(x + 3)(2x^2 - x - 4)$

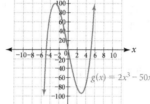

17. $-\dfrac{1}{2}$ (has multiplicity 2), $\dfrac{-1 \pm i\sqrt{15}}{2}$

19. -2 (multiplicity 3), $\pm i$ **21.** $f(x) = 2(2x - 1)^3(x + 3)$

23. Intercepts: $(-4, 0), \left(0, -\dfrac{4}{3}\right)$; asymptotes: $x = 3, -1$ and $y = 0$

25. $y = x + 4$

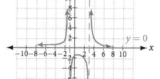

27. $f^{-1}(x) = \sqrt[3]{\dfrac{x + 4}{3}}$

29. $y = 18$ **31.** 4 seconds

CHAPTER 4

Section 4.1

1. Linear functions have a constant rate of change. Exponential functions increase based on a percent of the original.

3. When interest is compounded, the percentage of interest earned to principal ends up being greater than the annual percentage rate for the investment account. Thus, the annual percentage rate does not necessarily correspond to the real interest earned, which is the very definition of *nominal*.   **5.** Exponential; the population decreases by a proportional rate.   **7.** Not exponential; the charge decreases by a constant amount each visit, so the statement represents a linear function.   **9.** Forest B

11. After 20 years forest A will have 43 more trees than forest B.

13. Answers will vary. Sample response: For a number of years, the population of forest A will increasingly exceed forest B, but because forest B actually grows at a faster rate, the population will eventually become larger than forest A and will remain that way as long as the population growth models hold. Some factors that might influence the long-term validity of the exponential growth model are drought, an epidemic that culls the population, and other environmental and biological factors.

15. Exponential growth; the growth factor, 1.06, is greater than 1.
17. Exponential decay; the decay factor, 0.97, is between 0 and 1.
19. $f(x) = 2000(0.1)^x$

21. $f(x) = \left(\dfrac{1}{6}\right)^{-\frac{3}{5}} \left(\dfrac{1}{6}\right)^{\frac{x}{5}} \approx 2.93(0.699)^x$ **23.** Linear

25. Neither   **27.** Linear   **29.** \$10,250   **31.** \$13,268.58

33. $P = A(t) \cdot \left(1 + \dfrac{r}{n}\right)^{-nt}$ **35.** \$4,569.10   **37.** 4%

39. Continuous growth; the growth rate is greater than 0.
41. Continuous decay; the growth rate is less than 0.
43. \$669.42   **45.** $f(-1) = -4$ **47.** $f(-1) \approx -0.2707$
49. $f(3) \approx 483.8146$ **51.** $y = 3 \cdot 5^x$ **53.** $y \approx 18 \cdot 1.025^x$
55. $y \approx 0.2 \cdot 1.95^x$

57. $\mathrm{APY} = \dfrac{A(t) - a}{a} = \dfrac{a\left(1 + \dfrac{r}{365}\right)^{365(1)} - a}{a}$

$= \dfrac{a\left[\left(1 + \dfrac{r}{365}\right)^{365} - 1\right]}{a} = \left(1 + \dfrac{r}{365}\right)^{365} - 1;$

$I(n) = \left(1 + \dfrac{r}{n}\right)^n - 1$

59. Let f be the exponential decay function $f(x) = a \cdot \left(\dfrac{1}{b}\right)^x$ such that $b > 1$. Then for some number $n > 0$,

$f(x) = a \cdot \left(\dfrac{1}{b}\right)^x = a(b^{-1})^x = a((e^n)^{-1})^x = a(e^{-n})^x = a(e)^{-nx}.$

61. 47,622 foxes   **63.** 1.39%; \$155,368.09   **65.** \$35,838.76
67. \$82,247.78; \$449.75

Section 4.2

1. An asymptote is a line that the graph of a function approaches, as x either increases or decreases without bound. The horizontal asymptote of an exponential function tells us the limit of the function's values as the independent variable gets either extremely large or extremely small.   **3.** $g(x) = 4(3)^{-x}$; y-intercept: $(0, 4)$; domain: all real numbers; range: all real numbers greater than 0.
5. $g(x) = -10^x + 7$; y-intercept: $(0, 6)$; domain: all real numbers; range: all real numbers less than 7.

7. $g(x) = 2\left(\dfrac{1}{4}\right)^x$; y-intercept: $(0, 2)$; domain: all real numbers; range: all real numbers greater than 0.

9. y-intercept: $(0, -2)$ **11.**

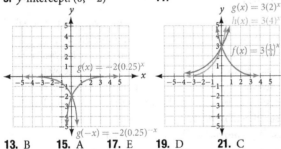

13. B   **15.** A   **17.** E   **19.** D   **21.** C

23.   **25.**

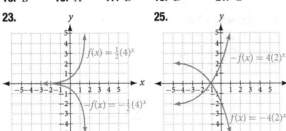

27. Horizontal asymptote: $h(x) = 3$; domain: all real numbers; range: all real numbers strictly greater than 3.

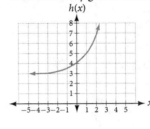

29. As $x \to \infty, f(x) \to -\infty$; as $x \to -\infty, f(x) \to -1$
31. As $x \to \infty, f(x) \to 2$; as $x \to -\infty, f(x) \to \infty$
33. $f(x) = 4^x - 3$
35. $f(x) = 4^{x-5}$
37. $f(x) = 4^{-x}$
39. $y = -2^x + 3$
41. $y = -2(3)^x + 7$
43. $g(6) \approx 800.\overline{3}$

45. $h(-7) = -58$ **47.** $x \approx -2.953$ **49.** $x \approx -0.222$
51. The graph of $g(x) = \left(\dfrac{1}{b}\right)^x$ is the reflection about the y-axis of the graph of $f(x) = b^x$; for any real number $b > 0$ and function $f(x) = b^x$, the graph of $\left(\dfrac{1}{b}\right)^x$ is the reflection about the y-axis, $f(-x)$.
53. The graphs of $g(x)$ and $h(x)$ are the same and are a horizontal shift to the right of the graph of $f(x)$. For any real number n, real number $b > 0$, and function $f(x) = b^x$, the graph of $\left(\dfrac{1}{b^n}\right)b^x$ is the horizontal shift $f(x - n)$.

Section 4.3

1. A logarithm is an exponent. Specifically, it is the exponent to which a base b is raised to produce a given value. In the expressions given, the base b has the same value. The exponent, y, in the expression b^y can also be written as the logarithm, $\log_b x$, and the value of x is the result of raising b to the power of y.
3. Since the equation of a logarithm is equivalent to an exponential equation, the logarithm can be converted to the exponential equation $b^y = x$, and then properties of exponents can be applied to solve for x.   **5.** The natural logarithm is a special case of the logarithm with base b in that the natural log always has base e. Rather than notating the natural logarithm as $\log_e(x)$, the notation used is $\ln(x)$.
7. $a^c = b$ **9.** $x^y = 64$ **11.** $15^b = a$ **13.** $13^a = 142$
15. $e^n = w$ **17.** $\log_c(k) = d$ **19.** $\log_{19}(y) = x$
21. $\log_n(103) = 4$ **23.** $\log_y\left(\dfrac{39}{100}\right) = x$ **25.** $\ln(h) = k$
27. $x = \dfrac{1}{8}$ **29.** $x = 27$ **31.** $x = 3$ **33.** $x = \dfrac{1}{216}$
35. $x = e^2$ **37.** 32   **39.** 1.06   **41.** 14.125   **43.** $\dfrac{1}{2}$
45. 4   **47.** -3 **49.** -12 **51.** 0   **53.** 10
55. ≈ 2.708 **57.** ≈ 0.151 **59.** No, the function has no defined value for $x = 0$. To verify, suppose $x = 0$ is in the domain of the function $f(x) = \log(x)$. Then there is some number n such that $n = \log(0)$. Rewriting as an exponential equation gives: $10^n = 0$, which is impossible since no such real number n exists. Therefore, $x = 0$ is not the domain of the function $f(x) = \log(x)$.
61. Yes. Suppose there exists a real number, x such that $\ln(x) = 2$. Rewriting as an exponential equation gives $x = e^2$, which is a real number ($x = e^2 \approx 7.389056099$). To verify, let $x = e^2$. Then, by definition, $\ln(x) = \ln(e^2) = 2$.   **63.** No; $\ln(1) = 0$, so $\dfrac{\ln(e^{1.725})}{\ln(1)}$ is undefined.   **65.** 2

Section 4.4

1. Since the functions are inverses, their graphs are mirror images about the line $y = x$. So for every point (a, b) on the graph of a logarithmic function, there is a corresponding point (b, a) on the graph of its inverse exponential function.　**3.** Shifting the function right or left and reflecting the function about the y-axis will affect its domain.　**5.** No. A horizontal asymptote would suggest a limit on the range, and the range of any logarithmic function in general form is all real numbers.

7. Domain: $\left(-\infty, \dfrac{1}{2}\right)$; range: $(-\infty, \infty)$

9. Domain: $\left(-\dfrac{17}{4}, \infty\right)$; range: $(-\infty, \infty)$

11. Domain: $(5, \infty)$; vertical asymptote: $x = 5$

13. Domain: $\left(-\dfrac{1}{3}, \infty\right)$; vertical asymptote: $x = -\dfrac{1}{3}$

15. Domain: $(-3, \infty)$; vertical asymptote: $x = -3$

17. Domain: $\left(\dfrac{3}{7}, \infty\right)$; vertical asymptote: $x = \dfrac{3}{7}$; end behavior: as $x \to \left(\dfrac{3}{7}\right)^{+}, f(x) \to -\infty$ and as $x \to \infty, f(x) \to \infty$

19. Domain: $(-3, \infty)$; vertical asymptote: $x = -3$; end behavior: as $x \to -3^{+}, f(x) \to -\infty$ and as $x \to \infty, f(x) \to \infty$

21. Domain: $(1, \infty)$; range: $(-\infty, \infty)$; vertical asymptote: $x = 1$; x-intercept: $\left(\dfrac{5}{4}, 0\right)$; y-intercept: DNE

23. Domain: $(-\infty, 0)$; range: $(-\infty, \infty)$; vertical asymptote: $x = 0$; x-intercept: $(-e^2, 0)$; y-intercept: DNE

25. Domain: $(0, \infty)$; range: $(-\infty, \infty)$ vertical asymptote: $x = 0$; x-intercept: $(e^3, 0)$; y-intercept: DNE

27. B　**29.** C　**31.** B　**33.** C

35.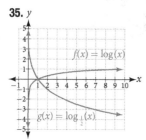

37.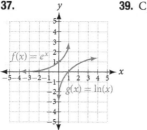

39. C

41.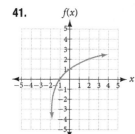

43.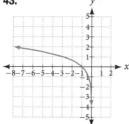

45.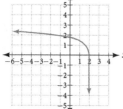

47. $f(x) = \log_2(-(x - 1))$

49. $f(x) = 3\log_4(x + 2)$

51. $x = 2$

53. $x \approx 2.303$

55. $x \approx -0.472$

57. The graphs of $f(x) = \log_{\frac{1}{2}}(x)$ and $g(x) = -\log_2(x)$ app the same; conjecture: for any positive base $b \neq 1$, $\log_b(x) = -\log_{\frac{1}{b}}$

59. Recall that the argument of a logarithmic function must be positive, so we determine where $\dfrac{x + 2}{x - 4} > 0$. From the graph of the function $f(x) = \dfrac{x + 2}{x - 4}$, note that the graph lies above the x-axis on the interval $(-\infty, -2)$ and again to the right of the vertical asymptote, that is $(4, \infty)$. Therefore, the domain is $(-\infty, -2) \cup (4, \infty)$.

Section 4.5

1. Any root expression can be rewritten as an expression with a rational exponent so that the power rule can be applied, making the logarithm easier to calculate. Thus, $\log_b(x^{\frac{1}{n}}) = \dfrac{1}{n}\log_b(x)$.

3. $\log_b(2) + \log_b(7) + \log_b(x) + \log_b(y)$

5. $\log_b(13) - \log_b(17)$　**7.** $-k\ln(4)$　**9.** $\ln(7xy)$

11. $\log_b(4)$　**13.** $\log_b(7)$　**15.** $15\log(x) + 13\log(y) - 19\log(z)$

17. $\dfrac{3}{2}\log(x) - 2\log(y)$　**19.** $\dfrac{8}{3}\log(x) + \dfrac{14}{3}\log(y)$　**21.** $\ln(2x^7)$

23. $\log\left(\dfrac{xz^3}{\sqrt{y}}\right)$　**25.** $\log_7(15) = \dfrac{\ln(15)}{\ln(7)}$

27. $\log_{11}(5) = \dfrac{1}{b}$　**29.** $\log_{11}\left(\dfrac{6}{11}\right) = \dfrac{a - b}{b}$ or $\dfrac{a}{b - 1}$　**31.** 3

33. ≈ 2.81359　**35.** ≈ 0.93913　**37.** ≈ -2.23266

39. $x = 4$, By the quotient rule:
$$\log_6(x + 2) - \log_6(x - 3) = \log_6\left(\dfrac{x + 2}{x - 3}\right) = 1$$
Rewriting as an exponential equation and solving for x:
$$6^1 = \dfrac{x + 2}{x - 3}$$
$$0 = \dfrac{x + 2}{x - 3} - 6$$
$$0 = \dfrac{x + 2}{x - 3} - \dfrac{6(x - 3)}{(x - 3)}$$
$$0 = \dfrac{x + 2 - 6x + 18}{x - 3}$$
$$0 = \dfrac{x - 4}{x - 3}$$
$$x = 4$$
Checking, we find that $\log_6(4 + 2) - \log_6(4 - 3) = \log_6(6) - \log_6(1)$ is defined, so $x = 4$.

41. Let b and n be positive integers greater than 1. Then, by the change-of-base formula, $\log_b(n) = \dfrac{\log_n(n)}{\log_n(b)} = \dfrac{1}{\log_n(b)}$.

Section 4.6

1. Determine first if the equation can be rewritten so that each side uses the same base. If so, the exponents can be set equal to each other. If the equation cannot be rewritten so that each side uses the same base, then apply the logarithm to each side and use properties of logarithms to solve.　**3.** The one-to-one property can be used if both sides of the equation can be rewritten as a single logarithm with the same base. If so, the arguments can be set equal to each other, and the resulting equation can be solved algebraically. The one-to-one property cannot be used when each side of the equation cannot be rewritten as a single logarithm with the same base.　**5.** $x = -\dfrac{1}{3}$　**7.** $n = -1$　**9.** $b = \dfrac{6}{5}$

11. $x = 10$　**13.** No solution　**15.** $p = \log\left(\dfrac{17}{8}\right) - 7$

17. $k = -\dfrac{\ln(38)}{3}$　**19.** $x = \dfrac{\ln\left(\dfrac{38}{3}\right) - 8}{9}$　**21.** $x = \ln(12)$

5. No solution   **27.** $x = \ln(3)$

49   **33.** $k = \dfrac{1}{36}$ **35.** $x = \dfrac{9-e}{8}$

n   **41.** No solution

x = 10   **47.** $x = 0$ **49.** $x = \dfrac{3}{4}$

51. $x = 9$ **53.** $x = \dfrac{e^2}{3} \approx 2.5$

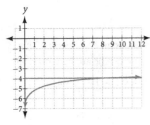

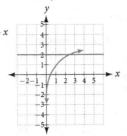

55. $x = -5$ **57.** $x = \dfrac{e+10}{4} \approx 3.2$

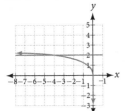

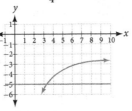

59. No solution   **61.** $x = \dfrac{11}{5} \approx 2.2$

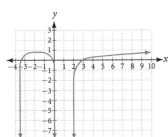

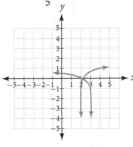

63. $x = \dfrac{101}{11} \approx 9.2$

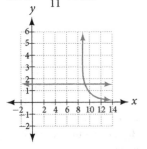

65. About $27,710.24

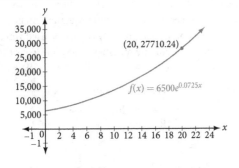

67. About 5 years

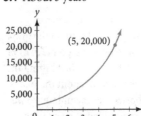

(5, 20,000)

69. ≈ 0.567 **71.** ≈ 2.078

73. ≈ 2.2401

75. ≈ -44655.7143

77. About 5.83

79. $t = \ln\left(\left(\dfrac{y}{A}\right)^{\frac{1}{k}}\right)$

81. $t = \ln\left(\left(\dfrac{T - T_s}{T_0 - T_s}\right)^{-\frac{1}{k}}\right)$

Section 4.7

1. Half-life is a measure of decay and is thus associated with exponential decay models. The half-life of a substance or quantity is the amount of time it takes for half of the initial amount of that substance or quantity to decay.   **3.** Doubling time is a measure of growth and is thus associated with exponential growth models. The doubling time of a substance or quantity is the amount of time it takes for the initial amount of that substance or quantity to double in size.   **5.** An order of magnitude is the nearest power of ten by which a quantity exponentially grows. It is also an approximate position on a logarithmic scale; Sample response: Orders of magnitude are useful when making comparisons between numbers that differ by a great amount. For example, the mass of Saturn is 95 times greater than the mass of Earth. This is the same as saying that the mass of Saturn is about 10^2 times, or 2 *orders of magnitude* greater, than the mass of Earth.

7. $f(0) \approx 16.7$; the amount initially present is about 16.7 units.

9. 150   **11.** Exponential; $f(x) = 1.2^x$

13. Logarithmic   **15.** Logarithmic

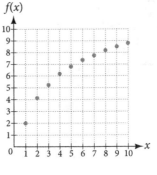

17.

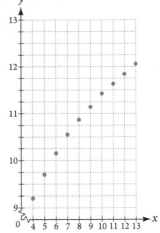

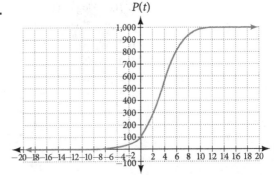

19. About 1.4 years   **21.** About 7.3 years

23. Four half-lives; 8.18 minutes

25. $M = \frac{2}{3} \log\left(\frac{S}{S_0}\right)$

$\frac{3}{2} M = \log\left(\frac{S}{S_0}\right)$

$10^{\frac{3M}{2}} = \left(\frac{S}{S_0}\right)$

$S_0 10^{\frac{3M}{2}} = S$

27. Let $y = b^x$ for some non-negative real number b such that $b \neq 1$. Then,

$\ln(y) = \ln(b^x)$

$\ln(y) = x \ln(b)$

$e^{\ln(y)} = e^{x \ln(b)}$

$y = e^{x \ln(b)}$

29. $A = 125 e^{(-0.3567t)}$; $A \approx 43$mg   **31.** About 60 days

33. $f(t) = 250 e^{-0.00914t}$; half-life: about 76 minutes

35. $r \approx -0.0667$; hourly decay rate: about 6.67%

37. $f(t) = 1350 e^{0.034657359t}$; after 3 hours; $P(180) \approx 691{,}200$

39. $f(t) = 256 e^{(0.068110t)}$; doubling time: about 10 minutes

41. About 88minutes   **43.** $T(t) = 90 e^{(-0.008377t)} + 75$, where t is in minutes   **45.** About 113 minutes   **47.** $\log_{10} x = 1.5$; $x \approx 31.623$

49. MMS Magnitude: ≈ 5.82 **51.** $N(3) \approx 71$ **53.** C

Section 4.8

1. Logistic models are best used for situations that have limited values. For example, populations cannot grow indefinitely since resources such as food, water, and space are limited, so a logistic model best describes populations.   **3.** Regression analysis is the process of finding an equation that best fits a given set of data points. To perform a regression analysis on a graphing utility, first list the given points using the STAT then EDIT menu. Next graph the scatter plot using the STAT PLOT feature. The shape of the data points on the scatter graph can help determine which regression feature to use. Once this is determined, select the appropriate regression analysis command from the STAT then CALC menu.

5. The y-intercept on the graph of a logistic equation corresponds to the initial population for the population model.

7. C   **9.** B   **11.** $P(0) = 22$; 175

13. $p \approx 2.67$ **15.** y-intercept: $(0, 15)$ **17.** 4 koi

19. About 6.8 months.

21.
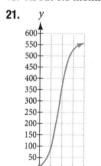

23. About 38 wolves

25. About 8.7 years

27. $f(x) = 776.682 (1.426)^x$

29.
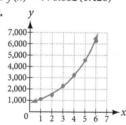

31.
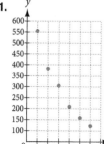

33. $f(x) = 731.92 e^{-0.3038x}$

35. When $f(x) = 250$, $x \approx 3.6$

37. $y = 5.063 + 1.934 \log(x)$

39.
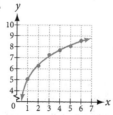

41.
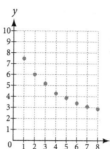

43. $f(10) \approx 2.3$

45. When $f(x) = 8$, $x \approx 0.82$

47. $f(x) = \dfrac{25.081}{1 + 3.182 e^{-0.545x}}$

49. About 25

51.
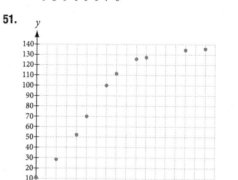

53.
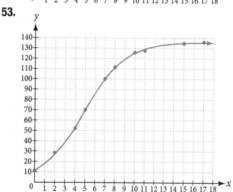

55. When $f(x) = 68$, $x \approx 4.9$ **57.** $f(x) = 1.034341 (1.281204)^x$; $g(x) = 4.035510$; the regression curves are symmetrical about $y = x$, so it appears that they are inverse functions.

59. $f^{-1}(x) = \dfrac{\ln(a) - \ln\left(\frac{c}{x} - 1\right)}{b}$

Chapter 4 Review Exercises

1. Exponential decay; the growth factor, 0.825, is between 0 and 1.

3. $y = 0.25(3)^x$ **5.** \$42,888.18   **7.** Continuous decay; the growth rate is negative

9. Domain: all real numbers; range: all real numbers strictly greater than zero; y-intercept: $(0, 3.5)$

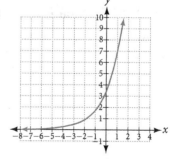

11. $g(x) = 7(6.5)^{-x}$; y-intercept: $(0, 7)$; domain: all real numbers; range: all real numbers greater than 0.   **13.** $17^x = 4{,}913$

15. $\log_a b = -\dfrac{2}{5}$ **17.** $x = 4$ **19.** $\log(0.000001) = -6$

21. $\ln(e^{-0.8648}) = -0.8648$

23.

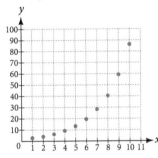

$g(x)$

25. Domain: $x > -5$; vertical asymptote: $x = -5$; end behavior: as $x \to -5^+$, $f(x) \to -\infty$ and as $x \to \infty$, $f(x) \to \infty$

27. $\log_8(65xy)$

29. $\ln\left(\dfrac{z}{xy}\right)$

31. $\log_y(12)$

33. $\ln(2) + \ln(b) + \dfrac{\ln(b+1) - \ln(b-1)}{2}$ **35.** $\log_7\left(\dfrac{v^3 w^6}{\sqrt[3]{u}}\right)$

37. $x = \dfrac{5}{3}$ **39.** $x = -3$ **41.** No solution   **43.** No solution

45. $x = \ln(11)$ **47.** $a = e^4 - 3$ **49.** $x = \pm\dfrac{9}{5}$

51. About 5.45 years   **53.** $f^{-1}(x) = \sqrt[3]{2^{4x} - 1}$

55. $f(t) = 300(0.83)^t$; $f(24) \approx 3.43\, g$ **57.** About 45 minutes

59. About 8.5 days

61. Exponential

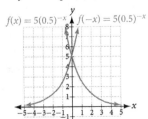

y

63. $y = 4(0.2)^x$; $y = 4e^{-1.609438x}$

65. About 7.2 days

67. Logarithmic $y = 16.68718 - 9.71860\ln(x)$

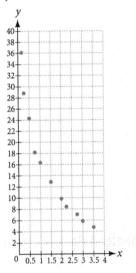

y

19. $x = \dfrac{\dfrac{\ln(1000)}{\ln(16)} + 5}{3} \approx 2.497$ **21.** $a = \dfrac{\ln(4) + 8}{10}$

23. No solution   **25.** $x = \ln(9)$ **27.** $x = \pm\dfrac{3\sqrt{3}}{2}$

29. $f(t) = 112e^{-0.019792t}$; half-life: about 35 days

31. $T(t) = 36e^{-0.025131t} + 35$; $T(60) \approx 43°F$

33. Logarithmic

35. Exponential; $y = 15.10062(1.24621)^x$

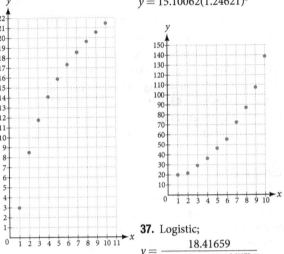

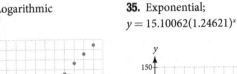

y

37. Logistic; $y = \dfrac{18.41659}{1 + 7.54644\,e^{-0.68375x}}$

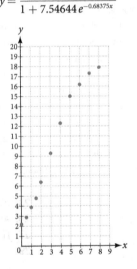

y

CHAPTER 5

Section 5.1

1.

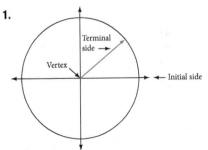

Terminal side

Vertex

Initial side

3. Whether the angle is positive or negative determines the direction. A positive angle is drawn in the counterclockwise direction, and a negative angle is drawn in the clockwise direction.

Chapter 4 Practice Test

1. About 13 dolphins   **3.** $1{,}947

5. y-intercept: $(0, 5)$ **7.** $8.5^a = 614.125$ **9.** $x = \dfrac{1}{49}$

11. $\ln(0.716) \approx -0.334$

13. Domain: $x < 3$; vertical asymptote: $x = 3$; end behavior: as $x \to 3^-$, $f(x) \to -\infty$ and as $x \to -\infty$, $f(x) \to \infty$

$f(x) = 5(0.5)^{-x}$ $f(-x) = 5(0.5)^{-x}$

y

15. $\log_t(12)$

17. $3\ln(y) + 2\ln(z) + \dfrac{\ln(x-4)}{3}$

5. Linear speed is a measurement found by calculating distance of an arc compared to time. Angular speed is a measurement found by calculating the angle of an arc compared to time.

7.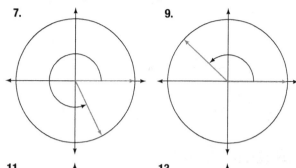

9.

11.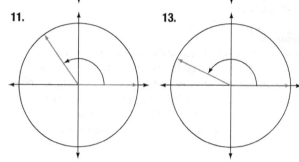

13.

15.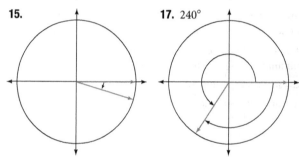

17. 240°

19. $\frac{4\pi}{3}$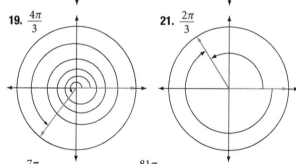

21. $\frac{2\pi}{3}$

23. $\frac{7\pi}{2} \approx 11.00$ in² **25.** $\frac{81\pi}{20} \approx 12.72$ cm² **27.** 20°

29. 60° **31.** −75° **33.** $\frac{\pi}{2}$ radians **35.** −3π radians

37. π radians **39.** $\frac{5\pi}{6}$ radians **41.** $\frac{5.02\pi}{3} \approx 5.26$ miles

43. $\frac{25\pi}{9} \approx 8.73$ centimeters **45.** $\frac{21\pi}{10} \approx 6.60$ meters

47. 104.7198 cm² **49.** 0.7697 in² **51.** 250° **53.** 320°

55. $\frac{4\pi}{3}$ **57.** $\frac{8\pi}{9}$ **59.** 1320 rad/min 210.085 RPM

61. 7 in/s, 4.77 RPM, 28.65 deg/s

63. 1,809,557.37 mm/min = 30.16 m/s **65.** 5.76 miles

67. 120° **69.** 794 miles per hour **71.** 2,234 miles per hour

73. 11.5 inches

Section 5.2

1. The unit circle is a circle of radius 1 centered at the origin.

3. Coterminal angles are angles that share the same terminal side. A reference angle is the size of the smallest acute angle, t, formed by the terminal side of the angle t and the horizontal axis.

5. The sine values are equal. **7.** I **9.** IV **11.** $\frac{\sqrt{3}}{2}$ **13.** $\frac{1}{2}$

15. $\frac{\sqrt{2}}{2}$ **17.** 0 **19.** −1 **21.** $\frac{\sqrt{3}}{2}$ **23.** 60°

25. 80° **27.** 45° **29.** $\frac{\pi}{3}$ **31.** $\frac{\pi}{3}$ **33.** $\frac{\pi}{8}$

35. 60°, Quadrant IV, $\sin(300°) = -\frac{\sqrt{3}}{2}$, $\cos(300°) = \frac{1}{2}$

37. 45°, Quadrant II, $\sin(135°) = \frac{\sqrt{2}}{2}$, $\cos(135°) = -\frac{\sqrt{2}}{2}$

39. 60°, Quadrant II, $\sin(120°) = \frac{\sqrt{3}}{2}$, $\cos(120°) = -\frac{1}{2}$

41. 30°, Quadrant II, $\sin(150°) = \frac{1}{2}$, $\cos(150°) = -\frac{\sqrt{3}}{2}$

43. $\frac{\pi}{6}$, Quadrant III, $\sin\left(\frac{7\pi}{6}\right) = -\frac{1}{2}$, $\cos\left(\frac{7\pi}{6}\right) = -\frac{\sqrt{3}}{2}$

45. $\frac{\pi}{4}$, Quadrant II, $\sin\left(\frac{3\pi}{4}\right) = \frac{\sqrt{2}}{2}$, $\cos\left(\frac{3\pi}{4}\right) = -\frac{\sqrt{2}}{2}$

47. $\frac{\pi}{3}$, Quadrant II, $\sin\left(\frac{2\pi}{3}\right) = \frac{\sqrt{3}}{2}$, $\cos\left(\frac{2\pi}{3}\right) = -\frac{1}{2}$

49. $\frac{\pi}{4}$, Quadrant IV, $\sin\left(\frac{7\pi}{4}\right) = -\frac{\sqrt{2}}{2}$, $\cos\left(\frac{7\pi}{4}\right) = \frac{\sqrt{2}}{2}$

51. $\frac{\sqrt{77}}{9}$ **53.** $-\frac{\sqrt{15}}{4}$ **55.** $\left(-10, 10\sqrt{3}\right)$

57. (−2.778, 15.757) **59.** [−1, 1] **61.** $\sin t = \frac{1}{2}$, $\cos t = -\frac{\sqrt{3}}{2}$

63. $\sin t = -\frac{\sqrt{2}}{2}$, $\cos t = -\frac{\sqrt{2}}{2}$ **65.** $\sin t = \frac{\sqrt{3}}{2}$, $\cos t = -\frac{1}{2}$

67. $\sin t = -\frac{\sqrt{2}}{2}$, $\cos t = \frac{\sqrt{2}}{2}$ **69.** $\sin t = 0$, $\cos t = -1$

71. $\sin t = -0.596$, $\cos t = 0.803$ **73.** $\sin t = \frac{1}{2}$, $\cos t = \frac{\sqrt{3}}{2}$

75. $\sin t = -\frac{1}{2}$, $\cos t = \frac{\sqrt{3}}{2}$ **77.** $\sin t = 0.761$, $\cos t = -0.649$

79. $\sin t = 1$, $\cos t = 0$ **81.** −0.1736 **83.** 0.9511

85. −0.7071 **87.** −0.1392 **89.** −0.7660 **91.** $\frac{\sqrt{2}}{4}$

93. $-\frac{\sqrt{6}}{4}$ **95.** $\frac{\sqrt{2}}{4}$ **97.** $\frac{\sqrt{2}}{4}$ **99.** 0 **101.** (0, −1)

103. 37.5 seconds, 97.5 seconds, 157.5 seconds, 217.5 seconds, 277.5 seconds, 337.5 seconds

Section 5.3

1. Yes, when the reference angle is $\frac{\pi}{4}$ and the terminal side of the angle is in quadrants I or III. Thus, at $x = \frac{\pi}{4}, \frac{5\pi}{4}$, the sine and cosine values are equal. **3.** Substitute the sine of the angle in for y in the Pythagorean Theorem $x^2 + y^2 = 1$. Solve for x and take the negative solution. **5.** The outputs of tangent and cotangent will repeat every π units.

7. $\frac{2\sqrt{3}}{3}$ **9.** $\sqrt{3}$ **11.** $\sqrt{2}$ **13.** 1 **15.** 2

17. $\frac{\sqrt{3}}{3}$ **19.** $-\frac{2\sqrt{3}}{3}$ **21.** $\sqrt{3}$ **23.** $-\sqrt{2}$ **25.** −1

27. −2 **29.** $-\frac{\sqrt{3}}{3}$ **31.** 2 **33.** $\frac{\sqrt{3}}{3}$ **35.** −2 **37.** −1

39. $\sin t = -\dfrac{2\sqrt{2}}{3}$, $\sec t = -3$, $\csc t = -\dfrac{3\sqrt{2}}{4}$,

$\tan t = 2\sqrt{2}$, $\cot t = \dfrac{\sqrt{2}}{4}$ **41.** $\sec t = 2$, $\csc t = \dfrac{2\sqrt{3}}{3}$,

$\tan t = \sqrt{3}$, $\cot t = \dfrac{\sqrt{3}}{3}$ **43.** $-\dfrac{\sqrt{2}}{2}$ **45.** 3.1

47. 1.4   **49.** $\sin t = \dfrac{\sqrt{2}}{2}$, $\cos t = \dfrac{\sqrt{2}}{2}$, $\tan t = 1$, $\cot t = 1$,

$\sec t = \sqrt{2}$, $\csc t = \sqrt{2}$ **51.** $\sin t = -\dfrac{\sqrt{3}}{2}$, $\cos t = -\dfrac{1}{2}$, $\tan$

$t = \sqrt{3}$, $\cot t = \dfrac{\sqrt{3}}{3}$, $\sec t = -2$, $\csc t = -\dfrac{2\sqrt{3}}{3}$

53. -0.228 **55.** -2.414 **57.** 1.414   **59.** 1.540

61. 1.556   **63.** $\sin(t) \approx 0.79$ **65.** $\csc(t) \approx 1.16$ **67.** Even

69. Even   **71.** $\dfrac{\sin t}{\cos t} = \tan t$ **73.** 13.77 hours, period: 1000π

75. 7.73 inches

Section 5.4

1.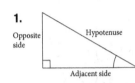

3. The tangent of an angle is the ratio of the opposite side to the adjacent side.   **5.** For example, the sine of an angle is equal to the cosine of its complement; the cosine of an angle is equal to the sine of its complement.

7. $\dfrac{\pi}{6}$ **9.** $\dfrac{\pi}{4}$ **11.** $b = \dfrac{20\sqrt{3}}{3}$, $c = \dfrac{40\sqrt{3}}{3}$

13. $a = 10{,}000$, $c = 10{,}000.5$ **15.** $b = \dfrac{5\sqrt{3}}{3}$, $c = \dfrac{10\sqrt{3}}{3}$

17. $\dfrac{5\sqrt{29}}{29}$ **19.** $\dfrac{5}{2}$ **21.** $\dfrac{\sqrt{29}}{2}$ **23.** $\dfrac{5\sqrt{41}}{41}$

25. $\dfrac{5}{4}$ **27.** $\dfrac{\sqrt{41}}{4}$ **29.** $c = 14$, $b = 7\sqrt{3}$

31. $a = 15$, $b = 15$ **33.** $b = 9.9970$, $c = 12.2041$

35. $a = 2.0838$, $b = 11.8177$ **37.** $a = 55.9808$, $c = 57.9555$

39. $a = 46.6790$, $b = 17.9184$ **41.** $a = 16.4662$, $c = 16.8341$

43. 188.3159   **45.** 200.6737   **47.** 498.3471 ft.

49. 1,060.09 ft.   **51.** 27.372 ft.   **53.** 22.6506 ft.

55. 368.7633 ft.

Chapter 5 Review Exercises

1. 45°   **3.** $-\dfrac{7\pi}{6}$ **5.** 10.385 meters   **7.** 60°   **9.** $\dfrac{2\pi}{11}$

11.   **13.**

15. 1,036.73 miles per hour   **17.** $\dfrac{\sqrt{3}}{2}$ **19.** -1 **21.** $\dfrac{\pi}{4}$

23. $-\dfrac{\sqrt{2}}{2}$ **25.** $[-1, 1]$ **27.** 1   **29.** $\sqrt{2}$

31. $\sqrt{2}$ **33.** 0.6   **35.** $\dfrac{\sqrt{2}}{2}$ or $-\dfrac{\sqrt{2}}{2}$

37. Sine, cosecant, tangent, cotangent

39. $\dfrac{\sqrt{3}}{3}$ **41.** 0   **43.** $b = 8$, $c = 10$ **45.** $\dfrac{11\sqrt{157}}{157}$

47. $a = 4$, $b = 4$ **49.** 14.0954 ft.

Chapter 5 Practice Test

1. 150°   **3.** 6.283 centimeters   **5.** 15°

7.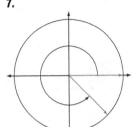

9. 3.351 feet per second, $\dfrac{2\pi}{75}$ radians per second

11. $-\dfrac{\sqrt{3}}{2}$ **13.** $[-1, 1]$

15. $\sqrt{3}$ **17.** $\dfrac{\sqrt{3}}{3}$

19. $\dfrac{\sqrt{3}}{2}$ **21.** $\dfrac{\pi}{3}$

23. $a = \dfrac{9}{2}$, $b = \dfrac{9\sqrt{3}}{2}$

CHAPTER 6

Section 6.1

1. The sine and cosine functions have the property that $f(x + P) = f(x)$ for a certain P. This means that the function values repeat for every P units on the x-axis.   **3.** The absolute value of the constant A (amplitude) increases the total range and the constant D (vertical shift) shifts the graph vertically.

5. At the point where the terminal side of t intersects the unit circle, you can determine that the sin t equals the y-coordinate of the point.

7. Amplitude: $\dfrac{2}{3}$; period: 2π; midline: $y = 0$; maximum: $y = \dfrac{2}{3}$ occurs at $x = 0$; minimum: $y = -\dfrac{2}{3}$ occurs at $x = \pi$; for one period, the graph starts at 0 and ends at 2π.

9. Amplitude: 4; period: 2π; midline: $y = 0$; maximum: $y = 4$ occurs at $x = \dfrac{\pi}{2}$; minimum: $y = -4$ occurs at $x = \dfrac{3\pi}{2}$; for one period, the graph starts at 0 and ends at 2π.

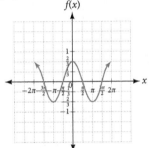

11. Amplitude: 1; period: π; midline: $y = 0$; maximum: $y = 1$ occurs at $x = \pi$; minimum: $y = -1$ occurs at $x = \dfrac{\pi}{2}$; for one period, the graph starts at 0 and ends at π.

13. Amplitude: 4; period: 2; midline: $y = 0$; maximum: $y = 4$ occurs at $x = 0$; minimum: $y = -4$ occurs at $x = 1$; for one period, the graph starts at 0 and ends at π.

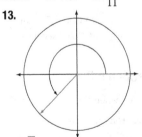

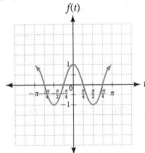

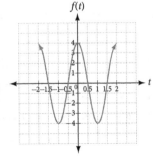

15. Amplitude: 3; period: $\frac{\pi}{4}$; midline: $y = 5$; maximum: $y = 8$ occurs at $x = 0.12$; minimum: $y = 2$ occurs at $x = 0.516$; horizontal shift: -4; vertical translation: 5; for one period, the graph starts at 0 and ends at $\frac{\pi}{4}$.

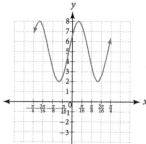

17. Amplitude: 5; period: $\frac{2\pi}{5}$; midline: $y = -2$; maximum: $y = 3$ occurs at $x = 0.08$; minimum: $y = -7$ occurs at $x = 0.71$; phase shift: -4; vertical translation: -2; for one period, the graph starts at 0 and ends at $\frac{2\pi}{5}$.

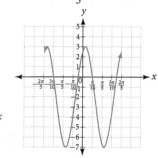

43. A linear function is added to a periodic sine function. The graph does not have an amplitude because as the linear function increases without bound the combined function $h(x) = x + \sin x$ will increase without bound as well. The graph is bounded between the graphs of $y = x + 1$ and $y = x - 1$ because sine oscillates between -1 and 1.

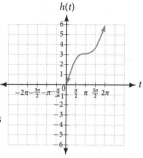

45. There is no amplitude because the function is not bounded.

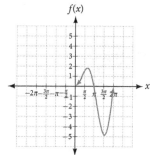

47. The graph is symmetric with respect to the y-axis and there is no amplitude because the function's bounds decrease as $|x|$ grows. There appears to be a horizontal asymptote at $y = 0$.

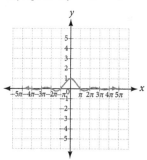

19. Amplitude: 1; period: 2π; midline: $y = 1$; maximum: $y = 2$ occurs at $t = 2.09$; minimum: $y = 0$ occurs at $t = 5.24$; phase shift: $-\frac{\pi}{3}$; vertical translation: 1; for one period, the graph starts at 0 and ends at 2π.

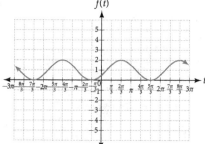

21. Amplitude: 1; period: 4π; midline: $y = 0$; maximum: $y = 1$ occurs at $t = 11.52$; minimum: $y = -1$ occurs at $t = 5.24$; phase shift: $-\frac{10\pi}{3}$; vertical shift: 0; for one period, the graph starts at 0 and ends at 4π.

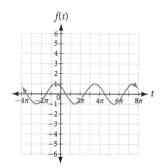

23. Amplitude: 2, midline: $y = -3$; period: 4; equation: $f(x) = 2\sin\left(\frac{\pi}{2}x\right) - 3$ **25.** Amplitude: 2, midline: $y = 3$; period: 5; equation: $f(x) = -2\cos\left(\frac{2\pi}{5}x\right) + 3$

27. Amplitude: 4, midline: $y = 0$; period: 2; equation: $f(x) = -4\cos\left(\pi\left(x - \frac{\pi}{2}\right)\right)$ **29.** Amplitude: 2, midline: $y = 1$; period: 2; equation: $f(x) = 2\cos(\pi x) + 1$ **31.** $0, \pi$

33. $\sin\left(\frac{\pi}{2}\right) = 1$ **35.** $\frac{\pi}{2}$ **37.** $f(x) = \sin x$ is symmetric with respect to the origin.   **39.** $\frac{\pi}{3}, \frac{5\pi}{3}$

41. Maximum: 1 at $x = 0$; minimum: -1 at $x = \pi$

Section 6.2

1. Since $y = \csc x$ is the reciprocal function of $y = \sin x$, you can plot the reciprocal of the coordinates on the graph of $y = \sin x$ to obtain the y-coordinates of $y = \csc x$. The x-intercepts of the graph $y = \sin x$ are the vertical asymptotes for the graph of $y = \csc x$.   **3.** Answers will vary. Using the unit circle, one can show that $\tan(x + \pi) = \tan x$.   **5.** The period is the same: 2π

7. IV   **9.** III   **11.** Period: 8; horizontal shift: 1 unit to the left

13. 1.5   **15.** 5   **17.** $-\cot x \cos x - \sin x$

19. Stretching factor: 2; period: $\frac{\pi}{4}$; asymptotes: $x = \frac{1}{4}\left(\frac{\pi}{2} + \pi k\right) + 8$, where k is an integer

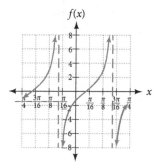

21. Stretching factor: 6; period: 6; asymptotes: $x = 3k$, where k is an integer

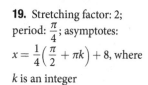

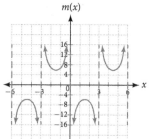

23. Stretching factor: 1; period: π; asymptotes: $x = \pi k$, where k is an integer

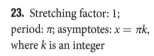

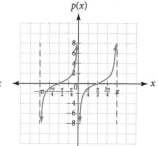

25. Stretching factor: 1; period: π; asymptotes: $x = \dfrac{\pi}{4} + \pi k$, where k is an integer

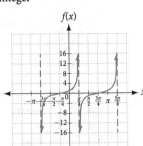

27. Stretching factor: 2; period: 2π; asymptotes: $x = \pi k$, where k is an integer

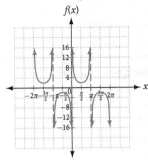

37. $y = \left(\tan 3\left(x - \dfrac{\pi}{4} \right) \right) + 2$

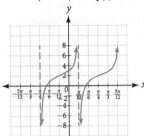

39. $f(x) = \csc(2x)$

41. $f(x) = \csc(4x)$

43. $f(x) = 2\csc x$

45. $f(x) = \dfrac{1}{2}\tan(100\pi x)$

47.

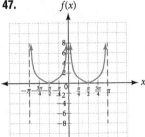

29. Stretching factor: 4; period: $\dfrac{2\pi}{3}$; asymptotes: $x = \dfrac{\pi}{6}k$, where k is an integer

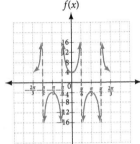

31. Stretching factor: 7; period: $\dfrac{2\pi}{5}$; asymptotes: $x = \dfrac{\pi}{10}k$, where k is an integer

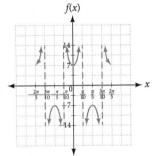

49.

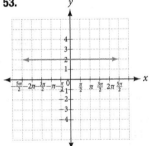

33. Stretching factor: 2; period: 2π; asymptotes: $x = -\dfrac{\pi}{4} + \pi k$, where k is an integer

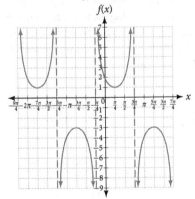

51.

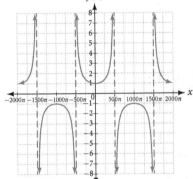

53.

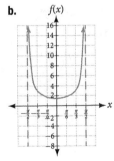

35. Stretching factor: $\dfrac{7}{5}$; period: 2π; asymptotes: $x = \dfrac{\pi}{4} + \pi k$, where k is an integer

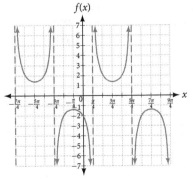

55. a. $\left(-\dfrac{\pi}{2}, \dfrac{\pi}{2} \right)$;

b.

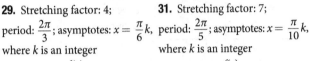

c. $x = -\dfrac{\pi}{2}$ and $x = \dfrac{\pi}{2}$; the distance grows without bound as $|x|$ approaches $\dfrac{\pi}{2}$–i.e., at right angles to the line representing due north, the boat would be so far away, the fisherman could not see it **d.** 3; when $x = -\dfrac{\pi}{3}$, the boat is 3 km away **e.** 1.73; when $x = \dfrac{\pi}{6}$, the boat is about 1.73 km away **f.** 1.5 km; when $x = 0$

57. a. $h(x) = 2\tan\left(\frac{\pi}{120}x\right)$

b. $f(x)$

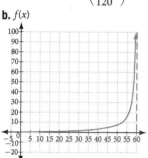

c. $h(0) = 0$: after 0 seconds, the rocket is 0 mi above the ground; $h(30) = 2$: after 30 seconds, the rockets is 2 mi high; **d.** As x approaches 60 seconds, the values of $h(x)$ grow increasingly large. As $x \to 60$ the model breaks down, since it assumes that the angle of elevation continues to increase with x. In fact, the angle is bounded at 90 degrees.

Section 6.3

1. The function $y = \sin x$ is one-to-one on $\left[-\frac{\pi}{2}, \frac{\pi}{2}\right]$; thus, this interval is the range of the inverse function of $y = \sin x$, $f(x) = \sin^{-1} x$. The function $y = \cos x$ is one-to-one on $[0, \pi]$; thus, this interval is the range of the inverse function of $y = \cos x$, $f(x) = \cos^{-1} x$. **3.** $\frac{\pi}{6}$ is the radian measure of an angle between $-\frac{\pi}{2}$ and $\frac{\pi}{2}$ whose sine is 0.5. **5.** In order for any function to have an inverse, the function must be one-to-one and must pass the horizontal line test. The regular sine function is not one-to-one unless its domain is restricted in some way. Mathematicians have agreed to restrict the sine function to the interval $\left[-\frac{\pi}{2}, \frac{\pi}{2}\right]$ so that it is one-to-one and possesses an inverse. **7.** True. The angle, θ_1 that equals $\arccos(-x)$, $x > 0$, will be a second quadrant angle with reference angle, θ_2, where θ_2 equals $\arccos x$, $x > 0$. Since θ_2 is the reference angle for θ_1, $\theta_2 = \pi - \theta_1$ and $\arccos(-x) = \pi - \arccos x$ **9.** $-\frac{\pi}{6}$

11. $\frac{3\pi}{4}$ **13.** $-\frac{\pi}{3}$ **15.** $\frac{\pi}{3}$ **17.** 1.98 **19.** 0.93

21. 1.41 **23.** 0.56 radians **25.** 0 **27.** 0.71 radians

29. -0.71 radians **31.** $-\frac{\pi}{6}$ radians **33.** $\frac{4}{5}$ **35.** $\frac{5}{13}$

37. $\frac{x-1}{\sqrt{-x^2 + 2x}}$ **39.** $\frac{\sqrt{x^2 - 1}}{x}$ **41.** $\frac{x + 0.5}{\sqrt{-x^2 - x + \frac{3}{4}}}$

43. $\frac{\sqrt{2x+1}}{x+1}$ **45.** $\frac{\sqrt{2x+1}}{x}$ **47.** t

49. Domain: $[-1, 1]$; range: $[0, \pi]$ **51.** $x = 0$

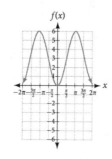

53. 0.395 radians

55. 1.11 radians

57. 1.25 radians

59. 0.405 radians

61. No. The angle the ladder makes with the horizontal is 60 degrees.

Chapter 6 Review Exercises

1. Amplitude: 3; period: is 2π; midline: $y = 3$; no asymptotes

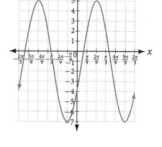

3. Amplitude: 3; period: is 2π; midline: $y = 0$; no asymptotes

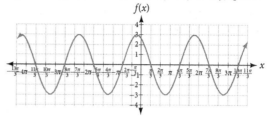

5. Amplitude: 3; period: is 2π; midline: $y = -4$; no asymptotes

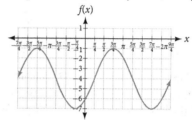

7. Amplitude: 6; period: is $\frac{2\pi}{3}$; midline: $y = -1$; no asymptotes

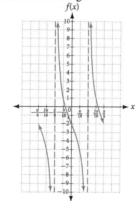

9. Stretching factor: none; period: π; midline: $y = -4$; asymptotes: $x = \frac{\pi}{2} + \pi k$, where k is an integer

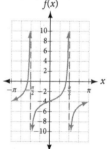

11. Stretching factor: 3; period: $\frac{\pi}{4}$; midline: $y = -2$; asymptotes: $x = \frac{\pi}{8} + \frac{\pi}{4}k$, where k is an integer

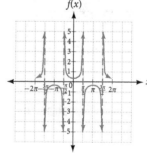

13. Amplitude: none; period: 2π; no phase shift; asymptotes: $x = \frac{\pi}{2}k$, where k is an odd integer

15. Amplitude: none; period: $\frac{2\pi}{5}$; no phase shift; asymptotes: $x = \frac{\pi}{5}k$, where k is an integer

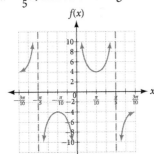

17. Amplitude: none; period: 4π; no phase shift; asymptotes: $x = 2\pi k$, where k is an integer

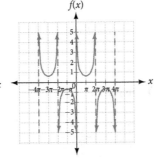

5. Amplitude: 1; period: 2π; midline: $y = 1$

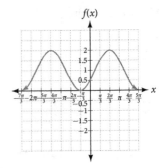

7. Amplitude: 3; period: 6π; midline: $y = 0$

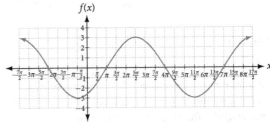

19. Largest: 20,000; smallest: 4,000   **21.** Amplitude: 8,000; period: 10; phase shift: 0   **23.** In 2007, the predicted population is 4,413. In 2010, the population will be 11,924.   **25.** 5 in.

27. 10 seconds   **29.** $\frac{\pi}{6}$ **31.** $\frac{\pi}{4}$ **33.** $\frac{\pi}{3}$

35. No solution   **37.** $\frac{12}{5}$

39. The graphs are not symmetrical with respect to the line $y = x$. They are symmetrical with respect to the y-axis.

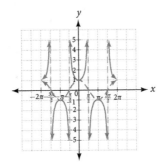

9. Amplitude: none; period: π; midline: $y = 0$; asymptotes: $x = \frac{2\pi}{3} + \pi k$, where k is some integer

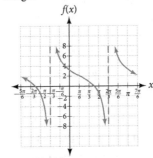

11. Amplitude: none; period: $\frac{2\pi}{3}$; midline: $y = 0$; asymptotes: $x = \frac{\pi}{3}k$, where k is some integer

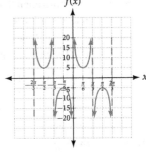

13. Amplitude: none; period: 2π; midline: $y = -3$

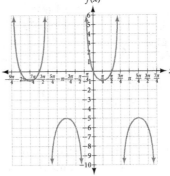

15. Amplitude; 2; period: 2; midline: $y = 0$; $f(x) = 2\sin(\pi(x - 1))$

17. Amplitude; 1; period: 12; phase shift: -6; midline: $y = -3$

19. $D(t) = 68 - 12\sin\left(\frac{\pi}{12}x\right)$

21. Period: $\frac{\pi}{6}$; horizontal shift: -7

23. $f(x) = \sec(\pi x)$; period: 2; phase shift: 0

25. 4

41. The graphs appear to be identical.

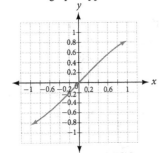

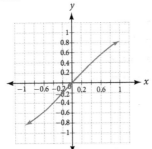

Chapter 6 Practice Test

1. Amplitude: 0.5; period: 2π; midline: $y = 0$

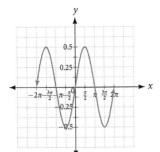

3. Amplitude: 5; period: 2π; midline: $y = 0$

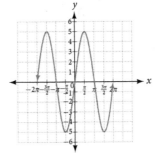

27. The views are different because the period of the wave is $\frac{1}{25}$. Over a bigger domain, there will be more cycles of the graph.

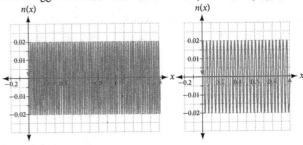

29. $\dfrac{3}{5}$

31. $\left(\dfrac{\pi}{6}, \dfrac{\pi}{3}\right), \left(\dfrac{\pi}{2}, \dfrac{2\pi}{3}\right), \left(\dfrac{5\pi}{6}, \pi\right), \left(\dfrac{7\pi}{6}, \dfrac{4\pi}{3}\right), \left(\dfrac{3\pi}{2}, \dfrac{5\pi}{3}\right), \left(\dfrac{11\pi}{6}, 2\pi\right)$

33. $f(x) = 2\cos\left(12\left(x + \dfrac{\pi}{4}\right)\right) + 3$ **35.** This graph is periodic with a period of 2π.

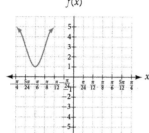

37. $\dfrac{\pi}{3}$ **39.** $\dfrac{\pi}{2}$ **41.** $\sqrt{1 - (1 - 2x)^2}$ **43.** $\dfrac{}{\sqrt{1 + x^4}}$

45. $\csc t = \dfrac{x + 1}{x}$ **47.** False   **49.** 0.07 radians

Index